D1200289

The Captain from Connecticut

The Captain
from
Connecticut

The Life and
Naval Times of
Isaac Hull

Linda M. Maloney

Northeastern University Press

BOSTON

HOUSTON PUBLIC LIBRARY

R0155772539
SSC

Northeastern University Press

Copyright © 1986 by Linda M. Maloney

All rights reserved. This book, or parts thereof,
may not be reproduced in any form or by any means,
electronic or mechanical, including photocopying,
recording, or any information storage and retrieval
system now known or to be invented, without written
permission from the publisher.

Library of Congress Cataloging in Publication Data

Maloney, Linda M.
The Captain from Connecticut.
Bibliography: p.
Includes index.
1. Hull, Isaac. 2. Admirals—United States—Biography.
3. United States. Navy—Biography. I. Title.
V63.H85M35   1986   359'.0092'4 [B]   85–10552
ISBN 0-930350-79-0 (alk. paper)

Designed by David Ford

Composed in Trump by Graphic Composition, Athens,
Georgia. Printed and bound by the Murray Printing
Company, Westford, Massachusetts. The paper is
Glatfelter Offset, an acid-free sheet.

MANUFACTURED IN THE UNITED STATES OF AMERICA
91 90 89 88 87 86   5 4 3 2 1

The Frontispiece is a portrait of Isaac Hull by Gilbert
Stuart, ca. 1809, from the collection of Mrs. Roger C.
Elliott. Courtesy of the New-York Historical Society,
New York City.

For Sharon, David, and Vincent

Acknowledgments

This book began more than twenty-five years ago when a young author, long on enthusiasm though short on experience, contacted the heirs of Isaac Hull for permission to write a new biography of their famous forebear. Mr. and Mrs. Haviland Hull Platt both welcomed and aided my first efforts, placing their collection of papers at my disposal. Their continued encouragement was essential to my work, and I regret only that they did not live to see its completion. Extensive private resources were also made available by Frederick Rodgers and by Arthur and Eleanor Tilton.

Among institutions whose staffs have been most gracious and helpful, particular mention should go to the William L. Clements Library of the University of Michigan, where I read my first Hull letters and whose collections acquired more and more valuable documents as the years went by, as well as to the National Archives in Washington, D.C., where I spent a year. In addition, I am grateful to the staffs of the Library of Congress, Manuscripts Division; the New-York Historical Society; the Boston Athenaeum; and the historical societies of Connecticut, Pennsylvania, Massachusetts, and Maine, as well as the New Hampshire State Archives. Documents from these collections are reproduced by permission of the respective organizations.

I owe a particular debt of gratitude to the Smithsonian Institution for granting me a year as Visiting Research Associate in 1969–70. During that year, with the advice and encouragement of my director, the late Howard I. Chapelle, and of Harold D. Langley and the rest of the Naval History Division, I completed virtually the second half of the research. Grants from the faculty research funds of the University of South Carolina at Columbia assisted the final research and writing of the book.

A word of thanks is due also to the dozens of other libraries that turned up lesser pieces of the mosaic, as well as to the many friends whose interest in Isaac Hull has endured since our high school and college celebrations of his 9 March birthday. My classmates wrote in the high school prophecy that I would be flying to South America to investigate newly discovered Hull memorabilia, and though my researches have not carried me quite so far, the mileage has been substantial.

I am grateful to William Frohlich, Deborah Kops, and Ann Twombly at Northeastern University Press; and to Bill Fowler, who brought the manuscript to their attention.

Finally and foremost, this book has been sustained from beginning to end by the expert advice and unflagging enthusiasm of Christopher McKee. The debt I owe him only the book itself can hope to repay. Its remaining faults are those he was unable to prevent.

Grateful acknowledgment is made to the following institutions for permission to quote from their collections: Library of the Boston Athenaeum, William L. Clements Library, The Historical Society of Pennsylvania, the Houghton Library, The Huntington Library, San Marino, California, Massachusetts Historical Society, Mystic Seaport Museum, and the New-York Historical Society.

Tübingen, West Germany
January 1985

Contents

List of Illustrations

List of Maps

Introduction

Isaac Hull is, for most of those who recognize him at all, a name in a history book. A majority of American history textbooks mention the naval victories of the War of 1812 and give a passing nod to the war's first victorious captain. The conquest of HMS *Guerrière* was a crucial moment in the conscious life of a new nation and certainly a turning point in the life of Isaac Hull. But it is in a sense ironic that Hull should be known for nothing but this warlike deed, since in his personal character he was one of the most pacific of men. It could be said that he embodied the ideals of a nation that cared to fight only under extreme provocation. That was the dream, at least; for Isaac Hull it was a lived reality.

He came from a prototypical New England context: a middle-class family of farmer-seamen, politically significant at the local level but with few aspirations beyond that. Whatever ambitions the family had for a legal career for him were thwarted both by his lifelong aversion to politics and law courts and by his undying passion for the sea. His early seafaring days were anything but unusual: he rose to command at about the usual age and was somewhat less successful financially than most. But he developed skills in those early years that were his mainstay for life: ship-handling skills unsurpassed in his time and a way of dealing with sailors that made him one of the most beloved as well as one of the most efficient naval captains of the early Republic.

It was in the navy, however, that Hull found his true career. There his ability to maneuver a ship combined in ideal circumstances with his skill at human relations. At the peak of his career, both his professional acumen and his amiability were legendary. Nevertheless, he might have remained an obscure figure but for the "good luck" of 19 August 1812. As is usually the case, he created his own luck. Had he not been the consummate seaman he was, the *Constitution* would have been gobbled up by a British squadron weeks earlier. And, had he not summoned the audacity to leave Boston without orders, he might have captained a blockaded ship for the rest of the war. As it was, he seized the moment, and the moment was his.

The battle of 19 August has been called a classic, though the balance of skill and luck may be disputed. What should be said is that Isaac Hull took no chances of losing. He knew his advantages: a heavy ship and a big, though inexperienced, crew against a less powerful opponent with a history of winning. Hull disdained carrying out a pirouetting combat at long range, despite his skill at maneuvering, lest his adversary escape. He chose instead a battle at close range where, should his ship's propulsion be disabled, he could still hope to overpower his enemy by boarding. The tactic was so successful that the opposing frigate was not merely defeated but destroyed. Hull's was the first combat, as he may have guessed, and it was vital that it be solid and complete to hearten a frightened and demoralized nation. Hull felt it important for the morale of a crew to "get them in heart." His victory did that for a whole nation, giving it the impetus to see the struggle through two more years. The War of 1812, taken as a whole, was hardly a chain of glorious successes, but in retrospect the defeats seemed to fade, whereas the victories, and Hull's especially, remained landmarks of both the nation's and the navy's history.

Hull's postwar life was like that of the nation as a whole in its absorption in domestic matters. His victory brought him not only fame but also a wife. It was an enduring love match on both sides, but Ann Hart Hull saw her husband from the first as a hero and an important man. As a result, she expected a certain social deference, and when in some situations it was not forthcoming, frictions arose that were a source of discomfort to Isaac Hull. These frictions added to the financial difficulties of supporting an enlarged family and even contributed to professional quarrels that enveloped Hull in the early 1820s. His letters from the postwar years show a steady dampening of the wit and sparkle of his bachelor days. His marriage had its benefits but also its burdens.

In national and local politics Isaac Hull was less than fortunate. Although, like every officer, he owed his original appointment to a good word spoken in high places, he believed from first to last that "the cloth has no politics." As a consequence of this conviction, Hull occasionally seemed to display a political naïveté. During the 1820s he was caught in a political cross fire in Boston between last-gasp Federalists and entrenched Republicans that was very nearly fatal to his professional reputation. He seemed at first to have been almost oblivious to the partisan complexion of the attack on him, and only the powerful advocacy of his naval friends at Washington, David Porter and John Rodgers, saved him from undeserved ignominy.

Although he was an efficient administrator—a fact obscured by the trials and charges at Boston—Isaac Hull in a navy yard was rather a fish out of water. More than twelve of his first fourteen years in the navy were spent on shipboard; of the thirty years after 1812, only about six were passed at sea. He made up for the lack in part by sailing and fishing with a private yacht at Boston, but by far his happiest later years were those spent in the Pacific squadron. There, at the climax of the Peruvian war of independence, Hull showed what could be accomplished by a combination of diplomatic skill and democratic sympathy. He left the United States a far better reputation in South America than it was later to enjoy.

Hull's last cruise, by contrast, was a sad episode. He carried out the duties of the Mediterranean squadron in routine fashion, but the personal costs were tragically high. For many years Hull had been a mirror of his times, but by the late 1830s the pace of change was accelerating too fast for him. He had become, almost without noticing it, "the old Commodore," an officer of "the old school." Old school indeed was this man who had dedicated his life to the navy without a backward look. How could he understand an officer like Sylvanus Godon, a lieutenant in his flagship, who wrote to a friend in 1841, "I am going, in future, to look out for myself a little, for it is thought at the Department, I find, that I am always ready and willing for sea service, good or bad. That, I find, is a convenient reputation, by no means however a profitable one."[1] That one could use the navy to one's own benefit was a thought completely foreign to Isaac Hull. He was, by the end of his life, doubly deaf to these younger men: he had lost his physical sense of hearing, but he had also lost, or had never acquired, the ability to listen to the voice of self-interest. These officers resented Hull for his fame, for his old-fashioned ideas of duty, and for his very existence as an obstacle to their promotion. They resented his wife and sister-in-law for their claims to social distinction. The disaffection was mutual, and because the unhappiness of this cruise was so well documented, and the personalities involved so famous, these years have seemed a gross failure at the end of Hull's career. But this period should be kept in perspective. Scarcely any American squadron in the Mediterranean was happy in those years: some were merely more publicly miserable than others. And Hull kept, to the end, the affection of his crew. From beginning to end of his career, the first objects of his concern were the sailors under his command, and they repaid him with steady devotion.

Isaac Hull believed that duty and honor—true honor, not the synthetic puff "defended" by pistols at dawn—were the best guides in life. He rejected the strut of Stephen Decatur's "our country, right or wrong," but prayed with a sincere religious conviction that was not merely for show that his country would find and follow the right path. If at the end he had some doubts, he also had hope. The country was, after all, the sum of people like Isaac Hull. In his life and times we can find part of our past, and much of the hope that he and his like had for us, and for our future. Be it example or critique, it is worth our attention.

The Captain from Connecticut

1

Choose the Sea

The winter of 1773 was a lull in the years of pre-Revolutionary agitation in New England. Toward the end of that calm before the storm, on 9 March, before the ice had begun to break up on the Housatonic, Sarah Bennett Hull was brought to bed of her second child in a house near the river at Derby Landing, Connecticut. Her husband, Captain Joseph Hull, the fourth of that name in America, was twenty-three years old and a rising man in Derby. His grandfather represented Derby in the General Assembly, as *his* father had before him, until his death in 1775. Grandfather Joseph had also served as collector of customs at New London in the 1750s. Joseph Hull, Jr., father of Joseph IV, was proprietor of an ironworks at the falls of the Naugatuck, justice of the peace for New Haven County, and described in the journal of the General Assembly as "one of the principal inhabitants of Derby." Joseph Hull IV traded out of the Housatonic in small vessels on Long Island Sound and to the West Indies; marriage had also brought him the prospect of the substantial "Bennett place" across the river at Huntington Landing. But it was in the house at Derby that his second son was born. The first, two years older, had been called Joseph after the four previous generations; the new boy was Isaac, so christened at the Congregational church at Derby on 6 June 1773 by the Reverend Daniel Humphreys.

On the death of his mother-in-law, Elizabeth Bennett, in 1783, Joseph Hull IV moved to Huntington Landing, giving rise to later belief that Isaac Hull was born on the Bennett farm. Confusion was increased by the fact that Isaac himself was unsure of his birth date, later setting it in 1775.[1] In that year, however, his brother Levi was born, adding to the total of Hull sons, which eventually reached seven.[2] All the boys grew up on the tidal river, and for Isaac the river was alive with the activities of war. Derby lay on the flank of British-occupied New York. In 1776 Joseph Hull entered the army as a lieutenant of artillery; taken prisoner at Fort Washington on the Hudson in November, he spent two years in one of the prison hulks at New York.[3]

A family tradition recorded in his later years says that during this period five-year-old Isaac was found conducting naval battles in the river with a flotilla of shingles, "whipping the British for keeping my father in their prison ship." This is the sort of tale that arises from hindsight on a great career; nevertheless, his father's activities and those of the other men of Derby, which was a considerable shipbuilding center during the war, could not help turning a boy's mind to the sea and the navy. Was Isaac Hull at hand when his grandmother, Elizabeth, served breakfast to General Rochambeau and his staff as they rode from Rhode Island to join Washington at White Plains in 1781? Exchanged in 1778, Joseph Hull tried to reclaim his army commission; when he was unable to do so, he took command of a flotilla of armed whaleboats fitted out to harass the enemy on Long Island Sound. His return to Derby with a prize, a British armed schooner surprised in a daring night boarding action, made a deep impression on Isaac. Subsequently Joseph Hull fitted out the armed boat *Rover* and, in 1782–83, sent in two prizes captured on the Sound.[4]

By that time the war was nearly over. The two prizes brought a tidy sum, which Joseph Hull invested in additional land at Derby and Huntington and in fitting out a succession of small vessels for the coasting trade.

Isaac had been too young to share in his father's Revolutionary exploits; now, at ten, he was chafing to go to sea. Another family tradition has him sailing the Housatonic with a pleasure party of ladies and rescuing all eight or ten passengers when the boat overset in a sudden squall. If true, this tale seems an early instance of Isaac's lifelong delight in female company; in later years, however, he was a much better seaman than he was on this occasion. Some of his seamanship may have been acquired in pursuit of whales with small boats on Long Island Sound, an enterprise in which his father engaged from time to time.[5]

It is unlikely that Joseph Hull objected to his son's desire to follow his own calling, but apparently he felt that the boy needed some schooling first. Young Joseph, destined to be a physician, had been sent to prepare with his uncle David Hull, a doctor in Fairfield, Connecticut. Now Isaac was dispatched, probably in 1784, to another uncle, the Revolutionary hero William Hull, who dwelt at Newton, Massachusetts. William Hull was a lawyer, so it is possible that Isaac Hull was also marked by his family for the law.

Samuel C. Clarke, a grandson of William Hull's, later recorded his mother's account of the arrival of the Derby cousin, a chubby boy with blue eyes and brown curls: "Colonel Hull was standing at his door when the stage coach drove up and a little boy jumped out with bundle in hand and came up. 'Why, what little boy is this?' 'Howdy do, uncle, I'm come to live with you.'" Isaac was not very big for his eleven years;

Clarke's story continues with an anecdote of a sea captain dining at Colonel Hull's and being asked to take the boy to sea. "'Why, he [is] so small that I should have to take a nurse to care for him,'" says the captain. "'Oh, no, Captain,' said Isaac, 'if I am little I can work—I will take care of the cabin if you will have me.'"[6]

It may have been with this captain that Isaac made his first voyage, which in 1842 he remembered as having been in the coasting trade, visiting "part of the ports from North Carolina to the East as far as Frenchman's Bay." He probably did not spend more than a year with his uncle; although he learned to read and write, his spelling and orthography were always uncertain, and a few years later he found it necessary to attend a night school at Boston to learn the mathematics needed for navigation.[7]

On 14 November 1785 Joseph Hull registered the sloop *Hawk* at New Haven. Early records are sketchy, but beginning in June 1787 are entries for a series of at least six voyages in which Joseph Hull commanded the *Hawk* to the West Indies, principally to Cap Français (Cap Haitien) in Hispaniola and to Martinique. It was almost certainly in the *Hawk* or a similar Connecticut "horse-jockey" that Isaac Hull made his first foreign voyages. The character of the commerce is suggested by a newspaper account of a minor disaster the *Hawk* met with on one of her voyages in 1788: "Captain Joseph Hull, of Derby, in a sloop, who sailed for the West-Indies about the 10th [of July] lost his mast, and part of his flock in the late gale [about 23 July in the zone from 35° to 38° north latitude] and returned to New-London, on Friday last."

Tiny vessels like the *Hawk*, which registered sixty tons and had a crew of six to nine—holds crammed with lumber, salt meat, meal, crockery, and dry goods; decks crowded with sheep, cattle, goats, chickens, and swine—must have combined all the worst features of the seafaring life and the farm. The manifest for the *Hawk*'s outward voyage of June 1787, for example, lists six thousand feet of lumber, thirty horses, five cows, twenty-five sheep or swine, twenty cases of poultry, and fifteen barrels of Indian meal. On the voyage of June–August 1788, she carried six thousand feet of lumber, twenty-eight horses, six oxen, and twenty sheep or swine. The daily routine of care for livestock, added to the normal chores aboard ship, was dismal enough, but when a gale came up the trouble began. With the tiny vessel pitching about in a storm, the few hands fully occupied at the sheets or the pumps, there was no way to secure the terrified stock, which added their laments to the din of wind and sea. Frequently the poor beasts, if not washed overboard, were so badly injured by falling that they later died. The return voyages with a cargo of molasses or sugar must have been a good deal more restful. But somehow Isaac survived his years as a sea-going herdsman with undiminished enthusiasm. By the time Joseph Hull sold the *Hawk* in December 1790, Isaac had risen from landsman to seaman and was ready to voyage farther afield.[8]

Like most merchant seamen, Isaac Hull is an obscure figure until he reaches the status of command. From memoranda written near the end of his life, it appears that after his West Indies voyages he sailed to Europe before the mast two or three times. On one of these voyages, possibly the first, his vessel was wrecked in the English Channel, and young Hull stayed afloat on the wreckage from nine in the evening until noon the following day. For that service he earned only five dollars and had to work his way home; next he made a voyage to Portugal, three and a half months at ten dollars per month, in the ship *Favorite*, Daniel Reed, captain.[9] From the month following his return to Boston, three letters survive that give a glimpse of Isaac Hull, eighteen years old and on the verge of becoming a ship's officer.

On 8 October 1791 Isaac wrote his father from Boston, assuring him of his health and rising prospects. Knowing that his parents were concerned about him and that his father had visited Boston in the spring to inquire after him, the young seaman wrote that "I think myself better off than at home. I have the offer of going second mate of a brig 160 tons but am at a loss whether to accept or not. The owner that I am with has two brigs and the ship." Isaac was then in a position of trust, acting as shipkeeper and selling at retail the ship's cargo of salt at a wage of nine dollars per month.

The following paragraph, reproduced as written, gives some idea of young Hull's appraisal of his relative professional prospects, as well as of the state of the New England schools:

> I under stand that Joseph has left my uncle David which in my opinion Is the worst thing he could do I shoud advise him not to spend his time in keeping school for I think that no business a tall my uncle Coud have got me in to a Chool at 10 dolers pr month. But choose the sea.

Promising frequent letters, the young mariner closed with an appeal: "I wish you to advise me how to conduct as to not forget that I have a father."

Captain Joseph Hull was a dilatory correspondent, however. Isaac wrote twice again, on 25 October and 9 November, indicating his desire for letters from home. In the interval he was going to a Mr. Colton's night school to improve his navigation; he mentions his need for sixteen dollars to purchase a Hadley's quadrant, having been at some expense both to outfit himself with "land clothes" and to pay the costs of his tuition and books. By the time he wrote the last of these three letters he had accepted a berth as second mate of a snow sailing for Europe in about a fortnight. "I have been but one voyage from here," he wrote, "but I think I have as good a prospect as any of my age can have. But it is impossible to tell how luck will turn but don't make yourself uneasy for I am as contented as at home and more so for I am in business, as I may say." With typical fraternal solicitude, he again inquired about Joseph: "I am more concerned about him than myself at present. . . . I shall I believe rub and go, which I think is a good pilot."[10]

After this letter Isaac Hull's movements are again obscure for a time. The snow apparently took him to either Cadiz or Rotterdam; after another voyage as second mate, he again sailed to Spain, this time as first mate. His European voyages may have been interrupted by one to the West Indies in the early spring of 1792, for on 10 March of that year he gave to John Lynch a receipt for $126.13 for cash sent to the West Indies.[11]

It was in the *Favorite* that Isaac Hull began to rise above a seaman's status; and it was from the *Favorite*'s owner, Thomas English of Boston, that he received his first command. She was the brand-new brig *Liffey*, 124½ tons, built at Rehoboth, Rhode Island, and obviously destined for the Irish trade. Her first register, issued at Newport, Rhode Island, on 11 March 1794, two days after her new master's twenty-first birthday, shows her as a square-sterned brig, 66 feet 3 inches long, 21 feet in the beam, and 10 feet 6 inches deep in the hold, with a quarterdeck, a straight waist, and no quarter galleries or figurehead. For the *Liffey*'s maiden voyage to Galway, Isaac Hull filed a manifest on 12 March showing a cargo of flaxseed and barrel staves, the whole valued at $3,087.16. On the same day Captain Isaac Hull swore himself to be an American citizen; *Liffey*'s sea letter was issued on 26 March, and Isaac Hull embarked on his first voyage in command.[12]

Hull said that he made two voyages in the *Liffey*, though the second is not recorded. In the summer of 1795, however, he left Boston and the European trade for good. Apparently, he wanted to return to Connecticut. He may also have felt that the West Indies trade offered him a better opportunity of becoming part owner of a vessel. It was in ownership that the real profits of seafaring were to be found. So it was that on 4 August 1795 he cleared from Norwich in command of the square-sterned brig *Nancy*, 178⁷⁷/₉₅ tons, owned by Park Benjamin and Jedidiah Kelley, merchants. The *Nancy* was bound for Turk's Island, in the West Indies, for salt. Her outward cargo was a standard one: corn, flour, beef, bacon, and crockery.

By 9 September the *Nancy* was reported at Turk's Island, preparing to sail in four days with her cargo of six thousand bushels of salt; on Thursday, 8 October, she blew into New London on the wings of a nor'easter, twenty days from her departure. It was a long passage, perhaps complicated by equinoctial gales—or maybe the *Nancy* was a slow sailer.[13]

There is no record of a second voyage in the *Nancy*, but on 19 November, when her permanent register was issued at New London, Isaac Hull was still in command. By 1 March 1796, however, he had shifted to a new and larger vessel, the 188½-ton ship *Minerva*, built at Bath in the district of Maine. The *Minerva* was a new ship, first registered on 29 December 1795. She was owned in part by one of the Norwich Kelleys, Hezekiah. When Isaac Hull registered her temporarily at Boston on 1 March, she was recorded as a square-sterned ship, 80 feet by 23 feet 3½ inches by 11 feet 7¾ inches, with no quarter galleries but boasting a figurehead—presumably that of a woman.[14]

Hull was back in the livestock trade. Boston records no clearance for the *Minerva* in 1796, but by November her captain had reregistered her at New London and filed a manifest for his voyage: ninety-eight oxen and one hundred hogs, hay, corn, hogsheads, hoops, beans, salt meat, potatoes, and bread. Whatever the destination of his cargo, he cleared on the return voyage from Barbados; stopped at Turk's Island; and returned to New London on Friday, 3 February 1797.[15]

In returning to the West Indies trade, Isaac Hull was gambling his rising fortunes in a risky sea. As all New England captains were aware, profits on West Indies commerce were high in the 1790s, but this was partly because perils were equally high. Britain and France were at war. While Napoleon's armies dominated the continent, Great Britain sought to make its might prevail at sea. Each of the great European rivals sought to cripple the other in the critical Caribbean area, without a great deal of nicety where neutral carriers were concerned. Particularly after Jay's Treaty (1795), in which the United States submitted to British wishes with regard to the laws of international trade, the outraged French made West Indian waters hot for American traders. Guadeloupe, Martinique, Saint Lucia, and Tobago had fallen to the British, but in late 1794 Guadeloupe was recaptured. The new governor, Victor Hugues, made Guadeloupe a base for French cruiser and privateer operations. By 1796 Holland and Spain had fallen under French domination and opened their island ports to French corsairs. Hugues and the French commissioners at Cap Français issued a series of decrees directing the seizure of American vessels bound to or from British ports or laden with contraband, and the French Directory, by a decree of 2 March

1797, made sweeping changes in France's international commercial practices. Contraband lists were extended to conform to American concessions in Jay's Treaty, and any goods belonging to an enemy were held to be seizable, even in a neutral ship; Americans serving in enemy ships were to be treated as pirates; and any American ship not carrying a *rôle d'équipage* (a crew list in designated form) was declared a lawful prize.[16]

Obviously, this situation was one in which an enterprising naval captain or privateersman could make prize of almost any American vessel that appealed to him. It may have been an attempt to circumvent these French regulations that led Isaac Hull to file, on 14 April 1797, a manifest for the *Minerva*'s next voyage, which gave her destination as Guadeloupe. As her movements and subsequent litigation reveal, she was in fact bound for British-held Martinique, with a typical cargo consisting of oxen, sheep, staves, hoops, soap, candles, and provisions. If the false manifest was in fact a ruse, it did not work. The voyage was unlucky from the start. On 16–17 April the *Minerva* rode out a heavy gale in which twelve of her sixty oxen were lost. Then, at about 9:00 A.M. on 3 May, three leagues from Martinique, she fell in with the 2-gun schooner *Bayonnaise*, Jean Baptiste Langa, captain. Captain Hull was taken on board the privateer, which put a crew in the *Minerva* and then bore up in chase of another sail. It was a mistake; this proved to be the British sloop-of-war *Cyane*. The pursuer became the pursued, and about 8:00 P.M. the Englishman overhauled the privateer, ending Hull's brief captivity.

Unfortunately, the *Minerva* escaped in the darkness and made Basse-Terre, Guadeloupe, the following day. There the ship was condemned without trial and, over the protests of Mate Benjamin Paine, was sold on the ground of having been bound to Martinique. Captain Hull was landed at Fort Royale, Martinique, on 5 May, and he filed a protest of his capture at Saint-Pierre before returning to New London in late June. Paine, after being confined sixteen days on board the *Minerva*, escaped with the connivance of the prize master and returned to the United States on 25 June. He reported that the prize crew had plundered the *Minerva* of everything, including Hull's quadrant, chest, and bedding.[17]

The *Minerva* had been insured for $7,000; her cargo, with an estimated value of $8,229, was secured for $8,000. But insurance premiums were high and payments low; how much the owners recovered from the voyage is uncertain. It would appear, in any case, that Hezekiah Kelley was not reduced to penury, for he was able to make another venture immediately: it was in partnership with Hezekiah and Jabez Kelley that

Isaac Hull now achieved the shipmaster's goal: he became an owner. Almost as soon as Hull returned to Connecticut, the three men purchased the 62-ton schooner *Beaver*.

The *Beaver* was a single-decked, square-sterned, unadorned vessel; three years old; 57 feet 6 inches long, 17 feet in beam, and 7 feet 4 inches deep in the hold: two-thirds the length and one-third the capacity of the *Minerva*. But she was his. Losing no time, Hull registered her at New London on 1 July, loaded her with forty-two mules and a cargo of barreled meat, butter, lard, herring, and barrel hoops, and cleared for Grenada on 6 July. The *Beaver* made her destination all right, but the French still had rules against trading with the enemy. On 15 November the *Connecticut Gazette* reported tersely: "The schr. Beaver, Hull, of Norwich, from Grenada, is taken and carried to Porto Rico."[18]

By the time that report was published Isaac Hull had returned to Connecticut after enduring several months of distress. Since he was homeward bound when captured, he was probably landed at San Juan sometime in August. Once again the predator was a French privateer. The *Beaver* was seized by the French consul at San Juan even before her formal condemnation, to be used as a cartel, which suggests that she was not looked upon as a very valuable vessel. Her captain, having been robbed of his personal possessions by his captors and, as he later reported, "inhumanely treated," was left penniless in the Spanish port, to find a way home as best he might.

In a letter written not long afterward, Secretary of State Timothy Pickering described the plight of the victims of French hostility:

> The numerous captures of our vessels in the West Indies by the French, and the forlorn and miserable situation in which their crews are turned on shore, without subsistence or clothing, claimed at once the commiseration and aid of the government. . . . The United States brigantine *Sophia* was therefore dispatched in August last to the various French and Spanish ports in the West Indies, where it was probable they might be found, to collect and bring home the sufferers.

Captain William Maley of the *Sophia* located Hull at San Juan and transported him, with eleven other captains and their crews, to the port of Santo Domingo in Hispaniola. Thence Hull obtained a passage down the coast to Les Cayes, where he was again stranded for a time. On this occasion he was succored by some twenty American traders who collected $380 for Hull and two other captains.

At last, on 14 October, Captain Hull boarded the brig *Peggy*, Captain Small commanding, homeward bound to Boston. As if to rub salt in his still smarting wounds, the French privateer *La Parelle* ran the *Peggy* down near Havana. She was sated, however, with her previous day's prize, a brig from New York. Perhaps the *Peggy*, crowded with passengers and short of provisions, was not a tempting catch. The privateer's captain contented himself with forcing three prisoners on board the already overloaded *Peggy* and dismissed her. She made Boston three weeks later.[19]

Isaac Hull was, it would seem, bloodied but unbowed. After less than three months at home, and presumably as soon as the *Beaver*'s insurance could be collected, he and Hezekiah Kelley ventured once again. This time their purchase was the schooner *Favorite*, single-decked, square-sterned, and unadorned. The *Favorite*, built at Hartford in 1793, was beginning to show signs of wear when her new owners looked her over in early February 1798. At 62 tons she was almost the same size as the *Beaver* but slightly shallower and more beamy, measuring 58 feet 3 inches by 18 feet 9 inches by 6 feet 8 inches. She carried a crew of seven.

On 8 February 1798 Hull registered the *Favorite* at New London and declared her cargo for Surinam: thirty-four horses and a hold full of barreled salt meat, fish, lard, beans, and cheeses. It is worth noting that the cargo of a small vessel like the *Favorite* might consist of the ventures of a number of shippers—in this case, the 206 barrels of salt provisions belonged to six individuals or partnerships from such diverse places as Windham, Norwich, and Hampton. This dispersal of cargoes may have been a device for spreading the risk of West Indies shipping.[20]

On this voyage Isaac Hull's downfall was not the French but yellow fever. Returning from Surinam via Martinique, he was forced to go on shore at Saint-Pierre to recover, sending the *Favorite* home. It was late May before he was able to take passage to New London in the schooner *Commerce*, F. Bulkley, captain, and he was not to leave the West Indies without one final encounter with the French. The story that appeared on 13 June in the "Arrivals" column of the *Connecticut Journal* (New Haven) told how the *Commerce* had fared. She left Tortola with a fleet of three hundred English and American vessels under convoy of a British ship of the line and three frigates. On 25 May the American vessels, about thirty in number, parted company, now protected only by the *Pigou*, a Philadelphia Indiaman, and some other armed merchantmen. But the *Pigou* was a fast ship and soon left the others behind. The next day the *Commerce* and a companion, the brig *Sterling*, were boarded by the 18-gun privateer *Mercury*, John LeBrun, captain, one of a group of six large privateers that had sailed from Bordeaux to seek American prizes. LeBrun seized the *Sterling*, which had a rich cargo of rum, but put some prisoners on board the *Commerce* and released her. The story concluded:

The Capt. of the Mercury made particular enquiry after the Pigou; and appeared to have a perfect knowledge of the fleet which sailed from Tortola. He told Capt. B. that he saved his men for more valuable prizes than his vessel. Came passenger in the Commerce, Capt. Isaac Hull. Capt. Hull, Capt. [Thomas] Evans [late commander of the sloop *Mary,* scuttled by the *Mercury*], and other gentlemen passengers speak in terms of warmest praise of the friendly and generous attention they experienced from Capt. Bulkley, while on board his vessel and wish thus publicly to acknowledge his politeness.[21]

Fate had one final blow for Isaac Hull, merchant venturer. When he reached home, presumably still convalescent from the fever, he learned to his dismay that Hezekiah Kelley had failed in his absence. Perhaps the *Favorite,* though she returned safely, had failed to make a "saving voyage," to secure a sufficient profit to redeem her owners' investment. Kelley had sold the schooner on 1 June 1798, but Hull was left with the unhappy prospect of paying her insurance bills.

Three West Indies ventures, three successive losses: It was enough to discourage a more seasoned captain than Isaac Hull. There is ample evidence to suggest that the young man was permanently soured on merchant voyaging. During the years from 1800 to 1812, and again after 1815, when the navy was not very active, a large proportion of the officers took leave of absence for periods of two to three years to make trading voyages, and most of them profited handsomely. Isaac Hull was one of the few who did not make such a venture. He never trod a merchant's quarterdeck after 1798, even though financially he was never more than moderately well off. He spoke of doing so in 1801 and again in 1807, but did not carry through on the idea, not even when he was desperate for enough money to enable him to marry. And he deprecated the ventures of his younger brothers, particularly in the dangerous years after 1810, preferring to see them in New York countinghouses rather than braving the risky fortunes of the sea. His love of the sea he never lost, but after three humiliations he preferred to do his sailing in the navy where he could fight back when attacked. To be made prisoner by a 2-gun schooner! Never again!

The opportunity to leave the merchant service was at hand when Hull reached Derby in mid-June. A letter from the War Department had been awaiting him there for three months. He broke the seal and read that on 9 March, his twenty-fifth birthday, he had been commissioned a lieutenant in the U.S. Navy. His appointment was to the frigate *Constitution,* then outfitting at Boston, and he made haste to join her.[22]

2

Lieutenant Hull

On the same day that Isaac Hull registered the *Beaver* for her fated voyage, Congress undertook to resist French depredations by force. The Act Providing a Naval Armament of 1 July 1797 authorized the president to fit out the three frigates *United States, Constitution,* and *Constellation,* whose construction had begun three years earlier in response to the piratical activities of Algiers. Construction of three other frigates— the *Congress,* the *Chesapeake,* and the *President*—had been suspended on conclusion of an Algerian treaty but would soon be resumed.[1] The captains of these ships had been appointed in 1794 and had been charged with superintending the building of the vessels, but no other officers had yet been chosen. John Barry of Philadelphia, the senior of the trio, a Revolutionary War veteran now in his declining years, commanded the *United States.* The *Constellation* was the command, one might well say the satrapy, of Thomas Truxtun, an officer whose ego was matched only by his remarkable ability. Barry does not seem to have been a strong political partisan, but both he and Truxtun were safely Federalist. Samuel Nicholson, commander of the *Constitution,* was of another stripe. The Nicholsons, a Maryland family, were strongly anti-Federalist. Three Nicholson brothers had been captains in the Continental navy; James, the eldest, ended the war as senior officer of the service. Samuel Nicholson's Revolutionary service had been honorable and successful, though, for reasons now obscure, at the very end of the war he had been relieved of his command, court-martialed, and acquitted. By 1797 the political polarization was such that his appointment to the U.S. Navy would have been impossible; James Nicholson's house in New York had by then become a rendezvous for the partisans of Thomas Jefferson and Aaron Burr. But in 1794 it was still thought proper to make a gesture of conciliation to this powerful family, and since James Nicholson was nearly sixty years old, the honor fell to Samuel, then fifty-one.

The appointment of Samuel Nicholson meant an opportunity to Isaac Hull, for prominent among the small group of anti-Federalists in Boston, where the *Constitution* was being built, was his uncle William

Hull. The younger brother of Joseph Hull had graduated from Yale, studied law at Litchfield, and was admitted to the bar just before he marched to the siege of Boston at the head of Derby's militia company in 1775. After arduous war service that brought him commendation both from General George Washington and from Congress, and promotion to the rank of lieutenant colonel, William Hull married in 1781 and established his law practice in Newton, Massachusetts, his wife's home. There he received young Isaac, and though he failed to make a lawyer of him, it was almost certainly William Hull who fostered his nephew's naval career by persuading Samuel Nicholson to request his appointment to a lieutenancy in the *Constitution*.

Records of the appointment process are fragmentary. The only surviving document relating to Isaac Hull's appointment is a memorandum from Secretary of War James McHenry to President John Adams from late 1797 or early 1798 listing possible appointees to the *Constitution*. Isaac Hull's name is second among the twelve listed (for four vacancies). Presumably these were, at least in part, Nicholson's selections.[2]

It is noteworthy that in an era when political partisanship was the breath of life to most public men, Isaac Hull was never warmly attached to a party. Although his uncle was a prominent Republican, Isaac seems never to have uttered any Republican sentiments; and though most of his later associates among the "best people" of New England were necessarily Federalists, he never delivered himself of any Federalist remarks either. In 1808 he observed to William Bainbridge, "you know the cloth has no politics"; and throughout his life he appears to have adhered to his extraordinary belief that a naval officer should not be a political man.[3]

It is most likely that Hull applied for his appointment before he sailed in the *Beaver*. Congress adjourned on 10 July without receiving any nominations from the president, and when it reconvened in November, soon after Hull's return from captivity, Adams was still not prepared to nominate officers. So Isaac Hull embarked in the *Favorite* and in his absence was named fourth lieutenant of the *Constitution*.

On receiving his orders, Hull lost no time in joining his new ship. Within a week of his return in the *Commerce* he was at Boston, where he offered Captain Nicholson his formal acceptance and was ordered to duty.[4] Although the frigate was nearly ready for sea, his messmates in the wardroom were not all present. Nicholson's choice for first lieutenant, Benjamin Lee, had declined the appointment, and the place had been offered to Edward Preble of the district of Maine, but Preble was in the West Indies and did not return in time for the ship's sailing. Second Lieutenant John Blake Cordis, acting for the time in Preble's place,

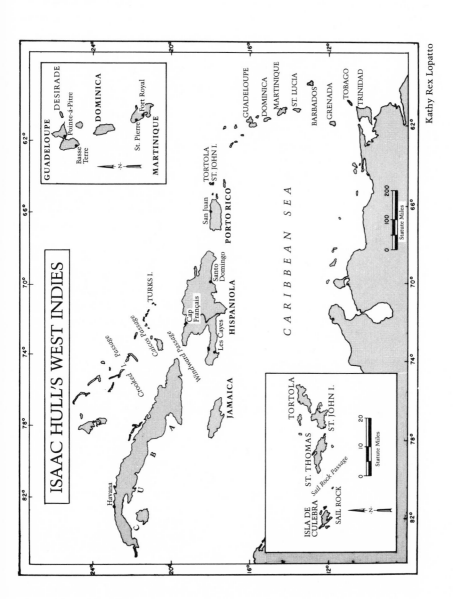

ISAAC HULL'S WEST INDIES

GUADELOUPE
DESIRADE
Pointe-à-Pitre
Basse Terre
DOMINICA
-N-
St. Pierre Fort Royal
MARTINIQUE

GUADELOUPE
DOMINICA
MARTINIQUE
ST. LUCIA
BARBADOS
GRENADA
TOBAGO
TRINIDAD

TORTOLA
ST. JOHN I.

San Juan
PORTO RICO

C A R I B B E A N   S E A

0   100   200
Statute Miles

TURKS I.

Crooked I. Passage
Caicos Passage
Windward Passage

Cap Français
Les Cayes
Santo Domingo
HISPANIOLA

JAMAICA

C U B A

Havana

TORTOLA

ST. THOMAS
ISLA DE CULEBRA
Sail Rock Passage
SAIL ROCK
ST. JOHN I.

-N-

0   10   20
Statute Miles

Kathy Rex Lopatto

1 5

was on shore attending the recruiting rendezvous. Cordis was from nearby Charlestown and had been a merchant officer in the China trade. His career included a voyage around the world as third lieutenant of the famous ship *Columbia.* Third Lieutenant Richard C. Beale was a Quincy neighbor of President Adams. Beale and Hull were the same age and had been merchant shipmasters for about the same length of time.[5] Marine Lieutenant Lemuel Clark, Purser James DeBlois, and Surgeon William Reed completed the mess.

The *Constitution* had been launched, after two abortive attempts, on 21 October 1797, and was now fitting for sea at what seemed to the government a leisurely pace. On 5 May the War Department had ordered Nicholson to "lose no time in completing, equipping and manning her for sea."[6] Within a week the *Constitution*'s rendezvous opened at the Federal Eagle tavern in Fore Street, kept by Mrs. Priscilla Broaders, to recruit 150 able and 95 ordinary seamen for one year's service. Lieutenant Clark was also present to engage 50 marine privates, seven petty officers, and a drummer and a fifer. By the time Isaac Hull joined the ship in mid-June, some 200 seamen had been recruited.[7]

In the week before Hull's arrival the Boston navy agent, Stephen Higginson, had written no fewer than four letters to Secretary of State Pickering in which he delivered himself freely of his opinions of the frigate's officers. Higginson's views are highly colored by his intense federalism. He thought Captain Nicholson

> a rough blustering tar merely, . . . a good seaman probably and . . . no doubt acquainted with many or most parts of his duty so far as relates to practical seamanship; but he wants points much more important as a commander in my view: prudence, judgment and reflection are no traits in his character, nor will he ever improve.[8]

Returning to the subject a few days later, he damned with faint praise:

> Captain N. is not intemperate that I have either seen or heard of; he has exerted himself all he could to man and get out the ship. His defects are more natural than acquired, they consist in want of natural talents rather than vicious habits; he is neither a Gentleman, nor a popular man with the sailors, as some rough men are; but I know of no criminal conduct or neglect, nor such a gross incapacity as would justify perhaps a dismissal from office in the public opinion.[9]

In saying Nicholson was not a "Gentleman," Higginson was really saying he was not a Federalist. He was clearly disappointed that there were no solid grounds for dismissing him. As for the junior officers,

Mr. Cordis, the second lieutenant, is a young man who possesses none of the requisites. He is deficient in every point essential to a good officer. He is said to be intemperate, and he looks like it. The surgeon, Reed, is the opposite of what he ought to be in morals, in politics and in his profession.[10]

There were two officers attached to the ship, however, who had correct political principles:

Mr. Preble, the first lieutenant, . . . is a smart, active, popular man, judicious and well qualified for his station, or for the first command; but I do not believe he will go in the ship when he sees his associates. . . . Mr. Beals [Beale], who is appointed third lieutenant is a smart young man, and will be a good officer.[11]

Higginson failed to comment on Purser James DeBlois, but this perhaps was superfluous, since Timothy Pickering himself had recommended DeBlois for his berth. Finally, on 9 June, Higginson observed darkly:

the more I reflect upon the subject the more I see the necessity of caution in our naval appointments, or else the public ships will become the receptacles, and the public money the support of those only who for want of principle, of capacity, of reputation or of energy are incapable of getting their living in the common pursuits of life. Such is literally and truly the case in the instance referred to; there is not a man appointed to the frigate, except Preble, who does not resort to the Navy from a necessity arising from some of the causes stated. Not one of them can find or has found employment in their respective professions adequate to their support, not even those who have none to provide for but themselves, which indeed is the case with all of these except the captain, I believe.[12]

That these remarks applied to Isaac Hull, late master on three disastrous voyages, was smartingly obvious.

The *Constitution* was in an advanced state of preparation for sea. About the time Isaac Hull entered on board, one of her midshipmen described her situation:

Our ship is now in a respectable state; we have nearly 300 men on board and shall shortly receive our full complement from Providence. A lighter has gone down to the Castle this morning to get our upper guns: we carry sixteen 18-pounders [long guns] on our quarterdeck and forecastle, and fourteen twelves on the spar deck. This you will allow to be very heavy metal. Our petty officers are very good men. Most of them, such as quartermasters, master's mates, gunners, master at arms, etc. are either English or Irish who have sustained the same berths on board British men of war. We have our topsails now bent; shall bend the topgallant sails today and expect to fall down into the road in the course of the week.[13]

On 2 July the frigate, still aswarm with workmen, got under way for the first time and dropped down to King Road.[14] Lieutenants Hull and Beale were fully occupied in stationing the new crew and supervising their work; even Captain Nicholson had to give attention to the boatswain's department. On 7 July the men began to exercise at the guns.[15]

The navy was no longer under direction of the War Department. From the newly appointed secretary of the navy, Benjamin Stoddert, came orders, dated 12 July, for the *Constitution*'s first cruise. For the time being, the frigate was to protect the east coast from Georges Bank to Long Island, that is, to prevent French cruisers from preying on the commerce of the eastern ports. An act of Congress of 10 July authorized the capture of all armed French vessels and the recapture of American ships from the French, but American commanders were cautioned not to retake American ships seized by "any nation at war, with whom WE are at peace," meaning, of course, Great Britain. All such cases would be handled through the courts.[16] Technically, of course, the United States was "at peace" with France—but in reality, the two nations were at war on the high seas.

The *Constitution* was nearly ready for sea when these orders were received, but she still lacked a first lieutenant. Preble had not returned, and the president offered the post to Captain Patrick Fletcher of Boston. But through a clerk's error Nicholson was told that Fletcher, being a late appointee, would have to serve as junior lieutenant. This Fletcher of course declined, and although the mistake was corrected at the Navy Department by 23 July, it was too late. The frigate had sailed.[17]

Late in the afternoon of Sunday, 22 July 1798, the *Constitution*'s crew bent to the capstan bars. Topmen lay out on the yards to loose her new sails to the fresh breeze, and Hercules at her bow began to lift and dip to the ocean swell as she stood down the harbor, bound to sea for the first time. The sun was setting beyond Boston Light as she took her departure—red skies and fair weather. There are worse assignments, after all, than a summer cruise on the New England coast.[18] The breeze freshened through the night; in the predawn chill all hands were called to strike the topgallant yards, light sails, and booms, and to set up the rigging and make all taut. Many of the crew would be sick for the first few days, but the officers remarked that the frigate worked easily and sailed remarkably well.[19]

The next month at sea was ideal for a shakedown cruise. With pleasant weather and few other sail in sight, the *Constitution*'s officers spent most of the time schooling her crew at the great guns and sails, agreeing that "they come on bravely."[20] Twice during the month the *Constitution* called, as instructed, at Newport, Rhode Island. There, on 21 August, Nicholson received orders to change his cruising ground, relieving Commodore Truxtun in protecting the coast southward from Cape Henry, in company with the revenue cutters *Virginia* and *Unanimity*.[21] Cruising to the southward, the *Constitution* began to find more action in the latitude of the Virginia capes. In the afternoon of 31 August she chased a ship that appeared to be armed; for the first time the drum roll called all hands to quarters. Three men resisted and were summarily punished, as the log records: "At 3 p.m. punished three men, viz., Dennis Carney, Jno. Brown and Richard Sullivan (all Irish) with one dozen each on the bare back for making use of mutinous expressions and fighting with the Master at Arms."[22] The chase, however, got away.

On 2 September the *Constitution* fell in with the Havana convoy, sixty-five sail under the protection of two armed merchant ships.[23] The next day she brought to an English privateer sailing in company with an American ship and carrying a number of American captains whose vessels had been captured by the French.[24] On the fourth Cape Hatteras was in sight;[25] next evening off Cape Lookout the ship encountered a heavy gale, a sharp reminder that the equinox was at hand, the season when hurricanes ravaged the Atlantic coast and ships must make for port.[26]

But the *Constitution* did not go into port without a prize. In the early morning of Saturday, 8 September, a ship was seen in the southwest that appeared to be a cruiser. Crowding sail after her and clearing for action, the *Constitution* overhauled the chase at 11:30. American colors were run up, and a shot was fired over the ship to bring her to. She hoisted English colors and fired a gun to leeward but kept on her course. The *Constitution*, continuing to outsail her chase, soon brought the ship close aboard, when the Americans could see that her decks were cleared for action and that the crew were at their guns. The two ships jockeyed about, training their cannon on each other. Nicholson hailed the stranger and received an impertinent retort in broken English from the boatswain. When he then ordered the captain on board the frigate with his papers and was refused, Nicholson grew thoroughly angry and swore that if they gave him any further trouble he would sink them and give them no quarter. This threat brought a boat with the first lieutenant and four men. Nicholson returned the boat filled with his own men and commanded by Lieutenant Beale, who drove the crew from their guns. It was reported that a powder train had been laid to blow up the ship.[27]

After some further delay the boat returned with the captain, George du Petit-Thouars. Both officers wore French uniforms; they told Nicholson they were Royalists and showed him English commissions for privateering against France and Spain. They were bound from Kingston,

Jamaica, to Philadelphia. Their ship was the 400-ton *Niger*, of 24 guns, a handsome coppered ship of cedar built by the Spanish government, captured by the British, and sold at Jamaica three years before.

Nicholson had already convinced himself that the *Niger* was a pirate, with or without official French authorization. Her register and clearance from Jamaica he dismissed as counterfeit. She had no ship's articles, log, or shipping papers. The crew of about seventy-five was a motley collection of French, Spanish, English, Portuguese, Italian, Dutch, and black men. Besides a cargo of sugar and rum, there was a large sum of money on board, and supposedly more hidden under the magazine. The crew seemed very well supplied with money as well, and with trunks of American-looking clothes. Moreover, one of the *Constitution*'s seamen, Martin Rose, recognized the *Niger*'s boatswain as boatswain of a French schooner that had sent his vessel into Guadeloupe seven months earlier.

Nicholson disarmed Captain Petit-Thouars on the *Constitution*'s quarterdeck and ordered him and his officers confined to the wardroom. There they were sympathetically received by the younger officers. Isaac Hull's opinion of this episode is not recorded, but bluster like Nicholson's was not his style. He and his fellows of the wardroom apparently treated their French captives with kindness, twice mentioned in Petit-Thouars's official statement of the affair. No doubt they shared with the rueful Frenchmen the "long splice in the main brace," which the frigate's officers took to celebrate the capture.[28]

Not so Lieutenant Beale, who continued in charge of the prize. On the afternoon of the ninth when the *Niger*'s boat brought him on board the frigate, Petit-Thouars was outraged to see that Beale was using the British ensign as a seat cushion. He remonstrated and was told contemptuously: "English flag, French flag, it is all the same to me; I pay no attention to it." Petit-Thouars then complained to Nicholson, who apparently viewed the Frenchman as a troublemaker. After pouring a torrent of verbal abuse on him, Nicholson had Petit-Thouars and the *Niger*'s officers confined aft with a sentinel guarding them night and day. A Baltimore merchant named Garts, a passenger in the *Niger*, protested Nicholson's treatment of the vessel, but another passenger, named Jackson, paymaster of the British Fifty-eighth Regiment, added to Nicholson's apprehension by intimating that the *Niger*'s officers had attempted to poison his wine.

Although he had removed the *Niger*'s entire crew, Nicholson affected to believe that the prize could not safely be sent into port alone and determined to accompany her. The *Constitution* and her prize accordingly shaped course for the Chesapeake, anchoring off Norfolk on 12

September.[29] Nicholson's report of the capture reached Secretary Stoddert at Trenton, where the government had fled for the duration of the fever season, ten days later. The secretary was much more inclined to believe Petit-Thouars's story than was Nicholson. He relayed the news, and his analysis of the incident, to President Adams at Quincy, Massachusetts, telling him that he believed the ship's officers to be French Royalists and that the suspicious circumstances mentioned by Nicholson could be accounted for in other ways than by supposing the *Niger* to be a French privateer. The train of gunpowder, for example, might be a precaution against falling into the hands of French revolutionists, and the motley character of the crew could be explained by the British refusal to allow Britons to be shipped at Jamaica in foreign vessels. Stoddert thought it strange that Nicholson was able to offer no direct evidence of the *Niger*'s engaging in privateering against Americans and also that he had failed to capitalize fully on the disaffection of passengers like Jackson. He concluded ruefully: "I fear the real truth has not been so much the object of his inquiries as might have been wished in an officer of his high rank in the American Navy."[30]

Soon after reaching Norfolk the *Constitution* had acquired a first officer, Lieutenant Charles C. Russell. With Russell to relieve him of the immediate duties of his command, Nicholson assiduously pursued the condemnation of his prize at Norfolk and at Williamsburg. In his absence, however, tragedy struck the frigate. It was the fever season everywhere on the East Coast, and when the ship had lain at Norfolk little more than a week the dreaded fever appeared on board. Among its first victims were Surgeon Reed and sixteen-year-old Midshipman Samuel Nicholson, Jr.[31]

Captain Nicholson returned on 24 September from Williamsburg where he had confided the *Niger* case to Littleton W. Tazewell, Jr., barely in time to bid farewell to his dying son. There is no doubt of the genuineness of the old man's grief, but his expression of it in an official letter, sandwiched between two paragraphs on the subject of the *Niger*, occasioned snide comments from Timothy Pickering: "Indeed the eagerness of Captain Nicholson to procure a condemnation savoured of rapacity. And in the very letter in which he informed of the death of his son (the consequence of this unfortunate capture) his thoughts seemed wholly engrossed with his prize and the means of ensuring, if possible, a condemnation."[32]

Secretary Stoddert was deeply disturbed by the outbreak of fever on board the frigate. He wrote Nicholson a sharp letter ordering him to land his sick and proceed to sea immediately.[33] Nicholson was willing enough to go out but delayed his departure till the equinox was safely past, for fear his consort, the revenue cutter *Virginia*, could not endure a severe gale.[34] Then he met a succession of adverse winds, which kept him in port for another week.[35]

In the afternoon of Monday, 1 October, while the *Constitution* lay at anchor in Hampton Roads, a merchant vessel was observed at anchor with her ensign hoisted union down—the signal of distress. Lieutenant Hull took the frigate's yawl to the stranger to investigate and was told there was a mutiny on board: the ship's crew refused to do their duty. After returning to the *Constitution* for the master at arms, Hull boarded the merchant and had four men put in irons. So ended his brief adventure and rare appearance in the frigate's log.

The *Constitution* sailed, with the cutter *Virginia* in company, on Sunday, 7 October, and ran to the southward. Near Charleston she met a convoy from Havana under charge of the sloop-of-war *Baltimore*, Captain Isaac Phillips commanding. Nicholson immediately attached the *Baltimore* to his command, to the chagrin of Commodore Thomas Truxtun, who arrived in Norfolk at the end of the month to find that one of the ships of his squadron had been purloined. The three ships called off Charleston on the nineteenth and remained for six days. The *Constitution* sailed again on the twenty-fourth with the *Baltimore*, bound to Havana at the request of the Charleston merchants with a new convoy of eleven vessels.[36]

In the Adams administration the rumblings against Nicholson continued. Secretary Stoddert, although not an intense party man, observed to President Adams, "I fear this gentleman will fulfill all the predictions of Boston concerning him."[37] Secretary of State Pickering was determined to make the Boston prophecies self-fulfilling by using the *Niger* case as a political weapon. On 22 October he wrote to Thomas Nelson, United States attorney for the trial:

> I expect it will appear on the trial that the capture was wholly unwarrantable. . . . Nevertheless, I have thought it expedient that the trial should be had, in order not only to prevent any complaint on the part of Captain Nicholson and ship's company, . . . but by clearly ascertaining the facts, to enable the President to form a correct opinion of Captain Nicholson's conduct.[38]

Nelson, who must appear at the trial on behalf of Nicholson and his officers, thus had his orders: the *Niger* was to be released, and Nicholson was to be made to look as bad as possible so that President Adams might be brought to favor his ouster. Early in November the *Niger* was released by the court, but to Pickering's chagrin the judge refused damages, for the ship's circumstances were thought to be suspicious enough to warrant her detention.[39]

Soon after the decision in the *Niger* case, the *Constitution* came to anchor in Nantasket Roads. Her return to Boston was caused by a sprung bowsprit, which occurred on 29 October and deprived her of the use of her headsails. Secretary Stoddert was pleased to find the *Constitution* at Boston, even if by accident. She was ordered to fit for a six-month cruise, a business that engaged her officers and men for the next six weeks. Meanwhile, a number of smoldering feuds broke into the open. Most of the trouble seemed to revolve around Second Lieutenant John B. Cordis. On Friday, 22 November, two men were arrested and put in irons. Master's Mate Ward was charged with "speaking seditious words tending to stir up the minds of the people,"[40] and Boatswain Connell was charged "for abusing Mr. Cordis, Second Lieutenant, for inspecting the storeroom." Midshipman James Pitts was arrested the same day for "unofficerlike conduct" and, on 1 December, was dismissed from the ship by Nicholson. At about the same time Cordis gave Seaman John Hunt twenty-four blows with a rope's end (twice the legal number) for real or supposed desertion.[41]

Midshipman Pitts was reinstated on 22 December. Two days later he and Seaman Hunt swore affidavits against Cordis. Pitts alleged that he had frequently seen Cordis drunk and sleeping on his watch, and he further swore that Lieutenant Hull, who had the watch before Cordis, had at least once had to send below for him, and that Lieutenant Russell had waked Cordis when the latter was sleeping on watch. These officers and others gave contrary affidavits, but under the circumstances Captain Nicholson had little choice but to arrest Cordis for trial. On 27 December he ordered the luckless lieutenant on shore to wait for the ship's return. First Lieutenant Russell and marine Second Lieutenant William Amory left the ship at the same time because Captain Nicholson had refused to deliver their commissions to them, an act for which he was roundly censured by his superiors. Thus, when the frigate weighed anchor once again on 28 December 1798, she had only two lieutenants—Richard C. Beale, acting as first, and Isaac Hull, now acting as second.

None of this was calculated to endear Captain Nicholson to the Navy Department. Stoddert had confided to Higginson as early as 3 December that he had hoped the offensive captain might be transferred on shore for the winter.[42] This wholesale dismissal of officers was a further irritant. The *Constitution* was now on her way to join Commodore John Barry at Dominica, and Stoddert wrote Barry to transfer Lieutenant Robert Hamilton to the frigate as third officer, adding:

I am sorry to observe that Captain Nicholson has excited great clamour against him, by his arbitrary conduct towards some officers he left behind. I hope, however, he will not justify by his conduct under your command, the predictions of his enemies, but that he will conduct himself with prudence and propriety and pay strict attention to your orders. Should he act in a different manner, you will know what to do with him.[43]

If Nicholson's head was about to roll, the position of his remaining junior lieutenant was none too secure. Higginson was on the warpath again, and this time the direct object of his wrath was William Hull. As commander of the Third Division of Massachusetts militia, Hull had offered President Adams the services of his unit in the French emergency. To Higginson and other Massachusetts Federalists like Francis Dana, this could only be a Jacobin plot to undermine the defenses of the United States. "It is a well known fact," wrote Higginson,

> that Hull and many of his officers are of the most inveterate grade of Jacobins in this state, perhaps in the United States. . . . Nor is there any doubt of there being deep laid schemes to defeat the measures of Government, by assuming the garb of federalism, and enlisting into the public service, with a view to acquire the confidence of the President and under his name and sanction to increase their influence with the people, and to have more and better means to poison their minds and excite opposition to the Executive. . . . [I]t will be a sad thing to have the military commands in the hands of men disposed to overturn rather than support our government. It is here believed to be an essential part of the Jacobin System to insert their devoted agents into the military as well as the civil department, and it was at once suspected that such was the design of General Hull in his addresses and tenders of service, etc., from the known characters of the men and the whole course of their conduct.[44]

Could the young infiltrator in the *Constitution* be long overlooked?

Meanwhile, the *Constitution* ran to the southward in such heavy weather that not until 2 January 1799 could her crew be mustered for the formal reading of the Articles of War. Midshipman Philip Jarvis and gunner Joseph Torrey were delegated to act as lieutenants, while Seaman James Moore moved up to the gunner's berth. On 11 January the ship crossed the Tropic of Cancer and hove to while King Neptune came on board to perform "the usual ceremonies, viz. blacking, ducking, shaving, etc." for neophyte sailors, "which among 400 people, produced a set of devils equal to any ever seen."[45]

On 15 January, near Guadeloupe, the *Constitution* had her grandest opportunity of the war. About one in the afternoon two sail were discovered in the northwest; giving chase, by four the Americans were able to ascertain that one was a warship. She was unable to answer the private signals and crowded sail to escape; the *Constitution* cleared for action and maintained pursuit. By eight the stranger was only five or six miles distant, but the weather had turned squally; the *Constitution* had to secure the great guns on her lee side and close the gun ports. Grimly she kept her way, but she was deep with sea stores, and her foremast, sprung during the gale, would not carry heavy canvas; about eleven-thirty the chase disappeared. Less than an hour later a sail again loomed up in the northwest. Thinking that they had stumbled on their quarry, the Americans fired several guns at the ship and brought her to. By this time it was evident that she was not the warship; the boarding party learned that she was the British ship *Spencer*, prize to the frigate *Insurgente*. It was the *Insurgente* that the *Constitution* had pursued. Three weeks later that frigate would fall prize to Thomas Truxtun and the *Constellation* in the most brilliant action of the war. It was bad luck for the *Constitution* and her hapless captain.[46]

Nicholson sent a prize crew on board the *Spencer* to secure her but left them there only overnight. He was still smarting from the accusation that he had been too hasty in capturing the *Niger* and was not inclined to take chances again. There was nothing in his instructions about recapturing the vessels of other nations; nor did the *Spencer* have sufficient weapons on board, he thought, to be considered a French armed vessel. If the administration wanted to be literal-minded, he could play that game as well. At nine o'clock the following morning he released the *Spencer* to her French prize crew.[47]

Of course, this action did not please the administration at all. As soon as he learned of it the secretary of the navy issued a circular to all naval commanders clarifying their responsibilities in this regard and making what amounted to a public reprimand of Nicholson. He explained, "A vessel captured by the cruisers of France must be considered as sailing under the authority of France. . . . To justify a recapture nothing is necessary but that the vessel be provided with such means of annoyance as will render her dangerous to an unarmed American vessel in pursuit of lawful commerce."[48]

On 19 January the *Constitution* joined Commodore Barry's squadron off Dominica, but on the twenty-fourth she was forced to go into Prince Rupert Bay to repair her damaged masts. A week later she sailed and commenced two and a half months of rather uneventful cruising near Dominica and Désirade. It was a frustrating business, for most of the French cruisers in the area were small vessels that could, when pursued, run into shallow water out of reach of the big American frigates. Two French frigates lying at Point-à-Pitre, Guadeloupe, refused to be lured out. But there were some diversions. It was evidently on 2 March that the famous race took place between the *Constitution* and a British frigate. James Fenimore Cooper, writing in 1853 and evidently drawing on recollections of the *Constitution*'s officers, probably including Isaac Hull, places this match at a later time, when the frigate was commanded by Silas Talbot, but there is no evidence in the log of such a contest during that period. James Pitts's journal for 2–3 March 1799, however, states:

> spoke the British frigate *Santa Margaretta* of 36 guns Captain Parker. Sent an officer on board for the night private signals. . . . At 9 a.m. brought to for the captain of the *Santa Margaretta* to pay his respects to Captain Nicholson. . . . [A]t 3 p.m. parted company with the *Santa Margaretta*. Captain Parker after sailing in company 16 hours and using every method to outsail us, being sensible of inability tacked to the Northward and shortened sail.[49]

Cooper's account is a good deal more dramatic:

> Just as the lower limb of the sun rose clear of the waves, each fired a gun, and made sail on a bowline. Throughout the whole of that day, did these two gallant ships continue turning to windward, on tacks of a few leagues in length, and endeavoring to avail themselves of every advantage which skill could confer on seamen. [Isaac] Hull sailed the Constitution on this interesting occasion, and the admirable manner in which he did it, was long the subject of eulogy. All hands were kept on deck all day, and there were tacks in which the people were made to place themselves to windward, in order to keep the vessel as near upright as possible, so as to hold a better wind.
>
> Just as the sun dipped, in the evening, the Constitution fired a gun, as did her competitor. At that moment the English frigate was precisely hull down dead to leeward; so much having Old Ironsides, or young Ironsides, as she was then, gained in the race, which lasted about eleven hours! The manner in which the Constitution eat her competitor out of the wind, was not the least striking feature of this trial, and it must in a great degree be ascribed to Hull, whose dexterity in handling a craft under her canvas, was ever remarkable. In this particular, he was perhaps one of the most skillful seamen of his time, as he was also for coolness in moments of hazard.[50]

Some of Cooper's details do not square with the log, but this is to be expected of stories told half a century after the fact. Alas for the fame of Isaac Hull, he was only second lieutenant of the frigate when the actual race occurred and cannot be credited with the victory. That he was a consummate seaman was later proverbial in the navy, and the fact that the story attached itself to him is evidence of the extent to which he was considered the navy's master of sailing.

On 15 March, Secretary Stoddert wrote Commodore Barry to detach the *Constitution* to defend the East Coast. Barry decided independently about the same time that he would return to the United States in mid-April with the *Constitution* and his own frigate, the *United States*.[51]

The secretary's stated reason for ordering the *Constitution* to Boston was not the real one, as he revealed in a letter to Stephen Higginson. He was sending her in, he wrote, so that Nicholson could be replaced as her commander, and he hoped the change could be made expeditiously, so that the frigate could be of service again before the year was out. The means and motive to be stated for Nicholson's removal remained a problem:

> He might be arrested for his conduct in relation to the ship *Niger*, but that ought to have been done sooner. Besides, I wish not to injure his family. If he could be brought to ask leave of absence for a month or two another captain would be appointed to the ship. . . . I have no acquaintance with any particular friend of his, through whose means this might be brought about. Can you do me [the] favor to manage it for me? [52]

The *Constitution* ended her West Indies cruise with the capture of two small prizes. On 27 March she retook the New Haven schooner *Neutrality* and sent her into Martinique.[53] On the morning of 2 April another strange sail was sighted, and a chase commenced that lasted thirty-two hours; during the latter hours of the chase the *Constitution's* men were at the fire engines, pumping up water to wet the sails and give the frigate extra speed. At 5:00 P.M. on 3 April the Americans boarded their prize, the British packet *Carteret* from Falmouth, which had fallen prey to a French privateer a week previously. Lieutenant Hull was sent on board with a warrant officer and eleven men to navigate the *Carteret* into Saint-Pierre—no great task, as the *Constitution* took the packet, which had lost her main topmast, in tow. On the morning of the fifth Hull anchored his prize at Saint-Pierre and delivered her to John Gay, a local merchant who would act as prize agent for the *Constitution's* captures. In the evening Hull and his men—less three deserters—returned on board the frigate, which proceeded to rejoin the squadron.[54]

The *United States*, the *Constitution*, and the brig *Eagle* sailed for home on 17 April, shepherding a convoy of thirty to forty American merchantmen. The *Constitution* anchored at Boston on the evening of 14 May, not without beating through another tempest off Cape Cod, which once again sprung the shaky foremast.[55]

By this time Samuel Nicholson's fate had been decided. On 25 February an act had passed Congress authorizing the building of six 74-gun ships for the navy. Nicholson was to be given the task of superintending the construction of one of these ships at Boston. This was, of course, a pretext for getting the old man on shore, as Stoddert candidly admitted in proposing the idea to President Adams.[56] The president agreed to the arrangement,[57] and since Stoddert was anxious to get the frigate back in service as soon as possible, Nicholson found himself hustled on shore within two weeks of his arrival. By 5 June the *Constitution* was under the command of Silas Talbot.

3

Saint-Domingue

The Quasi-War with France was, and remained, frustrating for all concerned. The commercial concerns that provoked it, and the bulk of the action, were confined to the Caribbean and to the trade routes leading from that sea to the North American coast. But the United States Navy, partly made up of new ships built to be the biggest and best of their class, partly scraped together out of whatever came to hand, was ill adapted to its assigned task. Most of the damage to American commerce was being done by small privateers, like the 2-gun schooner that had captured Hull's *Minerva*, and chasing them with frigates was like fighting jungle-based guerrillas with tanks. The little vessels simply disappeared into tiny harbors or hugged the shore where big ships dared not approach, then slipped out at night to seize more American merchantmen.

The naval officer corps was also ill fitted to its task. It was headed by a group of Revolutionary veterans, none of them terribly imaginative except for the peppery Thomas Truxtun, and most of them afflicted with the lethargy and timidity of advancing age. Below these in rank chafed a large group of eager young officers, whose only chance for glory was in actions in small vessels. Those assigned to such commands often did well; many others, unless—like Isaac Hull or Charles Stewart—they were made of exceptional stuff, lapsed into routine, took to drink, or resigned.

Secretary of the Navy Stoddert was perplexed in the face of this situation. He had some ideas about why the enormous expense of the navy was producing so little action, and he hoped to remedy the situation. Replacing Samuel Nicholson was a first step. Since he did not trust Nicholson, Stoddert had kept him under the command of Commodore John Barry, and this made the *Constitution* virtually useless, for Barry had most of the fleet crowded into one area, doing nothing but desultory blockade and convoy. If he could get a reliable commander into the frigate, Stoddert could create a separate squadron to operate off Hispaniola, while Barry or someone else cruised the smaller islands. He hoped that he had found the right man in Silas Talbot.

The *Constitution*'s new commander was a tall, active man of forty-eight. Silas Talbot, born in Massachusetts, had spent the greater part of his adult life in Rhode Island and New York, most recently as a gentleman farmer in Fulton County. He had been an officer of the Continental army but had seen more service afloat than ashore, winning successive promotions to major and lieutenant colonel for his daring exploits in defense of the coast. In 1779 he was commissioned in the Continental navy as well, but, failing to secure a command that suited him, he turned to privateering. He was shortly captured; confined in the prison hulk *Jersey*; and then shipped to an English prison, from which he was released in 1781. He had served a year in the New York Assembly and was congressman from his district for the 1793–95 term. Talbot was a man of dignity, courage, property, and proper Federalist politics.

He brought with him, however, a personal controversy that would shadow his naval service and eventually lead to his resignation. When the federal navy was reborn in 1794, in response to the Algerian depredations, six captains were appointed to command the six projected frigates. Talbot was third on the list and took charge of the *President* at New York. But when work was suspended on three of the ships in 1796, there was no employment for their commanders until the outbreak of hostilities in 1798. The question then arose: Had the captains' commissions ceased to exist with the cancellation of their ships? To be on the safe side, President Adams reappointed Talbot and Richard Dale in May 1798, but this placed them junior to the now third-ranking Thomas Truxtun. Dale was apparently acquiescent, but Talbot would not serve under Truxtun, and Truxtun would not serve under Talbot. Politicians in and out of government wrestled with the matter for three years. Secretary of the Navy Stoddert inclined to support Truxtun's claims; President Adams favored Talbot's. When the president decided for Talbot in July 1799, Truxtun resigned, but he was coaxed back into the service in October. Finally, in September 1801, Talbot quit the navy for good.[1]

If Talbot did not have troubles enough of his own, he could occupy himself with the quarrels of his juniors. As a result of Nicholson's high-handed actions, the *Constitution* was sadly short of officers. On 21 May the frigate's midshipmen wrote to the secretary, protesting their treatment at the hands of "those who are not authorized by the executive of our country, whom we cannot respect as equal in point of education or knowledge of naval tactics, and whose ignorance exposes them to the ridicule of the ship's company."[2] Their reference is evidently to Midshipman Jarvis and gunner Torrey, elevated to lieutenancies by Nicholson on the last cruise. Stoddert referred the matter to Talbot, observing:

The lieutenants of that ship, at least some of them, I fear, are not very worthy of their appointments. I wish it were possible for you to discriminate and by some means get clear of those who are not fit to be officers, before you sail, and get good men in their places. This, perhaps, will not be in your power until you have been in service with them. But . . . there always has been great uneasiness among the officers of the *Constitution.*[3]

Talbot, on his arrival in Boston, conferred with President Adams, with Navy Agent Higginson, and with John Coffin Jones, chairman of the committee for fitting out the frigate *Boston,* a gift of the city to the United States. They must have determined that the best interests of the *Constitution* would be served by the removal of controversial officers. Russell and Cordis were already on shore; Jarvis and Torrey would be removed as well, and so would Richard Beale. The reasons for Beale's transfer are unstated; apparently he was the subject of unfriendly gossip, perhaps resulting from his behavior in the *Niger* affair. Stoddert remarked to Adams, when recommending the change, that "Lieutenant Beale is said to be a young man, who promises well, but is too young and inexperienced to act as first lieutenant on board of such a ship."[4] But he wrote Talbot on the same day, apparently in response to Talbot's inquiry, "There are not lieutenants now in the country senior to Lieutenant Hull; he must therefore be the first."[5] Hull and Beale were, in fact, almost identical in age and experience. It seems that, on brief acquaintance, Lieutenant Hull had impressed his new commander and Lieutenant Beale had not.

President Adams was not happy about all this. Beale was the son of a neighbor, and Hull was, after all, politically unsound. The reasons Stoddert had assigned for removing Beale did not impress him:

If Beale is removed Hull who is a younger man will be first lieutenant and although I have a very good opinion of him, I see not why Beale should be removed to make way for him. If we could get [Edward] Preble or some other able captain to accept the place of second captain, a practice common in the English navy, I should think it would be better to leave Beale, Hull, Hamilton and Torrey in the order they hold as lieutenants.

Besides, the president's son Charles had told him that Talbot, "though an excellent brave man is not a regular bred sailor, and it is therefore necessary his second should be a perfect seaman."[6] There was serious doubt whether young Mr. Hull could handle the job.

Stoddert did not think a second captain could be allowed, but apparently at this time thought of remedying the lack of a senior lieutenant by having Talbot's son, Lieutenant Commandant Cyrus Talbot, act as his second in command. Cyrus Talbot was ordered to that post on 18 June.[7] But the secretary had doubts that the arrangement would prove amicable: "I have said to Captain Talbot that if he found it would excite no heartburnings, I should be pleased if he took this young gentleman on board, to act as second in command. The connection may create difficulty, not to be overcome."[8] Cyrus Talbot went to Boston, but evidently his father was satisfied with the capability of Lieutenant Hull, for Cyrus did not join the frigate. In the end, John Adams's Puritan conscience scuttled Lieutenant Beale. The harried president wrote on 8 July:

> The Constitution employs my thoughts by day and my dreams by night. Captain Talbot has written to you in his letter of the 7th of June, which I return, his candid and impartial opinions, according to the information he received. But Beale was absent by the advice of his physicians and Hull was present. I mean no insinuation by this against Mr. Hull, whose character is in my mind fair, and his conduct irreproachable. No lieutenant in the service stands fairer in my mind. But I see no reason for discouraging Beale, by turning him out of the ship, for I believe him to be equal to Hull in every respect, even in age. I believe Beale to have had great injustice done him by little passions and a miserable caprice, which I will not explain at present, because I shall probably, though not certainly, consent to his removal, more because he and his father, grandfather and great grandfather have been my neighbors, and to avoid suspicion of partiality, for that cause, than for any other reason.[9]

Isaac Hull, at twenty-six, was now the *Constitution's* first lieutenant. Second was Robert W. Hamilton, who had joined the ship in the West Indies. Filling the other two places posed a problem. Stoddert suggested two candidates, Peleg Tallman of Maine, and Joseph Doble, both of whom had good reports from Boston.[10] Talbot made his own inquiries about these two and concluded they would definitely not do. Tallman was said to have a foul disposition and had never ranked higher than midshipman during the Revolutionary War, and Doble was described as "dissipated."[11] The choice eventually fell to Isaac Collins, who became third lieutenant, and to Edward Boss, of Rhode Island, who became fourth. Boss, who had served at sea throughout the Revolution, was considerably older than the other lieutenants. He brought along his son, Edward, Jr., who entered as acting midshipman.[12]

One more piece of unfinished business remained before the matter of the officers could be laid to rest: John Blake Cordis had to be tried on the charges brought against him by Samuel Nicholson before the last cruise. The trial testimony is suggestive of the polarization within the ship under Nicholson. The captain's charges were supported by only four witnesses: Seaman John Hunt, the reputed victim of Cordis's cruelty; Midshipman James Pitts; and Acting Lieutenants Jarvis and Torrey. Hunt had since left the ship without permission but had not been charged with desertion. Jarvis and Torrey owed their elevation in rank to Nicholson. And Pitts had himself been arrested in November 1798 and was then reinstated and returned on board with Nicholson on the day of Cordis's arrest. No other member of the ship's company could be found to testify to the charges; it appeared that Cordis had given Hunt a dozen strokes with a rope's end in lieu of a formal flogging, at the direction of First Lieutenant Russell, and that Cordis perhaps drank "more than some, and less than others." He was acquitted and was subsequently ordered to the *Congress* but remained under a cloud in official opinion. Midshipman Pitts had already made a bad impression on Captain Talbot. He was persuaded to resign early in July, and the president "requested" Talbot to accept his resignation "so that the midshipmen will now be according to his mind."[13]

Meanwhile, preparations were going forward for getting the *Constitution* to sea once more. The secretary had hoped to send her out again by 15 June, but the combination of a change of command and the need to recruit a new crew proved too much for a speedy refit. Until Talbot took command, most of the responsibility for the ship fell to Isaac Hull. Almost as soon as the frigate made Boston in mid-May, and even before she reached her anchorage at King Road, Captain Nicholson and Lieutenant Beale went on shore, leaving Hull in charge of stripping the ship. Two weeks later Nicholson returned, and Hull went to Boston to organize the recruiting effort. He established his headquarters again at Mrs. Priscilla Broaders's Federal Eagle tavern, with William Hammond, fifer, and William Higgins, drummer, to play a siren song to wandering sailors and "to indulge and humour the Johns in a farewell frolic," as well as with a boat's crew to take the enlistees off to the ship. Bartholomew Broaders served up punch to the recruits. Business was brisk. By the middle of the month Hull had enrolled 113 men. There was always danger that these men would take their advance pay and abscond; Hull implored Talbot "that they may be kept on board as much as possible."[14] He had the assistance of several midshipmen in recruiting, but none was so valuable as John Delouisy, who knew the seamen and "the houses that they visit"; Delouisy was an asset both in drumming up business and in ferreting out deserters.

Desertion was, despite all precautions, a continuing problem. The ship could not be readied for sea without a constant procession of boats going on shore to fetch provisions and stores, fill water casks, and perform other services. Each of these occasions was a chance for a sailor with money in his pocket to slip away. Every man recruited had a "surety" who gave bond for him, and these bondsmen were understandably distressed when they saw their men on the streets. If a man escaped, the surety must either deliver him or forfeit the bond. The recruiting officer, however, wanted the man more than the money and so had a particular interest in catching the pesky seamen. Chubby young Mr. Hull, pursuing his errant men through the steamy Boston streets in early summer, found little time or energy for Boston social life. "I have been on the run since five o'clock," he reported on 2 July. "I think [the men sent in today's boat] meant to be off and I hope you will secure them. . . . I hope Mr. Haraden [the *Constitution*'s sailing master] will not let men come [on shore] who cannot be trusted as I hear it is his doings."[15]

These letters sent from the recruiting rendezvous show that Hull had already developed a warm working relationship with Silas Talbot. On 20 June, for example, Hull wrote: "I am very sorry that we are so unfortunate in our officers being sick. I think you must have a hard task on board, and wish it was in my power to come on board to duty, but fear I shall have a hard time in getting our men on board."[16] After mid-June the pace of recruiting, but not of deserting, slackened. Landsmen were plentiful, but qualified seamen were scarce. A group of recruits arriving from Providence included three blacks, and Hull observed that more such could be had at Boston, some of them seamen, if Talbot would authorize recruiting them. Many captains refused to receive black sailors, but being under pressure to get the frigate to sea, Talbot acquiesced.[17] One day Lieutenant Hull caught a deserter, Israel Southwork, who had been missing for thirteen months! But Southwork was lame, and when his wife produced a substitute, John Wilson, paying thirty dollars for his expenses, the *Constitution*'s officers were happy to make the exchange.[18]

By 15 July the roll was nearly full. Hull wound up his affairs at Mrs. Broaders's, leaving a list of deserters still to be apprehended, and returned on board the *Constitution*, which had dropped down to the outer harbor, four miles from the city.[19] Most of the provisions and stores for the cruise were on board, but the ship was still being supplied with fresh food from Boston for daily use. This "fresh" food was sometimes less than that: in the late afternoon of 19 July, Lieutenant Hull entered the captain's cabin to report that a load of beef just received was crawling with maggots. Talbot's orders were to have the daily beef killed less than twenty-four hours before it was served to the crew, but this ox had been slain on Thursday morning and delivered Friday afternoon—much too long a time lag in July. The meat was returned to the protesting suppliers, but Talbot remarked grimly: "On the whole it may be best not to send any more on board for the present. Let us make a cruise and when we return we shall be less delicate perhaps and of course more easily pleased. For the present we will subsist on salt provisions in full hope that every hour will provide us with a fair wind."[20] Three days later those hopes were realized. In the late forenoon of Tuesday, 23 July, the *Constitution* passed Boston Light once more.

Since the *Constitution* had been so long delayed in getting to sea, Secretary Stoddert had meditated a plan for sending her and the *United States* to raid the coast of France until the end of the hurricane season. But events in the West Indies forced him to scrap this foolhardy plan. As a result of the revolution in Hispaniola that had liberated the western half of the island from direct French control, the United States had accepted an offer from Toussaint-Louverture, the new ruler of Saint-Domingue (present-day Haiti), to reopen some of the island ports to American shipping. Toussaint had agreed to exclude French privateers from his ports and to protect American commerce. In return, an American presidential proclamation of 26 June permitted American vessels to trade with points between Montecristi and Petit Gonave, with Cap Français and Port Républicain (Port-au-Prince) designated as ports of entry. The rest of the former French ports, on the south and west coasts, remained closed because of the continuing conflict between Toussaint and the mulatto General André Rigaud, who held the southwestern peninsula. The effect of this regulation was to permit American vessels to carry food and also cannon, guns, powder, and other war materials, to Toussaint, while interdicting them to Rigaud.

The situation now demanded a strong American naval presence off Saint-Domingue, to protect the American vessels bound to and from the open ports from French privateers, from Rigaud's forces, and from other freebooters, and to prevent American traders from engaging in illicit trade with Rigaud. As it turned out, the American warships soon had a third assignment: to assist Toussaint in mopping up his rival. Active American involvement in the civil war in Saint-Domingue was not yet contemplated in Philadelphia, but it had occurred to Dr. Edward Stevens, American consul for Saint-Domingue and architect of the treaty with Toussaint: "if Toussaint should prove unsuccessful all the arrangements we have made respecting commerce must fall to the ground. The most solemn treaty would have little weight with a man of Rigaud's capricious and tyrannical temper. This circumstance points out the absolute necessity of supporting Toussaint by every legal measure."[21]

When the *Constitution* sailed on 23 July, the nature of her cruise was not resolved, so she was ordered to call at Hampton Roads for the new bowsprit she needed, there to receive further instructions.[22] The frigate anchored in Lynnhaven Bay at 7:00 P.M. on 14 August. Within the hour Lieutenant Hull was on his way to Norfolk, where his weary rowers landed him at 5:00 A.M. He went immediately to William Pennock, the navy agent, who promised to have the needed spars ready in forty-eight hours. Water and stores were also short; the *Constitution's* officers had condemned and discarded 155 pounds of bread and 80 pounds of cheese on the voyage from Boston, and the *Constitution* had been an unconscionable twenty-two days on that passage because of head winds.[23] The agent thought the provisions could not be furnished unless the ship were moved nearer to town, but this would mean further delay, and Talbot would have none of it: "I will not be delayed whether I receive anything or not. Let me therefore repeat that the spars for the yards may be brought whether finished or not, as we can illy go without them, for I now learn that the main topsail yard now aloft is also sprung, but that Mr. Haraden means to keep it a secret from me."[24]

This was a far cry from the dilatory Nicholson. Although his last remark suggests friction between Talbot and his officious sailing master, the *Constitution* was in general a much happier ship than she had been. The reports of Captain Daniel Carmick, commanding the ship's marines, show what a dramatic transformation had occurred under the new regime. On joining the ship early in July he wrote:

> I think it is not possible to produce such another shabby set of animals in this world. . . . The Marines on board the Constitution do not know how to hold a firelock. . . . Captain [Lemuel] Clark says Nicholson would not let him drill the men on board. . . . These men have been abused in a most cruel manner. . . . I shall bid adieu to the Marine Corps if these men go in the ship; it will be impossible to make them respectable.[25]

But by mid-August things were looking up:

> I have got the Marines on board this ship in a fair way of becoming respectable. I permit them to do no kind of work that will tar their clothes; the officers of the ship do not interfere with my men, and had they been clean when they came on board they would have been decent for some time yet. . . . At present I am perfectly contented and very pleased with the captain and all the officers.[26]

Midshipman John Roche affirmed that "a greater degree of satisfaction prevails than I have ever witnessed on board the ship."[27]

Unfortunately for Talbot's efforts to get to sea promptly, the *Constitution* lay windbound in Lynnhaven Bay until the evening of 25 August. The officers were doubly anxious to get out, as French frigates were reported in the West Indies; and although they doubted the truth of the report, they did not like to seem idle when the foe was at hand. Two sergeants of marines deserted, much to the astonishment of Captain Carmick, who thought them the last men who might be expected to run. The search for them was unsuccessful but turned up two deserting seamen who received a dozen lashes each. Carmick thought this much too lenient: "could I have had my will of them I should have given them five dozen." He also commented ironically on Truxtun's resignation: "I am sorry to hear of the resignation of Captain Truxtun but see in to-day's paper he will act as his own trumpeter."[28] By the next day the frigate was under way, bound for a short cruise off Cayenne and then, when the hurricanes were safely past, to take station off Cap Français.[29]

Isaac Hull was now executive officer of one of his navy's largest vessels. As such, he was primarily responsible for the ship's day-to-day routine, the more so as Talbot was a squadron commander and must give his attention to the overall management of the several vessels under his command. It was Lieutenant Hull's responsibility to set the watches and station the crew. He must see that the deck was properly officered and manned, day and night. During the day he must be on deck whenever the ship tacked or wore, when topsails were reefed, or when topgallant masts or yards were swayed up or down. His also was the duty of directing and supervising the work of the warrant officers: carpenter, sailmaker, boatswain, and gunner. Cleanliness and clothing of the sailors fell under his eye as well. When the great guns were exercised, he superintended the practice and personally commanded the quarterdeck and forecastle guns. Finally, although the education of the *Constitution*'s twenty midshipmen was primarily the responsibility of Chaplain William Austin, it fell to Lieutenant Hull to supervise their progress in navigation and to inspect their sea journals at regular intervals before they were transmitted to the captain. The midshipmen could not have found a better teacher, for in the business of practical navigation and ship handling no officer in the navy surpassed Isaac Hull.[30]

On Sunday, 15 September, not far from Saint-Domingue, the *Constitution* at last made a prize, the ship *Amalia* of Hamburg, taken ten days before by the French naval corvette *La Diligente*. Nathaniel Bosworth, a midshipman promoted to acting fifth lieutenant while the ship lay at Norfolk, was sent on board with a quartermaster and sixteen men to carry the *Amalia* into New York, where the disposition of the prize was consigned to Talbot's son George, a merchant in the city. The law of salvage provided one-eighth of the value to the captors, but the district court at New York ordered one half the value to be assigned, apparently because the *Amalia* had been in French hands for ten days, and might therefore be considered to have become French property. This was a great deal of money, for the *Amalia* was a large Indiaman homeward bound from Calcutta; her sale netted $194,000. The officers' twentieth of this figure, less costs and 10 percent for the prize agent, came to nearly $9,000, which must have loomed large indeed to a lieutenant whose pay was $40 per month plus rations. Divided among five lieutenants, the marine captain, and the sailing master, this would have yielded each officer some $1,250.

The *Constitution*'s ill luck with prizes, however, was not to be overcome. The owners appealed the decision to the circuit court, where the political rivalries at stake became clear: Alexander Hamilton and Richard Harrison appeared for the captors, Aaron Burr and Brockholst Livingston for the owners. Justice Bushrod Washington reversed the district court, awarding the whole proceeds to the owners, but Talbot and his officers carried a new appeal to the Supreme Court.[31]

The legal issues at stake in *Talbot* v. *The Ship Amelia* were large ones. The circuit court reversal had been won on the contention that, since Hamburg was a neutral trading port, the original capture by the French had been illegal and would have been reversed in the French court; the *Constitution*, therefore, had performed no service in recapturing the ship. In the Supreme Court, however, Jared Ingersoll ably argued that since the *Amalia* had cleared from an English-controlled port (Calcutta) and was laden with English goods, she was subject to capture and condemnation under the French decree of 4 January 1798, which authorized the capture of any vessel carrying English merchandise. This decree was considered contrary to international law, but the question was: To what extent was the United States entitled to enforce the law of nations by recapturing neutrals which had been illegally seized?

The issue interested Chief Justice Marshall, who continued the case until August 1801. In the final decision, the recaptors of the *Amalia* were awarded salvage but only "according to the just and equitable rules established by the general consent of nations," or one-sixth of the net proceeds: $26,405. Commissions, attorneys' fees, and other expenses further reduced the final figure to about $20,000, so that Lieutenant Hull's eventual share of the *Amalia* came to about $285. Even that was a fine figure compared to a seaman's share: the *Constitution*'s Jack Tars, if they had not already sold their prize tickets, realized about $17 apiece.[32]

The *Constitution*, after a brief visit to the Guiana coast, took up her station off Saint-Domingue on 15 October. The rest of Talbot's squadron was waiting at Cap Français: the frigate *Boston* of 28 guns, George Little, captain; the frigate *General Greene*, also 28, Christopher R. Perry, captain; and the 18-gun brig *Norfolk*, Lieutenant Commandant William Bainbridge commanding. The *Norfolk* was soon dispatched to protect the newly opened trade to Havana but was replaced by the ship *Herald*, 18, commanded by the *Constitution*'s former first lieutenant, Charles C. Russell. The squadron was further augmented from time to time by vessels coming from the United States.[33]

The *Constitution* and her consorts now began a routine of cruising off Cap Français. On the seventeenth Lieutenant William Amory of the marines, who had been ill for some time, was sent on shore, giving Talbot his first occasion to communicate with the United States navy agent, a Cap merchant named Nathan Levy. Levy was full of advice: a brig in the harbor, laden for France, might prove a good prize, but it would be better if the American ships did not cruise within sight of the land. He considered Cap Français quite safe as a port for American warships but on the whole thought this coast would not prove a fruitful cruising ground. Puerto Rico would be much better, as there were reports of privateers operating out of San Juan, as well as rumors that American ships were smuggling goods from Danish Saint John to Rigaud's forces in the south.[34]

As far as action off Saint-Domingue was concerned, Levy proved a good prophet. In the next six weeks of cruising the *Constitution* spoke only English warships and American and neutral traders. She chased several small vessels that appeared suspicious, but these always took care to keep close to the land, where the heavy frigate could not go. The only diversion was an occasional gam with a British warship or a trial of sailing: on 1 and 3 November the *Constitution* challenged the *Boston* both on and off the wind and beat her handily.[35]

The *Constitution* was beginning to be short of water and fresh provisions. Two or three men died of scurvy during October.[36] But Talbot was leery of taking his ship into Le Cap; he did not trust General Toussaint, and he feared the frigate's draft was too great for safety in entering the harbor. Levy sent off fresh provisions from time to time, which allayed the scurvy. To fill his water casks, Talbot, after investigating all other possibilities, finally decided to leave the *Boston* off Cap Français and take the *Constitution* to Môle Saint-Nicolas, at the northwest tip of the island, where she anchored on 2 December. Fifteen seamen whose enlistments had expired were discharged at the Môle, at their own request. Sailing Master Haraden summed up the preceding three months tersely in his journal: "From our last anchorage to this is one hundred days, which time we have been at sea. Three men we lost overboard and six died. Sent one commissioned officer and three midshipmen on the watering service."[37]

Commodore Talbot had been the more loath to leave his cruising ground because of the prospects of action there. Several vessels loaded with coffee for France were lying in the harbor, and of course the Americans hoped to seize them when they came out. The *Boston* and the *Norfolk* had already made a few small prizes. And there were bigger fish. In late November the French corvette *La Diligente,* late captor of the *Amalia,* slipped past the American vessels into Cap Français, where she was requisitioned by Toussaint to convoy some troops to put down a mulatto revolt in Jean Rabel parish, near Môle Saint-Nicolas. Under the circumstances, American Consul Stevens felt compelled to give *La Diligente* a safe-conduct, and Captain Little of the *Boston* reluctantly let her pass. On 7 December she sailed boldly into Môle Saint-Nicolas harbor and anchored directly under the *Constitution*'s stern. The American officers had every hope of catching her at sea after she had completed her convoy mission, when she would be fair game. Most exciting of all, there were rumors of a French delegation en route to Saint-Domingue in two or three frigates. The *Constitution* therefore filled her water casks with great dispatch and sailed again on 8 December.[38]

This close surveillance of their port, amounting almost to a blockade, was alarming to the merchants of Cap Français. They protested to Consul Stevens, who explained the matter at length to Secretary of State Pickering. Stevens, like Levy, thought the north coast of Saint-Domingue an unprofitable cruising ground, and the constant presence of American warships a source of ill will:

> much discontent has been excited by the constant appearances of our armed vessels so close to the harbour that nothing can either come in or go out without being subject to their examination. These clamors have been much increased of late by some injudicious firing of our ships on neutral vessels, even while entering the harbour. . . .
>
> our naval commanders . . . have been represented as hostile to the commerce of the island, and determined to capture all French armed vessels, with or without passports. It has even been reported that, while our ships were in the harbour, their boats were sent frequently to examine all the vessels bound out, and that they come into the port now by night, to ascertain whether any of them are preparing to leave it in the dark, that they may give intelligence to the ships that lie off. Though I know the prudence of our naval commanders too well to suppose that these reports are true, yet they will continue to have a very unfavorable influence on our commerce as long as they are believed and they will continue to be credited as long as our ships shall give them an air of probability by lying so obstinately off the harbour.

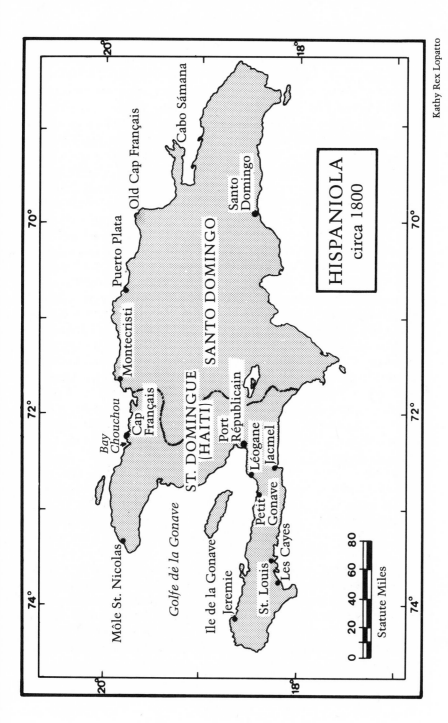

HISPANIOLA
circa 1800

ST. DOMINGUE
(HAITI)

SANTO DOMINGO

Cabo Sámana

Old Cap Français

Puerto Plata

Montecristi

Bay
Chouchou

Cap
Français

Môle St. Nicolas

Golfe de la Gonave

Ile de la Gonave

Jeremie

Petit
Gonave

St. Louis

Les Cayes

Léogane

Jacmel

Port
Républicain

Santo
Domingo

0	20	40	60	80

Statute Miles

20°

18°

70°

72°

74°

70°

72°

74°

20°

18°

Kathy Rex Lopatto

4 1

Stevens had said all this to Talbot before he left for Môle Saint-Nicolas and had suggested more proper cruising grounds for the American ships. There were no privateers at all, he said, on the north coast of Saint-Domingue, but there were plenty near San Juan, while in the Bight of Léogane (or the Gulf of Gonave) on the west side of the island there were numerous armed barges belonging to Rigaud, which preyed on American commerce. No American presence was needed on the south side of the island, because of the many English cruisers there.[39]

After conferring with Talbot again on 20 December, Stevens was full of praise: "I find him so candid, so prudent and liberal that I am convinced that he will do everything that can contribute to the good of the service and for supporting the dignity and interest of the United States. It is a happy circumstance for me to have a man of his character to cooperate with."[40] But Talbot was not being all that candid. On the night of 24 December, and again on the twenty-fifth, he sent Lieutenant Hull with an armed boat to reconnoiter the situation of a ship expected to sail from Cap Français soon, the very action Stevens had refused to believe American commanders capable of. Shortly after this, however, Talbot began to disperse his squadron. The *Herald* he ordered to Saint Thomas and the brig *Augusta*, 14, newly arrived in company with a storeship, he sent to Môle Saint-Nicolas. She was soon followed by the schooner *Experiment*, 12, under Lieutenant William Maley. These two small vessels were to cruise in the Gulf of Gonave to protect American shipping in that area. What this amounted to was the first direct American naval assistance to Toussaint, for protecting American commerce in the Gulf really meant the destruction of Rigaud's armed barges based in the small ports.[41]

The turn of the year and of the century was a critical time in the Haitian revolution. Toussaint was about to make his final drive against Rigaud, to bring all of Saint-Domingue under unified control. The chief mulatto stronghold was at Jacmel on the south coast; its capture would break the back of Rigaud's resistance. In December 1799 Toussaint had moved against Jacmel by land and by sea. In addition to *La Diligente*, now seized outright as a *batiment d'état*, the general had assembled a squadron of four schooners, three gunboats, a barque, two brigs, and two ships.[42] Some of these he loaded with men at Léogane and dispatched for Jacmel, while Henri Christophe's army invested the city by land. But on their passage the ships were captured by the British squadron and carried to Jamaica. The pretext for this was that secret agents were fomenting revolt in Jamaica, contrary to treaty pledges given by Toussaint. These men had been sent by the French agent in Saint-

Domingue, Phillippe Roume, but Toussaint had not found it politic to stop them and thus lost his fleet.[43]

But all was not lost. Toussaint appealed for American help and got it. Captain C. R. Perry of the *General Greene*, who had been ordered on a cruise around the island, was persuaded to employ his vessel as naval support for the assault on Jacmel. The frigate cruised off the port for some time to interdict supplies to the starving garrison and in the final assault bombarded the town and its forts. Jacmel fell on 11 March.[44]

In the Gulf of Gonave, Talbot's squadron was able to serve American and Haitian interests simultaneously. From late December 1799 the commodore kept two or three American vessels on constant patrol there, running fortnightly convoys from Môle Saint-Nicolas to Port Républicain. The great hazard in the Gulf was its frequent calms; when a sailing vessel lay helplessly becalmed, Rigaud's big barges, manned by forty or fifty men and armed with swivel guns and small arms, would row swiftly out of the many bays and inlets and overwhelm their victims. A graphic instance of the danger, even with a warship present, was the attack made by the barges on 1 January 1800 on a convoy led by the *Experiment*. Consul Stevens was on board the *Experiment* at the time. The vessels were becalmed near the island of Gonave when the barges set upon them; the fighting continued off and on from six in the morning until noon and resulted in the loss of two of the convoy.[45] From that time onward, most of the action for American forces on the Saint-Domingue station took place in the Gulf. Several small prizes were made, for the Gulf remained a cruising ground for French privateers as long as Rigaud held the ports of Jeremie and Les Cayes. One of these prizes was the schooner *Amphitrite*, which Talbot attached to the *Constitution* as a tender.[46]

The acquisition of the *Amphitrite* provided at least a partial solution to the problem of small vessels that escaped from the *Constitution* by working close inshore. (The Americans took the schooner's name to be *Amphitheatre*, and during her brief service as a naval auxiliary she bore that name.) Lieutenant David Porter, her commander, was instructed to keep the schooner close under the land near Montecristi and to stop every passing vessel. Commodore Talbot was careful to state in his instructions that the *Amphitheatre*'s crew was still considered part of the *Constitution*'s company and that her prizes were to be shared equally with the whole crew. He had already suffered frustration on that score from another subordinate commander, George Little. In January, while dispersing the squadron, Talbot had made an oral agreement with Little that the *Constitution* and the *Boston* would share equally in prizes made by each. This was to Little's advantage, since Talbot was entitled to one-twentieth of all prizes taken by his squadron, while Little had no claim on the commodore's captures. A few days later, on 27 January, while the *Constitution* was on a brief cruise in the Windward Passage between Saint-Domingue and Cuba, the *Boston* captured *Les Deux Anges*, one of the long-awaited coffee ships from Cap Français, and sent her to America. The net proceeds of *Les Deux Anges* were $53,929.59, but Little refused to share them with Talbot and his men. This case, like that of the *Amalia*, caused a long wrangle in the courts.[47]

By 1 April, Talbot had his eye on another quarry. The intended victim was a former British packet, the *Sandwich*, now operating as a French letter of marque mounting 8 guns. The *Sandwich* was then lying in the harbor of Puerto Plata in Santo Domingo (present-day Dominican Republic) loading a cargo of sugar and coffee for France, and Talbot intended to take her out. The chief difficulty was a legal one: Puerto Plata was a Spanish-controlled and therefore neutral harbor, so that captures could not legitimately be made there. Talbot reasoned, however, that Puerto Plata was not really neutral because the whole of Hispaniola belonged to France, by treaty of July 1795, although the French had never yet been able to take possession of the Spanish part of the island. Moreover, an act of Congress of 27 February regulating trade with the island seemed to adopt this point of view: "the whole of the island of Hispaniola shall for the purposes of this act be considered as a dependency of the French Republic."[48] Talbot therefore approached Stevens for information on the possibilities of getting the *Sandwich* out of Puerto Plata:

is it a fine open harbour, or is the entrance narrow, or otherwise difficult for strangers to go in and come out; what is the strength of their fort that protects the harbour, is it such as the Constitution need not value; what is the probable force or number of the inhabitants that can be brought to defend it immediately? These inquiries will naturally lead you to conclude that I meditate an attempt to capture the French ship lying at Port platt, and which is really the case. I have not yet made up my mind as to the most proper mode of making the attempt, whether by sending in boats or going in with the ship; indeed nothing can be decided on until I know more of the state of the harbor, of which I am quite ignorant, nor have I any draft or chart of it.

I have reflected whether it might not be practicable to go in with the ship, as if in want of water &c, and when in to take possession of the ship in question, but here again nothing can be determined on until I know from you whether it is likely they would admit the ship into port, and if they would whether it might be safe to trust them, especially if their battery is of force sufficient to stop her coming out. . . . I have not communicated these ideas to one of my officers, wishing to keep it a profound secret.[49]

Talbot was unwilling to hazard the enterprise until the *Sandwich* had loaded her cargo, so for the remainder of April he kept the *Constitution* cruising between Cap Français and Puerto Plata, observing the progress of lading.[50] By 1 May he had a good excuse for a close reconnaissance: a polacre loading at Puerto Plata with supplies for Toussaint's army in the south needed a convoy. The *Constitution* therefore proceeded to take station off the harbor and, early in the morning of 2 May, sent her small cutter into the port with Captain Carmick of the marines to inform the vessel's commander that the *Boston,* his intended escort, would be off the port in two or three days. Carmick would remain with the polacre until she came out, ostensibly to procure some livestock for the *Constitution.*[51] Talbot had not given up the idea of taking the *Constitution* into Puerto Plata to seize the *Sandwich.* He gave Carmick a letter of introduction to the captain of the port, indicating his ship's need for water and provisions and continuing:

> I have always been informed that vessels sailing under the American flag are freely admitted into port plate, in the same manner as Spanish ships are admitted into the ports of the United States. If this be really the case I should like to run into your port and anchor for one or two days, that is, if it be quite agreeable to you, and provided also that port plate affords a safe and convenient harbor for a ship of the size and magnitude of the Constitution. [Otherwise] I trust you will not have the smallest objections to grant leave for my boats to go in, and bring out wood and some small stock, such as fowls, pigs, goats, &c.[52]

But the commandant was not so easily fooled. The *Constitution* was welcome, "but there being several neutral vessels now anchored in this port which are at peace with my nation I beg the favour that you would give me your word of honour not to molest them in any way whatever, as they are under the protection of the Spanish colours."[53]

A bolder stratagem, then, would be needed. The officer of the returning boat reported, and Isaac Hull carefully recorded in his journal, that Puerto Plata harbor was formed by a small island and reef on the west and another reef on the east, the passage commanded by a small fort mounting four guns. The town itself contained about one hundred houses, mostly thatched huts. The *Sandwich* lay close under the fort, in shoal water, with her cargo largely on board, but stripped of her rigging.

Toussaint's ship came out of port on 5 May, and on the evening of the seventh she and the *Boston* proceeded on their voyage. The *Constitution,* with the tender *Amphitheatre* in company, was now left to deal with the *Sandwich.* Talbot's intentions could have been no secret to anyone by this time. He had probably decided, in concert with his officers, to send an expedition into Puerto Plata to cut out the prize. He would have to employ the ship's boats, perhaps escorted by the *Amphitheatre,* which would be a hazardous undertaking, since the intent would be so obvious. Just at this time, however, fate put into his hands a readier vehicle for his purpose.

On Thursday afternoon, 8 May, Lieutenant Porter brought the *Amphitheatre* alongside to report that he had discovered, inshore near Old Cap Français, a merchant brig, a French privateer schooner, and a barge. The *Constitution* reinforced the *Amphitheatre*'s company with a party of marines and manned four boats. By two-thirty Porter's little flotilla was in close combat with the French schooner, which ran aground. Three of her crew were killed and sixteen captured; the remainder escaped into the forest. The *Constitution* also worked inshore and fired several shots at the barge, a three-masted lugger, but she escaped while the Americans were securing the other vessels. The brig was an American merchant, the *Nymph* of Newburyport, captured the previous evening by the privateer schooner *Ester,* which had been operating in Saint-Domingue waters for some time.[54]

The *Amphitheatre* had three men wounded. She had lost her rudder and so was unable to pursue the fleeing barge. Two armed boats were therefore dispatched, about seven in the evening, under command of Third Lieutenant Collins, to seek her out. One boat returned the next morning, but Collins's was not heard from until the morning of Saturday, 10 May. When Collins reappeared he had, not the barge, but a sloop called the *Sally,* which he had taken out of Bay Chouchou.[55]

The *Sally* was a real find. She was from Providence, Rhode Island, measured 58 tons, and had a crew of six men. She had sailed for Turk's Island and from there to Puerto Plata, where she had been six days, and had then gone to Bay Chouchou with the intention of returning to Puerto Plata. The *Sally* was clearly an illegal trader, since Puerto Plata was not legitimately open to American vessels. And since she was known at Puerto Plata and was routinely expected to return, she was the perfect vessel to transport the men who would cut out the *Sandwich.*[56]

Isaac Hull's first opportunity for naval glory was at hand, and he lost no time in seizing it. That same afternoon he took charge of the *Sally,* with Captain Carmick and Lieutenant Amory of the marines and eighty men, and provisioned her for several days. By sundown the expedition was under way. During the night, as the *Sally* ghosted down toward the port with a light breeze, a shot whistled across the bow, and out of the darkness loomed the high yellow sides of a frigate. Lieutenant

Saint-Domingue

Hull and Captain Carmick were hustled on board HBM ship *Alarm*. Captain Robert Rolles was very polite, asking where they were bound. Hull replied coolly that they were in pursuit of a sugar barge inshore. Rolles remarked that he had met a small vessel off Montecristi with dispatches for Commodore Talbot. (He did not add that he had read the dispatches and kept copies of some of them, which occasioned a fierce quarrel when Talbot learned of it.) The two vessels parted, and the *Sally* drifted on toward the port. The sea breeze of the morning carried her down until by noon she had reached the harbor mouth. Now came the critical moments. Hull, dressed in common clothing, stood near the stern of the sloop, ready to let go the anchor. His helmsman had orders to lay the *Sandwich* aboard on the starboard bow. A half-dozen seamen lazed about the deck, keeping an eye on the *Sally's* master, Thomas Sandford, who was there for appearance's sake. Below, armed with cutlasses, crouched seventy-five men. Captain Carmick thought of the Trojan horse.

Isaac Hull made no record of his emotions at moments of crisis like this. It would not be unreasonable to suppose, however, that in the long dark hours on board the *Sally* he thought of the miserable months of 1797 when he had been a prisoner in the Spanish ports of San Juan and Santo Domingo. Now, in a Spanish port, a French privateer, like the ones which seized the *Beaver* and the *Minerva*, was about to be delivered into his hands.

In Puerto Plata, nothing stirred. Town, harbor, fort—all drowsed in the warm Sabbath afternoon. Suddenly the *Sally's* bow ground against the *Sandwich's* side. "Board!" shouted Hull as he leapt for the *Sandwich's* gunwale. The men sprang from the hold "like devils," firing their muskets in the air and wielding their cutlasses so vigorously that Hull and Carmick had all they could do to prevent bloodshed. As it was, no one was hurt on either side. The startled Frenchmen vanished over the opposite side of the ship or down the hatchway; Hull secured a total of twenty-four prisoners. Carmick and Amory, with the marines, manned a boat and rowed ashore to the little fort where, to make sure that their further proceedings would not be interrupted, they spiked the four cannon.

All this was accomplished within a half hour. But a great deal remained to be done before the *Sandwich* could be carried off. The schooner was stripped, with nothing but her lower masts standing and not even a rope over the caps. The breeze that had blown from the sea in the forenoon would blow off the land late at night; the "Constitutions" must catch it if they hoped to make their escape before the town had time to react. Through the broiling May afternoon the *Sandwich*

Cutting out of the privateer *Sandwich* at Puerto Plata, 11 May 1800. By Robert Salmon. Courtesy of the Trustees of the Boston Athenaeum.

swarmed with riggers. Lieutenant Hull was everywhere. Carmick and Amory, with no seamanly expertise, kept an eye on the crowd gathered at the beach and dealt with the bearers of several flags of truce who approached during the afternoon. The reply to all was the same: the Americans were merely executing their commander's orders. By 6:00 P.M. the *Sandwich* was rigged and ready for sea, royal yards athwart; moreover, her guns had been scaled, primed, and loaded, and men stood ready to use them if there were any threat from the shore. In the long hours after sunset Daniel Carmick had time to reflect that "On shore they were not ignorant that it was impossible for us to get out until the land breeze came off which you know is in the morning; [the commandant] concluded we must have been pretty determined before we undertook the business as we had no other alternative than to die or succeed." At midnight the breeze came up; the two vessels got under way and were in sight of the *Constitution* by 9:00 A.M.

Talbot immediately got the *Sandwich* and the *Sally* off to son George at New York and wrote a glowing letter to the secretary of the navy, describing the incident and concluding:

> Perhaps no enterprize of the same moment was ever better executed; and I feel myself under great obligations to Lieutenant Hull, Captain Carmick, and Lieutenant Amory for their avidity in undertaking the scheme I had planned, and for the handsome manner and great address with which they performed this dashing adventure.
>
> The ship, I understand, mounts four sixes and two nines; she was formerly the British packet *Sandwich*, and from the boasting publications at the Cape, and the declaration of the officers, she is one of the fastest sailors that swims. She ran three or four years (if I forget not) as a privateer out of France, and with greater success than any other that ever sailed out of their ports. She is a beautiful copper-bottomed ship; her cargo consists principally of sugar and coffee.

A rich prize! It is sad to have to relate that the *Sandwich* yielded her captors nothing but fame. The prize court ruled that Puerto Plata was a Spanish harbor and therefore neutral, so that the *Sandwich* must be returned to her owners. Moreover, the court costs, which the *Constitution* had to pay, pretty well ate up the proceeds of the *Amalia* and her other prizes. To a young naval officer, however, fame is sometimes worth more than material gain. Isaac Hull, throughout his long career, viewed the capture of the *Sandwich* as his first glorious exploit. He had matched his father's Revolutionary feat of boarding and capturing an armed schooner. So proud was he of the achievement, and of his captain's commendatory letter, that he had the letter printed as a broadside. Thereafter, whenever an admirer asked for a souvenir or some information on Hull's life, he was quite likely to receive a copy.[57]

Flushed with this success, Talbot determined on further aggressive moves against French privateers and the Spanish towns that sheltered them. On 1 June the *Constitution* again ran down the coast to the eastward, this time all the way to Cape Sámana at the northeastern tip of the island. The plan was to attack the settlement at the plantation of one Monsieur Petitant, fifteen miles west of the cape, where French privateers were not only outfitted but were actually built. The convenient *Sally* had been sent to the United States, so that the attack on Petitant's settlement had to be made with the ship's boats. This time the honor of command went to Lieutenant Robert Hamilton. But luck or skill failed him; his boats swamped in the surf, wetting the ammunition, and the attack fizzled.[58]

The *Constitution*'s cruise was nearly at an end. On 23 June the *Amphitheatre* was stripped of her armament and ordered to Philadelphia for condemnation as a prize. Three weeks later Talbot ordered Lieutenant Russell in the *Herald* to carry supplies to Toussaint's forces at Jacmel and then to cruise off Saint Louis in concert with the *Augusta* in an effort to catch out and destroy Rigaud's remaining naval force, estimated at four or five vessels of 14 to 20 guns each. With his forces and those of Toussaint cooperating so closely, Talbot now thought it prudent to pay a farewell visit to Cap Français, and so on the morning of 15 July 1800 the *Constitution* at last anchored in the port she had been patrolling for nine months. The next day Moyse, the commanding general at Le Cap and Toussaint's closest associate, made a ceremonial visit on board and invited Talbot and his officers to dine on shore with him. Unfortunately Lieutenant Hull had the duty that afternoon.[59] The harbor was jammed with shipping, most of it American: besides the *Constitution* and the *Herald* there were thirty-seven merchantmen, including one armed French ship.

The enlistments of the *Constitution*'s crew had expired and the men were growing restless. Eight deserted at Cap Français. But three days after she anchored there her relief, the frigate *Constellation,* appeared in the offing. It remained only to repair the shaky mainmast, take in water and fresh provisions, and then up anchor for home. Consul Stevens and the Cap merchants were effusive in their parting praise of Talbot, whose "dignified conduct while on the station has impressed the inhabitants of St. Domingo with a high idea of the American character, conciliated their affection, and produced an attachment to the government of the United States which in all probability will be permanent."[60]

Soon after midnight on Tuesday, 22 July, rang out the glad cry: "All hands, up anchor for America!" But Commodore Talbot had been right in his original doubts about the safety of Cap Français for a big ship.

Saint-Domingue

After the excitement subsided, Isaac Hull recorded the day's events in his journal:

> At 3 [A.M.] hove short on the best bower and made the signal for sailing by firing a gun and loosing the topsail. At daylight weighed and made all sail (winds vble) in order to proceed to sea. We had two pilots which were chosen by General Stevens. In entering the channel which is narrow and in depth 7, 8 & 9 fathoms and [was not] more than 4 cables wide it came on a dead calm. Came to with the best bower to prevent falling on the western breaker. At 7 a breeze sprung up from the westward. Weighed and stood along by the western reef which made the weather side. Near the north part of the western breakers and nearly abreast of the outer fort we were suddenly taken aback with the wind from the northward.
>
> Immediately the wind from the eastward. Came to with the two bowers as the reef afforded no room to veer away. Clewed up amain and furled sails. A swell from North brought her stern home to the reef. The ship then struck abaft, which shock was sensibly felt and violently repeated. Made the signal for assistance which was instantly obeyed by the American shipping lying in the harbour. We ran out the stream anchor nearly 200 fathoms to windward on which we hove. Transported the aft guns forward and hove off. Weighed the two bowers and hove nearly into the middle of the channel. Came to with the best bower and veered to a third of a cable. It was 17 minutes past 8 a.m. when we struck and 4 minutes past 9 when we hove off. At 10 let go the small bower and veered away on the best. The ship makes no more water than usual.[61]

After the frigate had cleared the reef two more days elapsed while Talbot conferred with his replacement, Alexander Murray, and gathered the twelve merchantmen to be convoyed home. On Thursday afternoon, 24 July, the *Constitution* and her little flock filled away through the Caicos Passage. On 6 August they made Charleston Light. It was politic to call at Charleston, whose leading citizens were not pleased by the thought that their navy was actively supporting a black revolution in Saint-Domingue. The *Constitution* sent in the ships bound to Charleston and purchased a few provisions: rice, flour, and four fat bullocks. These she sorely needed: an inventory of remaining stores on 12 August showed no beef, fourteen barrels of pork, and sixty gallons of rum. On her way up the coast she was forced to stop a number of merchant vessels in search of provisions: from one she obtained ten barrels of pork and a thousand bunches of onions; from another, two puncheons of rum. After parting with the last of the convoy on 12 August she spread her sails eastward and at last, on Sunday afternoon, 24 August, came to anchor in President Roads off Boston to wait out her quarantine. The latter seemed superfluous; there was not a sick man on board.

The sea-weary sailors were outraged at this further delay. About nine o'clock on Monday evening a group of them, egged on by Seaman John Hewett, assembled between decks and seized several officers. They met with instant resistance: Talbot, Hull, and the other officers marched boldly into the mob and seized four men, who were clapped into double irons. The mutiny collapsed. In any case, the quarantine expired at noon on Wednesday. Three days seems a remarkably short interval, and it is not unlikely that Talbot pressured the health officers to release his crew. The paymasters began to discharge the men on Thursday morning. In the end, only Hewett was punished for the mutinous outbreak, for which he received twelve lashes.[62]

The *Constitution* had been almost continually at sea for thirteen months, since 23 July 1799. During that period she had not spent more than a total of two weeks in port for watering and refitting. Her masts were shaky and her rigging and sails in tatters, but she had done yeoman service, both for American commerce and for the Haitian revolution. With the exception of the *Sandwich* exploit, it had not been an adventurous cruise, but it had been a worthy one.

The frigate's return to Boston was followed by the inevitable period of refitting, resupplying, and recruiting, which lasted until 14 December 1800.[63] During her stay she went through a change of officers once again. Hull and Hamilton remained and, in fact, received the highest praise from their commander: "Lieutenants Hull and Hamilton are expert seamen and men of gentlemanly manners, and I am confident they would do honor to any command that may hereafter be entrusted to them."[64] But the junior lieutenants, Isaac Collins and Edward Boss, had disgraced themselves on the cruise. With both of them, the basic problem was drink. Talbot had succeeded in getting rid of Boss by putting him in the *Experiment*. But Collins still had to be disposed of.

Lieutenant Collins had sealed his fate by exposing Talbot to public disgrace at Cap Français. On 16 July, when Talbot went on shore to dine with General Moyse, he took with him Lieutenants Collins and Hamilton, Captain Carmick, Purser DeBlois, and Surgeon Peter St. Medard. By the time the party were seated at table, Talbot discovered that Collins was loudly and abusively drunk; taking possession of the wine bottle, which he held in one hand while clutching his glass with the other, the lieutenant proceeded to get more and more intoxicated until, halfway through dinner, he was falling out of his chair. Talbot called Carmick to his side and whispered to him to get Collins out of the room, but Carmick protested that doing this would only enrage Collins. As soon as dinner was over the embarrassed company arose, and Talbot ordered Hamilton and Carmick to remove Collins. They half-carried him through the streets, with Collins calling Hamilton a "damned Scotch bugger" and threatening Carmick with his dagger. Now and then he would break away and run into a house to demand liquor. Finally the two officers deposited him in a sailors' coffeehouse and returned to the ship.

Talbot came on board in a towering rage and demanded of Lieutenant Hull why he had not told him that Collins was drunk before he went on shore. Hull, much embarrassed, said that he had in fact been on the way to Talbot's cabin for that purpose when Carmick dissuaded him, saying that if they informed on Collins there would be no living with him. Carmick had hoped that, since the French did not drink much at table, Collins might do all right.

Collins finally returned to the ship the following evening, after a day of gin slings, and made such a row in the wardroom that at eleven Hull told him to pipe down or be shut up in his berth. Collins kept himself drunk for three days, and on 20 July was at last advised by the long-suffering commodore to resign his commission rather than face a court-martial. Collins, suddenly sober, pleaded for forgiveness, but the next day Talbot put him under arrest. On 4 August, Collins bowed to the inevitable and submitted his resignation. He returned to a family of seven children in Boston, where he set up as a boardinghouse keeper, but he was already in debt and threatened with prison. In November he petitioned Talbot for a recommendation to Collector Benjamin Lincoln for a position in the customhouse, but it was not likely that Talbot would recommend him for a position of trust. He then disappeared from the record—possibly to debtors' prison.[65]

The vacancies among the officers were filled by the appointment of Joseph Saunders of Massachusetts, who had been third lieutenant in the *Congress* and the *Chesapeake,* and the promotion of Midshipman Joseph Tarbell, on Talbot's recommendation.[66] Talbot also received an application from Lieutenant Seymour Potter, but Hull thought the ship could do very well without him: "I should rather take the chance of any [officer in Boston] than to take Lieutenant Potter as I have heard and in fact seen some of his conduct that I am sure would not be pleasing to you. I wish you however not to mention those hints as from me."[67] This remark, and his conduct in the Collins affair, illustrate an aspect of Isaac Hull's personality. He was never inclined to "make waves" in personal relationships—which perhaps accounts for the fact that he never fought a duel.

Hull was often willing, on the other hand, to say a good word for someone, and so it happened that a midshipman's berth in the frigate went to Thomas Hunt. This young man's father, William Hunt, lived at Watertown, Massachusetts, and was probably a friend of William Hull. He applied to Lieutenant Hull for a recommendation to Commodore Talbot, and young Thomas, who was only fifteen, soon joined the *Constitution*'s steerage mess.[68]

A visit to his uncle William was about as much leisure as Isaac Hull was to have during this period. On 9 September he opened the rendezvous at Boston to ship the new crew, but the next day he had to return on board and take charge of the ship while Commodore Talbot went to visit his family in New York. Placing a good deal of confidence in his lieutenant, Talbot left him only a hasty and generalized order to "perform all and everything that is indispensably necessary to fitting the ship for another cruise." Talbot mentioned a number of essential repairs he wanted performed, but in general "your good sense and experience will suggest everything proper to be done as circumstances occur though not particularly herein mentioned and you will govern yourself accordingly."[69]

Talbot rejoined the ship on 1 October, and the next morning Lieutenant Hull was off to Boston to supervise recruiting again and to see to the preparation of new topmasts and spars. On the night of 5–6 October five seamen stole the ship's pinnace and escaped, so Lieutenant Hull had also to chase them. He caught them all within two days—one retrieved from a housetop.[70] He had then to take charge of the ship again while Talbot went to attend a court-martial in Rhode Island. When the latter returned, he took lodgings on shore and Hull continued in charge of the ship. He was far from idle. On 27 October he wrote:

> we are ready for every kind of stores that is to come from town and I've nothing on the part of the ship but we are nearly ready for sea. I have this day set up the main rigging, swayed up topgallant masts and blacked the ship round. We have every rope in the ship rove and are ready for our bending suit of sails. We have them to point on board, which will take a little time. Your stock came on board today; the doctor's comes tomorrow. The cooks have not come yet. . . . Everything that can be done to get the ship ready for sea in my power you may rest assured shall be attended to.[71]

The situation in the American government at this period was scarcely more tranquil than that of Saint-Domingue. President Adams had defied the wishes of the High Federalists by sending a new mission to France, and in May, after electoral reverses in New York clipped the Hamiltonians' wings and foretold the coming Federalist disaster, the president purged his cabinet of men loyal to Alexander Hamilton. Stoddert, the only member who was consistently an Adams man, remained.

Saint-Domingue

The High Federalists pinned their hopes for victory, which would include the replacement of Adams, on the failure of the Oliver Ellsworth negotiations in France. But the deliberations there proceeded smoothly. The French, now under the firm leadership of Bonaparte, conceded most of the American demands concerning neutral rights, and on 30 September 1800 the Convention of Mortefontaine was signed. By 7 November the news of peace was published in American newspapers, although the official version of the treaty would not be received for another five weeks.[72] Congress was assembling at the new capital in Washington to receive both the treaty and the crucial returns from the presidential election. In this atmosphere of uncertainty the *Constitution* once again departed for the West Indies.

Stoddert gave Talbot orders commensurate with the unsettled state of affairs:

> In the present state of uncertainty as to our situation with France, when unofficial accounts say that a treaty has been formed, though nothing official has been received on the subject, it is difficult to prescribe the conduct you are to observe towards French national ships, should you meet with any. It is deemed however by the President most proper that you should not seek any encounters with vessels of this description unless you find they are capturing American vessels, nor will it be proper to avoid engagements with them, should they show a disposition to attack you. As to privateers, and all armed ships sailing under French authority, except national ships, you will treat them as heretofore. But in the present state of uncertainty, it will be more desirable that you should employ the vessels under your command more in convoying our trade than formerly.[73]

Once under orders, Talbot was, as always, anxious to be at sea. The *Constitution* was supposed to take under convoy a storeship for the squadron and any other vessels bound for Saint-Domingue, but Talbot would accept no delay, especially since the weather had turned bitter,

> to that degree that a great number of the ship's crew were already frostbitten and we had lost great part of our stock by their perishing with the cold. Besides, the ice began to make and run very considerably, even so that two or three more such cold days as we had already experienced would likely increase the ice to that degree as to make it dangerous to the ship's cables and her copper.

The red sunset of Saturday, 13 December, promised fair wind for the morning, and word was sent to the storeship to get under way or be left behind. At 1:30 A.M. Talbot went on deck to find the west wind blowing; all hands were immediately called to unmoor ship. Up tumbled the sleepy tars. At 4:00 A.M. a gun was fired as a signal for sailing; by daylight the anchors were aweigh. The storeship did not budge from her moorings. The *Constitution* ran past the lighthouse at 9:00 A.M. and put to sea, accompanied by a lone merchant, the schooner *John* of Salem.

The frigate was snug for a winter cruise. Her topgallant masts were on deck, forward guns housed and ports shut in, and all the great guns well secured. The passage, however, was relatively calm.[74] On Friday, the nineteenth, the *Constitution* spoke the *Mehitabel* from Norfolk, whose master assured Talbot that there was peace with France. This was only report, however, for President Adams had presented the convention to the Senate just four days earlier. The *Constitution* continued her course, reaching Cap Français on 29 December.[75]

Affairs in the island were moving to a dénouement. In the late spring of 1800 the long-awaited frigates from France had reached Saint-Domingue, avoiding both the British and American cruisers. Toussaint, who had previously determined not to receive another commission from France, relented because of his respect for Napoleon Bonaparte. The First Consul's letter confirmed Toussaint as commander in chief for Saint-Domingue but ordered him to make peace with Rigaud and to reserve his forces for use against the English. Toussaint, who was not yet prepared to declare independence, had no choice but to obey, or at least to give an appearance of doing so. On 20 June he offered clemency to Rigaud, but when the latter refused to surrender, Toussaint ordered Jean-Jacques Dessalines to attack Rigaud's stronghold at Les Cayes. On 29 July, Rigaud fled to France, an unfortunate circumstance for Toussaint, since it put his bitterest enemy at the ears of the powerful. Dessalines was allowed to purge the southern provinces in order to crush any remaining mulatto resistance.

Toussaint was also under orders from Bonaparte not to meddle with Santo Domingo; but as long as the erstwhile Spanish portion of the island remained out of his control there was danger to his authority. An unoccupied Santo Domingo would be all too available as an invasion route should the French authorities again seek to reduce the island to their control. With the coerced approval of the French agent, Roume, Toussaint began to prepare for the invasion of the eastern province. By the time the *Constitution* reached Cap Français, Toussaint was ready. Early in January his forces, totaling eight thousand men, launched a two-pronged attack against the Spanish. Toussaint, regarding the appearance of the American commander as providential, appealed to him to assist the invasion by blockading the city of Santo Domingo.

Talbot was in a quandary. His instructions were to maintain friendly relations with Toussaint, but they were very cautious with respect to aggression against French vessels and said nothing about Spain. The commodore was on the point of declining to comply with Toussaint's request when the Spanish hastily capitulated, relieving him of the necessity. Toussaint entered the Spanish capital on 26 January after a virtually bloodless conquest.

The commander in chief devoted the first half of 1801 to preparing a constitution for his island. This document, apparently based on suggestions from Alexander Hamilton, made Toussaint governor general for life with power to name his successor. It did not declare Saint-Domingue independent of France but envisioned a kind of dominion status for the island. Toussaint, whatever his wishes may have been, was unable to declare independence because of the deterioration of his foreign support. Great Britain, now entering into peace negotiations with France, had little interest in supporting Saint-Domingue's independence, especially since it felt that black independence in Saint-Domingue set a bad example for its own colonies. The American position was similar. The difficulties with France being resolved, the only remaining attraction of Toussaint's island was its commerce. It was this that Toussaint had counted on as a binding tie between his country and the United States. But he reckoned without the changing American political climate.

There were two good reasons why the Republican party in America would be less friendly to Toussaint's regime than the Federalists had been: their supporters among the commercial classes were fewer, and their numbers in the southern states were greater. They were therefore less inclined to think of the profits of trade with Saint-Domingue and more apt to listen to complaints from slaveowners about the folly of supporting a republic of revolted slaves. There were, after all, other theaters of commerce that could well occupy the government's concern, especially the Mediterranean. Moreover, the new president of the United States foresaw as readily as did the governor general of Saint-Domingue that Bonaparte, once freed of his entanglements with England and the United States, would seek to reduce his rebel colony. Thomas Jefferson had no intention of being caught in the middle of that struggle. Toussaint asked sarcastically if the change of administrations had destroyed all the American armed ships; but he knew his doom.[76]

The new administration was a matter of concern to the American officers as well. By late December it was clear that the Republican ticket had been elected, but no one could be sure whether Jefferson or Burr would be president. Some Federalists hoped to prevent any election, as Consul Stevens told Talbot, but the latter thought this an unwise expedient. "I must confess I dread the consequence of an attempt at management to render the election void, for I think it very possible that was such an event to take place it would create a civil war in the country."[77] Most Federalists, luckily, agreed with him. Jefferson was elected on 17 February, and the Republican administration took office on 4 March. The Senate had already approved the Convention of Mortefontaine, with several reservations, on 3 February.

This is not to say, of course, that the members of the defeated party were pleased at the outcome. Even in the *Constitution* there was plenty of grousing about the turn of events at home. The chief concern was that the Republican administration would destroy or sharply reduce the navy. But it was not the Jeffersonians who initiated moves toward such ends. Jefferson, in fact, had been a proponent of a naval force since his service as minister to France, when he had proposed that a combined naval squadron of several nations could be employed to stop the commercial depredations of the Barbary States. As president, he was soon to resurrect that idea. But, as early as 12 January 1801, Secretary Stoddert had presented to the House Naval Affairs Committee a plan for reducing the navy to a peacetime footing. His recommendations were substantially adopted by the retiring Federalist Congress on its last day in office in an act that authorized, though it did not command, the president to sell all the navy ships except thirteen frigates, to keep six of these in constant service, and to lay up the remainder. The cruising ships were to be limited to two-thirds their wartime complement, and the officer corps was also to be reduced to 9 captains, 36 lieutenants, and 150 midshipmen.[78]

The lack of activity on the Saint-Domingue station seemed to give ample warrant for such a reduction in force. Talbot had seven vessels in service with nothing to do except a little routine convoy work. Having resolved its difficulties with the French tiger, however, the United States was in danger of being entangled with the British shark. The Mortefontaine stipulations with regard to neutral trade were by no means in accord with British policy. Furthermore, France was urging the United States to defend its rights by making common cause with the nations of northern Europe in the League of Armed Neutrality. There was some speculation on board the *Constitution* that America might do just that, and certainly there was ample provocation. Jefferson was not about to get involved in a struggle with Britain, however. The League of Armed Neutrality collapsed in April after the Danish defeat at Copenhagen, and in the following year the Peace of Amiens brought a temporary respite in the European war. But the *Constitution*, before she left the West Indies, had two brushes with the Royal Navy that were omens of future events. Early in March while the frigate was at Môle

Saint-Nicolas her officers saw a British frigate seize two American merchant ships that were beating up to the Môle harbor. About a week later the *Constitution* herself was convoying a group of vessels through Crooked Island passage in the Bahamas when she spoke the frigate *Andromache*. The English captain demanded that Talbot order his convoy to heave to and be searched for French property. Talbot refused and signaled the ships to disperse, but when the *Andromache* continued to pursue his charges he had no authority to resist. Luckily the British frigate chose to chase the swiftest American, the *Arethusa*, and both ships vanished in the gathering dusk. Talbot hoped that thus the whole convoy had escaped.[79]

On 23 March 1801 all remaining American warships were ordered home from the West Indies. Talbot received these orders via the *Herald* about 12 May. Five days later the *Constitution* left Môle Saint-Nicolas and, after calling at Cap Français for a last farewell, sailed for America. She reached Boston Light on 11 June and anchored before the town on 14 June. During the passage Talbot had formally inquired of his officers which of them wished to continue in the navy under the Peace Establishment Law. All expressed a desire to remain except Lieutenant Saunders, who had an offer of command in the East India trade, and two midshipmen. Talbot's regard for his senior lieutenants was undiminished:

> Lieutenant Hull and Lieutenant Hamilton were in the ship before I was honored with the command of her; they have been with me more than two years, and I can say with perfect truth and great pleasure that their conduct has been always such, and I may add without one exception, as to meet my most perfect approbation, and the unexampled cordiality that has ever existed between them and the commander, and also between every grade, and the good condition of the ship at this time is a proof that duty on board has been regularly and cheerfully performed by all.[80]

With such a recommendation Lieutenants Hull and Hamilton were certain to be continued in the navy. Hull was notified of his selection in July by Secretary of War Henry Dearborn, the Navy Department being temporarily without a secretary. Hamilton, however, resigned the following January. Talbot was equally enthusiastic in his recommendation of Acting Lieutenant John Delouisy, but Delouisy went down in the general slaughter, together with six of the *Constitution*'s thirteen remaining midshipmen.[81]

Talbot himself was on the way out, but the reasons for his resignation are obscure. He was selected as one of the nine captains to be retained under the Peace Establishment Law, and had been placed third on the list, after Barry and Nicholson. Thomas Truxtun had been in America since April and had apparently employed influence with the new administration through his friend Aaron Burr, but to no avail. Adams's decision on the rank question was to stand. Samuel Nicholson's place had been saved through the exertions of his nephew, the powerful Congressman Joseph H. Nicholson, but it was generally understood that he would never again have a command at sea. Everyone knew that Barry was old and ill; he would not go to sea again, either. Had Talbot remained, he would certainly have commanded the first or second of the squadrons soon to be sent to the Mediterranean, and his energetic nature would have made the history of the subsequent operations vastly different. It must have seemed to him, however, that opportunities in the peacetime navy were poor. Moreover, his son Cyrus had seen his career cut off with the abolition of the rank of master commandant. The new administration, anxious to keep the Talbots, made concessions: Cyrus was offered the command of the schooner *Enterprize*, the only vessel smaller than a frigate to be kept in service, and a continuance in the rank of master commandant, although this was bending the law pretty far. But Cyrus Talbot had commanded a sloop of war, and he apparently felt that the *Enterprize*, heretofore a lieutenant's command, was beneath him. Both father and son resigned in July 1801.[82]

Isaac Hull would have been the first to admit how much he owed to Silas Talbot. Talbot was undoubtedly the formative influence on Hull's naval career, the man after whom he modeled himself. Two points are particularly noteworthy: first, Hull, when in command, always gave his senior lieutenant great discretion and responsibility, thus tacitly acknowledging the importance of the opportunity Talbot had given him to become master of the working of a ship. Second, Talbot was a notably lenient man with his sailors, giving only twelve lashes for a serious crime like desertion. Hull took the same attitude of fatherly sympathy toward his men and was in his own generation the officer most noted for sparing the cat. Like Talbot, Hull was ever intolerant of delay, eager always to be at sea and in action. Talbot's daring balanced by prudence, combined with his willingness to grasp the initiative, appealed to Hull and called for emulation. Hull began his two years' service under Talbot a green lieutenant whose capacities were doubted by his superiors; he ended them a fully formed officer ready for command.

Talbot gave over the command of the *Constitution* to Isaac Hull in late August 1801.[83] His resignation became effective in September. He did not leave Boston, however, until late October or early November. The *Constitution* was undergoing a thorough repair under Hull's supervision. She was found to be quite rotten. By mid-January she had been rebuilt as high as the upper part of the bends; a new berth deck was laid; and some gun deck beams were going in. While the repairs went on the ship was uninhabitable, so Hull and the other officers lived in Boston at Dr. Peter St. Medard's house, where they shared a jolly mess they called "the wardroom."[84]

At this period occurred what appears from a perspective of two hundred years the most regrettable episode of Isaac Hull's life but which undoubtedly seemed to him at the time merely an act of courtesy for a friend. Isaac Hull turned slavecatcher.

Slavery was not legal in Massachusetts, but Talbot, a resident of New York, owned several slaves. At least three of them had been enlisted in the *Constitution* as Talbot's servants: Henry, Mungo, and a nineteen-year-old mulatto named William Roberts. Roberts was a native of Jamaica and was evidently a proud and troublesome young man. Soon after Talbot returned to New York in November, Roberts ran away, taking with him one hundred dollars in bank bills and a trunkful of clothes. Talbot immediately suspected the runaway would make for free Massachusetts, and he asked Lieutenant Hull to track him down.

Hull felt no compunction about the matter. He obviously did not like Roberts, who had been a sulky and ungovernable servant in the ship. For a few days he conducted a quiet search, having learned that the quarry had been seen in Cambridge. Finally in December he ran an advertisement in the *Columbian Centinel* offering a twenty-dollar reward. This bore fruit within the month; Roberts was captured at Dedham on 29 December by Edward Brewer and put into the Boston jail. There was some difficulty about this, since Roberts swore he was a freeman and of age and Hull could produce no contrary proof. But there is always a way; he charged the servant with theft and got him secured.

William Roberts had come close to freedom. He had managed to contact Boston's black underground and with its aid nearly managed to escape. When captured, he was in a stage bound to Providence, Rhode Island—"I suppose to stay," wrote Hull,

> as he had a letter in his pocket book from a black woman in this town to a woman in Providence wishing her to take him in and she would see her paid, by which I think he must have given her money as he had but one dollar with him. He says that his trunk is in Salem, that he owes three dollars and was obliged to leave it. I shall endeavor to get his things and find out more about him if possible, but he appears to be very sulky and when taken abused you very much, but when in my presence had very little to say. . . . I have desired Mr. Hartshorn, the gaoler, not to suffer any black people to see him for fear of their putting him up to something . . . as there are people enough in Boston that would be glad to get him clear.[85]

Poor William would languish in jail for nearly six weeks. Talbot sent on a bill of sale to prove his property in the man and instructed Hull to send him around by water or else sell him back to Jamaica. Hull thought the latter would be preferable, since Roberts was such a troublesome property, but it proved too difficult to arrange. It was almost impossible to get a shipmaster to carry him to New York, either. One agreed, then reneged when his passengers refused to go in company with the black man. Finally, on 8 February, the schooner *Jerusha* took him, in irons and "very sulky." To prevent another escape, Hull stayed by the schooner until a few hours before she sailed. The last note in the story is the saddest of all: William Roberts, chained in the tiny vessel in the dead of winter, froze some of his extremities on the passage. Hull's comment on this was merely to commiserate the owner of the damaged property: "I am very sorry that William was so unfortunate as to get frozen but hope he is not so bad as to disable him, or render him in any manner unserviceable to you."[86]

During these winter months Isaac Hull was growing discouraged with the navy. Talbot's resignation had been a blow. The uncertainty surrounding the change of administrations and the unsettled state of foreign affairs seemed to make prospects for a career in the service less bright than they had been two or three years earlier. In January 1802 Hull confided to Talbot that "I fear there never will be any permanency in the Navy and am almost discouraged and think of leaving in the spring." This elicited from Talbot a cordial invitation to join him and his sons in a new venture: a migration to Kentucky. Had the prize money from their cruises been greater, Isaac Hull might have been lost to the navy then and there. But he had no funds for such an enterprise:

> I assure you nothing would give me so much pleasure as to make a journey with a family I so much respect, and nothing should prevent my going but the want of funds sufficient to get me a comfortable settlement in that country. I feel how happy three or four such families as your sons must be settled down for life within a few miles of each other where they would have nothing to trouble them but their family concerns and what pleasure they must take in visiting each other with their families. The very thoughts of the journey [give] me pleasure and the more I think of it the better I like it.

There was a rumor afloat that Hull would be ordered to the *Enterprize* as second to Lieutenant Commandant Andrew Sterrett. Hull was sure the rumor was unfounded, as he actually ranked Sterrett by one place on the lieutenants' list, and

> the Secretary would not order two of the oldest officers to one ship. But should that be the case I shall either leave or get leave of absence for a year or

two. Let which will take place I shall have the journey in my mind and notwithstanding my want of funds to settle in the country I hope I shall be able to make a journey with you and perhaps have it in my power to settle in some future day.[87]

His old commander was so anxious to take the genial Hull along with him that he offered to stake him in the enterprise. But, whatever his romantic dreams of the Kentucky frontier, the attraction of the sea was, whether he admitted it or not, too strong for Isaac Hull to think of leaving it so irrevocably. By 3 March, Captain Richard V. Morris had arrived in Boston to take command of the *Constitution* and gave warm praise for Hull's efforts in repairing the ship. "He wishes very much to have me remain by the ship and not think of leaving the service but I have not as yet determined. I am very much pleased with Captain Morris and think him a gentleman and a good officer and have no doubt but should I remain I shall be happy with him should we be fortunate in our wardroom officers."[88]

Morris decided to have the *Constitution* careened for recoppering and Hull steeled himself for that ticklish job, but within three weeks everything changed. Truxtun, who was to have commanded the Mediterranean squadron, resigned the service,[89] and Morris was ordered to Norfolk to take over the frigate *Chesapeake* and assume the squadron command. Hull still hoped that the *Constitution* would go out as part of the squadron and that Morris might shift his flag to the larger ship.[90]

But Isaac Hull was about to part company with his old ship as well. The small frigate *Adams*, 28, was fitting at New York and was more urgently needed than the *Constitution*. Her commander, Edward Preble, was in very poor health. He suffered from chronic stomach ulcers, which made it impossible for him to attend to fitting out the *Adams*. Preble needed an experienced lieutenant who could relieve him of the details of duty. Isaac Hull was just the man. The secretary of the navy tried tactfully to soften the apparent demotion to a smaller ship:

Captain Preble's state of health requires that he should have a first lieutenant of the utmost professional skill. . . . From the rank you hold in the Navy, you must expect soon to have the command of a frigate. I wish you therefore to see as much active service as possible. This is an additional consideration in inducing the present order.[91]

Hull accepted this reasoning. It was a responsible position and promised immediate and active service in a new theater. In mid-April 1802 he left the *Constitution* to join the *Adams* at New York.

4

Keep Yourself Cool!

When Isaac Hull reached New York on 21 April, he found that Captain Preble was indeed a sick man. The duties of equipping the *Adams* for sea had so aggravated his chronic stomach disorders that a week earlier he had submitted his resignation from the service. He surrendered the *Adams* forthwith to Isaac Hull. As the secretary of the navy had written, he could soon expect "the command of a frigate"—and here she was! Hull surveyed his new command. The *Adams* had undergone a thorough overhaul, such as Hull had been giving the *Constitution*, and had been substantially rebuilt from the wales up, her spar deck raised four inches, arid her botton caulked and recoppered. Preble had given her a lighter armament than the 38 long twelves she had carried during the French war, and she now mounted 32 guns, more in keeping with her rating of 28. Still, she was a poor warship. Preble probably repeated to Hull what he had told the secretary of the navy in February:

> The *Adams* is not well constructed for a frigate. She is too narrow and sharp and draws too great a draught of water for a ship of her rate; she is over masted, and requires so much ballast to enable her to bear her canvas that she will not carry more than three months' provisions and stores and even with that quantity is very much lumbered. But to counterbalance those inconveniences she is said to be a remarkable fast sailer, and being a light frigate will answer well for the Mediterranean service.[1]

With all her defects, then, the *Adams* was a fast-sailing ship with which an active officer might do something. Preble, despite his illness, had her nearly ready for sea. In a week or two Lieutenant Hull could be under way, in command, bound for a new sea, facing a new enemy.

The dream was shattered abruptly on 25 April. On that day, to Hull's chagrin, there appeared in the *Adams*'s gangway the gilt epaulets of Hugh George Campbell, the lowest-ranking captain in the navy but one—and therefore only three places above Isaac Hull—now appointed to command the *Adams*. Campbell, like Cyrus Talbot, had been told in 1801 that he could remain in the navy only by losing rank and acting as commandant in a commodore's flagship, but the South Carolinian had somehow managed to hang on until the Mediterranean emergency led to an easing of the policy of reducing the officer list. Even so, the navy had not been overeager to put him on active service. He had been in Washington to obtain a post as inspector of naval timber when the secretary received Preble's letter of resignation. A captain was urgently needed; Campbell was unemployed; three days later he was on his way to New York.

Preble now formally resigned the command to Campbell and departed for his home in Maine. (His resignation from the service had been refused, and he was placed on furlough.) Isaac Hull thought over the matter for three days before concluding that his situation was intolerable. He had been demoted from executive officer and acting commander of the *Constitution* to first lieutenant of the smallest frigate and was to serve under one of the most junior captains! Though no hothead, he was hopping mad. His naval career was, it seemed, being wrecked before his eyes. There was only one thing to do. On 28 April 1802 he resigned from the navy. It might be the time to migrate to Kentucky after all.

Hull may have intended his resignation as a tactical move, but it is more likely that he was serious. After all, every officer in the navy had before his eyes the instructive example of Thomas Truxtun. The latter had tried to get his own way by threatening to resign and had been sorely dismayed when his resignation was summarily accepted. It was clear that Secretary of the Navy Robert Smith was not a man to trifle with. President Jefferson, seeking desperately to peddle the unpopular navy post in his cabinet, had finally settled the Department on this brother of the powerful Maryland senator, Samuel Smith, who had declined the position for himself. No one knew what to expect of Robert Smith, but they were beginning to find out: he was tough, audacious, and ardently devoted to the service he headed. The officers soon learned, with delight, that he could be a formidable advocate. But thus far he appeared only as a stern master.

Isaac Hull's letter of resignation no longer exists, so it is possible only to conjecture the contents from Smith's reply. Apparently, he based his resignation on old grievances having to do with the preferment of other officers. The loss of the letter is the more regrettable because it is almost the only evidence that during this period Hull was discontented with his relative rank in the service. Except for oblique remarks in his letters to Talbot the previous year, he never spoke of it. The most likely cause of his dissatisfaction was the relatively more rapid promotion that had come to lieutenants appointed to command the small vessels during the French war—men like Edward Preble and William Bainbridge, both of them now captains—as opposed to the slow advancement of the officers serving in the frigates. The same story was to repeat itself in the Tripolitan War: junior officers commanding small craft were in the heat of the action—and in the eye of the navy secretary—while frigate officers languished in obscurity.

Smith was not impressed with Hull's reasoning. If these were such weighty matters, he replied, Hull should have resigned when they occurred, and not now, years later and at a critical moment in preparations for a cruise. The secretary was understanding but scarcely consolatory:

> I know what the feelings of military men are, and that among them there always exists a jealousy on the subject of rank: this jealousy is by no means an improper one, but it sometimes leads men into hasty and intemperate decisions, incompatible with their own honor.
>
> I should not have ordered you to join the *Adams* but from absolute necessity. We had no other officer in the country in whose capacity . . . I could so confidently rely as in yours. The situation of Captain Preble's health required that one of the ablest lieutenants in the service should be ordered to join him, and as the probability was that you would never again be sent out in a station inferior to the command of a frigate, I wished you to see as much service as possible, and not intending to send the *Constitution* out, there was no other vessel to which you could have been ordered except the *Adams*. . . .
>
> If, upon receipt of this letter, you continue in the disposition expressed in yours of the 28 ultimo, you will communicate your determination to Captain Campbell and consider this as an acceptance of your resignation; otherwise you will remain on board the *Adams*.[2]

At the same time Smith wrote Campbell that he hoped Hull would not resign, since "he has been represented to me as a valuable officer"; should he remain adamant, the *Adams* must sail without him, and another lieutenant would be sent by the next provision ship. Above all, the frigate must get to sea.[3]

Sometime in that first week in May, Isaac Hull changed his mind. It was not the secretary's letter that made the difference; apparently he had made the decision before he received the letter, for on 5 May he was officially entered on the *Adams*'s muster roll as first lieutenant. His affection for the service was certainly the strongest factor. In a time of relative peace with few prospects for action, it took a strong attachment to naval service to keep a young man—especially a young man with grievances—in the navy. It is quite likely, also, that by the time a week had elapsed it had become clear to Hull that Hugh Campbell was a man he could live with. Campbell was, by all accounts, a pleasant man in peer relationships and one with whom Hull maintained a friendly correspondence for some years. But he was a terror to young officers, lacked judgment, and had practically no seamanship—all in contrast to Isaac

Hull. Subsequent events suggest that brief acquaintance with his new captain may have convinced Hull that Campbell needed him more than had the capable, if sickly, Preble. When the secretary's letter arrived, it again invoked "the probability . . . [of] the command of a frigate." Wait a bit, then. There was action in the Mediterranean; anything might happen. As it turned out, seven years elapsed before Hull trod a frigate's weather quarterdeck, but they were years of command, years of intense activity, years that shaped his life and the future of the service.

There have been many candidates for the title, "Father of the American Navy," but a case might be made for the dey of Algiers. It was, as noted, the menace of his fleet that drove the United States in 1794 to lay the keels of its first frigates. That particular threat was ended in 1796 with the conclusion of a treaty with the dey, and it was followed by a succession of agreements with the other North African principalities of Tunis and Tripoli. (A treaty with Morocco had been signed in 1787.) It was at best an uneasy solution, however. All the treaties acquiesced in periodic "presents" of one sort or another to be made to the Barbary states' rulers, and the consular representatives appointed to their ports were in a constant swivet over the nonarrival or nonacceptability of these "tokens," which included ships, naval stores, and even jeweled regalia.

Thomas Jefferson had believed at least since 1786 that the best solution to the United States' problems with the Barbary powers would be an aggressive naval policy. Now, in 1801, mandated by Congress to employ six frigates on active service and unwilling to fish any longer in Caribbean waters, he decided on a show of strength in the Mediterranean. In the spring a squadron of three frigates and the schooner *Enterprize* was ordered out under Commodore Richard Dale. Dale's instructions were to appear off Algiers, Tunis, and Tripoli; if he found any of them at war with the United States, he was to employ his squadron to protect American commerce by destroying the corsairs and blockading the ports of any offender.[4]

Dale reached the Mediterranean at a most opportune time, for on 14 May, six weeks before his arrival, the pasha of Tripoli had declared war on the United States by the dramatic device of chopping down the flagstaff at the residence of Consul James Leander Cathcart.[5] Yusuf Caramanli ruled the weakest of the Barbary states, but he was a shrewd and formidable adversary. He had not scrupled to murder his eldest brother, Hassan, and to drive another, Hamet, into exile in order to secure the throne of Tripoli for himself in 1796. One of his first acts as pasha had been the conclusion of a treaty with the United States, but when he was firmly settled in office he came to regard it as a bad bargain by comparison with those made by other Barbary rulers.[6] In 1800 he demanded a new treaty; the price for continued peace was set at $250,000 and an annual tribute of $20,000. When the demand was refused, Yusuf declared war.

The Tripolitan naval force consisted of ten vessels ranging in force from 32 guns to 1, mounting a total of 145 cannon, mostly light four-, six-, and nine-pounders. By a happy chance, Dale reached Gibraltar just in time to prevent two of the larger vessels, the *Meshuda,* of 26 guns, and a 16-gun brig, from escaping into the Atlantic. He left the frigate *Philadelphia* at Gibraltar to keep the two pinned down and proceeded up the Mediterranean, eventually to establish a blockade of Tripoli, which was effective enough to make Yusuf uncomfortable. Dale, however, felt that he lacked instructions to negotiate peace, or to cooperate with the Swedes, who were also at war with Tripoli. Lieutenant Andrew Sterrett, in the *Enterprize,* had the only serious action in the Dale squadron when he captured a Tripolitan polacre, stripped her, and sent her back to Tripoli, where her unfortunate commander was bastinadoed to complete his humiliation.[7]

Dale was, nevertheless, enthusiastic about an aggressive policy toward Tripoli, especially in combination with Sweden. He saw that an effective assault on the town and its shipping would require mortars and gunboats, of which Tripoli had now acquired more than a dozen. But, in preparing instructions for the relief squadron, the Jefferson administration continued to rely on the blockade, apparently for reasons of economy.

The Morris squadron, in which Isaac Hull was to make his Mediterranean debut, consisted of the frigates *Chesapeake,* 38, *Constellation,* 36, and *Adams,* 28, and the hardworking schooner *Enterprize.* An act of 6 February 1802 had effectively repealed the Peace Establishment Law, authorizing the president to fit out as many cruisers as he needed to "subdue, seize and make prize of all vessels, goods and effects belonging to the bey of Tripoli, or to his subjects . . . and also to cause to be done all such other acts of precaution or hostility as the state of war will justify and may, in his opinion, require." To facilitate effective Mediterranean cruising, the term of enlistment for seamen was extended from one year to two. Cathcart was empowered to negotiate peace with Tripoli, but no payment was to be made. Commodore Morris's instructions did not specify what action should be taken in the event that negotiations failed.[8]

Even with Hull and Campbell on board, another month elapsed before the *Adams* finally put to sea on 10 June. The other units of the squad-

ISAAC HULL'S MEDITERRANEAN
Political boundaries circa 1810

Kathy Rex Lopatto

FRANCE

SPAIN

PORTUGAL

Lisbon

Barcelona

C. Palos
C. Nao
C. Gata

Málaga
Cartagena
Cadiz
Tangier
Tetuan
Larache
Salé
Mogador

Marseilles
Toulon
Genoa
La Spezia
Leghorn
Piombino
TUSCANY
Rome
Trieste

ELBA
CORSICA
SARDINIA
Cagliari

BALEARIC IS.
MINORCA
MAJORCA
Port Mahon

Naples
KDM. OF THE
TWO SICILIES
Palermo
Messina
Syracuse
C. Passero
MALTA
Valetta

C. Bon
Tunis
Algiers

OTTOMAN

EMPIRE

Constantinople
Smyrna
Urla
Athens
HYDRA

CYPRUS
Beirut

CRETE

EGYPT
Cairo
Alexandria
Rosetta
Damanhur

C. Razatin
Tabarka
Derna
Bomba
Benghazi

TRIPOLITANIA

C. Misurata
Old Tripoli
Tripoli

Gibraltar
Europa Point
Cabrita Point
Algeciras

Statute Miles
0   200   400

N

ron were all in the Mediterranean. Once at sea, Campbell pressed all sail for Gibraltar. The *Adams* enjoyed pleasant seasonal weather, but the driving passage must have been wearisome for those on board. As Preble had said, the *Adams* was a fast sailer; many days on her outward passage she logged a sustained nine or ten knots. But one of her peculiarities, perhaps because she was so narrow and deep, was that she plowed straight through the waves instead of rising to them. It was a teeth-jarring cruise, and for all the speed on some days, light airs and calms on others made it a relatively long voyage. Twenty-six days from New York a landfall was made in the Azores, and two weeks later the African coast was sighted near Mogador. Finally, at 9:00 A.M. on Wednesday, 21 July, the *Adams* came to in Gibraltar Bay.

Had the *Adams*'s officers and men known what service lay in store for them they might have wished themselves pounding through the Atlantic waves once more. They would all get heartily sick of Gibraltar in the next nine months. At Gibraltar the *Adams* found Commodore Morris in the *Chesapeake*, accompanied by the *Enterprize*. The *Constellation* was on blockade duty at Tripoli, but Morris had been unable to go up the Mediterranean with the rest of the squadron because of a threat from Morocco. Sultan Maulay Sulaiman, with whom the United States had heretofore maintained cordial relations, had suddenly turned hostile. He had taken Tripoli's side in the war and had demanded that the *Meshuda*, still blockaded at Gibraltar, be released to him, asserting that he had bought her. (The brig had been sold to a third party, and the Tripolitan commodore, Murad Rais, had decamped with his men, leaving a skeleton crew in the *Meshuda*.) The emperor further demanded passports to send two vessels loaded with wheat to Tripoli. When his demands were refused, he declared war on 22 June. There was also a rumor of war with Tunis, but Morocco was by far the more dangerous because it had ports in both the Mediterranean and the Atlantic. Already a Moroccan frigate at Larache had been ordered to sortie into the Atlantic in search of American prizes.

Happily, the concentration of three American warships in the Straits had a sobering effect on Maulay Sulaiman. Early in August the sailing orders for the frigate at Larache were canceled and the war was called off, at least for the moment. But, when Morris proceeded up the Mediterranean on 18 August with the *Chesapeake*, the *Enterprize*, and a convoy of Swedish and American merchantmen, he prudently left the *Adams* behind for the dual purpose of keeping one eye on the *Meshuda* and the other on Morocco.

For two weeks after the departure of the commodore, the *Adams* lay at Gibraltar while her rotten mizzenmast was repaired. During this time Campbell received two letters from Consul James Simpson at Tangier, warning him that the emperor of Morocco was still pressing his claim to the *Meshuda*. On 1 September a crew, including the former commander of the Tripolitan brig and another Tripolitan officer, arrived from Tetuan and began to put the *Meshuda* in order for sea. Simpson was beginning to feel that he could not continue to refuse a passport in the face of the emperor's assertion that the *Meshuda* was his property, but Campbell insisted on seeing vouchers that would prove the sale before he would let the vessel pass.[9]

The boredom of Gibraltar was telling already. Some of the *Adams*'s officers relished the prospect of a fight with the *Meshuda* if she attempted to sail. But it was not only tedium that was fraying tempers in the *Adams*. Marine Lieutenant Presley N. O'Bannon commented cryptically: "Captain Campbell has conducted himself in such a manner as to forfeit all the respect of the officers on board his own ship and I believe it extends to all who know him."[10]

O'Bannon gave no further details of Campbell's behavior, but within the week occurred a long-remembered episode that fixed once and for all the relative standing of Hugh Campbell and Isaac Hull in the eyes of the *Adams*'s company. On Saturday evening, 11 September, the *Adams* weighed anchor and stood across the bay to Algeciras, where she anchored for about twenty-four hours. On Tuesday afternoon she again weighed and remained under sail through the night. At midnight Acting Lieutenant James Decatur took the deck. He had just joined the ship and was probably unfamiliar with the *Adams*'s sailing qualities. In tacking ship he missed stays, and the frigate was caught aback, drifting rapidly down toward the rocks of Cabrita Point. Shouts of "Breakers ahead!" brought Campbell on deck, closely followed by Hull, both in nightshirts. (Hull carried a pair of striped pantaloons he had grabbed up on his way.)

Campbell, seized with panic, stood frozen as the frigate slipped inexorably toward Diamond Rock on her lee bow. Hull brushed him aside, seized the speaking trumpet, and began giving orders. After sending the men to their stations, he turned to the still immobile Campbell and said: "Keep yourself cool, Sir, and the ship will be got off." This final piece of insubordination shocked Campbell into response, and he began to shout: "Cool! I am as cool as a cucumber! Do you see the rocks? Do you see the rocks?"

Hull, who had mounted one of the quarterdeck guns for a better view, said that he could hardly help seeing them and that something must be done at once. "You will be on the Diamond!" wailed Campbell. "You will be on the Diamond!" Hull turned on him in fury. "Damn the Diamond! We can't help it; the ship must be wore." He then turned his back on the stupefied captain and gave the necessary orders. Slowly, painfully, the *Adams* answered her helm. As she began to gather way on the new tack, Hull stepped down from the gun and, with great deliberation (for he was already a rather stout man), drew on his striped pantaloons while the crew watched in silent admiration. From then on, the *Adams* had a new watchword: "Keep yourself cool!"[11]

Soon after this incident the emperor of Morocco issued a formal passport for the *Meshuda* as his own property. With such a document Consul Simpson had no choice but to comply, and Campbell also, in the absence of Commodore Morris, was forced to accede. The *Meshuda* would be allowed to sail, but the Tripolitan-Moroccan crew seemed in no particular hurry to get her under way, and the *Adams*, having no new orders from the commodore, continued her vigil in the Straits.[12] She remained under sail through most of October, the better to watch the *Meshuda* and other vessels passing through the Straits, and also to prevent her crew from deserting to the British ships at Gibraltar. But late in the month the Tripolitan officers in the *Meshuda* quarreled over their relative rank, and both left the ship, so that she had to be laid up for the winter.[13] The *Adams* then anchored on the Algeciras side of the bay, where she lay for the greater part of November and December, her men engaged a good part of the time in overhauling her worn anchor cables and painting her sides. In mid-November the frigates *New York* and *John Adams*, sent to join the squadron as replacements for the *Chesapeake* and *Constellation*, arrived at Gibraltar and passed up the Mediterranean in search of the commodore. Finally, on 20 December, the *Adams* herself got under way and paid a two-day visit to Tangier to remind the emperor of her continued presence.

That, with another brief call at Tangier in February 1803, was the extent of the *Adams*'s cruising for the winter. Morocco appeared friendly for the moment, but Campbell had no orders to permit him to stir from Gibraltar. There was some diversion in watching the maneuvers of the great powers, as French or English warships passed the Straits almost daily. And there were the dark-eyed ladies of Algeciras, who could make even Lieutenant O'Bannon forget the dreariness of a winter at Gibraltar: "O'Bannon [is] one of the happiest fellows living. He has just returned from spending the evening with a brilliant circle of Spanish ladies, and by way of consolation for the loss of their company, philosophy and the fiddle is called to his aid. On the latter he is now playing 'Hogs in the Cornfield,'" wrote Campbell in December.[14] Isaac Hull was not to be outdone by a marine lieutenant when it came to gallantry; no doubt he, too, found some diversion on shore.

Keep Yourself Cool!

In mid-December, Captain Alexander Murray in the *Constellation* reached Gibraltar. He had been sent down by the commodore to load supplies for the squadron—a necessity because the Navy Department had failed to charter the storeships to go beyond Gibraltar. With the stores on board, Commodore Morris planned at last to take his squadron off Tripoli, where he had yet to make an appearance. But, en route to Gibraltar, Murray had received, unsealed, orders from Secretary Robert Smith to Morris to send the *Constellation* and *Chesapeake* home, and since his crew's enlistment was nearly up, Murray decided to proceed directly to the United States. Once there, he filled the administration's ears with accounts of Morris's inactivity, to which his own precipitate return was, of course, contributory.

Because of Murray's failure to bring stores, Morris felt it necessary, after one attempt to approach Tripoli in a January gale, to take the whole squadron back to Gibraltar. On the way he called at Tunis and Algiers, both of which were making menacing gestures toward the United States. Threats from several directions at once had a paralyzing effect on Morris. Instead of organizing his activities to meet the problems one by one, he became more vague and indecisive than ever. This sort of thing enraged one of the new subordinate commanders, Captain John Rodgers of the *John Adams*. While Rodgers fumed, however, the squadron proceeded to Gibraltar just as the spring season for cruising off Tripoli began. They anchored in the bay on 23 March 1803.

On his arrival at Gibraltar, Morris transferred his command to the *New York* and sent the *Chesapeake* to America as ordered. He was permitted to keep the *Enterprize* with the squadron; indeed, it was almost mandatory, since she was the only small vessel in service.[15] But the enlistment of the *Enterprize*'s crew was up, so volunteers were sought among the squadron to man her for another two-year hitch. The crew was made up mainly from the *Chesapeake*, with a few transfers from the *Adams*.[16] The *Enterprize* was also losing her commander. Andrew Sterrett had decided that two years in her were enough and was returning home to recoup his fortunes by a merchant voyage. There was, of course, only one choice for his replacement. On Tuesday, 5 April 1803, Lieutenant Commandant Isaac Hull lowered himself and his sea bags over the side of the *Adams* and was rowed to the anchorage where the *Enterprize* lay. Boatswain William Curtis piped the side as the new commander came on board. Isaac Hull had a navy command at last.

The schooner *Enterprize* was already a veteran of four years' service. Built in 1799 on the Eastern Shore of Maryland, she had the rakish lines of the famous pilot boat schooners of Chesapeake Bay and was notably fast and handy. She measured 60 feet on the keel, 84 feet 7 inches on deck, and had a beam of about 23 feet, with a depth of 9 feet 6 inches in the hold, an old-fashioned square-tuck stern, and considerable tumble home in her topsides. With these dimensions, she was a fine vessel for getting in and out of tight places, working inshore, and pursuing small craft, but of course she had very little firepower, mounting 6 long six-pounders in each broadside. By 1803 she had seen such steady and arduous service in the Caribbean and the Mediterranean that she was wearing out, quite rotten in places, and in need of a thorough overhaul. But she was too urgently needed. Isaac Hull must keep her running until she could be spared.[17]

At 135 tons, the *Enterprize* had about the same displacement as Hull's first merchant command, the brig *Liffey*, but instead of half a dozen sailors he now had to manage a complement of seventy-six.[18] He was a good manager. So far as the ship's journal records, there was not a single instance of public punishment in the *Enterprize* under Hull's command. At the age of thirty, he had formed an attitude toward discipline that would remain as a conviction throughout his career. Among naval officers, there were those who flogged and those who did not. Isaac Hull was one of those who did not. He thought the practice brutal and unlikely to produce good conduct. On rare occasions and in large ships it might be necessary, but only as a last resort. More than thirty years later he urged a young officer:

> above all let me advise you to treat the men and all under your command with as much kindness as you can consistent with your duty, and do not punish anyone except as the law directs. . . . [L]et me beseech you to be careful not to suffer yourself or any under you to punish the men unnecessarily.[19]

The officers' mess in a tiny vessel like the *Enterprize* was, of necessity, intimate. There were only Lieutenant James Lawrence; Acting Lieutenant Jonathan Thorn, whom Hull brought over from the *Adams*; Midshipmen George Mitchell and Walter Boyd; and Purser Samuel Robertson. But they were merry in the prospect of action, especially those who had been languishing at Gibraltar all winter. The *Enterprize* already had the reputation in the navy of being a lucky ship. The *Meshuda* having finally departed under her Moorish passport, the squadron, provisioned for the summer, weighed anchor again on 11 April for Malta. The *Adams* had sailed four days earlier with a convoy for Leghorn. Midshipman Henry Wadsworth of the *New York* wrote hopefully, "We may now date the commencement of our cruise off Tripoli, where we expect to pass the ensuing summer."[20]

The *New York*, the *John Adams*, and the *Enterprize* jogged up the Spanish coast with light breezes as far as Cape Palos. Isaac Hull tried the schooner's wings and found that he had to keep her under reduced sail to maintain position with the slower frigates. On 20 April the ships spread their sails eastward for Malta, making better time. But at about 8:00 A.M. on Monday, 25 April, off the south coast of Sardinia, the squadron was alarmed by a loud explosion on board the *New York* and by the signal "fire on board." The *Enterprize* and the *John Adams* hastily manned their boats and sent them to the flagship's aid. By ten the fire, which had resulted from mishandling of candles in the gunner's storeroom, was extinguished. It was only by luck that the explosion, which burst the door to the powder magazine, had not set off a chain reaction that would have detonated the frigate's whole store of powder. As it was, nine officers and men were badly injured, four mortally, and the *New York* was so heavily damaged that she must repair at Malta.[21]

The three ships anchored in Valletta harbor on the morning of 1 May; the *John Adams* remained only three days to take on water, and then Captain Rodgers, who for months had been chafing for action, was dispatched off Tripoli at his own request. The *New York*'s plight offered an opportunity for some badly needed repairs to the *Enterprize*'s bottom; between 6 and 12 May she was hove out at the British dockyard, cleaned, caulked, and recoppered. Although much of her topsides was still rotten, she at least had a tight bottom for the summer's cruising. The *Enterprize* and the *New York* were preparing to sail on 19 May when the *John Adams* entered the harbor towing a prize taken off Tripoli. Rodgers had sighted the city on 8 May and for the next several days amused himself by exchanging shots with the fort and gunboats. About sunset on the twelfth he ran down a large ship which was attempting to enter the harbor—none other than the old pest, the *Meshuda!* She was freighted with cutlasses, hemp, and other contraband and had twenty Tripolitans on board. The squadron officers decided that the whole business of a sale to Morocco had been a fraud. The *Meshuda* was left at Malta with a prize crew, and the squadron weighed for Tripoli on 20 May.[22]

Sunday morning, 22 May, was hazy and mild. The sun glinting on whitewashed walls and minarets brought Isaac Hull his first glimpse of Tripoli as the squadron approached the hostile port, and his first taste of action was not long in coming. At 10:00 A.M. the *New York* signaled the *Enterprize*, "chase to the westward." As the schooner went down along the land, all sail set, the batteries of the town and gunboats opened up, and as Hull maintained his course, at about noon, a previously undiscovered battery of two guns sent a salvo over the *Enterprize*'s deck. "Return the compliment, Mr. Lawrence," said Hull coolly, and the *Enterprize*'s six-pounders poured a broadside into the battery that put the guns' crew to flight. The *Enterprize*, making seven knots, continued to pursue the chase, which was now perceived to be a felucca of 25 or 30 tons. At about 2:00 P.M. the felucca ran on shore, and her crew fled, leaving the red flag flying on board. The *Enterprize* took station as near to her as possible and attempted to sink her by gunfire but without success. As the frigates approached the scene, the young officers of the squadron begged to be allowed to go in and capture the felucca, but Commodore Morris, after a brief hesitation, decided it was not worth the risk. Henry Wadsworth expressed the chagrin of the eager young men as the squadron hauled off:

> We were all very much disappointed at not being permitted to tow her off. . . .
> The Commodore said had she been armed, or an object worth taking, that he
> would have brought her off: however, had she been but an oyster boat t'would
> have been amusement for us to skirmish a little: I'm vexed.[23]

In the ensuing week the squadron found little action; there was just one exchange of broadsides with the Tripolitan gunboats, which did no damage to either side. On Thursday afternoon, 26 May, the *Adams* joined company. The next afternoon Commodore Morris and his squadron had an opportunity never offered an American vessel before or afterward—to cut off all the Tripolitan gunboats from the harbor. At about four a small vessel was seen to the westward, beating up for Tripoli. The Americans thought her a privateer, but she was actually one of Tripoli's eleven corsairs, a 14-gun xebec. All nine of the Tripolitan gunboats ran down to her assistance, as the Americans also made sail in chase. The *John Adams*, which had a pilot, took the lead as the ships neared shore, followed by the other two frigates and the *Enterprize*. The quarry were about five miles west of Tripoli, near the small battery that had fired on the *Enterprize* the week before. By six the ships were within long gunshot but just as the action got under way in earnest the wind died. The Americans were now at a disadvantage, for their enemy lay under the shadow of the land and could be made out only by the flash of their guns, whereas the attacking vessels, carrying all possible canvas in the light breeze, were brilliantly illuminated by the setting sun. Henry Wadsworth wished for a Joshua to make the sun stand still; but he admitted that the action was a "most elegant sight."

> The frequent flash and heavy report of the gunboats, the still more frequent
> broadsides of our squadron, formed the most sublime scene you can imagine.
> The shot from the gunboats whistled over us and struck all around, but none
> hit us.[24]

Keep Yourself Cool!

By eight the squadron gave up the action and hauled off, their sails now lighted by the rising moon. The gunboats of course did not offer pursuit but made their way into the harbor with the xebec. The *John Adams* had expended 108 shot, to no effect. The *Adams*, in the course of the action, fired a broadside over the *John Adams* and cut up her rigging. No one was injured, but this clumsy act earned Hugh Campbell a tongue-lashing from John Rodgers.[25]

On the day following this abortive engagement, Commodore Morris attempted to reopen communication with Tripoli. The pasha, however, had nothing to say to the American commander, who was obviously getting the worst of the contest thus far. The next afternoon the *Enterprize* ("who," said Wadsworth, "in light breezes and smooth water beats us all") was sent in chase of a tiny sloop leaving Tripoli. She proved to be a French privateer, *Le Vaillant Bonaparte*, bound for Messina. To the Americans she brought the lukewarm pleasure of knowing that they had inflicted a few casualties in their night engagement: three killed and five wounded, the latter including a brother-in-law of the pasha.[26] The captain of the privateer also told Morris that three Tripolitan cruisers were at sea and were expected to run into Tripoli soon. Morris posted his squadron at wide intervals off the port to wait for them.

The next three days saw the *Enterprize* in her hottest action of the summer. In the late forenoon of 31 May the *Adams*, stationed to the westward of Tripoli, made the signal "discovering strange ships to the west." The *New York* and the *Enterprize* made sail to join her, but as it was nearly calm only the *Enterprize*, powered by her sweeps, was able to come up with the chase. It proved to be a fleet of small merchantmen hugging the land near Old Tripoli. At 5:00 P.M. the *Adams* commenced firing her broadside, and at six the *Enterprize* was in position to follow suit. The schooner continued tacking back and forth in the dying light, firing broadsides, until about eight. At ten Hull brought his vessel to anchor in eleven fathoms and sent a boat in toward the shore, as did the *Adams*, to watch the movements of the enemy vessels.

Throughout the night the wind remained calm, and the crews of the *Adams* and the *Enterprize* watched, tensely alert lest their prey escape again. The *Adams* kept up a desultory fire all night, and in the morning of 1 June both ships anchored with springs on their cables, the *Enterprize* within musket shot of the small craft, and kept up a hot fire to prevent the crews of the vessels from carrying off their cargo by land. At noon the *Enterprize* weighed and stood out for the flagship, flying the signal "intelligence I have for the Commodore." Hull told Morris that the vessels, each between 15 and 25 tons' burden, were loaded with wheat and that assistance was needed from the *New York* if they were to be taken. He believed that eight of them were Tripolitan vessels, the other two Tunisian. By five both the *New York* and the *Enterprize* joined the action, the *New York* taking station about a mile offshore.

The plan was to send boats on shore, under covering fire from the frigates, to secure the wheat ships. But this began to seem a rather more desperate enterprise than it had earlier in the day, for during the afternoon a thousand or more men from Tripoli had come to the rescue. Many of them were now riding up and down the beach where the wheat ships lay aground, flourishing their guns and displaying the beauty of their horses. Nevertheless, a night reconnaissance was decided on, led by First Lieutenant David Porter of the *New York* and including the ardent Henry Wadsworth. Porter had wanted to make a night attack, but Morris hoped that he might persuade the Tripolitans to surrender the boats the next day, so permission to attack was refused. A second boat was sent from the *Enterprize*; the whole expedition mustered ten men. The boats set off about eight o'clock, but in the bright moonlight they were soon discovered. Much yelling and ineffectual shooting ensued on both sides; the Americans drew off out of range and landed on a large offshore rock. Wadsworth solemnly took possession of it in the name of the United States. At midnight the boats were recalled and a second watch was sent out.

Early in the morning of 2 June, no surrender being offered, preparations were made for a full-scale amphibious attack to fire the wheat ships. Lieutenant Porter was again in command, with two boats from the *New York*; three boats came from the *Adams* and two from the *Enterprize*, one under First Lieutenant James Lawrence and the other under Acting Lieutenant Jonathan Thorn, who reported in his journal that there were "at least 6000 armed men on shore." The boats' crews numbered about fifty.

At 8:00 A.M. the boats advanced, led by two carrying combustibles with which to fire the cargo ships. The Tripolitans, who by this time were well prepared to receive the assault, did not expose themselves on the beach but kept up a brisk fire from behind a stone building, from a barricade built of the ships' yards and sails, and from the surrounding hills. The first boats succeeded in penetrating the shipping and in starting fires while their compatriots laid down a protecting barrage of musketry; they took particular pride in bringing down a defiant rider on a black steed. But the Tripolitan aim was just as good; Lieutenant Porter was shot through both thighs, and several other men in the boats were wounded.

When they had exhausted their ammunition the boats pulled off, leaving the wheat ships ablaze; but as soon as they were out of musket shot the Tripolitans, despite the continued cannonade from the larger vessels, swarmed down the beach and extinguished the flames, which had been unable to gain much headway in the tightly stowed wheat. Only a few of the ships were seriously damaged. No follow-up attack was launched; as on the previous occasion, Commodore Morris thought the game was not worth the candle.[27]

The pasha of Tripoli, though not eager to treat with the Americans, had been persuaded to permit a conference on shore. Accordingly, on 7 and 8 June, Morris and six squadron officers went to Tripoli to confer with Yusuf through his prime minister, Sidi Mohammed Dghies. The Danish consul, Nicholas C. Nissen, and the French consul, Bonaventure Beaussier, were also active in assisting the negotiations. They proved useless, however. Tripoli demanded a payment of $200,000, a $20,000 annual present, and the expenses of the war; Morris was prepared to offer only a $5,000 consular present and $10,000 after five years for good behavior. The pasha was insulted; the negotiations were at an end.[28] Consul Nissen thought the Tripolitans, who had made peace with Sweden at a good price, were now in a very favorable position for continued resistance and that the American blockade was a weak weapon. He wrote Cathcart:

> Tripoli this year is well provided with provisions by a rich harvest. Here are plenty of European goods by the arrival of several ships and the Bashaw having the Swedish money has wherewith to maintain his people and defray his expenses. . . . Under such circumstances it seems, Sir, that a *simple* blockade is as expensive as useless, and that your navigation is not secure was seen last year![29]

On the afternoon of 9 June, as soon as the negotiations ended, Morris summoned the *Enterprize* to accompany him, and the two ships stood for Malta, leaving the *Adams* and *John Adams* to keep up the blockade. At Malta the *New York* was assigned two weeks' quarantine, during which time Mrs. Morris, who had remained at the island, gave birth to a son. No one in the squadron failed to notice the coincidence between Morris's hasty departure from Tripoli and the blessed event at Malta. Then, with the whole summer still before him, Morris dispatched the *Enterprize* to Tripoli once again to recall the two remaining frigates. John Rodgers's reaction when Isaac Hull gave him this news on board the *John Adams* can be readily imagined. Rodgers's impulse was always to attack. But Morris had what seemed to him logical reasons for his action: Morocco was probably angered by the recapture of the *Meshuda*, and Tunis by the attack on the wheat boats; the dey of Algiers was reported displeased with his annual present. These three powerful nations might be preparing to combine against American shipping. The *Adams*'s crew were due for discharge, and she must be sent home; but under the circumstances she could scarcely be sent to Gibraltar alone. Finally, the events of May and June had convinced Morris that he needed fewer frigates and more *Enterprizes* if he were to injure Tripoli significantly by destroying its gunboats and sealing the port. Therefore, there was little point in continuing the blockade with the vessels he had.

The *Enterprize* had one more shot in her locker before she quit Tripoli for the year. Morris's orders permitted the squadron to cruise for another week before lifting the blockade. Rodgers stationed the *Adams* to the west of the town, the *Enterprize* to the east, and kept the center with the *John Adams*. Two Tripolitan cruisers were still at sea. First light of Wednesday, 22 June, showed the *Enterprize*'s lookout a strange sail south-southwest, near the land. Signaling to the *John Adams* "discovering strange ships inshore," the *Enterprize* gave chase. At seven the stranger ran into a deep narrow bay east of the town and anchored. The Tripolitan gunboats began to beat up to her rescue, for she was, in fact, the largest and best of the corsair fleet, a polacre mounting 22 guns. At the same time, cavalry galloped from Tripoli to join the fight. The *Enterprize* was firing on the polacre when, at eight-thirty, the *John Adams* came up. The frigate anchored and fired her broadside at the Tripolitan vessel for three quarters of an hour, then hauled off to hoist out her boats for an attack. As she passed the *Enterprize*, Rodgers shouted to Hull to stand inshore and "amuse the enemy." The schooner closed the beach, all her guns firing round and doubleheaded shot. The polacre's crew were seen abandoning ship. A little before ten a boat was seen to return to the beleaguered vessel; immediately afterward her flag was hauled down, and she blew up with a shattering crash, discharging both broadsides and bursting her hull, the masts forced 150 feet in the air. The Americans congratulated themselves on this feat; they would probably have been a little deflated had they known that the polacre's crew, seeing the hopelessness of their situation, had fired the vessel on orders from the pasha to keep her from being captured by the Americans.[30]

On the morning of Saturday, 25 June, the *John Adams, Adams,* and *Enterprize* lifted the blockade of Tripoli and stood for Malta.

The day before the *John Adams* and the *Enterprize* engaged the polacre at Tripoli, Secretary of the Navy Robert Smith posted two letters to the Mediterranean. The first was addressed to Richard V. Morris and said succinctly:

You will upon the receipt of this consider yourself suspended in the command of the squadron on the Mediterranean station and of the frigate the *New York.* It is the command of the President that you take charge of the *Adams* and that with her you return without delay to the United States.[31]

This curt missive was enclosed in a letter to John Rodgers:

You will perceive by the enclosed the recall of Capt. Morris and after presenting it you will assume the command of the *New York* and of the squadron. To Capt. Campbell you must give the command of the *John Adams.* The term of the enlistment of the crew of the *Adams* having expired this month it is the desire of the President that she return to the United States and that Capt. Morris take charge of her for this purpose. . . .

If any provisions should be wanted by you before the arrival of the relieving squadron, you will, instead of going to Gibraltar for them, freight some merchant vessel to bring to you such supply. The relieving squadron will leave the United States about the first day of August. It will consist of the *Constitution* Capt. Preble, the *Philadelphia* Capt. Bainbridge, the *Siren* Lieut. Stewart, the *Argus* Lieut. Hull, the *Vixen* Lieut. Smith, and the *Nautilus* Lieut. Somers. The *Enterprize* is also to remain in the Mediterranean and will be there repaired. She will be commanded by Lieut. Decatur who will take out the brig *Argus* to be delivered to Lieut. Hull.[32]

The patience of the Jefferson administration with Richard V. Morris had run out. The cabinet could not know, of course, that Morris was again about to abandon operations off Tripoli at the height of the cruising season, but they had the unfavorable report of Alexander Murray before them and—most damaging of all—Morris's last dispatch, sent on 30 March before he left Gibraltar. Like all his letters to the Navy Department—few enough to begin with—this one was vague. It indicated that the vessels of the squadron would leave Gibraltar "as soon as possible" but did not say where they were bound; nor did it state any intention of engaging in active operations off Tripoli. This was the last straw, and when it reached the United States, a unanimous decision was taken to recall Morris, sending the letter by the newly acquired schooner *Nautilus,* in hopes that something could be salvaged of the summer season under the more aggressive Rodgers. The relief squadron, to be headed by Edward Preble (now restored to health), could not arrive before September or October; some elements of it were still on the stocks.

One particular cause of irritation with Morris is shown in the injunction to Rodgers that he not take the squadron to Gibraltar for provisions, as Morris had done, but have them sent up in merchant vessels, even at risk. It was a hint that John Rodgers was not likely to need. But there was bitter disappointment in the letter for Rodgers as well. He was to have only a temporary command, and the relief squadron would be led by Preble, an officer junior to himself. After months of frustration under Morris, Rodgers thought he deserved better than that.

Finally, the letter contained interesting news for Lieutenant Hull. A new and larger ship was on her way to him—the brig *Argus,* even then under construction at Boston.

None of this was known in the Mediterranean in June, of course. The squadron were assembling at Malta, preparing for a leisurely trip to Gibraltar. They weighed anchor on 11 July and crawled up to Messina, their progress impeded by the light summer breezes, but even more by the need to take with them the lumbering *Meshuda,* a singularly unhandy craft. She spent most of the voyage in tow of one or another ship. At first her escort was the *John Adams* or the *New York,* but for some reason as the squadron approached Messina she was handed over to the *Enterprize.* Hull and the "Enterprizes" did their best, but the *Meshuda* was too heavy for them. Even with sweeps out and all the squadron's boats towing, they could not get her into Messina harbor against the tide, and the trip through the Strait of Messina, with its baffling currents, was a nightmare. The frigates had a hard enough time making the passage on their own; Hull was forced to anchor twice in the two days and nights as the ships beat up past the erupting landmark of Stromboli, and finally cast off the *Meshuda* in the whirling confusion of the passage between Scylla and Charybdis. At last, on 27 July, the squadron anchored at Naples, where they remained, taking in water and provisions, until 4 August.[33]

The cruise was capped on 12 August by a comic-opera episode. As the squadron beat up for Leghorn, passing through the narrow channel between Elba and Piombino, the *Adams* tacked very close to a small islet near Elba and came under fire from the French garrison. Captain Campbell sent his boat on shore to remonstrate, whereupon the French commander seized First Lieutenant John H. Dent of the *Adams* and demanded that, before he could be released, Commodore Morris pay compensation for the three shots expended by the fort. The chagrined Campbell had to pay three guineas to get his lieutenant back.[34] Midshipman Wadsworth reflected the outrage of the other officers:

> Captain Campbell assumed great liberty in transacting any affairs directly under the nose of the Commodore—and through his damned foolishness our country is insulted and we pay for it, too. Blast him! if I were Commodore I'd arrest him and pack him off to the United States for trial.[35]

It was not Campbell, however, who was about to be sent home for trial, but Morris. On the squadron's arrival at Leghorn, Morris learned that the *Nautilus* was in the Mediterranean and sent Isaac Hull to find her and order her to rendezvous with him at Málaga. The *John Adams* and the *Adams* were also dispatched—Morris's fears of attack by Tunis, Algiers, and Morocco having somehow evaporated—the one with a convoy and the other to carry James L. Cathcart from Leghorn to Tunis. Hull never caught up with the *Nautilus;* her commander, Lieutenant Richard Somers, had been pursuing the squadron since 31 July from Gibraltar to Malta to Tripoli and back to Malta; on the second visit to Malta he missed the *Enterprize* by a day. He then headed for Leghorn, fell in with the *Adams,* and was deflected toward Barcelona, where Rodgers was bound. (The dispatches he bore, it will be recalled, were directed to Rodgers with enclosure to Morris.) On 11 September he blew into Málaga in a gale, found Morris there quite by chance, and delivered to him the unhappy letter of 21 June. The next day John Rodgers arrived to learn that he was now commodore. Alas for Rodgers! The very day he received the good news the frigate *Constitution,* flagship of Edward Preble's squadron, ran through the Straits of Gibraltar.[36]

After looking into Malta for the *Nautilus,* Isaac Hull and the *Enterprize* had carried out further orders from the commodore to cruise for Tripolitan corsairs. They sighted one soon after leaving Malta, a large vessel superior in force to the *Enterprize,* but she escaped into Tunis Bay. From there the schooner ran down to Cape de Gat (Cabo Gata), where she took up station to wait for two 10-gun Tripolitans expected to call there. The *New York* passed her on that station in early September. After two weeks of fruitless cruising, Hull turned his ship's bow westward once more, and on 18 September the *Enterprize* joined the other American warships at Gibraltar.[37]

There were now two American squadrons at Gibraltar, and there was enough trouble afoot to occupy them fully. The emperor of Morocco, disgusted at the loss of the *Meshuda,* had decided to make a hostile move. While denying that a state of war existed, he sent his cruisers to sea in late August with sealed orders to attack American shipping. But, as on the previous occasion in 1802, the emperor's timing was bad. One of his cruisers, the 22-gun *Mirboha,* had just seized her first prize, the brig *Celia* of Boston, near Cape de Gat, when the first major unit of the new American squadron hove in sight. This was the 36-gun frigate *Philadelphia,* William Bainbridge, captain, who had looked in at Cape de Gat for the same two Tripolitans that the *Enterprize* came searching for a few days later. Instead, he found the *Mirboha* and her prize and packed them off to Gibraltar. Commodore Preble encountered another Moroccan cruiser, the big frigate *Maimona,* in the Atlantic some two weeks later. He was suspicious of her, but after a thorough examination of her papers he found no proof sufficient to detain her. She was released but soon afterward put into Lisbon with a sprung mast and remained there until all the trouble was over.

Preble, surveying the situation on his arrival at Gibraltar, saw that he held all the cards at the moment and determined to act immediately before there should be some reverse. He had at hand his own ship, the *Constitution*, 44; the *Philadelphia*, 36; and the schooners *Vixen*, 12, and *Nautilus*, 12, with the *Enterprize* hourly expected. In addition, there were the ships of the departing squadron: the *New York*, 36, and the *John Adams*, 28, under Rodgers and Campbell, respectively. Morris was under orders to take the *Adams* home without delay. Besides, Preble had as prizes the *Meshuda* and the *Mirboha*, which the emperor badly wanted to recover. For the moment, Morocco held no American vessels except the brig *Hannah*, a Salem trader detained at Mogador. If the emperor could be brought to a negotiation before any other captures were made, he would have little to bargain with. Preble was determined that there would be no delay.

Before he could deal with the emperor of Morocco, however, he had to make peace with a man who could be even more difficult to deal with: John Rodgers. Rodgers was already seething with indignation at having lost the opportunity to show his valor before the new squadron arrived. When he entered Gibraltar Bay on 14 September, therefore, and saw Preble, his junior, flying a commodore's pendant, he was prepared to give vent to his anger. He sent Preble a hostile demand that the offending pendant be hauled down. Preble demurred, citing his orders as commander of an independent squadron. Rodgers was distinctly not satisfied but dropped the subject for the moment in "the interest of our country." Preble was in a tight spot, for if his negotiations with Morocco were to succeed, he had to persuade Rodgers to join him in a show of force at Tangier. To ask the already aroused Rodgers to act in concert with, and under leadership of, a junior captain, and one whom he personally detested to begin with, took considerable temerity. Luckily, Preble had it, and Rodgers had enough real patriotism to swallow his monumental pride for the nation's sake. The two men agreed to act together, although Rodgers hinted darkly at some future encounter—probably pistols at sunrise—when both had returned to the United States. (Fortunately, by the time that happened, Rodgers had found another object for his spleen.) Interestingly enough, in all this the dismissed Commodore Morris, though senior to both the other sparring commodores, was as thoroughly ignored as if he had taken flight to the moon.[38]

Unwilling to neglect the primary object of his mission while engaged with the immediate problem of Morocco, Preble sent off two of his vessels, the *Philadelphia* and the *Vixen*, on 19 September to resume the blockade of Tripoli. He had a special mission for the *Enterprize* as well. This was at Mogador, which had a brisk trade with the United States. The brig *Hannah*, seized by the authorities there, was the one American prize in the emperor's hands, but a number of other traders were daily expected. Hull was to provision the *Enterprize* as quickly as possible, then run down the Moroccan coast by Larache and Salé to cruise for fifteen days off Mogador, warning American vessels not to enter Moroccan ports. The other small vessels would be sent in the same direction if and when they arrived.[39]

That afternoon of 23 September, Hull and Preble had a brief opportunity to renew their interrupted acquaintance in the *Constitution*'s cabin. Hull was not the senior among Preble's subordinates, but he was the oldest, and the only one with whom Preble had previously served, albeit briefly. He was also the only other New Englander besides Preble among the squadron's commanders. The two men made a contrasting pair. Preble was tall, thin, pale, and sandy-haired; brusque and volatile in temper; and ordinarily of forbiddingly cool demeanor but given to demonic rages. Hull was short, stout, and ruddy, with a cap of brown curls done in the latest mode and a twinkling eye full of fun, open and pleasant in his manner, and ineffably cool in moments of excitement. Displays of temper were unknown to him. If opposites attract, then these two were drawn together like magnets; and, in fact, Hull admired Preble beyond all his other commanders, while Preble valued Hull more than the other young men of his command. It would take some time for the two fully to discover each other, but Preble was not long in assessing Hull's value. An incident on the morning following their meeting could have brought only delight to Preble, who so prized decision and skill: a strange ship appeared in the Straits, and the *Constitution* hoisted the signal for the *Enterprize* to chase. Midshipman Wadsworth gleefully reported: "The active Captain Hull was under way in eight minutes after the signal was made." There was seamanship! The chase was only a Baltimore merchant after all, but Preble marked Hull for an able commander.[40]

By the end of September the *Enterprize* was ready for sea and proceeded on her mission off Mogador—an entirely eventless cruise, as it turned out. Hull therefore missed the dramatic and colorful negotiations that took place at Tangier in the first week of October. The emperor arrived in full panoply, but so did Preble and Rodgers; the Barbary monarch was given full opportunity to contemplate the might of the

Constitution, the *New York*, the *John Adams*, and the *Nautilus* and the puniness of the *Mirboha* and the *Meshuda* alongside them. Perhaps he was not precisely "trembling in [his] shoes," as Midshipman Ralph Izard would have had it, but he was impressed. The result was that peace was restored between the two nations forthwith. The emperor got his ships back but nothing more; the *Hannah* was released, and the treaty of 1786 was confirmed. Preble dispatched the *Nautilus* on 12 October to carry the order for the *Hannah*'s release to Mogador and to recall the *Enterprize*. On the nineteenth the *Enterprize* reentered Gibraltar Bay, passing the *John Adams* and the *New York* outbound for America.[41] Now the work of the Preble squadron might begin in earnest.

Commodore Preble's first action after the reassembly of his squadron at Gibraltar was to take the *Constitution*, accompanied by the *Enterprize*, to Cadiz for water, provisions, and cables. During the two weeks spent in the Spanish port, Preble and Hull had ample time to discuss prospects for the coming year. Morale in the squadron was high in the wake of the Moroccan success, and Preble anticipated an equally speedy triumph at Tripoli. He had no intention of adopting halfway measures. The blockade of the city of Tripoli would be maintained through the winter, but when the summer cruising season of 1804 opened, the commodore projected an all-out attack on the Tripolitan coast; reduction of minor ports like Derna and Benghazi; and, if the pasha had not sued for peace by then, an assault on the capital.

If all this whetted Lieutenant Hull's appetite for action, Preble had dismaying words for him as well: the emperor of Morocco was not to be trusted, and one vessel must be left at Gibraltar to watch the movements of his cruisers and to remind him that American force was still at hand. For this independent service the most reliable officer in the squadron should be chosen: Who but Isaac Hull? If Hull groaned inwardly at the thought of another winter at Gibraltar, he was perhaps mollified by praise of the sort Preble expressed in his report to Robert Smith: "I have made choice of this vessel more particularly on account of the judgment, prudence and firmness of her commander, Lieutenant Commandant Hull, on whose discretion I rely with confidence."[42] Moreover, Preble promised Hull that he would be summoned to join the squadron before active operations commenced in the spring.

"This vessel" was not the *Enterprize* but the sleek new brig *Argus*, 16, built at Boston under Preble's supervision. She was on her way to the Mediterranean under Lieutenant Stephen Decatur, and since Hull was the ranking officer, he would take over the larger vessel while Decatur assumed command of the *Enterprize*. By the time the *Constitu-*

tion and *Enterprize* returned to Gibraltar on Sunday, 6 November, the *Argus* was at anchor there. On Wednesday morning the exchange of commands took place.[43]

The *Argus* was the last of Preble's squadron to reach the Mediterranean, but her delay was caused by construction and procurement problems, not by her own tardiness. Nearly every commander in the sailing navy claimed that his was the fastest ship afloat—if he was not complaining that she was the slowest tub in the fleet—but there seems some justification for the claim that the *Argus* was a smart vessel. Preble modestly called her "without exception the handsomest vessel of her rate that I have ever seen."[44] Ten feet longer than the *Enterprize* and, at nearly 300 tons, over twice the displacement of the schooner, the *Argus* was a full-bodied but rakish vessel, low in the water and sailing fast. For armament she carried 16 twenty-four-pounder carronades and 2 long twelves.[45]

The American squadron was anchored on the Algeciras side of the bay because of the much-resented British practice of enticing American sailors on board their naval ships at Gibraltar. For the same reason, Preble had decided not to base his operations at Malta but to establish a rendezvous at Syracuse. He sent the *Enterprize* there directly, in charge of a storeship, while the *Constitution* was to call at Algiers and take a look at Tripoli before proceeding to Sicily. The *Argus* would take a convoy to Marseilles and Leghorn, then assume her winter station. On 10 November she stood over to Gibraltar with the *Enterprize* to fill her water casks; the next day Preble made a visit of inspection on board. On Saturday night, true to the pattern, Seaman Robert Murray attempted to desert by swimming to HMS *Donegal*, but *Argus* eyes spotted him; he was fished out and put in irons. Hull disposed of another unsavory character, Marine Edward Madden, by sending him in irons on board the *Constitution*. That was bad luck for Madden; within three days he had accumulated enough offenses in the frigate (refusing duty, contempt of a commissioned officer, insolence to a noncommissioned officer, and attempting to desert) to net him forty-eight lashes. Edward Preble, unlike Isaac Hull, did not spare the cat.[46]

Hull was anticipating trouble higher up the line: his first lieutenant, William M. Livingston, arrived with a bad report, as Preble informed Robert Smith:

> Lieutenant Livingston of the Argus did while in Boston conduct very improperly and in a manner disgraceful to himself as an officer, and . . . there is not any probability of his amendment. He is extremely intemperate and exposes himself to observations on board and on shore. I have forbid Lieutenant Hull from suffering him to go on shore to disgrace the service, and the first formal

complaint that is made against him I shall arrest and order him home. This will be a painful task to me, but the service requires it.[47]

Sure enough, by the beginning of March, Second Lieutenant Joshua Blake of the *Argus* had presented formal charges against Livingston, which Hull forwarded to Preble. When the *Argus* rejoined the squadron in April, Preble demanded, and got, Livingston's resignation. "You may rest assured," he wrote Livingston with a kind of relish, "that your resignation will readily be accepted." This was Preble's favorite method for dealing with problem officers because it spared the ordeal of a court-martial—an ordeal, that is, not so much for the offending officer as for Preble. Some officers, like John Rodgers, were extremely litigious and relished a good court battle. But Hull was like Preble in this respect; he loathed sitting on courts; was known to catch up on his correspondence while supposedly taking down testimony; and would go to almost any lengths to avoid them, even overlooking offenses as long as possible to keep from bringing the culprits to trial.[48]

Before leaving the station Preble gave Hull written instructions for the winter. The spirit of these orders and of Preble's attitude toward his whole operation in the Mediterranean is succinctly expressed in the second paragraph:

> Experience has taught us that implicit faith cannot be placed in treaties with any of the Barbary states. You will, therefore, as often as possible, appear on the coast of Morocco and communicate with Consul Simpson at Tangier. If you learn that any of their cruisers are fitting for sea you will inform yourself of the object of such equipment, and take care that you repel the first aggression on their part with the greatest promptitude, as an ascendancy can only be obtained over these, or any other barbarians . . . by a determined mode of conduct towards them.

Since there was no *Meshuda* to blockade at Gibraltar now, the *Argus's* role would be considerably more active than the *Adams's* had been. Hull was instructed to convoy American vessels up the Spanish coast at least as far as Cape Saint Martin (Cabo de la Nao) and to keep a good lookout off Cape de Gat; to cruise for and capture Tripolitan vessels and to give all possible aid to American ships that might be attacked; and to call regularly at Gibraltar, Cadiz, and Málaga as well as at Tangier. At the same time, he should be careful to respect the rights of peaceful nations and not violate their territorial waters.

Preble was confident that the Navy Department would honor his request for another small frigate to be sent him in the spring. He therefore ordered Hull, as soon as that ship should reach Gibraltar, to leave her on that station and bring the *Argus* to rejoin the fleet. Meanwhile, "much must depend on your own judgment and prudence," but every opportunity should be taken to write to both Preble and the Navy Department.[49]

On the morning of Sunday, 13 November, the American vessels got under way for the eastward.[50] Within a few days, the *Constitution* and the *Nautilus* were out of sight. The *Argus*, frequently towing one of her convoy, plodded slowly up the coast to Leghorn, where she anchored early on the morning of 22 November. Hull was disgusted to find that the *Argus* would be kept in quarantine eight days because of a fever at Málaga—where he had not touched—but any vessel coming from that direction was held suspect. Even his letter bag could not be sent on shore. The weather was bad, too; in four days at anchor Hull was unable to communicate with Charles Stewart of the *Syren*, also in Leghorn harbor. He decided not to wait out the quarantine, and since no ships were waiting for convoy, sailed again for Gibraltar on the twenty-seventh. In the morning he held a trial of speed with the *Syren:* the two brigs unmoored at 5:30 and raced one another out of the harbor. By 6:30 Hull was satisfied he had beaten his rival and hauled into the anchorage again. The *Argus* went to sea at 8:00 P.M. The next afternoon she again encountered the *Syren* and tried her mettle at sea: "find we easily outsail the *Syren*," recorded Sailing Master Humphrey Magrath in the log.[51]

The next month was a seaman's hell. The *Argus*, for a few days accompanied by the *Syren* and then alone, clawed her way toward Gibraltar in the teeth of a series of westerly gales typical of the Mediterranean in the winter. Off Corsica heavy seas and winds threw the *Syren* on her beam ends; the *Argus* was "laboring very hard and shipping a great deal of water." From a landfall at Majorca, the *Argus* was driven south to the African coast, and it was not until 15 December that she was able to make Cartagena. Here she paused long enough to overhaul her rigging. Hull had decided, after watching the brig's performance in the storm, that the mainmast needed more rake. That accomplished, he sailed again on the nineteenth without having communicated with the Spanish shore. For a week he cruised off Cape de Gat. The crew were now on short allowance of water, but another week of vigilance off Málaga elapsed before the *Argus* put into Tangerole to refill her casks. Finally, on the morning of 4 January 1804, she anchored at Gibraltar.

Despite his three days' quarantine, due to the call at Tangerole, Hull was immediately in touch with Richard Somers of the *Nautilus*, just arrived from Syracuse, where Commodore Preble had established his base of operations. Somers's news was devastating: the *Philadelphia* had run aground off Tripoli on 31 October; worse than that, her captors had refloated her and carried her safely into port. All her officers and crew were prisoners in Tripoli. A letter from Preble, dated 10 December, confirmed the dismal tidings.

Hull knew that this event would force a radical change in Preble's plans. With his effective force halved, he would be unable to carry out the assaults on the city he had projected; moreover, the pasha now had a bargaining counter in the *Philadelphia* prisoners. Still worse, this disaster to the American squadron might make Morocco, Tunis, and Algiers restive. If the hoped-for additional frigate from America were to arrive by spring, however, something might yet be salvaged. In his reply to Preble, Hull tried to strike this consolatory note: "I have been informed by Captain Somers that men were shipping for one of the frigates; if so she may be soon expected on this station, so that I hope I shall be able to join you [by early April]." He also bolstered Preble's pride in the *Argus:* "I find the *Argus* to be an excellent sea boat, and I believe when in trim will sail very fast by the wind, but have not as yet had an opportunity of sailing with anything except the *Syren,* and I believe Captain Stewart will be candid enough to acknowledge she beats her."[52] Stewart must indeed have told Preble as much, for scarcely a week later and before receiving Hull's letter Preble wrote the secretary that "the *Argus* . . . is the best vessel in our service for cruising in these seas. She sails wonderfully fast, has been tried with the *Syren,* and sails more than a third faster and will certainly outsail the *Vixen* as much."[53]

Hull was anxious to be under way again. In his letter Preble had inquired about affairs at Morocco, but the long passage from Leghorn had prevented the *Argus* from visiting there yet. After two weeks of refitting and reprovisioning, therefore, Hull crossed the strait to Tangier. Within four hours he was in the harbor. All was quiet in Morocco. The cruisers were laid up for the winter at Larache and Salé. The next day, therefore, the *Argus* recrossed the strait to Gibraltar and, as soon as the wind was fair, ran to Cadiz to check on a rumor that difficulties had arisen with Spain over the transfer of Louisiana. Happily, it proved false.[54]

Thus, the *Argus* wore out the remainder of the winter cruising back and forth between Gibraltar and Cape de Gat, calling at Tangier from time to time. Late in February the schooner *Citizen* arrived with a present of one hundred gun carriages from the United States to the emperor of Morocco, and since she was shorthanded (her mate had been impressed by HMS *Amphion*), Hull took the *Argus* to Tangier to assist in unloading the cargo. With this sweetening, the Moorish disposition was pleasant indeed, although Preble disapproved of the transaction: "We ought not to give those barbarians the means of defense or annoyance."[55]

Returning from Tangier, Hull took the *Argus* to Algeciras for a thorough cleanup to prepare her for the cruising season ahead. "You will not be at a loss to know the reason of my anchoring on [the Algeciras] side," Hull told Preble, but even at that distance from Gibraltar a group of the *Argus*'s men attempted to desert, provoking one of the rare instances of flogging in Hull's brig: "At 8 a.m. [12 March] corporal punishment inflicted on the following vizt. John McKinley, 24 lashes, Francis Orange, 36 lashes, John Smith, 24 lashes and Robert Barney, 12 lashes as accomplices for desertion."[56] These were heavy sentences: Hull must have intended them as a deterrent example. Nevertheless, Francis Orange had to be hauled up to the gratings again the next morning "for mutinous behavior and publicly asserting that he intended to desert the first opportunity."

It was time to get away from Gibraltar. Preble had not yet summoned the *Argus* to join him, but on 21 March the storeship *Woodrop Sims* arrived from Norfolk with provisions for the squadron and two letters for Hull from Secretary Smith. The first, dated 24 January, ordered the *Argus* to convoy the storeship to Malta; the second, dated 9 February, said that there would be, after all, no need for convoy since the *Woodrop Sims* had an Algerian protection. But the secretary left the matter open: "the subject, however, is still committed to the discretion of yourself and [Consul John] Gavino."[57] It was a small loophole but big enough for Hull. "I have . . . consulted Mr. Gavino on the subject of giving her convoy, and have determined, as everything is perfectly tranquil on this station, and the *Argus* ready for sea, to sail immediately for Syracuse, with the ship under convoy, and shall make every exertion to return to my station as soon as possible."[58] The next evening the wind came fair and the two ships were under way. On Sunday morning, as they passed Cape de Gat, Hull mustered his crew and read the Articles of War; the *Argus* was bound for the fighting.

The Active Captain Hull

The *Argus* made a short passage to Syracuse and brought her convoy safely to anchor on 1 April. The schooners *Vixen* and *Nautilus* were in the harbor, but the commodore was absent on a visit to Tunis. From John Smith of the *Vixen* or Richard Somers of the *Nautilus* Hull learned that part of the *Philadelphia* disaster had been recouped when, on 16 February, Stephen Decatur had led an expedition into Tripoli harbor to burn the frigate. With that much of the threat removed, Preble was free to go ahead with offensive operations, but the prisoners remained in the pasha's hands.

Hull had no doubt hoped that once he was in the eastern theater, Preble would order him to remain, but he could not stay without orders. On 6 April, therefore, he again made sail for the west. As luck would have it, however, a strong gale from the westward made it impossible for the *Argus* to weather Cape Passero. After beating against the wind for twenty-six hours, Hull turned back to Syracuse. There he was joined by Somers in the *Nautilus*, which had been heavily damaged by the same gale while blockading Tripoli. Two days later the *Syren*, which had accompanied Preble to Tunis, returned with word that the *Constitution* was at Malta en route to Syracuse. Hull busied himself with raking the *Argus*'s mainmast a little more.[1]

On the afternoon of 14 April the *Constitution* appeared in the offing. Hull's hopes were realized, for Preble decided to "keep the *Argus* aloft" because of the threatening situation at Tunis, which made it unsafe for her to return to Gibraltar alone.[2] The *Argus* and the *Syren* were ordered to proceed immediately toward Tripoli, where the prime season for operations was just beginning. Hull sailed the next day and was in sight of the Barbary shore by Thursday, 19 April. The next evening he joined company with the *Vixen*, which was keeping up the blockade, and on Saturday morning Captains Hull and Smith treated their crews to an exchange of cannon fire with one of the Tripolitan forts.[3] By the end of April all the brigs and schooners except the *Nautilus* were assembled off Tripoli. Charles Stewart of the *Syren*, as senior lieutenant, was in nominal command. He had Preble's orders to station the *Argus* and the

Enterprize to the west of the town, the *Syren* and the *Vixen* to the east. On the afternoon of the twenty-ninth the *Argus* made her first capture by sending her boats inshore after a tiny Tunisian sloop. The vessel and her cargo of earthenware were so worthless that Hull set her adrift the next day; even so, she formed a pretext for a complaint by the bey of Tunis on Preble's next visit there.[4] The slight excitement of the capture of the sloop was the only relief from a monotonous succession of gales that lasted for two weeks. Then, on 12 May, the squadron let off steam by attacking the Tripolitan forts again and challenging the gunboats that were defending the harbor. A furious hour-long cannonade caused no damage on either side. The next day Stewart and Smith led a plundering raid on the shore twenty miles east of the city, which, however, produced no plunder. When Preble reached the station, he disapproved of these activities in the strongest terms: they used up ammunition; they gave the Tripolitans experience under fire; and they risked the loss of more of the squadron. It was disappointing to the young men who were finding war so surprisingly dull, but the commodore was adamant: raids and shooting matches must stop.[5]

The *Argus* made two more captures that spring. The first was a Spanish bombard, or ketch, *La Virgine del Rosario*, which had entered Tripoli with a passport from George Davis, American chargé at Tunis, and bore an embassy from the sultan of Turkey. When she left the port on 31 May, she was carrying several slaves that Hull believed were the pasha's property; he therefore put Midshipman William G. Stewart and a crew in her and ordered her to Malta, which was her destination in any case.[6] The *St. Jean Baptiste*, another ketch, was overhauled on 4 June and sent to Syracuse. Both vessels were subsequently set free. *St. Jean Baptiste* was a French vessel captured by the Tripolitans two years earlier and had been released only recently. *La Virgine del Rosario* was found to be in violation of her passport by bringing fourteen more persons out of Tripoli than she carried in, but Preble released her to keep good relations with Spain and with the sultan.[7]

Commodore Preble had almost completed his preparations for attacking Tripoli. Through the spring he had been engaged in negotiations to obtain gunboats and bomb vessels from the king of the Two Sicilies. These vessels were now being prepared for him at Messina. It remained for him to make two more calls on the Barbary shore: one at Tripoli, to offer negotiations once more before attacking; a second at Tunis, to try to quiet the bey and lessen the possibility of having a second antagonist on his flank. The *Constitution* appeared off Tripoli on 12 June, and negotiator Richard O'Brien was sent on shore the next day, but the meeting was abortive. Preble hoped to get the prisoners back for next to nothing; rather, he was confident enough of the success of his forth-coming operations to be unwilling to offer a reasonable ransom. On the fifteenth the *Constitution* made sail for Tunis, accompanied by the *Argus* and the *Enterprize*. The bey was restive, but Preble satisfied himself that no attack would be made, especially if the assault on Tripoli were successful.[8] By 27 June the ships were again at Syracuse.

The *Argus* rejoined the squadron off Tripoli on 6 July, just in time to participate in the most exciting episode of the blockade. It was a small-scale replay of the actions the *Enterprize* had taken part in during May and June 1803. Again a blockade runner, a galliot, was seen close under the land and, when pursued by the squadron, ran herself on shore. Again the squadron sent boats to the attack, but the Tripolitans repelled them with small-arms fire from behind rocks. The results were less satisfying than the *Enterprize*'s and the *John Adams*'s attack on the polacre had been; although Henry Wadsworth was sure that the galliot had been left "a riddling sieve" by the *Vixen*'s fire, the Tripolitans were able to save her and her entire cargo of wheat.[9]

The monotonous but effective blockade wore on until first light of Wednesday, 25 July, when a squadron appeared in the offing: the *Constitution*, with the *Vixen*, the *Nautilus* and her little flotilla of six gunboats and two bomb ketches. The attacks were to begin at last.

The assaults on Tripoli in August and September 1804 have been meticulously described by Christopher McKee in *Edward Preble: A Naval Biography*. It remains only to notice Isaac Hull's particular part in those actions. As commander of the *Argus*, he was not allotted a very active role. Preble's intention seems to have been to attempt a reduction of the Tripolitan gunboat force with his own gunboats while bombarding the town with shells from the bomb ketches and with shot from the *Constitution*'s heavy guns. If the gunboats could be eliminated, the brigs and schooners could advance into Tripoli harbor to attack the shipping and the town itself. But their light carronades were useless against the forts guarding the harbor and lacked the range to reach the city, so that in this first phase of the action their only role was to act as mother ships to the gunboats and the bombards. And, since the Tripolitan gunboats were never eliminated, the light vessels never took any greater part in the fighting. Two of the commanders, Decatur of the *Enterprize* and Somers of the *Nautilus*, commanded on board the gunboats themselves as heads of the two divisions of boats, but Hull and the other captains who remained in the small vessels took no part in the close fighting.

The *Argus* was mother to two gunboats: No. 2, commanded by Lieutenant James Decatur; and No. 3, commanded by Lieutenant Joshua Blake. In the first assault, on 3 August, both these boats were unlucky in different ways. Gunboat No. 2 forced a Tripolitan boat to strike its flag, but James Decatur was treacherously shot down as he was boarding his enemy to take possession, and the prize escaped as Decatur fell dying into the sea. Gunboat No. 3, after advancing to the attack with Stephen Decatur's division, unaccountably failed to follow when the other boats bore away after a group of Tripolitans and remained out of the action. Blake said afterward that he had seen a signal from the flagship to break off action and that by the time he discovered it was a mistake he was too far out of position to bring his clumsy boat into action. This may have been the case, for there was a good deal of confusion about signals, and many of the boats' officers, intent on the attack, failed to observe the flagship after the action began. However, Richard Somers, to whose division Blake's boat properly belonged, loudly denounced his junior as a coward. Blake gave up the command of Gunboat No. 3 to the *Argus*'s sailing master, Samuel B. Brooke. Subsequently he asked for and was granted a court of inquiry, but the squadron's movements prevented it from completing its work. Blake's career was ruined; he resigned from the navy in 1809 after being passed over for promotion. It seems certain that Isaac Hull did not believe the charge against his lieutenant. Hull detested cowards, but he and Blake remained warm friends.[10]

The attack of 3 August resulted in the capture of three Tripolitan gunboats, which Preble added to his flotilla, and in some minor damage to the city's defenses from the *Constitution*'s cannon. On 7 August a second attack was launched from westward of the city, in which bomb Ketch No. 1 dropped two dozen shells on the town, but one of the captured Tripolitan boats (No. 9) blew up, killing ten of her crew and wounding six. While this action was under way, a large sail was sighted on the northern horizon, and Preble hailed the *Argus* to investigate. Hull hauled off to the northward. By 6:00 P.M. he had spoken the vessel and hoisted his signal for the commodore: "Strange ships in sight are friends." It was the long-awaited frigate from America, the *John Adams*.

By 10:00 P.M. the squadron was at anchor and the officers had gathered in the *Constitution*'s cabin to greet Isaac Chauncey of the *John Adams* and to hear the news from home. The first piece of news was all-important and devastating: Preble was being superseded in command of the squadron. In the wake of Richard V. Morris's failure and the loss of the *Philadelphia*, the Jefferson administration had decided to strike a decisive, final blow in the Mediterranean. Four frigates besides the *John Adams*, which was primarily a storeship, would be sent. But there were only two captains junior to Preble in the United States—James Barron and Hugh G. Campbell. Senior captains must therefore be put in command of the other two frigates. Samuel Barron would succeed to command of the squadron. Second in command would be Preble's hated rival, John Rodgers.

Apart from the loss of their respected commander, the junior officers received good news about promotions. The good news was a little mixed, however, for while Hull, Stewart, Somers, Smith, and Chauncey had been advanced to the re-created rank of master commandant, Stephen Decatur, as a reward for his gallantry in burning the *Philadelphia*, had been promoted over their heads to captain. Hull was then the oldest of the masters commandant, though he was outranked by Charles Stewart. He left no record of his reaction to Decatur's promotion at the time, but rank had been a sore point with him in 1802 and would be again in 1815 and later.

Preble was determined to make the most of the time he had left. Using the *John Adams*'s arrival as a bluff, he once more offered negotiations, but the pasha's attitude was unchanged.[11] Preble's next device was a night attack, but since this required a particular combination of wind and sea, it was not possible to act until the night of 23–24 August. The *Argus* and the other light vessels played no prominent part either in this action or in a subsequent attack on the night of 27–28 August except to mother the gunboats. These assaults, though spectacular, had no serious effect on Tripoli, since the mortar boats proved ineffective and the Tripolitan gunboats declined to engage again in close combat with the Americans. On 29 August the *Argus* carried another peace offer to Tripoli that was again rejected. On 2 September a final attack on the town was mounted, with inconclusive results, and next night Preble played his last card by sending the ketch *Intrepid*, the vessel Decatur had used on his expedition to fire the *Philadelphia*, into Tripoli harbor once more, this time as an infernal. Now commanded by Richard Somers, the *Intrepid* was loaded with five tons of powder and other combustibles. She was to take station in the midst of the Tripolitan shipping and be set afire; if she exploded in the right place, she might destroy the entire defensive flotilla. She didn't. While still in the western passage through the reef the *Intrepid* blew up, apparently by accident, at 9:47 P.M. on 3 September. Somers, Midshipmen Henry Wadsworth and Joseph Israel, and the ten crewmen were killed instantly. No serious damage was done to the town, the forts, or the shipping.

So ended the summer campaign. On 5 September the *John Adams*, the *Syren*, the *Enterprize*, and the *Nautilus* sailed with the gunboats for Syracuse, while the *Constitution*, the *Argus*, and the *Vixen* remained to keep up the blockade. On Sunday, 9 September, the *Argus* once again went in chase of strange ships to the north and spoke the frigates *President* and *Constellation*, sixty-six days from America. Samuel Barron had arrived; Preble's command was over.[12]

Isaac Hull was about to become a principal in the most bizarre episode of the Mediterranean war. Barron had brought with him William Eaton, former American consul at Tunis, with discretionary authority to employ him if it seemed practical to do so. Hull had probably met this fellow Connecticut man at Gibraltar in April 1803, when Eaton was on his way home after being expelled by the bey of Tunis. During his consulship Eaton had encountered among the hangers-on at the Tunisian court Hamet (or Ahmed or Mohammed) Caramanli, who styled himself "the rightful Pasha of Tripoli." Hamet was the elder brother of the reigning pasha, Yusuf, and since he was in Tunis in 1796 when Yusuf seized the throne, Hamet had prudently elected to remain there, leaving his wife and children in Tripoli as hostages.[13] As early as December 1801 Eaton had conceived a scheme for establishing Hamet on the throne of Tripoli, thus assuring, he believed, a friendly regime and perpetual peace for the United States with that regency. Eaton should have seen from the outset that Hamet was a weak reed, and in his private journal there is some evidence that he did; still, the idea of setting up a compliant regime in Tripoli was attractive. Moreover, its successful execution would mean that the hero of the Tripolitan War would be ex-captain Eaton of the army, not some hated naval commander like Alexander Murray (Eaton's particular bête noire) or Richard V. Morris. Having made no progress in interesting Morris in his plan, Eaton returned to the United States to urge the idea in person at the seat of government. In March 1804 he gave President Jefferson a sketch of the grand operation:

> E. —will go forward in the first frigate to the Mediterranean. After an interview with the Commodore, will proceed, in one of the small vessels, to Derne to aid the motions of the legitimate Bashaw of Tripoli in order to bring him in the rear of the enemy. Thence to Naples and negotiate a convention as the President shall direct. Then be at the rendezvous on the arrival of a reenforcement, to assist the Commodore in any expedition which may require, on shore, a *coup de main*, at Tripoli—or at Tunis in case of hostilities commenced. Or to seize any favorable opportunity to treat of peace with either of those regencies.
>
> E. —still believes the project of dethroning the usurper practicable, if suitable advantage be taken of actual positions.[14]

To begin with, then, Eaton needed one of the small vessels of the squadron to carry him in search of Hamet. The latter had moved from Tunis to Malta, where he was contacted in late 1802 by Yusuf with an offer of the governorship of Derna—a spot where Yusuf could keep close watch on him. Eaton had tried to dissuade Hamet with money and threats ("Remember that your brother thirsts for your blood"), but Hamet had gone to Derna, only to flee a few months later, in terror of assassination, to Alexandria in Egypt.[15] He still had agents at Malta, and these had negotiated at length with Commodore Preble during 1804. The proposals had been essentially the same as Eaton's plan: given enough money ($80,000 to $90,000) and arms, Hamet would march to Derna and Benghazi and then cooperate with Preble's squadron in an assault on Tripoli. Alternatively, Hamet could go by ship to Derna or Benghazi, where the populace would rise in his support and his desert followers would join him. Preble liked the plan and encouraged Hamet's agents, but in April 1804 he shelved the idea. When Eaton arrived in the Barron squadron, Preble again threw his support behind the Hamet scheme.[16] He probably suggested to Barron as well that, if a small vessel were to be sent on detached service, the *Argus* would be the best choice.

On the afternoon of 12 September a council assembled in the *Constitution*'s cabin: Preble, Barron, Hugh G. Campbell, Eaton, and Isaac Hull. After a general discussion of the plan, Barron handed Hull a covering order to take the *Argus* to Syracuse for refitting and to proceed from there to Alexandria or Smyrna to convoy any American vessels that might be in those ports. The real orders, which he gave orally, were quite different:

Sir, the *written* orders, I here hand you . . . are intended to disguise the real object of your expedition; which is to proceed with Mr. Eaton to Alexandria in search of Hamet Bashaw, the rival brother and legitimate sovereign of the reigning Bashaw of Tripoli; and to convey him and his suit[e] to Derne or such other place on the coast as may be determined the most proper for co-operating with the naval force under my command against the common enemy: or, if more agreeable to him, to bring him to me before Tripoli—

Should Hamet Bashaw not be found at Alexandria, you have the discretion to proceed to any other place for him where the safety of your ship can be, in your opinion, relied upon.

The Bashaw may be assured of the support of my squadron at Bengazi or Derne; where you are at liberty to put in, if required, and if it can be done without too great risque. And you may assure him also that I will take the most effectual measures with the forces under my command for co-operating with him against the usurper, his brother; and for re-establishing him in the regency of Tripoli. Arrangements to this effect with him are confided to the discretion with which Mr. Eaton is vested by the Government.[17]

Throughout the Wednesday afternoon while this conference was going on the squadron was in chase of three blockade runners. At sundown the meeting broke up as the *Constitution* brought to and boarded two of the vessels. Barron and Campbell rejoined their ships, but the *Argus* was in chase of the third ship, so Hull was forced to remain on board the *Constitution*. He spent a pleasant evening with Preble and Eaton talking over the proposed campaign. After retiring late, the conferees were rudely awakened at 4:30 A.M. by a tremendous shock running through the frigate. Gaining the pitch-black upper deck, they found that the *Constitution* had been taken aback and had fallen foul of the *President*, crashing into her larboard bow. The *President*'s damages were minimal, but the *Constitution* had smashed her jibboom and cutwater and had crushed to pieces her figurehead of Hercules. This accident occasioned the *Constitution*'s departure for Malta next afternoon. Hull and Eaton transferred to the *President* and finally overtook the *Argus* on Saturday morning. By Monday night the *Argus*, too, was at Malta.[18]

Eaton was in high spirits and eager to be off to Egypt,[19] and "the active Captain Hull" was not inclined to shilly-shally. But Commodore Barron had not fully decided on the plan. The *Argus*, with Preble and Eaton as passengers, went on to Syracuse and then to Messina for repairs. When she returned to Malta on 24 October, Barron had been there for several weeks, seriously ill. He had a liver disorder that from this time on would keep him out of action, sometimes near death. Barron's physical condition reacted on his never ebullient spirits as well. He grew more and more pessimistic and less and less inclined to try new methods. Now he ordered Hull to return to Tripoli to relieve the *Nautilus* on the blockade, promising Eaton vaguely that the *Argus* would go to Alexandria when she returned.[20] At Malta, Barron was also under the influence of Tobias Lear, who was commissioned to negotiate a peace treaty with Tripoli and who thought little of the Eaton scheme. Lear apparently believed that he had quashed the plot this time: He wrote Secretary of State Madison on 3 November:

> I presume the co-operation of the brother of the Bashaw of Tripoli will not be attempted. Our force is thought sufficient to compel him to terms without this aid, and in any event it is very doubtful whether he has it in his power, with any reasonable pecuniary assistance we might give, to render us service. He is now in Egypt, driven by his brother from Derne, where it is presumed he might have made a stand, had he been a man of any force or influence; which, from the best accounts I can collect, he is not. Indeed, I should place much more confidence in the continuance of a peace with the present Bashaw, if he is well beaten into it, than I should have with the other, if he should be placed on the throne by our means.[21]

But Eaton, as events were to prove, was persistent. He enlisted Commodore Preble to sway Barron the other way, and when the *Argus* unexpectedly returned to Syracuse on 6 November because of an outbreak of smallpox on board, Barron reluctantly ordered her to proceed to Alexandria.

There remained some misunderstanding about the nature of the *Argus*'s mission. Although Barron's orders to Hull clearly allowed him to carry Hamet "and his suite" to Derna or Benghazi, it appears that Barron's real expectation was that, if Hamet could not be peacefully reinstalled at Derna, he would be brought to squadron headquarters where plans could be concerted for further action.[22] His mistake, of course, was in giving Eaton so much latitude. Eaton knew full well, in face of Lear's opposition, that if he brought Hamet back to the squadron the likelihood that there would be any further action to place him on the throne of Tripoli would be small indeed. Only the most extreme intransigence on Yusuf's part would drive Barron and Lear to employ Hamet, and everyone in the Mediterranean expected that the mere appearance of Barron's full force off Tripoli in the spring would force the pasha to make peace. William Bainbridge, writing in invisible ink from his prison in Tripoli on 11 November, was less sanguine about the squadron's success but echoed Lear's opinion of Hamet: "I can't conceive the most distant hope of any utility to be derived to the U.S. from pecuniary or other aid given the poor effeminate fugitive brother of the Bashaw of Tripoli. . . . What can be expected from such a pusillanimous being?"[23] Lear, of course, did not require convincing on that score, but before he received that letter the *Argus* had sailed for Alexandria, taking on board Eaton and Richard Farquhar, an Englishman who had been promoting Hamet's cause at Malta for several years. Heavy winter gales lashed the brig all the way up the Mediterranean. On Sunday afternoon, 25 November, she made her landfall near Alexandria and signaled for a pilot but was forced offshore again; finally, on Monday afternoon, she entered the harbor of the old port. Hull made a brave show with his little vessel as he came up, exchanging a seventeen-gun salute with the admiral of a Turkish squadron of a ship of the line and six frigates. As soon as the *Argus* was moored, the British consul, Samuel Briggs, came on board. Eaton presented a letter of introduction he had secured from Governor Sir Alexander John Ball of Malta and was promised the full cooperation both of Samuel Briggs, consul, and of the firm of Briggs Brothers. Eaton bestowed on Briggs the office of navy agent for the United States at Alexandria, an office whose chief duty was to supply the American expedition with whatever funds were asked, on distant promises of repayment.

The following morning the *Argus* changed her mooring to a spot nearer the town and, by prearrangement, exchanged a fifteen-gun salute with the castle. Then Hull and Eaton paid a ceremonial visit to the admiral, the governor, and the supervisor of the revenue. But conversation over the sherbet elicited news that would have dismayed anyone but William Eaton: Hamet was not in Alexandria; he had joined the rebel Mameluke chieftains and was somewhere in the interior of Egypt. Even if he could be found, he would not be able to enter the cities controlled by the Turkish authority. Not daunted, Eaton secured two river craft and embarked immediately for Cairo, taking with him Lieutenant Blake, marine Lieutenant Presley N. O'Bannon, and Midshipmen George Washington Mann and Eli Danielson (Eaton's stepson), as well as Richard Farquhar and a retinue of servants.[24] He assured Isaac Hull that he would return in two weeks, with or without Hamet.

If Hull was skeptical of Eaton's promise, it was well for him. He and his ship were about to spend two and a half months at Alexandria. It was not an unpleasant stay, on the whole, apart from his anxiety about keeping the *Argus* supplied with provisions—eventually furnished by notes on the firm of Briggs—and his felt duty to return to the squadron. Hull was convinced that Eaton's plan was a good one, and he was willing to exercise initiative in supporting it. He disliked inaction, but Alexandria was a good harbor and the Briggs brothers were pleasant company. An English Christmas was a delight to the Connecticut Yankee; unfortunately, by the New Year, Hull was laid low by a bad cold and so missed the festivities.[25] He did dress the *Argus* on 2 January and fire a salute in honor of the Muslim feast of *id al-Saghir*, closing the fast of Ramadan. In mid-December he made a short voyage to Rosetta and back, probably visiting the battlefield at Aboukir Bay where the British and French had fought in 1801, which Eaton had found "covered with human skeletons, ghastly monuments of the savage influence of avarice and ambition on the human mind."[26]

Hull spent most of the time waiting. At intervals, missives from Eaton erupted from the interior. He had reached Cairo; had had the good luck to meet Dr. Francisco Mendrici, an old friend from Tunis and now chief physician to the Turkish viceroy at Cairo; by his influence had secured an interview with the viceroy and persuaded him to give Hamet a safe-conduct out of Egypt. He had sent messengers to Hamet with these joyous tidings. He suspected French intrigue against him.[27] On 17 December, Eaton reported his success in obtaining the safe-conduct and advised Hull to "expect therefore an addition to your crew of about three hundred, rather passengers, all Bashaws and *Bashees*."[28]

Two days later Eaton had scaled down his request for accommodations in the *Argus* to a hundred; the remaining three hundred to five hundred would travel overland. But this was still outlandish. The *Argus* could not accommodate a hundred passengers, let alone the food and water they would require. Hull was beginning to doubt the rationality of the enterprise. He tried to persuade Eaton to drop his bold venture and return with Hamet to Syracuse:

> The plan you have formed of taking Derne I think rather a hazardous one, unless the Bashaw can bring into the field from eight hundred to one thousand men, particularly as we are destitute of every article necessary for an expedition of the kind. I am willing to grant you that a very few men will take the place, and hold it, yet they must have the means, they must have and be sure of supplies, which is out of our power to promise them. I think the most we can do is to get the Bashaw, make as many friends in this country as possible, and make the best of our way to Syracuse, get some little addition to our force, and make arrangements for our being supported, when we have got possession, and set off anew for Dern or Bengaze as may appear most proper. From the information you must have gained, however, at Cairo, you must be better acquainted with the dispositions of the people than I can possibly be, and consequently a better judge.

For Hull the difficulties of the situation had been clarified by the long delay at Alexandria:

> You must be satisfied that it is my wish to do every thing in my power before we return, but when I look at the situation we are sent here in, I lose all patience. With a little vessel, without friends, without authority to act, without a single friend except such as we have by our own good fortune procured— in short, without everything that is absolutely necessary to insure success to an enterprise.

This letter makes it clear that Eaton had already decided to make an attack on Derna without further reference to Barron. Hull, in writing to the commodore, was careful to say nothing of Eaton's plans, only cautioning that he would probably be detained in Egypt for several weeks or even longer.[29]

Hull was also growing anxious about the bills Eaton was running up. The account with Briggs Brothers eventually amounted to $13,000, in addition to other bills Hull drew on the squadron's London and Malta agents for $4,000. As the days dragged on without word from Hamet, the expedition began to disintegrate. Purser Robert Goldsborough of the *Argus* got into a fistfight with Richard Farquhar at a Cairo gambling table. Eaton accused Goldsborough of bilking a courtesan and of insulting Egyptian women on the streets by lifting their veils.[30] Hull ordered Goldsborough under arrest. Goldsborough protested that he was being persecuted by Eaton out of ill will, but since his brother was the powerful chief clerk of the Navy Department, he suffered no lasting bad effects. Eaton then quarreled with Farquhar, whom he accused of cheating in his accounts, and dismissed him as well.

Not until 5 February did the timid Hamet appear at a rendezvous near Damanhur. If he was frightened, so were the officials at Alexandria. The nearer Hamet and his followers came, the more nervous were the governor and his advisors. Whether because of French Consul Bernardino Drovetti's influence or simply from their own caution, at the last minute they decided that Hamet should not enter the city. That being the case, he could not go on board the *Argus* at Alexandria. Hull and Samuel Briggs went to the governor on 5 February and found him in a panic. He shouted at them that the viceroy would not allow Hamet to enter the city and that Hamet was wearing Mameluke dress and had five hundred or six hundred men with him. Hull and Briggs remonstrated; the argument waxed hot; and the governor rushed out in a rage. Hull told Eaton that he had better avoid the city and either fix a point of embarkation to the westward or resolve to travel by land.[31]

As it turned out, the latter was Hamet's wish. He realized that, if his followers were left to march to Derna while he went by sea, they would disappear.[32] By 14 February he had skirted Alexandria and established his camp at a marabout, or shrine, near Burg el-Arab, about thirty miles west of the city. But when Eaton rejoined Hull on board the *Argus*, he surprised Hull by announcing that he, too, would march through the desert. Eaton had his prize puppet at last and would take no chance of losing him. At Cairo, Rosetta, and Alexandria he had recruited a cadre of about fifty Christian cutthroats, mainly Greeks, who would be essentially his bodyguard, and he asked Hull to let him keep some of the *Argus*'s people: O'Bannon with a marine sergeant and six privates and Midshipman Pascal Paoli Peck. Altogether, his party numbered about four hundred.[33]

Hull carried with him to Syracuse a letter from Eaton to Barron, requesting two more vessels and a bombard to meet him off Bomba, plus two fieldpieces, a hundred stands of arms, and a hundred marines with bayonets. Another $10,000, Eaton thought, would come in handy and would immediately be repaid by Hamet when he got his hands on the coffers of Derna and Benghazi. Furthermore, he outlined a treaty to be executed between himself and Hamet whereby the United States would guarantee to install Hamet as pasha of Tripoli. In return, Hamet would release all the American prisoners; make a perpetual peace with the United States; and agree to indemnify the United States out of the tribute received from Sweden, Denmark, and Holland.

With these messages and with Hamet's "secretary of state," an elderly and dignified gentleman named Mahomet Mezaluna, the *Argus* left Alexandria about 19 February. She entered Syracuse harbor on 8 March. Commodore Barron had again gone to Malta, but his younger brother, Captain James Barron of the *Essex*, had just arrived at Syracuse en route to Trieste. Hull reported to the younger Barron.

"Where is Eaton?" asked Barron.

"With the Bashaw," said Hull.

Barron stared. "And where is *that?*"

Hull then explained at length Eaton's trials in locating Hamet and told Barron that the party was now on its way to Derna. Barron, of course, still supposed that Eaton was to have brought Hamet to Syracuse. Why had he not done so?

"Because the Bashaw would not leave his people," said Hull. "But he has sent his principal secretary to the Commodore."

James Barron asked Hull to spend the evening on board the *Essex* and went over with him the whole correspondence directed to his brother. He then asked Hull for his opinion of the affair. Hull was loyal to Eaton. He praised his honesty and perseverance and said he believed that the expedition was likely to succeed, at least as far as Derna, if it were adequately supported. Barron accordingly wrote his brother that the support should be given. He then departed for Trieste, and Hull left for Malta, where he arrived on 10 March.[34]

When Hull saw Samuel Barron, he was shocked. For most of the four months since Hull had sailed for Egypt, the commodore had been bedridden and unable to keep food in his stomach for weeks at a time. He was now slightly better and was able to go for short carriage rides, but his body was terribly wasted and his spirits were correspondingly low. Eaton's letters, particularly the plan for the treaty, alarmed him. Eaton must have been the only man in the Mediterranean who did not realize the the United States was using Hamet Caramanli as a tool to further its own interests. Even Hamet had occasional glimpses of that profound truth. Barron, when writing to Eaton on 22 March, spelled it out plainly in three or four different ways. Rumors from Tripoli and anguished letters from William Bainbridge made clear that American cooperation with Hamet, if it showed any signs of succeeding, was likely to provoke Yusuf to execute the prisoners. Barron was fully aware of the risky game being played. The main object of the squadron's efforts since the capture of the *Philadelphia* had been to secure the release of her crew without paying ransom. There would be little point in "winning" the war for the benefit of Hamet and losing the prisoners. Eaton seems neither to have grasped this point nor to have believed that Hamet would not be supported to the limit; hence his outrage at the peace settlement. This is the conclusion that must be drawn from his writings; yet it is hard to see how he failed to appreciate Barron's message:

> I wish you to understand that no guarantee or engagements to the exiled prince, whose cause, I repeat it, we are only favoring as the instrument to an attainment and not in itself as an object, must be held to stand in the way of our acquiescence in any honorable and advantageous terms of accommodation which the present Bashaw may be induced to propose. Such terms being once offered and accepted by the representative of Government appointed to treat of peace [Lear], our support to Hamet Bashaw must necessarily be withdrawn. . . .

Barron reiterated his hope that, with the supplies and support now being sent, Hamet and his force could capture Derna and Benghazi. Beyond that, they were definitely on their own.[35]

By the date of this letter Hull was nearly ready for sea again. He was to rendezvous with Eaton at Bomba in early April. Barron had assigned the sloop *Hornet* to accompany the *Argus* and had loaded them with provisions for the desert army. The fieldpieces needed for assaulting Derna were a problem, since the squadron had only naval guns, but Stephen Decatur in the *Congress* had been sent to Messina to try to buy them. The hundred marines Eaton wanted were out of the question. Barron must have felt that the only bright spot in the gloomy picture before him was the steady coolness of Isaac Hull. He gave Hull his sailing orders on 23 March, with repeated praise of his "judgment and discretion," and closed on a dark note: "In case of any unfortunate event having happened to Mr. Eaton and his companions, and you can obtain no satisfactory intelligence of them, it is left to you to act as you may think most advisable."[36]

Hull immediately ordered Lieutenant Samuel Evans in the *Hornet* to get ready for sea and to follow the *Argus* to Bomba. The two vessels met bad weather but managed to get within sight of Derna by 4 April. Seeing no signs of activity there, Hull concluded that Eaton had not yet pressed on to his object, and so he coasted on to the eastward to anchor in the Bay of Bomba. On the sixth he sent a boat on shore but found the place deserted. He pushed on to the eastward in search of the port of Tabarka (Tobruk), another possible rendezvous, but could not identify it. Thus, he retraced his course to the west, calling at Cape Razatin above Derna on the ninth. Here a man was found who claimed to know the whereabouts of Eaton's camp, still nearly forty miles to the east. Hull sent him to Eaton with news of his arrival. Three other men came down on horseback to the boat's landing place and announced that they had been sent by Hamet to supply the vessels with beef. But Hull decided that they were spies from Derna and had Mahomet Mezaluna, Hamet's minister, send them away. The *Argus* then sailed again for Bomba. The season was not good for lying in the open roadstead, so Hull sent word to Eaton by the messenger that he would stand offshore and call at Bomba every two or three days. That was Tuesday. On Monday night of the next week, 15 April, the *Argus*'s lookouts spotted fires on the headlands above Bomba. By 8:00 A.M. the brig was standing into the bay, where a tatterdemalion array waited to greet her.

One can only wonder what Hull must have felt on seeing Eaton, O'Bannon, Peck, and their retinue and on hearing the story of their march. By foot, horse, and camel they had crossed three hundred miles of the same grim desert through which Field Marshal Bernard Montgomery would one day pursue General Erwin Rommel. Some days they had been without water; on others they drank fetid sludge or drew water from cisterns in which corpses lay. Their food rations had given out three days before the *Argus* was sighted. The officers had traded the buttons from their uniforms to Bedouin women for dates. And day by day there had been the threat that someone would mutiny or desert— the Bedouins, the Greeks, the camel drivers, and as often as not, Hamet. The closer they got to Derna, the more nervous the "rightful Pasha" became. Once he rode away from camp and was gone for days. As the caravan neared the rendezvous he was attacked by terrible stomach cramps. But Eaton—unshorn, weary, but incredibly stubborn—had brought him and his retainers to Bomba. Here they could rest, refresh themselves from the provisions in the *Argus* and the *Hornet*, and prepare for the assault on Derna.

The army camped at Bomba for a week. Daily reports reached them of a Tripolitan force marching to the relief of Derna. Eaton knew he must get his reluctant pasha in motion soon, with or without cannon, lest he lose his nerve altogether. Hull agreed to bring up his vessels to bombard the town in support of Eaton's attack. Midshipman Peck had seen enough of the great Hamet campaign; he returned to the *Argus* and was replaced by Midshipman Mann, while Lieutenant O'Bannon continued in command of the marine detachment on shore. The camp was in motion again on 22 April, and the *Argus* beat out to sea in chase of a sail that had appeared in the offing. Hull brought his quarry to at 3:00 P.M.—a 30-ton boat under Ottoman colors from Alexandria bound to Benghazi with a number of prominent citizens on board, including the captain of a Tripolitan gunboat. The breeze was steadily freshening to a gale, making it impossible to search the tiny boat for contraband, but Hull decided to send her in as a prize anyway. Although he was not sure whether Barron considered this part of the Tripolitan coast under blockade, the presence of Tripolitan passengers seemed reason enough to condemn the boat.

By the evening of 24 April the army was within striking distance of Derna, but the *Argus* and the *Hornet* had been blown off the coast by the gale. A courier had reported that Yusuf's army was also near the city and was likely to get there first, especially if Hamet waited for his naval support to return. "Alarm and consternation seized the Arab chiefs, and despondency the Bashaw," Eaton noted in his journal. After a night spent in consultation, from which Eaton was excluded, Hamet's forces struck camp at dawn and began to return to Egypt; Eaton ranted, pleaded, and promised $2,000—which at last turned them again in the direction of Derna.[37] That afternoon he camped on a height above the town and surveyed the situation. Derna lay on a sheltered inlet, the water to the south and southeast of the town. Here was a battery of 8 nine-pounders and a populous quarter of the city that was loyal to Yusuf and fortified against attack. There were loopholes in the walls of the houses, and the governor had a ten-inch howitzer mounted on his terrace. Men coming out from the town to meet Hamet told him that the governor could bring eight hundred men into battle, besides the reinforcements that were hourly expected from Tripoli. The other two parts of the city were the home of Hamet's friends, but the governor held all the strong points. "I thought the Bashaw wished himself back to Egypt," commented Eaton.

Luckily for the expedition, on that same day John H. Dent in the *Nautilus* arrived with the two brass fieldpieces. He spoke the *Argus* off the coast, and Hull ordered him to stand in to Cape Razatin and contact Eaton.[38] At 8:00 A.M. Eaton sent up a smoke signal to guide the ships to his camp, and that evening he conferred with Dent, announcing that he would attack the next day if the other vessels arrived in time. He had already sent a proclamation to the governor of Derna:

> Sir, I want no territory. With me is advancing the legitimate sovereign of your country. Give us a passage through your city. . . . and for the supplies of which we shall have need you shall receive fair compensation. Let no differences of religion induce us to shed the blood of harmless men who think little and know nothing. . . . I shall see you tomorrow in a way of your choice.

The governor was a man of few words. He returned this missive succinctly endorsed: "My head or yours."[39]

At dawn on Saturday, 27 April, the *Argus* and the *Hornet* appeared off Derna. Seeing the *Nautilus* at anchor near the shore, Hull stood down and spoke to Dent, who told him of Eaton's plans to attack. The *Argus* hoisted out a boat and loaded the two fieldpieces, but when the boat neared shore it was found that the guns would have to be hauled up a twenty-foot cliff. For an hour or two the crewmen sweated and swore at hoisting the guns up the rock. They got one of them up by noon, and Eaton told them to take the other back; he would go forward with one cannon rather than risk any more delay.

By two o'clock Eaton had his army in motion. He had placed the least reliable troops in the position of least danger. Hamet and his forces were sent to the left, behind the town, to the areas not fortified and supposed to be occupied by his supporters, while the brunt of the attack on the defended part of the city was borne by the Christian troops under Eaton and the naval vessels led by Hull. As Eaton's men advanced to the attack, Hull ordered his ships to anchor (with springs on their cables for best maneuverability) as close to the town as they could get. These little ships had few cannon capable of reaching the town, but they made good use of what they had. The *Hornet* came to anchor at two within a hundred yards of the land battery and opened fire. The *Nautilus* followed, anchoring to the eastward of the *Hornet* and half a mile from shore; the *Argus* dropped anchor still farther to the east and near enough to pour twenty-four-pound carronade shot into the town and battery.

The naval guns drove the Tripolitan cannoneers from their battery within an hour, whereupon the ships wound on their springs and turned their fire on the beach, where a force was advancing to meet Eaton's troops, moving up under a hail of musketry from the fortified houses. Hamet, with the cavalry and most of the Muslim force of about two thousand, had taken possession of an old castle in the southwest quarter of the city. There, safely out of the battle, they awaited the outcome. Eaton had with him only the officers and marines from the *Argus* and his band of fifty Greeks. He also had the field gun, but it was put out of action early when an excited cannoneer shot away the ramrod. Seeing his troops in danger of giving way under the punishing musket fire, Eaton ordered a sudden charge against the force on the beach, which numbered several hundred. The Tripolitans gave ground slowly, firing tenaciously from behind walls and trees. Eaton was shot through the left wrist and so lost the use of his rifle. O'Bannon and the marines pressed stubbornly forward until, at three-thirty, Hull, watching from the *Argus*'s quarterdeck, saw his lieutenant rush into the fort, closely followed by Midshipman Mann. Down came the Tripolitan flag, and up went the American ensign. The Tripolitans had left their cannon primed and loaded for firing; by turning them on the town O'Bannon soon quieted all resistance. Hamet and his followers now emerged in time to cut down and capture those who tried to flee the city. It was four o'clock.

As soon as the firing subsided, Hull ordered the boats on shore to bring off the wounded. Predictably, it was the *Argus*'s people and the Greeks who had suffered most. John Wilton, marine, was dead; two of his fellows were wounded, one mortally; and nine Greeks and a Maltese were also hurt. There were no reported casualties among Hamet's followers. At five-thirty Eaton came on board to have his wound dressed and to exchange accounts of the day's events. Meanwhile, on shore Hamet reoccupied the palace he had once held as governor, while Mustapha, the recent incumbent, took sanctuary in a harem. Eaton wanted to fetch him out, but the owner reminded Hamet that he himself had taken refuge in the same harem when he fled from Yusuf; Mustapha remained unmolested until he escaped from Derna three weeks later.[40]

With his immediate objective accomplished, Eaton prepared an answer to Samuel Barron's strictures on the Hamet operation. Writing via the *Hornet*, which was returning to the squadron, he pleaded for more money on several grounds: first, the government had originally promised $50,000 for the operation, and expenses to date amounted to nearly $30,000; second, Hamet must have funds to pay his troops, and "it would not be good policy in Hamet Bashaw to levy contributions during the contest with his brother, lest it should alienate his friends"; third, cash would go a long way to smooth Hamet's path toward Tripoli and reduce the amount of fighting necessary. Eaton felt able to boast a little of his accomplishment—"We are in possession of the most valuable province of Tripoli"—and was more convinced than ever that success was within his grasp, yet his experience of the past months had finally forced him to acknowledge a weakness in Hamet and his associates. Certainly Hamet had a great following, Eaton thought: he had attracted two thousand supporters on his march, while Yusuf's army had been able to gather only a few hundred as they approached Derna from the other direction.

> I have no doubt, but he may proceed to the walls of Tripoli. But while I offer this opinion, I cannot conceal my apprehensions, grounded on experience, that when arrived there he would effect little, without more military talent and firmness than exists either in himself or the *hordes* of Arabs who attach themselves to him: . . . If therefore the cooperation is to be pursued with him and its direction is to be confided to me, it must be on condition that detachments of regulars may be occasionally debarked from the squadron, or procured elsewhere, to aid and give effect to such operations as require energy.

Finally, Eaton turned to Barron's stated intention to abandon Hamet if peace were made. To Eaton, this appeared dishonorable. "I cannot persuade myself that any bonds of patriotism dictate to me the duty of having a chief agency, nor indeed any, in so extraordinary a sacrifice." At the very least, he believed the government was obligated "to place Hamet Bashaw in a situation as eligible as that from which he has been drawn, out of the power of an incensed and vindictive enemy." Probably Yusuf could be made to offer Hamet his old post at Derna or Benghazi. (Why Eaton thought Hamet would be any more capable of holding his position than he had been before is not evident.) But now, at the moment of victory, was not the time to think of giving up: "Any accommodation savoring of relaxness would as probably be death to the Navy, and a wound to the national honor."[41]

Hull's view of the situation was the obverse of Eaton's. The late battle had enabled him to take the measure of Hamet and his followers, and he had found them wanting. He wrote Barron that, since the loyalist party in Derna still numbered about a third of the inhabitants, "many of them men of influence," he believed it essential to keep the *Argus* and the *Nautilus* on the station. With naval support and the guns of the fort trained on the town, the Christian troops could expect to hold their own, "as the inhabitants are very much afraid of Mr. Eaton's great guns . . . and are well convinced what ours from sea can do, by the sample they received on the 27th." But future operations were another matter:

> Should you think proper to keep possession of this place until you are made acquainted with the effect that our having it will have on the Bashaw of Tripoli, it may be easily done with supplies sufficient for the support of the few Christians that have the fort, and a vessel kept cruising off the town, but I am clearly of opinion that three or four hundred Christians, with additional supplies will be necessary to pursue the expedition to Bengaze and Tripoli. I presume Mr. Eaton will write you fully on this subject, and inform you what provisions are necessary for the expedition—should you think proper to have it pursued.[42]

Clearly, Hull did not believe anything was to be gained by pressing the adventure further.

While awaiting Barron's reply, the Americans and Greeks spent the time strengthening their position against the expected counterattack by Yusuf's approaching army. They raised a parapet around their battery and built a wharf at which supplies from the ships could be landed. Part of the *Argus*'s crew went on shore daily to work at these tasks.[43] On 8 May the hostile army appeared and took up a position on the ground formerly occupied by Eaton's force. Efforts were first made to persuade or bribe the people of Derna to rise up against Hamet, but after ex-governor Mustapha escaped to the camp on the night of 12 May with a full account of the occupiers' strength (or weakness), the Tripolitan commanders felt confident enough to attack. They chose the rear of the town, held by Hamet's cavalry, as the point of initial contact. Skirmishing began about 5:00 A.M., and surprisingly, the cavalry held its ground until badly outnumbered. Then the horsemen retreated rapidly into the city, pursued by the attackers, who by noon had overrun the town and surrounded Hamet's palace, despite a heavy fire from the *Argus* and the *Nautilus*. As a last resort, Eaton turned his battery on the town, firing into the courtyard of the palace, where a shot struck two men from their horses. This panicked the attacking army and started a rout; the cavalry chased them under the naval guns, and these in turn sped their flight. By 3:00 P.M. the city was clear again.

Thus rebuffed, Yusuf's commanders settled down to watch Hamet and his people in Derna. While Eaton still dreamed of marching on Tripoli, it was apparent that the Tripolitan army would keep his force pinned down at Derna indefinitely. On 18 May the *Nautilus* sailed for Syracuse, bearing Eaton's desperate plea to Barron for supplies merely to hold the position.[44] But the commodore had already decided that the adventure was at an end. Tobias Lear was preparing to embark for Tripoli to open negotiations for peace, and on the day the *Nautilus* left Derna Barron was dictating orders to Eaton to evacuate the town. To Lear, Barron maintained the view that the expedition had been beneficial.[45] But to Eaton he turned a face of stone: ". . . whatever, Sir, may have been once the intentions of government on this subject, and whatever your ideas touching those intentions, I feel that I have already gone to the full extent of my authority."[46] To Hull he gave positive orders to evacuate Eaton and his followers and to return immediately to Syracuse.[47]

All this was welcome news to Isaac Hull when the *Hornet* joined him on the morning of 30 May. For four days that week the sirocco had blown steadily, making breathing difficult and heating the very stones, so that work on the entrenchments had to be stopped. Hull was already concerned about his anchor cables, which were being chafed to pieces on the rocky holding ground; now he had to muster the carpenter's gang to caulk the seams of the *Argus*, which suddenly opened in the parching blast.[48]

Eager to get his vessels off the coast before something worse happened, on 4 June Hull gave Eaton formal notice that he must evacuate Derna. But Eaton refused to budge. He was writing a long serial letter to Barron, to be sent via the *Hornet*, detailing his reasons for disobeying the order, pleading for justice to Hamet, and sneering at the cowardice of Lear: "It is possible that he may have better information from whence to form an opinion of its issue than we who have thus far accompanied the expedition, but it is not probable: has he any agency in the war?"[49] Before he had finished the letter, on 9 June, the besieging army made a second attack on the town. Eaton was only a spectator of this battle. Yusuf's mounted forces, advancing at noon through the rocky defile that was the only avenue for horsemen to approach the city, were met by an outpost of Hamet's cavalry. Hull, seeing the advance and hearing musket fire, immediately hove up his anchor and brought the *Argus* to within half gunshot of the fort. He was still too far away to bring his carronades to bear, but by shifting the starboard bow gun to the larboard after port he got two long twelves into action. The *Hornet* also hauled close to the beach and opened fire, but she was too close to the high cliff, which masked her guns. On shore, reinforcements galloped to the aid of both sides until Hull estimated that five thousand men were engaged. After a fierce battle lasting nearly four hours the attackers retreated, closely pursued by Hamet's men, who secured a number of horses left behind in the flight. Casualties on both sides were about equal, amounting to fifty or sixty. O'Bannon and the marines and Greeks had wanted to join the battle, but Eaton was afraid to leave the fort unguarded; besides, he remarked petulantly to Barron, "I confess I had doubts whether the measures lately adopted by our commissioner of peace would justify me in acting offensively any longer in this quarter. Had the aids come forward seasonably which we hoped to receive here we might now have been at Cape Mensurat and in fifteen days more at Tripoli."[50]

During the night after the battle the wind and sea rose from the northward. At 4:00 A.M. Hull turned up his crew to make ready for sea and at 4:30 slipped his cables and stood to the eastward. The gale blew for twenty-four hours and carried the *Argus* past Cape Razatin. When Hull put about for Derna again on the morning of 11 June, he found that he had to beat against a strong current from the westward. Not till near sundown did he catch sight of Derna; a large ship was lying offshore. Still another night and day passed before the two vessels were near enough to exchange signals. Hull now learned what he had suspected, that the ship was American, but not until daylight of 13 June was he able to speak her. It was Hugh G. Campbell in the *Constellation*; he had come directly from Tripoli with news that the war was over.

After learning that Eaton, Hamet, and their followers were on board the *Constellation*, Hull stood into the bay to look for the anchors he had left behind when he went to sea. Neither of the buoys was to be seen. The jolly boat was sent to the *Hornet* to ask if they had been found; Hull then learned, to his disgust, that Lieutenant Samuel Evans in the *Hornet* had moored to one of the buoy ropes in the gale and parted it and had broken the other by using it as a kedge anchor while taking off Eaton's party from the beach. Both anchors were lost.[51] Hull refrained from giving Evans his opinion of such sloppy proceedings and instead went on board the *Constellation*. Chaos reigned in the frigate, her decks crowded with disconsolate Muslims and their baggage. Poor Hamet was deep in depression, but Eaton's anger sustained him. Hull learned the details of the evacuation: the *Constellation* had come in on the evening of the eleventh, and Campbell had immediately sent word to Eaton of the peace. Eaton and Hamet both knew that, if they let the desert army find out that it was being abandoned to Yusuf's mercy, they would be killed. So, counting on the supposition in both camps that the *Constellation* had brought reinforcements to Hamet, Eaton made mock preparations for an attack on the besiegers; then, as soon as it was dark on 12 June, he embarked the Greek cannoneers, then Hamet and his retinue, and finally the marines. Eaton was in the last boat. He was barely off shore when the betrayed soldiers and townspeople appeared on the beach, shrieking and cursing. The refugees were all on board by 2:00 A.M., and before daybreak those left behind had fled into the desert.[52]

Hull also learned from Campbell that Samuel Barron, at length abandoning hope of recovering his health, had resigned the command of the squadron to John Rodgers shortly before Lear opened the peace talks at Tripoli. The treaty, signed on 4 June, provided for an equal exchange of prisoners and a payment to the pasha of $60,000 for the two hundred Americans he held in excess of the number exchanged. Yusuf also engaged to deliver Hamet's family to him, but a secret article allowed him to delay as much as four years.

It was a much more favorable settlement than the pasha had ever offered Edward Preble and better than some that Preble would have accepted. Yet there were many who felt that a squadron as powerful as Barron's could have forced a peace without payment. Whether such a humiliating settlement imposed on the proud Yusuf would have endured was seldom considered. The most outspoken opponent of the treaty, predictably, was Eaton. He never doubted that his own operations had been most influential in bringing Yusuf to negotiate; nor did he doubt that he could have subjugated Tripoli in a month's time with adequate support. He had not left the Mediterranean before he began a violent polemic campaign against "Aunt Lear," John Rodgers, and the Barrons. In the United States he enlisted the support of Edward Preble and lobbied hard, though unsuccessfully, against ratification of the treaty. John Rodgers stood somewhere between the Eaton and Lear camps: he was bitterly disappointed that, when he had gained command of the squadron at last, the war had been snatched from him; still he held Eaton and Hamet in contempt, and of course he despised Preble. Isaac Hull's role in this hubbub is remarkable and revealing: he was and remained the friend of every one of the principals. His warm associations with Preble, Eaton, Lear, and Rodgers endured through the lifetime of each and were never interrupted. It was earlier noted that he was apolitical, but his maintenance of friendly relations simultaneously with all these towering egos while they were battling one another almost to the point of physical combat reveals him as a man of supreme tact and perfect sincerity. "Hull is as fat and good natured as ever," William Bainbridge wrote some years later, and whatever the tinge of patronizing in the remark, it nevertheless summed up the sunny nature of this man who, like the apostle Nathanael, had no guile.

As for Hamet Caramanli, he was landed at Syracuse with his followers and there abandoned, drawing an allowance of $200 per month from the United States for all of them. Not until October 1807 did his family rejoin him. Soon afterward Yusuf reinstalled his brother at Derna, but Hamet took flight for Egypt again in 1810, and there he died.[53]

6

The Gunboat Navy

The conclusion of peace with Tripoli did not mean that the American squadron could go home. The expansion-minded Jefferson administration had decided that American interests required the presence of a continuous force in the Mediterranean. Although the large squadron then on station would be gradually withdrawn, it was not all to return until a small replacement force was sent out. The *President* was to return to the United States immediately, carrying Commodore Barron and most of the liberated prisoners from Tripoli. For the time being, the rest of the force was committed to Commodore Rodgers, who, balked of action at Tripoli, was preparing for a show of force at Tunis in response to renewed threats from the bey.

But Isaac Hull was not going with the squadron to Tunis. The United States still owed the long-suffering Messrs. Briggs of Alexandria some $14,000. Soon after Hull brought the *Argus* to Syracuse on 22 June, Rodgers ordered him to Malta to pick up the money and deliver it to Briggs Brothers. By the time the *Argus* rejoined the ships in Tunis Bay on 13 August, the bey had been frightened into meekness and had agreed to send an ambassador to the United States to adjust all claims.

Owing to the loss of Hull's personal correspondence for this period, we have no way of knowing how he felt about his situation in the navy during this time. In the squadron at Tunis he could contemplate Stephen Decatur, lately his junior, now a captain in command of a frigate, and two other masters commandant, Charles Stewart and John Shaw (the latter below Hull on the list) commanding the frigates *Essex* and *John Adams*, respectively. The *Argus* was a handsome brig, but she was a small vessel. Had Hull, and Stewart for that matter, known what had happened in Washington in the spring, the gloom might have been deeper still.

In March 1805 Secretary of the Navy Robert Smith had made a strong plea for the promotion of the two senior masters commandant, using the return of Commodore Preble as leverage. Writing to President Jefferson at Monticello, Smith employed all possible nuances of persuasion, including political ones:

Commodore Preble has in the most importunate and impressive manner entreated me to recommend to you the promotion of Masters Commandant Charles Stewart and Isaac Hull to the rank of Captain in the Navy. Mr. Stewart I personally know. His manners are those of a well bred Gentleman. He has had the advantage of a classic liberal education and is considered by all an elegant officer. Mr. Hull I do not personally know; but his character in the Navy is remarkably high. He is admired by all who know him. He is a favorite nephew of our good friend General Hull, who interests himself much in his advancement. These two gentlemen have commanded the two brigs in our Mediterranean squadron and have upon all occasions so distinguished themselves for their bravery and judgment that in the opinion of their Commodore they have just claim upon their country for promotion. By this kind of manifestation of our good will to the officers of the Navy we not only strongly attach them to us but we inspire them with a zeal that will lead them on to the most glorious deeds. Indeed I fear unless we do something of that sort we will lose these two very valuable officers. They are both too far advanced in life to remain in their present grade. And let me suggest to you that I have learned since I have been in the Navy Department, that it requires many years experience and attention to make such officers as these gentlemen are.[1]

Smith even enclosed two commissions, made out for the president's signature, which he hoped to forward by a storeship ready to sail for the Mediterranean. But the young captains-to-be were victims of "strict construction." Jefferson signed the commissions but instructed Smith not to send them unless he was certain that the law allowed an addition to the list of captains. In reply Smith said that whereas "I have not considered the *peace*-establishment act the rule of our conduct with respect to the number of officers or men in the prosecution of the war against Tripoli," the letter of the law allowed only nine captains. Thus, Jefferson pocketed the appointments.[2]

One important point that emerges from this incident is the secretary's assessment of Isaac Hull. His career at this point rested on two firm bases: competence and political preferment. He did not have the education and polish of an "elegant" officer like Stewart or Decatur, but he had a well-deserved reputation for skill, and he had an uncle whose steadfast Republican politics now stood him in even better stead than they had in 1798. The political side, however, had carried him about as far as it could. The rest was up to Hull.

There was not much opportunity to gain distinction in the now peaceful Mediterranean. Hull's principal duty for the winter of 1805–6 was to supervise the squadron base at Syracuse with the gunboats and small craft laid up there. After a brief visit to the city of Tunis, he sailed for Syracuse on 1 September with the *Hornet* and eight gunboats, and with an injunction from Commodore Rodgers to keep a fatherly eye on the junior officers:

> As the officers commanding the gun boats are generally very young, and at an age whose prominent trait is not stability, I have to desire that you pay great attention to have regularity and system maintained in everything belonging to and under their respective commands. . . . I shall much rely on your discretion and judgment in maintaining that strict subordination and general harmony throughout the squadron without which we cannot be respected.[3]

This was an assignment that promised to be more nerve-wracking than exciting. The thirty-two-year-old shepherd's flock included Lieutenant David Porter, twenty-five years old, newly released from Tripoli and commanding the *Enterprize;* Lieutenant James Lawrence, twenty-four, Hull's old subaltern in the *Adams* and the *Enterprize;* and Lieutenant Ralph Izard, Jr., twenty, who had been a midshipman under Preble. On the other hand, there was Nathaniel Haraden, five years older than Hull, who had been sailing master of the *Constitution* for six years and was now, belatedly, a lieutenant. All the gunboat officers had brought their little craft, newly built in the United States, across the Atlantic and were feeling the cockiness of a first command. Perhaps none gave Hull so many gray hairs as James Lawrence, whose pride was such that he quarreled with Porter over a ship's carpenter and wrote Hull that "the Secretary of the Navy honored me with the command of No. 6 [and] of course attached to me every prerogative of a command of a gunboat."[4] But Rodgers had chosen his superintendent well. Hull, who from his earliest days in the navy had taken a fatherly interest in younger officers, smoothed over such disputes and ran the station in his own easy, diplomatic way. He had no problems with insubordination or dissipation.

In addition to looking after the young officers, Hull had to set up an arsenal and superintend two storeships and a hospital.[5] Considering that six of the eight gunboats were laid up for the winter, leaving their officers and men idle, a remarkable tranquillity prevailed at Syracuse. In October there was an outbreak of smallpox among the boats' crews, and a round of inoculations was ordered. The *Argus* made a brief visit to Tunis about that time and found all quiet. On his return to Syracuse, Hull learned that six men had deserted—an example of a constant annoyance. Although he sent the *Enterprize* to Messina in search of the wanderers, suspicion fell heavily on a group of British transports in the harbor. Hull approached their commander, Lieutenant Richard Cheeseman, and met what must have been a unique response in Anglo-

American encounters: Cheeseman ordered his commanders not to receive any deserters from the American vessels and to return any they might already have received, threatening to report the vessels short of complement according to the number of deserters found on board.[6]

Britain's bankers were not so sympathetic. In mid-November they inexplicably began refusing to pay the bills of the squadron's Malta agent, William Higgins. The resulting scramble for specie to meet current charges led to the Argus's being sent to Naples. There Hull spent Christmas riding out a gale that prevented him from going on shore during most of his stay,[7] so that he had ample time to reflect both on the events of the past year and on his progress, or lack of it. He had discussed his situation with Commodore Rodgers, who was nudging the secretary on the subject: "Captain Hull has been four years in the Mediterranean, and has requested of me to solicit your permission for his return to America, on the reduction of the Mediterranean Squadron; should there be any vacancies to cause promotion permit me to remind you of his claims."[8]

Smith needed no urging. He had already sent to Congress his recommendation for a peace establishment that included the promotion of the five senior masters commandant, "the greater part of whom I fear we shall lose, if they are not promoted." He had also sent Rodgers instructions to return the Constellation, the Congress, the Essex, the John Adams, and three of the small vessels in the spring, the Argus to be one of the latter.[9]

Winter society at Syracuse, except for the pre-Lenten carnival, was none too lively, but the officers did find respite, as Ralph Izard noted, in visits to Malta, Messina, and other Italian cities. Hull enjoyed the society of George Dyson, the squadron's agent at Syracuse, and of various foreign officers who drifted through the Neapolitan city. He frequently dined at Palermo with Sir John Acton, former prime minister of the Kingdom of the Two Sicilies. Malta was especially pleasant, with its vigorously British society and the hospitality of Navy Agent William Higgins and of Governor Sir Alexander John Ball.

This delightful social round was interrupted with the coming of spring 1807 as Commodore Rodgers began to prepare the squadron to return home. He would not go, however, without rattling the saber against Tunis once more. On 10 March he ordered the Argus and the Hornet to cruise off the city "in order to prevent the possibility of injury being done to our commerce before peace with that nation is permanently established."

Hull was at Tunis by 24 March, and since he had orders from Rodgers not to show more than one of his vessels at a time, he sent the Hornet to cruise off Cape Bon. His intention was just to touch at Tunis, communicating with James Dodge, the American consul, and then to run to Sardinia to assess the harbor at Cagliari for use as a possible naval base. But before the *Argus* could get under way on Wednesday evening, 26 March, Hull received a report that a single-masted American vessel had gone ashore near Cape Bon. It was the *Hornet*. Hull had visions of another set of American prisoners in Barbary hands. On Thursday the *Hornet's* boat arrived with a hysterical report that the cutter was breaking up. Hull was all activity, preparing boats to go to her assistance, when she suddenly appeared in the offing, apparently undamaged. She had lost her anchors and cables and jettisoned her guns and so had to tie up to the *Argus* to survive a hard overnight gale. The rest of the business was merely tedious: getting up the *Hornet's* guns and preparing her to return to Syracuse. Most gratifying was the friendly cooperation of the bey of Tunis, who gave Hull every possible assistance in saving his consort and her equipment, even supplying her with an anchor and cable. But so much time had been lost that the visit to Cagliari had to be deferred.[10]

The Rodgers squadron reached Gibraltar, homeward bound, on 21 May. A week later, at sunrise, the *Argus* and the *Syren* weighed anchor for America. Isaac Hull had arrived in Gibraltar Bay on 21 July 1802 and had been in the Mediterranean three years and ten months. The next day, at sea, he gave the customary order to his first lieutenant that "agreeable to law, each lieutenant, master and midshipman keep an exact journal of the ship's way, and report the same daily to me." He added: "I should recommend to them that each one keep his reckoning according to his own judgment, without communicating the result to anyone except as above directed."[11]

Hull carried home with him Commodore Rodgers's letter to the secretary of the navy, detailing his movements since 3 April and describing the bearer of his letter as "an officer of merit . . . whom I beg leave to recommend to your notice."[12] Happily, these encouraging hints were no longer necessary. On 21 April, Congress, having ratified the treaty with Tripoli despite the lobbying of William Eaton, enacted a Peace Establishment Law for the navy, setting the number of captains at thirteen. Within three days Robert Smith had made out commissions for Charles Stewart, Isaac Hull, and Isaac Chauncey. Stewart and Chauncey were in America, but not until he anchored in the Potomac on 13 July did Hull receive the good news that he was a captain at last.[13] Two days later, mounting his new epaulets, he received the president and department heads on board the *Argus*. The brig was dressed in all her flags and saluted the party as it came and went. "The state of this vessel indicated the utmost order and cleanliness," wrote the *National Intelligencer* approvingly, "which is further evinced by her not having a sick man on board, although directly from the Mediterranean."[14]

After settling his accounts at the Navy Department, Isaac Hull was free to visit his home for a few days. Major changes had taken place there. His mother had died in November 1803, aged fifty-one, and in the following year Captain Joseph Hull had married the widow Lucy Smith Wheeler. Mrs. Wheeler was a substantial person, aged fifty at the time of her second marriage and heiress to her late husband's prosperous tavern at Derby. Captain Joseph Hull had left his first wife's farm at Huntington Landing to the care of his son Levi and established himself at the tavern. Isaac's elder brother, Joseph, was now a doctor in New York City, and his brother William, now twenty-five years old, was in business in the same city, a partner in the firm of Hall & Hull. The three youngest brothers, Daniel, twenty-two; Henry, eighteen; and Charles, fourteen, were either still at home or made their base there; Daniel and Henry were beginning to make merchant voyages.

Lucy Wheeler had brought one great innovation to the Hull family: a daughter. Mary Wheeler was a young woman of considerable spirit and some education and occasionally worked as a schoolteacher. Her entry into the all-male household was a source of mutual joy, for she immediately became a friend and confidante of the younger boys. When Isaac reached home he welcomed the girl, whom he had doubtless known in the village, as the sister he had never had. They soon began a witty and intimate correspondence in which they exchanged gossip and confidences about their affairs of the heart.

Hull's visit home was short. By the first week in August, he was off to New York to see his brothers and friends; from there he went to Newport, Rhode Island, to consult with Decatur about his new assignment: superintending the construction of gunboats. Intrigued by the success of the Tripolitan gunboats, and eager to find a means of maintaining an inexpensive defense force, the Jefferson administration had determined to build a flotilla of gunboats to protect American waters. One of the most attractive features of the gunboat program was that the plums could be spread widely: whereas a large ship could be built in only one place, a dozen gunboats could be laid down in a dozen places. Scarcely a state was without at least one gunboat contract, not even those without coastlines, for there were always the rivers and lakes to be considered. Eventually some 177 boats were built.

Connecticut's share of the boats for 1806 was four. One of Hull's first acts before beginning to build was to get in touch with Commodore

Preble at his home in Portland, Maine. Preble had been designing and building gunboats for the past year, and Hull wanted to take advantage of his expertise. He also wanted to see his old commander again. By 1 September he had closed his contract, with William Van Deusen of Middletown, to build the four boats at $1,750 each. About a week later he left for Portland, calling on his way at Brimfield, Massachusetts, the home of William Eaton.

Both at Brimfield and at Portland the prime topics of discussion were two: the quarrel between John Rodgers and the Barron brothers and the suspicious activities of former vice-president Aaron Burr. Hull had written to Eaton before leaving Middletown:

> I hear nothing of Commodore Rodgers since I left Washington. I calculated on hearing of at least half a dozen fights before this. He wrote to [James] Barron from the Capes and informed him of his arrival and that he expected to hear from him. Report says that Barron was sick.[15]

His information was correct. Rodgers, who nursed a grievance against James Barron for having, he believed, encouraged his brother Samuel not to give up the command in the Mediterranean to Rodgers, had heard at Gibraltar that Barron was spreading scurrilous rumors about him in America. He was barely in sight of the coast before he fired off a scarcely coherent letter to his adversary:

> From an honorable motive I am induced to acquaint you that I have at length arrived in America. I am now on my passage to Washington, and as it is full likely that I shall not remain many weeks in the United States, in justice to your reputation, I take this method to inform you that I shall hold myself ready to account to you at any time from the present immediate epoch to the same date of the ensuing month; and as I possess a mind superior to giving you any unnecessary trouble, permit me to add that in case I leave Washington it will only be for a few days.[16]

Barron was sick in bed at Hampton, Virginia, and he so informed Rodgers on 29 July. He was willing to fight, however, and the two men appointed seconds. But, since Barron continued to be too ill to leave Hampton, and Rodgers would not go there to meet him, the affair fizzled. Rodgers's marriage on 21 October certainly damped his enthusiasm for dueling. By the end of the year the threat of violence was ended, though bad feelings between the two men persisted.

The Burr affair was also interesting, since it promised to involve the navy in some sort of fighting. Eaton was a good source of scandal, for he had been approached by Burr to join his expedition on the presumption that his wrongs in the Mediterranean had made him angry at the

government. They had, but Eaton recoiled from Burr's treasonous proposals. He told Hull and Preble that Burr's secessionist uprising in the
Southwest would bring the navy into action. When the threat subsided
in November, Hull wrote: "I fear our affairs in the West are blown over.
I am, however, ready, let what will come."[17]

There was also minor gossip to be exchanged about Mediterranean
friends and naval associates. Hull reported Master Commandant John
H. Dent "the same good fellow that he was when with us." Master
Commandant Samuel Evans, like so many others, was making a merchant voyage, out of Baltimore as first mate under the unpopular ex-
lieutenant Andrew Sterrett. Hull thought it "rather an Irish hoist"—
meaning that the roles of captain and mate should have been reversed.[18]
Master Commandant John Smith was at Newport but incommunicado:
"I suppose he has something [more] to occupy his mind than that of
writing. I think he will moor himself there for the winter, and perhaps
for life." Decatur reported that Smith "was in close siege of Miss Gibbs
and that he thought she would soon surrender at discretion."[19] Miss
Gibbs, however, must have escaped the siege, for Smith was still single
in 1813. Many of the officers married in the next several years—Rodgers, Porter, Decatur, Stewart, and Dent. Bainbridge and Preble were old
married men, and while at Portland, Hull was able to admire the
Prebles' little son, seven-month-old Edward Deering Preble. Hull spent
a good deal of time on "gallantry" in these years and even approached
marriage once but was driven off by the adverse wind of poverty. He had
no resources except his navy pay, which was quite insufficient to support a family, and in this period even the continued existence of the
navy seemed uncertain. The speaker of the House of Representatives
had recently proposed that, in the event of a foreign war, the American
ships be lent to another nation at war with the same enemy, which
could probably manage them better.

In mid-October, Hull was back at Middletown, regretfully declining
a proposal by Preble and Eaton that he join them on a fishing trip. By 8
November his gunboats were planked and the carpenters were laying
decks. Hull expected to have them complete by 10 December; he had
been ordered to replace Decatur at Newport, but he begged permission
to revisit his boats at Middletown in the course of the winter. "As I have
superintended them thus far I wish them to be finished in such a manner that when they are ordered where there are other boats they will
not be pointed at as boats built under my direction and the worst in
service."[20]

Hull remained at Middletown until 21 December, by which time the
boats there were nearly complete, and then moved on to Rhode Island.

There he met a surprising situation. Constant Taber, the navy agent at Newport and an ardent Jeffersonian, wrote a poison-pen letter to the president accusing the officer in charge of building there (apparently without giving his name) of awarding contracts to Federalists. Jefferson passed the letter on to Robert Smith, who replied:

> The officer complained of by Mr. Taber is Hull, the nephew and protege of General Hull, and has been therefore considered by me correct in his political principles. However, he and all others act in such cases under instructions to employ those who work upon the most reasonable terms and who at the same time are capable of the work. I will have the necessary enquiries made in this particular case and will communicate to you the results.

Since he did not wish to write such a letter himself, Smith assigned the task to the chief clerk, Charles W. Goldsborough. Hull's response has been lost, but apparently it was satisfactory, for Jefferson pronounced his "ideas on the subject of the persons to be employed . . . perfectly correct. We have the comfort of having inquired, as was our duty, of finding all right, and jogged the attention of the officers to keep them on their guard."[21]

Hull spent the spring of 1807 shuttling between Middletown and Newport. It was tiresome duty. Like his fellows, he was thinking of asking for a furlough to make a merchant voyage. He mentioned this to Eaton, who proposed sending his stepson, Midshipman Danielson, under his old commander. (It would have been a good thing for Danielson, who got himself killed in a pointless duel not long afterward.) But a crisis intervened that shook the navy—and the country—to its roots and drove away all thoughts of merchant voyaging.

On 22 June 1807, off Cape Henry, the frigate *Chesapeake* was attacked by HMS *Leopard*, which took from her four alleged deserters. The *Chesapeake* had been bound to the Mediterranean under James Barron to relieve the *Constitution* as flagship of the Mediterranean squadron. There was a national outcry; although the administration hoped to avoid war, it was compelled to prepare for it. The Mediterranean squadron was ordered home; it would not be reconstituted until 1815. The gunboats were hurried to completion. Hull rushed his boats to New York to join the flotilla and, as soon as that was done, transferred from New England to Hampton Roads, Virginia, to take charge of the gunboats there. He had thirteen ready for service by 3 September but found the general state of things very unpleasant. For one thing, the gunboat crews were poor; many were Frenchmen who spoke no English. For another, prices were atrociously high, and the manner of southern workmen did not please him. The boats had been twice as long in preparation and had cost nearly twice as much as he had expected. Living in the cramped cabin of Gunboat No. 10 was nearly unbearable. The weather was disagreeable, too: the boats had had to be caulked twice because the hot sun had opened their seams.[22] He even recommended that provisions be shipped from the North because of their high cost and low quality locally. To cap it all, a fever had appeared in Norfolk, causing him to order all communication stopped between the boats and the shore. Hull never did learn to like the South. To his Yankee way of thinking, it seemed the haunt of laziness and disease.

On 8 September, Hull received news of the death of Commodore Preble at Portland on 25 August. "Our Navy has certainly lost one of its most valuable officers," he wrote, "and a man whose examples every officer ought to be proud to follow." He ordered his officers to wear crepe for a month in honor of the dead hero.[23]

A court of inquiry convened at Norfolk on 5 October to determine the cause of the *Chesapeake* incident and to decide whether courts-martial were in order. Alexander Murray was president of the court, and Isaac Hull and Isaac Chauncey were members. It was a kind of duty Hull detested, and it lasted a month. On 4 November the court reported its findings: that Barron, Master Commandant Charles Gordon (the *Chesapeake*'s first officer), Gunner William Hook, and marine Captain John Hall were culpable in not preparing the ship for an emergency and that they should be tried by a general court-martial. The findings of the court of inquiry were damning: they used terms like "neglect," "indecision," and "prematurely surrendered." The resulting court-martial was headed by John Rodgers. Surprisingly, Barron objected neither to being tried by the man who one year earlier had been intent on killing him nor to the presence on the court of Stephen Decatur, who had made public anti-Barron statements and had asked to be excused. On 6 February 1808 Barron was found guilty of negligence in failing to clear his ship for action on the probability of an engagement and was suspended from the navy for five years. Gordon and Hall were reprimanded, and Hook was dismissed from the service. Barron went to Europe for the duration of his sentence and sat out the War of 1812 there as well. Although he remained in the service and ended his life as the navy's senior captain, he never went to sea in a navy ship again.

Hull remained in command of the Norfolk gunboats until the court-martial ended and then asked for a new appointment in Connecticut. He was making efforts in the Navy Department to get his father on the federal payroll. Joseph Hull was tired of tavernkeeping. He had leased the tavern and was looking around for a new means of earning a livelihood. Isaac's idea was to get his father an appointment as navy agent for Connecticut, which would give him a percentage of all funds spent by the navy in the state. He was also interested in a suggestion by Charles W. Goldsborough that Joseph Hull be made purser for the gunboat flotilla and thought that if the old man could be both purser and navy agent it might be worth his while to move to New London.

Isaac further recommended that his father be given a contract to build six or eight gunboats, which he could do with the assistance of his son William, whose firm built its own vessels in the Connecticut River. He gave an amusing assessment of his fellow Connecticut Yankees:

> I should recommend some person to superintend the boats, let who may build them, for I am well acquainted with the carpenters of that country and should not be willing to trust to any of them. . . . [William Van Deusen] wrote to me some time since to endeavor to get the building of some of the boats for him. He is very close and will be very apt to screw the carpenters so close after having made his own contract as to oblige them to slight their work unless they have good looking to. I believe him honest but hard in a bargain and will make the most of everything.[24]

The result of Isaac Hull's persuasion was an appointment for his father as navy agent for Connecticut and orders for himself to that state as well. Joseph Hull held the agency for many years, and Isaac, predictably, did most of the work. He was constantly prodding the old man to keep his accounts straight and to get his returns in on time. But the appointment is a clue that the Hull family's politics were, despite the Taber incident, still considered "correct."

In December 1807 Congress, in response to the *Chesapeake* incident, had ordered an embargo on foreign trade and authorized the building of an additional 188 gunboats. Isaac Hull was to oversee construction of 4: 2 at Norwich, Connecticut, and 2 just over the border at Westerly, Rhode Island. In addition, he had secured another boon for the family and the state: Joseph Hull nominally (but really Isaac) was to contract for two thousand boarding pikes, two thousand cutlasses, and two thousand pistols for the navy. The two Hulls met at Middletown on 8 April to discuss the pike-and-sword contract with Nathan Starr. Isaac thought Starr a good and honest workman, with a large family to support, and hoped to see him get the contract. But something Starr told him about William Van Deusen changed the opinion he had expressed in December and provoked a rare angry outburst. He wrote Robert Smith:

> Mr. Van Deusen has this day shown me a letter from Mr. [Gideon] Granger informing him that he had called on you agreeable to his request relative to the building of gunboats and had received assurances that if any more were built that Mr. Van Deusen should have the contracts. I think it my duty to

inform you that from what I have seen of late of Mr. Van Deusen and from an advantage which he took (or which I think he took) of Mr. Blodgett's inexperience in fitting out the boats built here that his only object is gain and that almost any advantage would be taken by him to obtain that object. I am the more induced to think so from what I heard from a man of the first respectability in this place: that when Mr. Starr was about to send forward his proposals Van Deusen advised him to put on a good price, that the government were able to pay. This, I suppose, was to induce Starr to set his price so high as to leave room for him to underbid him and take the business out of his hands.

I have also been informed by Starr this day that Van Deusen had been several times at him to endeavour to be concerned; at one of those interviews Starr told him what the terms were that he had sent forward. Van Deusen told him that if it had been left to him to have made the contracts that he could have got two dollars for the pikes, which would have paid Starr much more than he had offered to do them for and . . . a handsome sum to him.

Van Deusen is not concerned in any business whatever, consequently any contract he may make must be executed by a third person and he will be sure to take the last farthing from that third person so that it will be impossible for them to do their work faithfully.

This is the first letter I ever had occasion to write to the injury of any person nor should I be induced to do it now were I not compelled so to do by what I consider my duty.[25]

This letter offers an important clue to Hull's personality and to his attitude toward government service. He never said a derogatory word about anyone if he could honorably avoid it. But he would not put up with chicanery.

By the next day he had recovered his good humor and wrote a playful letter to William Bainbridge, who had been ordered to build gunboats in Maine and who hated the cold New England spring as much as Hull had loathed the hot Virginia summer. Hull wrote that he had sent Bainbridge three letters since he last saw him and that this was the fourth and last unless he received a response: "I shall leave [Middletown] in three days for New London and if I do not find at least three letters from you I shall be as angry as I was when you asked me if we had fire in this charming place in winter. So be on your guard." He continued with a political comment, an exceptional thing for him. Blows from both European belligerents had rained hard on the United States that winter. January had brought word of the British Orders in Council of 11 November 1807, forbidding all trade with French-controlled ports. In March the Milan Decree was received, whereby Napoleon forbade all trade with British ports. Later that month President Jefferson sent to Congress the record of fruitless negotiations with British emissary George Rose, along with the past year's communications with the

French government. The latter contained some highly offensive messages from the French minister of foreign relations, to which Hull refers:

> What do you think of the times? Mr. B[onaparte] appears to dictate to us in high style. Will not those communications change the minds of the people of this country very much? Shall we not have war with France, or shall we suffer them to go on with their insolence? You know the cloth has no politics, but I wish to see this country take a position and stick to it, let what will be the consequence. If we do not, our nation will dwindle to that of Spain. I think we shall all be in Washington in a few months quarreling for old junk to fit out the ships, etc.

But he concluded lightly: "Steady habits, I am going to church. God bless you." And he addressed the letter to "William Bainbridge Esquire, Commanding the U.S. Squadron Down East—Have you had fish for dinner?"[26]

Although Hull was well aware of the effects of the current embargo, he was not directly involved with its enforcement. His business for the time being was gunboats, pikes, cutlasses, and pistols. Nathan Starr closed his contract for the pikes and cutlasses on 18 May but not before Isaac had dickered down the price to $2.50 per cutlass and $0.75 for each pike. The contract was completed by 29 October, to everyone's satisfaction. Hull pronounced the cutlasses "the best we have in the Navy."[27] Meanwhile, the Hulls had executed a contract on 30 June with Simeon North of Berlin, Connecticut, for two thousand pistols to be delivered within eighteen months at $11.75 per pair, or $5.87½ per pistol. The secretary had allowed $6.00. Hull had planned to get them for $5.75 but eventually split the difference.[28]

Through the spring and summer of 1808 Isaac Hull was crisscrossing the state of Connecticut from Westerly, Rhode Island, and Norwich to Middletown to Derby and back again, but as he told Robert Smith, "I wish to be actively employed." The Norwich gunboats were put in the water by the end of July. Those at Westerly were not so far advanced because the building timber had not been seasoned to begin with; since they were not finished until mid-November, they were allowed to remain on the stocks until spring. Hull took one of the Norwich boats for a spin in the Sound in September: "I found that she worked and sailed much better than I calculated. They are well built and good looking vessels."[29]

With the gunboats disposed of, the pikes and cutlasses shipped, and the pistols being made, Isaac Hull had wound up all his business in Connecticut. He asked to be ordered to Washington to settle his accounts and to seek a new assignment. The gunboats and small craft had proved ineffective in enforcing the embargo during the past year. The big cruisers were about to be ordered out again for coastal patrol, and Hull hoped to get command of one of them. In the first week of December he visited Derby and picked up thirty yards of the best cloth from Colonel David Humphreys's woolen mill, to be made into suits at the request of Secretary Smith and Chief Clerk Goldsborough. Also visiting at home was his brother Joseph, with his wife and three small children. With his bundle of cloth and a sample of North's pistols in his luggage, Isaac paused briefly at New York to see William, who now had Henry, Daniel, and Charles with him, then continued his journey to Washington for the holiday season.[30]

While closing his accounts at the Navy Department, Isaac Hull had ample opportunity to enjoy a festive month at the nation's capital. On 11 January, Robert Smith gave him orders to fit out the *John Adams* at the Washington Navy Yard; this extended his stay in the capital, but three weeks later he was transferred to the *Chesapeake*, which was ready for sea at Norfolk. Thus, he left Washington on 2 February 1809 and missed James Madison's inauguration in March. His orders were to take the frigate to Boston to enforce the embargo, but he was there scarcely a month before the law was repealed. That was good news for Hull, since Boston of all places was the center of antiembargo feeling. With repeal there was little to be done, for the moment, except to reship the *Chesapeake*'s crew and make minor repairs to the ship.

Hull was in high glee at the prospect of spending a summer in Boston without pressing duties. He was in love but was so coy in his hints to friends that it is impossible to say who the young lady was. He wrote to Hugh G. Campbell in South Carolina:

> When you see my letter dated at Boston I am confident you will envy me my station. We have the same good society as when you [were] here, the Embargo notwithstanding. I was in company a few evenings since with Isaac P. Davis, who asked for you, as well as many others. They often speak of you, particularly the ladies. The season for pleasure in the country has not yet arrived. I promise myself much pleasure in the summer with my friends here, but I fear the pay and rations will suffer. You left such an impression here on the minds of the ladies that I shall not get off without giving them a few parties. This I shall do for the honor of the flag. . . . I found all our friends well at Norfolk, but not so gay as when we were there. They have suffered much from the Embargo.

The Massachusetts Federalists would not have believed that Virginia could be suffering, as Hull said. To their minds, the entire onus of the embargo fell on them. Even repeal of the law did not mollify them. The new administration was prepared to offer more carrot and less stick by reopening American ports to trade, excluding only commerce with Britain and France. Hull thought, however, that the shift to nonintercourse and the change of administrations might prove favorable:

> The Embargo is off, but I assure you the merchants here will do but little. They are not yet satisfied. Several vessels are fitting out for the East Indies, but few for Europe. . . . Doctor [William] Eustis leaves this today for Washington as Secretary at War. You know him. He is our friend. Pray, do you know our Master [the new secretary of the navy, Paul Hamilton of South Carolina]? I can find no one that is acquainted with him here either by reputation or personally. I hope we have a gentleman.
>
> Say you intend coming here this spring and take rooms with me in the new hotel. I have stylish lodgings, I assure you, and you shall share them with me.
>
> Our friends at Washington are well. I think you will not do better than strike whilst you can. I had much conversation there and I thought you were a great pet, indeed so much so that I did not like it.

Finally came the mysterious allusion: "I think her ten times more interesting than ever. A most lovely woman, be assured."[31]

Hull commanded the *Chesapeake* for seven months, but it was not the active kind of service he enjoyed. Throughout the spring the ship lay at Boston for small repairs, and Hull concerned himself chiefly with another responsibility, the gunboats at Portland, which were to be stripped and laid up. The most perplexing problem was disposing of the officers attached to these boats. Many of the sailing masters who once commanded them had been dismissed from service, but the midshipmen were "young gentlemen," and most of them had influential patrons. They could not be so cavalierly disposed of. Hull ordered several to the *Chesapeake*. She now had more than a dozen of these young officers on board, and this situation caused Hull to suggest to the Navy Department on 4 June the propriety of sending the *Chesapeake* on a summer cruise in Long Island Sound to acquaint the midshipmen with sea duty and with the coast. He took the frigate to sea on 1 July and made a leisurely run to Newport, then moved on to New London. From New London he had hoped to run still farther up the Sound and make a visit home, but on 27 July he received unexpected orders to lay the *Chesapeake* up at Boston again and disperse her crew to other vessels. He was back at Boston by 6 August.

The recruiting service had gone on through the spring and summer, briskly while the embargo lasted, and then more slowly. When the *Chesapeake* sailed on her cruise, Hull left Midshipman Alexander Wadsworth in charge at Boston and placed two of the junior midshipmen, Joseph Smith and Seth Johnson, Jr., on board Gunboat No. 81 to receive and guard the men recruited. On his return he learned of a dereliction of duty that set his temper boiling: Smith and Johnson had left the boat unattended and had allowed two out of three of their men, with two months' advance pay in their pockets, to desert. Hull noted bitingly that "had I not taken the precaution to have left in the boat [as a crew] men that were disabled and good for nothing . . . they would not have had one remaining on my return." The deplorable situation in the gunboat was not merely a matter of report. Hull saw it with his own eyes on 14 August. He wrote:

> I happened to be looking at the boat, and saw men beating each other, and the officers looking at them and suffering them to go on. I immediately ordered the officers and men on board [the *Chesapeake*], punished the men and turned two of them on shore as being unfit for service. The remainder are now on board this ship. . . . Midshipmen Smith and Johnson I sent out of the boat, with orders to settle with the purser and go where they pleased . . . not thinking them worth the trouble of an arrest and a trial by court martial.[32]

Hull much preferred this sort of Preblesque solution to such problems. He had already tapped Johnson as a troublemaker, and the young man's behavior after the dismissal confirmed his opinion: going on board the *Chesapeake* to settle his accounts with the purser, Johnson contrived to insult First Lieutenant William M. Crane and caused Crane to order him out of the ship. He then wrote Crane a letter saying that he despised him; it was the kind of thing that could lead to a duel had not Crane declined to notice it. Hull thought Johnson's father had put him up to it, "for if I may judge from his appearance he possesses as little good breeding as his son."[33]

At the Navy Department, however, there were fears that Hull was being too high-handed. Smith had been recommended for his appointment by a congressman; Johnson, by Secretary of War Eustis and the Boston navy agent, among others. Goldsborough, writing in Secretary of the Navy Paul Hamilton's absence, advised Hull to consult with these men before showing their protégés the door. Hull complied to the extent of seeing Eustis, who thought that misbehavior among men with powerful friends ought to be punished more severely than usual to prove that there was no favoritism in the service. That sealed Johnson's fate. But soon afterward Hull received a penitent letter from Joseph Smith, apologizing for his neglect and saying that he had been tricked into leaving the boat by Johnson; Eustis also received an appeal from the lad's father, which he passed on to Hull. Hull was skeptical about Smith's innocence, but he always had a soft heart for a gentlemanly young officer: "I have no doubt myself but they were both to blame," he wrote Hamilton, "yet it's possible (as Mr. Smith is very young in service) that his error was not a wilful one, and as his father is a man of respectability and the son rather promising than otherwise, may I be permitted to suggest the idea of giving him another chance?"[34] Smith was reinstated.

By 30 August, Hull had turned the *Chesapeake* over to the navy yard. He did not particularly regret leaving her. She was an unpopular ship, at least in part because she was considered unlucky, but also because she was a dull sailer. Hull suggested some minor alterations, with which he thought "she [might] be made to sail with common cruising ships, but a first rate sailer I fear she never can be."[35] When he relinquished the *Chesapeake*, he expected to be given command of the *Constellation*, which, even though she was a smaller frigate, he called "a command more to my mind."[36] Secretary Hamilton hinted that he might have the *Congress*.[37] But, as it turned out, he was to be "on the beach" at Boston for the better part of a year, with very little duty except to oversee recruiting.

Life at Boston was expensive; in April, Isaac asked his father to sell his horse and carriage at Derby rather than send them to him, for "I am now getting rid of more than my pay."[38] In the fall he sent home his servant James as well, and for most of his stay on shore he dispensed with a clerk, writing all his letters himself. But Boston had continuing charms: "constant parties among you know who," he told Campbell in August. Still, he disclaimed a serious love affair: "I am still as far from taking a rib as ever. I cannot concentrate my love for the ladies."[39]

It was probably during this winter at Boston that Hull had his portrait painted by Gilbert Stuart. In 1835 he remembered the year as 1807, but since he spent half of 1807 in Middletown and Derby and the other half in Virginia, his recollection may have been mistaken. The winter of 1809–10 in the lively society of Boston was a likely occasion for a sitting with the famous portraitist. The picture is one of Stuart's luminous likenesses: the sitter is poised, charming, a trifle portly, with snapping blue eyes, modish brown curls, and the ruddy complexion typical of a Stuart painting. The fair brow, contrasting with the rosy cheeks and chin, reveals that Isaac Hull was careful to wear his hat when on deck. The portrait was a great improvement over the miniature done sometime earlier (but after 1806, for the subject has two epaulets) in which Isaac looks more than a little dubious about something. Stuart, however, who knew Hull for many years, thought that David Edwin had caught his expression better than he himself had. "You have Hull's likeness," he told Edwin. "He always looks as if he was looking at the sun and half shutting his eyes."[40] This suggests that as he approached forty

Miniature of Isaac Hull, ca. 1807–1811. By an unknown artist. Collection of Mrs.
Roger C. Elliott. Courtesy of the New-York Historical Society, New York City.

Isaac Hull was beginning to show some signs of nearsightedness. The
noise of naval guns also literally deafened him. By 1813 he had some
symptoms of hearing loss, and by 1820 his hearing was seriously impaired.

From Boston, Hull was able to make frequent visits to Derby. He had
assumed by this time an essentially paternal attitude toward his father.
When Isaac's ne'er-do-well uncle, Daniel, died in May 1809 ("I lament
much that he should have been taken off so unprepared, but to society
or to his country he can be no great loss"), Isaac urged his father to
settle his financial affairs so that he could live quietly in retirement.
"For God's sake," he admonished the old man,

> don't let your usual goodness lead you to dispose of any of your property or
> lend money to those who never intend paying it. . . . You ought also to be
> careful in hiring your help to get men that will earn their wages, and such as
> you can discharge and get rid of when you please. Otherwise you will get the
> same set of idlers and loungers as that you have formerly had trespassing on
> your goodness and picking your pocket. . . . You find those that you owe will-
> ing to call on you. Why not call on them that owe you?

Later in the summer he chided: "I am told you are quite a farmer. Pray let me beseech you not to let your industry injure your health. There can be no occasion for your own labor—your superintendence is sufficient."[41]

Isaac made a long visit home in September and October 1809 after disposing of the *Chesapeake* and squired Mary Wheeler to New York City. On his return to Boston he wrote her that "I had not left the stage before I received an invitation to the most splendid party I have ever been at in America. We supped upwards of two hundred, at least one hundred of them *ladies.*" The letter continues with playful hints about his love affair: "I have made my *bow* and find everything as when I left. No arrival from Europe as yet but hourly expected. What will then take place is very uncertain, but I believe there are many chances to one against anything serious."[42]

After some hesitation Mary had accepted a teaching post at Litchfield for the winter, perhaps at Miss Pierce's famous school for girls. Her move disrupted the correspondence, for which her brother chided her: "I calculated to have at least one letter a week and as many more as you found time to write." Although he had welcomed the chance for "a resting space" when his ship was laid up in August, by late November inactivity was beginning to pall:

> I am spending my time as jelly, as when I last wrote you: nothing to do but eat, sleep, gallant. . . . [A]nd as a proof of my gallantry I . . . choose to sit at home and write to you in preference to attending a very gay *ball.* At least two hundred people will attend it and many fine girls as you may suppose. I shall now threaten you for not writing: you shall have no more hints, though I have many to dispose of, until you become more punctual in your correspondence. This much, however, I will tell you—that I am now more persuaded than ever that you [were] once in *love* by your predicting so accurately the feelings of others. An effort has been made and [many] resolutions, but to no effect. All would not do—as you foretold in New York.

He promised to send her some books but, "not being acquainted with the taste of ladies in what they read," asked her instructions for the purchase. He also promised her a visit, for "I am tired of this place for want of something to do."[43]

Isaac's affairs reached some kind of crisis at the turn of the year. On New Year's Eve he poured out his heart in a letter to William Bainbridge, who had taken the frigate *President* to Norfolk and endured a terrific storm off Cape Henry that he described in a letter to Hull. Isaac sympathized with his friend, so often the victim of hard luck: "I can easily conceive your anxiety when riding with three anchors down and the sea breaking over you. . . . I think you must have begun to think that damned jade misfortune never would leave you. I hope, however, notwithstanding the slipperiness of Mr. *Fortune* you will be able to hold on upon him and leave Misfortune in the lurch in future."

Then he turned to his own problems:

> I thank you, my dear sir, for your kind wishes for my happiness in the matrimonial state, but I must assure you that you are months and I do not know but years ahead of me. I did not intend the hint I gave you should have led you to believe that I was near marrying. I will now, however, tell you what you might have inferred from it: that your friend is very fond of a charming woman, or (I should say) and that a charming woman is fond of an old *bachelor*. Thus much is *true* but MONEY MONEY where art thou? For want thereof and some other obstacles that are in the way I fear all must end in smoke, however much the parties concerned may suffer in their feelings. *Come, come,* give us a little comfort. You know I was always fond of the advice of my friend and I never wanted it more than on this occasion. Can we fetch when we beat at the years, and without a tide under our lee? If not, and a tide is necessary, how strong must it run? If a person is to starve . . . had he better starve alone or in good company, &c. &c. Answer me these questions and perhaps you will give me courage. If so, you shall know more in my next.

In a lighter vein he continued:

> So much for *love.* I am as usual out at dinners and balls often, indeed too much so as I have caught a bad cold and have a cough. To begin the year anew we have a ball at a friend, R. C. Derby's tomorrow night, and I suppose it will be very brilliant. All your friends will be there, which will give me an opportunity of saying you are well, as I am sure I shall be asked about you. All our friends are in town and as gay as the times will admit of.

Hull's phraseology reveals how intimately his personal and professional fortunes were bound up. The state of the navy and therefore of his career affected the most intimate aspects of his life. At the moment, everything was in question. Optimists were predicting a general peace with France and England, which would mean the laying up of the ships—not a pleasant prospect for the navy men. Pessimists, including the secretary of the navy, were doing their best to prepare for a possible war, even without the necessary appropriations to strengthen the fleet. Hamilton was still an unknown quantity to many people, even to many naval officers. Hull asked Bainbridge:

> What do you think of Mr. P. H.'s report? I think we shall pass over another Congress without getting anything done for us. Indeed, I fear another and another. . . . [I am] tired and think more and more how necessary it is to begin to look out for a stormy day.

As the bells began to toll for the New Year of 1810 he concluded his letter:

> My good sir, I have not read this letter nor do I intend to. It's for you to read if you can make it out. It's now dark and damned cold, as you may suppose as it's snowing. Happy New Year to all my friends. God bless them.[44]

The impecunious Bainbridge was so discouraged with the navy's prospects that he was about to take a leave of absence to make a merchant voyage to Russia. Whatever advice he gave Hull must not have been encouraging. Isaac was still ebullient and full of gossip, despite another cold that kept him from attending a ball, when he wrote to David Porter on 23 February. He deplored the resignations of young officers that were rife in these years but twitted Porter ironically on his good wishes to the older officers:

> I notice what you say of us old codgers. If I thought you serious when you wish I may live a thousand years I would thank you, but I believe you would say with [John] Smith, the devil take the old ones if by his doing so we can get *aloft*.

A letter from Isaac Chauncey, just back from Washington, had filled him with optimism:

> I think that the Navy stands fairer than it has for nine years. The bill for fitting out all the ships has passed the Senate and it's expected it will pass the House with a large majority. The *Congress* is fitting out for Chauncey; the *Constellation* is to be sent to New York to repair for your humble servant. . . . This is the present arrangement but God knows whether some change will not be made before Congress rises. They are much against making any appropriation for war measures until they hear from Europe, which must be soon, as it's now a long time since we have had anything new.[45]

But by the end of March he was chafing to be on the move. Mary Wheeler wrote to brother Levi on 3 March that "Miss R. G." (Rebecca Gracie) at Derby was probably wrong in suspecting Isaac of matrimonial intentions: "He writes me that he is tired of Boston."[46] He could not bring himself to marry on the strength of his meager prospects, so that the involvement of his heart had become painful. "Boston is as dull as ever," he told Mary,

> and my time passes without doing any good to myself or anybody else, which you know is tiresome to me that has always been actively employed. . . . I have employment for this evening at the theater. . . . We have now a play that has brought full houses for many nights, and continues to do so: the *Forty Thieves* very handsomely got up. The scenery is enchanting.

He was concerned about his younger brothers—Daniel, who had been captured at sea more than once in the past few years, and Henry, who was again at loose ends, as well as about Mary's brother Joseph Wheeler, also unemployed. "What would I give for money," he cried, "*not to squander*, but to do good with." He concluded wearily:

I am, my dear sister, as when I last wrote you: neither one thing nor the other, neither on shipboard nor on shore, neither married nor single, neither engaged nor entirely free from it, neither rich nor poor. In short, I am nothing that I might rather, nor do I expect to be soon.

Miss J. goes to Europe . . . to remain two years or perhaps longer. How will her mind be? Can you tell? I have some doubts about its being at ease but it cannot be helped.[47]

With that the mysterious Miss J. sailed out of Isaac Hull's life. He never mentioned her again.

As spring began, preparations were under way to fit out the frigates for cruising. Hull was still attached to the *Chesapeake*, though he had asked for a transfer. Apart from his other objections to the frigate, he feared that the business of preparing her for sea at Boston would be particularly troublesome because of the mismanagement of the navy yard. His old captain, Samuel Nicholson, had been beached there since 1799 and had treated the post as a sinecure. The yard was a wreck, and Nicholson devoted most of his remaining energy to carrying on quarrels with Francis Johonott, the navy agent, and Caleb Gibbs, the naval store-keeper. Hull therefore asked for very precise instructions about fitting the ship, and to whom he should apply for particular articles and services. "I regret to state that these quarrels are of long standing," he wrote,

and that they frequently carry the parties to lengths that do great injury to the service. I pray you to be assured that I do not offer this as a complaint against any particular person, but merely to ask of you such instructions as will enable me to carry your orders completely into effect, without involving myself in the quarrels of other people.[48]

But Secretary Hamilton was already excited about another letter Hull had written him concerning the seamen being recruited at Boston. On 1 April he had asked sanction for fitting out one of the gunboats to anchor in the harbor as a receiving vessel, because it was so difficult to keep the recruits from deserting from the *Chesapeake*, which was at the wharf. He had written, "we . . . have been obliged either to lock them up in the storerooms, or put them in irons every night to prevent their getting away."[49] Hamilton was shocked at this apparent brutality, and he wrote Hull a stiff letter admonishing him to stop mistreating the men in that fashion:

> Such proceedings must surely tend to excite disgust and prevent good men from entering the public service. . . . Precautionary measures may and ought to be taken, to prevent desertion from the public service, or to prevent the commission of any offense intended to be committed, but such measures may be humane and effectual too, as is illustrated in the case of the men under your command on board of a gunboat moored in the stream: they will no doubt be as safe as they would be loaded with irons on board the Chesapeake. . . . Degrading punishments are calculated to produce debasement of mind, which in time dries up all the springs of honorable action, and renders man callous to every generous impulse and a fit instrument for the basest purposes. . . . Penal laws are intended not to aggravate, but to alleviate the condition of human nature, by the salutary effect of exemplary punishment.[50]

The gentle Hull was hurt by this reprimand, which might be thought to come with ill grace from a slaveholder. "I . . . am extremely unhappy," he replied, "that my letter . . . should have given you impressions so unfavourable towards me as a man of feeling and humanity." He had not meant, he said, to intimate that the men were confined, except for being kept on board ship.

> Those men mentioned as being in irons were men who had shipped in merchant ships and run from them after having received an advance, and shipped with the recruiting officer of the Chesapeake without informing him that they had run from the merchant.
>
> With the two months' advance from the merchant ship, and the advance and bounty from the recruiting officer and other expenses brought them in debt from fifty to eighty dollars. This being the case, and they having shown by deserting from the merchants that they were not to be trusted, I should certainly have thought myself wanting in duty and zeal for the service if I had not taken every proper and necessary precaution against desertion a second time.

At 8:00 P.M. the recruits were all put into the sail room, he explained, as much for their comfort as for safekeeping, for, having few clothes or blankets, they were able to get some protection from the cold by rolling up in the old sails. Hull thought his record as a commander spoke for itself when it came to compassionate treatment of seamen. To Hamilton's flatulent homily on punishment he replied crisply:

> I am aware that every attention ought to be paid to the happiness and comfort of men that enter the public service and that punishment ought not to be inflicted before a crime has been committed, and then only in proportion to the offense. Ever since I have had the honor of commanding men I have pun-

ished with great caution and have ever made it a rule not to punish a man before I had informed myself perfectly as to his guilt.[51]

Within two weeks after this letter, the specified number of recruits had all been enrolled, and the Boston rendezvous closed. On 1 May, with the expiration of the Nonintercourse Act, Macon's Bill No. 2 came into effect. This bill prohibited the entry of British and French armed vessels into American waters; enforcement would depend on the navy. It was now organized into two cruising squadrons: a northern division under John Rodgers and a southern one under Stephen Decatur.

There were fourteen captains on the navy list in 1810. The top three (Samuel Nicholson, Samuel Barron, and Alexander Murray) would never go to sea again. Of those in active service, John Rodgers ranked first, followed by James Barron (suspended), William Bainbridge, Hugh G. Campbell, Stephen Decatur, Thomas Tingey, Charles Stewart, Isaac Hull, Isaac Chauncey, John Shaw, and John Smith. Campbell and Tingey were also permanently on shore, the former in Charleston, the latter at the Washington Navy Yard. Chauncey was at the New York yard, and Shaw was being posted to New Orleans. Stewart was on a furlough, making merchant voyages, and when Bainbridge also left for a merchant cruise the frigate *President*, 44, was without a commander. Hull was ordered to her on 7 May.[52]

He dallied a week in Annapolis before joining the *President* at Norfolk. "I was quite delighted with the ladies," he told Mary, "and I assure you there was no scarcity of them. I, however, took care of the main chance in that I yet have my heart, however much you may doubt it, or at least I did not leave it at Annapolis."[53] But he had scarcely made a turn of the *President*'s quarterdeck before he was out of her again. Rodgers had brought the *President* and his own ship, the *Constitution*, from New York a few weeks earlier and had been very dissatisfied with the *Constitution*'s performance. She had seen much hard service since her last overhaul in 1803. Her bottom was foul, and she sailed miserably. Rodgers, being senior in command, was determined to have the best ship. He told Hull on his arrival that he wished to take the *President*, and so on 17 June the two captains exchanged frigates, each taking his officers and crew with him. Hull was not sorry. Twelve years earlier to the day he had joined the *Constitution* as a lieutenant. He called her "that favorite frigate." Now she was his own.

7

That Favorite Frigate

At home again in the *Constitution,* Isaac Hull was jubilant. Even though the old frigate had come to him because she was defective, he believed he could make her again what she had been. His officers and crew had been serving for some time under Bainbridge in the *President* and were well disciplined. The first lieutenant was Charles Morris, whom Hull had known as a midshipman in the Mediterranean. Morris was also a Connecticut man. He was one of the most skillful junior officers in the navy, and one of the shrewdest. When the exchange of ships was made, Commodore Rodgers had praised the good order of the *President* and asked him to remain as her first lieutenant. Morris had declined, partly because he preferred to remain with messmates he knew and a crew he had broken in, but more importantly because of the character of the two prospective commanders:

> [Commodore Rodgers] is passionate, and we should soon disagree. I conceive I appear better at a distance than on close inspection, and have no doubt should have lowered myself in his estimation were we in the same ship. Captain Hull . . . gives his first lieutenant every opportunity of displaying taste or talent that they can desire.[1]

Isaac Hull as commander of the *Constitution* modeled himself on Silas Talbot in giving the management of the ship largely to his executive officer, thus preparing the younger man for future command.

A few days before the exchange of commands took place, Rodgers had received a bombastic letter from Secretary of the Navy Paul Hamilton, exhorting the navy to righteous anger against Britain and France:

> You like every patriotic American have observed and deeply feel the injuries and insults heaped on our country by the two great belligerents of Europe, and you must also believe that (calculating by the past) from neither are we to expect either liberality or justice; but on the contrary, no opportunity will be lost of adding to the outrages to which for years we have been subjected. . . . What has been perpetrated may again be attempted; it is therefore our duty to be prepared, and determined at every hazard, to vindicate the injured honor of our country, and revive the drooping spirits of the nation. Influenced by these considerations, it is expected that while you conduct the force under your

command consistently with the principles of a strict and upright neutrality, you are to maintain and support at any risk, and cost, the dignity of your flag, and that offering yourself no unjust aggression, you are to submit to none: not even a menace, or threat, from a force not materially your superior.[2]

This style, of course, was more than congenial to Rodgers. He ordered Hamilton's letter read on board every ship in his command, with his own added comment that in case of such an insult again being offered to an American ship the eyes of the country would be on the navy; if they failed to retaliate, the people would "be active in consigning our names to disgrace, and even the very vessels composing at present our little Navy to the ravages of the worms, or the detestable transmigration to Merchantmen." Therefore, he would expect his commanders to return two shot for every one fired at them, or should a shot actually strike an American vessel, "it ought to be considered an act of hostility, meriting chastisement to the utmost extent of all your force."[3]

Hamilton's letter was duly read on board the *Constitution* on 24 June. Midshipman Henry Gilliam understood the secretary to say that "it is highly probable . . . if we should happen to fall in with any ships of the belligerents, they would insult us; if so, we are to defend ourselves to the last, let their force be ever so superior to ours."[4]

This was very big talk for 1810, when the antagonism between England and America was dormant. Hull was more concerned with the immediate task of getting the *Constitution* into sailing trim. When the squadron sailed on 27 June for a short cruise up the coast, she made a poor showing. Rodgers crowed to his wife that "I am this moment passing the poor old Constitution and feel I do assure you much distressed to see how much we are beating her. The President sails like a witch."[5] The *President* passed the *Constitution* at 6:30 A.M.; by 4:00 P.M. Rodgers's ship was eight miles ahead.

The *President* put into New York, while the *Constitution* was ordered to Boston to take in water and three months' provisions, and to return to Hampton Roads by 15 July. Her sailing was so bad that she did not arrive off Boston until the sixth. Hull then met contrary winds that forced him at last to get out the boats to tow the ship up to an anchorage in Nantasket Roads on 8 July, and to get his water and provisions from Boston, six miles away, by means of lighters. This occupied six frantic days and nights; although Hull knew he could not possibly make the rendezvous on the fifteenth, he did not lose an hour at Boston. On the night of the twelfth he found time to write a brief letter to Mary Wheeler reporting that he had been too busy to visit more than one or two families in Boston. "I however have about thirty to dine with me tomorrow, but no ladies. My ship is too far from town for them to come on board." His conclusion gives a clear picture of his state of mind: happy, exultant, engrossed in the ship that was, to this date, the great love of his life:

> I have now one of the best ships in our Navy and a crew of 430 men, which you will think a large family, it's true; but being a good housekeeper I manage them with tolerable ease. I however scold sometimes and now and then get angry.
>
> Mary, I have not a word of news to tell you. Indeed, I am so much rapt up in my ship if half Boston was to burn down I should not know it unless I got a singe.[6]

The *Constitution* was at sea again on 14 July. It was already clear to her captain what the trouble was. The frigate had been in salt water continuously for seven years, and her bottom had acquired an incredible load of oysters, mussels, and barnacles. A few days out of Boston she struck a calm, and Hull took the occasion to send down divers. They gave a conservative estimate of ten wagonloads of shellfish on the ship's bottom. Hull sent a sample to the navy secretary, which must have been in a malodorous condition by the time it reached Washington. He had examined the ballast and the set of the masts and rigging—which Rodgers had seen to personally and which Hull did not presume to change in any material way. The mussels were hanging from the ship's bottom like bunches of grapes, with thousands in each bunch. The only solution was to take the ship into fresh water to kill the shellfish.[7]

Accordingly, the *Constitution* left Norfolk again on 4 August and ran up the Delaware River. Hull promised himself some pleasure on the occasion in visiting David Porter, just returned to his home in Chester, Pennsylvania, after a tour of duty at New Orleans. By 10 August he had gone as far as Wilmington, where he found that the water was not deep enough for him to go farther in safety. He anchored below the mouths of Brandywine and Christina creeks to get the benefit of their fresh flow. So good was the water, in fact, that he had a hard time keeping the crew from drinking it, "which I do not wish them to do, believing it to be unwholesome until it has been some time in casks." Hull was a devout believer in the medical wisdom of his time. He also thought that night air, freshwater fogs, and fresh fruit were unhealthful.[8]

The mussels died readily in the fresh water, but the oysters were stubborn. On the passage from Norfolk, Hull devised an iron scraper to drag under the ship's bottom. With this he got off ten or twelve bushels of shells on 11 August. Vigorous scrubbing and scraping continued for two weeks, by which time the mussels were nearly gone, though the copper remained closely covered with oyster shells. The divers reported that the copper was rough and loose in some places, but after it was given a final scrubbing with river reeds, Hull hoped that the *Constitution* would sail nearly as well as formerly, which, he confessed to Hamilton, would "give me great pleasure as she has always been a favourite of mine and her dull sailing has been a source of great mortification to me."[9]

The *Constitution* was off New York by 3 September. In spite of the remaining oyster shells, "she has been going eight knots all morning by the wind with single reefed topsails, with topgallant sails handed, which is not bad sailing, but" Hull told Rodgers, "I dare not yet give you a challenge after seeing your ship sail off Hampton."[10]

From New York, Hull was ordered to run to Boston to lie over the equinoctial storms. There he broke out the *Constitution*'s hold and substituted shingle for some of her iron ballast. He also received on board Midshipman James Reilly, a nephew of Thomas English, who had been the owner of the *Liffey*, Hull's first command. English had particularly requested that his nephew be ordered to Hull's ship: "as I have long acquaintance with Captain Hull I am particularly anxious that he should be in his care."[11]

The *Constitution* sailed again on 30 September to make a circuit of her cruising ground. She touched at Hampton Roads from 6 to 9 October and reached Sandy Hook in thirty-six hours from the capes. While she was lying off New York awaiting further orders from Rodgers, on 16 October, Midshipmen Charles W. Morgan, Richard Rodgers, and Archibald Hamilton, and Surgeon's Mate Samuel Gilleland asked permission to go on shore to shoot. Hull should probably have noted that there were four of them and asked: Shoot what? But he gave them leave to go. Not long afterward he learned that Rodgers and Morgan had fought a duel, the other two serving as seconds; Rodgers had been killed and Morgan had been wounded in the chest. Hull ordered Morgan under arrest and the other two suspended from duty. But, since naval regulations did not specifically forbid dueling, there was little more he could do. He even had to stretch a point to arrest Morgan under Article 15 of the regulations, "which says that no person in this Navy shall quarrel with any other person in the Navy etc."[12] Commodore John Rodgers thought the law inadequate to punish dueling and recommended that the miscreants be let go with a talking-to. Secretary Hamilton was on the spot, since his own son was among the guilty, but on reading the Act for the Better Government of the Navy he convinced himself, too, that there was nothing there that could subject the participants to a court-martial. With relief, he instructed Rodgers and Hull "to reinstate the survivor and the two seconds, without subjecting them to further inconvenience than a suitable reprimand."[13] Hull made the reprimand as stiff as his orders allowed. He strongly reprobated dueling, particularly among junior officers, and he was not sorry when Midshipman Hamilton was transferred out of the *Constitution* soon afterward.[14]

The frigate next made another run up the Delaware, and Hull, taking advantage of the layover at Newcastle, spent a few days in the "gay city" of Philadelphia. From there he wrote to Mary Wheeler, reproaching her over a bit of gossip that had come to his ears, to the effect that the real cause of Mary's unhappiness at Litchfield the previous winter had been her absence from his brother Levi at Derby.

> I notice what you say of the matrimonial madness that's going about our neighbourhood, and from hints that I have I am apt to think it will extend its ravages not far from our house. I think it's a good one that with me I can tell you a thousand things that there is no truth in and [you] at the same time keep from me a secret in which I am so deeply interested . . . and one that I am led to believe is true. You know I once made you a confidante and you ought to have been assured that was I about to enter into any new engagements you would be made acquainted with it amongst the first. It's you that keeps all in the dark; yes, Mary, who I expected would have told me everything, but I find I am mistaken. Time, however, will tell me all, and if nothing else will do, patience must.[15]

With ice beginning to form on the Delaware, it was time for the squadron to select a winter rendezvous, and Isaac Hull rendered another service to Connecticut—and incidentally to Navy Agent Joseph Hull— by persuading Commodore Rodgers to choose New London. On 3 November he suggested:

> was it not a delicate thing for me, I should most certainly name New London, as being by far the safest and most convenient port for wintering. . . . [B]ut being from that part of the country and my friends living not far distant, I should much rather . . . that you should form your own opinion from a visit there, or from such information as you can get in New York, as it might be thought I wish to get there to be near home.[16]

The *Constitution* sailed for New London on 17 November and anchored there on the twenty-eighth. She had lost three men by drowning in the Delaware: Midshipman Sylvanus Sprogell on the way up, and two seamen, Samuel Francis and Caleb Martin, on the passage down. Hull had learned that Francis was the only support of a widowed mother, so he opened a subscription for the mother among his crew. "In doing this," he said,

I reminded them that from the number that would subscribe a small sum from each, say twenty-five cents to one dollar, would amount to a considerable sum, and after advising them to take time and reflect and be sure not to put down more than on reflection they could afford, so that they would not repent when they come to be paid off, I ordered their names taken and the sum put against each man as named by himself.

When the list was complete, he was astonished to find that it totaled $1,000, or an average of about $3 per man. At this time a sailor's pay in the navy was from $6 to $12 per month, depending on his status. This incident found its way into the newspapers in January 1813 as yet one more noble deed of the *Constitution*'s crew.[17]

By mid-December the whole squadron was assembled at New London: the *President* and the *Constitution*; the *Argus*, now commanded by James Lawrence; and the schooner *Revenge*, Oliver H. Perry commanding. Some of the young officers were less than enchanted at the prospect of spending the winter in such a social backwater as New London, so that Rodgers and Hull had to devise means to keep them occupied. Hull recommended that Chaplain Montgomery of the *Constitution* be asked to set up a school for midshipmen, which was done. Courts-martial of seamen and petty officers for accumulated offenses took up a few days. Rodgers also put the midshipmen and lieutenants to work sounding and mapping the harbors of New London and Newport and the adjacent coast. While on this duty in January the *Revenge* was wrecked on Watch Hill Reef and lost. Some of the *Constitution*'s midshipmen again found less wholesome diversion in quarreling. On 19 February, Midshipmen Joseph Brailsford and Charles M. Fowle fought a duel, with Midshipmen William Laughton and John Packet as seconds. Fowle died of his wounds on 13 March.[18] Hull was particularly disgusted with Brailsford and Packet, whom he had suspended previously for unofficerlike conduct. He therefore asked Rodgers to remove the pair as an example to the other midshipmen, "that they may be assured that for similar conduct they will receive the same treatment."[19] With Hamilton's sanction, Brailsford and Packet were transferred to the *Argus* as a mark of the navy's displeasure.[20]

Now that he commanded the *Constitution*, Hull was more zealous than ever about the care of his young officers and men. He deplored the wrist-slapping meted out to duelers, and he took great pains to ensure that his junior officers would become a credit to the service. When leaving the ship to spend Christmas in Derby, he gave Charles Morris orders to "attend (as much as circumstances will admit of) to the comfort of the officers and crew, and give them such indulgences as the nature of the service will admit of, and in your judgment they merit." Nothing should, if possible, interfere with the midshipmen's school,

> as I wish the young men to improve every leisure moment to their studies. And should any of them be so neglectful as not to attend to the opportunity given them to attend school, you will take such measures with them as may appear to you most likely to make them more attentive, either by imposing the harder parts of the ship's duty on them, or by suspending them from duty and keep them below.[21]

When he returned to the ship, however, he was unhappy to learn that the officers had taken it on themselves to punish the men in what he thought was an excessive manner. He ordered Morris to make it known to the officers "that it is my positive orders that they do not punish any seaman, marine, or any other person on board in my absence, and that the punishment for missing muster, or any other trifling offense, shall not exceed three lashes with a small rope over the shirt."[22] Rodgers's ideas were very different. On 24 February he approved the sentence of a court-martial that meted out one hundred lashes each to Seamen John Loring and Samuel McClary of the *Constitution* for desertion. This sentence, intended as a deterrent example, was carried out at the *Constitution*'s gangway the next morning.

There was sadness at the Hull home that Christmas, for Isaac's older brother, Dr. Joseph, had died in August, leaving his widow with a nine-year-old son, Joseph Bartone Hull, and two little girls, Eliza and Sarah Ann. Isaac now assumed the role of eldest son. He offered to take little Joseph on board ship, but his mother could not part with him yet.

Isaac returned on board the *Constitution* on 3 January to enjoy the winter social season that, for New London, was hectic. Isaac told Mary on 24 January, "we are out almost every day either on dining parties or hot water parties. Last evening I attended the assembly for the first time; found many pretty girls. Some of my Middletown friends were there, say Miss Sages and Miss Chandler, etc." While at home Isaac had apparently smitten one of the young ladies of Derby, but not being attracted himself, he asked Mary to let her down gently: "I think it will be well to undeceive Miss Gracie and quiet her mind, as you may prevent her making herself very agreeable to some one *else* that may be pleased with her." Mary had at last confessed her engagement to Levi; and Isaac, in case he should be abroad when the marriage took place, wished her "all the happiness of a double sister and all that the marriage state is capable of giving."[23] At that time he expected the *Constitution* to be ordered on a foreign cruise, but the *John Adams* was sent instead, so that he remained at New London until the rendezvous was broken up in March. He had continually to prod his father to carry out his duties as agent for the ships and, in February, got the old man to pay a visit to New London. Isaac organized a party for a hundred people during his stay, but Joseph claimed to be too fatigued by his trip in the stage and would not attend. It seems that Isaac was the only member of the clan who enjoyed consistently good health. William had chronic respiratory problems that forced him to go south nearly every winter, and this year Levi had also made a voyage to Charleston, South Carolina, for his health. Daniel, Henry, and Charles, too, were often sick in the winter.

In February, New London society was even livelier. Isaac claimed that not a single night except Sunday was without a ball or a party, and usually a large dinner party took place at midday as well. "You will, however, readily suppose I joined those parties out of politeness," he teased Mary, "and not because I am fond of them." He was amused by the continual rumors from home that he was about to be married to this or that person. He was, he said, still single, the visit of one Miss Williams notwithstanding. "I carried her to Norwich and took leave without shedding a tear." As for "Aunt Hull," the wife of his uncle David, who was forever trying to marry him off, "tell her I have been waiting for Eliza [her daughter] to grow that I might make love to her. I think now she will about do for a man of my age and she may expect to see me this summer." Eliza was then in her teens, her prospective suitor thirty-seven.

"My ink is frozen, my pen worn out and myself nearly asleep, as the sentry on post is singing out 'All's well, eleven o'clock.'"[24] But all was not so peaceful on board the *Constitution*. Some thirty of the men, led by Boatswain's Mate John Nease and Seaman John Read, had written to the Navy Department, without Hull's knowledge or permission, complaining that their enlistments had expired and that they ought to be discharged. Hull, on investigation, found that they had entered at Philadelphia between 10 February and 4 March 1809 and had signed articles obliging them to serve two years from the time the ship weighed anchor for sea—a common stipulation. This would make the enlistments run until September. Further inquiry showed that the men had been incited by some person in Philadelphia who had assisted in recruiting. Hull thought that "if there is any law to punish scoundrels like him it ought to be done . . . as this letter is calculated to stir up mutiny and everything that is disorderly in the ship."[25] He took the course, unusual for him, of punishing some of the rebellious men: nine of them received twelve lashes apiece; one got ten; four more had nine; and Lanson

Marks, who had deserted twice, received twenty-four. Nicholas Fountain, a gunner's yeoman, and John Emmings, a cook, were reduced to the rank of seaman as well. The ringleaders, Nease and Read, were arrested and turned over to Rodgers for trial.[26]

Over one hundred of the *Constitution*'s crew would legitimately be entitled to discharge by 1 May, and since most of them had shipped at Boston, Hull asked Rodgers to let him take the ship there to pay them off and recruit replacements. He was particularly anxious not to be ordered back to the Delaware, which he thought was much too shallow and dangerous for such a large frigate.[27] The squadron broke up its winter quarters on 20 March, and the *Constitution* anchored at Boston on the twenty-eighth. She was there six weeks and could replace only sixty or seventy of the one hundred men discharged. Hull was very particular to order his recruiting officers to engage men to serve from "the first day of May next" to avoid any future disputes.

On this visit to Boston, Isaac was able to see his uncle William's family at Newton, though William Hull was in Detroit as governor of Michigan territory. Isaac had not seen him since before he went to the Mediterranean in 1802. He invited his cousin Samuel Clarke, husband of William's daughter Rebecca, and their little son Samuel C., aged six, to spend a day on board the *Constitution*. Isaac particularly asked that the little boy come, and S. C. Clarke remembered all his life "sitting at dinner in the cabin opposite two big guns which projected from the stern windows." The Clarkes, despite their Hull heritage, were Federalists. When little Samuel said he was a Federalist, he was asked by the gentlemen at table to define it. "A Federalist," he replied, "is one who votes for Governor Gore." The little boy was gratified by the burst of approving laughter.[28]

By the spring of 1811 it seemed increasingly likely that the United States would soon find itself at war with England or France, if not with both at once. American commerce was both the lifeblood and the prey of the two great belligerents now locked in total war with one another. The international situation had grown so tense and the fate of commercial shipping so precarious that the government could no longer depend on chance merchant sailings for communication with Europe. The naval vessels were now being sent across the Atlantic in relays every few months with official dispatches. The *John Adams* had gone in February. Now, suddenly, on 3 May the *Constitution* was ordered to close her rendezvous and sail for Annapolis to prepare for a European cruise. The ship was being painted, and Hull was visiting at Medford on 8 May when he received the order. He wrote Morris a hasty scrawl:

You will use all possible dispatch in getting the ship ready for sea. Do not paint any more. Get the officers and men on board as soon as possible, and give no more liberty. I shall be on board in the morning and shall order the provisions down immediately. . . . Bend all the sails for sea.[29]

A week later the ship was at sea, though she was thirty short of her complement of able seamen, and Hull had to station marines at the great guns to complete their crews.

One of the men shaking off his "dissipation on shore" on that run to Annapolis was a young seaman named Moses Smith. In his old age Smith published his reminiscences of life in the *Constitution* as *Naval Scenes in the Last War*. He shipped at Boston on 10 April and was stationed on the larboard fore yardarm, or in battle as sponger to Gun No. 1. Smith remembered the troublesome men in the crew who thought they should be discharged, and another countryman, named John Brown, shipped at Boston because his wife wanted him out of the grogshops. He had been persuaded to enter as the "captain's gardener." Brown came on board half sober and asked to be shown to the captain's garden; he was told to wait till the captain came, when he repeated the same question. Hull turned him over to the boatswain for a half-dozen strokes of the rope's end. The amused Smith reported that Brown became a good member of the carpenter's gang instead of a gardener.

The *Constitution* anchored at Annapolis at five-thirty on the evening of 24 May, having had a pleasant run of four days from Boston to the Chesapeake capes and then being forced to beat the whole distance up the bay against northeasterly breezes. Off the Virginia coast the ship had averaged ten knots before the wind. Hull thought that he could be ready to sail again in a week except for the state of his crew. Besides being shorthanded, he was still having trouble with the thirty men who claimed to be eligible for discharge. At Annapolis on 9 June he received the sentence of the court-martial on Nease and Read and read it aloud to the crew. But the agitation did not stop.[30] The center of dissension now was Quarter Gunner Thomas McCumber; indeed, most of the men claiming discharge were quartermasters, quarter gunners, and other valuable petty officers and able seamen.[31] At Annapolis they wrote to Justice Samuel Chase for a writ of habeas corpus to compel their release; Hull was able to quash the writ only at the last moment by presenting his case to the state's attorney. McCumber was court-martialed as a result. His trial turned on the question of the legality of shipping men for more than the two years stipulated by law; Hull and the members of the court were all in doubt, but after securing another legal opinion, this time from William Pinkney, former minister to England, they convicted McCumber. He was sentenced to receive one hundred lashes and be reduced to the rank of ordinary seaman for the remainder of his service, but the court recommended to the secretary that the whipping be remitted, and it was.[32] McCumber and the rest of the men who disputed their enlistments were offered the opportunity to transfer to other ships before the *Constitution* left for Europe, and though Hull tried to talk them into staying the extra time—for they were the most experienced hands—all but one chose to transfer so that they could be discharged in September.[33]

In addition to those men, there were others who were foreigners, including Hull's cook, whom he could not take with him to Europe where they might be arrested as deserters or impressed into British or French service. Thus it happened that the *Constitution* had to go to Europe in that perilous year with a crew short of experienced men. Hull estimated that one-third of the sailors had never been on board an armed ship, much less a warship. Relations with England and France were tense, and particularly with England. Pinkney had recently closed the American mission in London, and no replacement had been named, so that diplomatic relations between the two countries had been effectively broken. On 16 May, while the *Constitution* was on her way to Annapolis, Commodore Rodgers in the *President* had fired into the British sloop of war *Little Belt*, which, he said, he mistook for the frigate *Guerrière*, not far from Cape Henry, thus creating another international incident somewhat like the *Chesapeake* affair in 1807. Hull had to expect possible retaliation on the *Constitution* when she met British ships at sea. The crew were kept busy with gun drills, even at Annapolis. Hull did not feel at ease about going to sea with his raw crew, yet he was pleased at Rodgers's exploit, because "I consider the event of that importance that it will be the means of bringing our affairs with that nation to a close, one way or the other."[34]

The *Constitution* had a dual mission: to carry to France the new American minister, Joel Barlow, and his suite, and to convey to the Netherlands a debt payment of $220,000 in specie. The latter gave Hull a good deal of uneasiness: "that sum is worth quarrelling for and I am not sure that I shall escape it." Soon after the ship reached Annapolis, Hull went to Washington to meet the future minister; he may have known him already, since Barlow was from Connecticut. In addition to Barlow and his wife, there would be David Baillie Warden, appointed consul at Paris and agent for prizes; the Reverend Francis Parkman of Boston; Barlow's secretary, John Mason; William Lee, secretary of legation; the usual assortment of servants; and Mrs. Barlow's sister Clara Baldwin, a young and charming widow. This fact Isaac Hull did not overlook. "I find I am to take out a *buxom widow. Take care:* at sea is a dangerous place to be with ladies."[35]

Preparations for sea continued through June and July. Hull advised the Barlows on what provisions to prepare for a crossing that might last from thirty to sixty days, but he told the minister he had better not try to take his carriage, as "we have not one inch of room below and it would be much in the way on deck and very much exposed to the salt water and being injured by the ropes."[36] He himself laid in a stock of wine and other delicacies with which to entertain his guests, besides providing a goat (for fresh milk) and some crates of turkeys, geese, and chickens. He was besieged by businessmen who wanted him to carry money to Europe, to avoid the nonintercourse law, but was hesitant unless he was sure the money belonged to American citizens. Secretary Hamilton advised him not to take such money unless he were given a commission. Aside from that, he decided to do a little enterprising of his own and entered into an agreement with Charles Stewart to buy some goods in France to import; Stewart apparently to put up most of the capital, as he had about £1,500 credit with London merchants.[37]

Hull's correspondence in June was impaired when he burned his right hand badly, but as soon as he could hold a pen with two fingers he wrote his good wishes to Levi and Mary on their marriage: "now then let me congratulate you (as I do myself) on having taken to yourself a Hull." He went on in a blithely nautical-punning vein: "Tell Levy he ought to be a happy fellow and that I yet have hopes some day not far distant to be made so by Hulling some charming girl myself." He was pleased that the elder Hulls seemed inclined to settle down with the young couple at Huntington Landing. The house and farm at Derby were, he thought, too much for the old people to manage; they would be better off across the river.[38]

Although he denied feeling any difference in affection for any of his brothers, Isaac was probably most closely drawn to William. He felt uneasy if a week passed without a letter from him. Levi was not a faithful correspondent, but fortunately his new wife made up for it. She wrote in July that Levi was planning a voyage to southern Europe, which made her uneasy. Isaac agreed: "I think our affairs so unsettled with the continent of Europe that it cannot be visited with safety in a merchant ship and I do not feel easy at visiting it in a ship of war."

Meanwhile, he was enjoying the society at Annapolis: "I am here in the gay world, sometimes with ladies of seventy and sometimes with those of sixteen. I am now in love with one of seventy—Mrs. [Elizabeth Tayloe] Lloyd, mother of the governor of the state."[39] He visited at the homes of the first citizens of Maryland, including the Carrolls, with

David Baillie Warden, and the *Constitution* was honored by a visit from Governor Lloyd. If Hull's social contacts were mainly with Federalist families, it may have been because the *Constitution*'s officers were excluded from Republican gatherings on principle, as presumed enemies. Warden was invited to a public dinner given for William Pinkney that was restricted to Republicans. He "thought it would have been more polite to have presented to Federalists the subscription list, and to have invited to the fete, the captain and officers of the Constitution frigate. This I hinted to one of the committee. He replied, that between Republicans and Federalists assembled together, on such an occasion, it was impossible to preserve harmony."[40]

The *Constitution* left Annapolis on Thursday, 1 August, and anchored in Hampton Roads on Saturday evening, passing and speaking the British frigates *Atalanta* and *Tartarus*, which had come on a dispatch mission. They seemed disposed to be friendly; as the *Constitution* passed, the *Atalanta*'s band played "Hail Columbia!" But Hull sent Morris on board the *Atalanta* to question her captain, and both frigates departed the next day. Hull was not to be caught like James Barron. When he went to sea, he would be ready for anything. The *Constitution* stayed two days in Hampton Roads exchanging men with the *Essex* and the *Nautilus* and getting fully prepared for sea. The crew with which she finally sailed was a few hands short of full complement, but Hull had made up for it by taking more than his share of able seamen. He took Warden on shore to introduce him to Norfolk society and to attend the marriage of Lieutenant Thomas R. Swift, the *Constitution*'s chief marine officer, at Portsmouth. When returning to Norfolk in the gig with two ladies, they were overtaken by a terrific thunderstorm. They got the ladies home before the rain began, but since Hull recognized the storm as a portent of a fair wind for sea, he hustled Warden back into the boat at 10:00 P.M., and the two were rowed through the torrential downpour for four hours to reach the frigate. Hull was on board at 2:00 A.M.; by 6:00 A.M. he had everything in order for sailing. The frigate weighed anchor at 6:30 A.M., dropped her pilot at 6:00 P.M., and stood to the eastward.

On the first afternoon at sea the crew were mustered and assigned their watches and stations. Thereafter, when the weather permitted, there were daily sail drills or gun drills. The ship was not twenty-four hours outside the Chesapeake capes before she struck a spell of squally weather that laid all her cabin passengers (except Warden) low with seasickness. Many of the green hands were also stricken; even First Lieutenant Charles Morris confessed to Warden that, no matter how long he had been at sea, he always felt queasy when the ship's motion was heavy. The sufferers were scarcely on their feet again when the frigate encountered a real storm in the earlier hours of Sunday, 11 August, off Georges Bank. Sheets of rain, thunder and lightning, and heavy gusts from the westward buffeted the ship. Canvas was shortened, and shortened again. The *Constitution* was going at nine knots but was rolling and pitching so much that the sea poured in through her ports. The men were sent aloft to strike the topgallant masts and yards, and the ship kept away under a storm staysail. In the afternoon it fell calm and the light of the electrical phenomenon known as the "come-pleasant" was seen on the masts, but at daylight on Monday the gale renewed its fury until, before noon, the ship was brought under bare poles. As she scudded away before the wind, Captain Hull came on deck, "as calm as ever in sunshine, and gazing placidly around, while all nature seemed upturned about him," as Moses Smith observed. He spoke to Lieutenant Alexander Wadsworth, who had the deck:

> "She labors hard, Mr. Wadsworth; very hard, sir."
> "Yes, sir, but she makes fair weather of it."
> "Ay, ay, indeed she does. She'll give us at this rate a good appetite for dinner."
> "She comes up like a top, sir, and she's as steady, too."
> "Just so. What vessel have we there to leeward, Mr. Wadsworth?"
> "A square-rigger; she's lying to, sir."
> "Anything on her?"
> "Not a stitch, sir. Nothing could stand this blow but masts."
> "Keep the frigate so, Mr. Wadsworth. I'm thinking this will hang on some time yet."[41]

The groaning passengers did not find their appetites improved by the storm. One of the sheep died, and the poultry looked bedraggled. Warden wryly observed that "man and the hog are the only animals which thrive and fatten on board a ship." Mrs. Baldwin lay on her couch while Warden read "La Roche"[42] to her; suddenly a sea filled the after gallery and drenched the poor chambermaid. Warden forgot the pathetic tale and rocked with laughter. Worse was in store for the sick; early the next morning the frigate's drums beat "to quarters" as a strange ship with gun ports appeared, and in a few minutes the cabin bulkheads, beds, trunks, and all the niceties were swept aside. After speaking the merchant (the *General Greene* of New York), Hull ordered the guns secured and the topgallant masts swayed up, and the sailors brought their drenched clothes on deck to dry. The storm had nearly blown itself out, and for the remainder of the voyage there was fair summer weather.

Once the gales and the seasickness were past, the passengers began to enjoy their voyage. They had brought books and backgammon and even pet animals for amusement. Warden and Mason had caged squirrels; there was a raccoon that took up its abode in the wardroom; and Mrs. Baldwin had two mockingbirds. These birds did not finish the voyage: one flew out the cabin window and drowned; the other died in its cage two weeks later.

Isaac Hull played the genial host to perfection. In Moses Smith's view from the main deck, he was

> full of animation. He had not then been married, and he took delight in showing his gallantry and respect for the ladies on board. He became quite a favorite with them, and appeared as familiar with the requirements of polite intercourse, as with the command of our stately frigate. He devised various means of amusing his gentle guests; and after all it is not so difficult for refined females to dwell upon the deep, as would at first appear.[43]

Hull and Warden seemed at times to be vying for Mrs. Baldwin's attention, and if Warden had the advantage of being constantly by her side, Hull certainly appeared in a favorable light as the master of the *Constitution*. He showed his prowess, too, as a fisherman, bringing up a shark and, on the Grand Banks, several cod. Other diversions for the passengers were provided by ships spoken on the passage and by performing scientific observations of the temperature of the water and of the velocity of the Gulf Stream. Warden, who was a distinguished student of natural philosophy, made extensive notes of the variation of color and temperature of the water as affected by the Gulf Stream, the Grand Banks, and other phenomena. For the male passengers there were always the pleasures of dining with the wardroom officers (mock turtle soup, claret, and madeira were featured), of smoking on the forecastle, or of venturing up the rigging for a broader view, but the ladies led rather a confined existence. The sailors provided some sport; one evening the passengers witnessed a game of "goose" on the spar deck.

With a fine wind, the *Constitution* was bowling along day by day under her royals and studding sails, logging nine, ten, or eleven knots. Not a day passed without some exercise involving the great guns, the sails, or boarders and small arms. One evening the crew were called to quarters after dark to practice placing the lanterns for a night action. The passengers were impressed with the speed, order, and silence of the drill.

In the night of 28 August, Warden went on deck to admire a phosphorescent sea around the ship; the next day the *Constitution* was surrounded by dolphins, and a small land bird lighted in the rigging. By 31 August the ship was on soundings. Just after noon on 1 September the lookout at the main topmast head sighted Lizard Point, the southernmost tip of England, nine leagues to the north. In the morning the *Constitution* passed Eddystone Light, and her officers counted sixty sail at Torbay. Then the wind shifted to the east and continued obstinately to blow that way for several days, forcing the *Constitution* to beat slowly up the Channel for her intended port of Cherbourg. On the afternoon of 5 September the sails of the British blockading squadron were sighted at last: two frigates and two line-of-battle ships. Hull ordered the *Constitution* cleared for action as she bore away for the blockaders; he spoke the patrolling frigate and then the flagship, the *Royal Oak*, which sent a boat on board. After a polite exchange of identification, the *Constitution* stood off shore for the night. At dawn she again closed the port and sent the second cutter in for a pilot; at 10:30 the frigate came to in Cherbourg harbor, thirty days from Hampton Roads. Hull was pleased with the short passage and with the restoration, at least partially, of the *Constitution*'s sailing reputation.

The *Constitution* drew only twenty-four hours' quarantine. Thereafter came the round of formalities and ceremonies. First the frigate saluted Admiral Aimable-Gilles Troude with fifteen guns and received a salute in return, after which Hull and Warden visited the admiral on board the *Courageux*, 84. Troude and Hull talked shop: the French officer demonstrated to his American visitor a new method of mounting carronades by which they could, he said, be fired twice as fast and by half as many men as was usual. Hull was interested, but since the French navy had a reputation for firing with great speed and equally great inaccuracy, he may have taken the advice with a grain of salt.

At 1:00 P.M. on Saturday, 7 September, Minister Barlow and his train left the *Constitution* as a salute of seventeen guns was fired and the crew manned the yards and gave three cheers. Hull accompanied his friends on shore to the Hôtel d'Angleterre, then returned to receive a visit from Admiral Troude on board the *Constitution*. There began a hectic round of dinners, first by the American consul, then by the admiral on board the *Courageux*, and so on. Besides, there were wonderful things to see at Cherbourg: the Tivoli with its baths, the lace factory ("for the education and support of poor female children"), the forts and huge dike under construction, the Gothic church, and the marine hospital. Most interesting to Isaac Hull were the shipyard, with two line-of-battle ships on the stocks, and the two large marine basins under construction, one able to receive ten ships at once.

But the *Constitution* did not linger at Cherbourg at this time. Hull dreaded the equinoctial weather in the North Sea and was anxious to take care of his business with Holland as soon as possible. He and Morris left the Hôtel d'Angleterre early on the morning of 11 September; as soon as they were on board, the frigate got under way and began again the tedious process of beating up the Channel. The wind stubbornly remained ahead for a week; the *Constitution* was forced to anchor at Dover on the sixteenth and did not get sight of the Texel until late on the nineteenth. But the frustrations were only beginning. When the Helder pilot came off, he told Hull that there were but nineteen feet of water on the bar; the *Constitution*, drawing 23 feet 6 inches, could not possibly enter the port. She must, in fact, lie eight or ten miles off the land, and the $220,000 in gold and silver would have to be lightered over that distance. Nor was that all: the complications of politics interfered. Since the Netherlands had been subsumed in the Grand Empire, permission must be sought from Paris before the money could be received. Hull sent his purser, Isaac Garretson, on shore to communicate with the firm of Willink & Van Staphorst at Amsterdam, which was to receive the funds, but Garretson was detained by the police, and only his letters were forwarded.[44]

On Sunday morning, 22 September, Hull received a reply from Willink & Van Staphorst saying that, although they could not receive the specie and give a receipt until permission came from Paris, they would arrange to have it removed into boats so that the *Constitution* would not be kept waiting. Hull could not agree to this, since he would be responsible for the money until it was in the bankers' hands. He resolved instead to return to Cherbourg with the specie. But then the wind, which had remained obstinately in the east as the frigate came up the Channel, suddenly hauled into the west and began to blow a gale onshore. The *Constitution* was obliged to claw off the lee shore. She was in sight of the Texel again at 9:00 A.M. on Tuesday when Hull, now almost frantic with anxiety for the ship and his mission, wrote a hasty letter to David Baillie Warden: "you yet find me floating about the shoals of the North Sea. Indeed, my good sir, you can have no idea of the trouble and anxiety I have in this very unpleasant cruise. . . . We are all well on board but some of us have long faces at being detained here so long."[45] Again, before he could send his letters on shore the wind veered around, and the ship had to beat off. This storm was much worse. For five days the *Constitution* beat about the shoaly waters, sounding every half hour. The seas were so heavy that the shot from the gun deck had to be sent into the hold. It was again Sunday before Hull added a final postscript to his letter to Warden and sent it off at dawn with Lieutenant Octavius A. Page to the Texel.

But there was good news at last. While the *Constitution* was enduring the storm, the permission had come from Paris, so that the specie could be landed if the weather would cooperate. Hull and the pilots lost no time. By 1:15 P.M. marine Lieutenant Swift was on his way to the Texel in the pilot boat with the kegs and boxes of specie, with instructions to go on to Cherbourg by land with Purser Garretson if they should be unable to return to the ship. Sure enough, the wind began rising again almost immediately. Hull dashed through his letters, including another one to Warden: "my mind is at this moment so under torment and harassed with this cursed specie and gales of wind that I hardly know what to say. . . . If I have time I shall write you again but at this moment I have a dozen letters to write and a gale of wind at my heels."[46] The *Constitution* could not keep on the coast until the officers returned from Amsterdam, so Hull bore up for Deal on Wednesday, and anchored there on Thursday afternoon.

With the war between England and France at a peak of ferocity, passage from one warring nation to the other was difficult. The regular Channel boat from Morlaix was dirty, dangerous, and uncertain. Part of Hull's mission, therefore, was to ferry Jonathan Russell from France to England. Russell had been chargé d'affaires at Paris and was transferring to the same post in London, but he flatly refused to go unless a public vessel would transport him. He was not alone in his feeling. While beating about off the Texel, Hull had received an appeal via Warden to take passengers across the Channel and even to America. Madame de Staël and her son were among those who wished to go to America in the frigate; at least twenty others desired passage from Cherbourg to Portsmouth.[47] Hull, distraught with his detention at the Texel and not looking forward to a winter passage of the North Atlantic (especially with his cabin full of sick landlubbers), made a tentative refusal. "The passage will probably be long and very cold, which will make it unpleasant both to them and to me. I must acknowledge that it is not very gallant to refuse a lady a passage, yet I believe I must for once deviate from being the gallant."[48]

But there was no way to avoid taking the cross-Channel travelers. Near midnight of the day the *Constitution* anchored off Deal the American consul, Edward Iggulden, brought off three passengers for Cherbourg: Sir James Jay, the distinguished physician and brother of John Jay; Judge William A. Thompson of New York; and one Barney Smith of Milton, Massachusetts. Hull made them welcome and entertained them bountifully with the best of wines and fresh meat for what turned out to be so long a stay that Smith gave up and disembarked. The *Constitution* was windbound in the Downs until dawn of Tuesday, 8 October. After beating all the way up the Channel, she now had to beat back down. The passage was not uneventful. At 2:30 A.M. on Wednesday a brig of war ran down for the *Constitution* and fired two shot at her, one striking her quarter and the other amidships. Whatever the captain of HMS *Redpole* thought he was doing, he changed his mind when the drums rolled through the *Constitution* and her ports flew open, revealing a broadside of 15 long twenty-fours and 12 thirty-two-pounder carronades. An officer from the British ship was on board by 3:00 A.M. to apologize for the attack. According to Moses Smith, Hull shouted at the British lieutenant: "How dare you fire on us?"

"O—we beg pardon," was the reply; "we mistook you for French." "French! French!" retorted Hull; "you've been in sight all night, and yet can't tell who we are! I've a good mind to sink you on the spot."[49]

Had he been Rodgers, he would have carried out the threat, but Hull was too temperate to create another *Little Belt* incident, particularly in that locale. He let the *Redpole* go.

Another three days passed in tacking down the Channel before the *Constitution* spoke the blockaders of Cherbourg again on Saturday morning. It was raining as she stood into the harbor, and whether because her identifying flag was obscured by rain or through some other error, the French forts opened fire on the frigate. Two of the four shots struck the *Constitution*, one passing through the hammock nettings and smashing the stern of the second cutter, the other bouncing off the water and striking the ship's side abaft the forechains. Hull kept coolly on his course, confident that when the officers at the forts saw he intended to enter the harbor they would know he was not an enemy. Within half an hour the *Constitution* rounded to her larboard anchor.

Eager to get away and home before the winter gales in the Atlantic began, Hull had asked Barlow to get Jonathan Russell to Cherbourg in time for the *Constitution*'s return. But despite all the delays Russell was not there, and Hull learned that he could not expect him for several weeks. Jay and Thompson persuaded him to use the interval by accompanying them on a trip to Paris. That it was an important episode in Hull's life can be inferred from the fact that for the first and only time he kept a diary, covering the two weeks of his journey to Paris and his stay in the city, with extensive jottings on his trip to Versailles.

The travelers set out at dawn on 15 October in the Paris coach, passing through Valognes, Sainte-Mère Église, Carentan, and Saint-Lô. Hull took note of the character of the country—poor as far as Valognes, and thereafter lush, "the most beautiful country that can be imagined, every foot being under cultivation or used for grazing." He was told that the land sold for $250 to $300 an acre. All this was remarkable indeed to a New Englander, whose native farms averaged one hundred acres (at $10 to $15 an acre) with only 10 to 20 percent under cultivation or pasture, and grazed by scrawny beasts quite unlike the fat cattle, sheep, and hogs of Normandy. He noted also the small factories for pottery and lace and the home manufacture of cloth in the region, as well as the ambitious canal projects to connect the Cotentin towns with the sea. The roads were unlike American ones, too—"very good, and carriage easy and smooth."

On the second day before sunrise the diligence entered Bayeux. Hull had a fleeting glimpse of "a large and very ancient town, the streets narrow and the houses high" before being whirled on through "a perfect garden" to Caen. He recorded the distinctions of that city in proper tourist fashion: the famous churches, "particularly the church in which William the Conqueror was buried"; the lace factory (with prices noted); the canal under construction; and the famous building stone. Hull took note of the half-timbered houses in the old towns, and of dirt and beggars as well. The road on which they now traveled was full of Danish and German conscripts marching for Brest to embark. Hull was distressed at the sight: some of the boys were not more than fourteen.

The party arrived in Paris at 1:00 P.M. on 18 October. Hull and Judge Thompson engaged the best rooms at the Hôtel d'Orleans; they were bemused to find that the servants spoke no English. After much gesticulating, matters were settled to reasonable satisfaction, and Hull fared forth to call on the Barlows. By eight he was off to the opera with two Bostonians. He was dazzled with the performance.

The ensuing week at Paris was spent in giving and receiving calls, in visiting the "sights," and in transacting business. While at Deal, Hull had obtained part of Charles Stewart's funds in gold from his English agents, and he intended to invest them, with some money of his own, in goods for speculation, as well as buying presents and articles requested by his American friends. He hoped to invest $3,000 to $6,000, depending on the availability of funds, for the most part in satins, laces, cambrics, gloves, ribbons, watches, and razors, and "one handsome clock with ornaments for a room, price from 100 to 150 dollars"—perhaps a bridal present for Mary and Levi.[50] He had also "a memorandum as long as my arm" from Dr. John Bullus, the New York navy agent, to purchase articles for Governor Daniel Tompkins, including a sword belt and sash.[51] Therefore, on his first morning in Paris he went with Warden to meet Luke Callaghan, a merchant who would act as agent in collecting the goods, and on two subsequent afternoons he accompanied Callaghan's wife to inspect silks, cambrics, and artificial flowers. But most of his time was devoted to sightseeing: the Luxembourg, the Louvre, the Tuileries, the site of the Bastille, Notre Dame, and on the twenty-fourth a whole day at Versailles. The paintings he saw at the

Luxembourg and the Louvre were "elegant beyond description. . . . [I]ndeed, they exceed all the paintings I have ever seen." On his visit to Versailles he was so overcome by the palace, "though in ruins and disorder," that he could only repeat "elegant . . . elegant" again and again. Even the "necessary" was "very elegant, all gold." On many of his excursions he was accompanied by Clara Baldwin; after a visit on Sunday, the twenty-seventh, to the Louvre galleries from the thirteenth to the nineteenth century he noted that he "was much gratified by this visit." Was his gratification with the paintings or with the lady? Another highlight of his stay was a dinner with some Americans who had formed a shooting club. The meal, "served up in high style," began at five-thirty, and Hull left the company at ten o'clock. Like so many Americans in Paris, Hull was limited by his lack of French. Thus he spent most of his time in the company of Americans and never really made the acquaintance of the Parisians.

Jonathan Russell, the ostensible object of Hull's search, was at Dunkirk when the captain reached Paris. He returned to Paris on the twenty-fifth, and the two agreed that, rather than wait for Barlow's dispatches, which could not be prepared until he saw the emperor, Hull would take Russell to England and return once more to Cherbourg for the letters.

It was not what Hull would have preferred, as he was still hopeful of getting home before the worst of the winter, but it was the best that could be done. By the following Sunday afternoon he was on board the *Constitution* again, preparing to receive Russell and the half-dozen or more other men he had agreed to transport across the Channel. Late in the week Russell's baggage arrived, and so did some of Hull's Paris purchases, but he found to his chagrin that Callaghan had mixed them up with some goods he was exporting, and the customs officers were unwilling to let Hull take his own things without paying tonnage duty on his ship as if she were a merchant. Hull was despondent: the delay of the ship and the powder-keg situation between the United States, England, and France, signaled by the incidents with the *Redpole* and the Cherbourg forts, put him in a mood to fear some catastrophe. He wrote Warden before sailing to ask that "should anything happen [to] me my friends may find in you a friend."

On Saturday afternoon, 9 November, Hull welcomed his passengers on board: Jonathan Russell (to whom he gave his own cabin and bed) and his traveling companion, Dr. Robert M. Patterson of Philadelphia; the Reverend Francis Parkman, who had come on the voyage in August and had been since at Paris; Judge Thompson again; a French major named Montflorence; John Purviance; and one William F. Cutter of

Cambridge, Massachusetts, a "mechanist"—plus perhaps a few more. Fortunately, this time it was a quick passage. The *Constitution* was under way by 4:00 P.M. on Saturday and anchored in St. Helen's Roads by three the next afternoon. Hull had laid in provisions for six days, just in case, but Judge Thompson later recalled that "the passengers endeavoured to lessen the quantity of wines as much as they could." Near the end of this convivial journey the passengers consulted on what would be a proper recompense to Hull for his hospitality. He had refused to take anything from Jay and Thompson for their passage to Cherbourg, but this crowd was a strain on his generosity. He was persuaded at last to take ten guineas apiece, though he refused anything from Russell, who was on official business.[52]

On Monday evening, after exchanging salutes with Admiral Sir Roger Curtis, Hull left with Russell for London. The *Constitution* was taking in stores and adding to her complement about thirty distressed American seamen who were stranded in England and looking for a way home. Hull explained to the secretary that "the British are taking our vessels daily and the crews either turned on shore to starve or detained on board their ships."[53] His apprehension of a confrontation with the Royal Navy was about to become a reality. On Tuesday evening after dark a British officer came on board the frigate to say that a deserter, Thomas Holland, had swum on board HMS *Havana,* 44. The next morning a lieutenant from the *Constitution* went to demand Holland's return but was told that the decision must come from Admiral Curtis. Lieutenant Morris went in person to the admiral, only to be told that Holland claimed to be a British subject and would not be surrendered.

It was an old and all-too-familiar situation, but this time with a twist. At midnight between Saturday and Sunday a swimmer was picked up by the *Constitution.* He cheerfully identified himself as William Wallace, alias John Burns, a deserter from the *Havana,* but who, according to his papers and his own statement, was an American. The captain of the *Havana* sent to ask if Wallace was in the *Constitution* and was told that he was; no immediate demand was made.

So matters stood when Hull rejoined the ship on Monday. He wrote a formal demand for Holland immediately to Sir Roger Curtis, which in turn was given a formal response: "the man in question has declared on oath that his real name is Charles Davis, and that he is a subject of His Britannic Majesty."[54] Although William Wallace's return had not been asked—perhaps Sir Roger saw the irony of that, or at least the inevitability of a refusal—there was talk in Portsmouth that the *Constitution* would be pursued and forced to give him up. Hull was fully alert to the possibility. He told his passengers (Leonard Jarvis, John

Spear Smith, Nathaniel Heyward, with Thompson and Montflorence returning) that, much as he regretted the inconvenience to them, the ship would have to be cleared for action. To Russell in London he wrote an account of the incident as the frigate was unmooring, concluding: "I am now getting ready and hope to be able to give them a fight for [Wallace]. There can be no doubt but he is an American and belongs to New York; at any rate he is ready to make oath of it and that is more than they asked of the man they detained of me."[55]

Before the *Constitution* was out of the roads two more men deserted from one of her boats while fetching provisions. Though his crew was full with the American seamen enlisted from the beach, Hull was outraged at the behavior of the British officers in enticing his men away. When the boat returned short, he exploded: "The insults of these cursed British are more than flesh and blood can bear!" Moses Smith and his mates were impressed with the impassioned address Hull delivered at the ship's muster: "The aspect and language of our commander upon that occasion can never be forgotten." Hull said: "'Boys, are you ready to fight? I don't know but they'll be after us with a frigate. Are you ready for 'em?' This was a home appeal, and it was answered by a tremendous cheer from all on board."[56]

In the afternoon of Wednesday, 20 November, the *Constitution* prepared to quit British waters, her men at their guns, "expecting a disturbance on account of William Wallace who Capt. Hull refused to give up, he claiming our protection," Midshipman Frederick Baury recorded in his journal. At dusk, after dropping the pilot, Hull ordered a general exercise at quarters. The *Constitution* ghosted along with a light breeze, lanterns aglow, matches burning, tense faces watching for a pursuer or a waylaying ship. None appeared. The *Constitution* entered Cherbourg without incident on Friday morning. Hull, obviously relieved, indulged in a little prideful reflection: "I have again had my troubles in England but luckily got off with flying colors. . . . [I]t was whispered about on shore that they intended taking [the deserter] out at sea, but they made no attempt of that sort. If they had, we were ready for them."[57]

All things English seemed bad. The weather was terrible and had given everyone colds: "about forty of my crew are barking and I am hardly able to speak"; the prices were atrociously high: "indeed I cannot imagine how one half get bread to eat. My expenses from Portsmouth 70 miles and stay in London seven days was more than traveling to Paris and remaining three weeks [that had cost him about $350] with the same living, indeed the living at Paris is better than what I found in England"; and the government was arrogant: "they . . . are full of war but I believe the people at large are heartily tired of it."[58] All in all, the cruise seemed "the worst I ever made," and Hull was eager to be gone. He sent Charles Morris off immediately to Paris for Barlow's dispatches, but by 1 December a letter from the capital showed that they were still not ready. The minister was confident that the emperor would soon give him a suitable reception. Hull was skeptical: "Great bodies move slow."[59]

He was to be detained seven weeks. The cold, wet, windy weather made life on shipboard unpleasant, yet when he lodged on shore he suffered anxiety because in the worst weather he could not get off to the ship. And the whole time he was besieged with appeals—demands, in fact—to take goods and passengers to America. He was forced to give in on the passengers, though the famous lady had changed her mind about going. Among those he accepted were Abbé José Francisco Correa da Serra, F.R.S., a Portuguese scientist and diplomat; John Rodman, whom Hull had seen at Paris; and four or five other Americans.[60] Hull stipulated that the passengers pay fifty guineas for the expenses of the passage and bring nothing on board but their clothes, for he was at wit's end over the bales, boxes, and barrels of goods being pressed on him to carry.

Carrying goods from France to America was legal but unsafe except in a warship, which could not be molested by British cruisers. Consequently, every American in France wanted to send something home in the *Constitution*. Hull had already angered Jonathan Russell by refusing outright to carry a flock of Merino sheep that the former empress Josephine had offered as a gift to the United States. His memories of the horse jockeys were too strong. Now he found he must leave behind dozens of boxes, as well, that Russell had shipped to Cherbourg. Russell's disgust over this is perhaps the reason why, in the fall of 1812, he started some scurrilous rumors that Hull had been profiteering on passages across the Channel. The rumors would dog Hull for thirty years.

Warden was sending down from Paris box after box of goods purchased on order for friends in America. Mrs. Eliza Parke Custis's orders occupied three cases, one quite large, and with orders for Mrs. Elizabeth Patterson Bonaparte "would fill cases of sufficient bulk to load a common merchant ship . . . I could not suppose that any lady would give orders to such an amount, particularly for articles that would take so much room. I have sent down for Mr. Russell boxes sufficient to load a ship of sixty tons, all of which I must leave behind. I am sure he will be angry. Indeed," Hull noted prophetically, "I find I am about to make many enemies by endeavoring to serve my friends." It seemed to him after a time that people in Paris think that I have nothing to do but to take on board whatever they wish to send. They will, however, find that I am tired of endeavoring to please those I know nothing about and those who, when I was in Paris, did not find out I was there. . . . Some send wine in great hampers; some send things without any direction . . . and all expect that their things must go, although I do not believe one in ten would go the length of my ship to serve me.

Hull was in the last stages of exasperation: "Indeed . . . I have everything to trouble me: detained far beyond my calculation; fifty men on the sick list; constant bad weather; a cold and unpleasant passage to make, &c. &c. &c. &c. If I get home safe you need not calculate on seeing me soon on a voyage of this sort."[61]

The dark days of the winter solstice brought Hull to the nadir of his cruise. On Thursday, 19 December, he had to have two men flogged for smuggling rum into the ship. The next morning Midshipman William C. Pierpoint and Abraham Harding, the cabin boy, died of the influenza that had attacked the crew in England. The ship was littered with boxes, and Hull's own purchases were lying on deck while other people's goods were stored in the hold. Hull was sure that he would be censured by the government for carrying goods and that the people for whom he incurred the displeasure would not be satisfied either. "I would not again, was I to come on to this or any other country," he swore, "take the value of a pin from anyone, not even the President."[62]

Isaac Hull spent a lonely Christmas writing a letter to his brother William, detailing all his monetary transactions in Europe, to be sent by another ship—again a precaution in case he did not return alive. The wind had begun to blow from the east; if the ship could only get under way she could go booming down the Channel. Hull was disconsolate at losing the rare chance of an east wind. It continued to blow that way for a week; on 30 December a ship came beating up against it under American colors and answered the *Constitution*'s recognition signal. It was the sloop of war *Hornet*, Captain James Lawrence commanding, come for the next relay of dispatches from France and England. Hull and Lawrence were able at least to regale one another over the New Year before the *Hornet* sailed again for England the next day. Soon after that Charles Morris arrived from Paris, at last, in weather so thick that thirty-six hours passed before he could even let Captain Hull know of his arrival. Morris, Barlow's letters, and the passengers were on board on 6 January, but by then the wind was unfavorable. The *Constitution* finally weighed anchor at sunrise on 9 January and stood out of Cherbourg with her men at action stations as she bore down for the blockading frigate *Hotspur*. Captain Percy sent his boat on board and was satisfied that he did not want a quarrel with this frigate. The *Constitution* bore up for Alderney and secured the guns.[63]

Hull's fears of a long passage home were, happily, not realized. The *Constitution* was forty days from Cherbourg to Hampton Roads, compared with thirty days on her outward passage. But forty days in the North Atlantic in January and February had less to recommend them than a month in the same waters in August. There was only one bad storm, 29–31 January, but the weather was cold and damp throughout and the crew continued sickly—fifty-eight men were on the surgeon's report on 2 February. Those who were well were kept continually at work setting, reefing, and altering sails until by the end of the voyage Isaac Hull had the expert crew he wanted. There was little else to break the monotony. The *Constitution* did not sight a single ship from the time she left the Channel until 11 February. By this time she was in Bermuda waters, and the temperature was a pleasant sixty degrees. A week later she was on soundings, and at 10:00 A.M. Hull made his landfall, as neatly as could be, within five hours' run of Cape Henry Light. Lieutenant Morris went off in the pilot boat with the letter bag. The wind tantalized the frigate with calms for another night and day till the anchor splashed in Lynnhaven Bay at 11:00 P.M. on 19 February. The *Constitution* had been out six and a half months.

Hull had first to get his sick into the Norfolk naval hospital, then to discharge the passengers and baggage. He had seen enough to convince him that, if there were not war between the United States and one of the European empires soon, there should be. "In my opinion," he wrote a friend at Boston, "no good can be expected either from France or England."[64] But he was undecided what should be done to prepare the *Constitution* for the eventuality. Her copper was in very bad condition, "so that she sails dull and will not be fit to cruise until she is hove out. And whilst that is doing," he mused,

> it would be a pity that her upper works should be left in a state that they would cause her to be laid up again in a year or two to repair them, and on the other hand it would be a pity to take her to pieces and lose the year or two of service that the upper works would bear.

Besides, the *Constitution* needed a complete suit of sails and running rigging: "many of her spars are bad and those that are not are much too heavy." Hull would have liked to take her to New York for repairs, but he pointed out that many of the crew were now to be discharged, and it would not be safe to take the frigate outside the Chesapeake capes without recruiting more men.[65]

After a month's hesitation, Secretary Hamilton finally made up his mind to have the *Constitution* repaired at Washington. On the morning of 25 March, Hull got her under way and stood up the bay, accompanied by Gunboat No. 69. Three days later she entered the Potomac. The great drawback of the Washington Navy Yard was its location. In all seasons the Potomac was too shallow for heavy vessels like the *Constitution* to go up or down with their guns and stores on board. Soon after she entered the river the frigate anchored and loaded most of her shot into the gunboat. The next morning she got under way again but within an hour found only six fathoms of water. Hull moored ship and dispatched the gunboat to Washington for lighters to take out the guns.[66] It took three days and four lighters to make her shallow enough to go on. On Thursday, 2 April, Hull had to call a halt again off Quantico Creek and send away two more lighter loads of provisions and ballast. By Saturday she had reached Fort Washington, and Hull left her with a deep sigh of relief. But the next morning, as Lieutenant Page was edging up toward the navy yard, she grounded on the bar and had to be hauled over it with a kedge anchor.

Once the *Constitution* was secured to the navy yard wharf, her men began clearing everything out of her and preparing for the ticklish task of heaving down.[67] For the time being her crew were quartered in the hulk of the old frigate *General Greene,* and her captain took up residence in the city. About this time he suffered a badly bruised ankle in a fall and was confined to his room for a few days. This gave him a chance to catch up his neglected correspondence with sister-in-law Mary.

> How now, Mary? You are by this time acquainted with matrimony. Do you yet advise me to get married, or have I been all this time in the right by living single? . . . How is Rebecca [Gracie] and the girls? Tell them how much I love them and long to be in the bushes for a few months, but fate appears to have doomed me to a ship and to a *bachelor*'s life.

He had at least been accumulating some household goods on his travels: "three handsome counterpanes . . . elegant furniture sufficient to furnish two rooms, and two elegant clocks, presents." These he asked Mary to collect and care for. "I may yet want them for keeping house."

Several of Isaac's brothers were on foreign voyages, and he was worried about them, particularly Charles: "he will be gone so long that I fear we shall have trouble before he returns."[68] Congress had just passed a ninety-day embargo on American trade, which some, at least, recognized as a prelude to hostilities. Washington was full of war talk, and there was little society. Isaac's uncle William was in town to accept an appointment as brigadier general in command of troops in the Northwest. The two men had not met for ten years. William Hull wrote to Isaac's father on this occasion that "you have reason to be proud of him. I am myself, tho' more distantly connected. No officer's fame is greater."[69]

By Saturday, 2 May, the frigate was ready for heaving down, and from this date on Isaac Hull was totally absorbed in fitting her. His first inspection showed the copper somewhat better than he had thought, but it still took nearly a week to patch the starboard side, the ship being hove out each morning and righted again each evening. By the following Tuesday the larboard side was done. After that the work was routine, but it went on without pause, even on Sundays, except for an hour off for divine services in the navy yard. On 1 June, President Madison asked Congress for a declaration of war against Great Britain. A week later the *Constitution* was bending sails. On 10 June she was towed to Greenleaf Point to be hauled over the bar; the next day she anchored off Alexandria to take in stores. The capital was full of intrigue; congressional votes on the war resolution were secret. Hull wrote his father: "We have nothing here but wars and rumors of wars. There is no doubt but the House have passed a bill to make war against England. The business is now before the Senate and will come near passing . . . if there is not a *tie* there will not be more than one majority."[70]

Secretary Hamilton made a last visit to the *Constitution* on 13 June. She was now in good order, though her topsides were worn and her crew still deficient. She was short of lieutenants as well. Charles Morris had been detached at his own request, because he thought it time he had an independent command; then on 2 June he was ordered back to the frigate. He had not yet rejoined her and was protesting the reappointment. Morris knew that in wartime frigate lieutenants usually did not rise so fast as those with their own vessels, however small. Page had been replaced by Beekman V. Hoffman of New York. Wadsworth was recruiting in Boston. It would still be necessary to go to Annapolis to complete the crew, and the *Constitution* weighed for Annapolis on the morning of Thursday, 18 June. She was anchored off Mud Creek at 11:30 P.M. when her fifth cutter brought a letter from Washington. Hull broke the seal and read:

> This day war has been declared between the "United Empire of Great Britain & Ireland" and their dependencies and the United States of America and their territories and you are with the force under your command entitled to every belligerent right to attack and capture, and to defend. You will use the utmost dispatch to reach New York after you have made up your complement of men etc. at Annapolis. In your way from thence, you will not fail to notice the

British flag should it present itself. I am informed that the Belvidere is on our coast, but you are not to understand me as impelling you to battle, previously to your having confidence in your crew unless attacked, or with a reasonable prospect of success, of which you are to be at your discretion the judge. You are to reply to this and inform me of your progress.[71]

8

By Heaven, That Ship Is Ours!

As Isaac Hull read the declaration of war in the *Constitution*'s cabin that soft June night, he experienced both the animal fear of physical danger and the mental exultation that his country had at last taken a position against her enemies. No more insults! The insufferable "Lords of the Ocean" would now be made to pay for every seaman impressed, for every cargo seized, for the *Chesapeake*, for the sneers at Portsmouth. But how does a navy of eighteen vessels contend with a fleet of hundreds? The senior captains had offered plans: Rodgers would take the lot in pursuit of the rich West India convoys, lie off the British Isles, sink and burn; Stephen Decatur and William Bainbridge would prefer to lead smaller units on wide-ranging cruises. Where did Isaac Hull and the *Constitution* fit in? They were part of Rodgers's squadron; they were to make haste to join him at New York. Yet Hull knew his friend too well to expect him to linger in port when war was declared. Rodgers would be at sea within a few days. Would he stay on the coast? Perhaps. The merchant fleet was flocking home; the war news would be at Halifax soon, and the English frigates would be out in search of prizes. Rodgers might linger to protect the trade, to await the challenge. Hull's task, at any rate, was clear: to get the *Constitution* to New York as quickly as he could. Hamilton's orders were timorous, quite a retreat from what he had written in 1810. But they were vague. Hull could make the most of them.

He thought about the state of his crew: there were many new hands, and more coming on board every day. Few knew their stations or their tasks well. With hard work, they would do—hard work and good officers—but Morris, at Washington, had talked his way out of the ship again. Hull asked the secretary if he might have Nathaniel Haraden instead. The old sailing master was rough but a better seaman than most officers. But Hamilton had already changed his mind again: Morris joined the ship at Annapolis.

The *Constitution* was a cosmopolitan ship, but she had three officers from "the land of steady habits": Captain Hull; First Lieutenant Morris; and the new purser, Thomas Chew of Middletown. Alexander

By Heaven, That Ship Is Ours!

Scammel Wadsworth of Massachusetts (district of Maine), George Campbell Read of Pennsylvania, Beekman Verplanck Hoffman of New York, John Templar Shubrick of South Carolina, and Charles W. Morgan of Virginia completed the wardroom mess, with a new surgeon, Amos Alexander Evans of Maryland, and the marine lieutenants, William Bush of Delaware and John Contee of Maryland.

At the evening muster on 19 June Third Lieutenant Read read the declaration of war to the crew. The men asked permission to cheer; Read gravely granted it, and the crew responded with three loud "huzzas!" These men were mainly Americans, born or naturalized, from all over the seaboard. After the declaration of war was read, a dozen or more approached Hull to say that they were deserters from the Royal Navy and that, while willing to serve on shore, they feared going out in the ship because if taken prisoner they would be hanged. Hull relayed their appeal to Hamilton, who took a high line: "The men who *say* they are deserters from the British service, are not to be discharged from the *Constitution*. If they apprehend any serious consequences from being taken, such apprehensions will excite them to additional exertions— for such exertions may insure their safety."[1] Sober second thoughts, however, caused him to show Hull's letter to President Madison, and the president ordered the men discharged.[2] How would it look to force foreign seamen to fight a war against impressment? As it turned out, only two men persisted in their request; they were transferred on shore. The rest would take their chances with the *Constitution*. One of the "men" who shipped for the war cruise, if her own testimony be accepted, was one Lucy Brewer West, who published her memoir in 1816 under the title, *An Affecting Narrative of Louisa Baker.* In it she spoke of "my good fortune in having for my commander one of the most humane and experienced officers in the American Navy . . . as the respect entertained for him and the under officers caused the utmost harmony to prevail among the ship's crew."[3] Apparently Miss West, who served as a marine, felt that in a rowdy ship she would have been in more danger of discovery than in the orderly *Constitution*. If her messmates did know her true character, they didn't tell. It was no unusual thing, after all, for women to be in the ships; the only odd feature in this case was the disguise.

It remained only to get the crew ready for war—no small task. The *Constitution* was still working up the bay to Annapolis on 27 June when a gunnery exercise was called, and it was kept up for two hours. That was to be the daily routine henceforth. Sometimes a cask was floated for a target. Hull passed along the deck among the toiling crews: "I'll risk you now, my boys!" he told them at the end of the week. "If it were an enemy's boat you had there, you'd cut it all to splinters!"[4] The bay pilot, one Welsh, was not so zealous. He was shivering—with fear or ague, Hull couldn't tell—and begging to go on shore. Hull asked the Baltimore navy agent to send him a pilot boat and a *good* pilot, for once.[5]

By 2 July, Hull was ready to try his men at sea. "[I]n a few days," he assured Hamilton, "we shall have nothing to fear from any single deck ship; indeed, unacquainted as we now are, we should, I hope, give a good account of any frigate the enemy have."[6] He was anxious to be out of Chesapeake Bay, which was so easy to blockade. There was supposed to have been heavy cannonading heard off the Capes already. (The coast was edgy that summer: similar firing was heard off nearly every port at one time or another, but they must have been ghost ships that fired the guns.) The *Constitution* fired a last salute on Saturday, 4 July, in honor of American independence, and on Sunday morning sailed to vindicate it. Hull had received a final set of orders even more shrinking than the last: "If . . . you should fall in with an enemy vessel, you will be guided in your proceeding by your own judgment, bearing in mind, however, that you are not voluntarily to encounter a force superior to your own. On your arrival at New York, you will report yourself to Commodore Rodgers. If he should not be in that port, you will remain there till further orders."[7]

Soon after leaving Annapolis, Isaac wrote a last note to his father:

> Constitution Chesapeake Bay
> 5th July 1812
>
> My Dear Father
>
> My Ship is now underway from Annapolis and standing down the Bay. you will ere long hear from me some where to the Northd unless I fall in with superior force in that case you may Probably hear of my being in hallifax or Bermudas. I left William a statement of all my matters in case of accident and I have no doubt but he will dispose of what little I have as he ought to do. My most earnest wish is that you and our good Mother has the use of it as long as you have occasion after which I have no doubt but a proper disposition will be made of it   Should anything happen [to] me I leave but little but it may be sufficient to make you comfortable during your stay in this Troublesome world.
>
> be pleased to make my love to all the Family and accept for them & your self my most fervent Prayers for your health & long life.
>
> your Son
> Isaac Hull[8]

In hot, breathless weather the new pilot, Mark Carroll, carried the *Constitution* slowly down the bay. Thirty or more of the crew (now

numbering 440) were sick with dysentery and other hot-weather mala-
dies. Hull anchored his ship off Cape Henry Light on 10 July to take on
board some spars, sending the pilot boat with a midshipman out to
scout for enemies. The sickness made his force less than it appeared to
be, by numbers, but he believed in the efficacy of sea air: "I am in
hopes, however, the moment the ship gets to sea, to give them rest, and
get them in heart, after which I shall have a tolerable good crew."[9]

At sunrise on Sunday, 12 July, the *Constitution* ran out to sea with a
fine southwesterly breeze. Hull wrote a farewell to Hamilton by the
pilot at 9:00 A.M.: "I shall run to the eastward under easy sail all this
day to get everything as clear as possible for action. The cables are now
unbent, anchors stowed, and the ship as clear as the few moments we
have been out would allow of."[10]

The first few days at sea were peaceful. On Monday afternoon the
Constitution spoke a Spanish privateer from Santiago and a brig from
New Orleans; on Wednesday, a schooner from New Bedford. Twice a
day there were gunnery exercises. Winds were light and the frigate
crawled slowly up the coast. On Thursday afternoon, 16 July, she was
in 39°18′ north latitude, off Little Egg Harbor, New Jersey, in soundings
of eighteen to twenty-two fathoms. Hull expected to be in New York
the next day. At 2:00 P.M. the lookout sighted a sail—no! four sail in
the northwest. It was probably Rodgers's squadron, but not to be too
forward in meeting them, the *Constitution* tacked to the east at 3:15
P.M. By 4:00 another large ship was made out in the northeast, and the
vessels inshore were seen to be three ships and a brig. This must be
Rodgers: the frigates *President, Congress* and *United States*; the brig
should be the *Argus* or the *Nautilus*. The ship in the offing might be
the *Hornet* but looked too large; perhaps she was a stranger. The wind
was light and shifting, the air hazy with heat. At 6:15 the *Constitution*
got a breeze from southeast. Hull wore and stood for the sail to windward, setting studding sails and keeping the chase a little off the larboard bow. The men went to quarters at 7:30. Still the wind was light;
the two ships closed very slowly.

Hull strolled up on the forecastle among the men at the bow chasers.
He turned to Boatswain Adams:

"Adams, what do you think of that vessel?"
"Don't know, sir," replied the veteran tar, with his deep voice.
"I can't make her out, sir. But I think she's an Englishman."
"So do I," added Hull. "How long will it take to flog her, Adams?"
"Don't know, sir!" replied the boatswain. "We can do it, but they're hard
fellows on salt water."
"I know that," continued the captain. "They are rather a hard set of fellows,

sure enough. But don't you think we can flog them in two hours and a half, Adams?"

"Yes, sir!" said the boatswain, with all the coolness imaginable.

"Yes, sir! we can do it in that time, if we can do it at all."[11]

Hull turned away with a smile and, as it was now dark, ordered the private night signal hoisted. For three quarters of an hour the lights remained aloft, but there was no answer from the ship in the northeast. Hull grew more thoughtful. Either the lone ship was an enemy, and thus unable to answer his signals, or else, if she understood him, she was declining to answer because she believed the ships inshore to be enemies. In either case, it would be well not to approach any nearer in the dark. At 11:15 the *Constitution* hauled by the wind to the southeast, with her starboard tacks on board.

As the dawn watch on 17 July began at 4:00 A.M. the ship in the northeast wore, threw a rocket, and fired two guns. The light from the rocket, and the growing daylight, revealed a chilling sight: there were now three ships in the northeast and three astern, about ten miles distant; by 5:00 A.M. another sail was made out astern, and the whole force of the pursuers was all too evident: four frigates, a ship of the line, a brig, and a schooner. From every truck fluttered the cross of St. George. As Hull viewed the ghastly sight, the little breeze that had held through the night dropped away altogether; the *Constitution* lost steerageway, and her bow swung slowly around toward her pursuers while they, with wind still in their sails, came bounding toward her. The boats were swung out to tow the frigate's head around again. In preparation for a stern chase, one of the bow chase guns was trundled aft and a long twenty-four was swayed up from the gun deck. Carpenters hacked away part of the taffrail to make room for them while crews ran two other guns out the cabin windows below.

By 6:00 the *Constitution* was headed southeast again, with every sail set but no wind to power them. Three of the pursuing frigates had drawn within five miles of the *Constitution*, and now one of them opened fire. Escape seemed hopeless, and Hull had little taste for being run to earth like a rabbit. Moses Smith heard him say to Lieutenant Morris: "Let's lay broadside to them, Mr. Morris, and fight the whole! If they sink us, we'll go down like men!"[12] But Morris had a last-ditch suggestion: since the water was relatively shallow, it might be possible to warp the ship ahead with her kedge anchors. The lead was thrown: twenty-six fathoms. It was deep, but not too deep. By 6:30 an anchor was being carried out ahead while the crew roused up the cables. At length, three hundred or four hundred fathoms of line were spliced to-

1 Nautilus
2 Constitution
3 africa
4 prise
5 Johanon
6 Eulus
7 la Guerriere
8 belvedere

Escape of the *Constitution* from a British squadron off New York, June 1812. Sketch by Michel Corné. Courtesy of the New-York Historical Society, New York City.

1 7 3

gether and two anchors were set working alternately, one being carried forward as the other was hauled in. By this expedient the *Constitution* began to gain some headway, eventually making two or three knots. At 7:30 Hull showed a little bravado by ordering the colors hoisted and personally firing one of the stern chasers at the enemy.

Still the wind favored the pursuers. While the *Constitution* remained becalmed, her antagonists kept a light breeze and drew inexorably up on her. One of the lighter vessels was using sweeps. Some of them had six or eight boats ahead towing, and when they discovered the *Constitution*'s kedging maneuver they were quick to imitate it. By 9:00 the nearest frigates were kedging and were also being towed by the combined boats of the other ships, to bring them within range so that they might cripple the *Constitution*'s spars. The nearest opened fire on her with her bow guns, and fire was returned from the *Constitution*'s stern chasers. At least one of her shot, though spent, went on board the pursuing frigate; Dr. Evans, watching through a spyglass, saw the crowd of officers on her forecastle hastily scatter. Firing the chase guns gave the ship a little boost through the water, but it quickly appeared that, because of the rake of the stern, the explosion of those in the cabin threatened to blow up the quarterdeck. Hull ordered firing to cease.

Just then, at 9:09, sharp eyes in the *Constitution* spotted a breeze coming across the sea from the southward. In a moment the yards were braced, and as the wind reached the ship, she came to on the larboard tack, heading southwest. The boats ran alongside and were hoisted clear of the water by purchases on the spare spars outboard, a tricky maneuver which Hull directed with such skill that not a foot of advantage was lost. One of the pursuers, seeing the quarry getting ahead, came to and fired a broadside at the *Constitution*, but the shot fell short. The men in the boats, dangling above the water only a few feet from the falling shot, replied with raucous shouts and impolite gestures.

The advantage of the breeze was all too brief. By 10:00 the boats were again sent ahead to tow, and a part of the *Constitution*'s water (2,335 gallons) was started and pumped out. This was only a fraction of the 39,634 gallons on board, so that the purpose was not to lighten but to trim ship. There were now six ships off the starboard beam, the ship of the line lagging a little behind. The boats of the whole squadron were towing the nearest frigate, and as the rowing contest went on through the forenoon and afternoon she continued to gain. This ship had all her sails furled to lessen resistance, but the *Constitution* kept her canvas set, and with an occasional cat's-paw of wind she just held her own. At 1:53 P.M. there was another exchange of gunfire. The *Constitution*'s sole advantage was that, should the enemy's boats come within gunshot while towing, they could be driven back by her chase guns. But the range was still too long.

The ships in pursuit, as Hull and his crew learned much later, were a squadron from Halifax under the command of Captain Philip Bowes Vere Broke, who flew his pendant in the frigate *Shannon*, 38. The *Shannon* was the frigate towing so hard to catch up. The other frigates were the *Aeolus*, 32; the *Belvidera*, 36; and the *Guerrière*, 38 (the ship the *Constitution* had first pursued); the ship of the line was the *Africa*, 64; and the brig was the former USS *Nautilus*, captured off New York a few days earlier. The squadron had already burned several American merchantmen, whose crews were prisoners in the fleet. The master of one, Captain James Brown, was on board the *Shannon*, and he endured agonies as the English officers discussed what they would do with the Yankee frigate (they could only guess she was the *Constitution*) when they got her. A prize master and crew were told off to carry her into Halifax. But Brown kept up a brave front. "Gentlemen," he told them coolly, "you will never take that frigate."[13]

Brown looked like a poor prophet that afternoon. The *Constitution* took advantage of every wind, but the *Shannon* kept towing up in the calms. The American boats worked in relays, commanded by the excited midshipmen. Young Frederick Baury shook his fist at the enemy ships and vowed to defend his cutter to the last with his pistols. Late into the night they toiled until, at 10:53, a breeze sprang up from the south. The *Shannon* had to abandon some of her boats as she came to the wind, but the *Constitution*'s gig and green cutter hooked on and were swung up as before without a moment's lost time. Hammocks were not piped down that night; officers and men slept on the decks at their battle stations.

From midnight of 18 July there was enough wind to keep the ships under sail, and what had been a towing contest turned into a sailing race. Now Isaac Hull would find out, once and for all, whether two years' work on the *Constitution*'s bottom had been fruitful. At daylight there were still six sail in sight from the deck, the smallest frigate (the *Aeolus*) only two or three miles off the lee beam. It would soon be necessary to tack, for the *Constitution* had been running southwest all day and night; she would risk being trapped against the land. Moreover, the *Guerrière* had forged ahead during the night and, when ahead of the *Constitution*'s beam, tacked, so that to continue the present course would bring the *Constitution* down on her.[14] But to tack to the east meant bringing the *Aeolus* within gunshot. No matter, it must be done; at 4:20 A.M. the *Constitution* tacked and passed the near frigate at 5:00. As she did so, Hull supervised the hoisting in of the last of the boats.

Abel Bowen, who collected reminiscences of the war in *The Naval Monument*, comments on Hull's skill and daring in this maneuver:

> So coolly however did he proceed, that he would not suffer one of his boats to be cut adrift, but, though pressed by a pursuing enemy, attended personally to hoisting in his launch and other boats, while the ship was going nine or ten knots through the water. This is a fact which will appear astonishing to a sailor; and he seemed to be the only person in the ship who conceived it feasible:—the British squadron cut adrift all their boats, and, after they abandoned the chase, spent two or three whole days in cruising to pick them up.[15]

Though the *Constitution* passed within easy long-gun range, the *Aeolus* did not fire. Hull conjectured that Captain Townshend was afraid of becalming his ship in the light airs, but certainly he lost a chance to disable the American. The *Aeolus* merely tacked in the *Constitution*'s wake. The "Constitutions," with their boats secured, now prepared for some sailing in earnest.

If Isaac Hull had once helped to sail the *Constitution* against a British frigate in the West Indies, he now had a race on his hands with much more at stake than a cask of Madeira. But if anyone knew how to handle the *Constitution*, it was he. Sailmakers had been busy the previous day making skysails, and these were now set on the topmost masts. Men seized the handles of the fire engine and raised water to wet the sails, closing the canvas for maximum draw. For one not involved in the outcome, the scene must have been dazzling: five frigates on a smooth sea, clouds of canvas from truck to water line. As the wind freshened, the *Constitution* gathered speed: five knots at 10:00, six knots at 12:00, eight knots at 1:00. At midmorning another sail was sighted ahead, apparently a merchantman, standing for the squadron. All the English ships set American colors to lure her down; the *Constitution* promptly raised a British jack. The stranger got the message and hauled her wind.

Lieutenant Wadsworth recorded in the log at noon: "rather leaving the frigates in chase." The nearest pursuer, the *Belvidera*, was now about three and a half miles dead astern, the *Africa* falling behind and hull down. By 4:00 P.M. Lieutenant Read thought the nearest ship was about six miles distant. The Americans began to breathe easily again, or as Lieutenant Morris phrased it: "Our hopes began to overcome apprehension, and cheerfulness was more apparent among us." The *Constitution* was indeed the sailing witch she once had been. Hull continued to watch for every advantage. About 6:30 a squall approached, and he prepared to turn it to account. The men were stationed on the yards and at the halyards, ready to let everything go at a run. The *Constitution* kept all sail set till the last moment; then at 6:45 as the squall struck, the order was given to "clew up and clew down." The *Constitution* took in staysails, topgallant sails, and flying jib, reefed the mizzen topsail and spanker, and took the force of the wind. The pursuers, seeing her suddenly shorten sail, began to prepare for a blow. But as soon as rain hid the *Constitution* she sheeted home her topgallant sails again and went bowling away at eleven knots. Half an hour later she got sight of her pursuers; they were steering in different directions, and two of the frigates were hull down!

The *Constitution* carried sail hard all night. Hull knew the enemy were still behind him. At 10:30 P.M. he heard them fire two signal guns, and one ship could just be seen in the *Constitution*'s wake. At daylight on the nineteenth only four sail could be seen from the masthead, the nearest twelve miles astern and all hull down, but John Bull held on tenaciously. Hull was determined to lose him. Again the sails were wet from the trucks down, the men pumping the engine and carrying the fire buckets aloft. "We soon found we left the enemy very fast," Hull recorded with satisfaction. The enemy found that out, too. At 8:15 A.M. they gave up and hauled off to the northeast. Broke was sorely disappointed. He reported to the Admiralty that "we had an anxious chase after an American frigate supposed to be the *Constitution*, but she escaped by very superiour sailing, though the frigates under my orders are remarkably fast ships."[16]

The *Constitution*'s weary tars were piped from quarters for the first time in sixty-one hours. "Now," Hull told them, "we'll take a cruise by ourselves. But if I come across one of these chaps alone, depend on it he shall pay for this."[17]

This escape of the *Constitution* has been long and justly acclaimed. George Coggeshall, in his *History of the American Privateers*, called it "a chase that has become celebrated for its length, perseverance, coolness, and activity, and stands unparalleled on the pages of nautical history."[18] For sixty-six hours the frigate had been in sight of an overwhelming enemy force and for most of that time was actively pursued by them. Except for a fraction of her water, jettisoned to give her better sailing trim, she had lost nothing—not a gun, not a boat, not a man. Officers and crew had displayed skill and determination in devising and executing means of escape, as well as great courage and steadiness in face of almost certain capture. Isaac Hull had secured his already considerable reputation for seamanship, yet characteristically he bestowed the credit elsewhere: in reporting the chase to the secretary he scrupulously indicated that the kedging that saved the ship in the initial crisis was done "by the suggestion of that valuable officer Lieutenant Morris," and he heaped praise upon his ship's company: "I cannot (in justice to the brave officers and crew under my command) close . . . without expressing to you the confidence I have in them, and assuring you that their conduct while under the guns of the enemy was such as might have been expected from American officers and seamen."[19] As soon as he was in port, he posted a public notice to the same effect:

> Captain HULL, finding his friends in Boston are correctly informed of his situation when chased by the British squadron off New York, and that they are good enough to give him more credit for having escaped them than he ought to claim, takes this opportunity of requesting them to make a transfer of a great part of their good wishes to lieutenant MORRIS, and the other brave officers, and the crew under his command, for their many great exertions and prompt attention to orders while the enemy were in chase. Captain HULL has great pleasure in saying, that notwithstanding the length of the chase, and the officers and crew being deprived of sleep, and allowed but little refreshment during the time, not a murmur was heard to escape them.[20]

Purser Thomas Chew had been an all-too-interested spectator of the escape. He commented: "We have had a narrow escape from Admiral Sawyer; he was too strong for us and we too fast for him. For twelve hours I would scarcely have given a dollar for the rights of the U.S. to this ship; nothing but superior management and unheard-of exertion preserved her."[21] Charles Morris was more philosophical: "The result may be remembered as an evidence of the advantages to be expected from perseverance under the most discouraging circumstances, so long as *any* chance for success may remain."[22]

More than anything, the episode was important for its effect on the *Constitution*'s men. Through the ordeal they had endured together the crew, the ship, and the commander had become one. If Hull had gained confidence in his officers and crew, and regained faith in the "favorite frigate," he in turn had become a hero in their eyes, a leader to whom they would confidently entrust their lives. The "Constitutions" were now prepared to go to war.

Isaac Hull faced a difficult decision. He obviously could not carry out his orders to enter New York, and he did not know where Commodore Rodgers was. The *Constitution* had taken on only eight weeks' provisions, in expectation of going to New York, so he could not make an extended cruise off the coast. He determined, at length, to run for Boston and to try to communicate with the Navy Department if it could be done in a short time, or at least learn if instructions had been left for him at New York. He sent word of his proceedings to Hamilton by the *Diana*, bound for Baltimore, which he spoke in the afternoon after losing the British squadron. The *Constitution* was nearly a week on her passage to Boston, chasing and speaking all the merchant vessels she saw and warning them of the squadron off New York. On Wednesday afternoon two sail were seen in the northwest, then three more. It looked like the same old gang, and Hull declined to investigate closely this time. Earlier that day the *Constitution* had spoken a Spanish ship four days out of New York and from her obtained a newspaper that indicated that Rodgers's squadron was at sea. This information confirmed Hull in his decision to make for Boston.

By Saturday afternoon the *Constitution* was in Boston Bay. The wind was unfavorable for getting up to the city, so Hull brought the ship to anchor off the lighthouse and dispatched Purser Chew and Lieutenant Morgan to town in the gig. On Monday morning, 27 July, the boats got out again to tow the ship up to an anchorage in President Roads. The town was abuzz with the *Constitution's* exploit; she was a local favorite, since Boston was in a sense her home port. The *New York Evening Post* had reported that she had gone to sea without powder, and it was rumored as definite that she had been taken. A friend of one of the officers had gone so far as to send letters of credit for him to Halifax.[23] There was great relief in Boston, then, to see the old frigate come up the bay. When Hull landed at noon and walked up State Street to the Exchange Coffee House, people lined the street to cheer him. One of the papers printed an offering by the *Constitution's* resident poet:

'Neath Hull's command, with a tough band,
And naught beside to back her,
Upon a day, as log-books say,
A fleet bore down to thwack her.
A fleet, you know, is odds or so,
Against a single ship, sirs;
So 'cross the tide her legs she tried,
And gave the rogues the slip, sirs.[24]

But the Boston Federalists were disgusted at the war. Surgeon Amos Evans found the bookstores full of pamphlets excoriating "Madison's ruinous war." After talking with the merchants at the Exchange he was moved to wonder: "Will the United States receive any assistance from the eastern states in the prosecution of the present war? Judging from present symptoms, I fear not. Good God! Is it possible that the people of the U.S. enjoying the blessings of freedom under the only republican government on earth, have not virtue enough to support it!" The Bostonians seemed shocked at reports that the British were destroying American merchantmen on the coast. Evans thought that, since these merchants had deliberately evaded the prewar embargo, they had no cause to blame the government now if their ships were seized.

Hull didn't take much time to argue these matters with his Boston friends. He was working night and day to get the *Constitution* to sea before British cruisers appeared to blockade the port. He aimed to sail in three days, and he wrote the secretary that

> Should I not by the time she is ready get instructions from New York, or find some at this place I am at present under the impression that I shall proceed to sea and run to the Eastward, and endeavour to join the squadron, and if I am so unfortunate as not to fall in with them I shall continue cruising where (from information I may collect) I shall be most likely to distress the enemy. Should I proceed to sea without your further orders, and it should not meet your approbation I shall be very unhappy, for I pray you to be assured in doing so I shall act as at this moment I believe you would order me to do, was it possible for me to receive orders from you.[25]

As Hull well knew, if he acted without orders and his action was not approved, he would be more than unhappy—he would be court-martialed. But he was convinced that, having failed to blockade Rodgers in New York, the British squadron would now separate and send pairs of frigates off the other ports. His belief was supported by reports, within three days of his arrival, that the frigate *Maidstone* was in Boston Bay. Hull suggested to Hamilton that it would be well to have instructions for the cruisers sent to all the ports to avoid dilemmas such as the one he faced. Luckily he did not know that two letters were already on their way to him from Washington. One was written on 28 July:

> On the arrival of the Constitution in port, I have ordered Commodore Bainbridge to take command of her. You will accordingly deliver up to him the command and proceed to this place and assume the command of the frigate Constellation.[26]

The second was written the next day, after Hamilton had received word of Hull's escape:

> Your letter of the 20th instant just received has relieved me from much anxiety. I am truly happy to hear of your safety. Remain at Boston until further orders.[27]

There is no doubt that Hull expected some such orders as these. With two senior captains, Stewart and Bainbridge, clamoring for commands, it was unlikely that he would long be left in the *Constitution*. Bainbridge, who was commanding the navy yard at Boston, may even have told him that he had asked for Hull's ship and expected to get her. If Hull had received the letters he would remain a minor figure in navy annals; the *Constellation* was blockaded in the Chesapeake throughout the war.

By Saturday, 1 August, the *Constitution* awaited only a fair wind to sail. The post had brought nothing from Washington, and there were no orders from Rodgers in New York. But there was one letter from New York for Isaac Hull that made him sick at heart: his brother William was dying. A few hours before he sailed he wrote to his father; the letter shows the troubled state of his thoughts at that critical hour:

Boston 1st August 1812

My Dear Father

It is with extream Pain I hear that William is dangerously ill. I can Easily anticipate your felings and I fear unless you keep your spirits up and bare misfortune as becomes a Parent under distressing Circumstances you will suffer in your health and constitution. Let me beseech you not to let his sickness or even the loss of him (which god forbid)—Trouble your mind so as to occasion your spirits to leave you. At your time of life with a slender Constitution it cannot be expected that you can bare as much as in former days will you then Console yourself in thinking that whatever is is right that we have but a short time to stay & be assured my good Father that as long as I have health you will command me and what little I have.

I have some things with William which in case of accident I wish you & Mr. Griswold to look to. my Papers will shew how my affairs stand as it is Possable I may not return for some time I give you this information. for heaven sake Cheer up William take from him that gloom that hangs over him say and do all you can to give him spirits.

Indeed my mind is in such a state I hardly know what I am writing—nor will it be at Ease untill I hear from you and god only knows when that will be as I sail in the morning.

your Son
Isaac Hull

My love to all the family.

I have this day a letter signed S. C. Gracie dated in Northcarolina. the letter contains a few unconnected words and on the outside I am informed that the Person who is supposed to have written it is a stranger and that he has cut his Throat and will probably not live. it must be Shelden Gracie of our Place.[28]

Thus, as he prepared to sail, Isaac Hull was burdened with the news of his brother's mortal illness, fear for his father's reaction, and a report of the apparent suicide of an old friend. At the same time he faced a decision that could affect not only his own future but the fate of his country.

The wind was getting around to the southwest, favorable for sailing. Hull had made up his mind. He would go out without orders and risk the consequences. The lack of orders was an opportunity to a bold man. Hull seized it, disclaiming the while, perhaps even to himself, his willingness to do so. At 3:00 A.M. on Sunday, 2 August, he gave orders to unmoor. At the same time he sent the third cutter to town for one last inquiry at the post office. At 5:15 the frigate was under way; at 7:00 she hove to outside the lighthouse, hoisted in her boats, and unbent her cables so that she would be completely unencumbered when she got into the bay. Then she waited for the boat. Hull wrote to Hamilton in the interim:

> The wind for the first time since the ship came in has hauled so far to the westward as to enable us to fetch out, and as this harbour is so difficult to get to sea from I have determined to run out, having great hopes that my boat which is now at the post office may bring me letters from you. If she does not I shall indeed be at a loss how to proceed, and shall take a responsibility on myself that I should wish to avoid, but to remain here any time longer I am confident that the ship would be blockaded in by superior force, and probably would not get out for months.

He described his cruising plans: he would run eastward between Georges Bank and Cape Sable and go onto the Grand Banks to intercept convoys from Canada to England. But he must have planned to go farther afield if need be: on 29 July he had purchased from Bemis & Eddy of Boston charts not only of the American coast and the Gulf of St. Lawrence, but also of the Gulf of Mexico, the Spanish Main, Demerara and Cayenne, Brazil, La Plata, and the coast of Africa. His letter to his father, too, suggested that "I may not return for some time." Clearly he meant to cruise on his own until he found a lone frigate or until he had done maximum damage to British trade. He felt sure of his ship and his crew, if given a few days' shakedown at sea:

> My crew is now strong but want exercise. If I can keep from action a few days I promise myself that we shall be able to see any frigate. I have great confidence in the men, and they appear in good spirits. How the ship will sail I have doubts. I fear that being obliged to fill her up with provisions and water will make some difference, but she will soon grow light.

Once more he justified his dubious action and outlined his own thoughts on appropriate strategy for the American fleet:

> Should I not get letters from you, and should proceed as above, I pray you to be assured, that I have done so, with a view of being useful to my country, and of taking a direction that I supposed you would give me, had I your orders. The force of the enemy is so superiour on our coast that it is impossible to cruise with any hope of escaping them, and if we should, they have no vessels that we could take, nor should we have any means of annoying them, where by cruising off the coast we may do them great injury. These, Sir, are the motives that have led me to take the step I have, and should they not meet your approbation I shall be truly unfortunate.[29]

By Heaven, That Ship Is Ours!

By the time Hull's clerk had copied the letter, at 8:30, the boat returned from town. Hull took the packet from the midshipman and riffled through it: there was nothing for him. He scrawled a note on the back of his own letter: "The boat has returned but without letters from you. I cannot account for it as there is one for Mr. Morris directed to him at Boston from the Navy Department" and handed it to the commander of the attendant gunboat. He turned on his heel: "Make sail by the wind, Mr. Shubrick."

It is not difficult to imagine that Hull's feelings were mixed. He was taking a terrible risk in sailing without orders, yet it would be worse to be blockaded, or peremptorily ordered from the *Constitution*. He was probably a bit disingenuous in saying repeatedly that he was acting as he thought Hamilton would have him do, for he well knew how timid and despondent the secretary was. Only a few days earlier Hamilton had written to a friend in South Carolina: "In our Navy men I have the utmost confidence that in equal combat they will be superior . . . but when I reflect on the overwhelming force of our enemy my heart swells almost to bursting, and all the consolation I have is, that in falling they will fall nobly."[30] But Isaac Hull and the other naval officers did not think that way. They, perhaps alone among Americans, believed they could meet the "Lords of the Ocean" on equal terms and come off best. Hull would risk everything for a chance to prove them right.

The *Constitution* ran off to the northeast, passing Cape Ann amid crowds of small craft. At 1:00 p.m. the crew were assembled to hear the Articles of War. Everyone on board was on edge, eagerly looking for the *Maidstone* or other enemy ships. Even Lieutenant Wadsworth was nervous: at 1:30 a.m. he saw a strange light in the southeast which he took to be signals. He had the crew called to quarters; Hull came briskly on deck only to be greeted by the rising moon and a sheepish lieutenant. The next few days were routine and helped the ship's company to settle down; carpenters worked at repairing the taffrail that had been cut away during the chase, and the rest of the crew made themselves boarding helmets. The frigate was deep and, as Hull had anticipated, did not catch many of the vessels she chased; they were mainly small brigs and schooners, though one looked like a sloop of war.

In heading for the Grand Banks, Hull was actually on Rodgers's track, though much too far behind to have any chance of catching up with him. He was also on the track of his old foes from New York. One of Broke's officers was dating a letter on 4 August: "Shannon: Banks of Newfoundland." The British then thought that Rodgers was about ten miles ahead and looked forward to catching him: "We have the Africa of 64 guns, Aeolus, Belvidera, Guerriere and Shannon frigates, as fine vessels as ever swam, particularly the Guerriere. As 'we love the Americans dearly,' you may expect the American squadron at Plymouth very soon."[31] About a week later, having failed to catch Rodgers, Broke divided his squadron, as Hull had expected he would. The *Guerrière* he detached alone, to go into Halifax for repairs to her foremast. A few days after the separation, the *Guerrière* fell in with a small merchant vessel, the *John Adams*, bound from Liverpool to New York. Instead of destroying her, Captain James R. Dacres sent her on her way with a contemptuous endorsement on her register:

> Captain Dacres, commander of His Britannic Majesty's frigate Guerriere, of 44 guns, presents his compliments to Commodore Rodgers, of the U. States frigate President, and will be very happy to meet him, or any other American frigate of equal force to the President, off Sandy Hook, for the purpose of having a few minutes tete-a-tete.[32]

On Monday afternoon, 10 August, the *Constitution* ran down a brig just south of the Grand Banks. Two warning shots failed to bring her to, so Hull ordered English colors hoisted, whereupon the brig raised an English jack and ran down for the frigate. Lieutenant Morris soon disappointed her master's hopes; after taking him, the supercargo, and the crew of five men out, he set the brig on fire. She was the *Lady Warren*, from St. John's, Newfoundland, bound to Cape Breton in ballast, and not worth the risk of sending in. Hull well understood that his task was to hurt the enemy by destroying their commerce. Considerations of prize money must be secondary, and only a very valuable ship was worth the risk of recapture. The next day a second brig was burned, the *Adeona* of New Brunswick, laden with timber. From the masters of these prizes Hull received reports of several frigates supposed to be nearby. It was certain that David Porter of the *Essex* had already sent a cartel of prisoners into St. John's.[33]

At daylight on the fifteenth five sail were discovered to windward. The *Constitution* made all sail and came up with them fast. One was seen to be a sloop of war, and at 6:15 A.M. she set fire to one of the other vessels and fled. At 8:00 one of the merchants, a sharp-sterned barque, tacked between the *Constitution* and the sloop; the *Constitution* closed with her and brought her to. The boarders found she was a prize to the American privateer *Dolphin* of Salem and had been saved by the *Constitution*'s timely arrival from recapture by the sloop of war *Avenger*. The barque, in tacking, had been trying to rejoin the privateer schooner, which was standing off to the southeast. The brig on fire was a New York ship, prize to the *Avenger*, as was the other brig in sight. Leaving the barque, the *Constitution* stood after the *Avenger* and her remaining prize. The fleet sloop was soon out of sight, but the frigate quickly overhauled the brig, which was the *Adeline* of Bath, Maine. Hull took the British midshipman and her crew of five as prisoners. Since she was an American ship, he did not burn her but sent Midshipman John R. Madison and five of his own men on board to carry her into port. As the ships parted, Cape Race in Newfoundland could just be discerned to the north.

The *Constitution* now ran southwest in cold, windy weather. If the prisoners could be believed, the Grand Banks were alive with enemy frigates, including Broke's squadron. Hull had decided to change his cruising ground, pass near Bermuda, and take a station off the southern coast. At 10:00 P.M. the drum and fife sounded battle stations, but this time the light proved to be the burning brig. On Monday evening, the seventeenth, the ship passed what appeared to be the hull of a capsized vessel. It turned out to be a dead whale; on close approach, the smell confirmed it. At 9:00 P.M. the call for quarters sounded again. This time there was a ship ahead. The *Constitution* overtook her at 11:00 and sent a boat on board. She was the privateer brig *Decatur* of Salem, twelve days out with no prizes. Captain Nichols reported that he had been chased the evening before by a frigate and, supposing the *Constitution* to be the same vessel, had used every means to get away, throwing overboard twelve of his fourteen guns. At Nichols's request, Hull gave him some leg irons. Nichols was so glad to have saved his ship that he made light of the loss of his guns; two cannon were enough to bring merchantmen to, he said. After standing by the *Constitution* all night, he hauled up for Cape Race, planning to take ships by boarding.

Hull, having gotten from Nichols the direction in which he had encountered the strange frigate, stood off to the southeast. The eighteenth of August was foggy and rainy, and no sightings were made. The nineteenth brought fresh northwest breezes and flying clouds. The *Constitution* was running free before the wind at 2:00 P.M. in 41°42' north latitude and 55°48' west longitude when the lookout discovered a large ship ahead. Hull called Midshipman Lewis German to him. "Mr. German! Take the glass and go aloft. See if you can make out what she is." German scrambled up the mizzen shrouds and trained the glass on the distant ship.

"What do you think?" asked Hull.

"She's a great vessel, sir!" shouted the midshipman. "Tremendous sails!"

"Never mind, you can come down, sir," said Hull. He turned to the boatswain: "Mr. Adams, call all hands and make all sail for her!"[34]

There was no need to call all hands; they were already swarming to the upper deck and into the rigging for a glimpse of the stranger. By

3:00 the officers gathered on the *Constitution*'s quarterdeck could clearly make her out; she was a big ship under reefed topsails, close hauled on the starboard tack. In another half hour her high black sides and yellow stripe could be seen; she was a frigate, and her heavy, stubby spars proclaimed her British. An electric thrill ran through the *Constitution*. Hull kept steadily on his course, edging off southwest to cut off the chase if she tried to escape. The stranger made unintelligible signals, and when the *Constitution* failed to reply both captains knew they were in the presence of an enemy.

The British frigate was the *Guerrière*. If she was, as Moses Smith asserts, wearing her famous topsail, painted with the words "Not the Little Belt" in contemptuous reference to Rodgers's 1811 encounter, Hull recognized her at once. She had carried that message up and down the coast the previous year, seizing every American vessel she met. Captain Dacres was eager to meet an American frigate. He called one of his American prisoners, Captain William B. Orne of the *Betsey*, to the quarterdeck and handed him the spyglass, asking if he thought the frigate coming down were French or American. Orne, after studying the stranger's sails, said she was certainly a Yankee. Dacres sniffed. "He comes down too boldly for an American," he said, "but the better he behaves, the more honor we shall gain by taking him."[35] The English captain was elated: he told Orne that by taking the first American frigate on the station he would be made an admiral like his father—"Made for life!" Orne shook his head as he went below.

By this time Dacres had decided that the ship he faced was the *Constitution*. He had lost her off New York, but he would have her this time! Though shorthanded, he magnanimously permitted a few Americans to go below when they said they would not fight against their countrymen. The fewer the hands, the greater the glory! The drum rolled through both ships about 3:00 as they closed to within three miles of one another. Each was brought under fighting canvas: courses were hauled up and topsails were reefed. On board the *Guerrière* a part of the crew rolled out a barrel of molasses to make a drink of "switchel" for the Yankee prisoners when they came on board. The *Guerrière*, ready for action, backed her main topsail and waited for the *Constitution* to come down.

The *Constitution*'s crew went to quarters with three cheers. Boys raced up and down the ladders with shot and wads; sand was strewn over the decks to prevent slipping. Gunner Robert Anderson made last-minute checks. The midshipmen stood by their divisions, encouraging the men. Marines in their bright red coats manned the fighting tops and gathered in the gangway. According to Moses Smith,

By Heaven, That Ship Is Ours!

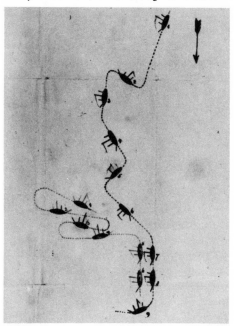

Isaac Hull's diagram of the Constitution-Guerrière battle, 19 August 1812. Courtesy of the New-York Historical Society, New York City.

Hull was now all animation. He saw that the decisive moment had come. With great energy, yet calmness of manner, he passed around among the officers and men, addressing to them words of confidence and encouragement. "Men!" said he, "now do your duty. Your officers cannot have entire command over you now. Each man must do all in his power for his country."

He cautioned the gunners: "No firing at random. Let every man look well to his aim."[36]

As soon as the *Constitution* was ready for action Hull ordered her sails filled to run directly for the *Guerrière*. But when the *Constitution* came within long-gun shot at 5:00 the *Guerrière* hoisted her ensigns, fired a gun to test the range, then delivered her whole starboard broadside. Shot splashed around the *Constitution* as she came on. The *Guerrière* wore round and fired the larboard broadside; two shot struck the *Constitution*'s hull, and the remainder whistled overhead.

Now the fifteen-striped flag blossomed from the *Constitution*'s mastheads and mizzen peak; the crew cheered again. Hull maneuvered his ship to avoid being raked (the enemy's fire passing the length of the deck), but he withheld the full power of his guns. The *Constitution* responded to the *Guerrière*'s broadsides by yawing slightly to receive the shot off her bow and by firing a few of the bow guns as they bore. Hull would not play at long bowls. He wanted close and decisive action. The shot that struck the *Constitution*'s hull at long range bounced harmlessly away, and the word ran through the ship: "Her sides are made of iron!" So she gained her name: Old Ironsides.

About 5:45 Dacres decided that the classic tactic of crippling the enemy at long range was not working; he ordered the *Guerrière*'s helm put up and ran before the wind, waiting for the *Constitution* to come down. Hull ordered the main topgallant sail set to close faster. Once more the crew cheered. By 6:00 the *Constitution* began to double on her enemy's larboard quarter. The *Guerrière* was firing as her guns bore, but the *Constitution* was silent. Below decks in the *Guerrière*, Orne wondered if another *Chesapeake* affair was happening. On the *Constitution*'s deck Lieutenant Morris turned to Hull with the question: "Permission to fire, sir?" "No, sir, not yet," said Hull. "Mr. Morris, I'll tell you when to fire, so stand ready and see that not a shot is thrown away."

At 6:05 the ships were fairly alongside, the *Guerrière* firing rapidly and high into the *Constitution*'s top-hamper. Hull gave a series of rapid orders to slow his frigate's headway: "Haul down the jib! Shiver the main topsail!" And then: "First division, fire! The next, sir! Pour in the whole broadside! Now, boys, pour it into them!"

The *Constitution*'s starboard guns were double-shotted with round and grape. With one tremendous crash, they delivered seven hundred pounds of metal into the *Guerrière*'s side at half-pistol shot. The *Guerrière* was firing as she came up with the waves, throwing her shot into her opponent's rigging to disable her means of propulsion, but the *Constitution*'s men fired, as they had been taught, on the down roll, sending their shot directly into the enemy's hull. With the first broadside, the *Guerrière* reeled as though in an earthquake and trembled from bow to stern. Again and again the iron throats bellowed. A cloud of splinters from the stricken ship flew as high as the mizzentop. Hull was standing on an arms chest for a good view; at the first broadside he knew the game was his. "By heaven," he shouted, "that ship is ours!" In his excitement he jumped up and down on the arms chest, oblivious of the fact that this furious activity had split his tight white uniform breeches from waist to knee.

The *Constitution* was taking very little punishment. One man, Robert Brice, was killed because of his own haste; he failed to sponge his gun before reloading it, and the powder charge ignited at the hot muzzle. One of the *Guerrière*'s high-flying shot cut the flag halyards on the foremast; the ensign fluttered downward as British tars cheered, thinking their foe had struck her colors. But a young American sailor named Daniel Hogan snatched the flag as it reached the deck and raced up the shrouds, through the iron hail, to knot it in place again.

After fifteen minutes of such fire, the *Guerrière* began to crumble. With a heavy crash, her mizzenmast, shattered a few feet above the deck, fell over her starboard quarter. Again the "Constitutions" gave three cheers, and Hull cheered with them: "Huzza, my boys, we've made a brig of her!" Someone took up the cry: "Give her another, we'll make her a sloop!"

The *Constitution* now pulled ahead of her crippled opponent and crossed her bow, pouring in two deadly raking broadsides. But the action of the *Guerrière*'s shot aloft told, as, with most of her braces shot away, the *Constitution* could not be maneuvered with precision. She shot up into the wind and lay dead in the water with her topsails aback as the *Guerrière* bore down to cross her stern and rake in her turn. Hull ordered the helm to starboard, and the *Constitution* swung back before the wind—slowly, slowly—and the oncoming *Guerrière,* unable to avoid her, crashed into the *Constitution*'s stern. There was a grinding impact, then the *Guerrière* fell into the *Constitution*'s wake, her bowsprit over the *Constitution*'s larboard quarter, resting on the boat davit and heavily entangled in her mizzen rigging.

On board both ships the trumpets shrilled for boarders. The *Guerrière*'s marines raced forward as First Lieutenant Bartholomew Kent prepared to lead the boarding party. Captain Dacres had just received a wound in the back, and Second Lieutenant Henry Ready was already dead. In the *Constitution* First Lieutenant Charles Morris headed the boarding sailors, and Lieutenant William S. Bush of the marines brought up his men. It was at this point in the action, with the ships locked together, that most of the casualties occurred on both sides. Small-arms fire peppered the decks. Kent was wounded by a large splinter, and the *Guerrière*'s decks were swept clear. Morris, while attempting to lash the ships together, was shot through the abdomen and fell from the taffrail to the deck. Bush, sword in hand, leaped to the rail shouting, "Shall I board her?" and instantly received a musket ball through the left cheekbone that shattered his skull. Below, the *Guerrière* had brought her starboard bow gun to bear through the *Constitution*'s cabin window, so close that the flaming wads set the cabin on fire. The shot killed two men at the *Constitution*'s after gun and wounded another. After Morris fell, Hull prepared to lead the boarders himself, but as he stepped up on the arms chest again, one of the sailors, throwing discipline aside, caught his arm: "Don't get up there, sir, unless you take off them swabs!" pointing to Hull's epaulets.

Boarding was impossible, anyway. The ships were plunging wildly in the heavy sea. Hull countermanded the order to board and directed the sails filled to get clear of the enemy. It was 6:30. As the *Constitution* drew ahead, the *Guerrière*'s bowsprit ripped through her mizzen rigging, smashing the spanker boom and tearing away the stern boat. Freed from the tangle, the bowsprit snapped upward, slacking the fore rigging; and the foremast, weakened by a double-headed shot, reeled and stumbled over the side, carrying the mainmast with it. The once proud frigate was a dismasted wreck, rolling in the trough of the sea and dipping the muzzles of her main deck guns under.

Since his prize was certainly not going to escape, Hull stood off to the eastward to reeve the broken halyards and braces, extinguish the cabin fire, and get the *Constitution* ready for further action in case her enemy had not surrendered. Seven men were killed—one of them John Brown, the erstwhile captain's gardener. Surgeon Evans tended the seven wounded while repairs were made aloft. Meanwhile, the *Guerrière*'s crew struggled to cut away the wreck of the masts and get their ship under control by means of a spritsail. But wind and sea were still rising; the sail was scarcely set before it carried away. The *Guerrière* was now completely unmanageable, and as the *Constitution* stood down for her at 7:00, looking almost as fresh as she had an hour earlier, the wreck fired a gun to leeward as a signal of surrender. She could not strike her flag, for all had gone overboard with the masts. The *Constitution* ran briskly down across her bow and backed her main topsail; Third Lieutenant Read, with Midshipman Henry Gilliam to command the boat, crossed to the prize to receive her submission. All the boats were quickly manned to bring the prisoners on board. Sailing Master John C. Aylwin, though slightly wounded, went with a hawser to get the prize in tow, and a surgeon's mate went to assist Surgeon Irvine of the *Guerrière* with her wounded: the British dead numbered fifteen; the wounded, sixty-two; and two dozen more were missing, probably lost overboard with the masts. At 8:00 the first boat returned, leaving Read in charge of the prize, and Hull walked quickly to the gangway to receive his chief prisoner. In the gathering dusk he bent to offer his arm to the wounded Dacres who, on reaching the deck, executed the stiff little ceremony of surrendering his sword. Hull politely refused to receive it from a gallant foe but conducted Dacres to the cabin as his guest. The Englishman was crestfallen. "You are a set of tigers!" he exclaimed. "I have lost a hundred men."[37]

By Heaven, That Ship Is Ours!

The *Guerrière*, rated 38 guns, mounted 49; her main deck battery was 30 eighteen-pounder long guns, her spar deck having 16 thirty-two-pounder carronades, 2 long twelves, and a twelve-pounder howitzer.[38] The *Constitution*, rated 44, mounted 56 guns: 30 twenty-four-pounder long guns on the main deck, 24 thirty-two-pounder carronades on the spar deck, and 2 long eighteens at the bow. The weight of her broadside was greater than the *Guerrière's* by about 3 to 2, and her men very roughly in proportion: 440 to 302.[39] But the execution done was out of all proportion to the relative force. The *Constitution* had demolished an opponent of equal rate, whose commander had been eager to fight and confident of victory.

The victors found it impossible to keep their prize in tow because of the heavy sea, so through the long, sleepless night the *Constitution* lay by her, the boats coming and going to bring the prisoners on board, beginning with the wounded. Surgeons Evans and Irvine worked all night dressing, splinting, and cleansing. The scene of carnage in the British ship was terrible. Midshipman Gilliam, who spent the night on board, thought he had

> one of the most convincing and awful examples of the effects of mortality and the tyranny of kings, in contemplating upon the scene which her decks presented; pieces of skulls, brains, legs, arms and blood lay in every direction and the groans of the wounded were enough almost to make me curse the war, but when I recollected that we were fighting under the banners of a republic and in the cause of liberty it was a complete solace to my mind, and I considered it as the inevitable decrees of fate.

The men in the *Constitution* also worked through the night making essential repairs. At 1:00 A.M. a sail was seen in the northwest, but she did not approach. Had she been another enemy, the *Constitution* was ready. At 9:30 A.M. Lieutenant Read hailed from the *Guerrière*. She had five feet of water in the hold, and the leaks were gaining on the pumps. The *Constitution's* shot had penetrated the hull the length of the larboard side, and six feet of the plank below the bends had been completely shot away. The English prisoners remaining on board, many of whom had broken into and helped themselves to the ship's liquor supply, refused to man the pumps. In this situation Hull had little choice but to destroy his prize. During the forenoon all the *Guerrière's* crew were brought on board the *Constitution*. Meticulous attention was paid to salvaging their belongings; Hull made a special point of sending for a Bible belonging to Dacres, a gift from his mother that he did not want to lose. (Later it was discovered that the *Guerrière's* men had in their bags some cloth that had been rifled from American prizes; this was confiscated and distributed to the *Constitution*'s crew.) Hull secured a few souvenirs: some powder horns and the one remaining flag, a jack found bent to the flagstaff at the bowsprit.

While this work was going on Hull went among his crew to see how they were faring. The steadfast commander was a gentle man. "I do not mind the day of battle," he told a friend later. "The excitement carries one through: but the day after is fearful; it is so dreadful to see my men wounded and suffering."[40] One of the wounded, a young seaman named Richard Dunn, was about to have his leg amputated. He made no outcry, only muttering at Evans and Irvine, "You are a hard set of butchers."[41] Hull promised the lad he would look after him, and he was as good as his word: he collected a subscription of $1,000 for Dunn and invested it in interest-bearing notes, secured him a naval pension, and found employment for him in the navy yards for the rest of his life. He also got a reward of a month's pay for Daniel Hogan, who had lashed the flag at the foretopmast head. Moses Smith saw his commander passing among the men in the sick bay and thought that "he even looked more truly noble, bending over the hammock of a wounded tar, than when invading and conquering the enemy."

The battle had also given Hull a new respect for the blacks in his crew. He confessed to a friend that "I never had any better fighters than those niggers. They stripped to the waist and fought like devils, sir, seeming to be utterly insensible to danger and to be possessed with a determination to outfight the white sailors."[42]

By 1:00 P.M. all the boats had returned from the *Guerrière* except Read's. He and his crew were laying the powder train to blow up the ship. Hull and Dacres stood on the quarterdeck watching the *Guerrière*. Each regretted her loss for different reasons. She had served six years in the Royal Navy, having been captured from the French on 19 July 1806. Now she was finished. At 3:00 Read's boat was seen pulling away from her side. Within five minutes the hulk was wrapped in flames, and her guns, heated by the blaze, began to discharge for the last time. Before the boat reached the *Constitution*'s side, at 3:15, the *Guerrière* shuddered; a flash like lightning ran along her gun deck, and as the roar of the explosion reached Hull's ears she burst in two. The quarterdeck, directly over the magazine, rose in a mass and shattered. Then, with a rumble and a sigh, the remnants of her hull sank below the waves. Surgeon Evans pronounced the sight "the most incomparably grand and magnificent I have experienced. No painter, no poet or historian could give on canvas or paper any description that could do justice to the scene."

The *Constitution* was not so badly injured that she could not have continued her cruise, but she was filled with more than three hundred prisoners. And it was important to bring home the news that a British frigate had been destroyed. Hull shaped a course for Boston. The homeward run was uneventful. Hull's dispatches for the Navy Department contained a detailed account of his cruise up to 19 August, and a second letter, relating the action with the *Guerrière,* concluded with his usual magnanimity:

> I want words to convey to you the bravery and gallant conduct of the officers and the crew under my command during the action. I can therefore only assure you that so well directed was the fire of the Constitution, and so closely kept up, that in the short space of thirty minutes from the time we got alongside of the enemy (one of their finest frigates) she was left without a spar standing, and the hull cut to pieces, in such a manner as to make it difficult to keep her above water, and the Constitution in a state to be brought into action in two hours. Actions like these speak for themselves, which makes it unnecessary for me to say anything to establish the bravery and gallant conduct of those that were engaged in it. Yet I cannot but make you acquainted with the very great assistance I received from that valuable officer, Lieutenant Morris, in bringing the ship into action, and in working her whilst alongside the enemy, and I am extremely sorry to state that he is badly wounded, being shot through the body. We have yet hopes of his recovery, when I am sure he will receive the thanks and gratitude of his country, for this and the many gallant acts he has done in its service.
>
> Were I to name any particular officer as having been more useful than the rest I should do them great injustice. They all fought bravely and gave me every possible assistance that I could wish.[43]

Captain Dacres was also preparing his official report. In it he gave full credit to the Americans for their humane treatment of himself and his crew but ascribed the *Guerrière's* loss entirely to the "accident" of losing her masts, and he boasted that he would gladly undertake the same contest again with the same crew. His court-martial solemnly confirmed that the lamentable loss was "from the accident of her masts going, which was occasioned more by their defective state than from the fire of the enemy, though so greatly superiour in guns and men." It was a curious judgment: the Americans were of superior force, yet that could avail them nothing; a British frigate could be defeated only by, as it were, an act of God. The *London Times* offered an acid comment on this sort of rationalizing:

> We have been accused of sentiments unworthy of Englishmen, because we described what we saw and felt on the occasion of the capture of the Guerriere. We witnessed the gloom which that event cast over high and honourable minds; we participated in the vexation and regret; and it is the first time we have ever heard that the striking of the English flag on the high seas to any-

thing like an equal force, should be regarded by Englishmen with complacency or satisfaction. If it be a fault to cherish among our countrymen "that chastity of honour which feels a stain like a wound;" if it be an error to consider the reputation of our navy as tenderly and delicately alive to reproach—that fault, that error, we are likely often to commit; and we cannot but consider the sophistry, which would render us insensible to the dishonour of our flag, as peculiarly noxious at the present conjuncture. It is not merely that an English frigate has been taken, after what we are free to confess may be called a brave resistance; but that it has been taken by a new enemy, an enemy unaccustomed to such triumphs, and likely to be rendered insolent and confident by them. He must be a weak politician, who does not see how important the first triumph is in giving a tone and character to the war. Never before in the history of the world did an English frigate strike to an American; and though we cannot say, that Capt. Dacres, under all circumstances, is punishable for this act, yet we do say, there are commanders in the English navy, who would a thousand times have rather gone down with their colours flying, than have set their brother officers so fatal an example.[44]

That was the point, after all: it was unheard of. It could not happen. But it had.

Hull, on his part, had second thoughts after sending off his own account of the affair to the Navy Department. Perhaps it was too long, too boastful. Certainly it credited the officers, but it did too little to praise the men of the *Constitution*. He drew up a second, shorter letter which he sent to the secretary, saying: "I have written you an account of the action in detail, but as it's my opinion that the less that is said about a brilliant act the better, I have therefore given you a short sketch which I should prefer having published to that in detail." This was the letter sent to the newspapers, with its famous peroration:

> After informing you that so fine a ship as the Guerriere commanded by an able, and experienced officer, had been totally dismasted, and otherwise cut to pieces so as to make her not worth towing into port, in the short short space of thirty minutes, you can have no doubt of the gallantry, and good conduct of the officers and ships company I have the honor to command; it only remains therefore for me to assure you, that they all fought with great bravery; and it gives me great pleasure to say that from the smallest boy in the ship to the oldest seaman not a look of fear was seen. They all went into action giving three cheers, and requesting to be laid close alongside the enemy.[45]

It was Saturday morning, 29 August, ten days after the battle, when the *Constitution* made her landfall at Cape Cod. She ran up the bay under full sail and got a pilot at dusk. The southwest wind that had carried her out of Boston now kept her from getting in; after beating up all night she anchored at the lighthouse on Sunday morning, 30 August. At 8:30 Purser Chew and Lieutenant John T. Shubrick left in the boat for Boston. Shubrick was to go on to Washington with Hull's letters, and to give an eyewitness account of the battle to Hamilton. In the afternoon the ship got up to Nantasket Roads; the crew spent the day washing clothes and cleaning ship to prepare for the inevitable swarm of visitors. By this time, Chew had spread the news of victory on shore, and the boats of the curious and the well-wishers were coming out to the roads. Large numbers could be expected in the morning. There was also the task of transferring the wounded prisoners to the hospital on Rainsford Island.

Isaac Hull, thinking himself safe in port at last, went to his stateroom for his first night of uninterrupted sleep in months. He was still sound asleep at 6:30 A.M. when an excited lieutenant burst in on him, shouting: "Captain! The British are upon us! An armed fleet is entering the harbor!" Groggily, Hull groped for his trousers, while ordering the lieutenant to unmoor and clear the ship for action—"determined," as he said, "to sell our lives as dear as possible." In a few minutes he was on deck, as cool as ever. Four ships and a brig were rounding Point Alderton. The *Constitution* could not pass them to get to sea, so the only course was to run for the inner harbor and the protection of the forts. But the ships were coming up so fast, with a northeast breeze, that by the time the *Constitution*'s anchors could be weighed they would cut her off from the harbor also. Hull gave the order: "Cut!" A few minutes of hacking at the two heavy cables freed the ship; by 6:45 she was beating out of the roads. At 7:30 the squadron made signals that Hull could not understand. The *Constitution* continued to strain everything to get up the harbor, but still the enemy drew nearer. Hull trained his glass on the leading ship. At 8:00 he shouted with relief. The American flag was flying on board! It was Rodgers! The *Constitution* now became the leader of a grand procession. Proclaiming her victory by hoisting the *Guerrière*'s jack beneath her own, she stood up the roadstead, followed by the *President*, the *United States*, the *Congress*, the *Hornet*, and the *Argus*. The other ships anchored in President Roads, but the *Constitution* ran all the way up to Long Wharf, where she moored at 9:45 A.M.

Boston was wild with fervor at the triumph of the favorite frigate. Partisan politics and hatred of the war were thrown aside in the general rejoicing. Isaac Hull was overwhelmed with congratulatory calls that day: Captain Bainbridge came from the navy yard, Decatur from the *United States*, James Lawrence from the *Hornet*, and Arthur Sinclair from the *Argus*. Other officers from Rodgers's squadron came as well. Rodgers did not make a formal visit until Wednesday. The crew went on scrubbing clothes and cleaning the ship, and sightseers gaped in astonishment that she could have been in an engagement at all. Arrangements were made for Hull's formal reception on shore the next day. At 11:00 A.M. on Tuesday, 1 September, he stepped ashore at Long Wharf, as the Washington Artillery Company fired a "federal salute" of seventeen guns (for the seventeen states). The *Constitution*'s yards were manned with sailors dressed in their best, and her guns boomed seventeen times in answer. The streets were decorated with flags, and citizens crowded the housetops, wharves, and shipping to cheer the new national hero. Women waved handkerchiefs and threw wreaths of flowers at Hull as he passed slowly up State Street among throngs of cheering people.

Hull was glad to get out of the crowds to a room in the hotel where Morris had also been moved for his convalescence. The letters waiting for him at Boston had brought the news he dreaded: William had died two weeks earlier. This left Isaac more than ever the man in charge of his family. As soon as the public reception was over, he posted a painful letter to Washington:

> Having had the misfortune to lose a brother since my departure from this place, on whom depended my father's family, and with whom all my private concerns had been left ever since I joined the Navy, makes it absolutely necessary that I should take a short time to make provision for my younger brothers, and to see my father placed in a comfortable situation. I have therefore to request that you will be pleased to order a commander to the Constitution to take my place.[46]

It was generally believed that Hull gave up the *Constitution* to allow the other officers a turn at cruising, but this is quite doubtful. Decatur did not surrender the *United States* after he took the *Macedonian*, and Bainbridge apparently quitted the *Constitution* after his cruise because of his wounds, and because he expected to build a line-of-battle ship at Boston. Successful sloop commanders were promoted to frigates. If Hull was setting an example of magnanimity, he found no followers. But it seems more likely that he gave up the command, as he said, because he was needed at home. It would have been terribly hard for him, otherwise, to surrender his "favorite frigate." He would never sail in her again.

Bainbridge's letter requesting command of the *Constitution* was not twenty-four hours behind Hull's resignation. He suggested at the same time that "Captain Hull could be appointed to the command of this Navy Yard, during my absence from it."[47] Bainbridge already regarded the Boston yard, which he had taken over on the death of Commodore

Nicholson a year earlier, as quasi-private property that he was entitled to hold whenever he wished. On 9 September the secretary acceded to both requests, assuring Hull that "this appointment [to the navy yard] is given to you under the impression that it will in no degree prevent your giving the requisite attention to your private concerns."[48]

In the two weeks required for the exchange of letters, Hull was swept up in a whirl of public celebration. On Saturday, 5 September, an enormous public dinner was given at Faneuil Hall, attended by over five hundred of Boston's leading citizens. President for the occasion was John Coffin Jones. Hull was escorted in procession to the hall, which was decorated with flags, cannon, flowers, a model of the *Constitution*, and—as a delicate political reminder—a portrait of Washington. A band of musicians played in the gallery, and each of the many toasts was answered by an artillery salute from the street. Hull was also voted the thanks of the Massachusetts legislature, and gifts of swords and plate and votes of congratulation poured in from as far away as Charleston, South Carolina. (Hull's own state was too adamantly Federalist to honor its son until the war was over. In 1817 the Connecticut legislature belatedly extended its thanks and voted Hull a sword and a pair of pistols.) The Washington Benevolent Society of Massachusetts, a Federalist club, voted him a testimonial, not without political overtones:

> We are happy for ourselves, and for our country to see, from actual experiment, that such a Navy as the United States are already competent to create, will secure to this great commercial nation the full enjoyment of all their rights, upon the ocean so long as the skill and bravery of our mariners is directed by the example which draws forth this testimonial of gratitude and respect.[49]

Hull's response was carefully nonpartisan:

> Permit me . . . Gentlemen, through you to make known to the Society, of which you are members, my feelings of gratitude: and I pray that they may be assured, that if my feeble efforts have contributed toward the advancement of a naval establishment, or have in any way been serviceable to my country, I feel that I am more than compensated by the strong testimony I have received from my fellow citizens of their approbation.[50]

There were also letters of congratulation from Hull's friends all over the country, and even those in Europe like Mrs. Joel Barlow, all of which had to be acknowledged. To Caesar A. Rodney he wrote with typical modesty:

> I have indeed been fortunate, but not more so than I am confident my brother officers will be if they fall in with the enemy. Where there is anything like

equal force you will find that they are not invincible. They are not now fighting Frenchmen and Spaniards. My friends in all quarters are too good. They have more than paid me.[51]

Sir James Jay, his old passenger and traveling companion, wrote from New York:

Nothing certainly which it is in the power of a grateful and spirited people to bestow can be withheld from a man who has so eminently exalted the national honor. It is the only instance that I ever heard of an English ship of war being taken by a single ship of the same force.[52]

But, despite the outpouring of feeling for the *Constitution* and her commander, there were many Federalist diehards still to curse "Madison's ruinous war" and to abuse the naval officers or, as Lieutenant Hoffman said, "pour cold water down their backs." The officers of the *Guerrière*, in fact, were more liberally entertained in Boston than were their captors. Surgeon Evans wished "all His Majesty's loyal subjects would return to their own much loved, dear old England, and not hang like a wen or excrescence on the back of our government, thwarting all its views, and trying to pull it under water."

Meanwhile, Isaac Hull had more distressing news to cope with: his uncle William had surrendered his army at Detroit and laid bare the entire Northwest to British attack. There was plenty of talk about it in Boston; even at the public dinner one celebrant was heard to remark that "we have a Hull up and a Hull down." The old man was on his way home, on parole, to face a court-martial that would sentence him to be shot. Reprieved by the president, he spent the rest of his life trying to vindicate his conduct. At the moment, however, the antiwar party in Boston was treating the surrender as a kind of heroic act. The irony of seeing William Hull a Federalist hero was not lost on Isaac. His was an unhappy situation: he certainly would not abuse his uncle, yet defending him would be tantamount to siding with a group that was cursing his own action and the cause for which he fought. The situation called for all his native tact, yet he managed to remain on good terms with all parties.

There was, besides the social round, plenty to do in getting the *Constitution* ready for another cruise. On 11 September a cartel came from Halifax with Lieutenant William M. Crane and the crew of the *Nautilus*, and also Midshipman Madison and the men from the *Constitution* who had gone in the prize brig *Adeline*. They had been retaken by the frigate *Statira*. Madison reported that the British captain had taken his proffered sword, stamped on it, and thrown it into the sea, snarling:

"There's one damned Yankee sword gone."[53] Crane told Rodgers that Admiral Sawyer at Halifax had detained six of the *Nautilus*'s men as British subjects and had sent them to England for trial. Rodgers thereupon stopped the cartel that was getting under way with the *Guerrière*'s crew for Halifax and removed twelve men with a promise to treat them just as the six from the *Nautilus* were treated. There was news from farther south that day as well: Porter in the frigate *Essex* had captured the British sloop of war *Alert*, of 20 guns, and brought her into New York.

Tuesday, 15 September, was a brisk fall day. At four in the afternoon Captains Hull and Bainbridge went on board the *Constitution*. Mustering the crew, Hull read them a letter from the secretary of the navy:

> I have it in special charge from the [president of the United States] to express to you, and through you, to the officers and crew of the frigate Constitution the very high sense entertained by him of your and their distinguished conduct in the late action with his Britannic Majesty's frigate, the Guerriere. In this action, we know not which most to applaud, your gallantry or your skill. You, your officers and crew are entitled to and will receive the applause, and the gratitude of your grateful country.[54]

Hull added a few words of his own, and the men gave him three hearty cheers. Then, at a signal, Hull's long captain's pennant came down at a run from the masthead, and Bainbridge's broad red commodore's pendant was hoisted in its place. A murmur ran through the crew. Discipline broke, and they pressed forward around Hull. "The scene altogether was affecting," Evans noted in his journal. "This whole crew had a great affection for him. They urged him to remain: said they would go out with him and take the Africa, and finally requested to be transferred on board any other vessel." Hull was touched. He had to blink back tears and make his voice stern as he ordered the men to their duty, then quickly stepped over the side to his boat. Bainbridge, meanwhile, grew red in the face. He strode up to the men:

"Who here has ever sailed with me before and refuses to go again?"

"I have!" sounded from several quarters.

"One man said he had sailed with him in the Philadelphia and had been badly used," wrote Evans, "that it might be altered now, but he would prefer going with Captain Hull, or any of the other commanders. Several others said they had sailed with him before, and did not wish to sail again."

According to Moses Smith, who was among the discontented though he knew Bainbridge only by report, "we had become personally attached to Captain Hull, and hated to have him leave us. Such was the state of feeling that it almost amounted to a mutiny."[55] Sailing Master Aylwin coolly entered his own observation in the log: "At 4 p.m. Commodore William Bainbridge superseded Captain Isaac Hull in the command of this ship . . . at which the crew expressed their dissatisfaction. The armourer, Leonard Hayes, for mutinous expressions was sent on board of Gun Boat No. 53." The wrathful Bainbridge asked for a court-martial of Hayes, "on the charge of insolent and mutinous language."[56] The "Constitutions" never became fond of Bainbridge—no crew ever did, for he was a moody man and a savage martinet—but they were reconciled to serving out their time with him, and in the subsequent engagement with the *Java* they came to respect him.

Hull had arranged with Bainbridge that the latter would continue in charge of the navy yard until the *Constitution* was ready to sail, when Hull would return to take over. That would give him a few weeks to visit home. Before leaving, however, he had to chair a court of inquiry into the loss of the *Nautilus*—a cut-and-dried formality, since she had sailed out of New York into the jaws of Broke's squadron. Hull spent his time during the testimony apparently taking notes but really writing letters to his friends in Europe that were to go by a vessel that was about to sail. One went to David Baillie Warden. Hull sent greetings and news from various acquaintances but referred only obliquely to his recent feat: "you will see by the papers this vessel brings what is going on by sea and land and how we progress in the war."[57]

Hull never talked or wrote of his exploits, but he had one weakness in that regard: he liked to see them depicted on canvas. Years earlier he had ordered a painting of the cutting out of the *Sandwich* in Puerto Plata. Now he asked the portraitist Gilbert Stuart to recommend a marine artist who could render views of the *Constitution*'s recent adventures. Stuart named Michel Corné, who had done a large painting of the attack on Tripoli for Commodore Preble. Before Hull left Boston he arranged for Corné to paint the escape of the *Constitution* from the British squadron, as well as a series of four views of the engagement with the *Guerrière*. Thomas Chew, who had transferred to the pursership of the navy yard, was to keep an eye on the progress of the work.

Hull left Boston about 20 September and spent a few days at Derby before going on to New York to settle William's business affairs. He refused the offer of a public dinner in the city because of his bereavement. As it turned out, he was to spend nearly two months at New York, for on 15 October he received orders to take command of all the gunboats and naval vessels there, the previous commander, Isaac Chauncey, having been ordered to Lake Ontario.

It was a frustrating service. Chauncey had taken all the men, guns, and movable stores to the lake, leaving New York to be re-equipped from nothing. The *Alert,* Porter's prize, was to be purchased into service and fitted up as a block ship, as was the old frigate *John Adams.*[58] Hull was annoyed at being ordered to take on such a demanding assignment when his family affairs were still in chaos. He chided Hamilton:

> When you [were] pleased to order me to take charge of the Yard at Boston I had hopes of getting a few months' leisure to attend to my private concerns. I came here for that purpose, and having commenced on the settlement of my brother's estate must suffer great inconvenience by being confined at this yard. I have to make arrangements for the comfort of a large family and provide for them against the winter. My young brothers depend on me to settle my brother's estate and to provide for them. I hope, therefore, situated as I am, if the service will possibly permit of it you will be pleased to consider me attached to the Boston station, or should you have given that Yard to some other officer you will give me a station in Connecticut, or if there is none there [will] grant me a furlough for a few months. . . . The season will now soon be such that the enemy will hardly attempt to enter our ports, so that there will be little for the officers to do here.[59]

Hull seemed oblivious to the contradiction in his letter: the New York assignment was too confining, yet there was little to do. Willy-nilly, he was stuck with it until mid-November. Family affairs were continually on his mind. On Sunday, 18 October, he called on his sister-in-law Susan, widow of Dr. Joseph, and found her comfortably settled with young Joseph and her two daughters. But it was time for Joseph, now eleven years old, to be sent to school, and Isaac thought that Eliza, the older girl, should also be at school, perhaps at Middletown. "They are very fine children," he told his father, "and must be taken care of."[60] Moreover, his young brothers were a source of great concern. All three—Daniel, Henry, and Charles—had gone or were going on trading voyages, war or no war. Daniel and Henry were captured before the end of the year.

This continued activity of the merchant fleet, plus the fitting out of privateers, made Hull's task of preparing naval defenses for New York all the more difficult. Service in the gunboats, with no prospect of prize money, was a poor alternative to privateering. Hull was forced to offer a bounty and shorten the enlistment to one year in order to induce men to serve. The men were enlisted, not as seamen, but as "sea fencibles," who would not be subject to being drafted into seagoing warships. Use of this method attracted sailors from the coasting trade who were unwilling to go to sea. By the end of October, Hull had twenty-seven gunboats ready for service except for their crews, the *John Adams* armed, and the *Alert* under repair but short of gun carriages. The navy agent, Dr. John Bullus, was a close friend of Hull's, so there was easygoing cooperation between them. Hull had secured the appointment of Midshipman Samuel Bullus as an acting lieutenant to assist him, particularly in setting up a system of semaphore telegraphs between the city and Sandy Hook to warn of the distant approach of enemy ships. Meanwhile, some of the gunboats were kept patrolling off the harbor. Hull was convinced, though, that naval forces alone, without cooperating shore batteries, would be ineffective. On 4 November he prepared a list of the forces available but cautioned Hamilton:

> I much fear that all the force we can muster here will not be adequate to the defense of the harbour should the enemy make an attempt to come in, particularly if they come with heavy ships. I should thereby recommend a strong battery being erected at the Hook.[61]

By mid-November, Hull had the vessels at New York equipped, although they were still nearly devoid of men. But at Washington, meanwhile, the effects of his victory over the *Guerrière* were being felt in the halls of Congress. The wave of patriotic exultation and of gratitude to the navy seemed about to wash up, at last, some bounty for the navy itself, in the form of an appropriation for new ships. Another bill, no less interesting to Hull and his crew, would provide prize money to the captors of the *Guerrière*. Secretary Hamilton was anxious to have as much lobbying support as he could muster for the naval appropriation. Charles Stewart was already in the nation's capital and was preparing an elaborate statement on the best type of naval force for American needs. On 12 November, Hamilton summoned Hull and Morris, the heroes of the hour, to Washington to help put the proposal through.[62]

When Hull left New York, he believed that something would be accomplished for the navy this time. Burwell Bassett, chairman of the naval committee of the House, had written him that "[we] are determined to have a Navy." He was still concerned about the chaotic state of his personal affairs in Boston, Connecticut, and New York, but he left many of them in the capable hands of Purser Thomas Chew. Chew was asked to send the *Guerrière*'s flag and some of the powder horns to Washington for presentation to the Navy Department; to look after Richard Dunn, who had been given a job in the Boston Navy Yard; and to keep an eye on the subscription funds being raised for him, as well as to keep Corné on the right track with the paintings. Dunn was a subject of continuing concern to Hull: "Let me know how the poor fellow behaves. I feel an interest in him and hope his conduct will be correct." As for Corné, Chew seemed finally to have "brought the painter to his bearings." Hull wanted him to go ahead quickly with the series of paintings from the first sketches he had seen: "they were in most parts correct." Finally, but far from least, there were affairs connected with their mutual friends in Connecticut that were unsettled, at or near Mrs. Chew's home at New London:

> I am happy that you are about to visit our friends and if it is possible I will be with you before you leave. I am anxious to find the way to the farm. Mrs. Chew has been with me a part of the way several times but for some reason never would recommend my going all the way. Tell her I will now exchange interests with her: if she will say pretty things for me at the farm I will say pretty things for her at Washington.[63]

By the time Hull reached Washington, Bassett's committee had reported a resolution to give Hull a gold medal for the *Guerrière*'s capture, with silver copies for his officers, and to award $50,000 in lieu of prize money to the captors. Charles Morris was to be made a captain, skipping the grade of master commandant as Decatur had done in 1804— and causing similar hard feelings. Hull and Hamilton went before the committee to testify that the frigate had been worth at least $300,000 and that a just award of prize money would be $100,000, noting that the *Constitution* had also destroyed or forced the destruction of three British brigs. Bassett altered the bill accordingly. Meanwhile, in the Senate, an authorization to build four line-of-battle ships and six frigates passed without a dissenting voice, "so that they appear now to have a disposition to do something for us. The Navy is now up," Hull believed, "and if nothing is done this session it never will be worth remaining any longer."

Hull was, of course, the social lion of the season at Washington. He was a frequent visitor at the White House, where he was rumored to be courting Maria Mayo, a friend of Dolley Madison's. Hull knew better than to believe the rumors: he wrote his old lieutenant, Theodore Hunt, who had left the navy and established himself at Lexington, Kentucky: "I have called now and then but not often, so that, my friend, I fear you will never see her Mrs. H." He had much more important interests nearer home: "The little Connecticut friend had not arrived at New York when I left there but she must be there before this. I shall see her on my return." That there was something serious afoot is hinted again at the end of the letter: "let me know how you are pleased with the country. Pick out a good spot for me by the side of you that we may join in raising *mariners.*"[64]

Obviously Hull was anxious to be away, but social and political obligations kept him in Washington another week. There had already been a grand ball for five hundred people on board the *Constellation,* and on 8 December the citizens of Washington gave a return fête for the navy officers. At about 9:00 P.M. there was a stir and a shout at the door of the hall, and Midshipman Archibald Hamilton, the secretary's son, entered bearing a British battle flag. Hamilton was hoisted on the shoulders of some of the other officers, while Hull and Stewart took the corners of the flag and bore it to the dais. Hamilton announced to the cheering crowd that Decatur in the *United States* had captured the frigate *Macedonian* and brought her into New London. This triumph ensured the passage of the naval appropriation, but it was costly to Hull in the long run. Faced with the necessity of purchasing the *Macedonian* into the service at a fair valuation of $200,000, the naval committee again cut back on the money for frigates destroyed, so that Hull and his crew got only $50,000, as did Bainbridge for destruction of the *Java*. Hull was bitter about it: that Decatur, who seemed to be truly fortune's child, should receive four times the sum granted for the *Guerrière* simply because he had brought his antagonist into port rather than destroying her seemed rank injustice. Decatur had, in fact, done what Hull had refused to do: instead of seeking a quick, decisive, and certain victory by closing with the *Macedonian*, he had played the British game of long-range combat and had outgunned his opponent without crushing her. Hull's three-twentieths of the money voted for the *Guerrière* amounted to $7,500; Decatur's share was $30,000. The *Macedonian* ran for twenty years in the American navy and was a valuable ship; but what dollar value could be placed on that first crushing victory over a foe believed to be invincible?

Hull foresaw political upheavals in the months to come. President Madison had been reelected and was preparing to reshuffle part of his cabinet. When Secretary of War Eustis resigned on 3 December, it was clear that Paul Hamilton must follow shortly. Poor Hamilton had been appointed mainly for sectional reasons. He knew nothing about naval business, and the difficulties of administering the Navy Department in such times had led him to indulge his weakness for the bottle. By 1812 he was seldom sober after noon. The naval officers did not dislike him personally but thought he made a poor leader. Hull, with his hatred of politics, was glad to be leaving town: "Great changes must soon take place in our Department and report says that they will begin high up. Thank God I shall not be here to witness them." It was difficult even to know what the general policy of the government would be: Hull wrote John Bullus that he was uncertain about investing in a trading venture Bullus proposed: "all appears to be war, yet I should not be surprised should a peace be patched up in the spring."[65]

While at Washington, Hull had talked Hamilton into appointing Jacob Lewis commander of the forces at New York and reassigning him to the Boston yard as a sinecure. Thus, when he returned to New York in mid-December, he was free to enjoy the pleasures of the season. Although he had declined public honors in the fall, he was now forced to accept joint celebrations being prepared for himself, Decatur, and Jacob Jones, who had defeated the sloop-of-war *Frolic*. There was a regular routine of awards, as "The Croaker" described them in the *Evening Post:*

> The board is met—the names are read;
> Elate of heart, the glad committee
> Declare the mighty man has said
> He'll take the "freedom of the city."
> He thanks the council, and the mayor,
> Presents 'em all his humble service;
> And thinks he's time enough to spare
> To sit an hour or so with Jarvis.[66]

Just so, on Monday, 28 December, at 11:00 A.M. Hull appeared before Mayor De Witt Clinton and the Corporation in the Common Council chamber to receive the "freedom of the city" in a gold box, with a view of his battle in enamel on the lid. Mayor Clinton made a speech embellished with such statements as: "Deeds of valor and achievements of glory are at all times cherished by patriotism and rewarded by true policy." Hull's response was in character: "Captain Hull in a few words, and in a low and modest tone of voice, expressed the deep sense he felt at the honors thus conferred upon him." After taking the freeman's oath, Hull walked down the stairs amid a crowd of a thousand cheering New Yorkers. The following night there was a grand naval dinner at the City Hotel, attended by four hundred or five hundred gentlemen, with Hull, Decatur, and Jones as honored guests. The two senior captains, seated to the left and the right of the mayor, presented an interesting contrast. Hull, according to a contemporary observer, "was easy and prepossessing in his manners, but looked accustomed to face 'the battle and the breeze.' Decatur was uncommonly handsome, and remarkable for the delicacy and refinement of his appearance."[67] According to the newspaper report of the dinner, "the company retired at about eleven o'clock, *in good order* [after thirty-seven toasts!], and perhaps never was more sincere satisfaction evinced on a similar occasion."[68]

Both Hull and Decatur had also to "sit an hour or so" with John Wesley Jarvis for the full-length portraits that had been commissioned for city hall. When the portrait was proposed to him in the fall, Hull was determined that Gilbert Stuart should do it, and he had nearly persuaded Stuart to come from Boston for the purpose when he was ordered to Washington in November. In the meantime, Thomas Sully had proposed to Stuart that they collaborate on the series: Sully would do the backgrounds, which Stuart hated, and Stuart would do the heads. But Stuart did not take up Sully's proposition, and in the end the commission for Hull's portrait was given to Jarvis, who did a distinctly inferior job. The head is not bad, though it lacks the vitality of Stuart's likeness, but the body was evidently done by an assistant who botched the proportions, particularly of the right leg.[69]

Finally, on New Year's Eve, the season of celebration was capped with a gigantic ball, again at the City Hotel. The cotillion began at nine o'clock; Hull and Decatur made grand entrances to musical salutes. At eleven the ladies were conducted to the supper room, fitted up like the cabin of a warship. But, as there were more than three hundred female guests, escorts, except for the honored guests, had to be left behind. Dancing continued until one or two in the morning of 1 January.[70]

Isaac Hull found time between balls and dinners for more private society, particularly the company of "the little Connecticut friend." Her name was Ann Hart. She was the second of seven daughters of Elisha Hart of Saybrook, a village at the mouth of the Connecticut River. How long Hull had known her is uncertain, but in the intimate society of Connecticut at that period there was little chance of overlooking the existence of any well-connected family. Ann was twenty-one in 1812. Almost certainly she, and perhaps her younger sisters Mary Ann and Jannette (twenty and eighteen, respectively, in 1812) had been participants in the sparkling social season at New London in the winter of 1810–11 when the squadron was there. She was evidently a friend of Hortensia Chew's, and Hull's November letter to Thomas Chew suggests that he had seen her at New London or Saybrook a number of times.

There is an old family legend that Ann Hart had visited the *Constitution* as a schoolgirl and that Lieutenant Hull had given her a souvenir piece of rope made into a necklace, that after his triumph she had unearthed the tarry treasure and worn it to a ball where it caught his eye and sparked a renewed acquaintance, and that romance followed. The dates do not work out well, however; Ann was only ten when Hull left the *Constitution*, and she was nineteen when he returned to her. The kernel of truth in the story is probably that Ann had overlooked the charms of the portly young captain until he became a national hero and that she then saw him in a new light. Whatever her reasons, she certainly fell in love with him in the fall of 1812, and he with her. She had come to spend December in New York with her married older sister, Sarah Jarvis. On Saturday, 2 January 1813, Sarah's husband, the Reverend Samuel F. Jarvis, opened his little suburban church, St. Michael's, at Bloomingdale and, in a quiet ceremony, joined Isaac Hull and Ann Hart in marriage.

The newly married pair went to Derby the next day, and then to Ann's home at Saybrook. It would be hard to find a more ecstatic bridegroom than Isaac Hull. From Saybrook he wrote to John Bullus at New York in ebullient nautical metaphor: "I find the last frigate I had the good fortune to capture as tight a little boat as I could wish and suits me to a marlin-spike. I only wish you could have seen more of her before I took my departure. Had you I am sure you would have liked her construction."[71] To John Rodgers he said: "I am indeed happy, and if possible shall be made more so by making you acquainted with Mrs. H. . . . I am anxious to see you and shall of course improve every moment to get on but you know one can move faster than two."[72]

How did Ann Hart like being compared to a captured frigate? She seems to have taken her husband's navalisms in good part. She was certainly a beautiful and intelligent woman; many years later Admiral David D. Porter said that "of all the beautiful and brilliant women he had ever met in any country, Mrs. Hull surpassed them all."[73] On the other hand, Congressman Elijah H. Mills in 1819 thought her "too insipid and too much like wax-work," though she was then said to be the reigning beauty at Washington.[74] This comment has the flavor of sour grapes, as does the sneer of Joseph Hillhouse that "Miss Ann Hart bestowed her hand last winter on Victory as personified in our little fat captain, Isaac Hull, who is now reposing in the shade of his laurels."[75] For Isaac and Ann, however, it was the beginning of thirty years of mutual devotion.

Ann had made a good impression at Derby and had won the approval of Mary Wheeler Hull. So Mary wrote to Henry, who returned to New York early in January from his captivity in Bermuda. The whole family were amazed that, after so many years of false rumors, Isaac had married at last. Henry wrote:

> Am told she is a charming woman. I a few days since made Mr. Jarvis a visit; had the pleasure of seeing his lady and Miss [Jannette] Hart. She is a charming looking young lady, an amiable countenance and a fine black eye, and a very fine complexion. She is what I call a *beauty*; Mrs. Jarvis is not so handsome. I should like very much to see Isaac's lady, having heard so much of her. Little did I think when I left this that Isaac would be married so soon; was surprised when I heard of it at Bermuda; would not believe it until having seen it published.[76]

Jannette was in fact the most striking of the Hart sisters. In the 1811 season she had captivated Samuel F. B. Morse, and she continued to have a following among the Connecticut and New York literati. But she never married. Perhaps Isaac Hull had not yet guessed that in marrying Ann Hart he had taken on another set of family responsibilities. Besides his own younger brothers and Joseph's children, from 1815 on he would be continual host to one, two, or more of Ann's five younger sisters.

The Hulls were at Boston by the beginning of February, where Isaac again took charge of the navy yard. Rodgers had returned from a second cruise at the New Year—still without an important prize—and had brought his wife and children to Boston for a visit. Ann Hull and Minerva Rodgers quickly became friends, and Ann doted on the Rodgers children. With Susan Bainbridge it was quite otherwise. Apparently she and Ann hated each other on sight and, in the years ahead, seldom lost an opportunity to make catty remarks about one another. Since Mrs. Bainbridge and her children remained ensconced in the commandant's house at the navy yard, the Hulls took temporary lodgings in the city.

On 15 February the Hulls and the Rodgerses were attending a theatrical performance when an announcement was made from the stage that the *Constitution* was off the lighthouse and had won another victory: on 29 December she had destroyed the frigate *Java* off the coast of Brazil. A few days later she was in the harbor, still looking little the worse for her battles. Bainbridge, wounded in the action, had nearly recovered. The usual round of entertainments for the victors followed. Isaac Hull still enjoyed parties. But Ann, after a month of continual entertainments, began to find the pace exhausting. On 27 February she wrote Mary Wheeler Hull:

> This is almost the first leisure evening I have had since I came to Boston. Indeed, I am ashamed to tell you how dissipated I have been, for fear of your supposing that it was my disposition. But it has been from necessity, not inclination—for it is hardly consistent with the character of a rational woman to lead a dissipated, fashionable life. And from motives of selfishness, if no better, I should never do it for you are obliged to sacrifice so much peace and quiet, for what will not yield you one moment's pleasure upon reflection.[77]

Ann was still a young woman who could playfully tease her sister-in-law about having Isaac's miniature, a none-too-prepossessing likeness:

> I am glad you have my husband's miniature. When you look at that I suppose I shall get a thought, too, as we are *one* now. . . . I will promise not to be jealous for it is not captivating enough to steal anyone's heart. . . . He sends you his love and a kiss—I suppose in return for those you gave his ugly phiz.

The young couple often visited General William Hull's family at Newton. They were there on the evening of 20 March when he returned

Mrs. Isaac Hull in her wedding veil (Ann Hart), ca. 1813. Artist American, unknown. Photograph by John Klein. Courtesy of the Wadsworth Atheneum, Hartford.
Bequest of Ellen A. Jarvis.

from a visit to Derby, and both took note of his praise of Mary: Ann
told her "the old gentleman seemed quite in ecstasies when he spoke
of your ladyship," and Isaac wrote his father to "tell Mary he is quite in
love with her, and he is not the only one."

William Bainbridge quickly made it clear that he expected to resume
command of the navy yard at Boston, and Hull amiably acceded. On 11
March he asked the new secretary of the navy, William Jones, to assign
him to the navy yard at Portsmouth, New Hampshire. That yard had
never had a regular naval commandant, but it had been designated to
build one of the new ships of the line, so a captain would have to be

appointed. It would be a good assignment, for the commandant who built the ship would presumably be her first commander. And, for a bridegroom, a shore station was desirable. Ann thought that she would "be satisfied with almost anything, provided he does not go to sea."

On 15 March, Hull received the Portsmouth assignment, with command of the harbor at Portsmouth and "all the waters of the U. States to the East thereof."[78] Isaac and Ann had already been planning their life at Portsmouth. William Hull had left behind, as part of his estate, a flock of Merino sheep at the Derby farm. Isaac thought he might be able to graze twenty of them profitably at Portsmouth, where the navy yard was located on an undeveloped island. He made plans for getting them there, with the rest of the things he had been collecting at Derby for his future housekeeping, and Ann, writing to Mary, envisioned herself a rural shepherdess, à la Marie Antoinette:

> I love the country and almost everything appertaining to it. My husband says he shall get some sheep, a cow, etc. So when you come to see us you will find us in the true country style. I shall turn shepherdess—but I cannot as the poets describe follow them with my crook over rocks and mountains, for upon the island where we shall reside in summer there is nothing of that description and only one solitary oak which for a great number of years has resisted the wintry blasts. *Isaac* is going to Portsmouth on Tuesday to make the necessary arrangements for our removal and will be absent three or four days. . . . If you can read this you will deserve credit for your patience, but you must excuse it for my husband does not furnish me with the *best of pens.*[79]

The preparations for the move were quickly made, and after a fond farewell to John and Minerva Rodgers, the Hulls left in their carriage for Portsmouth, where they received a public welcome. "The arrival of this distinguished citizen was announced by a federal salute at Wybird's Hill. As he passed down Congress into Daniel-street, he was welcomed to the metropolis of Newhampshire by the repeated cheers of a large collection of citizens."[80]

9

The Portsmouth Station

On the first afternoon after his arrival in Portsmouth, Isaac Hull inspected his new command, an island of some fifty-eight acres in the harbor near the Kittery, Maine, shore.[1] Portsmouth, with its good hinterland for timber, had long been a popular building place for the navy. Three public ships had been built by contract at private yards on another island, called Langdon's. In 1800 it was decided that it would be more economical for the government to buy and improve its own yards, and Naval Constructor Joshua Humphreys made a tour of possible locations. One of those he favored was Dennett's (or Fernald's) Island, the advantages of which included its nearness to Kittery, where the carpenters lived; the large quantity of stone available for building docks, wharves, and storehouses; and the fact that William Dennett asked only $6,000 for his island, while John Langdon wanted $25,000 for his.[2] The government accordingly purchased Dennett's Island and built some sheds and docks for storing about 45,000 feet of timber for a 74-gun ship.[3] Building ways for the ship were also laid out before work was stopped.

Commodore Edward Preble visited the island in 1806 and reported to Robert Smith that "the site . . . has more natural advantages than any other place I have met with for a Navy Yard."[4] Hull concurred with Preble's and Humphreys's assessment:

> I find this place well situated for a Yard, and that a [dry] dock can be made here at much less expense, and be more convenient than at Boston, or indeed any Yard belonging to the United States, on account of having but a very small distance to build out to get deep water, and in consequence of having the stone of a superior quality on the spot.[5]

A few days after his tour of inspection, Hull was asked to submit a report on the condition of the yard for transmission to Congress. From this report, and the accompanying map, one can obtain an accurate idea of the state of things as Hull found them. There were then attached to the yard Captain Hull; his clerk, Joseph Watson; the naval storekeeper, Tunis Craven; a cockswain; and three seamen and three ordinary seamen. The men were occupied in bringing stores from the mainland and

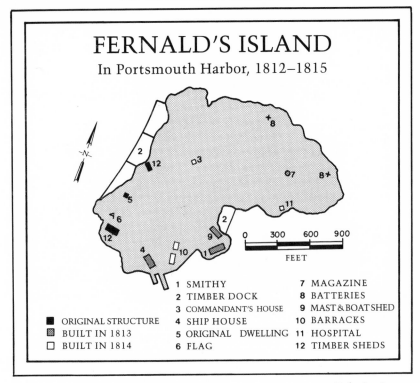

FERNALD'S ISLAND
In Portsmouth Harbor, 1812–1815

1 SMITHY	7 MAGAZINE
2 TIMBER DOCK	8 BATTERIES
3 COMMANDANT'S HOUSE	9 MAST & BOAT SHED
■ ORIGINAL STRUCTURE 4 SHIP HOUSE	10 BARRACKS
▨ BUILT IN 1813 5 ORIGINAL DWELLING	11 HOSPITAL
☐ BUILT IN 1814 6 FLAG	12 TIMBER SHEDS

Kathy Rex Lopatto

doing general laborers' work around the yard. There were also on the station Sailing Master Nathaniel Stoodley, a cook, four seamen, and two ordinary seamen attached to the six gunboats that were laid up at Portsmouth—a total of eighteen persons.[6] The "improvements" in the yard included a dwelling house which Hull thought "only fit for a master carpenter." This house was occupied by the numerous family of the storekeeper. There was a barracks for the seamen, a small house, a store, and a workshop (which should be removed), two timber sheds, a boathouse, three saw pits, and two water-filled docks for timber. A blacksmith shop was under construction on a small island 160 feet from the main island, a good location for such a fire hazard. There was a bellhouse, a flaghouse and flagstaff, and the ways for the 74-gun ship that had been laid down in Humphreys's time. In the docks were 17,050½ feet of live oak timber and 67,569 feet of white oak timber and plank. With these men and materials as a beginning, Hull was assigned the task of building a ship of the line and defending some three hundred miles of coast. It did not seem an auspicious beginning, but he set to work immediately and with vigor.

The Portsmouth Station

Building 74-gun ships was a new departure for Americans; only one vessel of that size had been built on this continent, and interestingly enough, it had been built at Portsmouth. She was the ship of the line *America*, built under the supervision of John Paul Jones and presented to France on completion to make up for the loss of the *Magnifique* in Boston harbor.[7] But the *America* was completed in 1782, and neither Jones nor the builders, James and William Hackett, was available to advise the constructors of 1813.

The only guide for the building of the four 74s now authorized—only three were actually built during the war—was a plan drawn by the then naval constructor, Joshua Humphreys, and his son Samuel, for the 74s that had been planned in 1799 and whose timber still lay in the navy yard docks. This draft was to provide the basic plan for the wartime ships, with certain alterations that proved to be generally for the worse.

Hull, on his arrival at Portsmouth, immediately applied for permission to begin building. The season was favorable for working, and there were constant applications from carpenters. With this advantage, plus the fact of having so much timber and the launching ways laid down, he hoped that the Portsmouth yard might be ahead of the others.[8] But, by the time he received the secretary's authorization to go ahead, Hull had discovered that the launching ways had been badly laid, partly on rock and partly on sand. "Had the ship been built on them she must have been ruined, as that part where the rock is would not have settled, when the part of sand must." The timber had to be taken up and the bed dug down to rock the whole length of the keel.[9]

Meanwhile, there was also the necessity of hiring a builder for the ship. The collector of the port, Joseph Whipple, had mentioned one William Badger to Secretary of the Treasury Albert Gallatin, as "the best constructor of vessels in this place," leading up to the fact that Badger had just finished the hull of a vessel of 200 tons suitable for a war brig or a revenue cutter that he wished to sell to the government. Jones suggested that Hull interview Badger; the two agreed on a contract to build the 74 with a salary of $1,800 per annum for Badger. This was later altered to allow $1,200 each for Badger and his son, the same terms given to Edmund and Edward Hartt, the builders of the 74 at Boston. At $1,200 per year, the builders were paid at nearly the same rate as the commandant.[10] The foreman on the job received about $3.00 per day, underforemen $2.00, while carpenters worked at $1.00 and laborers at $0.92.[11]

The builder being engaged, the next requirement was a draft of the ship by which to build. Copies of the Humphreys draft were supposed to be deposited at the various yards where frames had been placed, but there was none at Portsmouth. As it turned out, this lack was not particularly significant, for between 9 April and 17 May it was decided to alter the design of the ships so drastically that new drafts had to be drawn.[12] Meddling with a constructor's plan was an old tradition in the American service, as Howard I. Chapelle noted apropos of the building of the frigates in the 1790s, a passage that applies equally to the present episode:

> The relationship between the naval constructors and the ship captains was based upon the earlier idea that the man who played a piano was the best judge of the instrument. Hence the official correspondence, in the period under discussion, is marked by the freedom with which commanders of ships issued orders to the naval constructors and decided how the ships should be armed, fitted, rigged, and even built. From the perspective of the present, some of the American naval officers appear as surprisingly pompous and opinionated amateur ship designers, whose ill-judged decisions spoiled the reputation of many well-modeled ships.[13]

In this case, the chief meddlers were Bainbridge and Secretary William Jones. The latter had served in a privateer in the Revolution and had later been a merchant captain; he also seems to have regarded himself as an expert on ship construction.

Jones's chief contribution to the alteration of the plans was to straighten the sheer—the longitudinal curve of the ship—by raising it amidships and dropping it fore and aft, thus achieving a more nearly horizontal plane for the ship's lines.[14] This was a particularly bad idea. The tendency in the American navy had always been to build ships too straight, with the result that they were all hogged—that is, bow and stern drooped, giving the keel a "hogback" line. As soon as the ships began to take shape, Hull saw that they were much too straight, "and . . . they will be hogged in six months after they are launched, if they are not in launching itself, for no ship of the length of these can be built so strong as to prevent their hogging or straightening from five to eight inches and very often more. I therefore fear our ships have not sheer enough."[15] But his plea fell on deaf ears. This tendency to build too straight was not corrected by American builders until the 1820s; Hull was ahead of his time.

Hull and Bainbridge, on the other hand, persuaded the secretary that the ships were too narrow, and after a deliberation that lasted until early June and led to a third redrawing of the draft, the breadth was increased from 48 to 50 feet, and the straight part of the keel was lengthened from 150 to 155 feet, with the depth continued at 19 feet 6 inches.[16]

It would seem that nothing now stood in the way of rapid progress on the 74 at Portsmouth. But this was not the case. Hull was wrestling with an even more vexatious difficulty than the problem of the draft—

a shortage of timber. Over the years the timber stored at the navy yards for building 74-gun ships had been pirated for repairs of other ships. When Hull got the timber out of the docks in late April, he found only about two-thirds of the ship's frame.[17] This would not seem a particularly serious problem in a country so heavily timbered as northern New England. The problem was that the frame, for maximum durability, had to be made of live oak, which grows only in the South. Aside from the fact that the timber also had to be seasoned, there was no hope of getting it in any quantity from southern ports in the face of the blockade. The frame of the ship at Portsmouth therefore either had to be made up from the frames deposited at Boston or New York, or it had to be eked out with northern white oak.

Hull found that he was short 621 pieces of the frame. The most serious deficiency was knees, of which 411 were missing, and futtocks, which were short by 56.[18] The lack of these pieces was most likely to cause delay because they were more difficult to find in the first place and were therefore likely to be in short supply. The knees were the crooked pieces of timber used to connect the beams with the ship's sides, and thus secure and support the decks; they had to be hewed out of the angle of the tree with its root or, less commonly, of the angle between trunk and branch, and for a ship the size of the 74 they must be very large. The futtocks were pieces situated between the floor and the top timbers; the farther down in the ship they were located, the more crooked they must be.

Bainbridge was supposed to have two frames at Boston, but the inroads for repairs had been particularly severe there; Hull thought he would be lucky to make up one complete frame. Nevertheless, Jones ordered Hull to get whatever he needed from Boston or, failing that, from New York. Thus, Hull began a series of requests to Bainbridge to supply his missing frame pieces, a crescendo of pleas that netted but a grudging response. For the next few months Hull's hopes fluctuated with the reports from Boston. A week after his return from there with the draft, he made a sharp plea: "For God's sake give me all the timber you can, especially futtocks."[19] Soon after, some of the timber was reported on its way from Boston by water and the molds or pattern pieces by land. Hull was doing his part in the cooperative enterprise by having the white oak at Portsmouth sawed into plank for both ships; he was also engaged in seemingly endless negotiations for some cargoes of southern pine timber that had been cut for the Royal Navy but had been diverted to American ports at the outbreak of war. By playing hard to get he managed to buy up most of this timber for the navy yards and so ensure a plentiful supply of deck planking for the 74s.

Thirty-three pieces of the frame came from Boston in late June, and

Bainbridge said that these were all he could spare. Hull had the stem and stern of his ship raised, and he believed that his only course now was to substitute white oak for the missing live oak; otherwise, work would have to be halted.[20] But Jones would not consent to the substitution, which might lessen the durability of the ship, and on 24 July, Hull was forced to discharge his carpenters. He was depressed and was resentful of Bainbridge's selfishness:

> There is a large quantity of timber at Boston, and many pieces of it belong here, but there is such a deficiency in the frames that Commodore Bainbridge takes such as will not work into one place to make up another. . . . I shall visit Commodore Bainbridge again in a day or two and after getting every piece he will spare me I shall send a memorandum of the deficiency to New York, to meet your order for its being furnished from that place.[21]

In this letter Hull made two very important suggestions for the future of his ship and of ship construction in general. The first was that the lower deck beams be made of the well-seasoned white oak, which he had in quantity, instead of the customary pine beams; the second was the idea of building a cover over the ship to protect it from the weather and permit construction to continue during the winter. Both suggestions were adopted. The oak beams were undoubtedly stronger and more durable than pine, but they must also have made the ships heavier and contributed to their major fault, insufficient freeboard. As for the shiphouse, such structures became standard in the navy and were acclaimed as great improvements. Bainbridge's biographers have claimed the honor of suggesting the shiphouse for their hero, but in fact Hull voiced the idea almost a month sooner.[22]

Work at Portsmouth was now nearly at a standstill. Hull made another trip to Boston and wrung an additional sixty or seventy pieces of frame from Bainbridge, but his request for timber from New York was fruitless. He turned again to Bainbridge: "Allow me once more to be a beggar for timber."[23] This request netted a few more sticks, but some twenty pieces were still lacking. Jones, however, had at last given in on the use of white oak, although reemphasizing his desire to make the ships durable, to "remove the prejudice which has taken such deep root in consequence of the enormous repairs and loss of time which has so seriously impaired the resources and efficacy of the [naval] establishment."[24]

In September, Hull turned his attention to the shiphouse, an urgent matter with fall coming on. He had originally hoped to build it for $2,000, but five estimates taken ranged from $4,500 if the government supplied the construction labor to $5,975 complete. He submitted these estimates to Jones with some trepidation, but on 18 September received authorization to proceed. The house was up and covered by 6 December. Hull effected a saving by contracting for the frame and lumber separately and by having the seamen of the gunboats raise the building; still, it cost over $5,000. But it amply paid for itself. Not only was it a handsome structure; it was sturdy and durable as well. It was still in use in 1876; for forty-seven years, beginning in 1817, it sheltered the unfinished *New Hampshire*, 74, which was finally launched in 1864. There is still a "shiphouse" on its site—the largest enclosed building ways in the United States.[25]

By the end of September, Hull had about a hundred carpenters at work, and the ship was beginning to show her lines: all the frames, or ribs, were now in place. Hull didn't like the look of her; she was too straight, but he did not dare make alterations. He asked Bainbridge half-jocularly to "say whether you and myself have a right to have an opinion of our own, or whether we must conform precisely to the draft or be broke. . . . Do you plan the decks, or are we to get plans for everything from headquarters?"[26] In fact, most such matters were settled in consultation between Bainbridge and Jones, leaving Hull simply to go along.

Hull's perplexity over timber continued, and Bainbridge's continued intransigence unsettled his usual equanimity. His feelings burst out in a letter to Amos Binney, the Boston navy agent: "I find I am not to get any timber from the Commodore. I must therefore build one half of my ship and let the other stand unfinished."[27] Balked in another attempt to get timber from New York, he doggedly recurred to Bainbridge, "as you did not positively say [in] your last letter that you could not spare any." One has the impression that Hull had learned well the gospel lesson of the importunate friend.

Apparently, Bainbridge replied in injured tones that he was keeping back nothing that could possibly be spared, for Hull wrote soothingly on 13 October:

> I . . . feel assured that you have no disposition to keep from me what live oak timber you have that is not wanting for the 74 building under your direction. I know that all you have and more if you had it would work in, but whether live oak is more necessary in the bows of a ship as cants or in the hold as riders, I cannot pretend to say, or at least we might differ were I to give an opinion.[28]

Cants were pieces for the ends of the ship, and Hull was particularly short of these odd-shaped items. Riders were a sort of interior ribs, bolted to some of the principal timbers in the ship to strengthen them.

They were not generally used in war vessels unless the ships had been weakened by long service, and so it appears that Hull felt that by using the live oak to make riders in his ship Bainbridge was gilding the lily at his expense.

The "timber war" ended at last with an informal agreement between Hull and Bainbridge to exchange white oak plank for live oak timber. The frames of both ships were made up, and by mid-October work was going forward at a steady pace.

But Hull had another difficulty to cope with at Portsmouth: his constructor had disappointed him. When he proposed hiring the elder Badger, he had reported that "he is very respectable in all his transactions, honorable and correct. . . . Mr. Badger worked on the 74 that was built in the revolutionary war, and on the Congress and Crescent frigates, so that his experience is as great as any man we have in this part of the country." In their first weeks of association he felt that "the more I see of Mr. Badger the better I like him."[29]

But the honeymoon was brief. The first object of Hull's suspicion was the younger Badger. He initially questioned his competence as a draftsman; then demon rum entered the picture. Hull wrote Bainbridge on returning from a visit to Boston in October: "Indeed, my friend, the more I see of my ship after seeing yours the less I like her, and the more I see of young Badger the less I like him. He appears to me to be half in the wind at least half the time, yet not enough to enable me to charge him with it direct."[30]

In mid-October, with the passing of the timber crisis, Hull began looking for someone to replace the Badgers. He asked Bainbridge to send his master builder, Josiah Barker, to give his opinion of the work being done at Portsmouth, "for then I should know whether I complained without a cause or not."[31] He inquired of John Bullus whether Henry Eckford, the builder of Chauncey's fleet on Lake Ontario, was available. He was not, but Bullus learned that Noah Brown would come for ten dollars per day plus room, board, and traveling expenses. Hull evidently thought this too high, for he refused the offer. This was a mistake: Noah Brown, with his brother Adam, had built Perry's two fine brigs and five other vessels on Lake Erie; had recently completed the new sloop-of-war *Peacock*; and would soon be off to Lake Champlain where, among other feats, he built the corvette *Saratoga* in forty days and the brig *Eagle* in nineteen. His vessels were noted for speed, and he had a talent for showing the workmen what was to be done and why. Chapelle calls him "tireless and ingenious."[32]

By 24 November, Hull was nearing despair:

we have not progressed so fast as I could have wished with the ship, partly on account of the extreme bad weather we have had for some time past, and partly owing to a want of knowledge in Mr. Badger the Master Builder. I find he is but little acquainted with the draft, and as little accustomed to overlooking a great number of men. He has been accustomed to building only common country ships of the coarsest work, and employing a small number of hands, consequently is much at a loss in employing the number of men necessary on a ship like the one we are building. I have long been dissatisfied with him as a carpenter, but as he is a man of good character and very respectable I had hopes of getting on with him, but I fear I shall not be able to.

The ship is planked up to the orlop clamps inside and will be shut in on the outside in eight or ten days so that we shall soon begin to work about the ports. I fear that Mr. Badger will be *more* at a loss in finishing the ship than he has been in doing what we have done.[33]

Two days later Hull cut the Gordian knot by firing the Badgers. Bainbridge had quarreled with the Hartts in June and had thrown Edward Hartt bodily out of the yard, whereupon he and his father had both quit. Hull, better at human relations than Bainbridge, was willing to hire young Hartt for Portsmouth, but by this time he had gone into partnership for private building. Hull went to Boston once more, and when he left on 15 December he had talked Bainbridge out of the services of his second carpenter, Thatcher Magoun, a well-known Massachusetts shipbuilder. The work went on smoothly thereafter.[34]

One more major alteration was made in the plan for the 74s: at Bainbridge's insistence, and after some hesitation, Jones authorized building the ships with bows like a frigate's instead of the traditional 74 design of a "beak head bulkhead." Hull had doubts about the change, for he thought the European nations would not have followed the old practice so long unless they found it advantageous, but the new style was adopted in the American navy thereafter with success. With their ships housed in, Hull and Bainbridge were able to keep a force of ninety or more carpenters at work throughout the winter months, so that the new ships progressed steadily toward launching in the summer of 1814.

Portsmouth, the "metropolis of New Hampshire," was a town of seven thousand people in 1813. The Hulls found that it did not offer the social amenities of Boston or New York, but for the first several weeks of their residence they were caught up in a round of courtesy visits. Their hopes of living at the navy yard were dashed, for the only house on the island was the ramshackle affair occupied by the navy storekeeper. The Hulls took rooms in Portsmouth at the home of a widow. This left Ann Hull without housekeeping duties, a situation she did not lament.[35] It was now Isaac's turn to hymn the joys of a quiet country life: "We now have a little rational pleasure to ourselves, but are out too often for me. Indeed, Ann wishes as well as myself that we could be suffered to live more retired. We probably shall at this place after having received and returned our first visits."[36]

As the summer waxed and with it the pace of work at the yard, Isaac was away at the island for longer and longer hours, and Ann became very lonely and bored. "There is good society here," she wrote Mary,

> and the inhabitants have treated us with every kindness and attention, but I feel no inclination to form any more acquaintance, and the retirement which we have here is a luxury after a gay winter. I am left alone a great deal and often sigh for the society of some of my Connecticut friends. . . . My husband is very much engaged at the Navy Yard. He goes over at eight, returns at one and goes again at three and stays until dark. I have nothing particular to do and the time passes very heavily with me. I get fatigued with reading, sometimes mend my husband's stocking, read again and then go to [the] Island and follow him about the Yard. I expect soon to become a sailor and ship builder, for I have become familiarized to all the nautical phrases and hear the directions to the carpenters about the 74. I suppose with all the expedition that can be used it will be more than a year before the ship is built, and ere that time I hope with you that we shall have peace and then if my husband went to sea he would *take me*. If he should be obliged to go before, I know not what I should do. But I never anticipate trouble and always look on the bright side of the picture.[37]

By this time, though, there was diversion in the shape of Henry Hull, who, being put out of work by the tightened blockade south of New England, was paying Isaac and Ann a visit. He amused himself at Portsmouth by riding and fishing—and perhaps other things, as his brother darkly suspected: "Henry is . . . a little wild. He has been out two nights, but I hope he has spent them innocently." Isaac was relieved when Daniel and Charles got safely into port, and he urged them to stay put for the rest of the war. Now definitely the head of his family, he assumed a sage tone in advising Charles, who was twenty-one:

> Portsmouth 19th May 1813
>
> My Dear Brother
>
> I have heard with great pleasure your arrival in our happy country. And I fondly hope that your voyage has been a successful one and at least as much so as will pay your way and show you that to endeavor to be doing something is better than giving up to the hard times. . . . Look for something to do if it only enables you to live and save what you have got. You will find the benefit of it when the times are better. You will then have a little something to begin with, and I have no doubt but by industry and good management you will

soon rank with the first merchants in New York. Follow, my dear Charles, our good brother's example and you have nothing to fear. You will have friends that will assist you in all your undertakings. . . .

We have lost all that was dear in William and it now remains for us to endeavor to make his place good to our good parents and society, and to you I look for that station, and I pray God that he will in his infinite goodness place you in the same situation he did our good brother. . . . Write me soon and God bless you.

I. Hull[38]

Ann's thoughts often strayed to the Rodgers family, particularly Minerva and her three little boys. All the way to Portsmouth, whenever the carriage reached a muddy place in the road, she exclaimed: "How will Mrs. Rodgers get to New York with such bad roads?" Isaac chuckled as he wrote the commodore: "Indeed, she appears as much in love with your wife as I am with her; not a day passes but she speaks of her and the children. If she was in a family way I am sure the child would look like some one of them."[39]

News of a British raid on Havre de Grace, Maryland, in May made Ann even more anxious for Minerva and her children. Alone all day on 25 May, she sat daydreaming about them for a long time before taking up a pen:

I am as much the child of anticipation as before I learned from my own experience and that of others the fallacy of it. . . . [M]y memory dwelt on many a happy hour I had passed with you and in looking to future days fancy painted our meeting which would not be dimmed with tears as was our parting. . . . I write now to inquire after your well being, hoping that this will find you well and with such an increase of *courage* as the times call for, as all you thought you possessed must have been called into exercise, I think.

In fact, forty of the sixty houses in Havre de Grace had been burned, the Rodgers home among them.

Ann filled her letter with news of mutual friends and a tidbit of gossip about Susan Bainbridge:

Captain L[awrence] is in Boston to sail in a day or two in the Chesapeake. Mr. Chew and the Commodore [Bainbridge] do not *harmonize* and he is going out with Captain Lawrence. His wife returns to her friends at New London. My husband was at Boston last week. While [he was] there Mrs. B. took a whim to go to Philadelphia with Mr. Ludlow, and unfit [i.e., pregnant] as she was, set out in the mail stage! I should not be surprised if her form grew *genteel* by the jaunt.

She was then packing for a visit to Connecticut, escorted by Henry. "My heart beats with delight when I think of returning to my 'own my native home,'" she told Minerva, "yet that delight is mixed with pain, for my husband will not accompany me. Heigho, this love is a strange transmuting power, is it not? But I would not throw off the shackles if I could."[40]

A few days later she left Portsmouth, accompanied by Henry and by Eliza Hull McClellan, one of General William Hull's daughters who lived at Portland. Isaac went with them as far as Boston, where he had business with Bainbridge. He returned to Portsmouth on 5 June and, busy as he was at the yard, sighed for the return of his "charming little wife." Like many longtime bachelors, he had become a uxorious husband. His waiting was almost over when he wrote Mary on 20 June:

> I would have given all the world if I could have made you a visit with Ann but I could not leave my ship. I had letters from her last evening. She left Saybrook yesterday and spends this day, Sunday, at Middletown and in the morning comes on. Happy shall I be, Mary, when she arrives, for I am tired of being alone. I have not visited since she left me nor have I seen any company. . . . I am indeed happy, Mary, in having so charming a woman for a partner, and I thank heaven that I am so, for had I been unfortunate in the choice of a wife I should have been miserable.

Aunt Nancy, the widow of the unlamented uncle Daniel, maintained a lively interest in Isaac's love life. "Ann writes me she saw Aunt Nancy," he added:

> Tell her that Ann wanted to box her ears for saying that she was glad that someone had taken pity on me and become my wife, for she did not believe anyone would have taken me. Ann says, "I had a mind to box the old woman's ears." I suppose she will not like being called old.[41]

The traveler returned on Friday, 25 June, "and received a very cordial and welcome embrace from 'Sweet,'" as her sister reported.[42] She was accompanied by her mother and Charles Hull. Mrs. Hart settled down to keep her daughter company for the summer; Isaac dispatched Charles for an educational tour to Bath and Wiscasset with the master of the navy yard.

The summer days were bustling ones in the yard, for not only was the ship to be built, but many buildings had to be erected on the long-neglected island. In the course of the spring and summer Hull built a smithy of brick and stone on the small detached island with room for six forges, a powder magazine that he pronounced "the handsomest building of the kind in America," and a mast shed. He asked for authority to put up a two-story building to house storerooms; a rigging-and-sail loft; and the ship's molds, which were being warped by lying out— and also to build a dwelling house for himself. He assured Jones:

I should be willing to undertake to build a comfortable small house for one half of what they cost in other yards. It appears to me that it is absolutely necessary for the commanding officer to live on the island. Indeed, every man attached to the Yard ought to live in it. . . . At Washington and the other places they board out, for which they are allowed at the office full what the interest of the money for building would be here, and this yard being on an island no such accommodations can be had.[43]

He was willing to forgo the house for the present if he could build the storehouse. However, by the time he wrung permission from Jones to contract for the store, in August, it was too late in the season; the mortar would not have time to dry well before the first frost. He would collect the materials and be ready to begin in the spring.

The coming of cold weather slowed the pace of work and afforded Hull a little time once more for the pleasures of society. In a town the size of Portsmouth, select society was so limited that it was easy for the Hulls not only to know all the "best people" but to be on quite friendly terms with them. Senator and Mrs. Jeremiah Mason were regularly callers and were regularly called upon; so were Major and Mrs. John Baptiste de Barth Walbach, Colonel and Mrs. Tobias Lear, former navy agent Jacob Sheafe, and of course the other naval and military officers. Major Walbach, a German baron who had emigrated in 1797, was intermittently in Portsmouth between campaigns; his wife and their young son John, who later entered the navy, lived there throughout the war. Other army officers who were assigned to Portsmouth from time to time included Lieutenant Colonel Abraham Eustis, nephew of the former secretary of war, and Lieutenant Colonel Timothy Upham who, together with Walbach, was decorated for bravery at the battle of Crysler's Farm in November 1813.

Hull's closest personal friend in Portsmouth was probably Joshua Blake, whom he appointed master of the navy yard. The two men were near contemporaries. Blake had been Hull's lieutenant in the *Argus* and had been the controversial commander of Gunboat No. 3 in Preble's attack on Tripoli in August 1804. When the rumors that he had acted in that engagement in a cowardly manner would not stop, Blake had resigned from the navy in 1809, but he and Hull remained on good terms. The Blakes were a prominent Massachusetts family; Joshua's brother George was United States attorney for the District of Massachusetts. Hull evidently persuaded Joshua to come to Portsmouth in June 1813 to run the day-to-day operations at the navy yard. The two men were also interested jointly in the venture of the Merino sheep; Blake was the immediate overseer of the project. The beasts were driven from the Derby farm in the spring of 1813 and turned to summer pasture on the navy yard grass. They wintered on General William Hull's farm at Newton and returned to Portsmouth the following spring. Blake was also Hull's general troubleshooter, charged with such tasks as visiting Maine and Massachusetts ports to survey and appraise timber offered for sale to the government, and working closely with the builders of the 74. As the construction neared its end, Hull recommended Blake's services to the secretary of the navy in the highest terms:

> Mr. Blake was formerly a lieutenant in the Navy and known as [an] intelligent and able officer. He has been in the Yard nearly a year, and has been of great service to me as he is perfectly acquainted with every thing that relates to the building or fitting for sea of a ship of war. Should you be in want of someone to superintend the ship at Philadelphia, or any other one that is building I am confident you would be pleased with him as a *Gentleman*. His brother, George Blake, Esquire, of Boston, I presume you are acquainted with.[44]

Evidently the secretary did not take the hint, but Blake pursued a long and successful career as a merchant captain. He was elected to the Boston Marine Society in 1816 and served as its president in 1826 and 1827.

Another favorite in the Hull household was Thomas Chew, former purser of the *Constitution*. The Hulls and the Chews were lifelong friends. Chew had left the Boston yard, as Ann Hull told Minerva Rodgers, because he could not get along with Bainbridge and, going out in the *Chesapeake*, had been promptly captured by the frigate *Shannon*. After being exchanged, he was assigned to the *Congress* in April 1814. He spent some time in Portsmouth with the ship, then left for Lake Ontario when her officers and crew were reassigned there. But, when Captain John Smith decided not to go to the lake, Chew requested and received a transfer back to the *Congress*. He returned to Portsmouth in November but left again almost immediately for Washington to settle his accounts; while there, in December 1814, he served as Hull's eyes and ears in the capital.

The Hulls were also on cordial terms with the efficient purser of the yard, Nathaniel Lyde, who was appointed to the station soon after Hull's arrival. Lyde had been Commodore Edward Preble's right-hand man when Preble was building gunboats at Portland. Their relations with Navy Agent Henry S. Langdon were less friendly. Langdon had served as superintendent of the navy yard as well as navy agent before Hull's appointment, and he seems to have resented his drop in pay and prestige. On several occasions he tried to out-Yankee Hull, a business that always raised the captain's dander, particularly when it involved attempts to defraud the government.

Another of Hull's associates at Portsmouth was perhaps more the object of pity than of friendship. Tunis Craven had been a merchant at Alexandria, Virginia, but had failed, whereupon he resorted to the public service. His wife, Hannah, was the daughter of Captain Thomas Tingey, commandant of the Washington Navy Yard. Doubtless through his father-in-law, Craven had obtained an appointment as purser and had borrowed $300 to move his family to Portsmouth, installing them in the old house on the island. Secretary of the Navy Paul Hamilton had promised him a further appointment as storekeeper when the Portsmouth yard was activated, but before this could be accomplished, Hamilton resigned and was replaced by William Jones. Craven was dismayed to learn, in February 1813, that his appointment as purser had not been sent to the Senate and was about to be revoked. He began writing anguished letters to any and all persons he thought might say a word on his behalf—the accountant of the navy, Thomas Turner, for example: "God alone knows what will become of us. Poverty in its most terrific aspect will be our portion—then shall I be among strangers, with an inestimable wife and five helpless children"—the youngest, Tunis Augustus Macdonough Craven, was less than a month old—"destitute of the common necessaries of life, nearly 400 miles from any friends, and without the means of returning to them."[45]

Craven occupied an anxious month in writing more appeals to Secretary Jones, to President Madison, to anyone he could think of. On 6 March, Jones wrote coldly that Craven's appointment as purser was revoked, but on the fifteenth he granted him the job of storekeeper, and disaster for the Craven family was staved off once more. When Hull arrived, his heart went out to the hapless family, especially to Hannah Craven, whom he had undoubtedly known in her father's household:

> To see a charming, amiable woman, delicately raised, wanting the necessaries of life and at a distance from all her friends is indeed distressing. Before I came here Mrs. C. had not been off the island for five months nor had a single person visited her. In this situation you, sir, can judge what her feelings must be. Mr. C. is now making up his accounts and will soon forward them to the Department, and I hope he has not from want been obliged to make use of the public money for the support of his family.[46]

Although he had brought his personal clerk, Joseph Watson, with him, Hull gave Craven the appointment of clerk of the yard. The dual appointment of clerk and storekeeper kept Craven busy enough, but the combined salary of $700 per annum barely provided subsistence for so large a family. It must have been nearly impossible to like Craven, who can only be described as a Uriah Heep manqué—he lacked Heep's deviousness but had his obsequious manner. But Hull had compassion on him and worried that Craven's circumstances might lead him to dip into the public till. In January 1814 he sought and received permission to increase Craven's salary to $1,000. Apparently Craven, with this inducement, was able to keep to the path of righteousness. He served as storekeeper at Portsmouth throughout Hull's tenure and later obtained a similar post at the New York Navy Yard. His two sons, Thomas Tingey Craven and Tunis A. M. Craven, became prominent naval officers.

On the night of 22 December 1813, former navy agent Jacob Sheafe played host to the officers of the navy yard and of the frigate *Congress*. But the gay evening was barely under way when the cry of "Fire!" rang through the streets. The fire had begun about 7:30 P.M. in Mrs. Woodward's barn, at the corner of Church and Court streets. The citizens collected to put it out, but it was a cold, windy night, and by 8:00 the flames had enveloped the nearby home of Daniel Webster. Burning shingles, blown before the wind, scattered on roofs as much as one-sixth of a mile distant from the source of the blaze. By nine-thirty the Union Bank had caught fire, which spread steadily until at 11:00 every house in State Street a quarter of a mile east of the origin of the blaze was aflame—except Jacob Sheafe's house. There on the roof, surrounded by the flames of the neighboring houses, stood Captain Hull, Captain John Smith of the *Congress*, and their officers, beating out burning fragments that fell on the shingles. But it was no use; the fire swept in through the windows below them, and the house was lost.

Not until 5:00 A.M. on 23 December did the fire spend itself at the shores of the Piscataqua. Fifteen acres of ruins remained, studded with chimneys, broken walls, and charred trees; 108 houses, 64 stores, and 100 barns and outbuildings had been consumed. The Portsmouth library had perished. One hundred and thirty families were left homeless, but no lives were lost.[47]

The blazing town lighted the sky as far away as Salem and Newburyport. About forty men from Salem arrived at Portsmouth at 3:00 A.M. to assist in putting out the fire, and a detachment from Newburyport came in the next day to guard against looting. William Gray, the Salem merchant who was ostracized by his fellow Federalists for supporting the war, sent $1,000 for the relief of the sufferers in Portsmouth, and the officers and crew of the *Congress* collected $700. Captain Hull ordered a daily distribution of one hundred pounds of fresh beef and a like amount of potatoes, which, according to the *Gazette*, "has been a seasonable relief indeed to those who lost their little all, it has made glad the heart of many a poor widow, and caused numberless orphans to leap for joy." The surrounding towns also took up subscriptions for the sufferers: $300 and a quantity of corn were collected at Dover.[48]

This calamity served to bring the townspeople together for a time, but during most of Hull's tenure at Portsmouth they were bitterly divided politically. Portsmouth had enough Republicans to support one paper, the *New Hampshire Gazette*, but the Federalists had two organs, the *Oracle* and the *Intelligencer*. The *Gazette* was, however, larger and better edited than either of its competitors. Insults flew freely back and forth in the news columns, as when the *Intelligencer* printed the following item:

> JEFFERSON COMMERCE
>
> Friday, Oct. 14 — *Arrived* the regular trading four horse waggon, capt. Shaw, 2 days from Boston, cargo sundries, *to order*, had good weather, saw no cruisers, spoke nothing. In the latitude of Seabrook, saw a Shaving mill privateer, on the stocks; supposed her to be building, to cruize on the Salem turnpike. Saturday, Oct. 16 — *Sailed* four horse waggon, capt. Shaw for Newburyport.[49]

On the Fourth of July the two parties righteously conducted separate celebrations, each with appropriate speeches denouncing their rivals' policies, politics, and personal character. Captain Hull managed to get along with everyone, though he was frequently exasperated at the unwillingness of the people to act in their own defense.

In the fall of 1813 Hull had requested a midshipman's warrant for his nephew, Joseph. He renewed the request in December:

> This lad with two sisters were left in my charge to educate, and having no other means of doing it than that which my pay affords, it would be a great relief to me, independent of the great desire I have to have him in the Navy, as I think him well calculated for that life. He has a good constitution, is very active, and has an excellent disposition.[50]

Such requests by naval officers were almost always granted, and in January 1814 the warrant was issued. Hull had asked for leave of absence, but the arrival of the *Congress* made too much work at the yard for him to leave in January, as planned. Finally, about 1 February 1814, he and Ann set out. They spent a few days at Boston where they visited the family of General Hull, whose court-martial was then in process at Albany. Proceeding to Connecticut, they called on family and friends, collected twelve-year-old Midshipman Hull, and returned to Boston about 20 February. They found the family there much agitated because, as Isaac wrote his uncle:

> they had been informed that you were in close confinement and that much was to be apprehended from your situation. I told them I had nothing to fear, that I was confident that all would be well, that they might possibly find that

you had been guilty of an error in judgment [in the surrender of Detroit] but nothing more, and if even that appeared it was an error on the side of humanity.[51]

A conversation with former secretary of war William Eustis had apparently given Isaac cause for optimism; in the event, General Hull was found guilty of cowardice and sentenced to be shot, but the president remitted the death sentence because of the general's advanced age and Revolutionary War service. His prominence in Republican politics over so many years didn't hurt either.

Before leaving town on 21 February, Hull wrote a quick note to John Rodgers, who had just returned to New York from his last cruise of the war. Ann would have written, he said, except that she had callers, "so that you may soon expect to hear from her ladyship."

> It is well you have kept so far South, for had you arrived at Portsmouth I am sure I should have been jealous for not more than three days since a lady was heard to say that there was not a man on earth she loved more than Commodore R.—"*except* my *husband*" came out after a little pause. Joking aside, she feels a great interest in your fortune and that of Mrs. R. and I hope and pray that they may never feel less friendship for each other.[52]

The Hulls also called at Boston on the Bainbridges; Bainbridge commented to Rodgers after their departure that "Hull is as fat and good natured as ever."[53]

In addition to building the ship at Portsmouth, Isaac Hull was responsible for Portsmouth's defense as well as all the coast of Maine to the eastward. The ship herself was, of course, a tempting target for naval raiders. Hull was discomfited when he surveyed the state of the harbor defenses in the spring of 1813. There were no cannon on the navy yard island. The two passages into the harbor were commanded by defense works left from the Revolution, but little attention had been paid to these forts since that time, or as Hull put it, "nature has done everything that could possibly be done for this place, but we have done little."[54] Forts Sullivan and Washington together commanded the approach to the navy yard and the back passage by Little Harbor, but they were in total disrepair. The main entrance to the harbor was guarded by Fort McClary, mounting 10 guns, on the Kittery side (unoccupied), and by Fort Constitution, with 36 guns, on Great Island near the lighthouse. Fort Constitution contained a token force. Hull feared that, with these forts unmanned and not even a marine guard at the navy yard, the enemy could come up in boats by night and do as they pleased with the ship. Secretary Jones, in response to Hull's appeals, allowed him to man and outfit two gunboats and promised to inform the president and the secretary of war of the need for land defenses at Portsmouth, while expressing a naïve surprise that they should be wanted: "This was a subject of solicitude before I determined to build there, but the gentlemen from that quarter assured me there was not the least danger."[55] Hull suggested that he consult Senator Nicholas Gilman of New Hampshire, and also Representative Daniel Webster. He softened his criticism somewhat, saying the harbor at Portsmouth was "one of the best . . . in the United States for building, and easier defended than most of our Yards." But in the same letter he reported an incident that boded ill for the successful defense of Portsmouth if reliance were to be placed on the local population: a large privateer from Salem, Massachusetts, had that same day been chased ashore just east of Portsmouth by the British sloop of war *Rattler* and one or two smaller vessels. Three hundred or four hundred militia collected at the spot, but the *Rattler*'s commander sent in a flag of truce, with an offer to release the crew of the privateer if the militia would not resist the seizure of the vessel. To this the troops had supinely assented.[56]

New Hampshire politics affected the progress of defense preparations. The outgoing Republican regime of Governor William Plumer ordered some men and supplies to Portsmouth in May, but the incoming Federalist administration under Governor John Taylor Gilman adopted a do-nothing posture, not even supplying rations for the militia detachment.[57] Hull concluded that "I see no disposition on the part of the people to secure their harbour. We must therefore endeavour to defend ourselves."[58] He scoured the seaboard for cannon. Bainbridge reluctantly turned loose a few four-, six-, and nine-pounders, and Hull jollied him to be generous: "In sending the guns I hope you will spare the shot. You see, give me the ship, I want the longboat." He urged Joshua Blake, then at Boston, to take whatever could be had while Bainbridge was in a giving mood: "You ask whether I am to have shot, rammers and sponges, &c. &c. Beggars must not be choosers; I therefore wish you to get everything for them that the Commodore will give you out of the Yard."[59]

By 23 June these guns had slipped around from Boston in a fishing vessel, and 2 fine twenty-four-pounders were on their way from Portland. Hull had recommended that these guns, which were only barrels without carriages, be laid in the bottom of a fishing boat and covered with cordwood. A resourceful local captain, Daniel Fernald, put the guns, with some powder, shot, pikes, and cutlasses, in his schooner *Sally* and heaped spruce wood over them, piling more on the hatches. Crawling along toward Portsmouth, he was becalmed off Saco and boarded by the tender of the *Spencer*, 74. The British lieutenant ordered his men to take out the cargo and got within one tier of the guns before deciding that it was in fact nothing but a load of wood, not even worth condemning as a prize. Over the objections of his crew, he let the *Sally* go,

> "a bone prize for John Bull," said Capt. Fernald, "if he had but known it." The interview was seen, and news reached Commodore Hull at the Portsmouth Navy Yard that the vessel was captured by the *Spencer*, and the guns and powder were of course supposed to have "gone off." But ere long the *Sally*, slow and sure, appeared below, and the surprised Commodore speedily sent down his boats to tow her up to the Navy Yard, where, after the other wood was removed, the *"big logs,"* and *"kindlings"* were rolled out.[60]

Hull mounted all the guns, a total of 30, in batteries on the navy yard island. By early July he thought he would almost feel safe if he had men to fire them. He again asked for marines and that he be allowed to fit out the four remaining gunboats. There were plenty of men in the vicinity who were willing to enlist for gunboat service so long as they were not required to go to sea. A marine guard was finally constituted in the fall under Lieutenant Charles Hanna, but the boats were not fully manned before spring. The people of Portsmouth in their August town meeting petitioned the governor for a guard and some artillery, and the legislature appropriated $10,000 for the defense of the state, most of which would go to Portsmouth.[61]

If the defense of Portsmouth harbor was so troublesome a problem, protection of 250 miles of coastal Maine was an impossibility. Though Secretary Hamilton had fitted out the gunboats in the district in 1812, Jones had reversed the orders in March 1813 and ordered all the boats laid up at Portsmouth. Now, in response to repeated pleas from Maine citizens, Jones ordered two small brigs, the *Enterprize* and the *Syren*, to quit their cruising ground on the southern coast and report to Hull at Portsmouth. Hull made haste to publish this news, but the local people considered it only a gesture. William Widgery of Portland was especially eloquent. He wrote to Secretary of State Monroe that Portland, "the metropolis of Maine," had a harbor all too easy to enter and desperately needed three or four gunboats. "This town," he said reproachfully,

> has furnished about 350 seamen for the navy, the district of Maine about 4000 troops for the army, which would be its full proportion of one hundred thousand men; the friends of the administration in this quarter, amidst the opposition of Tories and bitter Federalists, with whom they are surrounded, have [striven] hard to support the union, and to be forsaken by the government at last would be still harder.

The Portsmouth Station

District of Maine

KITTERY

Navy Yard
dock (Fernald's) Island

Kittery Point

Fort McClary

Fort
Sullivan

Piscataqua River

PORTSMOUTH

Fort Washington

NEW CASTLE

Fort
Constitution

New Hampshire

The Harbor of
Portsmouth, New Hampshire,
1812–1815,
from Maps of the Time

Little   Harbor Passage

0   1/4   1/2   3/4   1
MILE

Kathy Rex Lopatto

As for the two brigs "ordered to cruise on the Eastern Station, if by that is meant off Portsmouth, they might as well be in Boston for all the good they will do us."[62]

Hull had every intention of sending the brigs to Maine if he could once get them, but the *Enterprize* did not reach Portsmouth until 13 June and the *Syren* never came. Her commander, Joseph Bainbridge, took her into Boston instead, where she was found to need extensive repairs. She was replaced by a brig purchased at Boston, renamed the *Rattlesnake*, and commanded by John Orde Creighton, but the replacement did not make Portsmouth until 10 September.

By that time the "lucky *Enterprize*" had, as usual, stolen all the glory. Although the altering of her rig from schooner to brig had turned the once handy vessel into a dull sailer, she was still reckoned a lucky ship, and indeed she must have been, for of all the small cruisers of the prewar navy—the *Argus*, the *Syren*, the *Enterprize*, the *Vixen*, and the *Nautilus*—she was the only one to survive the war and the only one to capture a naval opponent. Though chased by larger ships several times, she was never overtaken. To Isaac Hull, of course, she was in some way special, for she had been his first naval command. Her captain when she came to Portsmouth in June was Master Commandant Johnston Blakeley. Blakeley was an active and intelligent officer, but he disliked the *Enterprize* because she was too slow to catch privateers and too small to have much chance of meeting a naval vessel she could fight. He was glad to be transferred in August to command of the new sloop of war *Wasp* at Newburyport.

Hull, too, was worried about the *Enterprize,* for British forces on the coast that summer, though relatively small, were vastly superior to the little brig. She could meet the brigs *Boxer* or *Young Emulous* (formerly the USS *Nautilus*) but not the sloop *Rattler* or the big privateer *Sir John Sherbrooke;* nor could she be a match for any two of them. Blakeley made one run as far as Portland and was lucky to get back unscathed. Hull pointed out that such a small force was no use as a convoy and could be positively dangerous to the eastern ports, since by going into them she might invite enemy raids. He recommended that the little brigs be sent instead to cruise on the Grand Banks, but Jones preferred to keep them in Maine at least for the summer, "as the call for protection on that coast was very loud."[63]

Part of the brigs' duty was enforcing a naval general order of 29 July to stop the trade between American and British ports, as well as the supplying of British blockading ships by American vessels. On 21 August, Blakeley brought in the privateer *Fly,* whose log recorded boarding an American schooner from Boston bound to St. John, New Brunswick, with corn and flour, sailing under a British license. Hull disgustedly transmitted this information to H. A. S. Dearborn, collector of the port of Boston. "What can be done with such scoundrels?" he fumed. But this was only one of hundreds of such illegal traders who hampered the war effort by keeping the enemy fed.

When he brought the *Enterprize* to Portsmouth with the *Fly* as prize, Blakeley found his replacement waiting. He and Hull left the next day for Salem to act as pallbearers at the funeral of Captain James Lawrence of the *Chesapeake,* leaving Lieutenant William Burrows to fit the *Enterprize* for another cruise along the coast. When Hull got back, Burrows reported the brig ready to sail, and Hull sent her off on 1 September to cruise as far as the Kennebec River. She was supposed to return in two weeks.

Hull may have had misgivings as he watched Burrows sail away. The young lieutenant—Burrows was a month short of his twenty-eighth birthday—was known as something of an odd fish in the service. He was a Pennsylvanian, the son of William Ward Burrows, first commandant of the U.S. Marine Corps. Burrows was quiet, reserved almost to the point of being secretive, yet he had a gift for deadpan humor. One of his greatest peculiarities, from the point of view of his fellow officers, was his fondness for disguising himself as a common sailor and visiting the seamen's haunts. Yet he had gained considerable insight into the sailor's life by this practice, and he was a favorite with the men.

But Burrows had a penchant for trouble. In 1811 he had been ordered under arrest for writing an insulting letter to the secretary of the navy; released after an apology, he asked for a furlough to make a merchant voyage. Isaac Hull, then at Boston, located a first mate's berth for Burrows with an old friend—probably Thomas English—but Burrows was scarcely in the ship before he was turned out by the master for being drunk during duty hours. Somehow he had gotten another mate's berth and had been captured on his return voyage, shortly after the outbreak of war. While on parole and waiting for exchange, he had threatened to resign from the service because some of the midshipmen junior to himself had been promoted over him on the lieutenant's list. Burrows was still brooding about this injustice when he was ordered to the *Enterprize,* and it is probable that beneath the taciturn countenance there smoldered a fierce resolve to distinguish himself in his first command.

Burrows found distinction, glory, and death. On Sunday morning, 5 September, the *Enterprize* found the brig *Boxer* alone off the Kennebec and forced her surrender in half an hour. Both commanders were killed in the action. Burrows, lying mortally wounded on the *Enterprize*'s deck, clasped the sword of Captain Samuel Blyth and sighed, "I am satisfied. I die contented." Four others of the *Enterprize*'s wounded died, including Midshipman Kervin Waters, who lingered for two years and twenty days before succumbing to his wounds.

News of the battle reached Hull at Portsmouth late Monday night. Hastily relaying word to Washington, he left early the next morning for Portland with Mrs. Hull and Portsmouth's most distinguished citizen, Colonel Tobias Lear.[64] The next day, Wednesday, was completely taken up with the elaborate public funeral of the two captains. Six-year-old Henry Wadsworth Longfellow was a spectator at the parade, and years later he romanticized the whole affair in a stanza of "My Lost Youth":

I remember the sea-fight far away,
  How it thundered o'er the tide!
And the dead captains, as they lay
In their graves, o'erlooking the tranquil bay
  Where they in battle died.

After the procession ended, Captain Hull made a speech of thanks to the escort of the day and also published a card in the papers honoring the people of Portland for their generosity in providing such a handsome funeral for the young heroes. He was, then, understandably chagrined to learn, a month later, that the town of Portland had sent the United States government a bill for over $300 for Burrows's funeral expenses and a like bill to the agent of prisoners for Captain Blyth's. Had he not supposed that the citizens wanted to honor the dead at their own expense, he said, he would have buried them plainly, with only the naval officers and crews in attendance, both because the personal finances of the two captains did not warrant a lavish burial, and because "it would ill become the officers of the Navy to make such a display in burying one of their own officers. It would look too much like sounding their own praise."[65]

Hull recommended taking the *Boxer*, a stout, well-built brig, into service, but Secretary Jones had a fetish for speed, and no one praised the *Boxer* on that ground. He therefore ordered her sold. She brought her captors a total of $9,755. Burrows's heirs complained loudly because Hull claimed the commodore's twentieth ($487.75), yet they never got around to marking the young man's grave. The simple monument that now stands there was erected years later by "a passing stranger."[66] The crowning irony of William Burrows's career was that, when Congress voted a medal for his victory, no likeness of him could be found, and no one could sketch his profile well enough for even so crude a representation as a medal. The emblem finally struck bore an urn.

Hull left Portland on 11 September; the *Enterprize* remained there for repairs until early October. On 1 October her new commander, Lieutenant James Renshaw, passed through Portsmouth on his way to Portland. He may have come down from Boston with Captain Hull, but it is not very likely, for Renshaw seems to have been one of those few persons whom Hull disliked. On hearing of his appointment Hull, who was not given to sarcasm, remarked drily: "The Enterprize I presume will not be very enterprizing."[67] Apparently Renshaw was a martinet and was incapable of getting along with either superiors or inferiors. The brig's new officers began to arrive about 20 October; by 22 November the two lieutenants, the acting lieutenant, and the sailing master were requesting to be transferred because "we have all found it impossible to please our present commander. . . . We are much pleased with this little vessel, . . . but under Mr. Renshaw it is impossible for any officer to sail, with any degree of comfort."[68] Although he could not sanction the transfer of the officers, Hull sympathized with their plight. "I am led to believe," he wrote carefully to the secretary, "that the conduct of Captain Renshaw is not at all times as correct as it ought to be as a commander in the Navy, but perhaps a cruise or two will give him a more correct idea of service than he now possesses."[69] Hull had learned to dislike Renshaw when the latter was his subordinate in the *Chesapeake*. He also had doubts about John Orde Creighton of the *Rattlesnake*. When the squadron was at New London in the winter of 1811, Commodore Rodgers had put Creighton on shore for beating a seaman with his fists. But Creighton was not complained of in 1813; on the contrary, he wrote Hull a formal remonstrance about one of his own officers which at this distance seems amusing, though apparently the matter was profoundly shocking to those concerned. According to Creighton, he had in the *Rattlesnake* "one of the most extraordinary cases of uncleanliness that I ever heard of in an officer during fourteen years that I have served in the Navy." The unfortunate man was Acting Surgeon Donaldson Yeates, who was found to be "covered with vermin, and by sending his clothes on shore to wash, has nearly filled a whole neighborhood with the same." Yeates was removed from the brig.[70]

With the coming of winter the weather on the New England coast became too boisterous for the little brigs, so after repairs at Portsmouth in December, they sailed on 10 January to cruise in the West Indies. No naval vessels were sent to patrol the New England coast for the rest of the war, for in the spring of 1814 the British blockade was extended to New England and was kept up through the year with heavy frigates and line-of-battle ships.

Two other navy ships visited Portsmouth during the winter. First was the frigate *Congress*, returning from a cruise. She entered the outer harbor on 14 December 1813 but, because of contrary winds, did not get up to town until the twenty-seventh. Captain John Smith came up right away, however, to call on the Hulls. Smith and Hull were old friends from Mediterranean days. Smith was six years younger; he had his thirty-fourth birthday on New Year's Day of 1814. Born in England, he had been brought to Charleston, South Carolina, by his parents when he was five years old. He had had a creditable career in the navy but was one of those unfortunate men who seem never to be in the right place to join in the heroics. When he reached Portsmouth he was already seriously ill with the complaint, apparently consumption, that ended his life in 1815.

Smith was looking to transfer from the *Congress*, for although she was a sound vessel, her 36-gun rate would make her inferior to the new ships the Royal Navy was building to combat the big frigates like the *Constitution*. Those new frigates were expected to be on the coast in the spring. Hull agreed that Smith would do well to ask for command of one of the new American frigates under construction. The *Congress* could not sail again because the enlistment of a large part of her crew had expired; although she was in good condition and could easily have gotten to sea while bad weather kept the enemy off the coast, she was never able to make up her crew. The bounties being offered for army enlistment and for service on the lakes, the prospect of prize money for privateering, the dropping of the embargo in April 1814 that allowed the merchant fleet to fit out again—all these factors made navy recruiting difficult. The trickle of enlistments for the *Congress* barely kept pace with discharges. The ship was still more than fifty men short in May when Secretary Jones gave up trying to get her out and ordered her officers and such men as she had to go to Lake Ontario to take over the new frigate *Mohawk*. Smith had a choice of going to the lake or taking the uncompleted frigate *Java* at Baltimore. He started for the Ontario base at Sackett's Harbor in June but decided en route that his health would not stand it and returned to Boston, where he had business of a romantic nature.[71] As for the *Congress*, Hull took her guns out at the yard and sent her four miles up the Piscataqua, where she remained until November.

In February 1814, while the *Congress* was still at the yard, the new sloop of war *Wasp* came in. She had been built at Newburyport, but Johnston Blakeley brought her to Portsmouth to take in her guns and stores, because with them she was too deep to cross the notorious Newburyport bar.[72] Her stay at Portsmouth was uneventful except for an incident involving two of her midshipmen, William Burley and Ebenezer Clough. On 17 April, Burley was reported for drunkenness by Frederick Baury, Hull's old midshipman who was now an acting lieutenant in the *Wasp*. Two days later Clough was reported for a similar offense. It was not the first time for either, and Hull ordered them both on shore. Clough was immediately dismissed from the service, but Burley's entreaties won him one more chance in the navy yard. He blew it. Within a week Sailing Master Nathaniel Stoodley reported that Burley had been inebriated for three days and had "given himself entirely up to Bacchus."[73]

Burley and Clough had lost their warrants but saved their lives. The *Wasp* sailed from Portsmouth on 1 May, took her station in the English Channel, and there on 28 June met and destroyed the sloop of war *Reindeer*. The *Reindeer* lost an incredible twenty-five killed and forty-two wounded, nearly half the crew, but the *Wasp* also suffered. Among those killed in her were Midshipmen Frank Toscan and Henry S. Langdon, two Portsmouth men who had been sent into the ship to replace Burley and Clough. After repairing at L'Orient and destroying another sloop, the *Avon*, in the Channel, Blakeley took the *Wasp* southward. On 9 October, off the Azores, she spoke the Swedish brig *Adonis*. She then vanished into the South Atlantic and was never heard from again.

During the winter and spring of 1814 Hull was occupied with the thousand details of the 74. There were hundreds of fittings and castings to be ordered, as well as the plank and beams to be prepared. One of the most frustrating obstacles he faced was Isaac Ilsley, collector of the port of Portland, who interpreted the embargo of December 1813 so literally that he would not allow even ships loaded with government stores to leave the harbor. Otherwise, the business went on briskly. By 1 March the 74 was beginning to look like a ship. She was planked up to the gunwales; her orlop deck was in; and beams were being prepared for the gun decks. Hull viewed her with pride: "The work is well done, and I do not feel willing to allow that we shall be outdone in point of beauty and strength even by the Charlestown ship, and I am confident that the 74 here will outlast that [one] by years, owing to the plank and timber being much better seasoned here than at that Yard."[74]

The one shortage continued to be knees, the crooked pieces of timber that supported the beams. Lacking oak, Hull substituted hackmatack, a local wood. Two hundred to four hundred knees were needed, and it was July before a sufficient supply was collected. A large part came from Maine, and again there was a problem of transport. The American embargo was off by that time, but the British blockade was on. Captain Daniel Fernald, the man who had brought the guns from Portland in 1813, sailed from the same place in July 1814 with forty-eight knees and a breast hook, the knees hanging over the sides of his schooner, the *Sally*. Keeping close inshore, he was chased by the frigate *Tenedos*. As he approached Portsmouth, Fernald took his course so near the land that his men warned him he was among the kelp. "No matter," said Fernald, "throw over a few knees, and we will bring all up right directly." Over went four knees, and the *Sally* sailed nimbly between the rocks and over the bar while the *Tenedos* ran fast aground. Two shots were fired at the *Sally*, but both missed. When she was out of range, Fernald went on shore and picked up one of the eighteen-pound shot. The *Tenedos* lay on the rocks till high tide; by then the *Sally* was safe in Portsmouth. When she came up to the yard, Hull asked Fernald if he had been fired upon, whereupon the captain silently presented the round shot.[75]

During the spring Hull was also doing some building in the yard. In December, no doubt after a cold drenching in the boat one morning, he reminded the secretary about building a house for himself: "I have ever since [my last letter on the subject] lived in town and without much inconvenience, but the weather is now getting so cold that I find it very difficult crossing, and not unfrequently endanger the lives of the men that are in the boat."[76] In February he got at last a grudging assent, "upon the special understanding and pledge that the cost shall not exceed *$5000* Dollars including labour, materials and finishing, complete of the house, out houses and all improvements on the premises."[77] He was also permitted to build a small hospital.

During the spring, while the 74 was taking shape, building on the dwelling house beginning and work being done for the *Congress* and the *Wasp*, the days and weeks at the yard followed a predictable routine.

The length of the workday varied with the season. In February and March the men probably began work about seven or seven-thirty, as soon as it was light enough to see. The hired workmen brought their breakfast with them and took a break to eat it about nine. The sailors were summoned from barracks before sunrise, and they too began the day's tasks before breakfast. If it was Sunday, muster day, the hired workmen of course did not come, but the seamen and marines were mustered about ten o'clock by their respective officers. Purser Nathaniel Lyde took the roll of seamen, Lieutenant Hanna the roll of marines. During this period the Portsmouth yard mustered between ninety and two hundred seamen and officers, the total steadily increasing as spring came on. The roll of marines was kept separately and is no longer extant. Since the yard had no assigned chaplain, divine services, if held, were probably conducted by Joshua Blake. It was also his task to read the Articles of War at muster from time to time as well as any general orders that might be given. If it was a work day, the men went immediately to their various tasks. The portion of the crew of the *Congress* that had been assigned to the barracks for the time being went to the mast shed where they worked at overhauling the ship's masts, sails, and rigging. The seamen belonging to the yard dispersed, some to work as laborers at the shiphouse and others at the dwelling or hospital. They did the fetching and carrying for the carpenters and assisted with the heavy work. Some went in the boats to fetch provisions and water from town both for the yard and for the *Congress*. Storekeeper Tunis Craven, assisted by Stewards Richard Dunn and (after 1 March) John W. Fernald, had to receive each boat on its return and make a record of its contents. He also had to keep an account of the provisions consumed each day and the amount remaining on hand, as well as of supplies used by the carpenters and other workmen, down to the last hammer and pound of nails.

A boat was sent to Portsmouth for Captain Hull about eight. His morning would be spent in receiving reports from the surgeon and other officers; inspecting the work at the ship and the various buildings; and writing letters, which he drafted in longhand and gave to Joseph Watson, his clerk. Watson made a fair copy of each letter for sending and copied the draft again into his letterbook.

These letters covered a great variety of topics, for every order or transaction of any importance must be recorded in writing. One interesting series in the summer of 1813 concerned a seaman named James Brown who had served in the *Constitution* and who had been refused his prize money because he had been marked "Run" in the books of the Boston yard. Brown apparently had been arrested by the civil authorities on some charge and imprisoned; when he did not appear for duty he was thought to have deserted, but on his release he sought Captain Hull and told him the sad story. Hull took him into the yard, but Brown, a good man on board ship, proved worthless on shore, and Hull directed Purser Chew to discharge him and mark him "Run" in order to be rid of him. When it appeared, however, that Brown, as a deserter, would lose his prize money, Hull explained the circumstances to the Navy Department and asked that the money be paid. Commodore Bainbridge, now commanding at Boston, apparently balked at the settlement, and it had to be explained to him again:

> As he had behaved well during the cruise and knowing him to have several small children to support I did not feel that he ought to lose his prize money, and I am sure you will not feel less than I do. It is true that Brown was worthless but taking into view his family and that paying him his prize money would take nothing from Government I see no injury in doing it. Perhaps, however, I may err on the side of lenity. If I do it is an error in feeling and not from a wish to injure the service.[78]

Hull therefore signed Brown's prize ticket, but he cautioned John Shirley Williams, who had brought Brown's case to the Navy Department: "Knowing Brown as I do, I should recommend it as being an act of charity for some person to receive his money for him and see that it was applied to the use of his family, as he is not capable of taking care of it himself."[79]

This kind of solicitude for the men he had commanded was the usual thing with Hull. He was always quick to give employment to men who had been injured in the service, and to none did he extend the helping hand more often than to Richard Dunn, the young man who had lost his leg in the battle with the *Guerrière*. Dunn had become steward of the yard at Portsmouth, and he continued for years to move from place to place with Hull as he changed commands. Hull also encouraged the men injured in the *Enterprize* to serve again when they were able. But someone—apparently Bainbridge—frowned on this practice, saying that men who received a pension from the government should not draw wages as well. Hull brought the matter to Thomas Turner, accountant of the navy:

> As for myself, I have but one opinion on the subject, which is, that the pension is given for the injury received, and not intended to interfere with his again filling any station in the service that his health and wounds will allow him, and receive pay for his services independent of his pension. I now have a man in the Yard that lost his leg in the action between the Constitution and Guerriere, acting as Steward; indeed, he does the whole duty as Steward of the gunboats and Navy Yard, and ought no doubt to have the pay of Steward, yet he is only rated as Seaman.

Turner concurred in Hull's opinion but said he had heard from Commodore Bainbridge that Secretary Jones thought differently. Turner and Hull evidently kept the matter under their hats, and Seaman Dunn went on drawing his pay at Portsmouth as long as Hull remained.[80]

After a morning of this kind of work, Captain Hull returned to Portsmouth for dinner at one and remained there until three. The sailors and workmen also took at least an hour for dinner, and the workmen may have taken their meal at home. In the course of the afternoon there were one or two grog breaks for sailors and hired workmen. During the dinner hour, Joseph Watson probably visited the post office and collected the incoming mail, which he deposited in the letter box in Hull's office. When Hull returned to the yard, he would go over these letters as well as any that might have been placed in the box by officers or men at the yard. The volume of this correspondence was quite large. Winter months were always slower, but in March alone Hull sent some fifty letters on service. Besides these, he was required to receive and forward any letters from his subordinates to the government, sometimes with a covering letter. The government's letters to his subordinates were also directed to Hull for transmittal. Hardly a day went by without a request from some officer for a furlough, a transfer, a promotion, or an adjustment of his accounts. Seamen had to have their pension tickets signed; men who had been reported as deserters from other stations or from the army had to be returned. Friends wanted themselves or their sons recommended for positions in the government, midshipmen's or purser's warrants, or government contracts. Other friends wanted to borrow cannon to fit out their privateers. There were correspondence or personal interviews to be held with men who had timber, coal, oakum, or other articles for sale and with those who hoped to supply the yard with ship's stores, blocks, ironwork, cordage, and a thousand other things. Occasionally Captain Hull must make a call in town, as on the day he visited Greenleaf's copper foundry. A crusty workman named Richard Fitzgerald was roughing out some ironwork for the 74.

The Commodore, in his way, turning the rough pieces of iron with his cane, remarked, "What bungling fellow has been at work here?" The son of Vulcan was a little touched, and turning his face up to him who had looked down his thousands, replied: "I don't know what bungling fellow you mean; you may have bungling fellows in your ships, but there are none here. That is just as much as you know about it." The Commodore thought best to make no reply to an old man of the revolutionary stock, and retired. A day or two after he returned to the shop again, and finding Mr. Fitzgerald surrounded by the well finished pieces of shining iron, each neatly adapted to its purpose, the Commodore, touching them with his cane, remarked: "O, this looks finely." "That is just what I told you the other day," said Mr. Fitzgerald, "we have no bunglers here." The Commodore, instead of being displeased, replied with an oath, "You are a good fellow for standing up for your craft."[81]

The workday at the navy yard ended at sunset. This would have been about four-thirty in March, but in summer work went on until eight or eight-thirty. Then the sailors and marines retired to supper, and Captain Hull and the workmen returned to Portsmouth and Kittery. At about eight (nine in spring and summer) a cannon was fired to mark lights out, the marines loaded their muskets, and all was made secure for the night.

Unfortunately, the nights were not always peaceful. The Portsmouth Navy Yard, like all military installations, had a problem with people who smuggled liquor onto the post. To meet this difficulty, Hull ordered the marine sentries on the island to prevent any boat from landing on or leaving the island without being passed by an officer, except for the boats of the carpenters and those belonging to the island. The arrival of the *Congress*, with several hundred thirsty men on board, had further complicated the situation. Night was the preferred time for smuggling, but sometimes there were daylight incidents, as on Sunday, 20 February. On that day a boat with three men in it attempted to leave the navy yard wharf; when hailed by the sentinel, the boat did not stop. The marine, Aaron Smith, hailed again but got no response. Finally, he fired at the boat and killed one of the occupants, Joseph Gavett of Portsmouth. The next day a coroner's inquest returned a verdict of "willful murder." Thus, when Hull returned to the yard on Tuesday from his leave of absence, he was immediately confronted with an angry civil authority demanding the surrender of the marine.

The case grew more and more complicated, for a little research showed that the navy yard island, though purchased by the United States, had never been formally ceded by Massachusetts. The action therefore came within Massachusetts jurisdiction, and on 16 March, Hull surrendered Smith to the civil authority. To make matters worse, only a few days before a trigger-happy sentinel in the *Congress* had fired into a nearby house, narrowly missing a woman inside. Hull sternly ordered Lieutenant Joseph J. Nicholson, who was in charge of the ship, to see that the marines did not load their muskets before the evening gun and that no loaded gun be fired except

> at some person attempting to come on the island at night and will not answer after being hailed three times at least. You are aware of the difficulty we are now in, and another accident of the sort would make it appear to be something more than doing our duty and would much endanger the life of the poor fellow now under arrest. You will please send an officer on shore to see what damage is done and explain how the thing happened, and assure them that it shall not take place again.[82]

At the arraignment it appeared that the marine had only followed his orders, and so he was bailable at $1,000, which Hull put up and removed the man to the yard once more. The trial came before the Supreme Judicial Court of Massachusetts at York in May. The record does not survive, but apparently Smith was released. His service record shows that he was only eighteen years old. In December, using his age as a pretext, Hull had him discharged "as being a minor."[83]

In April, Hull tentatively suggested to the secretary that some further improvements be made in the yard but was told that "the first object to which the resources of the government must be applied is the efficient means of prosecuting the war, to which all improvements not absolutely necessary at present must give way."[84] Three weeks later came a crushing blow: all contracts, even for the 74, must be suspended. As Jones, who was now acting also as secretary of the treasury, knew only too well,

> it has become necessary to reduce the expenditure as much as possible in the Eastern section of the Union owing to the obstacles opposed to the fiscal operations of the government in that quarter, and to the artificial obstruction to the credit and circulation of the paper of the government, as well as of the banks of the middle states.[85]

The financial crisis was serious, and it would grow steadily worse for at least a year. The flow of specie toward the New England banks, continuous since 1810, had been increased as a result of the wartime embargo. These banks, by the beginning of 1814, held nearly two-thirds of the country's specie and were calling on the banks of New York, Philadelphia, and Baltimore for more. Moreover, the New England states were unblushingly obstructing the collection of the direct tax enacted to finance the war, and the New England banks, refusing to make loans to the United States, were buying British Treasury notes and shipping coin to Canada in payment. As a result, the government had no means of financing its operations in New England—the Treasury notes issued in February 1814 were heavily discounted or refused there—and the Portsmouth contracts became casualties.[86]

The secretary did authorize the completion and launching of the hull of the 74, and finishing the masts, spars, gun carriages, water casks, and blocks, for which the materials were already prepared. But the fitting out of the ship would certainly be delayed. Hull was deeply disappointed, but naturally he could not know that the war would be over before any of the new 74-gun ships would be ready for sea. Thus, any delay that promised to keep his ship in port was a cruel blow to him.

Hull accepted the decision philosophically. He even took the occasion to extol the merits of the shiphouse in cases where vessels must be left unfinished for a long period:

> I had no idea of the benefit of a ship house in building ships. There is no question in my mind but it will pay for itself more than double in building this ship, and should circumstances make it necessary to let her remain on the stocks there is no doubt but she will be a much better ship ten years hence than she now is.[87]

Moreover, he thought his shiphouse better than Bainbridge's, "being much wider at the ground than above. This I think an improvement, not only on account of the strength but it gives us much more room on the sides and under the bottom of the ship." Hull was right: in late July a tornado struck the New England coast and demolished the shiphouse at Boston, but at Portsmouth, although several barns were blown down and three boats capsized, the shiphouse stood—and continued to stand for over sixty years.[88]

Luckily for Bainbridge, he had already launched his ship, the *Independence*, on 23 June. Hull went on with construction as best he could, occasionally "teasing" the secretary, as he said, to be allowed to build a wharf, order rigging, and so forth.[89] He was all the more anxious to get his ship into the water because of the threat of attack; she would be so much less vulnerable if she were afloat.

He had been planning for defense since January but had met with little cooperation either from the state or the national government. An appeal to the Navy Department on 3 January 1814 for cannon, men for the gunboats, and funds to build a fast-sailing lookout boat received a reply that was like a slap in the face:

> When the intention of the government to build the 74s was known, all the intelligent men from the vicinity of Portsmouth represented the place to be so strong by nature, as to require very little protection from art; but to create and maintain the force contemplated in your letter would be an effectual bar to building at Portsmouth, as the expense of defending the ships while building, if the means of defense natural and artificial are really so feeble as represented, would cost more than the ships would be worth when built. . . . I doubt whether any very material force may be expected for this object.[90]

So began what must surely have been one of the most frustrating years in Hull's naval career. He observed gloomily, on receipt of Jones's letter, that he expected no assistance from the town; "nor do I believe ten men would come on the Island was it to be attacked, so that we have only to look out for ourselves."[91] Forts Constitution and McClary had not more than two men to each of their guns. They were so easy to pass in the night, and the alternative passage by Little Harbor was so unprotected that it was imperative to repair and man the old works nearer the town (Forts Sullivan and Washington.)[92] He wrung from Jones an order to man the remaining four gunboats. "I regret to learn," said the secretary, "that so little is to be expected from the patriotism of the people at Portsmouth."[93] Hull did not lose a minute. By the time the blockading squadron appeared in April he had all six boats fully manned and equipped with furnaces for heating shot.

Hull's friend and fellow Portsmouth resident, Major Walbach, was in Washington for the winter, acting as adjutant general of the army. In March Hull urged him to press the needs of Portsmouth on the War Department.[94] That same day he wrote to New Hampshire Senator Jeremiah Mason, touching the political aspect:

> As this is the only seaport in the state of any magnitude I cannot conceive that a request that the forts at the mouth of the harbour should be fully manned and kept so during the summer by the United States would be an unreasonable one, when we take into view the immense number of fine ships now lying at the wharves and other valuable property that is in danger of being destroyed by a very small force.

Some pressure on the state government to arm Forts Sullivan and Washington would also be in order, he thought. The news that Captain Sir Thomas Masterman Hardy, who had been Nelson's flag captain at Trafalgar, would command on the New England coast in the coming summer gave Hull particular cause for apprehension:

I hope I am not unnecessarily alarmed, nor do I feel any other than what my duty as commanding officer on this station obliges me to feel, but when I know we have an army about to enter Canada, and that the enemy have selected one of their most active officers to command on this coast, I cannot but believe the war will be carried on very differently from what it was last summer, and I see no reason why we ought to calculate that our seaport towns will be left unmolested, nor have we any right to expect lenity of this sort.[95]

The same day he wrote to Governor Gilman in almost the same words, asking the loan of some unmounted and rusty cannon reposing in the Portsmouth gunhouse.

That Hull was not whistling in the dark seemed confirmed on 10 April when he received the following note from a recent arrival from Bermuda:

An immediate attack is intended to be made on Portsmouth. I am acquainted with most of the enemy's plans, and hope, for your own sake, and the welfare of the place you are stationed at, you will not neglect this intelligence. *Your* force is well known, and the arrival of three 74s is only waited to determine the fate of the 74 building in Portsmouth, the other armed vessels [lying] there and the town. I am, Sir, Yours and a friend to America.[96]

Copies of this went off to the governor and the secretary, with desperate pleas for action. Nothing could be expected from the state government, Hull told Jones; despite repeated requests,

no measures have been taken to meet a force, nor *will* there be, in my opinion, until they see the enemy entering the port. I am extremely sorry that my opinion should differ so widely from those who informed you that this harbour was secure by nature; they could have had but little knowledge of the enterprise of the enemy, and much less of what ships of war can accomplish; and I will venture to say, before the summer is over they will come much nearer to me in opinion than they have heretofore.[97]

The warning of impending attack had at last aroused some local interest in defense.[98] Army headquarters at Boston dispatched Lieutenant Colonel Abraham Eustis of light artillery to get the Portsmouth defense works in order. He was directed to put Forts Constitution and McClary in complete repair, and in case of the appearance of an enemy fleet, Eustis might call on the entire force of the army in the vicinity. Should there be an attack, Eustis should command one fort and Lieutenant Colonel Timothy Upham of the Twenty-first Infantry the other.

Those two forts were by no means ideal works; Fort Constitution in particular was ill-designed and was commanded by a nearby height. Hull was pleased, therefore, when, after a tour of inspection by Governor Gilman, recruiting was opened for forty-eight militiamen to man

Fort Washington. The *Gazette* trumpeted: "We are happy to find our citizens are not waiting to be aroused to a sense of danger, by the thunder of British cannon, or the bayonets of the enemy at their breasts." The town meeting of 22 April also displayed zeal for defense preparations. It asked the governor for eight hundred men for the harbor batteries, one thousand pounds of powder, shot, barracks, signals, and the like.[99] All this cost the town nothing, of course, and Hull was not convinced that the townspeople had any will to defend themselves. "Very little is doing here by the people of the town," he wrote on 25 April, "nor has it yet been in my power to convince them that we are in a state of war." The average citizen's impulse was to run. Merchant vessels and boats of all kinds were winging up the Piscataqua to Dover, Durham, and Exeter, loaded with family belongings and merchants' stocks. Two frigates had appeared off the harbor, making regular calls every two or three days. These were the *Junon* and the *Tenedos*, which had been stationed for the summer to cruise between Boston and Portsmouth.

By the beginning of May, Forts Constitution and McClary were in fair order and manned and the six gunboats in readiness. On 11 May came a second warning of impending attack, this time from Lockwood De-Forrest, a New Haven merchant and acquaintance of Captain Hull's. He had talked with a man just back from Bermuda, who said that an expedition was preparing or perhaps under way, to be joined by forces already on the coast, expressly for an attack on Portsmouth. There was already, said DeForrest, a considerable additional force off New London, and some of the ships were said to have traveling carriages for their guns. It was uncertain whether Captain David Milne of the *Bulwark* or Captain Hardy of the *Ramillies* was to command. Hull thanked him for the warning but said grimly, "I shall make one more effort to arouse the people, and if I cannot, I must stand as long as I can, but you must not be astonished to hear that they have done all they wish in this quarter, and have taken themselves off, as they did in that shameful affair at Pettipague."[100]

Hull's "one more effort" was a vigorous one. He sent copies of DeForrest's letter to all the military authorities and also "leaked" it to the newspapers. From the local army command he got nothing; even the one hundred men in Fort Sullivan were ordered to march away, but General Henry Burbeck at Boston assured Hull that "should the enemy appear, under a frowning aspect, everything shall be done for you, which the limited force under my command will justify."[101] One is impressed by the aspect of this which so exasperated Hull: the easy assumption that the British would be so leisurely in their attack as to allow reinforcements to assemble from as far away as Boston.

The best news from Washington was that Major Walbach was being ordered to take charge of the troops at Portsmouth. These were reinforced late in May by two companies of the Fortieth Regiment, rather than the one company that had been promised, and on 24 May, General Storer ordered out eight companies of New Hampshire militia, to total about five hundred men. Hull had asked for twice the number, but still it was an improvement.[102]

Although no attack was launched against Portsmouth, it would be wrong to see this as a false alarm. DeForrest's information was substantially correct. On 22 May the *Ramillies*, flagship of the New London blockading squadron, joined the ships off Boston, and on the twenty-seventh her commander, Sir Thomas M. Hardy, went on board the frigate *Nymphe* for a cruise to Portsmouth. The reason is given by one of the *Nymphe*'s lieutenants: "Sir Thomas Hardy came on board for the purpose of reconnoitring the coast, particularly Portsmouth, *preparatory to an expedition being sent there.*"[103]

On the morning of Sunday, 29 May, the frigates *Junon* and *Nymphe* rounded the Isles of Shoals and anchored within three miles of the Portsmouth lighthouse. Lieutenant Napier of the *Nymphe* made notes on the day's activity:

Fort Independence [Constitution] appears very strong, but low, and commanded by Fort Kittery [McClary], which however could rake any ship engaging it. There is, besides these, another fort [Washington] which commands the harbour, on Pearce's Island, lately put into repair. The people in a great fright and all the militia concentrated there expecting an attack. . . . Sounded the southern passage [Little Harbor] and found it quite safe. . . . Gunboats seemed disposed to try our fire but second thoughts appeared to have weight and they returned without coming within gun shot. . . . We understand there is a fire ship ready in case of an attack by the English. The seventy-four gun ship, which is building, quite concealed by an immense wooden shed, is to be launched in August.[104]

Needless to say, the near approach of the two frigates spread alarm in the town. Fright was greatly increased on Monday when one of the *Junon*'s boats chased a schooner ashore at Rye Beach, but this incident afforded the militia a chance for a small success. About fifteen men secreted themselves behind a wall near the shore and, when the boat's crew attempted to take possession of the schooner, opened fire with muskets, wounding two men. The boat, having only a few muskets and lacking the customary boat carronade, retreated. Once the danger had passed, about three hundred of the local inhabitants assembled at the spot. The British had their revenge, however, as Napier described: "Made a few signals with guns to alarm the coast by way of a frolic, which succeeded. They, conceiving the British Fleet to be off the port, assembled all their militia and regulars to repel the invasion."[105] After this demonstration the two frigates weighed anchor in the evening and stood for Cape Cod.

The summer that followed was one of extreme frustration, anxiety, and occasional panic. Hull suggested despondently that if a drawing were to be made of the 74, it should be done soon, or there would be nothing from which to make it. His continued appeals to the secretary evoked either cold denials or heavy sarcasm:

> The want of seamen has, as you have seen, compelled the Department to strip from ships that were ready for sea to man those on the lakes. Are we to strip the remainder in order to defend those that are building in the Atlantic ports? If so, policy and economy would dictate the burning of the latter, in order to remove the temptation, rather than to defend them at an expense far transcending their value.[106]

Having failed to arouse the national government to action, Hull turned again to the state and local authorities. He had gotten a fairly good response thus far from Gilman, considering that the latter was a Federalist, but Hull had the misfortune to command a point at the junction of two states, and he was about to meet the immovable object in the person of Governor Caleb Strong of Massachusetts. The navy yard island was still a part of Massachusetts. So was the nearby Kittery shore and all the territory to the east; so also was Seavey's Island, the site of Fort Sullivan.

Caleb Strong was an extreme Federalist. His conduct during the war would have been ridiculous had it not been so dangerous. He had refused to call out the state militia in 1812 to defend the coast of Maine; when he finally called them on 6 September 1814, a week after Castine had been occupied, he placed them under a state major general so that they might not be made part of any national force. His reference to Great Britain as "the bulwark of our holy Protestant religion" afforded much merriment in the Republican press, especially after HMS *Bulwark* appeared as flagship of the blockading squadron off Boston. A key supporter of the Hartford Convention and the movement for disunion, Strong was willing to sacrifice a large part of Maine in order to preserve the fishing rights of the people of Massachusetts; he could scarcely be counted on to aid in the defense of national property at Portsmouth.[107]

More cooperation was forthcoming from the Regular Army after the *Bulwark* staged a raid at Saco on 16 June. But on the night of 21 June occurred the worst alarm of the war, and it served to convince Hull that no force but the regular troops and seamen was to be relied on. There had been reports of an attack at Bath and Wiscasset the previous day, and during the night the guard at Rye, a few miles south of Portsmouth, saw suspicious boats and raised the alarm. The town flew to arms, and the *Gazette* beamed: "It was gratifying to observe the order and regularity with which the militia assembled, and that no confusion ensued, although the alarm was made at midnight." But Hull, after spending a night on the island with his seamen on guard, observed bitterly to Walbach: "As I expected, my friend, not a soul came near me last night from the town so that you see we must take care of ourselves."[108]

As a result of this scare, the six gunboats were divided into two units, one division to be constantly at the lighthouse on guard. Three days after the alarm the New Hampshire legislature appropriated $50,000 for the defense of Portsmouth, but Governor Gilman had received a letter from Secretary of War John Armstrong blandly stating that the army and navy forces at Portsmouth were adequate to defend the harbor against boats—"the only mode of attack to be apprehended"—and Gilman promptly disbanded the militia. By 20 July they had marched away, leaving Forts Sullivan and Washington empty. Even the Federalist *Oracle* remarked: "The *Tenedos* frigate visited us on Thursday, '*To see the neakedness of the land have ye come?*'"[109]

In August the citizens convinced themselves that no attacks would be made during the peace negotiations, but Hull was now at the yard day and night to supervise the defense and to hurry the ship to completion. Ann was partially consoled in his absence by a visit from her mother and three of her sisters. She left on 20 August to accompany them home. Isaac was almost too busy to be lonely, for as he told Mary:

> If you knew what I have to do you would write me often and not look for an answer to all your letters. My time is not, as you say, devoted to Ann but to my ship and three or four hundred men at work on her. I see but little of Ann as she lives in town and myself on the island; you may well suppose how unpleasant her situation is when among strangers, not a female that she visits on terms of intimacy, and you well know how much an intimate friend is wanting in such a lonely situation. I am now building an elegant house where I hope she will soon be able to join me and then my time may be more with her. You must and ought to love her, Mary, for she is all that can possibly be wished for by man. I am indeed truly happy in getting such a woman.

Even young Joseph was suffering from his uncle's devotion to duty: "Joseph is growing very fast and would do very well if we had a school for him, but now Ann is gone he has no one to take care of him and he appears much disposed to play."[110]

Having made up their minds that no attack would come, the citizens of Portsmouth received with shocked dismay, on 2 September, the news of the British invasion of the Penobscot. That enemy occupation would be extended along the coast seemed certain. A town meeting the next day called on the governor for protection; on 5 September the great man himself arrived to take command of the militia. Hull still believed that "no dependence can be placed in the inhabitants of the town to defend anything more than themselves," and perhaps not even that.[111] Every available man in the yard was at work removing the stores of the *Congress* and all the movable United States property from Portsmouth up the river to Exeter. The 74 still lay temptingly on the stocks, and she was the object of Hull's greatest solicitude. He could not possibly get her in the water in less than two weeks; paradoxically, the panic-stricken state of the countryside delayed her preparation because the carpenters and caulkers were being called away to join the militia. If he could get her into the stream and arm her, Hull thought she could not be destroyed unless the enemy brought another 74 alongside her. The guard boat reported the force off the harbor as three 74s, two frigates, and three tenders, "a force much larger than is necessary for merely blockading," Hull thought. "What their intention is I know not."[112]

Governor Gilman lost no time in calling on Hull for the loan of the shot, powder, and musket balls needed by the town. Word had been received that the British had forced the destruction of the *Adams* in the Penobscot. Hull remarked bitterly to Jones:

> Be assured, notwithstanding all that has been said to you about the security of this harbour, and the difficulty of taking the place, it is not safe, and so sensible are the inhabitants now of it, that they are moving off in all directions; and to their shame be it known they have not fixed ammunition sufficient to defend themselves with, for one half hour's close action. . . . General Dearborn has ordered out twelve hundred men. They will be here in six or eight days but probably without being half armed, or if they have arms not more than one to ten will be likely to have the same calibre, consequently will require different balls to suit them.[113]

That same day the Portsmouth defense committee received a letter from a Massachusetts legislator in Belfast, Maine, saying that the British had evacuated Belfast on the morning of 6 September with the avowed purpose of attacking Portland and Portsmouth. Governor Gilman, who by this time had removed himself to Exeter, ordered the whole of the state militia into readiness and even requested the exempts to organize. Several detachments were ordered to march for Portsmouth immediately. A company of artillery arrived from Concord, fifty miles inland. Even the ladies of the town turned out at the state house to make cannon and musket cartridges. It appeared that General Clement Storer of the militia was right, so far as New Hampshire went, when he trumpeted that "difference of sentiment on political questions was magnanimously merged in the all important object of prompt and energetic preparations for the DEFENCE OF OUR COUNTRY."[114]

But, while Portsmouth bristled with armed men, the Maine shore remained undefended. By 11 September the refugees from the late *Adams* were arriving in town; the roads to the interior were choked with wagonloads of furniture and fleeing citizens.[115] There were about 1,000 militia in and around Portsmouth, not all of them armed. Hull's confidence in them was not increased by the behavior of the militia at Hampden, Maine, whose flight had led to the destruction of the *Adams*. His greatest hope now was in her crew, some 230 strong, men who were trained to handle artillery and to face enemy fire. As they straggled in by twos and threes from Hampden, Hull sent them to man the forts and batteries. Great was his chagrin, then, when on 15 September, Captain Charles Morris, late commander of the *Adams*, told him that Commodore Bainbridge had ordered him to transfer 30 of the *Adams*'s crew to Boston. Hull wrote Bainbridge an eloquent letter, concluding:

> Will you then take another view of my situation and let these men remain, at any rate until they all come in, or until we can learn what has become of the force that threatens us to the Eastward. I shall most cheerfully join you with all my force, should you require it first, and feel assured that you will not let me want for your aid, if in your power to give it; but, my friend, I am ashamed of all around me, and blush for my degraded country; all is going, and God only knows what can save it from ruin, unless by the hand of him, we can raise the people. Let me hear from you, and for God's sake leave the men.[116]

This appeal, one would suppose, must have softened the stoniest heart, but it made no impression on Bainbridge. The men marched away on 19 September. Hull reported on the twenty-first that, although there were more than two thousand militia at Portsmouth, the service of half of them would expire in a week; there were none, of course, on the Maine side.

A week later the *Gazette* published two alarming letters. One, dated at Bangor on 12 September, said that a strong enemy expedition was fitting at Castine, and

> we think here they will pay you a visit very soon at PORTSMOUTH. I understand considerable public property is removed up the river; if that [is] the case

you may expect they will land at some out port and come on your backs before you are aware of it; they move with the greatest rapidity possible. I would have you be all on your guard. The troops here appear to be all veterans; they are part of Wellington's army, direct from Spain.

An attack of that nature was, of course, just what Hull feared. A second letter, from Lancaster, Pennsylvania, added the grisly report that the forces in the Chesapeake were also preparing to cooperate in the attack on the eastern seaboard.[117] Reassurance had come from the secretary, however, that the men of the *Adams* would be returned. Jones was incensed at Bainbridge for taking men from outside his own command on the pretext of being Hull's superior. He wrote the commodore curtly on 26 September to return the men immediately to Portsmouth. Bainbridge replied pettishly on 1 October: "I have received your order of the 26th ulto. and in obedience thereto, however injurious it may prove to the service, I instantly comply with it." But he was so peeved with Hull for having reported the incident to Jones that he refused to attend the launch of the 74 at Portsmouth, preferring to remain at Boston.[118]

For the ship was ready to be launched at last. Hull had been so preoccupied with getting her ready and with the exigencies of defense that he had forgotten to ask the secretary what name to give her; the fact that Jones did not receive his belated request until 22 September probably accounts for the launch being delayed a week beyond Hull's expectation. On the twenty-eighth invitations to the launching went out to the officers at Boston and to such dignitaries as Governor Gilman, former governor John Langdon, and the officers of the army near Portsmouth, but advance notice was kept out of the newspapers for reasons of security.

At sunrise on Saturday, 1 October 1814, the buildings at the yard, the forts, and the gunboats and privateers in the harbor blossomed with banners. Two of the ships dressed themselves out in a medley of European flags. By 11:30 A.M. a sizable crowd had gathered and all preparations had ceased. At 12:30 P.M. precisely the ship was christened the *Washington* and "started from the stocks and glided with the utmost majesty and grandeur into that element of which we trust she will be the pride and boast. The launch is said by connoisseurs to have been one of the most elegant and perfect ever witnessed."[119] As the *Washington* went down the ways, she was greeted by a "federal salute" from the navy yard, Fort Constitution, and the privateers *Harpy* and *America*, and by the cheers of the spectators and of those on her decks, including Lieutenant Thomas A. Beatty, who wrote: "She made a most glorious launch. . . . You can't imagine the pleasing sensation I felt at the time

Launch of the *Washington*, 74, at Portsmouth, New Hampshire, 1 October 1814. Collection of Nina Fletcher Little. Used by permission.

she was leaving the place where she was built for her element."[120] The workmen who had built the ship were served an "elegant collation," and the town congratulated itself on being the only port in America where *two* line-of-battle ships had been launched.[121]

It was a perfect launch and a happy day; Hull cloaked his emotions beneath a studied terseness when he wrote the secretary: "I have the honour to inform you that the Washington was yesterday launched without the slightest injury or accident and I am proud to say she is worthy of the name she bears." Two days later he allowed himself to say, "I most certainly think her one of the best ships in the world."[122] Within a week the ship's bottom had been coppered and the men and officers of the *Adams* sent into her as a temporary crew, with the guns of the *Congress* mounted on board for her protection. "I now think her safe from the enemy," Hull wrote, "unless they come up the river with something much heavier than she is, and I have my doubts whether they will attempt that."[123]

By the end of October the militia force at Portsmouth approached three thousand men, but soon thereafter the companies began to withdraw, as the cruising season was over. The state governments spent part of the winter trying to recover the cost of the militia from the national government, and the local citizenry were no less enterprising. But they had little hope of collecting, for the government was bankrupt. The October remittance to Navy Agent Henry Langdon was $25,000 in Treasury notes. These notes were already in a condition of acute depreciation, yet even the sum remitted, had it passed at face value, would not have been enough. The agents were being ordered to establish priorities for disbursement of funds: recruiting and transportation first, then pay "in part, if not the whole," provisions third, and last "other supplies of the most immediate necessity."[124] At Portsmouth, moreover, were the men of the *Adams*, who were due to be paid off between November 1814 and March 1815. They were not pleased at the idea of getting depreciated Treasury paper for their pay; still, it was better than nothing, as Captain Morris remarked: "Nor do I see how we shall be able to subsist ourselves much longer unless we conclude to bear the loss upon Treasury paper for our pay," he wrote to William S. Rogers, purser of the *Adams*. "I am sometimes almost tempted to fear they are better now than they will be hereafter and that it will be better to lose 15 than 20 or 30 percent."[125]

Hull wrote the secretary that he was being forced to discharge men without being able to pay them and that many of the seamen, needing ready money, were obliged to sell their pay tickets at a discount of 30 to 50 percent. Officers on the station did not have enough cash to pay for their washing or to purchase winter clothing—a particular problem for the men from the *Adams,* who had lost everything in the burning ship. The secretary's not very helpful reply to this appeal was a suggestion that, if the men were going to sell their pay tickets at a discount, it would be better to give them nothing at all. He had, he said, no money to send but hoped that new arrangements could soon be made. "In the mean time this state of things has cost me excessive anxiety."[126]

On the other end of the line the cost was something more than anxiety. The *Congress* was again fitting out, but Langdon could not purchase provisions for her cruise. Contracts for the *Washington* were in suspension for want of funds. Treasury notes were discounted at 20 to 25 percent by mid-November, and the merchants were setting their prices accordingly. Since the navy agents could not discount the government paper, being held accountable for the entire amount received, they were powerless to purchase many items.

The situation bore heavily on Isaac Hull. A letter he wrote to Mary Wheeler Hull at this time reveals the depth of his depression. Having put young Joseph in a situation to advance himself—he was now assigned to the *Congress*—he was concerned about the two little sisters at school in Middletown. He urged that great care be taken about their expenses, for their inheritance would be small and his own income was not sufficient to support them for long. Perhaps the constant stream of family visits was causing him to worry over his expenses as well. Ann's sisters were paying another call:

> My dear sister, if you could see me from day to day you would wonder that I write to my friends at all, for I come home so tired from the Yard that I am willing to go to rest. I am now alone. Ann and her sisters are out to spend the evening. They of course would not do that without me if I could go with them. . . . Joseph is well. . . . I hope he will make a fine fellow, but all I can do I cannot make him attend to his school. He had much rather be in the top.

A postscript to the letter reveals his uneasiness. "Where [are] Daniel and Henry that they do not write me? I dreamt that Henry hung himself not long since. I hope I may not hear bad news."[127]

While Ann had her sisters for society, Isaac Hull was more and more alone at this anxious time. Joshua Blake had gone home to Worcester soon after the *Washington* was launched. Thomas Chew was at Washington settling his accounts and keeping Hull au courant on doings at the capital. Major Walbach also left for Washington in late November. Hull forwarded him introductory letters to Secretary of the Navy Jones and to Secretary of War Monroe, together with assurances that his family were well despite an earthquake on the night of 28 November. Portsmouth had quivered for nearly a minute, but no substantial damage was done.[128]

The house on the island was still unfinished, and the men remained unpaid. Hull wrote Senator Jeremiah Mason that Mrs. Hull visited the senator's wife frequently, but he himself had gone but once, as he seldom left the island before dark. The financial situation was damaging to the local people as well as to the navy: "we are now owing almost every poor man within twenty miles of us, and cannot pay them. Something must be done soon or they must starve."[129]

The suspension of specie payments by the banks had made Hull fearful of losing his "little all," which he had invested in the Bank of America at New York. He wrote anxiously to Oliver Wolcott to ask whether he might hope to recover his investment. "As to a dividend, I do not expect any." Wolcott replied soothingly that, although the directors of the bank in question had treated him shabbily in the course of the last election (Wolcott had switched from federalism to republicanism, the ultimate crime in the eyes of Federalists), the institution was sound. The suspension of specie payments was, he thought, rather beneficial to the stockholders than otherwise. United States bonds, despite present dark prospects, he thought better security than bank stock. Land was safest of all but would yield little income.[130]

On 1 December, William Jones resigned his office as secretary of the navy; Hull's next plea for funds fell on the even less responsive ears of Chief Clerk Benjamin Homans:

> I need not inform you the distress the families of these poor men experience, by our not being able to pay them, particularly those that have left to their wives half pay allotments. . . . It would indeed be of the first importance to pay these men, and the carpenters who have been at work these three months past, if it could possibly be done. Many of them have left us to travel from sixty to one hundred miles without a dollar to pay their way. I have myself advanced to them three hundred dollars, each five and ten dollars to pay their expenses home, and you will readily conceive the feelings of those men when they are informed that they must be discharged, and return to their families without taking with them the means of providing for a long winter.[131]

Homans, however, was a man who apparently had great difficulty in conceiving the feelings of others. He returned no reply to this letter, nor to one of 10 December informing him that Langdon could purchase neither stores for the *Congress* nor the small items that the yard needed daily. Bainbridge expressed the common feeling of the navy officers toward the acting secretary when he wrote Rodgers: "I hope that B. Homans is not to be long continued in his present elevated station. He most assuredly is not qualified to fill it." Finances were in a bad state in Boston, too: "We cannot command in Boston one cent of either money in credit, or *Treasury* notes. The officers under my command are nearly ragged and almost starving. I never did expect to see our country brought to this *low ebb.*"[132]

But the war was dragging its weary length to a close. News of the treaty signed at Ghent on Christmas Eve did not instantly reach the United States, so an apprehensive winter of preparation for the war in 1815 was passed at Portsmouth as elsewhere. Purser Nathaniel Lyde thought that "if we do not have peace before the spring we shall have to run here, as we shall have nothing to defend ourselves with. Many families are now preparing to remove into the back country by March next. There has been here such a nest of privateersmen that they are alarmed, fearful of losing all they have gained."[133] Lyde was also "wearied out with the cry after money," but by the end of January the new secretary of the navy, Benjamin W. Crowninshield, was again dispensing Treasury notes. This is not to say that all was well: in mid-February Hull sent a letter which was calculated to be a home appeal to a Salem man like Crowninshield: the men from the *Congress*, he said were selling their pay tickets at a 50 to 75 percent discount; most of the men now to be discharged from the yard were from Salem and Marblehead and had large families to support. "As you are well acquainted with the characters and habits of the seamen from Marblehead, and well know how much the Navy is indebted to that little town for steady good men, I am sure you will pardon me for taking such an interest in their behalf." Crowninshield sent the money.

Within days came the welcome news of peace. A few, like John Rodgers, might "ever regret that anything occurred to prevent my trying [a new frigate's] *stings* on John Bull's hide,"[134] but Isaac Hull had had all—more than all—the war he wanted. He recalled with distaste the sleepless nights of that long September and the lonely weeks spent on the island with scarcely a chance to visit his wife in town. "I have to congratulate you on the news of peace," he wrote a friend on 21 February, "and I hope it will be many years before we are again involved in war."[135]

10

Commissioner and Commandant

In the winter of 1814–15 Isaac Hull watched with keen interest the news from Washington, as conveyed through the papers and by letters from friends like Chew and Walbach. In its sessions of that year, Congress began to give serious attention to putting the navy on a permanent and efficient basis. To naval men who had lived through the fifteen years before the War of 1812 it was never clear, from one administration to the next, whether the service would continue to exist. Its successes against the British seemed to assure its continuance as a major branch of national defense, but the strains put upon the establishment by the war also pointed to a need for better organization.

Two major areas were suggested for reform. One was the rank of naval officers; the other, the organization of naval administration. While the army had established ten grades for its officers, up to the rank of major general, the naval officer could hope for only three promotions: to lieutenant, master commandant, and captain. An officer might be promoted to the rank of captain when in his early thirties, but he had nowhere to go beyond that. The situation with regard to the title of commodore, used to designate a captain who commanded, or had commanded, a squadron on separate service, was chaotic. There was no such rank; nor was there extra pay connected with the honorific. But it was a distinction beyond captain, and as a result any officer who commanded more than one vessel, even if it was only a flotilla of gunboats, immediately mounted two silver stars on his epaulets; styled himself commodore; and was so called thereafter, whether in active command or not.

On 7 November 1814 Senator Samuel W. Dana of Connecticut introduced two resolutions on the subject of naval rank that were referred to a committee headed by Senator Charles Tait. The committee was asked to inquire "what provision should be made for the appointment of officers above the grade of captain," and also "what provision should be made for conferring naval rank by brevet, in consideration of meritorious service."[1] While the committee was considering the resolutions, Senator David Daggett of Connecticut forwarded a copy to Hull for his comments. The resolutions called forth one of Hull's most eloquent statements on the subject of naval policy, and also gave him an opportunity to air a private grievance or two. Hull was in the unfortunate position of being still a captain, while at least six officers junior to him—two of them masters commandant—called themselves "commodore," and he resented it.[2] In reply to Daggett's letter he wrote:

> As for myself, I am so low on the list [ninth] that I can have but little to hope for either by admirals being made, or even by brevet rank, yet I hope something in that way will be done. It has long since been my opinion that at least three admirals ought to be made, and that some arrangement ought to be made to prevent every midshipman that has command of a gunboat on a separate station taking on himself the name of *Commodore*. If the government wish a grade between a captain and an admiral let them either do away their commodores altogether and substitute *brevet* rank, or give out commissions for commodores and attach to that grade of officers pay and emoluments accordingly. You now see, not infrequently, three commodores' broad pendants flying when there are not more than four ships together. Indeed, we now have so many commodores, that to be a captain is rather of the two the most honorable.

Hull thought that if the navy were to have any future, "which I almost despair of," the rank of admiral must be created. This he said without personal ambition. But he thought that Congress was unlikely to grant so much, considering the treatment it had accorded the navy in the past. He recalled with anger the reception given to a request by the naval officers in 1808 that their families be allowed pensions such as were given to the widows and orphans of army officers: "our memorial presented to Congress a few years since was treated with so much indelicacy (I may say indecency) that every officer had determined never to ask again for anything." He suggested that Daggett review the debates on the memorial, in which case, "I am sure you will blush for some that spoke against it."

This was indeed a painful memory. The officers had petitioned Congress in 1808, and again in 1810, that the half pay of unemployed naval officers might include their rations and that the ration be computed at $0.28, as it had been before 1801. They also asked that the pay of masters commandant and of midshipmen be increased. The midshipman's salary of $228 per year did not suffice for his education and subsistence, as they pointed out, particularly when the young men were dispersed in the gunboats and unable to share expenses in a mess.[3] But it was the summary rejection of the appeal for a pension plan similar to that accorded the army that most rankled Hull:

They even went so far as to say that the daughters of officers killed fighting for their country, could when *fifteen* get a living for themselves, meaning, I suppose, that they could take in washing or something still worse. What men of feeling could bear such treatment, when the world will and must acknowledge what they have asked was asked respectfully and ought to have been granted?

Thoughts of the rejected memorial led Hull to reflect on another, more personal slight: the discrepancy between the prize money allowed for the *Guerrière* and that given for the *Macedonian* and other captures.

There has not been an action fought since, even by a sloop of war, but the commander has shared equal honors and more money. Look at the U[nited] States and Macedonian,—there Commo[dore] Decatur shared upwards of thirty thousand dollars, and for what? Because he was not *so unfortunate* as to shoot away her masts and got her safe in, for which he was allowed the whole of the ship, when the world knows that the Guerrière was a much heavier ship, [than the *Macedonian*] and the U[nited] States full as heavy, indeed heavier than the Constitution. Why these things are, I know not; but they are facts. I hope you will pardon my going aside from your inquiries, but when I am led to think on the subject of the Navy I cannot but feel hurt at many things relative to myself that have taken place.[4]

Secretary of the Navy William Jones supported the idea of a grade of rear admiral for the time being, with the addition of the grades of vice admiral and admiral when the navy increased sufficiently to warrant it. He pointed out in his letter to Senator Tait that Great Britain had more than two hundred admirals in active service. The committee in its report, presented to the Senate on 28 November, reasoned that brevet rank was not needed, since it had long been the policy in the navy to promote officers directly as a reward for meritorious service, but it favored the establishment of a permanent grade above that of captain. Such a rank would encourage the officers of the navy to greater attainments in their profession, especially in squadron tactics:

If you expect men to labor for the highest qualifications in their professions, it is necessary to open to them the way to the station requiring them. The surest means by which you will probably induce the officers to qualify themselves for an admiral's command, is to create that grade in the navy: thereby requiring in the same act great professional attainments, and offering a reward for them.[5]

Hull, on reflection, agreed with the committee on the subject of brevets. "Whatever may be done for us," he urged Daggett in a second letter, "let me ask of you to avoid brevet rank in the Navy. It must and will interfere when officers holding that rank meet at sea, which cannot as on land be avoided."[6] But the proposal for advanced rank, like all earlier attempts to establish admirals in the American navy, died in Congress. Nearly fifty years would pass before the navy boasted an admiral.

The second and more immediately important line of action was the reorganization of the Navy Department. The strains of the war had proved that the business of the navy could no longer be handled by one man, and as early as March 1814 a committee was appointed in the House to consider the question of reform. The report of the secretary of the navy, presented to the Senate on 16 November, contained a bill for this purpose. The most important feature of the bill was its proposal to establish a board of naval inspectors to advise the navy secretary and to handle the routine business of the navy. There were to be five inspectors: three naval captains and two civilians, the president to appoint one member to preside and the secretary of the navy to assign the members their duties. This proposal was circulated to the naval captains both by the Senate committee that received it and by Representative William Reed of Massachusetts, chairman of the House Committee on Naval Affairs.

Hull had already said in his letter to Daggett of 18 November:

> A Navy Board must be established and be composed of men capable of bringing every thing that relates to a Navy into some sort of system and make regulations for its government that will be sure to fit out our ships at the least possible expense. This can only be done by men who know what is necessary for the equipment of a ship of each class. When they have fixed on what is absolutely necessary, let them allow it and if the commander gets anything more, make him pay for it out of his own pocket, or be held accountable to the Department.

As this letter indicates, one of the chief abuses intended to be corrected by the appointment of a board was the practice of allowing each commander to fit and alter his ship to suit himself.

The day after writing this letter, Hull received from Daggett a copy of the secretary's report. In a letter marked *"Private"* he repeated his previous statement and went on to discuss another part of the document. The secretary included a recommendation for more 74s and frigates, but Congress had just authorized the purchase of a number of small craft to be organized into "flying squadrons" for raids on enemy commerce. Hull was much opposed to the small-craft policy and told Daggett that American successes to date were due to the fact that American vessels were in every case of the largest size for their class, which gave them an instant advantage over their British opponents. The vessels to be built or purchased for the flying squadrons, on the other hand, would disgrace a privateer.[7] He repeated his remarks the following week to Senator Jeremiah Mason of New Hampshire. Pointing to the career of the *Wasp,* which had destroyed two enemy sloops of her own rate and was able to continue her cruise, he urged continuing to build vessels that were of the largest size for their class. "Surely," he scoffed, "there can be nothing like a Navy in vessels of eight guns. I wish to God that nothing less than 22 or 24 had been built."[8]

The circular from Representative Reed of the House committee reached Hull a few days later. In his reply he assented generally to the secretary's proposals and suggested that the members of the navy board be immediately appointed, so that they, with the secretary, could formulate a complete plan for reform to lay before the next Congress.

> The board would have time to examine particularly into the establishment as it now is; they would, some of them, be able to visit the different naval establishments and inform themselves what improvements are necessary, and how far it will be expedient to occupy all the Navy Yards we now have, or rather whether it will not be advisable to fix on some two or three establishments as being important ones and only improve others for temporary purposes, such as repairing ships, or giving them an outfit should they fall in, and cannot without risk get to the larger establishments. In short, a Board appointed immediately and to commence on the duties of the office, would in my opinion, as I have before stated, lay before the government a system with such rules and regulations for the better government of the Navy as cannot fail to meet their approbation, and I am sure such as will save millions to the nation if we are to have a Navy of any magnitude.[9]

The replies of several of the captains were appended to the committee's report that was submitted to the House on 9 January 1815. There was a consensus among the officers that a board of three, rather than five, would be sufficient; that all should be naval captains; and that the senior captain should preside. These recommendations were followed in the legislation establishing the Board of Navy Commissioners, which was enacted on 7 February 1815. The distribution of duties between the board and the secretary of the navy was left vague. Each of the three members was to receive a salary of $3,500 and the franking privilege.

While these matters were still under debate, Captain Hull, accompanied by his wife, left Portsmouth on furlough about 2 January 1815. He passed through Salem en route to Boston and stopped to pay a call on the newly appointed secretary of the navy, Benjamin W. Crowninshield.[10] After spending a few days in Boston the Hulls proceeded to Saybrook and Derby, and from there to New York where, on 1 February, Hull was installed as an honorary member of the New York State Society of the Cincinnati. He also joined with six other captains in a testimonial to the New York navy agent, Dr. John Bullus. Shortly after his return to Portsmouth on 18 February, Hull wrote Bullus to say that he would be glad to have Lieutenant Samuel H. Bullus with him in the *Washington* if he should take her on a cruise. (Young Bullus, however, had had enough of navy life. He resigned from the navy in April.) Mrs. Hull had remained at Saybrook to nurse her mother, and Captain Hull, who did not relish bachelor life, was looking for an excuse to take her with him on a Mediterranean voyage. "What do you think of the times?" he asked Bullus. "Shall we have a lasting peace? Will you go out with Mrs. B. consul and agent at Gibraltar? Old [John] Gavino is too old. If you will go and I am ordered out I shall ask to take my baggage out also."[11]

Meanwhile, naval politicking went on unabated. The more ambitious officers were all eager to catch the ear of the new secretary. On 7 January, for example, H. A. S. Dearborn, the collector at Boston, wrote Crowninshield, though not without prompting from his old friend Bainbridge, that Commodore Bainbridge would be the perfect man to advise the secretary on the duties of his new office. "On first coming into office you will find great advantage to have near you an experienced officer with whom to confer for two or three weeks," he wrote. "I therefore recommend that you should order Com. Bainbridge on to Washington forthwith. I asked if he would like to go and tender his services in the way mentioned. . . . [H]e said he would go with pleasure."[12]

Crowninshield, however, had every intention of choosing his own advisors. His first major decision would be the selection of the members of the Board of Navy Commissioners. Hull had already expressed a concern about the selections, which he may have repeated to the secretary when they met at Salem:

> [The navy board] ought to be composed of some of the ablest and most active men such as Commodore Rodgers and Bainbridge, and many others that might be named, but if for the sake of getting rid of some of our oldest commanders they appoint them to the board they may as well not have it, and I much fear if care is not taken that some will make interest for the appointment that ought not to get it.[13]

He need not have worried. Soon after he reached Washington, Crowninshield applied to John Rodgers to accept the chairmanship of the board and to advise him on the selection of the other members. Rodgers, no shrinking violet, wrote Crowninshield a famous letter in which he gave his trenchant, if prejudiced opinion of the entire list of navy captains. He first declined the chairmanship for himself; but, while still writing the letter, he received news of the peace treaty, changed his mind, and accepted the appointment. His analysis of the "character, as well as of the pretensions of the several post captains of the Navy" dismissed from consideration eleven of the twenty-one, often with cutting descriptions; for example: "Captain [John] Shaw, although an amiable man, is by no means qualified for anything requiring the exercise of more than an ordinary share of intellect." Of Bainbridge he gave a diplomatic assessment:

> Captain Bainbridge is an excellent officer, uniting much practice with considerable theory. He is also industrious, and if there is any objection to him it is because he feels the importance of his own ~~consequence~~ abilities too sensibly to qualify him as well as he otherwise would be for a subordinate situation.[14]

He praised David Porter as "a man of far more than ordinary natural talents, indefatigable in whatever he undertakes and added to these, his acquirements, professional as well as more immediately scientific, are respectable." Charles Morris received a similar encomium. Rodgers described him as "a man of strong, discriminating mind, of considerable science, and unites perhaps as much if not more theoretical and practical knowledge than any man of his age in the service." His old friend Hull he included almost as an afterthought: "Captain Hull I had almost forgot to mention. He is nevertheless a man of most amiable disposition, and although he does not pretend to much science is however an excellent seaman and at the same time unites all the most essential qualifications necessary for such a situation." Rodgers concluded:

> [Were] I authorized to nominate the three captains to assist in the discharge of the duties of the Department over which you preside, I would name Bainbridge, Hull and Morris, otherwise, Hull, Porter and Morris. It is probable Bainbridge might prefer the situation he at present holds; out of respect to his rank and services it might be well, however, to make him the offer. If Bainbridge should refuse, Hull and Morris, neither of them having active commands at present, might be appointed without giving umbrage to any others. By this you see that I wish you to remain popular with the officers. You are certainly so at present with all I have conversed with.[15]

Two days later Rodgers requested a personal interview with Crowninshield to discuss the appointments; when the names of the first Board of Navy Commissioners went to the Senate the next week, they were John Rodgers, David Porter, and Isaac Hull.[16]

While John Rodgers was anything but an unprejudiced judge of his fellow officers, his assessments were, on the whole, accurate. In the case of Isaac Hull, Rodgers mentioned precisely his strongest assets: his good temper and practical good sense. He was a good colleague, neither quarrelsome nor overly "sensible of his own consequence." He had surmounted his lack of formal education by immersing himself in the practice of his profession. As his letters to Daggett, Mason, and Reed illustrate, Hull had given much thought to the subjects that were likely to come before the commissioners; he was well prepared for the work that lay ahead.

Within days after these events came news that Congress had declared war on Algiers in retaliation for depredations committed against American commerce during the previous three years. With the navy still in wartime fighting trim, it seemed an ideal time to strike a crushing blow against the old Barbary enemies. Two squadrons were organized. Decatur was to take one, with his flag in the new *Guerrière*, 44, and including two more frigates, two sloops, and five vessels of the "mosquito fleet" purchased near the end of the war with Britain. Bainbridge moved heaven and earth to get command of the other squadron. His ship, the *Independence*, was nearly ready, and he arranged to take her as his flagship, with two frigates, the new sloop *Erie*, and five small vessels.

Immediately after the declaration of war, and before the squadron assignments were made, Hull was uncertain how to act. He might ask to go in the *Washington* as part of a squadron but would do so only if Rodgers were the commander. He did not wish to sail under Bainbridge, much as he respected him. Moreover, Ann's mother was seriously ill. He did not want to leave his wife alone at Portsmouth, and should her mother die—which, in fact, she did in April—Ann could not remain at Saybrook. If Rodgers were commodore of the squadron, he would ask his permission to take her with him. It seemed a dubious service, at best: "I fear much that the expectations of our country could not be realized by sending out ships alone. They have no idea of the strength of the place and the difficulty of getting at them."[17] But on the following day he received a letter from Rodgers announcing the appointments to the navy board and the choice of Bainbridge to command the squadron. He was inclined to take the board appointment and remain with Rodgers:

> I notice, my friend, what you say about the command of the squadron and think of that service as you do: but little either of honor and glory, or the *other* thing will be gained. I am glad that our friend Bainbridge is to command. He will do honour to our country, and I am sure no country can boast of better men.
>
> Now then, my friend, to myself. I shall feel a pleasure in being appointed with you and our friend Porter and I know of a lady that will not have less pleasure in being near you and Mrs. R. I have a letter from her today wherein she mentions having received a letter from Mrs. [Tobias] Lear wherein she asks how her *dear* Captain Hull is. Mrs. H. proposes making a compromise: let Mrs. Lear call me what she pleases, and Mrs. H. call you what she pleases.

The main consideration for Hull, on deciding whether to accept the commissioner's appointment, was money. Though the salary of $3,500 was a substantial increase over a captain's pay, it would be more than offset by the expense of living in Washington. Rodgers and Porter, though not wealthy, were in more comfortable circumstances than Hull; both had income-producing property in land. Hull explained his alternatives to his friend:

> I have a fine ship under foot, or a pleasant shore station. To take the ship I must leave Mrs. H. lonely indeed, for we have no hopes of her mother's recovery, and [to remain] down here inactive, I should not like it. And to go to Washington I have no fortune to sport with and the pay will barely support us. What shall I do? I now want much your advice as a friend. . . . [S]ay what your arrangements are; whether you can be content to form a little domestic circle of our three little *ribs* and take in Mrs. Lear and live on our pay and be happy. Let me know your plans that I may make my mind up.[18]

At the same time, he wrote in similar vein to David Porter, promising that "I shall delay giving an answer until I know what you intend doing . . . and your acceptance as a member would go far towards bringing me with you."[19] Two days later he acknowledged a letter from Crowninshield, dated 20 February, informing him of his appointment. He wrote somewhat evasively: "I . . . duly appreciate the honor conferred on me by this appointment." But apparently he had by this time all but decided to accept, for he wrote the Portland navy agent on the same day that "I have orders to leave this for Washington in a few days."[20]

As a delaying measure, Hull had told Crowninshield that the state of the *Washington* required someone to superintend her; he would therefore remain at Portsmouth a short time, or until relieved by another officer. This gave him time to wait for Rodgers's and Porter's replies. By 15 March they had accepted their appointments, but Hull's acceptance was still awaited. Thomas Tingey, at the Washington Navy Yard, wrote to Charles Morris, who was at Portsmouth outfitting the *Congress* for the Mediterranean, that he hoped Hull would accept

> and thus add to our naval society in this city. If he has returned to Portsmouth ask him if I shall look out for a house for him, and until he gets settled, say to him he must quarter with me, and I'll give his good wife the first mess of green peas. I have them already three inches high.
>
> Our new Secretary is friendly to the Board, and I think very much so to the service generally, conducting his duty with an amiable demeanor, void of ambiguity and hauteur![21]

On 18 March, Crowninshield directed Hull to proceed to Washington immediately, "as your presence here is more indispensably necessary than at Portsmouth."[22] Hull was ill. As he wrote Crowninshield on the 20th, he had been confined to the house for three days but hoped to be on his way soon. He was well enough on Wednesday, the twenty-second, to attend a public dinner in his honor at 3:00 P.M. at Treadwell's Hotel, given "by a large and respectable number of the citizens of this town, (without distinction of party) as a public expression of their high sense of his brilliant achievements in the service of his country, of his correct and manly deportment while commanding here, and of his vigilance and activity in providing for the defense of this port." That was certainly deserved. More than one hundred men assembled for the festivities, including the army and navy officers, the French consul, and members of the clergy. Senator Jeremiah Mason presided in a hall decorated with portraits of the four presidents of the United States and paintings of the captures of the *Guerrière* and the *Macedonian*. "The greatest harmony and conviviality prevailed." Hull's volunteer toast was graceful: "The town of Portsmouth—may its prosperity equal its hospitality." As was customary, Senator Mason toasted Hull after his departure, and the French consul offered "The constructors of the Navy—may they bear in mind how much they are indebted to a strong and steady 'HULL.'"[23]

Returning home, Hull found a letter from John Rodgers, dated 16 March, urging him to accept the commissioner's appointment. Hull replied:

> I shall most certainly accept, indeed I suppose from what I have already said to the Secretary he will take it for granted that I have accepted, and I pray you to be assured that one of the greatest inducements I have in doing so is that you and myself and our little Charges may be near each other, and I know that Mrs. Hull has not now a wish ungratified.

It would not be surprising if Mrs. Hull's enthusiasm for the tall, black-browed Rodgers had provoked her husband to some jealousy, but he never expressed any doubts, except in fun:

> She has again and again repeated how happy she should be settled near you and Mrs. R. Indeed, the only fear I have [is] that you will be too near for Mrs. R. and myself. If, however, you do not behave we will pay you in your own coin—though I fear I am not so great a favorite with Mrs. R. as you are with Mrs. H.

In answering Tingey's letter, Hull had asked him to arrange lodgings at Mrs. Wadsworth's, but now Rodgers had approved his suggestion of 9 March that the Hull and Rodgers families lodge together. "Will you, then, fit me a room with you," Hull wrote. "[I]t will be much pleasanter not only for us, but Mrs. R. and Mrs. H. will frequently be obliged to be their own gallants and together they could do without us and we could do much in our leisure evenings, as I am sure you will not be tied down to office hours."

His illness, which resembled pleurisy, seemed nearly cured, and Hull expected to be on his way in two days. "At present I think I should come without Mrs. Hull and let her remain until the roads are better. Her mother is at the point of death and cannot be left as Mrs. H. is her all in sickness. . . . We have had two very heavy snow storms this month, and it is now snowing very hard and has been all night."[24] Rodgers was worried about the expense of keeping a carriage for his family at Washington, but on this point Hull was more expansive: "My dear Sir, your horses and carriage will not ruin you. I have had mine two years and have not yet stopped payment."

He was still confined to his room the next day. This illness may have prevented him from taking a last survey of the navy yard that, in the space of two years, he had transformed from a deserted island to a thriving, bustling establishment. His energy had added to the yard a shiphouse, a smithy, a mast-and-boat shed, a small hospital, a powder magazine, and the newly finished commandant's house—no mean feat in wartime. In short, he had founded the Portsmouth Navy Yard as an active station.

He had also built the *Washington*, which sailed for the Mediterranean in March 1816 as the flagship of Commodore Isaac Chauncey, to remain until 1818. It was her only major cruise. In her later years she was laid up as a receiving ship at New York and was broken up there in 1843. The *Washington*, the *Independence*, and the third wartime 74, the *Franklin*, were handsome ships, but their design was unsuccessful. They had a common fault: insufficient displacement. They did not carry their lower deck guns high enough above the water, in service condition, for them to be useful in any but the mildest weather. The *Independence* was worst of all, showing only 3 feet 10 inches freeboard between the water line and the sill of the lower gun ports when loaded for a six-month cruise. When Secretary Crowninshield learned of this in July 1815, he proposed that she be immediately razed to a frigate, but Bainbridge managed to get away to the Mediterranean before his darling could be mutilated. She was cut down at last in 1836 and thereafter was a very successful frigate. The tampering of Jones and Bainbridge with the draft of these ships certainly contributed to their failure, but they were useful to American builders as an experiment in design. By 1817 men like William Doughty and Henry Eckford were laying down ships of the line such as the *Ohio* and the *North Carolina* that rank with the best ships of that rate ever built.

Hull's lingering illness made the stagecoach journey nearly intolerable for him. He left Portsmouth at noon on Saturday, 25 March. By 5 April he had reached Philadelphia, where he hoped to break the land journey by taking a steamboat to Newcastle, Delaware.[25] But he was waylaid by old Commodore Alexander Murray, who had orders from Crowninshield to convene a court of inquiry at New York regarding the capture of the frigate *President*; Hull was designated a member of the court. Wearily he retraced his route to New York, not cheered by the ever distasteful prospect of sitting on a court. That duty consumed a week. Hull resumed his journey about 16 April but did not arrive in the capital until the twenty-fifth. Immediately he and the other commissioners met, formally constituted their board, and announced to the secretary that they were ready to proceed to business.[26]

The members had already had some correspondence about the appointment of their secretary. Rodgers recommended Littleton W. Tazewell, and he received Hull's hearty concurrence: "I should admire of all things to have him as a secretary and if he can in any way be prevailed on I should certainly recommend him. If his salary would not be enough it could be made up in some way." He tentatively mentioned his old friend Charles W. Goldsborough, who had lost his post as chief clerk when William Jones took over the Navy Department: "I find Goldsborough an applicant. I do not know how you like him. He is poor and wants help." At its first meeting the board chose Tazewell, but he declined the post and was replaced by James K. Paulding. Goldsborough and Charles Dewitt were made clerks.[27]

Already there was trouble brewing between the commissioners and the secretary. On the day Hull reached Washington the *National Intelligencer* published a front-page piece signed "D" (probably written by Porter) arguing that the commissioners "are not subject to the orders, nor under the control of the Secretary of the Navy, to the extent which some have supposed." The members of the board, said the correspondent, ought to be viewed as counselors to the secretary; they would operate under his superintendence but not under his control. "The truth is," the article concluded, "the Board have the right of managing all the concerns of the naval establishment of the United States, subject only to the superintendence, in certain cases, of the Secretary, and in others, of the Secretary and President of the United States."

That was far from being the secretary's opinion. Within weeks he and Rodgers were banging away at each other with verbal salvos, culminating in a blast from Crowninshield on 23 May:

> The tone and character of your correspondence with this Department are as unexpected as they appear, to me, extraordinary; I am not conscious that in

my official or personal conduct toward the members of your Board there exists any foundation for a course of proceeding which carries with it an air of hostility; but as I believe I know my duty and as I mean to perform it, with all the responsibility attached to it, I shall still abstain from entering into any altercation upon the topics of your letter, and submit it, with the rest of our correspondence to the President of the United States for his consideration.[28]

The law creating the board had been hastily drawn, and its language was equivocal. It said that the board "shall discharge all the ministerial duties . . . relative to the procurement of naval stores and materials, and the construction, armament, equipment and employment of vessels of war, as well as all other matters connected with the naval establishment of the United States." Interpretation of this passage turned on an understanding of the term "ministerial duties." In the view adopted by Rodgers and Porter—Hull is silent on the record—the law gave complete authority in all matters naval to the commissioners, leaving the secretary a ceremonial functionary whose only recognized duties were to attend cabinet meetings and to relay information to the board.[29] Naturally, Crowninshield did not see it that way. At the end of May the whole dispute was referred to President James Madison, and the commissioners huffily subsided into inactivity until his decision was received.

Being embroiled in such a controversy was the last thing Isaac Hull wanted. He was already unhappy at Washington on several counts: the weather was disagreeable in "this hot hole"; the expenses were astronomical; and with the board marking time until the limits of its authority were established, Hull was balked of any real activity. He was probably lonely as well, since Ann had not yet been able to leave Connecticut after her mother's death.[30]

Before laying aside their pens in late May the commissioners had made a promising start on gathering to themselves authority over the material aspects of the naval service. The groundwork thus laid remained a foundation for the future work of the board. They had set in motion inquiries into the state of naval hospitals and the feasibility of dry docks; had reported to the secretary, by request, on revenue cutters, with details of the number and size needed and the ports where they should be stationed; and had presented a thoughtful plan for regulating the recruiting service. They had also made a long report on navy yards, echoing the ideas that Hull had expressed to Congressman Reed in December. They declared that only the yards at Portsmouth and Boston were suitable for the reception of large ships at all seasons, though, with an eye to local political sensibilities, they recommended that the Washington Navy Yard be retained as a building site. The New York, Philadelphia, Baltimore, Norfolk, and Charleston yards, they thought, should be abandoned. Portsmouth and Boston were so close together that they favored closing the smaller yard and seeking two sites farther to the south—one possibly in Rhode Island or Connecticut, the other in Virginia—but not in Chesapeake Bay, which could be blockaded so easily. The recommendations in this report, however sensible, were politically impossible to implement; only the Baltimore and Charleston yards were phased out of existence in the following decades.[31]

This useful, if tedious work excited little public acclaim. Receiving a great deal more notice during May was the triumphant return of the *Constitution* from her last war cruise, with the corvette *Cyane* as prize. The newspapers were full of praise for "Old Ironsides." On 23 May a letter to the *Intelligencer* urged that she be made a national monument:

> Let us keep *"Old Iron Sides"* at home. She has, literally, become a *Nation's* Ship, and should be preserved. Not as a "sheer hulk, in ordinary" (for she is no *ordinary* vessel); but, in honorable pomp, as a glorious Monument of her own, and our other Naval Victories.

Hull echoed the same idea in his own idiom: "I do not know who will command old Iron Sides. . . . [T]he old ship ought to be hung up in a band box."[32]

By 12 June, President Madison had settled the dispute between the commissioners and the secretary in the latter's favor, and the four men held a reconciliation session at the Navy Office on the fifteenth. But Isaac Hull had already discovered an escape from these Washington doldrums. William Bainbridge was on the point of sailing for the Mediterranean, leaving the command of the navy yard at Boston vacant. Toward the end of June, Hull asked for the position, and by 3 July he was on his way north. Bainbridge's passion for the Mediterranean command had cooled slightly when he learned that Stephen Decatur was going out ahead of him, but he had convinced himself that Decatur would return as soon as Bainbridge arrived, leaving all his vessels under Bainbridge's command. The secretary's decision to survey the *Independence* with an eye to razing her to a frigate put the spurs to Bainbridge, and he sailed on 2 July, before the survey could be held. Hull took over the navy yard at Boston on 17 July and settled in with satisfaction for a long stay.

Isaac Hull found the Charlestown Navy Yard in considerable disarray.[33] Although Bainbridge had done a good deal toward correcting the chaos left by Commodore Nicholson, his absorption in the *Independence* had led him to neglect the yard itself. Hull learned that no recent inventory of stores on hand had been done. Three days before his arrival a large storehouse had burned, and since no one knew what had been in the yard beforehand, there was no way of telling exactly what had been lost. Moreover, after the fire was extinguished the yard's officers had allowed the poor residents of Charlestown to carry off the remnants of provisions that were left in the cellar. Hull, anticipating the disapproval of the navy commissioners, halted the plunder and salvaged about fifty barrels of beef, which subsequently sold for $300.

The remains of the great shiphouse, blown down the previous fall, were still piled about the yard, and the timber remaining in the dock was not in good condition. Hull put his officers and men vigorously to work taking account of timber, stores, and other articles on hand; sawing refuse timber into firewood for the winter; and tidying up the yard. In addition, he had the *Enterprize,* the *United States,* and the *Alert* to outfit for the Mediterranean. His old lieutenant, Alexander S. Wadsworth, was fitting a purchased hermaphrodite schooner, the *Prometheus,* to join the Mediterranean squadron. The *Constitution* was there, laid up for extensive repairs. And the *Washington* was daily expected to arrive from Portsmouth for final outfitting, to relieve the squadron commanders in the Mediterranean. Luckily, the *United States,* the *Alert,* and the small vessels had gone to sea before a hurricane struck the coast on the morning of 23 September. Six merchant ships and brigs, torn from their moorings at Boston, drove on shore at the navy yard and narrowly missed colliding with the *Constitution.* A gunboat was wrecked, the fences blown down, windows broken, and chimneys toppled. Hull was relieved that the damage was no greater: "We have suffered some, but nothing compared with individuals. Many ships were sunk at the wharves in Boston, and damage done to other property to an immense amount."[34]

By mid-November, Hull had the yard in good order, the stores accounted for, and his family comfortably settled in the commandant's house. Ann had two of her sisters with her now: twenty-one-year-old Jannette and the youngest, Harriet Augusta, now twelve years old. Isaac Hull had the responsibility of sending Augusta, as well as his two nieces, Eliza and Sarah Ann, to school. These expenses and the cost of furnishing his house and of moving his belongings from Portsmouth, Washington, and Derby caused him a good deal of anxiety. He had lost $1,000 on the Merino sheep venture; his speculations in French laces, begun on his voyage in 1811–12, were still not settled; and in the course of the winter he was threatened with another heavy loss, as he told Mary in December: "A friend of mine is now at the point of death who owes me about all I am worth. Should he be taken away I shall suffer very much. Indeed, I have all sorts of troubles, but at home—there,

William Bainbridge. Portrait by Rembrandt Peale. Courtesy of the New-York Historical Society, New York City.

thank God, I am happy."[35] Early in November he appealed to Secretary Crowninshield to make arrangements with Treasury Secretary Dallas to send his pay, and some money owed him by the Navy Department, in cash or other form rather than Treasury notes, which were still discounted 15 to 22 percent at Boston. He grumbled about the differential enjoyed by officers serving on the lakes: "they are allowed 25% more than the officers on this station, while treasury notes were with them at par and with us at 20 to 22% discount, making a difference of nearly 50% in our pay."[36] Crowninshield and Dallas found that nothing could be done, however.

Despite money worries, Isaac Hull was happy in the society of old friends at Boston. Hortensia Chew was there with her little son Lawrence, awaiting the arrival of her husband in the *Washington*. Johnston Blakeley's widow was also in Boston with her baby daughter, born after the *Wasp* sailed from Portsmouth and disappeared forever. She had given up hope of her husband's return. Charles Morris and his new wife were passing through. But when William Bainbridge came back to Boston on 19 November, Isaac Hull's tranquillity was shattered, and an unpleasantness began that would endure, under varying guises, for eight years.

Bainbridge had long before made up his mind that the Charlestown Navy Yard was rightfully his, that he had been forced from it unjustly to go to the Mediterranean, and that he had a prescriptive right to resume the command on his return. The *Independence* was scarcely in sight of Tunis on 6 September when he scribbled a private letter to David Porter expressing his chagrin at finding that Stephen Decatur had already shot up the Algerian squadron and forced the dey to sign a treaty:

> Peace having taken place prior to my arrival in this sea I have been deprived of the opportunity of either *fighting* or negotiating. . . . Could I have possibly foreseen it, most assuredly I would not now be here. I was ordered from a most desirable situation and receive as a compensation the mere trouble and anxiety of a four months' cruise in a *seventy four*. . . . Whether I shall be permitted to return to my old station at Charlestown I know not. But as I left it in obedience to orders without having my wishes consulted I think I have some claim to reassume the command.[37]

Bainbridge had already managed to obliterate from his mind all the importunings he and his friends had made to secure the squadron command for him. An attack of measles suffered in the Mediterranean did not sweeten his temper. He led his sailors a miserable life, as usual, and wrote the navy commissioners that the new rules for governing the navy should include a wider application of capital punishment. His only satisfaction was with the *Independence:* she was wonderfully fast and weatherly, regrettably about two feet too shallow in the hold, but with that tiny (and all-important) exception she should be the model, he felt, for all future line-of-battle ships.

Bainbridge's letter to Porter preceded the arrival of the squadron in the United States by scarcely a week, giving Porter no time to warn Isaac Hull of what was about to happen. On Sunday morning, 20 November, when he came downstairs to breakfast Hull found a note from Bainbridge on his chair. As he reported in an agitated letter to John

Rodgers, the note was "couched in not a very pleasing style; saying that he had been ordered from this station without his consent and that he now claimed it again, that he considered his removal merely temporary, to be held for him until his return."[38] Bainbridge had in fact already written curt notes to Crowninshield and to the commissioners asking (demanding would be more correct) his reappointment as commander at Charlestown. He did not even bother to argue his claim, "trusting . . . that you will readily consider my claim as a just one, . . . notwithstanding Captain Hull's present residence and also that you are fully acquainted with the exertions which I have made for the improvement of that place, makes it unnecessary to trouble you with a detail in support of it."[39]

Hull's friends were indignant. Hortensia Chew reported to her husband the arrival of "the *modest B*" and his outrageous behavior, that "Captain H. has called, but no return has been made." Purser Chew responded that "the conduct of Comr. B. is such as I should expect from him. I am confident he will not be gratified in his wishes this time, that he ought not to be is certain in my opinion."[40]

Isaac Hull was not so confident, but he was thoroughly angry. In 1812 he had given up his ship to Bainbridge and then had looked after the Charlestown yard, affably vacating the spot on Bainbridge's return. But the years at Portsmouth with Bainbridge lording it over him as commander of a supposedly "superior" station had changed his outlook, and his financial anxieties confirmed him in his resolution not to be shunted aside by Bainbridge again. After one attempt at a conciliatory call, he decided to fight for his position. He wrote a firm letter to the secretary:

> I cannot see on what grounds he can claim this Yard any more than he could the New York station or any other that he might take it in his head to fancy; for when he took the command of the squadron to the Mediterranean, he of course did it from choice and forfeited all claims to this place as much as to any other.

Hull pointed out that the squadron had been expected to be absent one or two years, during which time such an important post could not be held vacant, and he reminded the secretary of his recent decision in favor of Samuel Evans, who had taken command of the New York Navy Yard in 1812 when Isaac Chauncey was transferred to Lake Ontario. Chauncey had wanted to return to the yard at the end of the war, but Crowninshield had upheld Evans's right to remain there. Hull said he would consider his own removal, under these circumstances, a blot on his reputation, since it would appear that his services had been somehow unsatisfactory. He concluded, with some pardonable exaggeration:

> I have been at an expense in providing for my family for the winter and settling them that would subject me to great inconvenience were they obliged to remove, and as this is the first time I have been able to settle down for a month at a time since I joined the service, I shall consider it a hard case independent of the mortification I must otherwise feel.[41]

In his letter to Rodgers he spoke more freely, alluding to the preferential treatment that he felt some officers were given:

> Is it to be believed that the Secretary of the Navy would have offered the command of this station (as he did) to Commodore Decatur to hold as a temporary thing until Commodore Bainbridge returned? No, I trust not, and I do hope that he would not have given it to me under any circumstances that he would not to Commodore Decatur.

The stiffness of his resolve was apparent: "I had once before kept the station for him and I did not believe that he would now expect my family, which is as dear to me as his can be to him, to be made a convenience of; nor do I intend they shall be without I am compelled so to do from higher authority."

Why did the easygoing Hull suddenly, in 1815, make a stand on his right to command the Charlestown Navy Yard? He must have foreseen that Bainbridge would make his life unpleasant if he balked him—though perhaps he did not anticipate the duration and intensity of the commodore's wrath. The repeated references to his family supply the key to Hull's change of attitude. His precarious finances had been of no great moment to him before 1812—except in the painful case of his blighted romance—and he had been willing to move about at the will of the Navy Department as long as he remained active. But now that he was a married man, with not only a wife to support but three brothers, five sisters-in-law, a nephew, and two nieces, it was imperative that he have a settled situation. He did not want to go to sea; nor was there a good opportunity to do so since he had given up the *Washington*. He had tried the commissioner's job but left it as soon as it became clear he could not make ends meet in the capital. In Boston he had friends and connections who could help him to make some prudent investments of his prize money, so that he could look forward to supplementing his pay with rents and dividends; and at the yard he could hope to live frugally. As he saw it, he was defending not merely his own interest but that of the many helpless people who depended on him. For their sake he would fight.

One other factor probably entered the equation. The victory over the *Guerrière* had given Hull a sense of himself as a man of some importance in the navy. He had been acclaimed a hero, the *first* hero of the war. He had earned the right to some consideration from his government. He meant to be treated at least as well as Decatur or Bainbridge— and why not? Isaac Hull was not just nobody—not anymore.

Secretary Crowninshield agreed with Hull and copied his arguments into the letter he sent Bainbridge on 4 December. Having decided that Hull was to retain the navy yard, however, he had to find a suitable command for Bainbridge. He hit on the idea of allowing Bainbridge to remain at Boston as commander afloat. This solution, of course, was the worst possible one for Hull. Bainbridge, surprised that Hull dared to resist him, had concluded that Hull had fomented a conspiracy to deprive him of the navy yard. As time went by he convinced himself of this more and more. An insight into his frame of mind is afforded by a letter he sent to David Porter when the latter declined to support his claim:

> Although I decidedly differ with you in Hull's *just* claim to the situation of that station and also to the advantages of keeping up two establishments, one ashore and the other afloat, I nevertheless thank you, for the interest which you take in my welfare. Did you know all the circumstances relative to Hull's obtaining the command of the Yard and the pledges of friendship and honor he was under to me, to effect if possible a temporary successor appointed in my absence, and which was consonant to his own feelings and desires when he expected to go out in the *Washington* and leave the command of the Yard at Portsmouth. And he also knew that *after Decatur's departure,* that if the Secretary of the Navy *condescended* to ask me whether I wish to leave the Navy Yard for the Mediterranean command that I would decline it and remain in the Yard; but neither his friendship or candor induced him to inform the Secretary of it, and the Secretary had not regard sufficiently for my feelings, or standing as an officer, to consult me on the Mediterranean expedition—but *ordered* me from a station to the exclusion of my return.[42]

No doubt the guileless Hull had given Bainbridge some such assurances of support before he sailed, or at least it was enough in character that Bainbridge may have supposed he had; but when it became clear that the secretary intended to appoint a successor unconditionally, Hull had no reason to stand aside for Bainbridge's sake. Now his own good nature was to be used as a club to beat him with.

Under the circumstances, Bainbridge set himself to make Hull's life difficult in every possible way. As he candidly explained to Porter,

> Captain Hull and myself cannot be on friendly terms. It is therefore necessary for the good of the service that the Navy Department explicitly defines the

extent of my command, and authority on this station as Senior Officer. I require nothing but what my seniority entitles me to but to the *full* extent of that I shall expect and cannot recede the least from.

With this view, Bainbridge arrogated to himself as commander afloat every conceivable authority, forcing Hull again and again to appeal to the navy board to arbitrate disputes.

Perhaps the most audacious thing the commodore did during this period was to pry into Hull's correspondence, seeking ways to discredit him. He was able to do this because the navy yard commandant's clerk, Benjamin H. Fosdick, was his own appointee and close confidant. As soon as Bainbridge became station commander, he made Fosdick his confidential clerk. Not only Hull's official letters of this period but Bainbridge's as well are copied in Fosdick's neat, minuscule hand.

This fact takes the mystery out of an occurrence in December 1815. Isaac Hull had continued as a nominal member of the Board of Navy Commissioners and had drawn his pay as such until 1 December. Meanwhile, Crowninshield had been searching without success for a replacement. He had offered the post to Chauncey and to Stewart; finally, in late December, Stephen Decatur accepted the appointment on his return from the Mediterranean. With the vacancy filled, Crowninshield wrote Hull to send his formal resignation, dated 1 December, and prepared an acceptance, which he dated 8 December. Hull responded immediately, on the twenty-third, expressing his gratitude to the secretary and his hope "that the knowledge you have of my family and the situation of my private concerns (which would not enable me to live at Washington as a Navy Commissioner ought) will prevent you from considering my resignation hasty or improper." On the same day Bainbridge wrote the secretary a letter copied in Fosdick's unmistakable script, saying that

> although I retained the opinion of the justice of my claim, I should not have troubled you again on the subject had I not this day been informed that Captain Hull had been written to from the Navy Board informing him that he might send in his resignation as a member of the Board of Navy Commissioners.
>
> It therefore appears, Sir, that when my application was made to you for orders to reassume the command of the Navy Yard at Charlestown, that my request was *refused* in *favor* of an officer holding, inconsistently, *two* honorable and lucrative situations.[43]

This letter netted him nothing, but the fact is that Bainbridge could not have known the contents of a letter to Hull from the Navy Department, on the very day Hull received it, except through Fosdick. Hull, unfortunately, had no inkling of Fosdick's duplicity, and he would not discover it for five years.

Emboldened perhaps by being privy to his enemy's letters, the commodore proceeded to marshal all the influence he possessed to bring pressure on the secretary to indulge him. His efforts became so clamorous that David Porter expressed dismay at Bainbridge's behavior. A mutual friend relayed his remarks, when Bainbridge assumed an expression of astonished innocence:

> I perceive by Lt. Finch's letter that you think the measures I have taken relative to my claim to resume the command of the Navy Yard have the character of coercing the government. Pray, my dear friend, how could possibly such an idea exist? Who could ever dream of an officer *coercing* his government with any measure? Surely God! the justification of a claim, or the honesty of self defense does not deserve such a construction.[44]

Bainbridge's direct efforts to regain the command subsided for a year, but in February 1817, when the Monroe administration was about to begin, he traveled to Washington to appeal to the new president to reverse his predecessor's decision. Before going, he exhibited around Boston a letter to the Navy Department setting forth allegations which Hull indignantly rejected in a letter to John Rodgers:

> At the time the Washington and Independence were building I believe we in a conversation we had about the ships, &c. . . . said how pleasant it would be if we could, after having built them, make a cruise and return to our stations again, which might then have been done without setting a precedent other than what was then established—as Commodore Chauncey held the command on the lakes and at New York at the same time.

The other charge, that he had intrigued against Bainbridge, made him even more irate:

> Again the Commodore, I am told, reports that I was under a pledge to use my influence to have the place kept for him when I was on my way to Washington as a member of the Board. I have now forgot what passed on this subject but let it be what it might it was previous to the decision of the Secretary of the Navy in favor of Captain Evans on the New York station. That being the case, it would indeed have been presumptuous in me to suppose anything I might have said or done could have done away a decision so wisely made, and to prove to you my sincerity as his friend I now assure you that after I got to Washington and before I arrived there I advised him again and again not to [leave] the station, telling him that it had been offered to Macdonough and would be given to Sinclair if Macdonough did not take it; that in consequence of that point being settled (and I thought very verily) the place could not be kept and this was long before I had any idea of asking for it, nor should I had it not been that I was sure someone else would have it.

Hull averred that he could establish that when Bainbridge sailed he had no idea that the station would be kept for him and that he was not, "as he asserts driven to sea against his will, but that he made interest to get the command." Moreover, "I can also establish that I have been longer in the service than he has and more actively employed and I am not willing to allow that he has done more than I have for the good of the country, his opinion to the contrary notwithstanding." The unkindest cut of all was that Susan Bainbridge had been gossiping about the Hulls around Boston:

> Before he left here some days he wrote the letter that I sent you and handed it about to a number of friends . . . without telling that he had been trying to injure me more than twelve months and that his wife had at least for that length of time been relating all the vulgar abuse against me and Mrs. Hull that she could think of—but thank God the two women are too well known in Boston to have her injure us here and I presume anything she might say to strangers would not. . . .[45]

In fact, Ann Hull and her sisters were not such positive factors as Isaac supposed. The Hart ladies evidently considered Charlestown society a bit beneath their notice, and the resulting sense, in the ladies of that town, of having been snubbed by a set of provincials made them willing to listen to any and all gossip about the family.

Hull threatened to make a public case for himself if Bainbridge continued his campaign, but on Rodgers's advice he remained quiet for the time being. President Monroe, who had been party to the cabinet discussions in 1815, declined to reverse Madison's ruling in the case. Bainbridge returned to Boston to sulk. Through Fosdick, he was still able to monitor Hull's correspondence, but he needed a more apt tool than Fosdick to really injure Isaac Hull. Not for several years did he find it, but when it came to hand the commodore knew well how to use it.

The work of the Charlestown Navy Yard was similar to that of the yard at Portsmouth, though on a grander scale. During the years from 1816 through 1821, Hull's time was occupied for the most part with the same tasks that had engrossed him in New Hampshire: improving the navy yard, repairing and tending old naval vessels, and building new ones.

A series of new ships, including six line-of-battle ships and nine frigates, was projected as early as 1816,[46] but the continued shortage of money in the first postwar years delayed the beginning of this project. Besides, the navy commissioners, with the conservative Rodgers at the helm, proceeded with great deliberation. In their first year they gave most attention to establishing procedural details; drawing up forms for reporting the status of personnel and supplies; and, of course, establishing the bounds of their authority. They had already decided that they ought to reduce the number of building yards, concentrating resources at only three or four locations in the North, the Middle States, and the South. Despite their early preference for Boston's excellent harbor and the facilities of the great port city, the commissioners took alarm late in 1816 at a report that there was a sandbar at the harbor entrance that might limit access by deep-draft vessels. To quiet their fears Hull went off in a boat on Christmas Eve of 1816 with pilot Robert Knox to sound the channel: the least depth they could find was four fathoms. Hull promised to make a full survey of the coast in the spring; it was eventually carried out in the summer by the *Prometheus*. Until it was completed, however, the commissioners were reluctant to build so much as a shed at Boston. In February they were still in doubt where "the great northern depot" would be located in their master plan.

The idea of reducing the number of building yards went the way of most schemes for cutting the military establishment. When the smoke of political battle had cleared, all the wartime yards were still in action, and the new 74s were laid down, severally, at Portsmouth, Boston, Norfolk, Philadelphia, and New York. The Washington yard also continued work, but because of the shallow water there it built no more 74s after 1819.

Hull's greatest effort in the first two years of his tenure at Charlestown was, therefore, directed to improving the facilities of the yard itself and to caring for the ships under his charge. The most that could be obtained in 1816 was a set of brick stores and a new conduit to carry water from the upper yard to the wharf. The following year a small schooner was built for watering ships. Construction of a new wharf, requiring extensive landfill, went on slowly for more than two years. This work was carried out in great part by "Paddy" Shannon, a local entrepreneur who owned two scows and hired a gang of his countrymen as day laborers.

In December 1816 Hull sent the commissioners a detailed plan and statement of improvements that should be made in the yard. The chief need was a wall to replace the inadequate wooden fences and to discourage desertion and theft. He incorporated in the proposed wall a set of quarters for officers, a group of storage sheds, and a guardroom at the gate. In addition, he asked for leave to build a new smithy; the existing one was too small and stood only fifteen feet from the stores. These latter he wished to reroof with slate, to prevent another disastrous fire; another new set of stores was also needed. "In fine," he concluded, "all that is asked for is in my opinion absolutely necessary, or I should not have asked it."[47]

2 8 1

Hull can have had no idea of getting all that he asked, however necessary it might appear. In May 1817 the construction of the guardroom—but not the rest of the wall—was authorized. The roofs of the stores were slated. Sheds for boats and spars, of a temporary sort, were put up so that those articles could be moved off the building ways. The rest of the proposals, however, were shelved in late 1817 in favor of a more urgent undertaking: a new shiphouse to cover the 74 soon to be laid down. The *Independence*'s house having blown down in 1814 and most of the materials salvaged from it having been used for other purposes in the intervening time, Hull had to begin from scratch: he estimated that the building would cost $7,000 to $10,000, and in fact the lowest outside bid he could get was for $10,600. Collecting the material for so large a building took a long time: construction did not actually begin until November 1818, a year after the plans were drawn.

Soon after settling at Charlestown, Hull began to buy land near the navy yard. City lots were a solid investment; besides, he wanted to eliminate some disorderly establishments near the navy yard gate in which goods stolen from the yard were often "fenced." He also bought a piece of property adjoining the yard that was being sold to settle an estate after having made several appeals to the secretary to buy the land for the navy, all of which had proved fruitless. In August 1817, when it had been decided that the Charlestown establishment would be permanent, he sold the navy about five thousand square feet of this land, to straighten the southwest side of the yard, for a sum of $3,889.50. The transaction was legitimate, and there is no evidence that Hull profited inordinately; but a sale of land to the government by an officer was indiscreet and served Hull's enemies as a weapon later on.[48]

No other major buildings were erected in the yard until 1821, when a second shiphouse was begun to shelter another 74 then to be laid down, and a new smithy was at last authorized, the old one having decided the question of its replacement by burning down. The lion's share of work in the yard was done, in the earlier years, on repair and maintenance of ships and, in the period after 1819, on new ship construction.

At the end of the war most of the navy ships returned to port, some to be repaired for service and others to be "mothballed" indefinitely. When Hull reached Boston in the summer of 1815, he found the *Constitution* already in ordinary. By the following February he also had the *Guerrière*, the *Congress*, and the *Macedonian* and the brigs *Chippewa* and *Prometheus* to attend to. Of these he had full control; in addition, he was expected to supply the needs of the ships in commission, which were under Bainbridge's command. There was always a degree of tension in determining which vessels were commanded by whom. When there were a great many ships in the harbor, the routine of caring for them all was exhausting, as Hull remarked to his sister-in-law in December 1815: "We have now at the Yard two 74s and three frigates and about three thousand men and officers. You must therefore suppose that I am not idle."[49] At that time the *Washington* was in Boston, preparing for a cruise to the Mediterranean. She sailed in March 1816, taking Midshipman Joseph B. Hull on his first voyage, but the *Independence* continued to lie at her anchors, requiring daily supplies of food and water for several hundred men. The *Macedonian* was under nearly continuous repair from the fall of 1815 until April 1816, and again, after a short summer cruise, from October 1816 until August 1817, when she was hove out, coppered, and put in order for sea service. The six months when the *Macedonian* was not repairing were occupied with coppering and overhauling the *Congress*. The *Guerrière*, though a new ship, also needed work. The yard officers were particularly disgusted to find that the *Macedonian*'s bottom was largely of pine rather than oak—this in an English ship after the British had hooted at American vessels during the war as "fir-built frigates!" At one point Hull almost despaired of making her seaworthy. By contrast with the American frigates she seemed a flimsy craft, though beautiful in her lines. After making a survey of the ship with Bainbridge, Charles Morris, and Yard Constructor Josiah Barker, Hull remarked ruefully that "were it not that she is the only frigate we possess, taken from the enemy, I should pronounce her not worth repairing, for we cannot, after having given her the most thorough repair, calculate on her lasting more than five or six years, her timbers being of common oak and many of them already beginning to decay."[50] The *Macedonian*'s status as a trophy ship saved her. She underwent a repair that Hull estimated would equal the cost of a new ship, but her frame proved more durable than he had expected: she remained in commission until 1835.

The wartime frigate *Java* was an even worse case. When she came to the yard in April 1817, she was found to be rotting and falling apart. Her repairs were delayed until April 1818 because of the need to get the *Macedonian* ready. She went under the hammer at about the same time that orders also came to fit out the *Guerrière*. The *Guerrière* sailed in July, the *Macedonian* in September. Work continued on the *Java* until halted by cold weather and the need to overhaul the sloop *Hornet;* by the following spring attention was diverted to the new 74, and the *Java* settled into semipermanent status as seamen's quarters.

Even ships that were merely being maintained in ordinary required a surprising amount of attention. They had to be regularly pumped, and in winter their upper decks had to be swept clear of snow after every storm. Their cables, canvas, and rigging, whether kept on board or in the navy yard stores, must be regularly inspected and overhauled. Their sides and decks must be caulked from time to time, and they had to be painted or whitewashed every year or two, the standing rigging tarred, and the masts repaired. Each spring they must be moved into the harbor, and men must be stationed on board to care for them and keep an eye on the moorings; in the fall they must be hauled in to the wharf again for the winter, where careful attention must be paid to the fasts to ensure that they were not damaged and did not damage other ships. These routines went on day in, day out all the year round.

And there was much incidental work to be done: indoor tasks of caring for and repairing the ships' stores; outdoor work of scraping, painting, hauling wood, piling unused cannon along the fences, proving new cannon and powder, plowing the commandant's garden, planting trees, and generally keeping the yard tidy.

These were the tasks that fell to the officers and seamen attached to the navy yard. Other jobs, skilled and semiskilled, were done by hired workmen: sawyers, joiners, carpenters, and caulkers. But Hull found great difficulty in keeping enough sailors on hand to cope with the necessary work. At the beginning of 1816 there were nineteen officers and petty officers and twenty-five men on the books of the yard. At that time commerce was still depressed and men relatively plentiful, but these were none too many, for each officer had a servant drawn from the enlisted men, two of the men were cooks, and two were only boys. Only nine seamen were available to do the general work of the yard. Shore drudgery was unpopular with sailors in any case, and as the economy picked up in 1816 the numbers of men willing to work in the yard dwindled. By March 1817 Hull was forced to appeal to the commissioners to be allowed to enlist more men. He suggested that the excessive number of officers allotted to the station, each of them monopolizing a seaman as a servant, would be better sent on furlough. The navy would not only have their servants back at work but would also save their chamber money. Besides, "it is to be desired that the Establishment should have no more officers about it than are necessary, for where there are more than there is duty for they are not only in the way but from their idle habits injure those who have duty to perform." He continued with a description of the work he had to do, for which no fewer than a hundred men would be needed during the summer.[51]

But the commissioners, rather than allow more men to be recruited, or furloughing the officers, merely called on Commodore Bainbridge to furnish men from the *Independence* to work in the navy yard by the day. This was a wholly unsatisfactory arrangement: of the hundred men requested, only fifteen to twenty were sent, and those grudgingly and irregularly; when they did work, they did so only for a few hours in the forenoon, usually from ten to noon or one; and when several of them deserted from the unwalled navy yard, Bainbridge seized the excuse to stop sending them. To make the situation still worse, in April the commissioners decreed that all blacks and foreigners be discharged from the service. Hull let them go but appealed to be allowed to continue the civilian sawyers on the payroll. They were all Irish—some naturalized, some not, but "as there are but few labourers, and still fewer sawyers, except Irishmen, and as they are by far the best men we can hire for sawing and for labour," he hoped to be able to keep them. But the commissioners were inflexible; the Irish had to go.[52] By 20 May 1817 Hull had only twenty-three men to work for the yard and the ships in ordinary. "I am not ambitious to have a large number of men under my command," he told Rodgers, "but when I see things suffering for want of care that are placed under my charge, I cannot but feel anxious to have them taken care of as soon as possible."[53] He drew up for the commissioners a detailed list of the men on duty and how they were employed; by 10 June he was down to thirteen men available for general duty. Two of those were disabled men who had been wounded in the *Constitution:* Philip Brimblecom had lost an arm in the battle with the *Java,* and Hull's one-legged protégé, Richard Dunn, had followed his captain from Portsmouth to Boston.[54]

That was the nadir. Within weeks after this last appeal the commissioners made up their minds to continue the Charlestown yard as a major building yard and ordered the first of two new ships of the line to be laid down there. The numbers on the muster roll of seamen and civilians took a permanent upturn, and it seems plain that Hull did not inquire too closely into the citizenship of the men he hired.

The spring and summer of 1817 thus saw a marked increase in activity at the navy yard. At the same time, the Hull family was agitated by internal changes. In March, Lucy Wheeler Hull died, leaving Isaac's father again a widower. Not many months later, Isaac's younger brother Daniel died in Natchez, Mississippi, where he had gone to set up in business and cotton planting. Isaac's hope that Daniel's business would enable him to help with the education of their brother Joseph's children was dashed. Three of the seven Hull brothers were now dead, leaving only Isaac, Levi, Charles, and Henry, and the latter two did not give much promise of worldly success. Levi continued to work one of the family farms; care of the orphaned children and general oversight of family affairs fell on Isaac. In November 1817 Joseph's daughter Sarah Ann came up from Connecticut to join the Charlestown household, which still included Ann's sisters, Jannette and Augusta, the latter boarding at school nearby. The summer had afforded a long visit from Ann's older sister, Sarah Hart Jarvis, and her two young children, Jannette and John Abraham. Isaac delighted in the children, particularly little Jannette, who ran to him whenever he came home, crying "Hull! Hull!" and hugged him tightly. Sarah's husband, the Reverend Samuel F. Jarvis, had sat to Gilbert Stuart for his portrait. Late in July the family at Boston went to Stuart's studio to see the finished work. All were amused by the behavior of John Abraham, who seemed to think his father had been strangely immobilized by the painter. Hull, chuckling, asked him, "Is it not Papa?" but the little boy only scowled.[55]

Both the Hull and the Hart families were faced in 1817 with the prospect of parental remarriages. First Elisha Hart began paying court, in July, to a woman his daughters considered quite unsuitable, the sister of a shoemaker. Ann called her a "vulgar, disagreeable [and] ignorant creature."[56] This match was somehow averted. Then in October, Joseph Hull announced his intent to marry the widow Blakely, presumably the same lady to whose school Isaac's nieces had previously been sent. She was quite a different sort of person from Mr. Hart's inamorata. Isaac expressed his complete satisfaction: "You know I have ever had the greatest respect for her character and had I been called on to make the choice for him I could not have named a person more to my mind."[57]

But something went awry. In March 1818 Mrs. Blakely called the match off, alleging that Joseph Hull was too old for her and that Isaac had made disparaging remarks about her during his winter visit home. Isaac did not know what he could have said that was offensive, since he so heartily approved of the lady and the marriage. He felt gloomy when he regarded his family situation, his father becoming more of a charge on himself and Levi, his father's farm more an expense than an asset. Joseph Hull had just revived an old claim to Congress for Revolutionary services; it had been turned down in 1795, and it fared no better in 1818. He retained the nominal post of navy agent for Connecticut, but scarcely any navy business was done in the state, so that a commission was rare. Isaac was disturbed to think of Levi and Mary spending their youth caring for the old man but could think of no alternative. "I find my expenses very great," he told Mary,

and what I can do for those children I know not. Sarah Ann costs me now 70 dollars the quarter besides clothes, and when Joseph [returns] his expenses will be as much or more. I am told that he will not attend to his books. I am determined he shall do it or not remain with me.[58]

Sarah Ann found the adjustment to her new life difficult. She was sent to board at Miss Ivan's school, but on her spring vacation at the navy yard she was glum and silent. After the summer term, however, she found her tongue and gave her uncle greater hopes. He proposed, after the fall quarter, to bring her home to attend Dr. Park's school in Boston, "as long as I can afford it." He was a little worried about her younger sister, Eliza, whom Henry proposed taking to New York to school. A suburban or country situation would be better, he thought. "There are so many temptations to carry children astray in our large cities that I should have fears for her." Whatever feelings he had about Henry as a mentor for young ladies he left unrecorded.[59]

In addition to family concerns, Isaac Hull had to attend to the political and social obligations of a prominent citizen. In July 1817 President James Monroe reached Boston on his tour of the northern states that prompted the *Columbian Centinel* to proclaim an "era of good feeling," the phrase that incongruously stuck to his administration. Every hand in the navy yard was put to work to prepare for the president's visit. He arrived in Boston at noon on Wednesday, 2 July, attended by a glittering military escort; the navy arranged for a twenty-gun salute when he reached the Exchange. The weather was superb. The next morning Captain Hull, Lieutenant Samuel Macomber, and Sailing Master Robert Knox took the president and his suite for a sail down the harbor. Friday, the glorious Fourth, was devoted entirely to salutes, at dawn, noon, and sunset, interspersed with oratory and banqueting. Then, on Saturday morning at eight the president's entourage arrived at the Hulls' residence for a formal tour of the navy yard. Captain R. D. Wainwright paraded his marines before the house, and the naval guns boomed another salute. After inspecting the yard and ships in ordinary, the party of two hundred had an "elegant breakfast" at the commandant's house. Then they went on board the *Independence*, returned to the yard, and departed in procession through the town. By the time the great man left town on Tuesday the people at the navy yard had expended six barrels of cannon powder and were exhausted.[60]

In August there was another dignitary to be fêted when John Quincy Adams returned from London on his way to join the administration in Washington. On 19 August Hull called on the Adamses at Quincy, in company with several of Boston's leading citizens, to invite the two statesmen to a public dinner. The event was held at the Exchange Coffee House in Boston on the afternoon of the twenty-sixth, with about two hundred men in attendance. Merchant William Gray presided, and the guests included two Massachusetts governors, Chief Justice Parker of the Supreme Judicial Court and Justice Joseph Story of the federal Supreme Court, Generals Henry and H. A. S. Dearborn, President Kirkland of Harvard, and of course Captain Hull. The merrymaking lasted until 9:00 P.M. On Saturday morning, the thirtieth, John Quincy Adams visited the navy yard and toured the *Independence*.[61]

In October 1817 Hull made a week's visit to New Hampshire with his naval constructor, Josiah Barker, in search of timber for the new 74. The yard and the ships in ordinary were being snugged down for the winter, and Hull was looking forward to his December visit to Connecticut when he wrote to his old lieutenant, now Captain George C. Read,

> I am going on as you left me, fretting and scolding. . . . The Commodore and myself remain the same. He last winter made a most violent effort to get the yard by going on to Washington with all his force, but all did not do. He returned as he went. . . . If you see my old friend, Captain [Hugh G.] Campbell, make my best regards and respects to him. Tell him I expect yet to come in for all the property he leaves that you cannot shoulder. I should like much to see him with us; perhaps he will make us a visit next summer. Tell him we have a cot for him.[62]

Hull was perhaps feeling especially buoyant at this time because the Connecticut legislature had belatedly recognized his wartime victory. The Federalist power was waning in "the land of steady habits." Hull's old friend Oliver Wolcott was governor and, in his annual message to the legislature in 1817, prodded its members to do something for their native hero. As a result, on 9 October the legislature voted to have a gold-mounted sword and set of pistols made and presented to Hull. On 9 January 1818, a few days after returning from his month at Derby and in New York, Hull wrote Wolcott his thanks. He had already consulted with the artists Elkanah Tisdale and John Trumbull about designs for the ornaments on the weapons, and with Nathan Starr and Simeon North about their manufacture. The trophies would be completely Connecticut made.[63]

Hull was able to do a return favor for Governor Wolcott by keeping an eye on his son Oliver, a midshipman stationed at Boston. The young man was ill in the summer of 1818 and feared he would be unable to go out in the frigate *Guerrière* as ordered, but Hull went to see him in company with John Downes, who was preparing the *Macedonian* for a cruise to the Pacific in September, and the three agreed that young Wolcott could transfer to the *Macedonian* if he could not sail in the *Guerrière*. Hull assured the father that Downes was "one of our most respectable and amiable commanders" and that Oliver "promises to be an ornament to the service. . . . [E]very moment goes to show that he has not mistaken his profession," but the governor thought otherwise. Soon after receiving Hull's letter he withdrew his son from the service.[64]

The year 1818 was a busy one at the yard. First, both the *Guerrière* and the *Macedonian* had to be prepared for sea. The *Guerrière* sailed on 25 July to take Minister G. W. Campbell to St. Petersburg; her sailing was preceded by a ceremonial visit of the minister to the navy yard. There was some satisfaction in making a good ship of the *Macedonian*, which Hull had originally found in so bad a state. A few days after the *Guerrière*'s departure he reported proudly that the *Macedonian* "is admired by every one that goes on board and I think very justly so, for, in my opinion, she is the handsomest ship we have, and her accommmodations are not less comfortable and convenient. . . . Indeed," he added with a touch of irony, "she is the first ship that I ever fitted that the commander, when ordered to her, could not discover something to find fault with."[65] One of the improvements Hull had made in the *Macedonian* was to fit her with Baker's Patent Elliptical Pumps. These pumps were invented by James Baker, the carpenter of the navy yard; Hull, Navy Agent Amos Binney, Winslow Lewis, and several other men had bought shares in the invention, and in 1816 or 1817 Hull had effectively taken over the promotion of the device. In January 1817 he gave Baker leave to go to Washington with a model of the pump to secure a patent and to demonstrate the pump to the navy board. In April he detached Lieutenant John Percival from duty at the yard and sent him to London to arrange for the sale of British patent rights to the pump. On his return, Percival was assigned to the *Macedonian*, where he was able to testify to the efficacy of Baker's pumps. Hull promoted the pump assiduously to the navy commissioners and in December persuaded them to install a sample set in the *Columbus*, 74, nearing completion at Washington. This kind of dealing would certainly be called conflict of interest today, but in the nineteenth century such behavior was perfectly acceptable.[66]

Isaac Hull had several other business ventures afoot; although none of them ever made him rich, they at least helped to keep his expensive family solvent. He was erecting some "ten-foot tenements" on his lots near the navy yard. Wages were high in 1818, and as the working season came to an end in November the carpenters began to "call loudly for money," forcing Hull to press his creditors, including Senator Samuel Dana of Connecticut, to send him funds, even, if need be, in bank notes that would be discounted at Boston.[67] For pleasure, rather than business, he had built a little schooner yacht for the fishing trips he loved;

it was also handy when there were visiting dignitaries, as on 14 July 1818, when the governor of Massachusetts joined him on an excursion in the bay, or on 26 October, of which the yard log recorded: "this day the Vice President [Daniel D. Tompkins], with Com. Hull, Perry and Colonel [Caleb] Gibbs, visited the harbour of Boston." A week later the yard had a visit from Henry Clay.[68]

By the end of November the keel of the new 74 was laid, and the annual inventory had been taken of the contents of the yard. Three days later Captain George C. Read arrived in the *Hornet* after a long passage from England. Reequipping her would keep the yard men busy through the usually slack months of December and January but did not require the commandant's presence. Hull had already applied for orders to visit Washington. Earlier in the year he had solidified his position at the navy yard by assuring Secretary Crowninshield that he had exerted himself to retain the station not out of desire to shrink from more difficult service, but because he felt he was being unfairly shouldered aside. "It has ever been my opinion," he told Crowninshield, "that the services of an officer belong to his country, and that all private feelings should give way to the public good. To this sentiment I have made many sacrifices, and am ready to make more should it become necessary." The secretary's reply was reassuring:

> The principle having been established upon which you hold the command of the Navy Yard, no change will be made to your prejudice or without your consent, unless a change of the political relations of the United States should necessarily call you to other duty. Your services are duly appreciated; and your present observations, in regard to the calls of your country, do you honour, and are such as might be expected from an officer of your character and well earned reputation.[69]

If Hull knew that Crowninshield planned to leave office at the end of the year, he may have wanted to get all that into the record beforehand. Still, there was no knowing what a successor might do; Hull thought it prudent to mend fences at Washington during the winter of 1818–19. He left Boston with Ann on 28 December and tarried at the nation's capital until 25 January. It was on this visit that Mrs. Hull dazzled Washington society despite Congressman Mills's objection that she was "too insipid." Her husband found the capital as disagreeable as ever. As he prepared to return to Boston he grumbled that when he got there, "I . . . shall be not far from one thousand dollars out of pocket without being any wiser than when I left—except that of having found out that Washington of all other places is the most abominable." This was in a letter to William Bainbridge. Apparently the two old friends had drifted back, if not into intimacy, at least into civility; certainly Hull was willing to go an extra mile or two to conciliate Bainbridge. He *had* learned something new at Washington: a rumor reached him by way of Congressman Nathaniel Silsbee that Bainbridge would ask for command of the new ship-of-the-line *Columbus* to head a squadron to the Mediterranean. Hull was obviously alarmed that Bainbridge would again fancy he was being ordered from his chosen station when he wrote:

> I have no doubt but you can have her if you wish it, but, my dear Sir, would it not be better for you to take a passage to France, visit Paris, Rome, Naples, etc. and take the command of the station in the *Franklin?* You know the trouble and vexation you would have in fitting a ship out at this place; indeed, what with the heat of the summer and the trouble you would have your health would not stand it. I mentioned to the Secretary last evening that I understood you intended making the application, but he made no answer, only that he had not been informed that you wished it. They have not as yet determined what to do with her.[70]

Bainbridge did take the *Columbus* to the Mediterranean. He left Boston in November 1819, turning over the *Independence* and the command afloat to Captain John Shaw. Hull was surely not sorry to see Bainbridge go. But if he could have read the future he might have begged him to stay.

11

His Good Name

The 1820s seem in retrospect to have been one of the most troubled decades in the history of the navy. Ironically, peace, and the prospect of a long continuance of that peace, was devastating to the morale of a service that had known little but war from its inception. The officer corps, which had swelled from the peace establishment of 250 in 1801 to over 1,100 in 1815, found peacetime hanging heavy on its hands. Immediately after the War of 1812 had come the Algerian disturbance, which kept the fleet occupied through 1815. The next three years were bustling, prosperous ones in the country, when many officers left the service permanently or temporarily to take up business ventures; to go west; or, most often, to command merchant vessels. But the panic of 1819 and the period of depression that followed brought much of this activity to a standstill and left hundreds of naval officers unemployed or underemployed, on half pay or doing routine watch duty in some navy yard. Fewer than 100 officers were of command rank and drawing pay that afforded a decent family living. A lieutenant's half pay was a miserable pittance, twenty dollars a month, and a midshipman's was half that. And there seemed to be no hope of change. The navy was building new ships, but few of these were to be launched in the near future, and fewer still were to be sent on active service. What service *was* there, after all, for the navy of a peaceful minor nation whose immediate hungers were continental? In this climate, aggressions formerly expended on the national foe turned inward, and the navy seethed with quarrels between officers—with accusations, courts-martial, and duels—reaching a kind of crescendo of acrimony in 1825 and gradually declining thereafter.

At the eye of the storm, for a while, stood the improbable figure of Isaac Hull. Of all men who ever mounted an epaulet, Hull was the least litigious, yet in the 1820s he was sucked into a round of bitter trials that left him permanently scarred. All this stemmed from his quarrel with Bainbridge. But Hull, unhappily, played into the commodore's hands.

The first occasion of disturbance arrived in November 1819 in the person of John Shaw, Bainbridge's successor as commander afloat at Boston. Isaac Hull knew him only slightly. Shaw was a native of Ireland who had come to the United States in 1794 and immediately joined the militia to march against the Whiskey Rebels. After a couple of merchant voyages to the Far East, his good Federalist connections secured him a lieutenant's commission in the navy, and he compiled an enviable record in the French war in command of the "lucky *Enterprize*," capturing six prizes. He was retained as a lieutenant in the peace establishment, fourth on the list, below Charles Stewart, Isaac Hull, and Andrew Sterrett. Thereafter his career languished. He made another merchant voyage; went to the Mediterranean in 1805, too late for the fighting; then spent most of the years before the War of 1812 in command of the station at New Orleans. He helped build up the defense forces there but left before the famous battle, took command of the frigate *United States* at New London, and remained blockaded in that port until the end of the war. He then sailed for the Mediterranean as part of Bainbridge's squadron and was left in command of the remaining ships when Bainbridge went home. Shaw returned to the United States in 1817 and was station commander at Norfolk until Bainbridge recommended him as his successor at Boston.

There is much to suggest that Shaw's unspectacular career after 1800 was not entirely the result of bad luck. He certainly made no favorable impression on any of his seniors except Bainbridge, for whom Shaw was a useful tool. John Rodgers, in describing the qualifications of captains for possible appointment to the Board of Navy Commissioners in 1815, had gone out of his way to belittle Shaw, effectively calling him stupid.[1] Shaw's personal associates were other men of undistinguished record or worse: the perpetually unlucky Bainbridge; Captain Arthur Sinclair, who succeeded Shaw in command at Norfolk after a lackluster wartime service on the upper Great Lakes; and the sinister Captain Jesse D. Elliott, whose conduct at the battle of Lake Erie was still the subject of raised-eyebrow speculation.

In 1820 John Shaw stood eleventh on the list of captains, still two places below Isaac Hull and sixteen months junior in date of commission. But he had called himself "Commodore" since taking command of the station at New Orleans in 1806, when he was still a master commandant, and his pretensions to the title were reinforced when he was left in command of the Mediterranean squadron by Bainbridge. At Norfolk he had very pointedly insisted that he be addressed as "Commodore Shaw," and when he succeeded Bainbridge at Boston he broke out a blue broad pendant in the *Independence*.[2]

Hull had very decided opinions about the rank of commodore. He had expressed himself freely on the subject as early as 1814. The sight of Shaw, his junior, strutting about Boston with stars on his epaulets and flying a first-rate pendant in the *Independence* made him angry, but for the time being he made no open animadversions to Shaw. On 8 March 1820 he wrote to his friend Senator Samuel W. Dana of Connecticut answering Dana's request for an opinion on the future of the naval building program. Hull thought all the officers would agree that, above all, the navy needed dry docks, for "we have spent money enough every year for seven years past in heaving out ships to have built a dock yearly, and yet we pursue that plan." On other points he thought his brother officers would differ:

> Some of them I know wish to get as many 74s built and launched as possible. This is not my wish; that is, I do not think it for the interest of the country to do so. I should be for repairing and keep[ing] in commission the ships we now have afloat, and build and launch about twenty heavy sloops of war. . . . Continue to build now and then a line of battle ship and collect as much timber for that class of ships as you please and put it in dock. But such ships as you build and do not want afloat, build houses over them and let them stand under cover until they are wanted. They then can be caulked, coppered and launched before you could get crews for them.

He pointed out that if the heavy ships were built and launched in time of peace, "the moment they are in the water they become a great expense to the nation and soon go to decay, and become an eyesore to those that gave the money to build them." The sloops, on the other hand, would be much more useful for protection of commerce in peacetime and would serve as training vessels for young officers and seamen. In peacetime there was reluctance to spend money for repairing the heavy line-of-battle ships; then suddenly "you have the enemy at your door with a fleet and come to examine your ships: you find them all in a state that requires they should have a thorough repair before you can proceed to sea in them. . . . Whereas had those ships been left under cover . . . in two months you could launch and fit them." But, thinking that this sensible proposal would not go down well with officers who wanted bigger and more grandiose commands, and reluctant as always to create controversy, Hull asked Dana to keep the letter strictly for his own use, adding in a postscript: "I hope you will give us a lift in getting admirals and commodores by commission, for as we now are there is no knowing who are commodores or who are captains."[3]

Two months later, and apparently in response to a question by someone, Secretary of the Navy Smith Thompson issued a circular on the subject of broad pendants:

No officer of the Navy is to hoist a broad pendant who is not acknowledged by the Secretary of the Navy as holding the station of Commodore; in which case he is to wear one of the order corresponding to his rank, as specified in the Regulations of the Navy, page *seventy five* of the quarto edition of new regulations for the naval service of the United States.[4]

Hull immediately asked the secretary which officers were considered commodores. If he were among them, he wanted specific authority to take on the rank, "for I ever considered it very improper that an officer should assume any part of the uniform, even a button, that he has not authority for doing." He continued:

I should also be much pleased to be informed (if my station entitles me to the rank of commodore) whether you consider it military and proper that there should be two broad pendants of the first order hoisted in the same port. I am induced to make these enquiries to prevent any difficulty between Captain Shaw and myself. I must confess I have felt not a little mortified at seeing letters from the Department addressed to captains many years junior to myself, as Commodores; and in being in society with those captains when they have been addressed as Commodores and myself as a captain; and more particularly so, since the new regulations were promulgated.[5]

Hull foresaw trouble in any case: if he and Shaw were both commodores, he would have to ask Shaw, as his junior, to substitute a red pendant while he displayed the blue. If, on the other hand, neither of them was a commodore, Shaw would have to give up the distinction, and by this time Hull knew Shaw well enough to doubt that he would do so willingly. Smith Thompson's reply was very direct:

no captain in the Navy of the United States is considered by the Department as holding the station of commodore or entitled to wear a broad pendant of any kind unless he shall have been by the President of the United States or the Secretary of the Navy directly appointed to the command of a Squadron of vessels on separate service. From this definition of the term commodore, although I may regret its operation as respects yourself, you will perceive that you are not nor is Captain John Shaw entitled to display a broad pendant.[6]

It seems pretty certain that Hull made this letter known to John Shaw; it is even more certain that Shaw did not lower his pendant, remove his stars, or cease to be "Commodore Shaw."

There the matter rested for the time being. Hull had other problems to occupy him, many of them stemming from the restlessness and poverty of the younger officers. In 1818 the master commandant of the yard, Samuel Macomber, preferred a series of charges against one of the lieutenants, Philander A. J. P. Jones, the most bizarre of which was that Jones had cut off the mane and tail of Macomber's horse. The evidence was clear but circumstantial, and Jones merely drew a one-year suspension for leaving the yard when he was supposed to be on watch. But Jones was scarcely back on duty before Isaac Hull had him up on other charges, including the theft of a horsewhip. Hull thought that Jones was a troublemaker and no gentleman and that he should have been cashiered in the first place. This time he was.[7]

Jones seems to have been a bad character, but the basic trouble with many "difficult" officers was that they had too little to do and too little money. They took advantage of their status as naval officers in ways that Hull and other older officers considered shocking:

> indeed there are one or two more that are going on in the same way, getting in debt to tailors, shoemakers, grocers, etc., and when called on, if lieutenants they go to gaol for [a few] days, and come out on the poor debtors act; if Masters they laugh at the man who has been good enough to trust them and say they will pay him when they please: that they are warrant officers, [and] of course cannot be sent to prison. I should recommend a furlough to all such officers, and not allow them to wear any part of the uniform. If they then got in debt they would do it as citizens and not as officers belonging to the Navy.[8]

In order to alleviate the financial worries of the numerous unemployed lieutenants, the secretary of the navy permitted them to be nominally attached to the navy yards and to ships in ordinary. This allowed them to draw their full pay and rations, but in July 1817 the secretary, following the lead of Constant Freeman, accountant of the navy, had ruled that "officers not on duty, and who have been ordered solely to give them full pay, are not entitled to any allowance, besides their pay and rations."[9] That is, they were not allowed chamber money (two dollars per week) or sums for fuel, candles, and servants such as were given to the regularly assigned officers attached to the yards. Part of the controversy at Boston revolved around the phrase "not on duty." Isaac Hull believed that idleness was bad for young men and that officers drawing full pay ought to do some token service, so he ordered the lieutenants nominally attached to his yard and to the ships in ordinary there to stand twenty-four-hour watch on an average of twice a week. The officers then argued that they *were* on duty and were entitled to their chamber money. Hull was inclined to agree with them, but every inquiry to Freeman elicited a more negative, though still ambiguous response. Finally, in October 1820, Hull explained to Secretary of the Navy Thompson that he had stopped the officers and men attached to the ships in ordinary from living on board in the winter because the accommodations were so uncomfortable and because the ships were in danger from keeping fires on board. The seamen had since been housed in the yard, and since the officers were at lodgings in town he thought they were entitled to chamber money. But Thompson returned a firm negative. The *Independence* had recently been moored near the yard and could provide comfortable accommodations for any officers who wished to live on board; those who did not choose to do so would not be given any allowance for chamber money. After that, Hull had no choice but to stop such payments. A loud lament went up from the off-duty officers. The chief complainers were Lieutenants Joel Abbot and William M. Caldwell and Sailing Master James Ferguson. They addressed an aggrieved letter to the secretary, arguing that they were "*actually on duty* . . . and that the duty we perform, is the most arduous and unpleasant of any we have ever done since we have been in service." Thompson thought that was putting it a little strongly: he advised the complainers that they could remain on the station and draw their pay, "but I cannot consent to increase the expense by allowing you chamber-money without a special statement from Captain Hull, that the service required additional officers at the yard."[10] These were, after all, depression times, and Lord Keynes was far in the future. Caldwell and Ferguson then subsided, but Joel Abbot kept nagging Hull about the money, insisting that it was his commander's duty to write the secretary that additional officers were needed at the yard. He told anyone who would listen that Hull was unjustly refusing officers their allowances, and he began to keep notes on what he considered suspicious doings in the navy yard.[11]

Another discontented officer was one of the yard's two regular sailing masters, Charles F. Waldo. Waldo had lost a leg in the *Constitution* during the war and drew a pension of ten dollars a month in addition to his navy yard pay. Some question had been raised in Washington about such "double-dipping" while Hull was at Portsmouth, and he had defended the practice. He was certainly not inimical to Waldo on that score. As a master, Waldo drew $40 per month; two rations per day, each reckoned at $0.25; $10 a month plus one ration per day for a servant; twelve cords of wood per year; and one candle per day—all of which, with the pension, gave him a yearly equivalent of $1,084. When not housed in the yard, he was also entitled to chamber money, in which case his annual income was $1,188.[12] At that rate, Waldo was considerably better off than a half-pay, or even a full-pay, lieutenant. But he had a young and growing family, and he thought he needed more money.

Waldo's duties were not onerous. He kept the journal of the yard, did some copying of letters and orders, and after 1820 assisted with the daily muster of mechanics. In keeping the yard journal he often made coded notes in the margin, and Hull may have thought that Waldo was not entirely above board. But he did not dislike him. When Hull came to the yard in 1815, he found it inefficiently run, and part of the chaos he traced to old Major Caleb Gibbs, the naval storekeeper, a Revolutionary War veteran. Hull wanted to ease Gibbs out of office, but Secretary Crowninshield insisted he be kept on out of "regard for his former services, and respect for his personal merit."[13] Hull then asked that at least a clerk be appointed to assist the old man, and he recommended Benjamin H. Fosdick, Commodore Bainbridge's appointee as clerk of the yard, who had proved himself very efficient and industrious. Crowninshield authorized the appointment of Fosdick at an additional salary of $600 per year, provided he could manage both sets of duties. If not, the secretary thought that Waldo could be given the post. Hull did not believe that Waldo could do so much work because of his impaired health, and he told him so, but he gave Waldo the refusal of the post as assistant storekeeper. Waldo weighed the $600 salary against his existing allowances and refused the office. Fosdick was then appointed. But Waldo came to believe that he could have held both posts—after all, Fosdick had two—and that Hull had cheated him of a possible $600 per year.[14]

Caleb Gibbs apparently suspected that Hull wanted him removed. He was a man of violent prejudices, and he took an instant dislike to Hull. He confined his outward manifestations of distate to querulous complaints that Hull would not let him cut a window in his office, but he kept clandestine notes on activities at the yard that might make it appear that Hull was using navy workmen and property for his own profit. When Gibbs died these notes passed, through his son, to Lieutenant Joel Abbot.[15]

Benjamin H. Fosdick, clerk of the yard and assistant storekeeper, stood high in Hull's esteem, but Hull was not his only partisan. Unknown to Hull, Fosdick was on intimate terms with Bainbridge. In November 1818, when Major Gibbs died suddenly, Hull recommended Fosdick as his successor. This application was not successful; within a month the secretary chose George Bates for the post, but Bates eagerly sought, and obtained, Fosdick's retention as assistant storekeeper, saying that he knew "no man whose character is fairer, whose fidelity, intelligence, capacity and industry in the discharge of various duties is more worthy of confidence."[16] Every officer in the yard echoed Bates's encomium of young Fosdick.

Hull was glad to have trustworthy help in the office, for his family and financial worries were numerous. Between 1816 and 1821 he paid out about $8,000 for land in Charlestown. Rents from the houses and from the stores he had bought near the navy yard were beginning to yield him a supplementary income approaching $1,000 a year, but in the early years this was largely eaten up by expenses of building and renovation. His disastrous venture in French goods was still plaguing him: in September 1821 he received a demand for an outstanding balance of 7,759.27 francs. The original purchases had been 39,006.66 francs, and the creditor in France wrote angrily that by this date "the interest has absorbed the capital. I hope therefore you will discharge this small debt, your wealth and the station you hold in the government putting you above such a trifle."[17] Two years later Hull was still paying installments on this account.

Another investment that had not yielded much profit was Baker's Patent Elliptical Pump. Isaac Hull owned seventy of the five hundred shares. Sales of the pump in the United States were slow, although it had been adopted for use by the navy, and in 1817 Hull had sent Lieutenant John Percival, who was attached to the yard, as agent for the shareholders to sell the patent rights in England. Percival was absent from April 1817 to March 1818; he sold the patent to United States Consul Thomas Aspinwall, but the sum realized barely covered his expenses. Hull was annoyed because Percival did not write to him for six months, and then sent a letter full of vague allusions to his plans for alterations in the pump. Hull wrote him peremptorily telling him to sell out and come home. Percival was miffed, and when he returned to the yard he and Hull had further words about his accounts because Percival had charged the stockholders for his civilian clothes for the journey. Hull insisted that Percival deduct that sum, $126, before he would approve the account. At the same time, the purser of the yard, Lewis Deblois, questioned whether Percival should receive his full pay of $589 for the time he was absent on leave. Hull favored his being paid, as there were ample precedents for officers drawing full pay while on leave, but he advised Percival to get prior approval from the accountant of the navy. This approval was immediately forthcoming, and Percival drew his pay.[18]

John Percival was a man with a violent temper. Not for nothing did sailors call him "Mad Jack." When he was enraged, which was often, he was liable to say things he later regretted. Percival had not forgiven Hull for chiding him by letter, and his anger broke out again when his clothing bills were disallowed. He quarreled with Hull, and the following winter he told the story of the accounts to Dr. Samuel Trevett, the surgeon of the yard, lumping the two sets of accounts together and saying that Hull had refused to sign his pay voucher until he surrendered the $126. "In short," concluded the enraged Percival, "I bribed him!" Then, taken aback for once by his own vehemence, he cautioned Trevett: "But I tell you this as a brother Mason."[19] Trevett, who had a grudge against

Hull because he had not been allowed extra pay as medical purveyor at Boston—though Hull had repeatedly recommended him in the warmest terms—took careful note of Percival's words.

Percival soon sailed for the Pacific in the *Macedonian*, returning to Charlestown in April 1820. In 1821 he was made lieutenant of the yard with a comfortable income of $1,050 a year. Hull had a great deal of trust in, and regard for, Percival, which were to a degree reciprocated, but Mad Jack still had his own opinion about their financial dealings. In May 1821 he grumbled to Aspinwall that "I. H. is a Connecticut man, [and] of course will not let slip an opportunity of getting money. 'Get it honestly *if you can* but *get* money'—Good Lord deliver us from peculators!"[20]

In 1820 family and financial affairs for the Hulls seemed to be going from bad to worse. During the summer Isaac Hull was ill for three weeks, and Ann was also unwell. In order to avail himself of the standard remedy, a trip to the country, Hull had to call on Senator Samuel W. Dana for funds: "you are aware that it costs *money* to *travel* (at least the pay of a *member* of *Congress*), particularly if you have ladies under your charge."[21] He had already borrowed $500 from Rowleff Classen, a Charlestown laborer with whom he had real estate dealings from time to time. He was not able to discharge this note until 1825.[22]

The vacation tour lasted from the end of July to early September. Within two weeks after his return Hull suffered a leg injury when his carriage horses bolted, and he was again confined to his room. All this time he was also concerned about his father, who had been ill the previous winter and who had again contracted matrimonial fever. This time the object of his affection was a woman the whole family thought totally unsuitable: widow Freelove Nichols, whose name seems to have been descriptive of her character. Isaac was appalled at the thought of "a man of his age and standing living about in taverns, and being the cause of such scandal and uproar in the town." He had proposed that his father either live with Mary and Levi or move to his other farm across the river and have Joseph's widow keep house for him, offering to pay for any necessary renovations to either house. But the old man was determined, and Isaac was in near despair:

> I have for years been very unhappy about him and I now feel worse than ever for he is so good that I fear the power of this woman over him will be such as not only to injure his health and reputation but will cause him to spend the little all that he has and both of them come to want. God only knows how all will end.[23]

When Hull returned to Charlestown in September 1820, it was clear that a showdown between him and Shaw was in the offing. The Navy Department was inconsistent in sending orders to be executed by the commander afloat or the commandant of the station, and this was particularly true in the summer when Smith Thompson was vacationing at Poughkeepsie and Benjamin Homans ran the secretary's office. Homans also habitually addressed letters to Shaw as "Commodore," while the secretary was usually careful to address him as "Captain." While Hull was absent Shaw had been ordered to convene a court-martial to try a seaman under Charles Morris's command at Portsmouth. Morris had protested, and while the wrangling went on the seaman had deserted. A sailing master under Hull's command was ordered to duty under Shaw, without reference to Hull; then a midshipman was ordered to report to Shaw for duty on board the *Constitution*, which was in ordinary under Hull's command. Shaw ordered him instead to the *Independence*.

On 20 September, while nursing his injured leg, Hull received a letter from David Porter, who was still a member of the Board of Navy Commissioners, enclosing correspondence with the secretary about the business of broad pendants. Hull and Porter saw eye to eye on that subject. Hull was fearful that the Navy's esprit was being lost as a result of departmental vacillation: "indeed there now appear [to be] parties forming and the great strife appears to be who shall be *commodores* and who shall remain captains, who shall get commands and who shall be without them, and not who shall attend promptly and stoically to duty and mind their own business." He told Porter that although he and Shaw were still on friendly terms a clash was inevitable because he intended to take a stand on the issue, "and when I do I either stand or fall."

> In short, every day I see things going so directly contrary to good order and correct discipline that I am sick, and if I had fortune or had twenty years of my life back that I have spent in the service I should be tempted to leave it rather than suffer what I consider indignities that are daily shown me, and why it is so I know not. What I have done to deserve them I know not. Or what he has done to give him what is considered rank over me I am equally at a loss to conjecture. You may well judge what my feelings are when letters are directed by the department to Commodore Isaac Chauncey, Commanding Naval Officer at New York, or rather Commanding on the New York Station; to Commodore Charles Morris, Commanding the Portsmouth Station; to Commodore John Shaw and to a thousand other Commodores who are junior to me and for what? Because, as the Secretary informs you . . . I had modesty enough not to claim what I had no right to; in other words that I never had claimed the right to wear a broad pendant. . . . [A]nd because I did not claim a

rank that did not exist by law, am I now to see those who have sailed with me as midshipmen holding nominal rank over me?

Hull told Porter that he had written the secretary on the subject and had been told that neither he nor Shaw was entitled to a broad pendant,

yet Shaw's pendant is now flying in my presence, and that of the first order, and he is now wearing all the *stars* and *garters* of an admiral. Is it, then, for me to ask his arrest for so doing and bring on a quarrel between him and create a party, or is it for the department to regulate those things? Should I bear it much longer it may be said that I do it from fear, but be assured that I shall not hesitate doing what I consider my duty, let the consequences be what they may.

He asked Porter for his advice, expressing a wish that the older officers could meet and decide what ought to be done about the situation. He said he would not act hastily but concluded grimly: "I shall in a day or two ask the Board officially whether they or the Department have established a rule of service that the Commandant of a Navy Yard has nothing to do with the command of the station."[24]

True to his word, Hull wrote an official letter to Commodore Rodgers on 22 September, asking whether the department or the commissioners

have established any rule of service whereby the senior naval officer on a station is not considered the commanding officer of the station and held accountable as such; or in other words, whether it is considered by the Department and by the Commissioners that the commandant of a Navy Yard has nothing to do with the command of the station, let his rank and that of the officer afloat be what they may.[25]

Rodgers's reply was satisfactory to Hull. Within a few months this exchange resulted in a new directive from the Navy Department making it clear that the senior officer on a station, whatever the nature of his appointment, was entitled to give orders to all those junior to him. Hull candidly told John Shaw what he had done and stated that he intended to try to get the whole question of rank resolved once and for all. On receiving Rodgers's letter, he offered it to Shaw, but Shaw refused to read it. Hull then told him that if necessary he would carry the question to the president, or even higher. Shaw scoffed: "No officer would have the hardihood to pursue such a course." "*I* certainly shall," replied Hull.[26] As he later reported the exchange to David Porter, "the conversation then turned on some other subject and we parted, as I supposed, friends. In the afternoon of the same day, I suppose after he had seen some of his wise advisers, for he has several of them, he wrote me a letter, of which the enclosed is a copy."[27] This letter of Shaw's was truly venomous:

U.S. Ship Independence
October 7, 1820

Sir,

Your interference with flag officers and your intention as you have informed me, to use every exertion to destroy that grade in our service, has induced me to make known to you my intention of opening a correspondence on this subject with every flag officer in the service, together with the Hon. Secretary of the Navy to whom I shall give, in the fullest extent, my opinion.

I believe, Sir, it is well known that stationary naval yard officers are adding yearly to the intrinsic value of their estates, while the case is quite the reverse with a commanding naval officer afloat, and why, and upon what principle you have decided to oppose this grade, in my opinion, can emanate from no other motives but ambition, and a desire to deprive us of the emoluments, which by law, and our present naval regulations we are entitled to.

If, Sir, your ambition aspires to a broad pendant, allow me to assure you that the ship of the line, which I now have the honor to command, is entirely at your service in exchange for the command you now have the honor to hold. The same proposition I intend making to the Navy Department, for the purpose of meeting your views, and gratifying your feelings, as you were pleased to express to me this morning.

Allow me, Sir, to acknowledge my perfect satisfaction of the candour you made use of in mentioning your intention; in the same spirit I assure you that I shall make use of all my personal influence connected with the flag officers of the several stations, to suppress your position and opinion on this particular subject.

I am, Sir, with due respect, your obdt. servant

John Shaw

P. S. Enclosed I send you copy of my orders from the Navy Department to take command of this station.[28]

Hull thought the letter beneath contempt. As he told Porter,

This letter I consider so ungentlemanly and his allusions and propositions so unofficerlike, or I may say boyish, that I took no notice of it nor should I think it worth copying for you, was it not to show the ideas entertained by some of those self-created commodores, he to offer me his ship and his broad pendant, assumed and suspended by a thread as it is. The man is in his dotage; an allowance must therefore be made for him, and the rattle which he is so much pleased with, he may yet wear, though it be contrary to all rules of service.[29]

Shaw did undertake the correspondence he promised with other "commodores," though he seems to have confined himself to those junior to Hull. Isaac Chauncey, one place below Hull on the list, and one above Shaw, but securely a commodore because he had been appointed by the secretary to command ships on Lake Ontario in 1812–15 and to head the Mediterranean squadron in 1816, turned him aside coldly: "Not believing that any individual officer has sufficient influence to destroy a grade so long recognized by the government, I deem it unnecessary (at least for the present) for me to make any communication to the Secretary upon the subject."[30] But Shaw struck a responsive chord in his friend Arthur Sinclair, the "commodore" at Norfolk, sixteenth on the list of captains and placed in much the same situation as Shaw. Sinclair wrote immediately to the secretary and to Rodgers, defending the appointment of commanding officers afloat at least in the major harbors. To Shaw he directed a hint that should Hull "commence 'throwing stones' he must recollect that 'he lives in a glass house' . . . and that there are talents equal to his own that, if put in requisition, may do him a more serious injury than he imagines."[31]

Hull, on his side, was not lax. As promised, he wrote to members of Congress to urge that "if we cannot get a permanent grade, the nominal one of commodore must be done away; if not there will be as many affairs of honor, as they are called, as there are nominal flags. . . . Believe me, it is a subject that ought to attract the attention of both Houses. . . . In short," as he told Congressman Nathaniel Silsbee of Salem, "my dear Sir, it will be impossible to prevent duelling and all sorts of quarrels unless rank and command is better defined, understood, and practiced than it now is."[32] When the pacific Hull mentioned dueling twice in one letter, affairs had reached a point of high seriousness.

During the winter of 1820–21 the battle of the broad pendants faded into the background as a crisis developed that could have left Hull permanently disgraced. The first hint was received in mid-December 1820 when the commissioners notified Hull that wages at Boston seemed excessive; the ship of the line being built there had cost $2,087 more than the North Carolina at Philadelphia, and the latter was already launched while the Boston ship was far from complete. Accounts showed 26,478 working days on the Boston ship and only 22,881¼ on the North Carolina.[33] This was a disturbing report. Hull was unwilling to believe that the Boston workmen were inferior to those of Philadelphia; during the previous summer they had built and launched the schooner Alligator in record time.[34] He wrote to Commodore Alexander Murray at Philadelphia for confirmation of the figures and by the end of January received a reply that showed that his ship was indeed costing a great deal more than her sister.[35]

While waiting for Murray's reply, Hull showed the commissioners' letter to the naval constructor, Josiah Barker, and to Navy Agent Amos Binney. As Barker related the conversation, "Captain Hull appeared to be irritated . . . and said that the men did not work; that they would do more work anywhere else than we did."[36] Barker protested that there must be some mistake; probably the commissioners had added in the cost of the *Alligator* and of fitting out the *Constitution*. But Hull had checked the records; the figures quoted by Rodgers were indeed those he had sent in on the new ship. Barker still believed there was a mistake, but Hull reiterated that the men were not working hard enough, and over the next two weeks he frequently insisted to Barker that the deficiency must be made up by exertion. Barker was puzzled by this, and he was astounded when Francis Wyman, the purser's steward, told him soon afterward that Benjamin Fosdick, who had left the yard the preceding January, had carried off $30,000 or $40,000. "How?" asked Barker, to which Wyman replied, "You will find out by and by."[37]

Fosdick's integrity had never been questioned, but it was he who had paid the yard mechanics for most of the time from 1813 to 1820. Barker obtained from one of his quartermen (foremen) an account of the workdays of his gang of carpenters for the previous September and took it to Amos Binney. The two men compared the payroll with the quarterman's account and found that, while the men had worked an average of four and a half days on the ship each week, they were entered on the roll as having worked six! What had happened was clear: Fosdick had caused the men to sign blank payrolls, and after paying them for four or five days of work had entered six on the account and pocketed the difference. Barker now remembered that a workman named Leavitt had once complained to him of having to sign blank payrolls. Barker had questioned Fosdick about the practice: his explanation was that, in order to get Saturday afternoons free to visit his parents, he had to get the men to sign the payroll on Friday so that he could get the money and have it ready to pay at one o'clock on Saturday.

Binney also remembered that there might be other evidence against Fosdick. He sent for Fosdick's successor as assistant storekeeper, William Keating. Keating had suspected Fosdick as far back as July 1816, when Keating was a subordinate clerk in charge of recording the daily work. At that time he had thought Fosdick was altering his rolls, and being a good Catholic he took his problem to Doctor Matignon, a priest in Boston. The priest advised him to tell just one high official, and Keating decided to confide in the navy agent, Amos Binney, because Binney had the duplicate payrolls and was in a better position to detect the fraud than was Captain Hull. Keating may also have been afraid of Fosdick, who might explain himself convincingly to Hull and then take revenge on Keating. The latter's testimony at the later trials suggests that he was not overly intelligent; certainly he would have been no match for the clever Fosdick. Binney apparently thought that there was nothing to Keating's story; Keating was known to hate Fosdick, and he was also very close in his accounting: he would dock a man a quarter day's pay if he were not present when his name was called at muster, even if the man arrived before work began. Binney suggested that the clerk keep a duplicate of his muster book, and he compared the two from time to time. Once in April 1819 the two men read over Fosdick's roll alongside Keating's, but they found only a few quarter days' difference. Binney dismissed the matter. But, when Barker confronted him with the new evidence, Binney remembered Keating's charges and sent him with his book to Captain Hull. Fosdick's iniquity was fully established. Hull, as he looked at the documents, felt despair: If a young man of such apparent integrity were a villain, who could be genuine? In Keating's presence he groaned: "The country is ruined! Who am I to trust? I had as much confidence in him as in one of my own family!"[38]

Amos Binney was on the point of leaving for Washington, and when he got there the government would know about the fraud at Boston. Hull felt he had to take immediate measures. He went to Boston to consult United States Attorney George Blake and to see if Fosdick had property there that could be attached, but very little was found. On speaking with Charles Bradbury, a merchant who had been Fosdick's mentor from youth and who was as startled as Hull at the fraud, he learned that the young man had spoken of going to Cuba to try his fortune. Fosdick had been at odds with his wife, and there were rumors that he had been keeping a mistress before he left for New York, but generally his habits had been very abstemious and he had showed no signs of unusual wealth. It was possible, then, that the money was still available for recovery. Hull determined to catch Fosdick at New York if possible, or at least to seize enough of his property to indemnify the United States. In the meantime, he set Keating to work with the yard clerks, John A. Bates and John Etheridge, to check the payrolls throughout Fosdick's whole term of service to establish the total amount missing.

The fraud was discovered on Friday, 26 January 1821. On the following Tuesday morning, although the Hulls had a large dinner party scheduled for the afternoon, the captain took the stage for New York. Fortunately, the severe cold of the past several weeks that had sealed Boston harbor with ice had begun to moderate, but the hazards of the stage journey were still considerable. The veteran of three wars wrote the secretary of the navy that "I have been in more danger of losing [my life] three different times in pursuit of him than I ever was before."[39] On arriving at New York, Hull sought out his old friend Thomas Chew, purser of the *Washington*, which was now the receiving ship at the navy yard in Brooklyn, and Joseph Watson, his wartime clerk, who was acting chaplain of the ship. Chew and Watson undertook to find Fosdick's address and have him arrested. Hull took a room at Bunker's Hotel on Wall Street and sent for David B. Ogden to give him legal advice. He asked Ogden to meet him at the hotel, rather than risk letting word get around that he was in town, giving Fosdick a chance to escape. Ogden advised him to find out through Fosdick's broker what his investments were and to apply to the attorney general for Fosdick's arrest and for an equity bill to prevent transfer of his stock. By the next morning Hull had learned where Fosdick's money was invested; he called on Ogden, and the two men went to the various insurance companies and other places where the stocks were held to warn them not to allow transfer of the holdings. Hull then applied to District Attorney Robert Tillotson, who entered suit before Justice Brockholst Livingston in the United States Circuit Court to have Fosdick's property sequestered for the benefit of the United States. Chew and Watson were unable to locate Fosdick, though he was reported to be in New Jersey, but the searchers did learn that the clerk had legally changed his name; he was now Benjamin Hichborn.[40]

With the property secured, Hull started for Boston again, but not far from New York he was overtaken by a messenger from Tillotson. Hichborn had appeared at his banker's office in Wall Street; and Tillotson, tipped off by an informer, had called a United States marshal; the culprit was under arrest. Hull returned to the city. He confronted Hichborn, who was inclined to stand on his rights and contest the proceedings, since he was aware that very little could be proved against him in court. But Hull overawed him; finally, in return for his release, Hichborn agreed to put $80,000 worth of property under bond in the hands of Charles Bradbury at Boston, pending a final settlement of his debt to the United States. With this agreement in hand, Hull returned to Boston on 10 February 1821, after two weeks almost without sleep.[41]

From then on the process of recovering the lost funds was merely tedious. It took several months for the clerks to check more than two hundred weekly payrolls, and for many of them it was impossible to provide parallel accounts. John A. Bates, who had succeeded Fosdick as clerk of the yard, with William Parmenter, Binney's clerk, eventually reached a figure of $52,502.63 as Hichborn's debt to the United States. Hichborn professed himself surprised that the amount of money stolen was so large—"Modest scoundrel!" snorted Mad Jack Percival. Hich-

THE CAPTAIN FROM CONNECTICUT

born also said to several people that Hull, who had been charged with determining the amount of money to be repaid, in company with Amos Binney and George Blake, was squeezing him for several thousand dollars more than he really owed; at one time he threatened to bring a civil suit to recover the excess, but his friends persuaded him to avoid litigation. He eventually agreed to pay $55,000, plus $3,000 for the expenses of the investigation. Bradbury released that amount to Binney and returned the remainder of the property to Hichborn, who promptly vanished.[42] One of his friends remarked later that Hichborn "felt injured with Captain Hull because he was more persevering and insisting than either of the other commissioners; at least Fosdick considered him so, and he felt more injured by Captain Hull than by the others."[43] The secretary of the navy, on the other hand, gave high praise to Hull for his zeal in recovering the stolen money, as well as to Amos Binney. Binney and Hull, in turn, requested a pay increase for William Keating as a reward for his help in proving the fraud.

But, in spite of all this, there were those in Charlestown and Boston who chose to believe that Hull and Binney were implicated in Hichborn's theft. To one who did not know Hull's personal character, or to a deliberate enemy, there was a plausible case: Hull and Binney, so the story went, were privy to Fosdick's doings and received part of the boodle. Binney turned aside Keating's accusations, and when the discrepancy in the expenses was revealed, Hull put it down to lazy workmen. Confronted with the evidence by Barker and Keating, Hull and Binney at last took steps to have the matter corrected but without letting it get into court, where their part in it might be revealed. They connived with Hichborn again in restoring the money, though probably not as much was put back as had actually been stolen.

The only thing wrong with this scenario is that there is no evidence to support it, and there is a great deal against it. The only persons who believed it were those who, from personal or political motives, wanted to injure and disgrace Hull or Binney. All the testimony pointed the other way: that Hull and Binney had been genuinely surprised at the revelations and that Hull in particular had extended himself beyond all expectation to recover the government funds. So far from wishing to be one of the commissioners to decide on the amount of money to be repaid, he had requested the secretary to release him from that duty and had undertaken it only when ordered to do so. Most conclusive was the testimony given in 1822 by Dr. Asa Bucknam, a respected citizen with whom Hichborn stayed while the settlement was being negotiated. Bucknam, like Charles Bradbury, had known Fosdick/Hichborn from his youth and was shocked that he could be capable of fraud. He told

Hichborn that he had heard rumors that Hull and Binney were in the game with him and that, if that were the case, Hichborn should expose them. "[He] then said nobody should suffer for him"; Bucknam recalled

that neither Captain Hull or Mr. Binney, or any person knew anything of the business; that if he had been suspected of such a course he should have been dismissed from the Yard immediately. He said it was a transaction that only one could carry on. [I am] sure, from the state of Fosdick's mind at the time, and the motives [I] held out to him, that if Captain Hull or any other person had been concerned in the transaction with Fosdick, [I] would certainly have known it.[44]

The third commissioner, George Blake, was loud in praise of Hull and enthusiastic about the settlement agreed upon. As United States attorney, Blake was uncomfortably aware that there was no law under which he could prosecute Hichborn. His offense was against the federal government, which is not a common law jurisdiction, so that, in the absence of a specific law prohibiting fraud of this type, Fosdick's crime was not justiciable. "It is my opinion," Blake wrote to Hull,

that the amount which is proposed to be refunded by this delinquent is, in truth, quite as large as could, under any circumstances, be reasonably demanded of him, and it cannot, at any rate, be doubted that it exceeds very considerably the sum which we should be able to establish against him by any legal evidence that could be produced, in the course of a regular trial at law. . . .

Moreover, I consider it but as an act of justice which is due from me, as the attorney of the United States in this case, to express to you the strong conviction which I feel that, but for the promptitude, the zeal, and unremitted exertions which were made by yourself at the outset, in the pursuit of this delinquent, and in bringing him to a proper sense of his misdemeanors, the government must, inevitably, have been subjected to the ultimate loss of the greater part, if not the whole of the very important sum which is now to be realized.[45]

Should Hull have suspected Fosdick sooner? Perhaps; but if he had, he would have been the only officer in the yard, and the only gentleman in Charlestown or Boston, to suspect him; and whatever Isaac Hull's faults, suspiciousness was not one of them. Except for Fosdick, Hull never had a clerk who betrayed him. Joseph Watson, John Adams Bates, and John Etheridge, who served him, singly or together, for thirty years, all had untarnished careers in government service. Why should Hull have thought otherwise of Fosdick, who was appointed and highly praised by Commodore Bainbridge?

The incident is a classic example of the degree to which an administrator is dependent on subordinates for detailed information. Comparative figures were not regularly exchanged between navy yards at that time, and periodic audits were a precaution of a later day. Even with more sophisticated modern techniques, fraud is hardly a vanished art, and one may suppose that today Fosdick would be an accomplished computer thief. If Hull could in any way be called negligent or credulous, he certainly paid for that fault many times over during the next several years.

Not long before the Hichborn settlement was reached, the climactic battle of the broad pendant was fought. The navy commissioners—John Rodgers, David Porter, and Isaac Chauncey—decided to visit the northern navy yards in the spring of 1821. It seemed particularly important to inspect the Boston yard and to settle any remaining doubts about the state of things at that troubled station. They visited the yard on 14 and 15 May and pronounced themselves satisfied with what they saw; and they instructed Hull to begin immediate preparations to lay down another ship of the line, with a new shiphouse to cover her. The money refunded by Hichborn was to be applied to her and to new buildings in the yard.

On his arrival in Boston, Rodgers quickly cast a baleful eye at the broad pendant flying on board the *Independence*, in defiance of his own letter and of the secretary's instructions. Coldly turning aside Captain Shaw's invitation to the board to visit the ship, Rodgers wrote him a curt demand for his authority for hoisting the pendant. Shaw overreached himself. He cited Articles 3 and 5 of the Navy Regulations of 1817 but added: "I would, however, observe that I hold myself subject to the immediate order and directions of the Hon. Secretary of the Navy, otherwise would state many instances of officers similarly situated wearing broad pendants."[46] It was not prudent to defy John Rodgers to his face. At 11:29 A.M. the next day Lieutenant John Percival delivered his stinging reply to Shaw:

> The Board of Navy Commissioners are not acquainted with any existing regulation of the Navy of the U.S. which gives to you, in your present command, the right of wearing a broad pendant. On the contrary, they know from having drawn up the regulations themselves, that they neither concede nor were they intended to concede any such right except by express permission of the Secretary of the Navy.
>
> In the name therefore of the Board of Navy Commissioners, as well as under the authority I possess as your superior officer, I have to direct that you haul down the broad pendant now flying on board the Independence, and that you hoist in its place, a long pendant, such as is usually worn by our ships when commanded by captains.[47]

His Good Name

Shaw had no choice. The pendant came down. But he would not give up; he addressed to the secretary an aggrieved letter of protest against being given orders by the commissioners; this was followed by an even longer letter of self-justification ten days later, which reveals the direction of his thoughts:

> The injury done to myself although great I consider but trifling in comparison with the disrespect the Commissioners have shown towards you, who[m] I conceive to be the legal and prerogative power in the case referred to. . . . Their conduct in regard to me compels me, (without any intention of disrespect to you) to express to you my belief, that had I instead of *Captain Hull* been the officer under whose immediate command, and direction, a clerk had for several years persevered in the villainy and fraud of from 40 to 60,000 dollars reported to have been committed by Mr. Fosdick late clerk of the Navy yard Charlestown, no means would be been left untried to have secured a public investigation of my conduct, and in the event of a decision unfavorable the most severe punishment.[48]

At the same time, he sent Hull another venomous note:

> Allow me, Sir, to congratulate you on the signal victory you have latterly gained over the broad pendant which for several years has been flying from on board the Independence.
>
> The uneasiness and vexation it has so long occasioned to you is now happily removed and the Board of Navy Commissioners will no doubt receive your warmest gratitude and the poor old flag, were it susceptible of feeling and capable of expression, would no doubt before this have returned you its thanks for your kindness in being instrumental in its timely risque from destruction by the howling of the winds and pelting of winter storms.[49]

Hull sent the note to Rodgers with the remark that "I have . . . determined to treat him with the same contempt that I did on receiving his former letter, and have nothing to do with him except on service." But he wrote pointedly that the *Independence* would be better off in ordinary, and much less costly to maintain, as she now had assigned to her more officers and men than were in the yard.[50] In that event Shaw would probably have been transferred elsewhere and out of Hull's hair for good, but the affair was not to end so easily. Although the secretary wrote Shaw on 29 May in unequivocal language that he was not entitled to a broad pendant, Shaw remained on board his ship, brooding over his wrongs and on the lookout for a way to injure his foe.

Hull looked forward to an active summer when the Fosdick/Hichborn business was settled. On 14 July 1821 the three commissioners sent in their report on the settlement, and he turned with relish to the business of the navy yard. On shore as at sea, he was still "the active Captain Hull," on duty in the yard day and night, in all kinds of weather, keeping his eye on everything that was done. In the summer of 1821 the bounds of the yard were being extended to allow for new construction and to include the old naval hospital, now being converted to officers' quarters, so that, as Isaac Hull noted to his nephew Joseph, "it keeps me constantly walking."[51] Joseph was about to make a cruise to the Pacific under Commodore Charles Stewart in the *Franklin*, 74. He had passed his midshipman's examination, and his uncle tried to have him made acting lieutenant before he sailed, but to no avail. If he made a good record under Stewart, though, he would certainly be a lieutenant by the time he returned. Isaac Hull sent him away with plenty of advice, a writing desk, a half barrel of hams, and a pot of pickles. He would have sent money, but as usual his finances were precarious: "I have so many calls for what little I have and particularly at this time, having within a few days lost 2000 dollars which I have to pay a second time; [this] distresses me very much. I wrote a few days since to Charles for 1000 of it but received for answer that he could not pay it. What I shall do I cannot say." He told Joseph to ask an advance from the purser of the *Franklin*, however, "and say that I will be held accountable for any money he may advance you that is not refunded by [your] pay during the cruise."[52] Joseph's sister Sarah was keeping house for her uncle Isaac while Ann and Augusta Hart made a visit to Saybrook. They returned in September in improved health after their country ramble.

But Hull was not to be left to enjoy his family and his daily round of duty. A week after the settlement of the Hichborn case, the *Columbus* entered Boston harbor on her return from the Mediterranean. William Bainbridge was back. Within one week he was raising clamorous objections to the official report on Hichborn because his name had been introduced into it; not only that, but the secretary had also mentioned the name of Bainbridge in his letter ordering the investigation![53] Bainbridge demanded that the secretary explain himself and that he say whether he had used Bainbridge's name at Hull's suggestion. Secretary Thompson replied that it had only been a reference point for a complete review of Fosdick's activities and that Hull had not made any such suggestion.[54] Hull, Binney, and Blake, bending over backward to be accommodating, even withdrew their report and drew up a new and more detailed one to show that only a few hundred dollars had been stolen under Bainbridge.[55] Bainbridge claimed to be satisfied: "I have only to add that the evidence is very imperfect, that any, even the smallest part of Hichborn's fraud was committed during my command of the Navy Yard."[56] He knew, of course, better than anyone, how intimate he had been with Fosdick up to the end of 1819; at one time the clerk had even lived in his house.[57]

There remained, of course, the delicate question of what to do with the commodore. The commissioners, anticipating his return, had suggested to Thompson months earlier that he be offered the Norfolk Navy Yard, from which Captain John Cassin was being removed because of senility. Evidently, Bainbridge declined the post in hopes of something better. For the moment he was again senior officer afloat at Boston, leaving Shaw high and dry; the latter was on a few weeks' leave of absence. The secretary timidly asked Bainbridge whether he wished to remain at Boston. He could have anticipated the answer:

> I answer with candour, I do, and should be gratified on being restored to the command of the Navy Yard at Charlestown Masst. were I to hold it only "as long as Captain Hull has had the command there" I believe I use his own words on a similar occasion and which may be found among the records of the Navy Department. And as a recent removal at Norfolk has established a precedent thereon, I perceive no difficulty in the hope of realizing my wish. But I beg it to be explicitly understood that I do not in the least intend to dictate to the government, for my rule in the service is obedience.[58]

It was out of the question for the secretary to remove Hull from the navy yard: he was not superannuated, and his ouster at this time would look like disciplinary action for some involvement in the Fosdick affair. As it turned out, within two months death intervened to provide an acceptable berth for Bainbridge: Alexander Murray died in Philadelphia, and less than a week afterward the secretary offered his post as commandant of that navy yard to the restive commodore. Bainbridge refused it: he rehashed all his old "claim" to the Charlestown yard and added:

> The Philadelphia station I acknowledge to be a respectable command. But having my family, which is quite large, already established at Boston, and arrangements made there for the education of my children, I should prefer that station at Boston to the one at Philadelphia. Capn Hull has no family but his wife, consequently could move with less inconvenience than I could do.[59]

But when, a few weeks later, the Board of Navy Commissioners ordered the *Columbus* put in ordinary, leaving nothing for the commander afloat to be afloat in, Bainbridge suffered a change of heart and, however reluctantly, accepted the Philadelphia post.[60]

Meanwhile John Shaw, although he had spent a good deal of time on leave during the summer, had not been eating the bread of idleness. He had visited Washington to press his claim to command a new naval station projected for Pensacola, Florida. And, with the aid of Arthur Sinclair, he had been gathering any scuttlebutt about Isaac Hull that might come in handy. Sinclair was full of gossip about Hull's having charged exorbitant fees for passage in the *Constitution* across the Channel in 1811. Twenty-five guineas was the favorite figure mentioned; Hull was also supposed to have extorted a watch from some impecunious passenger. The more often Sinclair told the story, the more elaborate it got. Shaw also had Sinclair investigate (through a friend, to avoid being obvious) the customhouse books at Norfolk to see if they could prove that Hull had smuggled goods in the *Constitution*, but that inquiry proved fruitless.[61]

After returning to Boston, Shaw decided to be mulish. The new regulations made it clear that the senior officer on a station, whether he were afloat, commanding the navy yard, or whatever, was entitled to give orders to all the junior officers. But, when Hull ordered Shaw to convene a court-martial, as directed by the secretary, Shaw refused: he was under Bainbridge's command, not Hull's. Bainbridge was at that time on an extended visit to New York. Hull told the secretary resignedly: "As Captain Shaw has to consult Commodore Bainbridge before he can determine whether he will or will not obey your order passed through me . . . I . . . respectfully submit to you the propriety of Captain Macdonough's being ordered as a member of the court."[62] To David Porter he wrote more directly:

> You see that Shaw is still troublesome. . . . It is fully my opinion if Shaw should not obey the order the Secretary ought to order his arrest immediately. If not, I must, but I dislike to do it; as he and myself have had some sparring his friends might suppose I had taken an advantage.[63]

But Bainbridge advised Shaw to obey the order, and he grumpily complied.

Bainbridge and Shaw had more important matters to think about. From the time of Bainbridge's return, the aimless obstructionism of Shaw was converted into a program of purposeful and organized malice, and other junior officers at Charlestown were drawn in as well. Bainbridge never allowed his hand to appear, nor did he do anything that could bring him openly into the fray. But he guided his none-too-perceptive subordinates, allowing them to destroy themselves while they accomplished his purpose of injuring Hull. The commodore was accustomed to having his way, and those who balked him were in for trouble. His former friend, Stephen Decatur, had injured him, he believed, by grabbing all the glory in the Mediterranean in 1815. While he was at Washington before sailing in the *Columbus* in 1820, Bainbridge had helped to foment the fatal duel between Decatur and James Barron, acting as Decatur's second and refusing to permit a reconciliation between the duelists. Jesse D. Elliott, Barron's second, had acted a similar role; he, too, would take a hand in the Boston business. Now, in 1821, Bainbridge had decided to get rid of Hull by one means or another.

Hull had been at Boston for six years, long enough to make a number of enemies. In addition to Shaw and the disgruntled junior officers of the yard, there were a few workmen who had been dismissed or denied contracts because of pilfering, laziness, or shoddy workmanship. The selectmen of Charlestown were antagonistic because they believed that Hull had walled into the yard a strip of land that rightfully belonged to the town. And Charlestown society had been further affronted by the high-and-mighty bearing of Ann Hull and her sisters. Susan Bainbridge was at hand to throw oil on that fire. And on the larger Boston scene, Hull, though apolitical as ever, was drawn inexorably into the death struggle between the waning Federalist party and the triumphant Republicans.

Hull had always been identified with the Republicans by everyone but himself, and his closest associates were Republican party appointees like Amos Binney and George Blake and Republican congressmen like Nathaniel Silsbee and Timothy Fuller. His uncle William, a symbol of the old Jeffersonians, still lived at Newton. Hull and Binney, by default, represented the hateful national government and specifically the Monroe administration and its heir apparent, John Quincy Adams, making them almost equally anathema to Republican factions supporting William H. Crawford or Andrew Jackson. Binney was even more odious than Hull because he had succeeded, over local opposition, in keeping the navy going through the war.

Hull's foes, overt and covert, were mainly Federalists: Bainbridge, Shaw, and Joel Abbot were all men of that party, as were their associates. Hull had stepped on some Federalist toes in 1820 by opposing as too costly the adoption of a design for the *Alligator* offered by Joseph Lee, member of a powerful family and supported in his application by Harrison Gray Otis. Other prominent Federalists sided openly with Shaw: William Sullivan and Thomas Handasyd Perkins of Hartford Convention fame were among them. And it was the Federalist newspapers that took up the cry against Hull in 1821 and 1822: Nathan Hale's *Repertory, Daily Advertiser,* and *Weekly Messenger;* John Russell's and Samuel Gardner's *Gazette;* Benjamin Russell's *Columbian Centinel,* the grandfather of Federalist papers; and most vociferously of all, Joseph Buckingham's, Jefferson Clark's and Samuel Knapp's *New England Galaxy,* a paper both Federalist and Masonic. (Isaac Hull was one of the few prominent navy men of his day who was not a Mason.) Hull's chief literary defenders, on the other hand, were the administration mouthpieces, Joseph Gales and William Seaton of the *National Intelligencer*. But the *Intelligencer*, far away in Washington, had little impact on the Boston scene.

Hull breathed a sigh of relief when he heard that Bainbridge had accepted the Philadelphia yard, remarking ironically to Porter: "How he will leave here I know not, but I expect without bidding me goodbye. I have not seen him and I cannot call as I have done all and more than the service requires. I regret those things, my dear Sir, but I must take care of myself and family."[64] He was having trouble with the marines on the station, there being some doubt whether they fell under his command or not, and commented: "I have trouble on all sides, yet I thought I was a good-natured fellow."

In fact, Bainbridge had already discovered a new cause for complaint against Hull. The *Columbus* had returned from the Mediterranean in company with the brig *Spark*, one of the smaller vessels of Bainbridge's squadron. When the *Spark* went to the navy yard to be overhauled for service in the West Indies, Hull found that "her cable bitts, topsail sheet bitts, capstan spindle, bowsprit beds and everything except her masts and pumps that went below her gun deck were sawed off flush with the beams under the deck for neatness," with the result that she leaked about the bitts and the capstan did not have enough purchase to raise the anchor.[65] Other alterations had been made to make the *Spark*, Hull thought, more like a packet than a war brig, and he complained to the commissioners about these unnecessary alterations, which were contrary to regulations. The board welcomed his remarks and copied them into a circular to all captains, enjoining them to desist from making such changes. Before he left Boston, Bainbridge fired off a letter to Hull, demanding that he prove his allegations about the *Spark*. Hull did his best to be soothing: "I . . . have to inform you that I have not at this moment any other proof of the bowsprit, bitts etc. of the Spark being sawed off than the fact that they were flush with the beams and had the appearance of having been sawed off." He detailed the problem of the capstan and assured Bainbridge,

> when I made that report it was done purely for the good of the service and not in any manner whatever to injure the feelings or reputation of anyone. . . . I cannot but regret that any new subject should have presented itself calculated to keep alive the unhappy misunderstanding that has so long existed between us and I say without hesitation and repeat it that in making my report I did not intend to injure the feelings of anyone.[66]

He complained bitterly to Rodgers and Porter of their putting him thus on the spot. "You will see," he told Porter, "that [Bainbridge] has without a moment's delay seized on it" to keep their quarrel alive and that the commodore was sending copies to officers who had commanded the *Spark*, "and no doubt in a way that will cause them to have unpleasant feelings towards me." If, he said, no officer could make an official report without being put into conflict with all the other officers, "there must be an end to order and discipline—and to reports."[67] Hull proved by a battery of testimony that his statement about the *Spark*'s capstan was correct, and a few days later Bainbridge huffed off to Philadelphia.

In December 1821 Hull obtained permission to make an official visit to Washington to confer with the commissioners on future building in the yard, to witness a proposed experiment at the Washington Navy Yard in the use of steam power to haul ships out of the water, and generally to mend fences. "I must in some way have an understanding about many matters with the Secretary," he told Porter, "or I shall forever be in hot water, though a good-natured man." He left Boston on 26 December 1821 and returned about 1 February 1822. He did have "an understanding with the Secretary" about one very important matter. On 1 February 1822, only a few days after Hull left Washington, Secretary Thompson issued a circular letter to all captains:

> The laws of the U.S. not having established among Navy officers any grade above that of captain and great inconvenience having been found in the use of the nominal title of commodore, it is hereby made known that no such title will hereafter [be] recognized by this department until the same be established by law.[68]

From this date, for the remainder of Thompson's tenure of office, *all* captains were addressed in department correspondence as "Captain." The title "commodore" was administratively dead for the time being.

But, while Hull was away from Charlestown, events moved swiftly. On the day of his departure the *Mariana Flora*, a prize to the schooner *Alligator*, came into Boston with Lieutenant Joel Abbot as prizemaster. Abbot lost no time in conferring with Shaw, once again the nominal "commander afloat," and the result of their conversation was a series of letters from each to the secretary accusing Hull of every crime possible.

Hull had no more inveterate enemy than Joel Abbot. The lieutenant had been in the yard—or, more often, on leave from it—since he received his commission in 1818, and when there he was constantly complaining about his allowances. He nagged and whined at Hull about the subject in a way that must have been particularly exasperating, for by this time Hull was quite deaf. At one point, according to Abbot, he told the lieutenant to go to hell—which, if true, betrays an extraordinary degree of temper on the part of Hull, who was normally not profane, at least not to officers. From the time of the denial of his chamber money in 1820, Abbot had been the close confidant of Surgeon Samuel R. Trevett, who for his own mysterious reasons enjoyed retailing any and all mean gossip about Hull he could turn up. In February 1821 Abbot had returned six days late from a leave of absence and immediately asked for leave again. Both Hull and Master Commandant William B. Shubrick were out of patience with him; besides, it was the time of the annual survey of the contents of the yard, when all the officers were needed on duty. They refused the second leave. Abbot whined and begged; after a lot of pre-Victorian pussyfooting he finally came right out and said that his wife was near her confinement in Newburyport and that he *must* be with her. (On his previous leave he had been in Connecticut and Rhode Island, on business, as he said, for Lieutenant Raymond Perry. It was suspected that he was engaged in arranging a duel.) Hull told him that the service could not depend on the state of officers' wives, but after a few days he let him go. Abbot had a week's leave, from 15 to 22 February; when he returned on the twenty-second he said that his wife was still with child. She was delivered on 24 February, and on the twenty-eighth Abbot again got leave to go to her. Mrs. Abbot did not recover from the birth and died in mid-April of a "nervous fever." During her whole illness Abbot was permitted to remain on leave, and immediately afterward he obtained a certificate of his own illness from Dr. Trevett and continued to avoid duty in the yard through the summer.[69] By some private logic, Abbot decided that his wife's death was the result of anxiety caused by his absence; only Captain Hull had prevented his being at her side, and therefore Hull was responsible for her death. From that time he began assiduously to collect all the evidence he could find or fabricate to cause Hull's ruin.

There is no question that Joel Abbot had a disturbed personality. The whole course of his actions from 1821 to 1823 reveals a man in the grip of a persecution mania. He seems to have believed that his superiors at Boston were all thieves and worse, that they were out to get him because he might expose them, and that the Navy Department owed it to him to grant him all the funds, time, and extralegal leeway needed to bring the culprits to justice. Under questioning in 1822 he admitted that he was prepared to believe *anything* said against Hull and not to disbelieve any report unless it could be proved false. Of all the conspirators he was the most vindictive and the most clearly psychotic. Shaw and Bainbridge did have real, if petty reasons for hating Isaac Hull. Abbot's motives were only the dark fantasies that lurked in his mind.

After making desultory inquiries of various yard personnel about possible delinquencies of the commandant, Abbot hit upon the subject of copper as a likely point of attack. The navy yard kept a large supply of sheet and bolt copper for use in building and repairing vessels; much of it was imported in iron-banded crates weighting a half ton or more. In 1819 Hull had asked the commissioners whether he must have this copper all weighed and counted, sheet by sheet, at each annual survey. He was told that it was not essential to reweigh heavy articles every year, and so the copper was surveyed usually without weighing. It was easy, then, to accuse Hull of neglect on this score, and since a few copper bolts and bars had been pilfered from time to time—Hull had recovered some, on a tip, from Prudence Frost's boardinghouse in Boston—there was a possibility that a case for fraud could be made. At the very least, an unpleasant investigation might ensue. In October 1821 Abbot received orders to sail in the *Alligator,* and on the day she left Boston he wrote a brief letter to the secretary: "From various circumstances, the inference is so apparent to my mind, that the copper deposited at the Navy Yard Charlestown, if carefully examined and surveyed might so fall short of the proper quantity that I feel it a duty to make this communication."[70] Obviously, Abbot hoped that the investigation would take place in his absence and that he would not have to show his hand.

But his untimely return in the *Mariana Flora* put Abbot on the spot: there was a letter waiting for him from the secretary directing him to be more explicit, "in order that I may be the better enabled to direct my inquiries in relation to the matter."[71] He consulted Shaw and Trevett; the three decided that, since Abbot had been ordered by the secretary to make disclosures, he might now make broad accusations without fear of reprisal. Accordingly, he drafted a long letter, which he circulated to his friends before sending. It provides a good example of Abbot's devious style:

> In making this report of the copper, it is impossible to convey my impressions of things, without alluding to other subjects. The fact is, there has been a chain of proceedings, more or less intricate, by a variety of individuals, which altogether have occasioned me to think a great deal upon the matter of this communication; and even with all the pains I am able to take, it is impossible for me by writing to convey any thing like a full representation of things. I hope you will, therefore, indulge me in telling my story in my own way; and if there are any general expressions which you may think ought to be con-

firmed by facts, on intimation of your wish, I think there will be no difficulty in supplying them, of a nature to satisfy any reasonable mind.[72]

Joel Abbot was incapable of giving a straightforward answer to any question. His letter went on to say that he suspected deficiency in the copper because of rumors, because Fosdick *could* have had access to it, because he had heard that copper with the yard mark had been seen in Boston, and because "proper surveys" had not been taken. He then expanded at great length on the Fosdick case, saying that the clerk had lived in great extravagance, "kept two horses, servants, and a mistress," and generally spent beyond his means. These, of course, were outright lies. Fosdick had been far too clever to give an appearance of sudden wealth. Every witness subsequently called on the subject affirmed, without exception, that Fosdick had lived very frugally.

Fosdick, Hull, and Binney were, according to Abbot, "all equally suspected by the officers of the Navy Yard as being concerned in a game of peculation. . . . [E]very honest man in the Navy Yard was, in short, attacked by them." Caleb Gibbs and William Keating were the particular victims mentioned in this connection. In denouncing Fosdick as so obvious a villain, of course, Abbot was in danger of tarring his chief mentor with the universal brush, so he added: "except Commodore Bainbridge, of whom I entertain the most exalted sentiments, I do not believe there was another individual of the *officers* recommending Mr. F. who supposed him to be honest. Commodore Bainbridge, I believe, was circumvented and deceived, in regard to him, but the others knew him better." Abbot never explained why Bainbridge had been so gullible or why he must be presumed innocent while Hull was presumed guilty; nor could he ever produce a credible witness who could say that he had suspected Fosdick of the slightest malversation before the revelation of his guilt.

Abbot expatiated on William Keating's part in detecting Fosdick's fraud, putting the most sinister interpretation on the conduct of Hull and Binney, and declaiming that "the captors of André could not display more moral heroism, nor offer a more enchanting theme to the pen of genius" than did old Keating. After several more pages in the same vein, and two paragraphs on the irresistible subject of his chamber money, Abbot reverted to the copper: even if it were surveyed and found correct, it might not be so "because the mismanagement might have been in the accounts of receipts and expenditures of that article, which were for a long time entirely in the hands of Mr. Fosdick, and the book which he kept is lost or misplaced."[73] Thus, Hull was damned either way: if the copper fell short he was in the wrong, and if it was correct he was still suspect. Abbot could not end without another sweeping statement: "The most weighty and serious specifications I purposely withhold until your further orders to divulge them."

John Shaw could hardly wait to second Abbot's accusations: "It is with much regret," he wrote the secretary,

> that I inform you of a report which is now in circulation both in and outside the Navy Yard Charlestown. . . . As to myself I know nothing of the transactions, but will hazard an opinion that if *Fosdick's* conduct should be strictly investigated according to law, much real benefit might arise to the service, and much fraud be detected.[74]

Thompson passed this letter along to the commissioners, who advised him to demand of Shaw exactly what he meant. Before the secretary's reply reached him, however, Shaw was sending off a second letter, detailing all the gossip he had collected about Hull's carrying passengers in the *Constitution*.[75] The conspirators were feeling particularly encouraged by a visit from Bainbridge; Shaw had discussed the *Constitution* story with him, and Abbot showed him his letters as well. Abbot advised Bainbridge not to leave the management of his business affairs in the hands of Binney, and Bainbridge thanked him for the advice. On 19 January, Abbot wrote to Trevett at New York, enclosing a formal letter to the secretary in which he declared that he could prove Binney guilty of more fraud than Fosdick, and stated that Hull could not remain any longer at Boston "without being himself, or having others, disgraced."[76] He confided to Trevett that "the Elliot story," involving the purchase of medicine for Hull's family with public funds, could be substantiated and that "I am very confident there can be established a connection between Captain Hull and Fosdick, that must damn Captain Hull if he is brought to a Court Martial."[77]

Trevett cheerfully dispatched Abbot's letter to the secretary, with an offer to come to Washington himself, as "I think it would be in my power to impart nearly as much information as Mr. Abbot could do . . . and . . . I could reach Washington sooner by four or five days than he."[78] Three days later Shaw responded to the secretary's request for a more detailed report by naming Hull and Binney as the persons he believed connected with Fosdick's fraud.[79]

Secretary Thompson could only believe that where there was so much smoke there might be fire. Hull was still at Washington, but apparently without mentioning the matter to him, the secretary on 26 January ordered David Porter to go to Boston and, in company with United States Attorney George Blake, to investigate Abbot's and Shaw's charges to see whether Binney and Hull should be arrested. Trevett and

Abbot were directed to cooperate in the investigation. Porter was given authority to "act as in your judgment the urgency of the case demands, and you are hereby authorised to suspend from duty any officer . . . whose conduct in your judgment renders such step necessary and proper."[80]

Thompson intended to resolve the matter with the least possible publicity and, he hoped, the least grief to Hull if, as he supposed, the charges were unfounded. But he would have been better advised to order a full-scale public investigation. For one thing, the newspapers made a football of this semiprivate inquiry; for another, Porter was too impetuous to carry through an inquiry with enough patience.

Porter was at New York on 30 January and there found Abbot and Trevett. He questioned them closely and got an earful about their suspicions. Trevett, however, declined to make an affidavit or written statement because, he said, everything he "knew" had been told him by someone else. Abbot claimed to have documentary evidence, and he was ordered to return to Boston to present it, together with his witnesses, for the formal scrutiny of Porter and Blake. Porter's first encounter with Abbot and Trevett had already colored his view of the case. He wrote Secretary Thompson a report of the conversations that was laden with irony:

> Some it seems have got rich, no one can tell how, some with apparently slender means have lived with more style and expense than is usual among people so remarkable for their economical habits as those of New England, and putting together certain circumstances, and facts, collected from different people, and at different times, there seems to have been produced a conviction, of a regularly connected chain, formed for the purpose of defrauding the government, from the commandant of the establishment down to the workmen of the yard—the Grand Mover of which, it is believed is Mr. Binney the Navy Agent, who, it would appear, has succeeded in introducing into the establishment a system of corruption which has extended through every ramification of it, with the exception only of the few officers who considered themselves fairly entitled to extra allowances for firewood, chamber money, etc., which was refused to them, and which they seem to have no doubt has gone into the pockets of these conspirators. It is even intimated, notwithstanding the art with which these things are managed, that there is a bare-facedness in the thing that has disgusted these gentlemen, and occasioned them to talk very freely of Captain Hull's conduct, for it is declared that he has been actually seen, in the open day, and in the yard, conversing freely with the Master Sailmaker, Master Carpenter, and Storekeeper. This, if I recollect right, the Doctor has seen himself, and is, as far as I can understand, the most he would be willing to swear to.

Porter thought that if half what was said were true there was not an honest man connected with the navy yard, "with the exception of the before-mentioned gentlemen. There are some things said with regard to Captain Hull which, if true, render him unworthy of the trust he holds, and of the cloth he wears, and if untrue, worthy of every satisfaction within the power of the department to give or exact for him." Clearly, Porter leaned to the latter view. He remarked that Abbot claimed to have journals kept by

> persons both in and out of the yard, who have been secretly watching the conduct of those implicated. . . . One of these persons [Charles Waldo] I understand was a disappointed applicant for the office of storekeeper, the other [George A. Otis], whose attention has been more particularly directed to Mr. Binney, is, or has been, an applicant for the situation he holds.

The willingness of Abbot and Trevett to talk made Porter sure that the task of getting at the origin of the gossip would be easy: "there appears to be a confidence existing of the certainty of substantiating the charges against Captain Hull and Mr. Binney, and . . . those who are active in the business promise to themselves not only much honor but much satisfaction." One important fact he had learned already: "That Captain Shaw is acting understandingly with Lt. Abbot I have ascertained in conversation with Dr. Trevett, as also that it was desired that the fact should not be known."[81]

Isaac Hull returned to the navy yard by Saturday, 2 February, and found everyone busily at work on the *Macedonian*. Master Commandant Shubrick informed him that orders had been received a day or two earlier to fit her for a West Indies cruise. He also told Hull that, about a week earlier, Shaw had attempted to draw him into his activities by giving him copies of his letters to the Navy Department, under cover of a letter to Hull, all unsealed. Shubrick had returned the letters; Shaw had again sent them; and Shubrick had then sealed them in an envelope and put them aside. Hull looked at the covering letter, which read:

> As a brother officer, influenced by a respect for the individuals of our service and a sense of the duty which I owe both to my country and myself, I have been compelled to address letters to the Hon. Secretary of the Navy on the subject of reports in circulation, copies of which letters I do myself the honor to enclose, and have requested Captain Shubrick to hand them to you on your arrival here.[82]

David Porter reached Boston at midnight on 3 February and took rooms at the Exchange Coffee House. Early the next morning he summoned George Blake and Joel Abbot and began the investigation. Sending Abbot to fetch his witnesses, Porter and Blake went over Abbot's letters together, and Blake was able to clear up several matters. He assured Porter that, having been involved in the investigation of Fosdick, he was absolutely certain that Hull and Binney had not been parties to the fraud. He described Binney as an "honest, candid, fair-dealing man," by no means as wealthy as some people thought, much of his property being tied up in real estate speculation. The real cause of grumbling against Binney, according to Blake, was that during the war he had succeeded, sometimes by selling his own property to buy naval stores, in manning and outfitting the ships at Boston. Many Bostonians had hoped to bring the war to a halt by withholding funds, and Binney had frustrated their plan. Since then he had declined to enter into certain schemes whose promoters were now eager to injure him.

Blake then made a list of fourteen charges contained in Abbot's letters and, when the lieutenant returned at the appointed hour, asked him which of these he could substantiate on oath. Abbot, ever averse to particulars, began to object: the list was not a fair summary of his letter. Blake and Porter then produced the letters and compared them in detail with the list; Abbot had to admit the details were correct. He now said he could not swear to any of his charges but could prove them through witnesses, which would be a long and tedious process. Very well, said the interrogators: produce some witnesses. If just one charge could be proved against Binney, it would be sufficient to bring him to court; if only one allegation against Hull were substantiated, he could be arrested.

Abbot shuffled. Clearly matters were not moving as he had expected. He had evidently been advised that his letters would produce the arrest of Hull and Binney and that he could then act as prosecutor, bringing forward any and all evidence at public expense, and appearing as a public hero. It was unfair, he said, to carry on both the Hull and the Binney cases at once; Porter told him that he had himself mixed them together in his letter. Finally, Porter asked Abbot point-blank whether he would disavow any knowledge of fraud in both cases. Abbot said that

"he was not prepared to answer the question" "He wanted time to arrange the proofs he had," "he considered the letter of the 11th as a mere preliminary step and had no idea of being called on in this hasty manner." "Should like to consult friends." "had hoped to reach Washington where he had friends in Congress to whom he had supplied much information on the subject and through whom he had intended to bring the thing before the Secretary of the Navy," etc. etc.

Porter was disgusted, "finding that nothing could be got out of him, and firmly believing from his ignorance of the content of his own letters that he is acting by advice."[83]

The investigation adjourned until 4:00 P.M. At that hour Abbot returned with one witness against Binney, a former business partner who had quarreled with him. The two men were engaged in litigation at the time, and the charges the ex-partner presented against Binney had nothing to do with navy business. As for Hull, Abbot would have preferred to drop the matter entirely, but Porter would not let him off the hook: "I . . . told him that one of two things must be done before I leave Boston—recant altogether his charges against Captain Hull or furnish some evidence of their truth." Abbot wanted to bring in his lawyer, James T. Austin, but Porter scoffed at the idea: Blake could do what he wished in the Binney affair, but with regard to the naval service Porter thought himself competent to judge whether there had been a violation by either Hull or Abbot of naval regulations. He was, after all, one of those who had written them. The meeting broke up about nine, and Porter told Abbot to bring in a list of witnesses against Hull the next day or suffer the consequences.[84]

Abbot thought he saw an escape hatch. After leaving Porter he had a talk with John Percival, who made a fatherly suggestion that he drop the whole matter. What gratification could there be, he asked the young man, in breaking a man who had done so much for the country? Abbot made no reply except to disclaim any personal animosity toward Hull, but early the next morning he came to Percival's house and said:

> I have thought much of what you said to me last night. I have called to make a proposition; not such a proposition as you proposed last night. Take your pen and write, and I will dictate. I am willing to withdraw my charges against Captain Hull, on his effecting an exchange with Commodore Bainbridge, which, no doubt, . . . he can do; and thereby leaving the station. Capt. Hull is not to arrest me, nor try to have me arrested. If he does, it is further to be understood, I am to be considered in the same situation as I am, as if nothing had transpired; but application must be made for the exchange before tomorrow, twelve o'clock, and I be informed of the same, or it will be out of my power to have anything to do or say in it.

The source of this suggestion is not difficult to conjecture. Bainbridge was then in Boston; and Bainbridge had wanted Hull to go to Philadelphia so that he could take over again at Charlestown. The deadline at noon the next day was to forestall any action by Porter against Abbot, which appeared to be impending. The proposition also clarifies Abbot's motives: If he believed Hull to be a dangerous embezzler, why would he be willing for Hull to quietly remove himself to another navy yard to continue his peculations? At any rate, Percival didn't think much of the idea. He told Abbot it was not very chivalrous, to say the least, to require Hull to make an arrangement with his enemy. Abbot, perhaps thinking that he had been a little more public about the matter than

Bainbridge would wish, said that Percival could erase the commodore's name. As an alternative, he suggested that Hull could plead ill health and take command of the *Macedonian* for a cruise to the West Indies. Percival again asked Abbot why he wanted Hull removed, and Abbot offered a piece of curious reasoning: since he had made accusations against Hull, he felt it was "due to his character" that Hull should make some sacrifice. In other words, the mere fact that he had raised charges against his commanding officer obligated that commander to suffer for the sake of the accuser's reputation.

Percival shrugged and went out to carry the note to the commandant's house. He anticipated the result. "Indeed," cried Hull, "I might as well acknowledge myself guilty of the infamous charges at once!" As Percival put it, "Captain Hull was very indignant."

Seeing that Percival's views were not in accord with theirs, the conspirators next attempted to silence him by a poison-pen letter:

"Dat veniam corvis, vexat censura columbas."
"Latet anguis in herba"
Percival   Beware!!! be not seduced by false appearance. *Hull* is not your *friend.* he affects to be, to accomplish his own purposes which once effected, *your ruin is inevitable.* The moment he is honourable acquitted (should such be the case, which much I doubt) it is his intention to arrest you for having used disrespectful language in reference to him. The plea of *harrass'd feelings,* of *passion at the moment* &c. will avail you but little with him *hereafter,* tho' you serve him *now,* and are so strenuously his advocate. *He once secure, your ruin is inevitable.* Think not that *gratitude* or *justice* will bind him; he knows not those feelings. Be not flattered by the attention you and yours have *recently* received from that quarter. You and Mrs. Percival were invited to dine with Mrs. Hull in *consequence* of a letter she received from her husband whilst at *Washington after he understood* how things were going on. Did you ever receive such a mark of her attention *before?* and why not? were you less worthy *formerly* than now? "SAT VERBUM SAPIENT." Improve upon it for your own safety. "FAVETE LINGUIS"—be neuter, or you will be implicated.

A Spectator[85]

Percival was unimpressed. He passed the letter along to Hull.

After his meeting with Percival on the morning of 5 February, Abbot went to Porter's room, but the story was the same. Abbot said he had been ill all night, and besides, "he could not get any of the witnesses to appear before the Board: that they were in the fear of Captain Hull, and in the power of Captain Hull." Porter must have smiled at this ludicrous portrait of his mild-mannered little friend, but he assured Abbot that if any of the witnesses were in the navy he had the power to compel them to testify and that civil proceedings could be brought against civilians. Abbot still refused to name a single witness against Hull. Porter thereupon arrested him for violating Article 3 of the Act for the Better Government of the Navy of 1800, "By wickedly and maliciously conspiring with others to defame the character of Captain Isaac Hull."[86]

The investigation of Amos Binney plodded along, resting entirely on witnesses brought forward by Abbot, and producing little or no evidence of wrongdoing. As a precaution, Porter had placed a secret attachment of $150,000 on Binney's property, but after a week of work he was convinced that there was not "any circumstance which could justify the seizure of any part of his property. . . . [M]ost of the charges are frivolous and vexatious."[87] Abbot, who at first had accepted his arrest with equanimity, had now become alarmed. He had been led to believe that he could use his own trial as a forum to air charges against Hull, but he began to fear that it would turn out with Hull as it had with Binney. On 12 February he wrote the secretary of the navy, begging to be released from arrest and enclosing an opinion of his lawyer that Porter's and Blake's proceeding was improper. But the ground of the lawyer's recommendation for Abbot's release was that the lieutenant should now be allowed to comply with Porter's demand for witnesses, and this he continued to refuse to do.[88]

Outwardly, all was calm. Porter and Hull attended a farewell dinner for Bainbridge on 7 February and a second, given by the Charlestown mechanics and manufacturers, on the fifteenth.[89] Conspicuous by his absence from the second dinner was Captain John Shaw. On the previous day Hull, on advice from Porter, had arrested Shaw and asked that he be court-martialed on two charges: (1) "treating with contempt his superior officer, being in the execution of the duties of his office," for writing the sneering letters to Hull of 7 October 1820 and 22 May 1821; and (2) "unofficerlike and ungentlemanlike conduct," for spreading rumors about Hull; for writing the letters of 14, 22, and 25 January to the secretary; and for circulating these letters to other officers.[90] On 2 March, Secretary Thompson gave orders for the court-martial to convene at Charlestown on the twentieth.

Meanwhile, Porter was anxious to wind up the Binney investigation and get back to Washington. He had learned that his wife was ill, and when, on 16 February, Binney gave his explanations of the transactions Abbot had called into question,

> Lt. Abbot assured him that he had been altogether in error with regard to the transactions that gave rise to the rumours . . . stated his willingness to do justice to his character, and offered, as his apology for the course he had taken, the duty incumbent on him as an officer of the Navy to endeavour to detect

fraud where it existed, as he had firmly believed it did, from the information he had named of persons on whom he had the fullest reliance.

Mr. Abbot wished to withdraw himself from any further prosecution, but Mr. Blake, as various persons had been named to him to whom reference could be had for facts, very properly insisted on pursuing the subject while a shadow of doubt could possibly remain on the mind of anyone; consequently I shall be detained here some time longer. I am, however, of opinion, (and Mr. Blake agrees with me) that all the rest of the evidence and charges will prove as frivolous and groundless as those we have examined.

I do not hesitate to say that there has been a shameful combination to ruin the character of Mr. Binney. The persons concerned in it are hostile to him because he has been too faithful to his trust to serve their avaricious views. I consider Mr. Abbot their mere tool.[91]

One week later the investigators drew up their opinion in the Binney case, concluding that while some of Binney's ways of doing business could be called irregular, "we have not been able, after the most rigid scrutiny, to discover any instance in the conduct of Mr. Binney wherein the United States have sustained injury, either in respect to money transactions, or otherwise, by reason of any unfairness or infidelity of this officer."[92] Porter then returned to Washington, but since a few witnesses remained to be examined, and since George Blake was unwilling to act alone, Secretary Thompson ordered Captain Charles Morris, who was going to Charlestown as a member of the court-martial, to assist in completing the investigation. So Binney's quasi trial dragged along into the spring.

Before leaving Boston, Porter extended the limits of Joel Abbot's arrest to allow him to visit Newburyport. As soon as he reached Washington he drew up a charge against the lieutenant for "scandalous conduct, tending to the destruction of good morals," with twenty-nine specifications of instances, all summed up in the first: "In that, moved by a spirit of envy, or base motive, he hath, upon the Boston station, and within a year now last past, scandalously attempted to take from his superior officer, Captain Isaac Hull, his good name."[93]

12

Trials

The court-martial met on board the *Independence* on the morning of Wednesday, 20 March 1822. Old Captain Thomas Tingey had come from the Washington Navy Yard to preside; members of the court were Captains Charles Morris, Lewis Warrington, John Orde Creighton, Thomas Macdonough, Robert T. Spence, and John Downes. They would try Shaw first, then Abbot.

Shaw had made one attempt to avoid trial by appealing to the secretary of the navy, insisting that he had written his letters only out of a sense of duty; at the least he wanted paid counsel and "proper witnesses"—he had made up a list of ninety-two. But he could not resist adding that "my prosecutor . . . now stands as low in the opinion of the population of Charlestown as it is [possible] a man can when he is implicated by them of dishonesty and public peculation on the funds of the government entrusted in his charge."[1] Secretary Smith Thompson told him gravely that "some parts of [your letter] I think you will on reflection agree with me in opinion had better been omitted. All the witnesses you have named have been ordered to report to the President of the Court Martial. I presume you cannot expect the government to furnish you with counsel."[2] Isaac Hull commented to David Porter on the Monday before the trial that

> Shaw intends having a host of witnesses. What they can say I know not. Officers, of course, must attend if the Dept. thinks proper to indulge him to run up an expense equal to the building of a sloop of war; I say, indulge him, for one half must be indulgence for surely ten is as good as ten thousand to establish any one fact. I cannot now but believe that his object is to prove reports and not facts. How far he will succeed I know not. He has called on many very respectable people of this town as witnesses and I am informed that some of them will not attend. Whether those at a greater distance will do the same or not is uncertain.[3]

Shaw had already lost his flagship. A few days before the court opened the commissioners ordered the *Independence* put in ordinary; she was warped to the navy yard dock for the convenience of the court, and as soon as it closed she would be "mothballed." Prosecution testimony was brief. Hull was the arresting officer and prosecutor in this trial. With George Blake at his side to repeat the witnesses' words in his ear, he called only six men to prove that Shaw had put his mean reports in circulation. When Shaw opened his defense on 25 March, it quickly appeared that Hull had guessed right: since he could in no way hope to prove that Hull had bilked his passengers in the *Constitution* or had been in collusion with Fosdick, Shaw hoped to show that such gossip had been in circulation. His letters to the secretary had alleged only the *existence* of reports, not their veracity, he contended. If he could prove that such reports were in fact current, he thought that sufficient to clear him of the second charge, that of circulating gossip with intent to defame. He didn't get all his ninety-two witnesses, though some, like Captains Arthur Sinclair and William Crane, came all the way from Norfolk to testify that they had heard the rumors about the *Constitution* passengers and had told them to Shaw. Sinclair was sure that he had heard from several people that Hull had charged twenty-five guineas. But the *Constitution*'s officers, when brought to the stand, gave no credence to the report, and Hull secured depositions from seven of his passengers that they had paid nothing on demand, that they had given freely what they gave, and that the most anyone remembered paying was ten guineas. Leonard Jarvis sent a voluntary testimonial:

> Your conduct towards myself and the other gentlemen, at your table, was hospitable, kind, and gentlemanly. You extorted no money from me, either as a douceur for receiving me on board, or as the price of my passage; nor did I ever hear any thing of the kind respecting the other passengers. I go further, and say, you did not even make a claim upon me for any remuneration whatever. I have always felt that you conferred a favour by receiving me on board, and I know, that by so doing, you saved me a considerable expense of money and time.[4]

Shaw was unlucky that Nathaniel Heyward of South Carolina was dead. Quite a few people remembered that Heyward, one of the richest men in America, had made loud complaints about paying for his passage in the *Constitution*. But the only man who could be found alive to complain against Hull was a Cambridge mechanic, William F. Cutter. It appeared on examination that, although Cutter believed that Hull had demanded ten guineas of him (not twenty-five), it was in fact the other passengers who had told him what sum they had agreed among themselves to pay.

Shaw actually produced only twelve witnesses, though he tried unsuccessfully to persuade the court that his having told the secretary "that Captains Bainbridge, Crane, and Sinclair, and *others*" had given him reports against Hull should entitle him to call as many "others" as he liked. After some delay for the return of depositions from other cities, the court heard Shaw's defense on 11 April and on the following day pronounced him guilty of the first charge of "treating with contempt his superior officer" and, with regard to the second, guilty of "unofficerlike" but not of "ungentlemanlike" conduct. The sentence, six months' suspension, was very light.

On Saturday, 13 April, the court arraigned Abbot and prepared to begin hearing his case on Monday. This trial lasted a little over three weeks, until 7 May. It heard fifteen prosecution and thirty-one defense witnesses. Abbot's position was that he had merely acted out of a sense of duty in making known to the secretary that rumors were rife about Hull. In essence, his defense depended on showing that Hull was guilty of the charges Abbot had brought against him, so that from 16 April, when Abbot opened his defense, it was really Isaac Hull who was on trial.

Abbot's "charges" fell into four categories: (1) the fraudulent use of government property by Hull, including labor and building materials for his property and medicine for his family; (2) collusion in, or at least deliberate ignorance of, Fosdick's peculation; (3) neglect of proper supervision of government stores, allowing copper and other materials to be filched from the yard; and (4) oppression of officers by refusing them their allowances—the alleged extortion of money from Percival was also mentioned. Moreover, Abbot insisted "that all and singular the charges, suggestions, and intimations that I have made, except my letter of October 4, 1821, were made in consequence of orders received from the Navy Department."[5]

The next afternoon Abbot challenged Hull's right to sit by the judge advocate and propose questions for the witnesses. Hull was not the prosecutor in Abbot's trial, but he could not hear the witnesses unless he sat in front of the courtroom with someone to aid him. He took the court's ruling in favor of Abbot's objection as expulsion and angrily left the courtroom. He was thus spared the parade of witnesses, but the tension of those weeks and the knowledge that his character was being flayed by Abbot's lawyers caused him much anguish. Although he tried to carry on the business of the yard as usual, his thoughts were in the courtroom.

Finally, on 6 May, Samuel Knapp and William Sullivan presented their client's defense at tedious length, repeating again every charge and every shred of evidence produced against Hull. William C. Aylwin, the judge advocate, summed up for the prosecution, showing that Abbot had not proved one of his charges and defining his motives in terms of his resentment over the chamber money and the matter of his leave: "because he did not instantly have his request granted, he charitably imputes to Captain Hull the death of his wife. The Court . . . will decide whether the mind could be pure, whether the intentions of the prisoner could have been dictated by an honest zeal for the good of the service or not."[6]

They were not long in making up their minds. On the following day, after the reading of the record had been completed, the court judged Abbot guilty of twenty of the twenty-nine specifications of the charge and of parts of four more:

> the Court thereupon adjudge him, the said Lieut. Joel Abbot, guilty of the charge of "Scandalous conduct, tending to the destruction of good morals," preferred against him; and sentence him to be suspended from rank, pay, and emoluments, for the term of two years from the time of the approval of this sentence; and that the finding of this Court on the charge and several specifications exhibited against him, and also the sentence pronounced, when approved, be transmitted to, and publicly read, at each of the naval stations in the United States.[7]

This was hardly the end of the affair. If the official trial of Abbot and Shaw had ended, the newspaper trial of Isaac Hull had only begun. The Federalist papers opened the offensive a few days before the close of Abbot's trial. Although the leading paper in terms of age and respectability was Russell's *Columbian Centinel,* the shrillest and most scurrilous was the *New England Galaxy.* Abbot's lawyer, Samuel Knapp, was an associate publisher of the *Galaxy,* which, unhappily for Hull, delivered its barbs with a good deal of style and wit. Anticipating some of this, Hull wrote Thompson on 9 May to ask that a court of inquiry be ordered to examine his conduct since 1815, for

> During the trial of Lieut. Abbot I am informed that such parts of the administration of the affairs of this Yard have been inquired into as he thought would conduce most to the extenuation of his offence. And as I could not be permitted to appear before the court martial in any legal shape in my own vindication, it may be possible that some transactions require explanation.[8]

Hull did not particularly want a trial, but he hoped the secretary would reply in such a way as to express full confidence in him and thus put a stop to all the gossip. Already there were signs that the trials of Shaw and Abbot would be used against him. As soon as Shaw's sentence was made public on 3 May the *Galaxy* crowed:

> We understand that the court acquitted him from the charge of ungentlemanly conduct; and if we can understand the nature of the charge on which

the court passed their extraordinary sentence, it may be construed into a sentence of approbation rather than of censure. . . . [F]or his letter of congratulation he is to be relieved from duty for six months and to receive his usual pay, which will enable him to spend a very comfortable summer of rest and recreation![9]

There was also a report that Shaw planned to publish his own version of the trial. He was frequently at the Exchange Coffee House, closeted with Chaplain Cheever Felch, his secretary. Hull therefore asked for an official copy of the trial and sentence, in case he should have to make a counterpublication, for "of course I cannot expect that a correct copy of the whole proceedings will be laid before the public, as they will probably select such parts as will best suit their purposes."[10] In fact, the secretary sent Hull the official transcript of the trial before there was time to copy it in Washington, so that Shaw, who did not have a copy adequate to publish, had to wait until Hull finished with the transcript before he could use it. He finally got his book into print in October, with an appendix containing his private correspondence with Sinclair and others, but it was too late; there had been so much sensation in Boston in the preceding six months that Shaw's book was anticlimactic.[11]

David Porter had been up to Boston again for Abbot's trial; on his return to Washington he received word from Hull that "all remains pretty quiet since you left us except a little abuse in that respectable paper *Galaxy.* I have not seen the papers of last evening but am told that the story of the medicine is made a great handle of. That you know was their strong point."[12] The *Galaxy* had in fact reported that Abbot was going to publish the minutes of his trial as taken down by a "professional gentleman . . . who attended it daily." The gentleman was F. W. Waldo, one of Abbot's friends and counselors. It added:

We shall be disappointed if the testimony of Mr. Eliot [*sic*], the apothecary, who supplied medicines for a lady in Connecticut, *on account of the U.S. navy,* does not open the eyes of some people; and we shall be still more so, if the new way of getting rich, which has been so successfully practiced by almost every one concerned in the Navy-Yard, is not satisfactorily explained.[13]

Before the trial Hull had made vain attempts to get this matter of the medicines clarified. The charge went back to 1818, when Ann Hull's sister Jannette had joined the Charlestown family. Her health was poor, and Isaac Hull had called in a private physician, Dr. Danforth, to attend her. Danforth, pronouncing the navy yard medicines "swill," ordered Hull to have his prescriptions filled by Ephraim Elliot, a Boston apothecary. Over the next year Hull frequently sent his black servant, Isaac

Wheeden, to Elliot for medicines, and sometimes the Hart sisters called at the shop. Once, in September, they asked that the bottles be packed for traveling, since they were going on a visit to Connecticut. When the time came to settle the bill, early in 1819, Hull sent word to Elliot to make it out against the navy yard. Elliot indignantly refused and kept on refusing until finally, in September 1819, he decided that the money was better than the principle and signed a receipt to the navy agent for $53.54½.

At the time these purchases were made, and until an order from the Navy Department of May 1821, it had been customary for medicines to be supplied at government expense, either from navy stores or private apothecaries, for the families of officers. Dr. Samuel Trevett, who introduced this subject to Abbot and directed him to Elliot, knew this fact, but he may have felt threatened in his pretensions to be "medical purveyor" to the yard by Danforth's rejection of his medicines.

Thinking that Elliot did not know about the regulations, Hull had called on him and explained the situation, but Elliot remarked petulantly that he had been ill used.

"By whom?" asked Hull in surprise.

Elliot replied, "By you, Captain Hull."

"Why," said the astonished Hull, "you are one of the last men I would ill use. I never had any such idea."

Elliot told Hull then that he had had several visits from men inquiring about the case; apparently, he thought Hull had sent them. As he recounted the events at Hull's trial, he had been visited on one occasion by Thomas Waine, purser of the Java, and an unidentified friend. Waine had questioned him about the medicines and Elliot had refused to say anything. Waine died in December 1820, and so did not figure in the subsequent intrigues. Some time after his visit, probably in the early months of 1821, Abbot had come to his shop with Lieutenant Henry Ward. Ward alleged that he was in trouble because he had repeated the medicine story, and he asked Elliot to confirm it. According to Elliot's testimony,

> [W]itness told him that it was very unpleasant business to witness, that they were strangers, and witness did not chuse to say any thing about it; he then said I am like to be sued for defamation for what I have said, witness said if you are like to be sued for defamation, you have a right to summons me to Court in your defence if you think I know any thing that will be of service to you. Lieutenant Abbot said that is all we want Mr. Ward; Lieutenant Abbot said, I am much obliged to you Doctor, they bowed and went off.

Hull, when Elliot told him of these encounters, said that there was a combination against him, including Dr. Trevett, but that he would baffle them all. Robert Knox, master of the yard, was a distant relative of Elliot's, and he also called on the apothecary to explain the motives of his visitors. According to Elliot,

> he said there was a number combined together to injure Captain Hull, they would fail, for he knew all about it; he said they depend very much upon your evidence; they say Doctor Elliot says he is ready to come forward at any time; witness said, Robert, I have got one plain story to tell, I have told it a great many times, and if I am called upon, which I hope I shall not be, I shall tell it right straight off; he answered, damn it Doctor, Captain Hull is a fine man, and they are trying to ruin him, you can tell the whole truth and yet word it so that it will appear to advantage after all.

Elliot, at any rate, was consistent. He continued to tell his story, at Abbot's trial and again at Hull's inquiry. Somehow he was never able to accept even the assurance of the court that what Hull had done was proper according to regulations, and he continued to play into the hands of the opposition editors.[14]

Consequently, despite the outcome of the trial, Hull foresaw the need of good offices at the capital. As he told Porter,

> Shaw continues to associate with the same low trash . . . and I have no doubt but they will do all they can to ruin me. I shall therefore require a continuance of your friendly air and that of the [other] Commissioners. . . . [N]othing short of a letter from the Department expressing in the fullest manner the approbation of the government will make the good people of Boston quiet. God only knows when they will let me alone, nor can I determine on what measures I ought to take.[15]

Shaw, it seems, was being showered with attention, including a public dinner by the citizens of Charlestown. He also received plenty of condolence and advice, some of it positively sinister. Jesse D. Elliott wrote him on 11 May that "you had materials in your court . . . to have made your case a second Barron's, and it rests with you to say whether it shall be so or not."[16] Jesse Elliott (no relation to the apothecary) had been one of the engineers of the fatal duel between James Barron and Stephen Decatur; his glee at the prospect of another such tragedy is unmistakable. The *Galaxy* was still printing that "*Thus a brave and experienced officer is condemned to suffer a six months recreation at Nahant, Ballston, Niagara, and other fashionable places of resort, with no care upon his mind, and plenty of money in his pocket!*"[17] To this Hull commented that "Shaw's friends are endeavouring to make out that the court have in their sentence merely paid him the compliment of giving him leave of absence to visit the springs for a few months on full pay, etc. All this he pays Knapp and his private *secretary*, Felch, for."[18] But on this point Shaw was to be sadly disappointed. On 27 May, Purser Robert Ludlow told him he had orders from the fourth auditor of the Treasury to put Shaw on half pay for six months from 23 April, the date his sentence was approved. Shaw protested to the secretary that "several members of the court took occasion to remark to me, and to others, that their decision did not in any way affect my pay and emoluments," and he asked permission to write to the president for redress. The secretary himself showed Shaw's letter to President Monroe and was confirmed in his decision. He wrote Shaw coldly that

> The Act of Congress of the 21st of April 1806 expressly declares that officers shall receive no more than half their monthly pay during the time when they shall not be under orders for actual service. An officer under sentence of suspension cannot be considered subject to an order for actual service, and it has long since been the construction given to this law, that Officers in that situation received only half pay. I have the official opinion of the Attorney General sanctioning this construction.[19]

Shaw's friends professed shock at this unwarranted severity. William Bainbridge wrote him a letter marked "*Strictly Confidential*," suggesting a series of arguments that Shaw might use against the secretary's ruling, concluding that "if he should not [reconsider his decision] after a respectful representation of the case you have your alternative by memorial to Congress."[20]

Isaac Hull, immediately after the trial, was alternately hopeful and cast down. On 13 May he wrote Porter that "I understand that the tide is now fast turning, particularly in Charlestown. The respectable and thinking men now believe that there has been a combination and a plan laid to do me all the injury in their power." He thought that under the circumstances the conspirators might be unwilling to show themselves before a formal court of inquiry: "still . . . if there is any doubt in the mind of the Secretary as to the correctness of my conduct I am ready and willing to stand another investigation, notwithstanding what I have suffered."[21]

Mad Jack Percival expressed to Thomas Aspinwall his satisfaction at the outcome of the trial and also at his own adherence to Hull in spite of past slights:

> We have had a hot campaign of court martial here this season, and what will you say when I assure you I was the only Lt. which stuck fast and friendly to Hull in this trying time, notwithstanding all his unkindness to me in my London expedition and on my return? But justice is my motive. . . . He has been most ungenerously treated by a set of conspiring and plotting knaves. He has proved his innocence and implicated his enemies, but I will acknowledge

to you as my friend I felt a pride; I exulted to find I was the only Lieut. on his side. It will, I trust, be a source of grateful reflection to me that the only one he ever injured was at his side in the day of his trouble and persecution.[22]

Hull did feel grateful to Percival; nor did he forget the lieutenant's faithfulness in the years to come. His other rock of support in these dark hours was David Porter. Porter's letter of 14 May gave Hull the first news that Abbot's sentence had been approved by the secretary and that Thompson thought further investigation of Hull was unnecessary. He assured Porter that the news was a great relief to him, "not from any apprehension I was under in having a fair and impartial investigation into my conduct, but when I saw a set of men destitute of honour or principle determined to go all lengths to effect their purpose I could not but be anxious." On one point, though, he was still apprehensive:

I hope the Secretary, should he not think a court of inquiry necessary, will give as full an answer to my letter as is proper that he should give, and that my letter requesting the inquiry and his answer will be published as soon as it can well be. I am confident that it will be much better to have not only these letters but the sentence of the court made public by the Department than to have them sent here for the papers, for should they be promulgated by me the public would say that I had done it to injure Shaw and Abbot. . . . I cannot but hope that the Secretary will do all that he can and ought in Justice to do to quiet the public mind and to put a stop to the abuse these people are heaping up against everyone that has stood in the way of their abominable designs.[23]

Hull's fears were fully justified. Thompson replied officially to his request for a court of inquiry on 21 May, saying that

such a measure is thought to be entirely unnecessary. Your conduct appears to have undergone an examination on the late trial of Lieut. Abbot, in the particulars respecting which complaints had been made by him; and the result of that trial shows, that those complaints were groundless. The public good does not, therefore, seem to require a compliance with your request; and the frequency of courts martial, and courts of inquiry, is not only expensive, but extremely injurious in many respects to the public service.[24]

Hull's letter and Thompson's reply were published in the *National Intelligencer* the following week and were picked up by the *Boston Patriot*, the city's leading Republican newspaper, together with the *Intelligencer*'s comment:

The following letters will be acceptable to that numerous class of our readers by whom the name of Capt. Hull is held in great respect; and we believe that there is none of our readers who will not heartily coincide in the view which is taken by Mr. Secretary Thompson, of the frequency of courts martial and courts of inquiry.[25]

But the *Galaxy* also reprinted the exchange, and the *Intelligencer's* editorial note, with a much longer comment of its own:

We can assure the editors of the Intelligencer that there are a great many readers who do not coincide with the views of the Secretary of the Navy, and who believe that there is a much better reason than the Secretary has been pleased to give for refusing to appoint a court of inquiry on the application of Capt. Hull; which is, that HE DARE NOT DO IT. We repeat it—it is the firm belief of many readers and talkers too, that the powers at Washington have not the courage either to order a court of inquiry on Capt. Hull, or to remove Mr. Binney from the office of navy agent. Such a course would be attended with danger to the reputation of many public officers, and might possibly produce some difficulty in the Cabinet.[26]

This was just what Hull had feared; the secretary's response had not been full and positive enough to stop the talk; discussion of the question of a court of inquiry would not cease.

But for the moment attention had shifted to the publication of Abbot's account of his trial. The appearance of the book, on 9 June, was preceded by a letter from Abbot to the newspapers, printed in the *Galaxy* on 31 May and reprinted by the other papers. He asked the public to suspend judgment on him until they saw his version of the trial. He wrote:

I have always considered an enlightened community the supreme court of errors, which supervises, and often reverses judgements founded in prejudice, partialities or mistakes. . . . There are but few infallible organs of justice, and a court martial was never ranked among them. When my fellow citizens are in full possession of all the facts and circumstances relating to my trial, they will, I have no doubt, judge correctly of me and others. The difficulties and dangers which surround a junior officer, who attempts to investigate the conduct of his superiors, can never be known until seen and felt, and then this knowledge generally comes too late for him to profit by it.

This letter, with its open insinuation that the court had been prejudiced, furnished Porter with ammunition for a new attack. He had been disgusted that Abbot was let off with a two-year suspension, and on 3 June he wrote a long and impassioned letter to the secretary, asking that Abbot be given a second trial for writing the offensive letter or, better yet, dismissed from the navy forthwith. Porter pulled out all the stops:

having brought the charges against Lieutenant Abbot and thereby placed by the course of investigation the character of Captain Hull in jeopardy, I cannot consent that injustice should be done to him. . . . The character of the man who taught us that British ships were not invincible must not be unjustly assailed with comparative impunity, whatever may be the consequences to others.

He observed pointedly that Abbot had been represented by three lawyer-politicians, not known to

> gratuitously employ their time in the service of others. It was also currently reported in Boston and generally believed that the supporters of Lieut. Abbot and his conspirators had pledged themselves to indemnify him for any injury he might sustain by the sentence of the Court. I have never heard this contradicted, and my own knowledge of the obliquities of Lieut. Abbot, independently of the sentence of the Court, justifies the belief that he is base enough to sell himself to the worst of characters and for the most scandalous and wicked purposes.

Porter himself accused the court of irregularities, principally in allowing Abbot too much leeway in bringing witnesses against Hull on matters not contained in the charges. Had it been a civilian court he would have appealed, but since there was no appeal from a military court, all he could do was ask for a new trial.[27]

He sent a copy of his letter to Isaac Hull. Though grateful as always for Porter's efforts, Hull was dubious about the possibility of a second trial on the same charges; he did think Abbot's letter to the newspapers might be made the ground of a new charge or even for outright dismissal: "I should suppose was the President to see that letter that he would not hesitate to run his pen over Abbot's name on the list after his suspension is out."

Porter's job now was to counter the publication of Abbot's version of the trial by writing to the *National Intelligencer*, pointing out the discrepancies between Waldo's transcription and that of the judge advocate. "By doing so, the sale will be stopped and the book will remain on their hands, except the few that are taken by subscribers. . . . No one can place things in their proper light as well as you can," Hull assured him. Isaac Hull never wrote to the newspapers. Although he wrote a plain, forthright, and lively style that is much more appealing today than the florid periods of his contemporaries, he could not achieve a fashionable prose, and he dared not risk ridicule of his spelling and sentence structure. He left the newspaper offensive to his more cultured friend, with the old watchword from the *Adams* days: "As you said to me, keep yourself cool, until you get the book. Let them have a little more rope and they will hang themselves."[28]

Telling Porter to keep cool was like cautioning a river not to flow.

The newspaper war was, for him, a near substitute for the real thing. The *Galaxy* began publishing parts of Waldo's transcript on 7 June, two days before the book was issued, with abundant editorial comment:

> We . . . feel astonished, as we believe the public will feel, that a court-martial could be found in this enlightened age, and in this *free* and *happy* country, to pass such a singular and unrighteous sentence. It is even difficult to conceive why Lieutenant Abbot should have been tried at all. . . . [O]ne might suppose that it was Capt. Hull who was upon trial, and that Lieut. Abbot was merely a witness on the stand.[29]

By 24 June, Porter had his copy of the book and had prepared his counterblast. He pointed out that the judge advocate was under oath to keep a correct account of the trial, and the *Intelligencer* printed in parallel columns Dr. Trevett's testimony as recorded by the judge advocate and by Waldo to show how "the language of the testimony [has been] in general so altered, and the matter so interpolated, as to give a colouring to it entirely different from the true intent and meaning of the witnesses, when it was given in before the court."[30] Dr. Trevett replied, defending the Waldo version, and there was an exchange between the two officers. Meanwhile, the vituperation in the Boston papers continued. The *Galaxy*'s output was predictable, but in late June even the *Patriot* published a letter, signed "A Republican," attacking Hull. This letter brought from the *Intelligencer* an editorial headed "Caballing," which said, in part:

> There is, perhaps, no man wearing the uniform of his country who has rendered more valuable service to it than Capt. Isaac Hull. Not that he is entitled, by superior conduct, to a preference over others of the same standing, whose merit may be equal, but that he gained the first of our great naval victories, which inspired confidence and encouraged hope in the breasts of his countrymen. His modest bearing and personal worth added lustre to his professional merits, and placed him high in the estimation of his fellow-citizens.
> From some motive which we do not understand, an organized attempt has been made to undermine the character of this man, and deprive him of that reputation which is to all men—but particularly to such men as Capt. Hull, dearer than life. Such an attempt must eventually, we know, recoil upon its authors, and cover them with scorn and public contempt. But it ought not to receive countenance from any respectable quarter. . . . We see, by a communication in the Boston Patriot, that there is at least one man who blames the Executive for not granting a Court Martial to Captain Hull, when he requested it; and it is suggested that "public opinion" required that a Court should have been held upon him. Now, what may be the opinion at Boston we cannot say—there is no accounting for the freaks of fashion or of faction in any contiguous population; the very best man in a neighborhood is not seldom the most unpopular—but this we say with perfect confidence, that Cap-

tain Hull enjoys the undiminished confidence of his fellow-citizens elsewhere, and of his government, and that it is not in the power of any
combination to deprive him of it. His fame is the property of his country, and
his countrymen will not suffer him and them to be robbed of it.[31]

The editor went on to intimate that Abbot's appeal to the people from
the decision of the court-martial "is unprecedented on the part of an
officer intending to remain in service, contrary to the interests of the
country, and subversive of the principle of subordination."

This was the opening salvo of a full-scale war between the editors of
the *Intelligencer*, on the one hand, and those of the *Galaxy*, the *Columbian Centinel*, and other Boston papers, Federalist and Republican
alike, on the other. Porter's letters to the papers also grew longer and
more frequent, until, after he had delivered an attack on "license" in
the press and threatened to sue the offending papers for libel, he found
nearly all the editors in arms against him. Hull, the unwilling cause of
all this hubbub, was forced to suffer in silence except for the comfort of
his family and his anguished letters to Porter and a few other close
friends. Through Porter and Rodgers, he was able to get rid of some of
his enemies. Dr. Trevett was surprised and chagrined to find himself
ordered to sea in the sloop of war *Peacock* bound for the West Indies, a
post he considered beneath his rank. Cheever Felch also received orders
to participate in a survey of the coasts of Alabama and Florida, but Hull
thought the chaplain had made a lucky escape: on 12 June he received
a letter from his brother-in-law, the Reverend Samuel F. Jarvis, to the
effect that the Massachusetts Episcopal Church Convention planned to
try Felch the following week for "disorderly, scandalous and immoral
conduct." Jarvis asked whether Hull or any of his officers had specific
charges to prefer against Felch under that head, and it is not difficult to
imagine that Hull might have supplied some, but he was content to get
rid of the troublemaker. He told Porter that "I shall take no part in [the
trial]. It will not be long before he will disgrace himself in a way that
others will have to notice it. He cannot return to this station without
being arrested for debt."[32]

Hull was feeling particularly aggrieved at his fellow officers. John Percival was not quite correct in saying that he was the only one to remain
loyal. Although William B. Shubrick, Robert Knox, and the other yard
officers took no public stand and hoped to stay clear of the whole business, they consistently testified in Hull's favor. But Hull was bitterly
disappointed that they did not rally to him more strongly. He was be-
wildered: How had he acquired so many enemies after a lifetime of
being every man's friend? Was it true, as the *Galaxy* alleged, that Abbot

had been convicted by a bare majority of the court? That Thomas Macdonough, Charles Morris, and Robert T. Spence had favored acquittal?[33] Hull was convinced that Morris, at least, was against him, and it was a bitter cup to drink: "You know what I have done for him," he wrote Porter, "and there is no cause why he should not be friendly except a mean, selfish disposition he possesses and a wish to serve a great man that he would be very happy to see commanding on this station."[34]

Morris was innocent of the charge. He was not a warm person, and when his career was at stake he was not above an eye for the main chance. But he behaved straightforwardly throughout the whole Charlestown affair. After Porter's return to Washington, Morris, along with George Blake, had been designated to continue the investigation of Amos Binney's finances. He had carried out this task during intervals of the Shaw and Abbot trials, patiently enduring Abbot's complaints that he was being forced to conduct his own defense and Binney's prosecution at the same time—for Abbot still regarded himself as a self-designated "public prosecutor." As soon as he returned to his command at Portsmouth, Morris wrote a long report about the investigation. Since Binney had taken his vouchers with him to Washington in order to confer with the secretary in person, Morris felt he could not give a definitive opinion on all points at issue but contented himself with pointing out certain matters that seemed to him questionable and that he thought the secretary should ask Binney about specifically. The only point on which he was disposed to censure Binney was his not having taken Keating's suspicions of Fosdick seriously, and neglecting to compare Keating's duplicate payrolls with Fosdick's, except for one instance in 1819. George Blake, who knew Keating better, and who understood that Binney had ordered him to keep the duplicate roll in order to humor him, did not agree with Morris on this point. In his own report he wrote that

> Having been, myself, as you will remember, one of the Commissioners under your appointment to investigate the transactions of Fosdick, & witnessing, as I certainly did upon that occasion, a remarkable degree of activity and exertion on the part of Mr. Binney in the pursuit of this Delinquent and in bringing to light the whole series of his fraudulent transactions, it is utterly impossible for me to indulge for a single moment, the suspicion that Mr. Binney could, at any time, have been voluntarily and culpably remiss in regard to the conduct of this man.

When Morris returned to Boston in August, he and Blake conferred and agreed to withdraw their reports, substituting briefer statements that generally accepted Binney's explanations and that cleared him of all imputation of wrongdoing. But meanwhile Binney, who had announced that he would publish the documents in his case as soon as the commissioners' opinion was issued, suffered much at the hands of the Federalist editors, who scoffed at his delay and accused him of concealing the awful truth. For the most part, the Boston papers roundly denied the *National Intelligencer*'s assertion that the brouhaha at Charlestown was in whole or in part politically motivated, but in commenting on Binney's case the *American Statesman,* an old-school Republican paper supporting William H. Crawford for president, broke ranks and blasted the Federalists:

> COLONEL BINNEY
>
> In the case of this gentleman, we have renewed evidence of that disposition which always prevails among federalists, to attack upon every occasion and upon the slightest pretence, the reputation of every distinguished republican.... Clearly ... the persecution which is now directed against the Navy Agent is not with a view of ascertaining truth, but its object is to gratify party animosity, and to subserve party views, and it is a part of the old Federal system to destroy by all means fair or foul, the standing of every republican, holding a responsible station.[35]

To the sensitized feelings of Isaac Hull and the aroused wrath of David Porter, Morris's judicious course seemed temporizing, and a proof of unfriendliness. But it is clear that Morris was no friend of Abbot's. After the publication of Waldo's version of the trial, he wrote Porter that

> The whole appears to me an unfair and partial publication, almost the whole of the documentary evidence is omitted, certain notes are added, some of which are gross misrepresentations, and papers not connected with, or rather not officially known in the trial and investigation are published with it, such as Gibbs' memoranda, etc. I am told it has an extensive and rapid sale at a dollar each and that there were very many subscribers.

Morris thought that Hull had been wise to apply formally for a court of inquiry on his own conduct, but he believed that such a court would not be necessary unless Hull had additional testimony to bring forward. On the other hand, publication of the official proceedings of the Abbot court-martial might be a good idea, in order to counteract the effect of the Waldo version.[36]

Whatever their other differences, Morris, Porter, and Hull were fully agreed on the last point. Despite a little wishful thinking that Waldo's book would not sell, Hull was eager to have the correct version of the trial published. He could not afford the cost himself and thought the Navy Department owed him that much at least, after the secretary's refusal of his request for an investigation. "And what in the name of

God am I to do?" he burst out in a letter to Porter. "Heaven only knows what I can do more. After you have read the enclosed scraps taken from this morning's papers will you give me your advice? I need it much." This was the day on which the *Boston Patriot* published the first attack of "A Republican" on Hull, with a demand that the secretary order a court of inquiry. Hull was despondent about Thompson's apparent coldness and told Porter he would have returned the letter denying him a court, "but with a belief that you and Commodores Rodgers and Chauncey had seen it and thought it satisfactory I determined rather to suffer in my feelings than to cause any more trouble about it." But silent acquiescence, it seemed, would not do: "Is there no way of quieting the public? What can I do? I am willing to make any sacrifice rather than suffer what I now do. . . . It does indeed appear to me that the whole world is against me, and why it is so I cannot imagine."[37]

Porter was already applying to various publishers for their terms for printing the official version of Abbot's trial. Davis and Force of Washington agreed to take on the job, but the "correct" version never had the sale of the Waldo sensations.[38] Porter also published extracts from Morris's letter, naming him only as "one of the members of the naval court martial," though no one could have doubted his identity, to help quash the Waldo sale as well as the reports that Morris had favored acquittal.[39]

Even as Hull was writing his anguished letter of 29 June he was being subjected to a public insult not many blocks away. The Harvard Washington Corps, a group of upperclassmen, had marched to John Shaw's house in Charlestown at noon. They performed military exercises and fired salutes in front of the house and then went inside for a collation, "in company with a large number of the friends of Capt. S. of Charlestown and Boston." The "friends" included editor Benjamin Russell of the *Columbian Centinel* and Samuel L. Knapp, Abbot's lawyer and associate publisher of the *Galaxy*. Russell toasted "Arts and Arms"; Knapp, "The Halls of Harvard—where Justice has suspended her patent scales for the weighing of public character"; and another, unidentified guest, "The venerable father of the American Navy—in whose time there were no contracts for *ten-footers,* and no ten guineas paid for passage money." Afterward the corps marched back to Cambridge by way of Boston to give ample publicity to their act. Of course, the whole affair was widely reported in the press—with lip-smacking glee by the *Centinel* and the *Galaxy,* and with loathing by the *National Intelligencer,* in a column headed "Persecution":

> Would the reader believe (unless he had seen it) that even the *boys* about Boston have been incited to slander the character of the Commander of that

naval station? Not the rabble of boys either, but the youths of Harvard College. Their innocence is tampered with, and their minds poisoned so far as to make them also instruments of Persecution: and a toast is given by one of them at an entertainment where the whole of the elder classes were present, reflecting, in the grossest terms, on the personal character of Capt. Hull, and pretending to express an opinion on matters they could not possibly understand. . . . In another of the same papers, to the further disgrace of the city, a person who signs himself "the Reporter" accuses Capt. Hull of stealing a piece or two of timber, some nails and some paint, belonging to the Navy Yard! It is worthy of consideration for heads of families in the middle [and] southern states, whether they will send their sons to an institution where their better feelings are tampered with thus, to serve the purposes of faction.[40]

President Kirkland of Harvard was very upset by this ungentlemanly episode. He sent a notice to the papers (which the Federalist press did not see fit to print) that the college military corps was permitted to leave Cambridge only by invitation. Captain Samuel Manning had told Kirkland that the corps was invited to Shaw's house, concealing the fact that he had previously sent a note to solicit the invitation. Kirkland now denounced the affair as "highly improper" and said that he would have forbidden the corps' visit had he not been deceived. Hull remarked with satisfaction that "President Kirkland has come out as he ought and put the visit to Shaw as it ought to be. Ben Russell is outrageous about it and I am told threatens the government of the college."[41]

Meanwhile, the July Fourth celebrations had passed, providing Isaac Hull with another miserable day. He did not attend either the Federalist or the Republican festivities at Boston, though his friend George Blake presided over the latter. The Charlestown gala, widely reported in all the papers, featured Shaw as an honored guest, and the toasts included "Captain John Shaw—'When the righteous are persecuted the people mourn'"; "The Charlestown Naval Station—Its commander has *requested* an inquiry, and the public voice *demands* a thorough investigation"; and others similar in tone. The *Galaxy* offered its own toasts for the day:

Justice.
  Our courts of law such wisdom boast
    Beyond the courts of olden time,
  That those are punished now the most,
    Who *publish*, not *commit* the crime.
Our Navy.
  Employed in administering bitter doses to our enemies in War; in Peace, in physicking the *Harts* of our own country.[42]

By this time Hull had decided that he could no longer continue in silence. In the following week he took action on two fronts: first, on 13

July, he again put to Secretary Smith Thompson the case for ordering a court of inquiry:

> Conscious of my innocence as well as of the fidelity with which I have discharged my duty, it ought not to be required of me to remain a silent spectator. . . . I have always understood that it was the tacit if not express engagement of the government with its officers, that they should, of right, be entitled to an investigation of their conduct whenever it was made the subject of reproach. The expense attending an inquiry, ought not, I apprehend under these circumstances, to have the slightest weight.[43]

His second action was to introduce civil suits for libel against two of the anonymous scribblers in the press. Wisely or by good advice he ignored the outpourings of the more violent Federalist papers and directed the suits against attackers in the *Gazette* and the *Patriot*. The principal suit was against Joseph Ingersoll, a Boston merchant and author of the letters to the *Patriot* signed "A Republican"; the other was against "The Reporter" item of 1 July mentioned by the *Intelligencer* in its "Persecution" column. Ingersoll had published a second, longer letter on Tuesday, 16 July, in which he repeated all of Abbot's own assertions of high motive in provoking an investigation, and also the attitude of "heads I win, tails you lose" taken by the lieutenant's defenders in regard to his sentence: "If [the charges] were true in whole or part, Capt. Hull and Mr. Binney deserve the contempt and execration of every honest man; if they were false, Mr. Abbot has escaped without punishment adequate to his folly, wickedness and presumption." Porter's view of the sentence was proved correct: when the *Galaxy* and the *Centinel* had ceased lamenting that Abbot had received such a severe and undeserved punishment, they began to chorus that the *lenity* of the sentence proved that the court had been badly divided and unwilling to punish him; that if they had not believed his charges against Hull were true, they would have ordered his dismissal.

The Ingersoll letter called into question every part of the proceedings, both of the court-martial and of the investigation conducted by Porter and Blake, concluding:

> The government knew that fraud, to a great amount, had been committed in the Navy Yard by Fosdick, and we are not quite sure if this, of itself, was not sufficient cause for a court of inquiry on the superintendent of that yard. . . . [W]e shall examine in our next the following question: *"Did Captain Hull take and apply to his private use any part of the public property under his charge, for his private benefit, or did he avail himself of the services of men, who at the same time were in the employ and pay of government; and did he make compensation therefor to the government?"*[44]

But there was no "next," except for a meek note in Wednesday's paper that, since Hull's request for an inquiry had been granted, "We shall . . . suspend our remarks upon this subject, as we have no wish to prejudice or influence the public mind for or against this gentleman."[45] This was not true: Hull had requested the inquiry only four days earlier. The real reason was that Ingersoll had been served with process for libel. One measure of his position in the scheme of things is the fact that he immediately retained Abbot's lawyers, James T. Austin and Samuel L. Knapp, to represent him in the suit.[46]

This development marked the beginning of better times for Hull. He learned soon after that the court of inquiry would be ordered, to meet in August, and although he regretted that Porter would not be able to attend, he was in a more confident mood:

> You may be assured that those fellows will leave no stone unturned to ruin me, but I hope to weather the storm. I am anxious about the court. I fear very much that the Secretary will object to ordering Commodores Rodgers and Chauncey on the ground of their being Commissioners. I hope whatever officers are ordered will have independence enough to defy what they here call *Public* opinion. . . . I have commenced a suit against two prints. As to *whipping* Waldo—he is indeed too low and all my friends advise letting him alone, neither *sue* or *whip* him. Abbot is down in Maine with [Senator John] Holmes, I am told, with all his papers. He will, no doubt, do all he can to make trouble.[47]

Some Boston people had at last begun to speak out on Hull's behalf: the *Patriot* for 17 July contained two letters backing him. "Copp's Hill" wrote that "All this is *nuts ready cracked* to the Junto," and "Decius" commented, "I have read the trial of Lieut. Abbot, and for my own part can discover nothing but a combination of surmises, suspicions and conjectures. Who charges Capt. Hull with fraud or peculation among the whole host of witnesses? Not one." The *Intelligencer* also printed parts of a letter received from Boston:

> Nothing is further from the truth, than the assertion of the Centinel, that the sentiments upon this subject, expressed by that, with other papers, is the opinion "of a large proportion of the unbiassed citizens of Boston." Major Russell is very prone to believe his own to be the opinion of all thinking men, notwithstanding he has been repeatedly convinced by sad experience to the contrary.
>
> The Clamor which has been raised against the amiable and gallant Hull sounds much louder at a distance than near. As the parties on both sides are very well known here, so are they and their assertions justly appreciated. . . . The excitement against Hull is greatest in Charlestown, where some little contemptible jealousies, arising from the intercourse, or want of intercourse,

in private society, roused the ire of some of the notable dames of that town, and who, of course, inoculated their good men with the same disease.

To which the *Intelligencer* added: "Eheu! Jam satis!"[48]

At the end of July, two weeks before the court was to begin, Hull wrote Porter a long letter in which he summed up most of the political and personal involvements in the whole affair and laid his finger on the source of the agitation that, as he candidly admitted, was bringing public censure on the navy, to such an extent that there were even threats of a congressional investigation. Among the political personalities he named the two old-school Federalists William Sullivan and Thomas Handasyd Perkins. John Shaw was spending a lot of time at Perkins's newly opened resort hotel at Nahant. John Holmes, the Maine lawyer and senator, a Federalist turned Republican and now an ardent Crawfordite, described by Albert Beveridge as "a busy, agile, talkative politician of the roustabout, hail-fellow-well-met variety, 'a power-on-the stump' orator, gifted with cheap wit and tawdry eloquence," was another member of the cabal.[49] Dr. William Eustis, the former secretary of war, was partly suspect:

> I have only seen him once. He then appeared friendly, and said that I had now taken the proper course. He complained much of Trevett's having been ordered away and said that the Secretary in having done it had lost all his influence in this part of the country. I have no doubt but he will do us all the injury he can. The next session he however said that the business of Binney should not go before Congress if he could help it.

But Hull did not think Jonathan Russell, who had been implicated as a supporter of Shaw's charges, was involved in the present agitation. Since Russell was then engaged in a newspaper war with John Quincy Adams that threatened to drive the navy affair off the front pages, he was, no doubt, fully occupied.

The situation was a vehicle for the politicians, but the real cause of the scandals, as Hull well knew, lay elsewhere:

> You may rely on it that the first cause of all this difficulty originated in Commodore B. wanting this place, and I am sure things have been kept alive by him and his family. He held a correspondence with Shaw all the time that he was making his communication to the government, and his friend Captain Derby received and carried his letters to Shaw and you know that Shaw and Bainbridge were not on terms before. Captain Derby was at the [public dinner for Shaw] as was Ben Russell, Major, Waldo, Knapp and the editors of the Galaxy. Those are the respectable citizens from Boston.

Still, his regret and chagrin at having provoked Shaw in the first place underlay his hatred and contempt:

The man is a fool and if he does publish the trial it will do the Navy more injury than all that has yet taken place. . . . I see no end to the mischief that will grow out of his doing it for half the officers in the Navy will in some way be at loggerheads. I hope you will in some way put a stop to the ruin we are bringing on ourselves. Shaw has done and will do more to ruin the Navy than all the officers beside if suffered to be made a tool of as he now is. Knapp and Waldo are leading him by the nose and B. Russell is helping them. You recollect that Lieut. [Henry] Ward married a daughter of B. Russell's and Ward and Commodore B. are great friends. Ward is now on his way to Washington; look out for him. He will endeavour to get what he can out of the clerks of the office to make use of in favour of Shaw and Abbot. . . . I hope to heaven you will put Shaw on his back, for he is a disgrace to the service.[50]

It was a bitter reflection indeed that he had, in a sense, brought the storm on his own head by challenging Shaw about the broad pendant. Yet, if he had not, perhaps Bainbridge would have found another tool. He had found Abbot readily enough, and fair treatment had availed nothing with that one. In face of his implacable enmity, neither action nor acquiescence was of any use. Hull felt guilty for bringing his family into possible disgrace, and for once he almost wished himself single again: "Indeed, sometimes my spirits leave me and I am ready to give up. Was it not for my family I should bear up under my troubles better. My wife's sisters, however, keep up their spirits."[51] In the last remark there is a perceptible note of resentment.

By this time John Rodgers and Isaac Chauncey were already at New York en route to Boston. They were combining the navy commissioners' summer inspection tour of navy yards with the court-of-inquiry assignment. The two captains reached Boston on Saturday evening, 3 August, and continued on to visit the yard at Portsmouth. From there they returned, accompanied by Charles Morris, to begin the investigation on Monday, 12 August. Despite Hull's fears that Secretary Thompson would balk at ordering two of the commissioners to sit on the court, the secretary had little choice. He had to choose at least one captain senior to Hull to preside, and it would be inappropriate that the other two should be very far down the list. The senior captains were John Rodgers, James Barron, William Bainbridge, Thomas Tingey, and Charles Stewart. Of these, Barron had just undergone an inquiry himself, and he was unfriendly toward Hull as a result of the *Chesapeake* affair of 1807; Bainbridge was Hull's known enemy; Tingey had headed the Abbot and Shaw courts; and Stewart was in the Pacific. That left Rodgers. Next below Hull stood Chauncey, Shaw, and Porter. Shaw and Porter were obviously out of the question, leaving Chauncey as the logical choice. Charles Morris was nearby, so he was added to complete the panel. Of the three, only Rodgers was Hull's close friend, and as the navy's senior captain he could be counted on to guard its honor. Chauncey and Morris were certainly impartial, and both were knowledgeable about the running of navy yards.

Rodgers was given discretion in appointing a judge advocate for the court. Since some of the Federalist papers had called for an "acceptable" person in that office, he sought to placate opinion by appointing George Sullivan, a moderate Federalist. Naturally, this appointment excited grief-stricken cries from the Republican papers, especially the *Statesman*; and Sullivan was too moderate to please the *Galaxy*, either. Sullivan, in turn, sought to elicit all possible complaints against Hull so that no one could later say the investigation had not been thorough. Thus, he published a notice in the papers giving the date and time of the court and saying that "all persons who have any complaints to make, or know any facts or circumstances tending to implicate captain Hull . . . are hereby *required* to appear." But this was also found objectionable in some quarters. "Is the Court of Inquiry setting a trap," the *Galaxy* archly inquired, "to catch a few more of the officers, that they may be dismissed from the service, or is this advertisement the *gratuitous* suggestion of the *wisdom* of the honourable Judge Advocate?"[52] One way or another, Hull's trial was about to begin.

Monday, 12 August 1822, was a pleasant New England summer day. As the members of the court made their way to the courtroom in the navy yard they could hear the ring of hammers from the new blacksmith shop, where ironwork for one of the ships of the line was being fashioned, and they could see carpenters' gangs at work on sizing her live oak timbers. Joiners were finishing the huge second shiphouse to cover her, and painters were giving its walls a coat of white paint. Laborers in guernsey frocks, the working uniform of the yard, were wheeling gravel to fill in around the foundations. At 11:00 A.M. Isaac Hull entered the room, and the court began with the reading of its orders and the formal appointment of George Sullivan as judge advocate. Hull was asked if he objected to any member of the court; he said he did not, and the oath was then administered to each of the three captains. After these formalities the court was cleared and the members deliberated their mode of proceeding—although doubtless they had talked it over some time earlier. This was *not* a court-martial, though there was much popular confusion on that point. There were no formal charges against Hull. Rather, it was analogous to a grand jury proceeding: an inquiry to determine whether evidence existed on which charges should be brought before a court-martial.

Rodgers, Chauncey, and Morris decided to propose a series of five basic questions, or interrogatories, to each witness, covering all the subjects of rumor and accusation that had been spread. The first asked whether the witness knew, or had reason to believe, that public property had been converted to Hull's or anyone else's private use. The second asked the same thing about the employment of workmen. The third asked whether Hull had in any way neglected his duty as commandant, especially in examining accounts and caring for the public property. The fourth question was whether the witness knew or believed that Hull had been in collusion with Fosdick or had failed to take proper measures for detecting his fraud and recovering the stolen money; the fifth, whether Hull had oppressed any officer under his command. The court decided to question naval officers and yard employees first, and private citizens afterward, and summonses were issued to the prospective witnesses, including the two chief complainers: Shaw's was sent to Nahant and Joel Abbot's to Saco, Maine. With that the court adjourned until 10:00 A.M. the following day.

John Rodgers had predicted that the court proceeding would last two weeks. It went on for nine weeks, concluding its business on 15 October. In all, seventy-six witnesses were examined, some of them two, three, and even four times. Abbot took the stand no less than seven times, and his testimony accounted for more than 50 of the 244 pages of the printed version of the trial.

Shaw was one of the first witnesses called, but he refused to say that he knew of anything against Hull, although he thought that Abbot might have some evidence. Abbot made his first appearance on Friday, 16 August. He behaved as if the summons were a complete surprise to him, said he did not have his books and papers with him, and begged to be excused until Monday. The court granted his request. But the delay did not seem to make any difference. The books and papers never appeared. The testimony that Abbot gave, beginning on 19 August and lasting for three days, was rambling, occasionally incoherent, and based almost entirely on surmise, inference, and—as was obvious—hatred of Isaac Hull. Even the newspapers remarked on the irony of his beginning this outpouring on the tenth anniversary of Hull's victory over the *Guerrière*. Many of his allegations were based on statements he said had been made to him by others, but when these men were called to the stand they all—sometimes heatedly—denied ever making the statements Abbot attributed to them. Even his supposed friend, Lieutenant Henry Ward, denied everything Abbot said. Lieutenant William M. Caldwell went further: when he heard that Abbot had said on the stand that "Mr. Caldwell is apt to branch out and say things he does not mean, and speak in stronger language than he is aware of," he threatened Abbot severely enough to force him to agree to retract the statement. This was on the afternoon of Thursday, 22 August. After three days of testimony Abbot sent word that he was sick, and Surgeon John A. Kearney reported to the court that Abbot was suffering from "an attack on his brain producing mental alienation." Caldwell went to see him and confronted him with his remarks about himself; Abbot said "he believed he had said a good many things before the court that he wouldn't have said if he . . . had been in his right mind." He then asked Caldwell anxiously "if he didn't suppose the court thought him insane." Caldwell said "he didn't know what the court thought, but spectators in court thought so."[53] Did Abbot intend to avoid any further prosecution for the things he said by claiming insanity?

On that same afternoon Isaac Hull received a letter from Derby: his father was dying. On Friday morning he asked the court to excuse him, and leaving his counsel, Samuel Hubbard, to represent him, he departed hastily for Connecticut. He found Joseph Hull very ill indeed, so he said his farewell and advised the family on settling the estate before returning to Charlestown on Saturday evening, 31 August. In fact, his father rallied from this attack and lived for several years. But it was a painful time for Isaac, with the trial hanging over his head and the knowledge that his father might die thinking him disgraced.

By the time Hull returned, the major part of Abbot's testimony had been completed. It was painfully clear that what motivated him was his anger at Hull's refusal to grant him chamber money and his delay in granting Abbot leave to go to Newburyport to visit his wife in the winter of 1821. Midshipman George S. Blake, who was with Abbot in the prize, the *Mariana Flora*, testified that not a day passed that Abbot did not talk about his ill treatment by Hull, and say that Hull had been the cause of his wife's death. "When talking about Captain Hull he used to work himself up into a most tremendous passion, and always seemed to have a most violent prejudice against him."[54]

From this fixation of Abbot's had come the whole agitation, for when he returned to Boston he had found Bainbridge, Shaw, and a few other malcontents to assist him. Of the whole parade of witnesses only three or four had any concrete charges to bring, and each of them was discredited. Daniel Leman, a capstan maker, was sure that he had refused to sign blank payrolls and said that he had even then suspected Fosdick; but it was proved that the payrolls he signed had been made out by Purser Lewis Deblois and had not been blank. Leman, in fact, had been discharged from the yard for laziness and for refusing to abide by yard regulations. He admitted that he had discussed his testimony with Abbot beforehand. Other workmen who came forward had also been dismissed for unsatisfactory work and, in one case, for attempted theft. A few more believed that they had worked for Hull on government time, but the master workmen testified that in each case they had seen to it that the men's names were taken off the yard roll for the days and hours they worked on Hull's projects.

Isaac Hull had, in fact, been imprudent. As mentioned earlier, he had bought land near the navy yard, part of it on the advice of the secretary, so that the government might purchase it from him at a convenient time in the future, to straighten the boundaries of the yard. Hull had bought other land in order to remove disorderly tenants. There were, for example, some grogshops on the southwest side that the seamen attached to the yard could reach unobserved by wading through the timber dock at low tide. These shops received and resold stolen property from the yard. Hull bought the houses, ejected the tenants, and installed respectable people or even let the houses stand empty, at considerable expense, rather than lease them again to dishonest people. Most of this property he was unable to buy outright but held under mortgages to the people he bought it from.

When the yard was enlarged by purchase of the piece of land Hull had bought from the Woodward estate in 1816, it was agreed that the house on it would be moved at government expense and put in good condition after being relocated. It was this activity that old Major Gibbs had spitefully made memoranda of to show that yard workmen were employed on Hull's property. At other times, Hull had employed some of the same men who worked in the yard to repair his buildings and to erect a brick house and some "ten-footers" on his land near Chelsea Bridge. It all looked bad. Spectators could not always tell which payroll the men were on at a given time, and the men themselves were not sure because the yard clerk paid both the yard roll and Hull's accounts. Also, Hull had occasionally stored paint, putty, nails, and iron that he had bought for his own use in the navy yard, and he had bought undersized timber unloaded at the yard wharf and had it hauled to his buildings. Such practices, too, led to confusion in some minds, though it was shown that Hull had been scrupulously careful to account for everything. Sometimes his workmen had borrowed navy supplies when Hull's ran out, replacing them soon after with equal quantities of the same supplies. None of it would have caused any remarks if Hull had not had enemies, and why should he suppose that he had? Never in his life before had anyone wished to deliberately injure him, and this experience was both bewildering and embittering.

Moreover, the court of inquiry had barely begun before a new charge was raised against Hull: that he, with Shubrick and the other yard officers, had neglected his duty in preparing the *Macedonian* for sea. The frigate had returned from the Pacific in June 1821 and lay six months in ordinary. At the end of January 1822 orders came to fit her for sea with all speed; she sailed for the West Indies under the command of James Biddle on 2 April. On 5 August she returned to Norfolk with more than seventy of her crew dead and fifty more on the sick list. She had lain for a month in Havana harbor, and the crew were suffering from yellow fever. But, at that time, no one understood the cause of the disease, and Captain Biddle, to clear himself of any blame, accused the navy yard workmen of neglecting to clean the ship properly, thereby causing "noxious effluvia" to build up in the hold and cause sickness. He even mustered the *Macedonian*'s crew before leaving Havana and told them that they were suffering because of neglect on the part of the navy yard. As a result, the court of inquiry was ordered to investigate the *Macedonian* case when it finished with the other matter.

Testimony in the main inquiry was completed on 2 October, and the next day Samuel Hubbard read Hull's defense statement. It was an able summary of the testimony and refutation of the charges, with minute attention to Abbot. Hubbard employed a fine irony in his treatment of the lieutenant: "I declare, when I read his solemn professions, and then hear his proofs in support of his allegations, I am half inclined to believe that his reported alienation of mind during the session of this court, is an alienation of no recent origin: but if it be so, there is malice in his madness still."

Hull had engaged Daniel Webster along with Hubbard to argue his still pending libel suit against Ingersoll, and it may be that the "godlike Daniel" had a hand in composing the eloquent peroration to Hull's defense:

I have defrauded none of their property, injured no one in his person, nor treacherously wounded any man in his good name. I neither thrive on calumny, nor build my hopes of success in the expectation of blasting the reputation of brother officers. My course has been a straight one: I have been four and twenty years in my country's service; her faithful servant, as I hope, through evil report and through good report. I have borne the summer heat in pestilential climates, and endured the rigour of wintry seas, when no distinction awaited the discharge of duty. And I have laboured, in the superintendence of this Yard, to lay the foundation of her future glory, when other wars shall summon her navies to the ocean, and her gallant seamen be once more called to face their country's foes. In that day, when the calumnies of these times shall have passed into oblivion, I feel a just confidence that the noble structures which now adorn the place on which we stand, shall witness that I have been faithful.

But the part that impressed people most, and that seemed to clinch the conviction of Hull's innocence in nearly everyone's mind, was his solemn avowal that his total estate, including what was left of his prize money, was smaller than when he came to the yard, and totaled less than $18,000. That sum probably put Hull in Boston's top 1 percent, but it was little enough for twenty-four years' service, and it certainly did not indicate any enrichment at the public expense. The *Evening Gazette* editors wrote after the reading of the defense that "there can be no difference of statement hereafter, as to the perfect integrity of Capt. Hull, and the unsubstantial and groundless charges that have been preferred against his official conduct."[55]

The court then began to weigh its opinion, but by this time James Biddle was getting fidgety. He had been ordered back to the West Indies in command of the *Congress,* and he wanted the court to take up the inquiry about the *Macedonian* so that he could be on his way. After consulting the secretary for permission, they agreed, and on 7 October they put aside their work on the opinion and devoted a week to taking testimony on the causes of mortality on board the unhappy frigate. Reference to the journal of the yard and testimony of the yard officers and workmen all showed that the ship had been thoroughly cleaned, pumped, and whitewashed, and carefully stowed for her voyage, and that everything had been done to prepare her that men could possibly do in the bitter cold of a Boston February. Even the firewood taken on board had been barked so that there would be no excess vegetable matter to decay in the hold. Doctors testified about the probable causes of the fever: sudden transition from a cold to a hot climate; dampness between decks; tropical heat acting on weak constitutions (many of the crew had colds when they left Boston); letting water into the ship's hold at Havana and remaining so long in that port; want of suitable clothing, tea, sugar, and other amenities; sleeping on deck; fatigue from frequent exercise of the guns; despondency (occasioned by Biddle's speech to the crew); and error in treatment after the ship's surgeon died. The court decided that the doctors must be right—how could they disagree?—and concluded that

> the conduct of the officers of the Navy Yard at Charlestown, manifested great zeal and attention to the fitting out of the Macedonian for her late cruise, and that the prevalence of sickness and mortality on board the Macedonian is not to be ascribed in any degree to any omission of duty on their part; on the contrary, it is the opinion of this court that the hold of that ship was sufficiently cleansed.[56]

355

Hull had felt easy about this inquiry; and he thanked Thomas Chew for some tips Chew had sent him about the case, saying, "I have not made any defense as saw nothing to defend myself against. The evidence I brought before the court was so clear that the ship was properly fitted out and clean that I did not wish to detain the court."[57]

Rodgers, Chauncey, and Morris spent one more day in deliberation before presenting their opinion in Hull's case. The outcome had been beyond doubt for a long time; Rodgers had written Porter even before the testimony was completed that Hull would be cleared. Porter, who was at New York conducting the annual examination of midshipmen, was gleeful, but he warned Rodgers that Bainbridge was on the warpath again: Porter's and Blake's report on Binney's affairs had mentioned—because it was a fact—that Fosdick had begun to pay the workmen during Bainbridge's command, and his name had also come up frequently in the court of inquiry. Bainbridge was as anxious as ever that he should have no public connection with the scandals. Porter told Rodgers:

> I send you a letter I received yesterday from the prime mover in all the Boston business. Taken in connection with other things it may be of importance. He has until now kept himself concealed. Perhaps you had better show it to Blake and let him take a copy of it as it contains a threat against him. Don't lose the letter as I shall want it hereafter. . . . Knowing as I do that Hull will be acquitted and his enemies humbled I feel no anxiety on the subject. Query: ought those who have been instrumental in this persecution to remain in the service, ought not their dismissal to be recommended?[58]

On 15 October the court presented a detailed summary of its view of the evidence, and with it an opinion. The members disapproved, in general, of the loan or exchange of government property for private purposes, of the employment of yard workmen by private individuals, and of deviations from the prescribed methods of paying the men; but in each case they concluded that no fraud had been practiced and that no loss had occurred. They cautioned that Hull, in placing his property in the public stores and having men paid by the public paymasters for work done for him, "was indiscreet; inasmuch, as such conduct, though in itself innocent, may nevertheless give rise in the minds of persons, not acquainted with the real nature, and all the particulars of such transactions, to vague impressions of misconduct in public officers."

Percival's trip to England without prior approval of the secretary they regarded as incorrect, but they found that the United States had not suffered thereby. Hull's purchase of property near the yard was also indiscreet, but the court found that his motives had been upright and that the public interest had in fact benefited.

On other points the findings were positive: the charging of medicine to the government had been in accord with regulations at the time; the withholding of officers' allowances was justified by Navy Department orders; and Hull had not oppressed his subordinates—"on the contrary, he has, so far as was consistent with his duty to the United States, granted every proper indulgence." The court concluded:

finally, this Court is of opinion that, with the before mentioned exceptions, the conduct of Captain Hull, since his command of this Yard, for strict personal attention to the preservation of the public property committed to his charge, the judicious application of the means placed at his disposal for the public service, and for the faithful performance of all his other official duties, has been correct and meritorious.[59]

The opinion was not immediately made public, since it had first to receive the secretary's approval. But the members of the court left no doubt in anyone's mind that Hull had been cleared. Chauncey did not get to Washington with the documents before 26 October, but four days before that the *Intelligencer* had printed "from authority which we question not"—probably Porter—"that [Captain Hull] has been fully and honorably acquitted of each and every offense alleged against him." Both the *Intelligencer* and the *Boston Patriot* reprinted an editorial from the *Baltimore Morning Chronicle:*

We join most cordially in congratulating our countrymen that the naval court of inquiry called on Captain Hull, and at his own request, have terminated their session in a full, complete, and triumphant acquittal of that meritorious officer. . . . He appears now in a more splendid light, than he did when we beheld his laurels in the first verdure of their leaves. Bravery and valor become associated with stern probity, white handed faith, and radiant honor.[60]

The outcome of the court probably also had an impact on the trial of Hull's suit for libel against Joseph Ingersoll, which was heard before Justice Joseph Story and a crowded courtroom on 22 October. Hull's counsel, Hubbard and Webster, said that Hull was not interested in pecuniary damages but wished only to give Ingersoll a chance to prove his charges if he could. Knapp and Austin rejoined that their client, too, was merely seeking to bring about an inquiry on the charges circulated by Abbot. The case went to the jury at the end of the day, and at 9:00 A.M. the following day they reported the defendant guilty and awarded Hull $500 damages. The other suit he had entered had apparently been dropped. Amos Binney, meanwhile, had already won a suit against Lorenzo T. Hall, editor of the *Boston Castigator*, which resulted in a three-month jail sentence for the editor.[61]

Now that the tumult of trials and suits was ended—except for a little continuing abuse in the *Galaxy*—Isaac Hull was anxious to get away from Boston. In the longer run, he wanted to leave the place for good, after a proper interval, and he wanted to discuss with the secretary whether there was another assignment he might be able to have. Thus, on 26 October, he wrote to Washington for leave of absence "for ten or fifteen days to make a short journey into the country," and without waiting for a reply he set out with his family for Saybrook five days later. But, having left the ladies at their home, he continued on southward. By Friday morning, 8 November, he was at Baltimore, but there he learned that the finding of the court had not yet been made public because of Secretary Thompson's absence from the capital. He therefore halted at Baltimore and wrote to Porter for advice:

> I . . . think it may by some be thought that I had come on to have something to say in the business, or at any rate some of those fellows may make a handle of it. If you think so, will you inform me, and I shall return without making you a visit. I understand that the Secretary of the Navy is on his way to Washington and will be in Baltimore tomorrow. If so I shall probably see him but as he has not seen the proceedings of the court I could say but little to him on the subject. . . . I understand that *Trevett* is not expected to live. I suppose should he not recover his death will be charged to some of us.[62]

The court's finding was not published until 16 November, but Hull did see the secretary briefly at Washington before returning to Charlestown on 25 November. Meanwhile, his foreboding with regard to Dr. Trevett was realized: the unfortunate doctor succumbed to yellow fever at Norfolk on 4 or 5 November as a result of his cruise to the West Indies in the *Peacock*, and the opposition press in Massachusetts blared:

> By the arts of intrigue and malice, the secretary of the navy was deceived respecting his character, and was prevailed on to deprive Dr. Trevett of the station to which he was, by usage, justly entitled, by his services and merits, and to order him on a cruise in a pestilential climate, to which his enemies knew he had never been inured, in a vessel of an inferior class.[63]

There was still one officer at Charlestown that Hull would have liked to be rid of. Lieutenant Henry Ward, Benjamin Russell's son-in-law and the close friend of Bainbridge, Abbot, Felch and Waldo, was still very irksome. While Hull was absent, Ward had attended a large dinner party in Charlestown where he offered a toast: "Charlestown Hogs: may they root out all peculation and fraud from the land." Hull sent a copy of this toast to the secretary with the comment that Ward had previously applied for a transfer to Pensacola and that this might be a good time to gratify his wish.[64] To Porter he spoke more candidly: "I wish that fellow could be ordered from the station. He will not commit himself in a way that I can get hold of him, yet he does much mischief and great injury to the service. A cruise to the West Indies would be of service to him." Considering the recent fate of so many officers in the West Indies, Hull's feelings toward Ward must have been very hard indeed.[65] The *Galaxy* was still keeping alive the agitation against Hull as best it could by publishing a series of vituperative letters signed "Publius," but in most minds the case was closed. Charles Morris wrote to John Rodgers that

> it is some compensation for our irksome labours at Charlestown to find that the result has given general satisfaction. The papers have either spoken favorably or remained quiet. —one in *Newburyport* made a very full and handsome recantation of its former opinions—and I trust the business is now effectually at end unless some meddling person in Congress may choose for sinister purposes to agitate it further.[66]

But the bitterness of the affair would never end for Isaac Hull. The animus shown him by people he had supposed were his friends had shaken him to the core. He would never recover the open trust and sunny good nature of the years before 1820, and for the rest of his life he was marked by latent suspicion. His enemies had not destroyed his good name, but they had seriously wounded his good nature. At the end of the year he wrote to his nephew Joseph, who was still in the Pacific, that

> since you left here I have had much trouble with some of the officers on this station, some of them of rank. But thank God I have so far weathered on them, and hope they will now be quiet. I shall, however, leave this yard in the spring. What I shall do I cannot say—perhaps go to the Mediterranean. It is, however, uncertain what I shall do. . . . This yard is much improved and in fine order for whoever may take it. I am tired of this kind of life and particularly of this place, and have nothing but constant quarrels with the Charlestown people.

Joseph was making good progress. His uncle was pleased to learn that Commodore Stewart had made him an acting lieutenant and was confident his promotion would come soon, since nearly a hundred officers had died or left the service within the year. He was able to report that the family were all well. Old Joseph Hull had made an amazing recovery and could get about the house, and young Joseph's sister Sarah Ann was keeping house for him at the Huntington Landing farm. Levi and his family had the Derby homestead. Joseph's other sister, Eliza, was with her uncle Charles Hull in New York, but Charles had failed in business, leaving brother Isaac "in the lurch for what he owed me."

Miniature of Lieutenant Joseph B. Hull. By an unknown artist. Collection of Mrs. Roger C. Elliott. Courtesy of the New-York Historical Society, New York City.

Speaking of Joseph's dependent sisters and of his own business difficulties led Isaac Hull to caution Joseph that nowadays a naval career might not be enough to count on for support. He urged his nephew to cultivate the acquaintance of the American merchants in Chile and Peru,

> for we must look to something beside the Navy for a support and no country offers a greater field for enterprise than the one you are in, and few young men have a better opportunity to become acquainted with it than you have, and few young men have a greater stimulus to get forward than you have. You have only to call to mind the situation of your mother and sisters to make you make every possible exertion to place yourself in a way to support them.

Looking farther afield, he called Joseph's attention to the federal act for taking possession of the Columbia river:

> A governor will probably be sent out before long and no doubt but settlers will be flocking there as they have land given them. You may yet be ordered

to that part of the country. . . . By making yourself well acquainted on that coast and by getting surveys of all the ports you can will be of great service to you and may get you a command of one of our small vessels much sooner than officers who are strangers. Independent of that it will be of service to you should you think of taking a merchant ship.[67]

The ensuing winter was very cold and snowy, lingering well into May. Subzero weather in early March made Hull think fondly of a warmer climate, and on 4 March he wrote privately to Thompson to remind him of their talk at Washington in November. He had decided that he would like to go to the Pacific to relieve Commodore Stewart as squadron commander, "the more so as my health is not good, and I have reason to believe a change would be of service to me." Thompson was a little puzzled, for in their conversation Hull had expressed a preference for the Mediterranean, and the Pacific command had since been promised to Chauncey. Hull had to explain:

when I was at Washington my feelings were so alive to the wicked and outrageous transactions of the last summer, and the persecution myself and family had experienced, together with the loss of a considerable share of the little property I possessed that my only wish was to leave the place as soon as a proper opportunity offered, and believing that Captain [Jacob] Jones would be relieved some time before Captain Stewart I mentioned the command of the Mediterranean more particularly than that of the Pacific, notwithstanding my wish was to have relieved Captain Stewart had I supposed he would have returned as early as I now find he will. . . . I have suffered here all that man could suffer and you will readily imagine what the feelings of my family were during the last summer in seeing me thus persecuted and robbed of reputation and a large part of the little property I have for their support.[68]

He had already written to Chauncey, and he thought he would agree not to contest Hull's application for the Pacific command. It was now clear that Captain Samuel Evans, commandant of the Brooklyn Navy Yard, was insane, and everyone expected that Chauncey would resume his old post there. By mid-April it was settled that Hull would command the next squadron in the Pacific.[69] Bainbridge had the news within a fortnight and applied immediately for the Charlestown yard. No doubt the secretary sighed with relief at being able to gratify him at last.[70]

Hull had to endure one more painful experience before he quit the Boston station. A court of inquiry headed by Bainbridge had recommended a court-martial of Captain Samuel Evans at Brooklyn—notwithstanding poor Evans's derangement—on charges brought by the naval storekeeper, which were in many ways similar to Abbot's charges against Hull. The secretary, short of senior officers as usual, appointed Hull president of the court-martial. Hull was thunderstruck. He loathed courts-martial to begin with; and how in the name of humanity could he be asked to sit in judgment on another officer who was suffering the agony he himself had so recently endured? He begged to be excused, "as it would be the most painful moment of my life, should I be compelled to sit as a member of the court under these circumstances."[71] Since the court was to convene on 10 June, however, he had no choice but to go to New York, hoping to receive relief from the orders after he got there. First he entertained the navy commissioners at their annual visit to the yard, on 3 and 4 June; on the sixth he left for New York. There he received a letter from Thompson saying that by law a court should not have more than one half of the members, exclusive of the president, junior to the accused, "when it can be avoided without injury to the service," but "if you do not feel able to sit as President of the Court without injury to your health, you will hand over the order for the Court . . . to Captain Sinclair."[72] Hull seized on this excuse, and having prevailed on Cadwallader Colden to serve as judge advocate, he returned to Charlestown on 16 June.[73]

He immediately plunged into the pleasant task of preparing for his cruise. Although "not ambitious as to the class of the ship I may be ordered to," he had hinted that it would be good to give one of the newer 74s a try.[74] Nevertheless, what he was getting was the frigate *United States*, the "Old Wagon," so called for her stately behavior and pace. Mrs. Charles Stewart was in the Pacific with her husband, where she was dubbed "the Commodoress." This furnished a precedent for Mrs. Hull, and she had already received the secretary's permission to go out in the frigate, accompanied by Augusta. Hull was besieged with applications for positions in the squadron. On 18 June he gave the secretary a tentative list of officers he would prefer, naming William K. Latimer, James Armstrong, Joseph Smoot, Hiram Paulding, William C. Nicholson, and Josiah Tattnall as lieutenants but leaving the first lieutenancy blank. He particularly wanted Thomas Chew as purser, but evidently Chew declined making the cruise.[75]

Officers on the scene had a good chance of being selected. Hull eventually took with him from the yard Lieutenant Tattnall and Gunner James Bogman, as well as Midshipmen Albert E. Downes (brother of Captain John Downes), John Bubier, Harry D. Hunter, William H. Homer, Patrick F. Bradley, and Charles F. Davis. He also took along his trusted clerks, John A. Bates and John Etheridge.[76] John Percival he enthusiastically recommended for command of one of the small vessels in the squadron, but Percival's application was not immediately successful.

On 30 July a large public dinner was given for Hull at Boston by the mercantile community, burying the hatchet and, in the toasts, twisting the tsar's nose over his recent ukase on Pacific colonization—so much so that the Russian minister at Washington, Baron de Tuyll, carried the newspaper account of the dinner to John Quincy Adams in great alarm. Adams gave him an equivocal answer, for he was already planning the message on that subject that came to be called the Monroe Doctrine.[77] One week later Hull returned the compliment with a dinner at the navy yard. The party included the newly elected Republican governor, William Eustis, Federalist ex-governor John Brooks, the mayor of Boston, Justices Story and Davis, Chief Justice Parker of Massachusetts, and many other "distinguished characters." From eleven to noon the group toured the yard, admiring the shiphouses and the 74s beneath them, the brick stores, timber docks, and other improvements Hull had made in eight years. At noon they were led to the sail loft over the stores, where a banquet room had been made of flags "tastefully suspended." Here they dined, "and the whole company appeared highly delighted with the taste evinced in the design, and the hospitality of the gallant officer who took so pleasant a farewell of his friends."[78]

But Hull had not forgiven the officers of the yard for their lack of support. The day before this party he had politely but rather coldly refused their offer of a public dinner, even though the committee was headed by his old friend John Downes, alleging that "every moment of my time until my departure, will be occupied in arranging my private concerns and performing the necessary public duties of the station."[79] The bitterness of 1822 still lingered. Hull by now had his formal orders to the *United States* and permission to leave Boston, if he wished, before Bainbridge arrived. But Hull would not skulk away as if defeated. He remained until Saturday, 23 August, when Bainbridge arrived with a ceremonial public escort and formally assumed command. Thirteen guns were fired as he entered the yard, and thirteen more as Hull departed.[80]

Hull gathered his family and left Boston without regret. The city had been in many ways his home port for a long time. From Boston he had sailed on his first cruises in the *Constitution*. There he had lived in 1809–10 when he commanded the *Chesapeake,* and there he had loved and regretfully said farewell to his first romance. To Boston he had come after escaping from the British squadron in 1812, and to Boston he returned in triumph with the flag of the *Guerrière.* To Boston he had brought his bride on their honeymoon, and to Boston he had returned in 1815 to make what he had hoped might be a permanent home. But the people of Boston had, he felt, rejected him, and he in turn had now rejected them. He would seldom visit, and never live there again.

13

Commodore Hull

The United States Pacific squadron under Isaac Hull was pivotal in the history of United States–Latin American relations. The sailing of the flagship in January 1824 was preceded by the proclamation of the Monroe Doctrine, and it was during the cruise of the Hull squadron, from 1824 to 1827, that the independence of Latin America was finally secured by the Patriot victory at Ayacucho in December 1824, the fall of Callao in January 1826, and the conquest of Chiloé in the same month. The task of the squadron accordingly shifted, during the three years, from maintenance of the rights of American neutral commerce against warring powers, the assignment of earlier American naval forces in the Pacific, to the upholding of commercial law and the fostering of an expanding American commerce throughout the Pacific in time of peace, the charge of future squadrons. The fact that the period was transitional, added to the difficulty of communicating with a government several months distant, made the assignment a particularly delicate one. Hull, with his easy temper and self-command, combined with conscientious devotion to his countrymen, was a fortunate choice as commodore.[1]

Considering the magnitude of the tasks to be performed, the force assigned seems ludicrously small: the frigate *United States*, 44, as flagship, and the sloop-of-war *Peacock*, 18. The previous squadron, under Charles Stewart, consisted of the *Franklin*, 74, and the schooner *Dolphin*, 12. Stewart had found it necessary to add an auxiliary and had purchased a small schooner, the *Peruviano*, for use as a dispatch vessel. Hull expected to retain this vessel, and perhaps the *Dolphin* as well. Even so, it would be a minimal force for patrolling a coastline twenty-five hundred miles in length and protecting American neutral commerce in time of war.

After eleven years on shore Isaac Hull was elated at the prospect of going to sea again. But embarking on a three-year cruise in the nineteenth century required a lot of preparation. Before he could go to Norfolk to take over his command Hull had to arrange the affairs of his extended family in Connecticut. The party of travelers first stopped at

Saybrook to bid farewell to Elisha Hart and the sisters at home: Mary Ann, Amelia, and Elizabeth. While they were there Heman Allen, appointed minister to Chile, arrived to confer with Hull about the date of sailing of the *United States* and the arrangements for his passage. Allen was a bachelor at the vulnerable age of forty, and on introduction to the Hart household he fell instantly in love with Elizabeth, a spinster aged twenty-seven. His sentiments were reciprocated, and within a week it was agreed that the two would be married in time to go together to Chile in the frigate. There was a hurried reshuffling of the passenger list: with two couples and Augusta Hart, plus Allen's Secretary of Legation Samuel Larned, and the usual assortment of servants, the frigate would be overcrowded. William Tudor, the new consul to Peru, was regretfully told that he would have to find another ship.

The next stops on the road south were New Haven and Derby, where Isaac Hull said goodbye to his father, certain that the old man would not live to see his return. Four days were spent at New York in whirlwind consultation with the dressmakers before the party moved on to Philadelphia. There they sought recommendations for a boarding situation for Jannette Hart, who was a semi-invalid and needed the attention of the Philadelphia physicians. Finally, after a pleasant social interlude at Baltimore, Ann, Isaac, and Augusta reached Washington in early October 1823.[2]

The Navy Department was between administrations. Smith Thompson had been appointed to the United States Supreme Court in late August, and the new secretary of the navy, Samuel Lewis Southard of New Jersey, had not yet taken office. John Rodgers was acting secretary. As soon as he had the family settled at Strother's Hotel, Hull went to call on him. One of the first things he heard was that his friend Mad Jack Percival was in trouble at Boston. One week after assuming command of the navy yard William Bainbridge had summoned Percival to his office and read a statement to him:

> Lieutenant Percival, it is indispensable for the good of the public service that the executive officers of the Yard should be respected by their commanding officer and necessarily on terms of intimacy with him; as this can never be the case between yourself and me I recommend you to make application to the Secretary of the Navy for a transfer from this station.

When Percival asked Bainbridge his reasons, the commodore referred vaguely to Percival's testimony in Abbot's trial. This kind of revenge on Hull's most outspoken supporter was to have been expected, but the manner of it did not have a sedative effect on Percival's temper. Smith Thompson had left this hot potato to John Rodgers, and Rodgers was holding it for Southard. In the meantime, as soon as he heard of it, Hull wrote Percival to "keep steady along, do your duty and you have little to fear." There was still hope that Percival would be appointed to command a schooner. Meanwhile, "I repeat that you must keep steady along and *cool*. Do not say a word that can be taken hold of and you will do well enough. Take the advice of Captain Shubrick and you cannot go astray."[3] When Southard arrived Hull persuaded him, for the time being, to order Percival to report to the *United States* for duty, though he had chosen Beverly Kennon as her first lieutenant. Supernumerary officers and men would be carried to the Pacific for the vessels to be kept on station, and Percival could be one of those.

The original plan had been for the squadron to sail in October, but the commissioners had learned, to their chagrin, that Navy Yard Commandant Lewis Warrington at Gosport had underestimated the time necessary to prepare the *United States* for sea, and the sailing date had been put off till December. Ann Hull and Augusta Hart were reveling in society at Washington, though things were a bit dull with Congress not in session, and none of the cabinet officers was in town except John Quincy Adams and John C. Calhoun. But Isaac was eager to get to his ship, so he settled them with friends—Augusta with Frances Lear and Ann with the Chaunceys—and hurried on to Norfolk. By 25 October he had the ship ready to receive her officers and crew. Recruiting had gone very well at Boston: 278 men were already on their way from there, and another large group had entered at New York on the promise of going in Hull's ship, so that the frigate was actually overfilled and was able to spare quite a few men for the *Peacock*.[4] By early November most of the officers were on board, including Lieutenants Kennon, Smoot, and Armstrong; Purser George Beale; eight midshipmen; and the draft of seamen and petty officers from Boston.[5] The *Peacock*, which had been serving in the West Indies, had not yet arrived. She was a last-minute substitution for the *Hornet*, which was now to be transferred to the West India squadron in exchange for the *Peacock*.[6]

Hull was very pleased with the *United States*. She was a sister of his favorite, the *Constitution*, although reputedly not as swift. At times in her career she had carried a light poop cabin, or "roundhouse," which damped her speed and earned her the nickname "Old Wagon." The *Peacock* was a war-built sloop, fast and handy, but after ten years of steady service she was nearly worn out. This would be her last cruise.[7]

Hull wanted to sail the first week in December, both to escape the winter weather in Hampton Roads and to ensure a summer passage of Cape Horn. The ship was ready in all respects except that she had no surgeon. There were about forty sick men in the crew, the number increasing as cold weather came on, and no one to attend them but the navy yard surgeon, George Kennon, of whom Hull had no very high opinion. When he was ordered to join the ship for her cruise, Kennon resigned. Service doctors were, and are, hard to come by. By 30 November the *United States* had fifty-seven sick men and still only a temporary surgeon, who was enthusiastically bleeding and purging the sufferers. As he had already been twice to the Pacific, however, he did not care to go again.[8]

On Thursday, 20 November, the pilot carried the *United States*, now with 450 men on board, to an anchorage between the forts at Norfolk. The next day about noon Hull went on board for an important ceremony. He read his official orders to take command of the ship, and as her cannon boomed a thirteen-gun salute, his blue broad pendant broke from the main truck. He was officially Commodore Hull at last.[9]

The *United States* would be too deep to cross the bar with all her stores on board, so on Wednesday afternoon, 26 November, she was lashed between the steamboats *Norfolk* and *Richmond* and carried down to Hampton Roads.[10] Ann Hull and Augusta Hart were now at Norfolk, and Heman Allen and his bride were expected daily. Jannette, to everyone's surprise, had decided to leave Philadelphia and winter at Nassau in the Bahamas. Ann had inspected the frigate and found it to her liking. The after cabin was furnished in crimson silk damask with couches, ottomans, and bookcases; the dining cabin, with carpet, sideboard, and sofas—not much like Isaac Hull's spartan bachelor quarters in the *Constitution*! One of the petty officers' wives, Mrs. Elkins, a veteran of two previous voyages, would be Ann's servant, and she was very probably only one of a number of women in the 'tween decks. Hull's manservant, Isaac Wheeden, had taken charge of the pantry, and John Etheridge was on board as captain's clerk—a post he would retain in Hull's family for twenty years. John A. Bates had been elevated to chaplain of the ship—a common step for clerks—although the Hart sisters were saddened that there would not be an Episcopal clergyman on board.[11]

Ann Hull had changed a great deal in eleven years of marriage. She had put on weight, though she was still regarded as a handsome woman. More important, she had put on airs. She still referred to Isaac as "husband" or "Captain H." but had begun to sign herself "Anna"; by the end of the voyage her sisters were calling her "Doña" and she had begun to style Isaac "the Commodore" even to the family. Isaac, on the other hand, although scarred by his recent experiences, was an older version of his genial self. The younger officers, when out of earshot—which was not very far nowadays—called him "Uncle Isaac."

Early on 30 November the *Peacock* arrived and went up to the navy yard for repairs. She needed new copper and rigging, and this was expected to take three or four weeks.[12] Hull was chafing to get the *United States* to sea. On 10 December the crew were stationed, and the next evening the ship received her powder from the magazine. Hull wanted to sail on Sunday, the fourteenth, but he received orders from Secretary Southard to wait for the *Peacock*. This order was annoying, but Hull was so happy to be on shipboard again that he did not let it bother him much. He simply kept prodding the secretary every few days to let him sail. Mad Jack Percival had joined the ship as second lieutenant. He had had a personal interview with Southard on his way through Washington, but the most he had been able to wring from the secretary was an equivocal note:

> it is probable the Dolphin will return with Captain Stewart before you shall reach the Pacific. Lieut. Conner is now in command of the Dolphin, and he will probably remain in command after Capt. Hull arrives if she is kept there. Should Lt. Conner come home, and the Dolphin remain, Capt. Hull will place in command, *until her return*, the officer whose rank and services best justify it. My wish is, that the merchants and others who recommended you, may be gratified by your appointment.[13]

But two weeks later he ordered Hull to send the *Dolphin* home on his arrival. It looked as if Percival was out of luck.

By mid-December the *United States* still lacked a surgeon, but Surgeon's Mate John Fitzhugh was on duty. Hull expressed his lifelong concern for the seamen in some remarks about the state of navy medicine at Norfolk: "indeed the sick on this station are in a comfortless situation, so much so as to do great injury to the service; for the least a seaman can expect for long and faithful services is comfortable quarters and good attendance when sick."[14] Eventually, Fitzhugh was made acting surgeon of the ship, with two junior surgeon's mates to assist him. Hull liked his new surgeon well enough, but Fitzhugh's health was not robust, so that the state of the ship's medical department remained precarious. Captain William Carter of the *Peacock* was also having a hard time finding competent doctors for his ship.

About this time the *United States* was the scene of a curious little cloak-and-dagger incident. It appears that the guardians of a young Baltimorean named Daniel Campbell thought that a few years in the South Pacific would be curative for his chronic alcoholism. One of them, Thomas Cromwell, persuaded Henry Clay to take an interest in the young man, and he in turn obtained from Secretary Southard a letter to Isaac Hull asking him to take Campbell in the *United States* as a boy or ordinary seaman, "but if his conduct will justify it, you will assign to him the duties of a cadet midshipman." Obviously, the reason for sending Campbell away was being kept closely concealed by his mentors. Cromwell then sent Campbell down to Hampton Roads on Christmas Day "to hand a letter to Commodore Hull." It told Hull that "I will thank you to *detain him on board.* I have been obliged to use considerable strategem to get him there. His baggage will be sent by tomorrow's steam boat." Hull wondered a bit at that, but Cromwell was a friend, so he cheerfully welcomed Campbell to the ship and directed him to the midshipmen's quarters. The outraged Campbell, who had had no idea that he was being turned over to the navy, panicked and begged Hull to let him go. Hull adamantly packed him off to the steerage. But within twenty-four hours he received a letter of protest from six of the senior midshipmen:

> The elder officers of the steerage of this ship respectfully submit to your consideration the propriety of allowing Mr. Campbell (a person who lately came on board this ship) to mess in the steerage. He has acknowledged that he is addicted to intemperance and we fear the examples he may set will have a very pernicious tendency. We sincerely hope, as he is desirous of leaving the ship, that he may be allowed to do so, or at least that he will be removed from the *steerage.*

That was a horse of another color. It was all very well to do a friend a good turn, but if there was one thing Hull could not abide it was a drunken officer, particularly one likely to lead his young midshipmen astray. The next morning he sent Campbell packing. His relatives would have to find some other means of reforming his character.[15]

On 13 December the *John Adams* came down to Norfolk from Washington with David Porter on board. Porter, after a successful cruise against pirates in the West Indies the previous summer, had suffered an attack of yellow fever and had returned to his home at Meridian Hill, near Washington, to recuperate. He was now bound south again, accompanied by his family. Porter and Hull had a pleasant reunion, but within two weeks their friendship was marred by a bitter and senseless dispute over seamen belonging to the *Hornet* and the *Peacock.* Hull believed that he was authorized to make up a volunteer crew for the *Peacock* from men of both crews who were willing to serve the three years of the cruise, leaving those who only wanted to serve out their present enlistments in Porter's squadron. Porter was quickly apprised of this by First Lieutenant Dulany Forrest of the *Peacock*, who told him that Hull was "enticing" men properly belonging to Porter's squadron by offers of advance pay and shore liberty. The explosive Porter decided that Hull was "pulling rank" and taking the cream of the two crews, leaving the dregs for him.[16] He wrote Hull a scathing demand for the men. Hull was deeply hurt. "You may suppose," he told Porter,

> that after an acquaintance of upwards of twenty years and after having been associated in war and in peace, and having been in habits of more than ordinary friendship, at least those have been my feelings towards you, that I must suffer in my feelings to be obliged at this time of life to present to you the signatures of those who were children when we were in active service as testimonials of the correctness of my conduct in relation to the transfer of the crews of the Hornet and Peacock; and I only regret that my being under sailing orders prevents my bringing Mr. Forrest before a court martial. . . . I have therefore determined to lay the facts before the Secretary of the Navy, that he may take such proceedings upon them as to him may appear proper.[17]

Porter was determined to maintain his rights. He told John Rodgers that "I would have divided a world with him, but I will not allow him to make an encroachment on me the hundredth part of a grain of sand."[18] After Hull had sailed Porter repossessed himself of the seamen from the *Peacock*, but before that he struck back in another way by depriving Hull of his first lieutenant. Beverly Kennon had been in Porter's squadron the previous year, and the two men had had a falling out that eventually led to an acrimonious exchange in the newspapers. Now Porter had Kennon arrested for trial before a court-martial for his publications, so that the *United States* sailed without him. As things turned out, Kennon was fully acquitted, and Porter sacrificed the friendship of both Hull and Rodgers and the favor of Samuel Southard.[19]

Christmas came and went and the *United States* still rode at her anchors in Hampton Roads. More and more of her crew were catching colds, and on 23 December one of them was found to have smallpox. Hull quickly assembled the men and sent the fifty-odd who had not been vaccinated on shore to take the "kine pox," taking an equal number from the *Peacock*.[20] He wanted to get away before anything worse happened, but the cabinet discussions at Washington that were within a few days to issue in President Monroe's message to Congress—the "Monroe Doctrine" message—were also shaping the instructions to be given Hull and Heman Allen. At last, on 27 December, Hull received his official orders to "proceed round Cape Horn to Valparaiso as speedily as circumstances will permit." But the orders were undated. Did they supersede Southard's instructions of 10 December to wait for the *Peacock*, or had they been drafted earlier? Hull decided to straighten things out by going to Washington, and on Sunday morning, 28 December, he and John A. Bates boarded the steamboat for the capital. By

Thursday afternoon they were back with orders to sail immediately. The *Peacock* could catch up when she was ready.[21]

Hull had decided to sail on Sunday, 4 January 1824, if the wind was fair. On returning to the ship, he discovered that he had left his official instructions behind at Washington, and he asked Southard to send them down by Sunday's mail. The mail boat hove alongside about noon, just as the *United States* weighed anchor. Mad Jack Percival, now first lieutenant, got her under way before a southwesterly breeze. At sunset the "Old Wagon" dropped her pilot off Cape Henry and stood off to the southeast. It was an unpleasant night for the officers and crew; the ship proved to have a leak around the rudder coat that dumped nine inches of water an hour into the wardroom, steerage, and berth deck. The watch below bailed all night.[22]

For the first two weeks of the voyage the *United States* went off like a racehorse before northerly winds, running almost due east for ten days and then dropping south to pass near the Cape Verde Islands on 18 January. She was still leaking at the stern, and her new running rigging was poor—Hull thought the Norfolk rope was inferior and full of sand—but generally her captain was pleased with her. "The ship sails very fast," he reported with satisfaction, "and will be when in order one of the first ships in the world."[23] She had indeed made a remarkable run to the islands, and only a change to light airs near the equator lengthened her passage to Rio to thirty-seven days, still a very short voyage. Hull was in his element again. Like most captains, he loved a fast ship, and he drove his vessels hard. He enjoyed tinkering with the *United States* to get the best speed out of her, as on Sunday, 1 February, when he tried altering her trim by sending the crew first forward and then aft to trim her by the head or the stern—but, as the log recorded, he "found it made no perceptible difference." Ann Hull and Augusta Hart also proved to be good sailors, but poor Elizabeth, who was already pregnant, was seasick during the whole passage, as was Allen's secretary, Samuel Larned. The ship's schoolmaster, Edward Kenney, was worse than seasick. He died of consumption on 30 January and was buried at sea.[24] In general, however, despite the dampness on the berth deck, the crew grew healthier as the ship drove southward. They were happy, too, under the benevolent sway of "Uncle Isaac." Only one man was punished in January, and he got just a half-dozen lashes.

The weeks of greater leisure in the tropics gave Isaac Hull time to read his instructions in detail and to discuss them with Heman Allen. Since the orders drawn up by John Quincy Adams for the minister to Chile had been used by Southard as a model for Hull's instructions, the spirit of the principal author of the Monroe Doctrine brooded over both.

It was clear to everyone that the neutrality of the United States in the revolutionary struggles in Latin America was merely formal. The government hoped to keep the American merchant fleet from engaging in non-neutral acts, such as carrying contraband, which might cause it to fall forfeit to the belligerents, but the sentiments of Americans generally, as well as their economic hopes, lay with the Patriots. It was in this spirit that Southard advised Hull: "Our relations with the government of Chile and Peru are of the most friendly character, and the desire of our government that they should continue so is undiminished. Your conduct must, on all occasions, be such as those relations require; at the same time full protection must be afforded to our citizens and their interests."[25]

This demanded that the naval commander walk a tightrope between friendship for the revolutionary governments and protection for American citizens. Southard added a caveat: "complaints have . . . been made, both by individuals, and by the governments existing there, that our vessels have afforded improper protection to unlawful trade, and aided our own citizens, and those of other nations, in violations of the laws." As a matter of fact, the government of the United Provinces of Rio de la Plata, at Buenos Aires, had registered a formal protest against Charles Stewart's alleged protection of American gun runners who were selling arms to the Royalists. John Quincy Adams had vigorously denied the fact, but Hull knew from his conversations at Washington that Stewart was going to face a full-scale court-martial on those and other charges when he reached home. Hull certainly wanted to avoid any such difficulties for himself, but he was not likely to encounter that sort of charge, for he was definitely "neutral on the side of the Patriots" in his own sentiments. Stewart, on the other hand, favored the Royalists and had had a great deal of trouble in getting along with the United States agent in Peru, the strongly pro-Patriot John W. Prevost. Hull would have no such problems.

In directing the general course of the cruise the secretary displayed a curiously foreshortened view of Pacific geography; the *United States* was "at such time as you can most conveniently and safely leave the coast of Chile and Peru" to visit the Sandwich Islands, and the frigate was also to "visit the mouth of Columbia River and return by the Cape of Good Hope." Circumstances, however, prevented the carrying out of these ambitious plans.[26]

Southard exhorted Hull at length that the midshipmen "are to be the objects of your unceasing care, both as to their conduct and improvement in their profession." This was a subject dear to Isaac Hull and a matter that he was not likely to neglect. Before the ship reached Brazil he had instructed First Lieutenant Percival to give special responsibilities to the passed midshipmen. John Bubier, the senior, was to assist the sailing master and take charge of the logbook. William H. Homer and Harry D. Hunter would alternate in charge of the hold and the berth deck, and William H. Campbell would supervise the gun deck and be in charge of issuing the ship's stores and provisions. The twenty-five junior midshipmen would be assigned to regular deck watches. Among them was one on whom Uncle Isaac's eye fell with special benevolence: Thomas Tingey Craven, who had been a very small boy when Hull first saw him in the bleak home of his improvident father on the navy yard island at Portsmouth.[27]

The *United States* lay only a week at Rio de Janeiro, taking in water, caulking her leaks, and exchanging salutes and visits with the local worthies, including British Admiral Sir George Eyre. Isaac Hull was ill and did not go on shore during the short stay. Early on Tuesday, 17 February, the frigate weighed anchor again and stood out of the harbor bound for Cape Horn. While the ship drove southward across the Brazil bank and past the muddy mouth of Rio de la Plata, the crew were kept busy setting up stump masts, belly stays, and other storm gear. Cape Horn greeted them on 7 March in proper style: "fresh gales from the Sd. & Ed. with heavy squalls accompanied with snow and hail . . . at 5 split the main topsail . . . from 6 to 8 strong gales with a heavy head sea." At dawn on 8 March the Cape gleamed twenty miles ahead; by evening it was behind them. The remaining three weeks were relatively easy. The storm gear came down; the pole masts and light sails went aloft. The decks and paintwork were holystoned and scrubbed. On 22 March they caught an albatross, and on the twenty-sixth land was in sight. The anchor splashed in Valparaiso harbor the next forenoon, Saturday, 27 March, thirty-nine days from Rio and eighty-two days from Cape Henry. It had been a very swift passage.[28]

Isaac Hull was still suffering from the illness that had attacked him in January—probably a bronchial complaint—but there were, of course, visits and salutes and pleasantries to be exchanged at Valparaiso. On Sunday morning the Allens and their entourage were rowed ashore to a ceremonial welcome that was somewhat muted by the restrictions of Lent. The schooners *Dolphin* and *Peruviano* were awaiting Hull at Valparaiso, but the *Franklin* was not there, and Consul Michael Hogan told Hull and Allen the disturbing reason. When Hull left Norfolk, Peru had been in the hands of the Patriot government and the liberating armies of Simón Bolívar, but the general's illness in January 1824 had so weakened his position that a counterrevolution had seized Lima and its port of Callao in February. Stewart had taken the *Franklin* back to Callao to protect the American shipping there, and Hull had to cut short his stay at Valparaiso to follow and relieve him there.[29]

Once again the *United States* was only a week at anchor. She joined the *Franklin* and the *Dolphin* at Callao on Sunday, 11 April. There was a round of salutes before Charles Stewart and his wife made a formal call at 11:30 A.M. Mrs. Hull was not much impressed with Delia Tudor Stewart: "She is too selfish and odd. She has no communion of feeling with those who find their happiness in cherishing the sweet charities of life and those bonds which unite families in domestic love and tenderness. She lives for admiration and the follies of the world." There was a joyful reunion with nephew Joseph, who would be going home with the *Franklin,* and the Hull family was given a tour of Lima by Zachariah W. Nixon, a navy lieutenant on extended leave who had established a mercantile house in the capital.

One of the striking characteristics of the early nineteenth century is the intimacy of American high society. It is evident that the Hulls were acquainted with the "best people" in all the principal cities of the eastern seaboard, and when they reached the west coast of South America nearly all the Americans they found there were also personally known to them. These included the Hogans at Valparaiso; William Tudor; Z. W. Nixon; and Henry DeKoven of Middletown, Connecticut, captain of the ship *America*—all of whom they found at Lima—as well as Eliphalet Smith, merchant at Arequipa, and Washington Stewart, vice-consul at Coquimbo. Richard Alsop and William S. Wetmore, Lima merchants, were also among their acquaintances; in the fall of 1824 Alsop spent six weeks on board the *United States* for medical treatment. Many of these were Boston people. It is suggestive of the intricate network of kin connections in the upper reaches of American society that William Tudor, consul at Lima, was Mrs. Charles Stewart's brother and that Heman Allen, minister to Chile, was now Hull's brother-in-law.

The Peruvian countryside was in a dangerous state of upheaval with Patriot and Royalist armies in the field and roving bands of *montañeros* (freebooters) sometimes controlling the cities at night. But Isaac Hull found waiting for him at Callao something more dreadful than war: Stewart had been saving all his offending officers and men to be tried by a general court-martial when the *United States* arrived, and Hull was required to preside. This proceeding went on daily (Sundays excepted) from 15 April until 3 May, and as Ann observed: "The name of court makes him sick and he had not recovered from a violent illness when he arrived, and now is miserable."[30]

At the same time, Hull had to make some important decisions about

SOUTH AMERICA
Cruise of the Frigate
United States, 1824–1827

80° 70° 60° 50° 40°

San Blas

COLOMBIA

P A C I F I C

Guayaquil

PERU

Ayacucho

Arequipo
Quilca
Arica

Huamachuco
Trujillo

0 50 100 150
STATUTE MILES

Casma

Huacho

Ancón Chancay
Callao Lima
Chorrillos Chilca

BRAZIL

O C E A N

Rio de
Janeiro

UNITED
Huasco PROVINCES
Coquimbo

CHILE

Island of
Juan Fernandez

Valparaiso

Talcahuano

O C E A N

A T L A N T I C O C E A N

Chiloé

100 0 200 600
STATUTE MILES

Cape Horn

90° 80° 70° 60° 50° 40° 30° 20°

Kathy Rex Lopatto

the future of his squadron. Stewart told him that the schooner *Peruviano* was his own property; he had bought her with his private funds and had already resold her to the firm of Nixon & McCall. Hull, of course, had no such sums in his pocket. He could not afford to buy his own dispatch vessels, and if he sent the *Dolphin* home as ordered, he would be left on the coast of a country at war with only his frigate until the *Peacock* arrived. The captains and supercargoes of American ships at Valparaiso had petitioned Hull and Allen that the *Dolphin* might remain, and Allen had recommended her retention to Stewart. Hull determined, therefore, with Stewart's approval, to keep the *Dolphin* with him. There was, of course, another consideration: Mad Jack Percival wanted the command. The secretary's letter to him had said that *if* she remained and *if* her commander, Lieutenant David Conner, came home, Hull could appoint a commander for her, and it was a foregone conclusion that he would choose Percival. But Hull would have to think of a reason for detaching Conner, an officer he genuinely admired. His orders gave as reasons for the return of the *Dolphin* to the United States "the situation of her crew, the necessity for repairs, and for the presence of her officers to investigate certain charges which have been made against some of them." Hull had extra men and officers for one of the schooners, and he thought he could make any necessary repairs on the coast. The third reason, therefore, was the one he alleged, obliquely, to Conner in ordering him home: "believing . . . that it is [the secretary's] wish and intention that you should return to the United States, notwithstanding his not having given you orders to do so." Conner was wanted to answer charges preferred by Lieutenant Horace B. Sawyer, including an allegation that he had allowed silks to be displayed for sale in the *Dolphin*'s cabin. He was convicted on this charge and reprimanded. But he was not satisfied that the charges were sufficient to cause him to be removed from his command, and when he got back to the United States he protested Hull's action to the secretary. By then, though, it was too late.[31]

Hull had then to go another step beyond his instructions, which enjoined him to "make no *acting appointment of any description* except in cases of *absolute necessity*" and to make a group of acting appointments for the *Dolphin:* Midshipmen Bubier and Homer were made acting lieutenants, Midshipman Harry D. Hunter acting sailing master, and Surgeon's Mate Benjamin Tinslar acting surgeon. Hull's clerk, now chaplain, John A. Bates, received the coveted appointment as purser. Considerations of favoritism aside, Percival was the logical choice for this command. He was an old and experienced officer—at forty-eight a good deal older than most of his rank, since he had "come up through the hawse hole" from sailing master; he had been on the coast previously as a lieutenant in the *Macedonian,* and he spoke Spanish.

Compared with those of the Charlestown Navy Yard, and even with other contemporary squadrons, the officers of Hull's command were a peaceable lot. He was generally successful in keeping them happy, and his cruise was not marred by duels as his predecessors' had been. But Uncle Isaac had difficulty with some of the young men over the ever sore subject of rank. After detaching Percival to the *Dolphin,* he had William K. Latimer and James Armstrong as first and second lieutenant, respectively, in the *United States,* both of them hot-blooded southerners. Armstrong expected Latimer to move to the quarters vacated by Percival, but Latimer preferred the stateroom he already had. The two submitted the matter to Hull, who thought that two grown men could resolve that petty issue between themselves, and he refused to intervene. When Latimer kept pestering him about it he finally said, "I see you wish to make a difficulty," whereupon Latimer asked permission to resign from the ship and return to the United States in the *Franklin.* Hull let him go. When he got back to Philadelphia, Latimer went about saying that he had left the Pacific because "Captain Hull had commenced a smuggling system . . . similar to the one carried on by Commodore Stewart." That was, apart from being untrue, a miscalculation. Stewart, who was about to face a court-martial on charges of that sort— a court that fully acquitted him—forced Latimer to admit that his stories were all based on hearsay. Latimer was lucky to get off with only a red face.[32]

Hull's intended first lieutenant, Beverly Kennon, after being acquitted of Porter's charges at Norfolk, took passage in the *Peacock* to rejoin his ship. The *Peacock* had a gruesome voyage out. Off Bermuda she was struck by lightning that killed four men; while the ship was rounding Cape Horn in winter weather her crew fell ill with smallpox, and another dozen were lost. She did not join the *United States* at Callao until 15 August. The strains of the passage had played on the nerves of her officers. Hull was immediately informed that Lieutenant Albert G. Wall had preferred charges against Captain William Carter, including allegations that Carter was a habitual drunkard and incapable of managing the ship—charges so serious that he would have to be sent home to await trial, since there was no senior officer on the station except Hull who could try him.

Thus, Hull was forced to another breach of Secretary Southard's wishes, for in his instructions to Hull the secretary had inveighed against the practice of sending officers home for trial and had directed Hull that it "should only be used when no doubt of its *necessity* remains." Hull evidently did not think much of the charges against Carter; he declined to arrest him and wrote him that "since you joined my command your conduct has been such as to meet my approbation."[33] He chose Beverly Kennon, as senior lieutenant in the squadron, to command the *Peacock* for the time being, and he transferred Joseph Smoot to her as first lieutenant, removing Lieutenant William W. Ramsay to the *United States* in Smoot's place. Hull gave as his reason for this that Smoot was senior to Ramsay and that a number of officers in the squadron were hurt by seeing a junior lieutenant in so exalted a position, but it is probable that Kennon, who had sailed in the *Peacock*, told Hull he didn't want Ramsay as his executive officer. Carter asserted that Ramsay had engineered the charges against him in order to obtain command of the *Peacock* and that he had told Lieutenant James Armstrong of the *United States* that "I will do my damndest to obtain the command of her." Kennon evidently thought that Carter was right and that if Ramsay, balked of command of the *Peacock*, remained in her as first lieutenant, Captain Kennon might be the next victim.

At any rate, Ramsay refused to accept the new arrangement. He told Hull that, if he could not command the *Peacock* or at least be first lieutenant, he preferred to return home and lay his case before the secretary. He even boasted that he would have the *Peacock* ordered back to the United States. Hull wished him a pleasant passage and wrote Southard that "I consider Lieutenant Ramsay a most promising officer, but I cannot approve of the measures he took to obtain the command of the *Peacock* or his pretensions to remain as first lieutenant of her to the injury of other officers."[34]

Ramsay won that round, however. In March 1825 Secretary Southard sent him back to the Pacific in company with the *Peacock*'s newly assigned commander, Master Commandant Thomas ap Catesby Jones. He gave two reasons. The first was that Ramsay should not have asked to return. "His duty was to obey your orders, and await the decision of the Department on his case." The habit of officers' returning home to plead their cases must be broken. The second reason was that Hull had erred in depriving Ramsay of the first lieutenancy of the *Peacock*. "He was placed in that situation by the express orders of the Department; nothing but absolute necessity should have induced the placing any other over him. . . . The claims of seniority are always regarded when consistent with public interest, but the Department must be left at liberty to place officers according to its views of the interest of the service."[35]

Ramsay's basic problem, however, was that he didn't know how to quit when he was ahead. As soon as he returned to Callao at the end of July 1825 he wrote Hull an insolent note:

Herewith I have the honor to submit warranty of the Honbl. the Secretary of the Navy for reassumption of the station put in my occupancy and of which by your command I was deposed. In the proffer of this unsought testimonial of approbation, there has been an attainment of all that I could have desired, and with me the measure has amply sufficed. Now, Sir, notwithstanding such considerations and in combination too with circumstances under which I returned to your command, I cheerfully tender you the disposal of my order, to be disposed of, or bestowed upon, whomsoever your pleasure may fall.

Hull sent this along to Southard with the remark that

It has been usual to forward copies of papers relating to the public service, but this letter is couched in such language and the style of it is so new to me that I have forwarded the original. It will be seen that Lieutenant Ramsay considers that he has gained his object as he has returned to the situation which was given him, in which he charges me of having "deposed" him, as he is pleased to call it, and now he is ready to take any situation that I may please to order him to, and this too with a knowledge of my having your positive order for him to join the Peacock. This condescension on his part could therefore be only with a view to remind me that he was now out of my reach, as I could not order him to any other situation without violating your positive orders whatever injury might result to the service by my not doing so.[36]

He had no choice but to let Ramsay remain where he was, but he may have anticipated the sequel: Thomas ap Catesby Jones was a firebrand, and it was not long before Ramsay crossed him. The next thing he knew, the well-traveled lieutenant was under arrest. Rather than send him home again, Hull ordered a court-martial to try him, but Ramsay objected to having Jones preside—as well he might, considering that Jones had instigated the charges. That made it impossible to try him on the station, and Jones, who had no desire to keep Ramsay confined on board the *Peacock* for a half year or more while she cruised the Pacific, recommended to Hull that the lieutenant be sent to the United States. "Mr. Ramsay is a young officer, not without fair pretensions in many respects," wrote Jones, "but like all mankind has his faults; and a few more years, and a little reflection will bring them to his own view." Hull's resolution of this was to allow Ramsay to leave the *Peacock* and remain at Lima until she was ready to return home. Lieutenant Smoot again volunteered for, and was transferred to, the sloop as first lieutenant.[37]

Some of the young officers took advantage of the shakeup in the *Peacock* in August 1824 to seek assignment to the more commodious *United States.* One who succeeded in getting transferred was Midshipman Andrew Hull Foote, who was a cousin of the commodore's, and who considered his relative the beau ideal of an officer. But kinship did not prevent young Foote from being suspended from duty and censured in the log for one escapade on 1 June 1825: "The following gentlemen have this day been suspended from duty for wantonly cutting the throats of two hogs and heaving them overboard: Benj. R. Tinslar, Surgeons Mate, Andrew H. Foote, Wm. E. Hunt & Geo. P. Upshur, Midn., by order of Commodore Hull." Other "young gentlemen" were in hot water from time to time, some for borrowing money, others for displays of temper—Charles McBlair was particularly vulnerable on that score— but generally they got on well with Uncle Isaac, and he was pleased with them. Bubier and Homer were confirmed as lieutenants early in the cruise.

Two of the *Peacock*'s midshipmen, on the other hand, ended the cruise in disgrace. In July 1825 Lieutenant Commandant Kennon reported Samuel B. Phelps and John Quincy Adams Boyd to the commodore to be disciplined. Hull avoided trying them, as he always did when possible. Phelps "being a young man of uncommon promise and believing from his penitence and youth that there was yet a hope of reclaiming him," he permitted him to return home by way of Europe "in hopes he will see his error and yet be an ornament to his profession." Boyd was a harder case:

> Midshipman Boyd was left on the station by Commodore Stewart and had been shifted from ship to ship until he was considered an outlaw and totally unmanageable. Soon after I took command of this sea Mr. Boyd requested permission to return to the United States, urging as a reason that he had been out three years and that other officers had been suffered to return on making known their wish to do so. Believing it to be the wish of Mr. Boyd's friends that he should remain out and knowing them to be very respectable I did not listen to his request, and ordered him to the Peacock where for about two months his conduct was such as to induce Capt. Kennon to hope that he would in future conduct with more propriety, and return to his friends in a way that a favorable report might be made of him, but he soon returned to his former bad habits and abandoned himself to every vice as you will see by Capt. Kennon's letter.
>
> To restore him to his friends and with a hope that he might be saved to them I gave him permission to return home, but his conduct was such that no one would receive him and I have since understood that he had entered on board one of the Patriot vessels of war, but had been sent from her on board one of their transports, where he now remains, and I much doubt whether he will ever return to his friends.

Hull asked Southard to forgive him if he had been too indulgent to the young men; like a true uncle, he was always hoping that they would mature and become ornaments to society and a comfort to their families.[38]

The situation Isaac Hull had to confront after the *Franklin*'s departure on 4 May 1824 was confused and precarious both by land and by sea. The Royalists held Lima and the forts guarding Callao Bay, but Bolívar had established a headquarters at Trujillo, to the northward, and was himself in the cordillera at Huamachuco, assembling an army for a counterstroke. By sea, Vice Admiral Martin George Guise, the Englishman who headed the Peruvian naval forces, had proclaimad a blockade of the coast from 11°3' to 22°30' south latitude—in other words, the entire coast of Peru from Callao southward. Since Guise had just one frigate and three smaller vessels at his disposal, the blockade could be only a paper one. At the time of Hull's arrival the blockade of Callao was being conducted by the lone brig *Macedonian*. In fact, it was being used merely as an excuse for levying tribute on merchant vessels: if a ship were caught entering a prohibited harbor, she could be permitted to go in anyway provided that her master paid the Peruvian naval commander a fee of from 6 to 25 percent of the value of his cargo. All this was patently illegal. The United States in particular had been sensitive for years to the problem of illegal blockades, and Stewart had protested such blockades during his cruise. But Stewart's instructions, which were also given to Hull, had been very precise about the manner of dealing with illegal blockades proclaimed by the Patriots. With reference to such a blockade by the Chilean squadron in 1821, Navy Secretary Thompson had written:

> although . . . its legality is expressly denied, yet the nature of the controversy that is carrying on in South America, being a struggle, on one side, for liberty and independence, renders it peculiarly fit and proper for the United States to avoid any collision with them, or to do any act that may, in any manner, have the appearance, or admit of the construction of favoring the cause of Spain against such a struggle. . . . Act, at present, on the defensive only; and for all violations of our neutral rights, if any occur under your observation, let strong and spirited appeals be made, through our public Agent.[39]

Heman Allen had also advised Hull, with regard to the Royalists,

> on his arrival off Callao, to demand of the existing authorities in that place, the immediate surrender of all the American prisoners and property; and in case of refusal, to retake the whole by force, if in his opinion, his squadron should be competent to the undertaking. I advised him also, to make a similar demand of the Admiral [Guise], for the restoration of the ransom money, which he had unjustly exacted; but, not to make war upon him, as the cases, though both unwarranted, appeared to me, to be somewhat dissimilar.[40]

The Spanish naval force on the coast was for the moment no match even for Guise's squadron, but it had several small cruisers, including the *Quintanilla*, the *Constante*, and the *Moyana*, which were indiscriminately seizing merchant vessels on the coasts of Chile and Peru. Hull was inclined to regard these as pirates, since their commissions were issued by provincial commanders and were therefore of doubtful legality. On 4 May the English brig *Triton* came into Callao with a report that she had been boarded by the *Quintanilla* and that five of her men had been impressed; by mid-July the *Constante* had sent two American vessels, the *Nancy* and the *General Carrington*, and the Swedish brig *Sophia* into Callao as prizes. These captures caused an increasingly heated correspondence between Hull and the commandant at Callao, General José Ramon Rodil, leading ultimately to a complete severance of relations between them.

Hull continued to have a much better understanding with the Patriots. He found two ways of coping with the blockade, the legality of which he denied. One was to keep a lookout for American vessels approaching Callao and to send one of his ships outside to escort them through the blockade. The *Dolphin* was kept busy cruising the outports for the same purpose. The second was to remonstrate with Guise's superiors in the Peruvian government. This he did principally through the United States special agent in Peru, John B. Prevost, who was at Trujillo with the government. Prevost was a warm partisan of Bolívar's and was on excellent terms with him. That was decidedly not the case with the new consul at Lima, William Tudor. Tudor, founder of the *North American Review*, had not prospered in literary pursuits and had obtained his consular appointment in hopes of finding some better source of income, such as his ingenious brother Frederick had hit upon in developing the export of New England ice. William had already entered into business ventures with Nixon & McCall, including ownership of the *Peruviano* and the brig *Frederic*. The Hulls had known the Tudors at Boston, but Isaac Hull did not share William Tudor's patrician political views. Tudor had an extravagant admiration for the Spanish viceroy, José de la Serna, and his generals; his opinion of Bolívar and the Colombians was correspondingly low. He had established himself at Lima and presented his credentials to the Royalist government, making no acknowledgment of the Patriot government at Trujillo. Tudor was delighted when Guise exacted a 6 percent payment from the British trader *Thomas Noland*, and HMS *Aurora*, Captain Prescott commanding, was sent to remonstrate: "I offer you my congratulations," he wrote Hull,

> that chance has brought Admiral Guise on his own countrymen first . . . that Captain P. who is such a great admirer of what are here called Patriots, who thought St. Martin a Washington in his day, and takes up his successors in the

same way; and alas! there are Americans too, who from a sort of infatuation are thus willing to lower the character of the immortal patriots of America to the level of what we see here—. . . it is curious that Capt. P. should have to discuss the matter with the floating customhouse. . . . I am glad that the case is likely to be made so very clear for you.[41]

Although he was willing to assist Hull in opposing Guise's proceedings, Tudor refused to have anything to do with protesting Royalist seizures, for fear that doing so would jeopardize his business connections at Lima.[42] Prevost took a dim view of Tudor—which was reciprocated— and Hull was worried that the consul's behavior would cause him to be expelled when the Patriots came to power again; but for the moment it was clear that he would have to negotiate with the government at Trujillo without the aid of the American consul. He wrote to Bolívar at the end of May, protesting the illegality of the blockade, assuring him both that no protection would be given to vessels carrying contraband and that a legal blockade would be respected. In an accompanying letter to Prevost he remarked on "the trouble and vexation I have in nursing the commerce of our country, and with all I can do God only knows what will become of it." Lieutenant Hiram Paulding was sent with the letters in the *Dolphin*, to land at Huacho or Trujillo and to seek Bolívar in the mountains. The Liberator's cordial response reached Hull on 8 July. Bolívar, who had before him both Hull's and Prevost's protests, said that he would himself be answerable for any illegal pillage by Guise's fleet. He also made at least a gesture of goodwill by instructing Guise to maintain a legal blockade by keeping a ship before every interdicted port—which was, of course, impossible. He had, after all, very little control over his admiral, and he could not afford to alienate him at that critical moment, as Hull realized. He laid the situation before Heman Allen, commenting:

when I am instructed to conduct in a way to insure a continuance of the friendly feelings that now exist between the two Governments and at the same time to protect commerce, I am much at a loss how far I should be justified in using force when remonstrance is found to be unavailing, and I am the more at a loss from the peculiar situation in which the Protector is placed at this time with Admiral Guise, for there cannot be a doubt that he disapproves of the conduct of the Admiral towards neutrals, yet he cannot well at this time dispense with his services, and if he could, it would be difficult to get him out of the ship he commands, nor dare he attempt to remove him for fear of the consequences. Under these circumstances were I to use force and disable his ship and General Bolivar should fail in establishing the independence of Peru, it would be said that America was the first to acknowledge their independence and the first to injure their cause when endeavouring to regain it.[43]

In reply, Allen insisted that Hull maintain American rights against both warring parties, for should the independence of Peru depend on acquiescence by the United States in outrages upon its citizens, "as much as I should lament its failure yet I should say that, our country is not prepared for so great a sacrifice."[44] No further serious trouble came from the Patriots, however. It is worth remarking that, of all the American squadron commanders to date, Hull had the greatest success in persuading the Patriot leaders to acknowledge American neutral rights. This was due in part to the improving situation of the Patriot cause, but it was also due in large measure to Hull's tact and his evident approval of the Peruvian and Colombian revolutions.

European nations had much larger naval forces in the Pacific than did the United States. At the time of Hull's arrival the British squadron at Callao consisted of the *Cambridge*, 84; the frigates *Aurora* and *Tartar*; and the sloops of war *Fly* and *Mersey*, under the overall command of Captain Thomas James Maling. Hull and Maling acted in close concert throughout the cruise; old hatchets were buried in a mutual celebration of the Fourth of July on board the *United States*, where a banquet was served under an awning composed of the flags of both nations. But the British were not of much help in arguing the blockade question, since, being chronic violators of international law in that respect, they were not willing to protest its violations by others. Near the end of June, there were reports of a strong French force of two ships of the line, a frigate and brig, en route to the Pacific. It was also rumored that a Spanish squadron was coming out from Cadiz: Would these forces cooperate in attacking Chile and/or Peru?

Hull put one Spanish cruiser out of business. In late July he left Callao with the frigate to visit Trujillo, and on 22 July he ran down the privateer *Moyana* after an eight-hour chase. He searched her and kept her captain on board the *United States* all night. But he could find no evidence of her having preyed on Americans, so he reluctantly let her go the next morning. The *Moyana*, however, had lost her foretopmast and foretopgallantmast in the chase and had so strained her hull that she fell victim to one of Guise's ships not long afterward and was burned.[45]

Hull was very pleased with the result of his visit to Trujillo on that occasion. His reception by the officers of the Peruvian government, coupled with the friendly assurances he had received from Bolívar, made him confident that

our relations with Peru will continue to be of the most friendly character; and the moment the Dictator can leave the Army and attend to the complaints of neutrals, that strict justice will be done; but at this moment when he is on the eve of engaging the Spanish army it cannot be supposed that he has leisure to attend the numerous calls he must necessarily have upon other subjects.[46]

During the remainder of the winter Admiral Guise was able to keep one or two vessels in Callao Roads most of the time and to make the port a hot spot by mounting night attacks on Spanish shipping. Although Hull recommended to the American merchant captains that they keep their ships close to the *United States,* some of them preferred to anchor near the town to facilitate landing their cargoes, and as a result they were not always able to get out of the way of the warring parties. On 5 September one man was killed and another wounded on board the *General Clinton* during an altercation between the Peruvian squadron and Rodil's ten gunboats.[47]

As the Patriot armies gathered strength in the countryside, American and British residents in Lima became more and more fearful for their lives and property, since the Lima authorities were helpless to protect the city even against raids by *montañeros.* About the middle of August, General Rodil proposed to the British and American commanders that they send their own marines into the city to guard the houses of their countrymen. Captain Maling immediately sent up a large force, which was quartered and fed by the Spanish government. To Hull this seemed an unneutral proceeding. He offered to send some sailors and an officer, to be distributed among the houses of the Americans, but not to be in any way associated with the government. The Americans, however, were more afraid of the sailors than of the *montañeros;* they declined the offer.[48]

The war at sea reached its climax—or anticlimax—in September and October 1824. On 12 September the expected Spanish squadron arrived: the *Asia,* 64, and the brig of war *Aquiles,* 22. Admiral Guise, who had only the frigate *Protector,* 44, and a 10-gun brig, nevertheless offered to fight; the Spaniards ignored him and, taking advantage of a favoring wind and current, sailed into Callao harbor where they joined the privateers *Ica,* 28 (formerly the American *Esther*); *Pezuela,* 16; and *Constante,* 16. At the time the Spanish ships hove in sight around the point of the island of San Lorenzo, the *United States* was anchored in the fairway, where she would have been directly in line of the contending ships if a running fight had taken place. Hull sent his men to quarters and got under way, as did Captain Maling in the *Cambridge.* He was much surprised to see the Spaniards, as he said, "skulk into port," and expressed his contempt so openly that Midshipman Andrew Hull Foote thought "it would have taken little provocation . . . to have been complimented with a broadside from Uncle Isaac."[49] Hull was even more astonished, and disgusted besides, to learn a few days later that the Spanish commodore, Don Saint-Roque Guruzeta, had said he avoided engaging Guise because he thought the *United States* was a Peruvian frigate. Hull had a diagram drawn of the positions of the vessels in the bay and got Maling to certify that it was correct and that no unneutral implications should be drawn from the fact of their vessels being under way.[50]

The Spaniards, having saved face, settled down to refit their ships. Guise went off to collect more force, but the squadron with which he returned on 6 October was still vastly inferior to the Spanish force. The latter sailed out to engage him, and again the neutral warships got under way to witness the action. They didn't see much; a confused melee followed in a fog in which Guise managed to escape with his ships intact and unpursued.[51] While the Spanish ships continued preparing for sea, Maling decided to shadow them; Hull, who was worried that they would attack American traders for supposed violation of the Laws of the Indies (regulating trade with Spain's colonies), called in the *Peacock* and the *Dolphin* from Quilca and Valparaiso. Should the Spanish squadron attack American ships, he planned to pursue it with his entire force. The *United States*, at least, was ready; her crew had undergone gun, sail, and small-arms drills several times a week throughout their stay in Callao Bay.

At the same time, Hull pointed out to the secretary of the navy the futility of trying to guard so long a coast with his tiny squadron and the difficulty of acting at such a long distance from Washington:

> having the Spaniards on one side and the Patriots on the other, the former inveterate and extremely hostile towards us, and the Patriots jealous but friendly, every movement of mine is closely watched and seized upon to make difficulty where it can be done, so that barely a day passes that I do not have trouble with one party or the other, and as neither are governed by the laws or usage of nations or by common justice, and having no one to advise with or aid me in these difficulties, I feel a weight of responsibility which I must earnestly hope to be relieved from soon, by receiving instructions to meet the great changes that have taken place in this sea, and the present state of affairs.[52]

On 20 October the entire Spanish squadron left Callao, bound southward. The *United States*, together with the British ships, the *Cambridge* and the *Tartar*, got under way and followed them to sea to watch what might happen. At 1:30 P.M. the combined Colombian and Peruvian squadrons, six sail, were sighted, but they were powerless to stop

the Spanish, who made off without firing a shot. Guise had been expecting aid from the Chilean navy, but Admiral Manuel Blanco Encalada did not leave Valparaiso until 15 November. Even then, his four
ships were not equal to the voyage. He had to stop at Coquimbo to
repair the frigate *O'Higgins* and the brig *Moctezuma*. Luckily, he found
there the schooner *Dolphin;* Lieutenant Percival had brought her to Coquimbo to heave out and clean her bottom, and he willingly lent his
carpenters to Admiral Blanco.⁵³ Had the Chilean, Peruvian, and Colombian squadrons combined, they would have made a rather formidable
force, but they were too late. On 9 December 1824 came the crowning
Patriot victory at Ayacucho. Lima had already fallen. The *Asia* and the
Aquiles, the principal ships of the Spanish naval force, had so many
impressed Peruvians in their crews that news of the Patriot victories led
to mutinies on board. The *Asia* was surrendered to Mexican authorities
at Acapulco by her crew, and the *Aquiles* sailed to Valparaiso and joined
the Chilean service. The unlucky *General Carrington*, which they had
taken from Callao with them, was burned.⁵⁴

After seeing the Spanish ships over the horizon, Hull continued on
to Huacho for water, fresh beef, to give his men shore liberty and to
pick up a convoy to return to Callao on 28 October. His most critical
problem by this time was his rapidly deteriorating relations with General Rodil: Consul Tudor reported that "Com. Hull and General Rodil
are on the worst terms; the former has certainly some reason on his
side, and the latter accuses the Com. of insulting him with perpetual
threats and other irritations." Hull called Rodil "a total stranger to all
law and justice."⁵⁵ The condemnations of the *Nancy* and the *General
Carrington* had embittered these relations, but the real crisis occurred
in November with the Spanish seizure of the ship *China* in Callao
harbor.

On the night of 2 November the *United States* was lying at anchor
near the island of San Lorenzo when a boat from the Baltimore trader
North Point came alongside with the unwelcome news that the American ship *China*, James Goodrich, captain, had been seized by the Spanish authorities and carried into the inner harbor, where she was moored
under the guns of the castles. It appeared that Captain Goodrich had
attempted to transship some goods to the American brig *Rimac*. Both
vessels were in the outer harbor, near the island, five miles from the
town of Callao. The *Rimac*, which had arrived only the previous day,
was in fact lying under the guns of the *United States* while navy carpenters carried out some needed repairs. At ten-thirty the next morning
a Spanish officer boarded the frigate with a demand that he be allowed
to search the *Rimac* for the supposedly smuggled goods. The *Rimac*'s

captain appealed to Commodore Hull, and he sent the customs officer away with a letter to General Rodil saying that, while he would not countenance smuggling, he believed the outer harbor to be outside the limits of customs jurisdiction and that such transshipments were usual. In fact, the *China* had already landed part of her cargo for Rodil's own use, though she had not entered at the customhouse. She had also sold provisions to the *Asia* and the *Cambridge*.[56] Nevertheless, Rodil gave orders to proceed against the *China* and even had her cargo unloaded before the judicial process began. The ship and cargo were valued at over $150,000, but Hull was the more disturbed at the seizure because the *China* was a well-built ship that could easily be turned into a privateer.[57]

During the night that followed, one of the frigate's cutters rowed guard around the *United States* and the *Rimac*. The next day, 4 November, Hull sent Midshipman Pedro Valdez on shore to deliver a note to Rodil requesting that the *China*'s officers be allowed to come out to the frigate, as was proper under international law. Valdez and his boat's crew were insulted and stoned away from the wharf, and Midshipman John Calhoun and the boat's coxswain, who had gone into the town in search of some of the frigate's officers, were arrested and detained. When Hull sent a protest against this outrage by Lieutenant Hiram Paulding, he too was detained and insulted. Hull had to send the *Peacock* inshore to reclaim him. Rodil then cut all normal communication by ordering that no boats from the *United States* be allowed to land and threatened to seize all American property in Callao if the *Rimac* were not handed over.[58] Hull demanded as a right, under America's treaty with Spain, that he be allowed to communicate with the Americans resident on shore and threatened, if he were refused, to take his own ship and all the other American vessels away from Callao. On 10 November he summoned all the trading ships, ten in number, to anchor near the *United States*. He was even angrier when he learned that Captain Goodrich and his crew had been imprisoned and that the crew had been forced to do manual labor on shore. The next day he sailed, with all the American traders, for Ancón, intending to wait there until the Patriots entered Lima, which was expected to happen any day. The merchants could then land their cargoes at Ancón and send them up to Lima, avoiding Callao.[59]

Should Rodil attempt to seize any more American property at Callao or Lima, Hull was determined to sail against Spanish cruisers and merchant shipping. Unfortunately, these, and especially the latter, were few. His frustration was evident: he was faced with an enemy who, though weak, had plenty of prey ready to hand. His force, though relatively strong, could scarcely hope to find any vulnerable point for retaliation. On 29–30 November he looked in again at Callao and succeeded in interviewing Captain Goodrich, who on Hull's advice had slipped on board the *Cambridge*. What he learned made him furious: the crew of the *China* had been beaten to make them work, and the mate had been threatened with hanging if he did not testify against his captain. Hull warned William Tudor to prepare the Americans on shore for possible violence, remarking grimly:

> I think there is not an American in this country, knowing all things which have taken place, who would not be willing to sacrifice every feeling of interest, to have their rights respected, and that would not view resistance to the violations of them here upon more liberal principles than individual interest. Capt. Goodrich will tell you what are my intentions. I have no time, if it was prudent.[60]

He wrote the secretary of the navy that "I know of no other alternative but to make reprisals and to retain Spanish subjects until the Americans are released."[61]

But, since he could not communicate with the shore at Callao, he had to make a run to Huacho for water before he could carry out his threat. Before returning to Callao he touched at Ancón, where he picked up the *Peacock* and exercised the great guns. The two American warships returned to Callao on 11 December, and Hull sent in an immediate demand for the release of Goodrich, his crew, and the *China*. His officers were not allowed to land, though his letters were received. Goodrich and his men were not permitted to come near the wharf. Hull sent a second demand, then a third, then told Rodil that he would not write again but would proceed as he had threatened. At this critical moment, however, news was received of the battle of Ayacucho on 9 December; Bolívar was securely in possession of Lima. Rodil was cut off by land and would soon be blockaded again by sea. Hull, believing that these circumstances might cause the general to have second thoughts, waited.[62] Within a short time Rodil relented to the extent of releasing Goodrich and his crew, though he retained the *China* and still refused to allow boats from the *United States* to land.

Isaac Hull's reaction to the Patriot victory was anything but nonpartisan. On receiving the news of Ayacucho he wrote the secretary of the navy that "the war which has so long distracted this country appears now to be drawing to a close, in such a manner as will cause every lover of freedom and humanity to rejoice."[63] He thought the Spanish squadron might pick up the remnant of the Royalist army and take refuge in

Callao, but more probably, since "it is known to the [Spanish] Admiral that the Chilean fleet is to join the Peruvian, and as he has hitherto shown a disinclination for fighting, I think he will steer the shortest course for Chiloé. His vessels can there disperse and prey upon neutral commerce." As late as 17 December he apparently thought of pursuing them in reprisal for Rodil's actions, but as he wrote to Heman Allen, "The Spanish cause is now so desperate that I think General Rodil will make concessions and reparation rather than risk any interruption to his squadron."[64] At the same time he wrote Bolívar a note of congratulation on the victory, expressing regret at not being able to come to Lima because of the tension in Callao. He called the success of the Patriot armies "a consummation of the wishes of every lover of freedom and humanity, and a most brilliant termination to those stupendous efforts which you have so nobly made in the cause of liberty."[65]

On 2 January 1825 the *United States* went around to the harbor of Chorrillos, about twelve miles southeast of Callao, and from there on the following day Commodore Hull was able at last to go up to Lima to pay his respects to the Liberator. He took Ann and Augusta with him and established them for a month or more in the house of one of Bolívar's retainers, with the family servants as well as Lieutenant William C. Nicholson, and Midshipman Pedro Valdez to attend them. Hull thought that after a year on shipboard the ladies deserved some time on shore. Ann found it very pleasant except for the absence of "husband," for Hull was unable to remain in the city for long periods. As long as the political situation remained volatile, and as long as Callao was in Royalist hands, his place was on board the ship. Ann remarked that "he is one so scrupulous in the performance of his duty, that while one of his countrymen was in difficulty, he would not desert him. . . . [They], by the way, are the most ungrateful rascals."[66]

The ladies were enchanted by the profusion of fruit and flowers at Lima and by the pleasures of daily rides on horseback through the beautiful countryside. They were bemused by the hyperbole of the Latin American gentlemen, like the colonel who after a few minutes' conversation placed himself and his regiment "at the feet" of "Señora Commodora." And they were shocked by the high prices: American residents said it cost them $15,000 a year to live there, and officers from the *United States* going to Lima for a two-day leave lightened their pockets by $50 or more.

Ann and Augusta were eyewitnesses to the continuing struggle among Patriot factions for control of the new republics. Midshipman Pedro Valdez was a young Chilean, and a nephew of the Carrera brothers who had sided against the party of San Martin and O'Higgins in the early days of the revolution there. His mother, their sister, had fled to Brazil, and her son had been taken to the United States by Joel R. Poinsett for education. He returned in the *United States* to be reunited with his mother but elected to remain in the navy rather than settle in Chile. While in Mrs. Hull's household he met one of his family's old enemies, Bernardo Monteagudo, who had recently returned from Panama and was reportedly to become governor of Lima. Monteagudo visited the frigate and called on the Hulls at Lima; Mrs. Hull found him elegant but somehow chilling. But on 27 January 1825, just after Monteagudo had been the subject of an evening's conversation between the Hull household and some Limaneans, the latter came rushing back to the house to report that Monteagudo had been assassinated. Young Valdez started up from the sofa, crying "Ah! Now my uncles are revenged!" Such incidents did not bode well for the future stability of the southern republics, as the North Americans were uncomfortably aware.

With the junction of the Colombian, Chilean, and Peruvian squadrons the Patriots were able to put an effective blockade on Callao, the only port in Peru still in Royalist hands. Admiral Blanco, who superseded Guise in command, had at his disposal two frigates, the *Protector* and the *O'Higgins* (renamed the *Isabella*), and three to five smaller vessels, including at different times the *Moctezuma*, the *Macedonian*, the *Pichincha*, the *Chimborazo*, the *Limanean*, and the *Congreso*. On 7 January the vice-captain of the port surrendered all the Spanish gunboats to the *Pichincha*, and thereafter the blockaders were able to enter the harbor almost every night and exchange fire with the forts as, on the landward side, the siege lines crept daily closer to the battlements. Since Callao was now a legally blockaded harbor, and a pretty hot spot besides, Hull withdrew his ships. Throughout 1825 the *Peacock* and the *Dolphin* continued their patrols and convoy work, and the *United States* based most of the time at Chorrillos, which was temporarily the port of entry for Lima. But it was a very uncomfortable place, being an open roadstead with a constant heavy swell and so much surf that it was often dangerous for the ship's boats to land.[67] When the *United States* did go into Callao, she usually anchored under the island of San Lorenzo, as far as possible from the forts. Hull set up a temporary signal station on the island to notify him of approaching ships. The island was also used throughout the three years as a temporary depot for provisions and livestock and as a place to repair the frigate's boats and gear. But it had a serious drawback as a base: it was barren. All the food and water for the stock and workmen had to be brought from somewhere else.

After visiting Trujillo, Casma, and Huacho in January 1825, Hull took the *United States* and the *Peacock* back to Chorrillos to prepare for an important occasion. Washington's birthday, 22 February, had been chosen as the day for a ceremonial visit by Simón Bolívar to the American flagship. Sunrise on that day was greeted with a salute of seventeen guns from each warship. At ten-thirty the general arrived. The flagship's yards were manned, and a twenty-one-gun salute roared across the harbor. Then the drums beat to quarters, and a gunnery exercise was performed for the visitors' benefit, after which refreshments were served in the cabin. Bolívar offered a toast to the Marquis de Lafayette, who was then on his visit to the United States, and the assembled company—which included Consul Tudor, Vice-Consul Stanhope Prevost, and all the principal American merchants of Lima as well as the naval officers—passed a series of resolutions in praise of Lafayette. These resolutions, signed by Hull and Tudor as presiding officers, were sent to the Marquis. Such an act had political overtones, of course, and caused Hull to have some second thoughts, but Tudor reassured him that "no one is committed by them who was not present, and . . . our first object is to give pleasure to him for whom these resolutions were passed. . . . I have shown them to all our countrymen whom I have met and they have none of them objected." Lafayette received the resolutions before he left the United States, but it was April 1826 before his acknowledgment found its way to Lima, expressing to Hull, Tudor, Bolívar, and the others present his "gratitude, respect and affections."[68]

A week after the celebration the *United States* got under way for Valparaiso. When he left the Allens there in April 1824, Hull had intended to revisit Chile in four months and to spend part of the winter at Juan Fernández, but the changed political situation in Peru had kept him away nearly a year. Elizabeth Allen's daughter had been born dead in August, and the mother had suffered afterward from fever and engorged breasts, but she had recovered. Hull landed her sisters at Valparaiso for a visit and took his ship south to Talcahuano, where part of the crew went on shore and dug several tons of coal for the ship's galley. He returned to Valparaiso on 11 April, where he remained until the end of the month. During that time the port was visited by the French corvette *Diligence;* the British sloop-of-war *Eclair;* and eight American ships, six traders and two whalers. One of the whalers, the *Enterprize,* brought in the survivors of the *O'Cain,* a Boston ship wrecked on the Topocalma rocks about fifty miles north of Valparaiso. Hull left word for John Percival to investigate this shoal with the *Dolphin* on his next sweep up the coast. At Valparaiso, Hull also received word from William Tudor of the sudden death of John W. Prevost, who suffered a heart attack while traveling in the mountains near Arequipo. A few months later Tudor had a report from Thomas Handasyd Perkins that Prevost was being recalled to answer charges in the United States; the consul remarked wryly that he "has gone to render his accounts at another tribunal, where mercy as well as power is infinite."[69]

After leaving Valparaiso the *United States* stopped for four weeks at the port of Coquimbo in northern Chile, where Hull settled a dispute between the captain of the whaler *Tarquin* and one of his seamen. Mainly because of the greed of the whalers' owners, who habitually bought the seamen's shares in the catch before the ships sailed, the American whaleships were plagued by desertion. Since the men had no pay to look forward to, they readily jumped ship in the Pacific, where the Patriot navies and the American and British traders were always shorthanded.

When he returned to Chorrillos on 6 June, Hull found two more foreign warships on the station: the frigate *Briton*, commanded by Sir Murray Maxwell, and French Rear Admiral Claude-Charles-Marie Ducampe de Rosamel in the 64-gun ship *Marie Thérèse*. French forces in the Pacific now totaled five vessels, including the *Marie Thérèse*, the barque *Diligence*, the brig *Lancier*, and the schooners *Aigret* and *Quintinilla*. Maling had his ship of the line, three frigates, and two sloops of war. The United States force, in relation to these, was small indeed.

Hull also learned that Beverly Kennon had been having some hot words with Admiral Blanco over two American traders, the *Elizabeth Ann* and the *General Brown*. Before Hull left Chorrillos, both had been seized for carrying Spanish property and/or guns in violation of Peruvian decrees. The *Elizabeth Ann* was evidently not worth quarreling over, but the *General Brown* and her cargo were valued at $250,000, and Blanco was determined to have her condemned as a prize. On 6 April he ordered half of her crew transferred to the *Moctezuma* and her sails sent on shore. A lieutenant whom Kennon sent on board the *General Brown* told the prize captain, Thomas Espora, in language that Espora called "gross insults," what would happen if he carried out Blanco's order. Espora, though offended, got the point. Blanco reassured Kennon that his intention was only "the greater security of that ship, as the sailors were not destined for the service," but Kennon was not persuaded. He told Hull that

> it is out of the question to suppose that an American man of war will allow an American seaman to be pressed from alongside of her, as it were, as long as she can defend him. . . . The Admiral pretends to justify himself by saying that the men "were not destined for the service." But the vessel [the *Moctezuma*] was, and has since been under the guns of Callao. Suppose he had carried those men off and some of them had been killed or maimed, what satis-

faction would it have been to their friends to be told "they were not destined for the service?" His design was, I have not the most remote doubt, to press them; otherwise he would have desired me to take them if his object had been merely to weaken the crew of the ship, so that they could not run away with her. I immediately sent a boat and brought them on board this ship.[70]

The question of impressed American seamen continued to be a troubled one as long as the war continued. After that the Patriots were only too glad to be rid of them, and quite a few were enlisted on board the naval vessels or shipped in merchantmen. As for the *General Brown*, Hull was tempted to wash his hands of her when he learned the facts of the case. According to Kennon, he had warned the *General Brown* out of Callao in the first place, but her captain had ignored his advice; on coming out of the harbor the ship had anchored near Blanco's ships and ignored Kennon's suggestion to lie near the *Peacock*. Hull then interviewed Captain Copeland of the *General Brown* and told him he would try to get his ship sent to Chile for trial, since she had been taken by the Chilean admiral and since at Valparaiso she would have Heman Allen to represent her. But Copeland protested that everything was arranged between him and Blanco: the Spanish goods would be taken out and freight paid for them, and the ship and the remaining property would be released. If the ship were sent to Chile, he told Hull, she would be condemned "stock and fluke," for she had clearly violated the law.

Hull was dubious about the arrangement. He told Copeland that he had better get security from Blanco, but the American was confident that all would be well. Hull left him, and soon thereafter the Spanish property was landed, whereupon Blanco again seized the ship. She was cleared by two courts, but Blanco appealed each time, finally getting two judges ousted from the bench in order to secure a condemnation. Hull did everything possible to save the ship, demanding an appeal to the Peruvian Supreme Court and denouncing Blanco's role in the affair. When the Supreme Court finally condemned the ship in September, it urged the Peruvian government to make a formal complaint against the "interference" of a naval officer in a civil proceeding. Hull had had little choice, for William Tudor was so involved with his mining interests in the cordillera that he was seldom at Lima, and the vice-consul, Stanhope Prevost, son of the late agent, was "placed in a situation where interference on his part would injure him as a merchant." Hull was, then, the only United States official on the scene who could be effective in pleading the case. "So you see," he wrote to Michael Hogan, "I have difficulty on all sides. I shall, however, continue to interfere when I consider it necessary to prevent insults being offered to our citizens and the plunder of their property, notwithstanding the opinion of the judges."[71]

Hull had a low opinion of Blanco. He told Heman Allen that "I do not know of any situation that he would be at home in, other than that of keeping a dancing school, for I do not believe he is either a Sailor or Soldier, nor do I believe that he is a man of honour or honesty."[72] On the other hand, his relations with the British officers in South American service were good. From the first he was on cordial terms with Colombian Admiral John Illingworth, and after the blockade question was resolved he became friendly with Admiral Guise as well. The North Americans, with the exception of John Prevost, never seemed to be able to achieve real understanding with their southern associates. Most of them believed, with Heman Allen, that a Spaniard was a Spaniard wherever found and that most of the men in power in Latin America were "without honour and without character." Hull, despite his support for the revolution and his admiration for Bolívar, was not immune to those feelings.[73]

Except for the *General Brown* case, the winter of 1825 passed in agreeable quiet for the North Americans. In June news arrived from the United States of the election of John Quincy Adams as president; Hull remarked to Michael Hogan that "we have indeed enlightened and great men to rule us. God grant that they make proper use of their wisdom." In Peru and Chile, on the other hand, there were rumblings of discontent. The upper provinces of Peru were forming themselves into the independent state of Bolivia, and at Coquimbo Hull found a movement to form a new government independent of Chile.[74]

Hull was already thinking about returning home in 1826. He had observed in 1810 the ill effects of keeping men in the navy ships after their term of service had expired, and dilatoriness in this respect was chronic with Navy Department officials, who did not have to deal directly with disgruntled sailors. As early as December 1824 Hull had gently reminded Secretary Southard that his orders to return should be sent in plenty of time, particularly if he was still expected to visit the Columbia River and return across the Pacific. "The bad consequences of seamen being retained longer have been seen on this coast by the state in which the crew of the Franklin returned," he pointedly remarked.[75] In June 1825 he again brought up the subject, and at the end of July he mentioned it again in a letter to William Bainbridge, who now chaired the Board of Navy Commissioners, John Rodgers having gone to the Mediterranean as squadron commander. The commissioners could be expected to be more sympathetic than Navy Department clerks: "The

Commissioners are too well acquainted with the evils of keeping men on foreign service for many months after their term of service has expired to require any remark on the subject from me, as they have all seen the ill effects of it."[76] Hull was not being premature. It would take four months for his letters to reach Washington, four months for a reply to come back, and four months more for the frigate to return home. That was twelve months at a minimum, if the Navy Department sent orders immediately, which was unlikely; and in thirteen months, in September 1826, the crew's enlistments would begin to expire. Once their terms were up the men could leave the ship, and no one could legitimately stop them. The attractions of the Pacific were too many for that possibility to be taken lightly.

Hull recommended at this time that in the future the United States should send several small vessels to the Pacific, two to cruise on the coast of Mexico and California, two or three more to cover the South American coast and visit the Pacific islands. The danger to be apprehended after the end of the war, he believed, was that officers, seamen, and vessels formerly employed by both sides would turn to piracy, as was said already to be the case with the former Colombian sloop of war *Santander*, 22, reported to have taken several prizes on the coasts of Mexico and California. There was also a rumor of a Spanish three-masted schooner with an English captain on her way to the Pacific to privateer from the Spanish base at Chiloé.[77] Further reports had it that the French had a squadron of ten or twelve ships of the line in the Caribbean; in November it was rumored that they had seized Cuba in the name of the Spanish Crown and acknowledged the independence of Haiti, but this was denied in December. Hull thought "we shall yet have a war in Europe, if not in America," as a result of the influence of the Holy Alliance.[78] When he heard about the French movement, and also about the mysterious transportation of three thousand Colombian troops from Peru to Panama, he told Allen:

What the object is in sending the troops from Peru I cannot ascertain, some believe that an expedition is intended against Cuba, others that French and Spaniards are preparing an expedition against Colombia. The French, it is said, have a squadron in the West Indies of ten sail of the line, if so they must have some object other than that of exercising their men as stated by the French Admiral [Rosamel, commander of the *Marie Thérèse* at Chorrillos]. I much fear that in withdrawing the Colombian troops from Peru, this part of the country will again be involved in war, either between the remaining Colombians and Peruvians, or that Rodil will in some way get up a party and cause a revolution; indeed, he told Captain Brown of the Tartar that he only wanted arms.[79]

The troop movement, however, was canceled in October.

In this state of things Hull did not think he could properly leave the coast with the *United States*. But he had received orders from Washington that, if possible, he should detach a vessel to the western Pacific in search of a group of mutineers who had seized the whaler *Globe* of Nantucket and taken refuge in the Mulgrave Islands (Mili Atoll). It was also desirable that an American warship visit the Sandwich Islands, which were increasingly a resort for American whalers and traders, and where a hundred or more men who had deserted from American ships were supposed to be living in destitution and lawlessness. The instigators of the *Globe* mutiny had been shipped at Oahu from among these desperadoes. Hull chose the *Dolphin* for this service, and on 10 August he ordered Lieutenant Commandant Percival to estimate both the minimum number of men needed to work the schooner and her guns and the maximum amount of provisions she could stow for such a reduced complement. Percival thought he could manage with sixty-seven men and could stow provisions for six months. The schooner was prepared accordingly and sailed from Chorrillos a week later. There was a great demand among the squadron's officers for places in the *Dolphin* on this interesting cruise. Hiram Paulding of the *United States* went as senior lieutenant, and several midshipmen also transferred to the schooner.[80]

The *Dolphin*'s cruise was dramatic and eventful. She reached the Mulgraves in November and found that the mutineers had either killed one another or had been massacred by the natives. The only survivors were two young sailors, Cyrus Hussey and William Lay, who had not been party to the mutiny. Percival took them on board and proceeded to Oahu, where he anchored on 14 January 1826. There he quickly became embroiled in an ongoing dispute between the merchant community and the American missionaries, in which he sided with the merchants. He further alienated the missionaries by opposing the taboo they had instituted against prostitution—a restriction that led to a sailors' riot on 26 February in which some of the "Dolphins" joined. In addition, Percival made an enemy of Alfred P. Edwards, commander of the ship *London* which was wrecked on the island of Lanai soon after the *Dolphin* arrived at Oahu. Percival salvaged Edwards's cargo and specie, but they had an argument about reporting the specie to the underwriters, and eventually the two men came to blows. The result of all this for Percival was a court of inquiry in 1828 that heard testimony for six weeks but declined to order a court-martial. Secretary Southard, who was a friend of several of the missionaries, was chagrined at this outcome, and he wrote Percival a letter of censure anyway.[81]

Two days after the *Dolphin* sailed from Chorrillos, smallpox broke out on board the flagship. When it appeared that, despite the precautions taken at the beginning of the cruise, the disease was likely to spread through the crew, Hull engaged a house at the village of Miraflores, about four miles from Chorrillos, and sent some fifty men there to be inoculated. The shortage of doctors in the squadron was acute. John Fitzhugh, the senior, was soon to be invalided home, leaving the *United States* with only a surgeon's mate. The *Dolphin*'s doctor was in poor health, and the *Peacock* had just one acting surgeon and a mate.[82] A number of the men at Miraflores broke out with smallpox, and on 19 September, Henry Hanson died. When the disease continued to spread, Hull decided on 12 October to take the ship to Callao where he could set up a tent hospital on San Lorenzo. During the frigate's stay there he also landed all the provisions from her hold and gave it a thorough cleaning and whitewashing. Seven men died at San Lorenzo before the disease ran its course in November; among those who died was Isaac Wheeden, the Hull family's servant. He was sincerely mourned by them all.[83] During most of this period Mrs. Hull and Augusta were again at Lima, but Isaac was apprehensive about the state of things there once Callao fell.

> More than three thousand soldiers will be without employment and no doubt will indulge in every sort of wickedness and dissipation, and the officers will have but little control over the men, and not much more over themselves, so that we may, for a time, look for great confusion, and I have no doubt but frequent murders and robberies will be committed by the soldiers on the roads leading to Lima and in the villages near the city. The moment the castles fall I shall take my family on board ship, and remain quiet until they can land with safety.[84]

Hull was distressed at what he considered the neglect of American citizens at Lima by Consul Tudor, who had been in the mountains since August. He had said guardedly to Southard at that time that "soon after he was acknowledged [as consul] he became concerned in the mines and is now a long distance in the country where such as require his aid cannot communicate with him." Heman Allen remarked sardonically in October, with reference to the *General Brown* case,

> It is very true that in countries where consuls reside, and where there are no other publick agents, they are the proper organs of communication with the supreme government; but in this case I presume our consul was in the mines. . . . It is to be hoped, however, that our consul has, ere this, *arisen*, and will hereafter be found at his post, ready to advocate the rights of his countrymen.[85]

The hoped-for resurrection did not, however, take place before January; Hull then expressed the hope that "he will attend to his duty." He was blunt with Tudor about the state of feeling toward him among the residents:

> I think it of great importance to our commercial interest that you should be in Lima. I tell you with great plainness that there is much dissatisfaction among our countrymen that the consul should be absent and you know their proneness to talking. From the irregularities and impositions at the Custom House they have much trouble, and some one should be on the spot whom this government will allow has the power of interfering in their behalf. . . . The Consul General from England has arrived, and if you were in Lima I presume you might cooperate in some measures which would secure our Countrymen from such vexations and losses in future.[86]

Tudor's response, however, was not quite what Hull had in mind; he saw Hull's warning only as a friendly attempt to put him on guard against unjustified aspersions:

> I consider your frankness in telling me of the mutterings of my countrymen as a proof of friendship. But I assure you I am prepared to meet a court martial tomorrow and without counsel. I need not trouble you with the particulars of my justification which make me so fearless. . . . I am fond of my countrymen but as to giving them satisfaction, I am not vain enough to expect the least success.[87]

The arrival of a storeship in December brought Isaac Hull a letter from his uncle William. The old veteran was elated at the success, as he thought, of his recently published vindication of his conduct in the War of 1812, and the consequent discomfiture of Henry Dearborn. William Hull had been fêted at a public dinner in Boston and had also been honored by Lafayette on his visit there. He had plenty of family news to retail, some of it pleasant and some not. His daughter Julia was about to marry Mary Wheeler Hull's brother Joseph and go with him to Georgia, where another daughter, Maria Campbell, was also living. General Hull planned to accompany the Wheelers and the Campbells as far as Derby to visit Joseph, whose health was still bad. On the other hand, the Hulls' brother-in-law Dr. Jarvis was in hot water with the Episcopal church and had been "separated from the Society, and the Bishop and ecclesiastical council." There was navy gossip as well: David Porter had been court-martialed for his conduct in the West Indies and suspended for six months, as a result of which he had resigned from the navy and was about to become Admiral of Mexico. Charles Stewart's trial was about to begin. With all this, General Hull remarked almost casually that Amos Binney, as Isaac's agent, had asked him to pay his debts to his nephew's account, but "[I] wrote in answer that it was [not] in my power to pay them, at that time, and hoped it might be made convenient, without injury to you, to wait until your return." Isaac thought he would probably have to wait a lot longer than that.[88]

That was to be his last letter from Uncle William. In July 1826 he received, first from Heman Allen and then by belated letters from his brother Henry and from Jannette Hart, the news that both William and Joseph Hull had died, William on 25 November 1825 and Joseph on 27 January 1826; their mother, Elizabeth Clark Hull, had followed on 11 February. "We can only say, 'God's will be done!'" he told Allen on hearing of his father's death. "He has ever been a kind and affectionate parent and a truly good man and I hope and trust he is now receiving his reward. My only wish was to have returned in time to give him all the comfort and consolation in my power in his last days, but that happiness has not been my lot."[89] Only a few months later came the news of the deaths on 4 July 1826 of Thomas Jefferson and John Adams. On Sunday, 19 November, at noon, the crew of the *United States* went to quarters and stood uncovered while twenty-four minute guns were fired in their honor. The Revolutionary generation, in the Hull family as in the nation, was passing away.[90]

With the coming of 1826 the war between Spain and the Patriot forces was drawing rapidly to a close, to be succeeded by turmoil among factions of the Patriots themselves. On 29 December 1825, José LaMar arrived at Chorrillos from Guayaquil in the *Pichincha* to assume his office as president of Peru. Hull told Southard with satisfaction that

> he is said to be an excellent man and much good is anticipated from his government; I had the pleasure of landing him and his family with my boats and I have great pleasure in saying that I am on the best terms, not only with the officers of the government . . . but with the commanders of the foreign ships that are on this station. They inevitably treat our officers with attention and great respect. As yet not the slightest unpleasant occurrence has taken place between our officers and those of other ships of war.[91]

On 17 January the *United States* went to Callao, where white flags flying on the castle and the Patriot battery signified that negotiations were under way. Finally, at noon on the twenty-third, after a siege of thirteen months, the forts were surrendered. At nearly the same time news was received of the fall of Chiloé to Chilean forces; the last Spanish bastion in the eastern Pacific was gone. The foreign warships at Callao joined in twenty-one-gun salutes to the Peruvian flag, and Hull wrote that "I trust the subjects of Spain will never get a foothold in Peru again." Grisly rumors were afloat about the state of things in Callao. It was said that during the siege Rodil had frequently had fifty people shot before breakfast, that forty or fifty women had been shot— and that one, the wife of a deserter, had been tied to a stake at low tide mark and left to drown—and that of six thousand people within the walls a year earlier, only nine hundred remained alive. Allowing for hyperbole, General Rodil was nevertheless an unpleasant person, and there was great public indignation that he was allowed to leave Callao peacefully in the *Briton* with his flag and, it was said, seven barrels of specie. Hull reported to Southard the day after the surrender that "my officers that landed at Callao represent the town as being in a most deplorable state. Many houses are entirely destroyed and the Patriots are now burying the dead from their dwellings where they have perished for want of food; some of them appear to have been dead many days."[92]

With everything now quiet in Peru and the *Peacock* on hand to care for American shipping in Callao, Hull was able to make a second visit to Valparaiso. The *United States* sailed on 7 February and ran down within sight of Juan Fernández before hauling up for Valparaiso, where she anchored on the twenty-fifth. The Hulls enjoyed a pleasant four-week visit with the Allens, at the end of which Elizabeth tried to prevail on Ann and Augusta to stay with her until the *United States* called at Valparaiso on the homeward passage, but "to separate Mrs. Hull from her husband even for that term was impossible and to separate Augusta from her was equally difficult."[93] On 2 March the supreme director of Chile, Ramon Freire, arrived in triumph from Chiloé and was saluted with twenty-one guns from the *United States*. The only thing that marred the visit was a quarrel with the Hogans. Mrs. Allen and Mrs. Hogan severed relations in mid-March when Mrs. Hogan was found to have been retailing some gossip about the commodore to the effect that he spent so much time in Peru because he was making money there. Hull traced the original rumor to the last visit of the *Peacock* to Valparaiso; specifically, it would appear, to the troublesome Lieutenant Ramsay. It was soon after the frigate's return to Callao that Ramsay was arrested by his captain and sent on shore to await trial.[94]

Hull did not, in fact, have any business ventures afloat in Peru. He was making a fair amount of money by the legitimate, government-sanctioned, and highly necessary act of accepting specie from American merchants for deposit. The volume of these transactions had been much greater during the war; since then the merchants were less fearful of capture and less eager to use the warships as floating banks. Since Peruvian exports were few, most of the traders sold their cargoes for cash; hence, there were immense sums in specie going up and down the coast at all seasons. From March 1824 to July 1825 the *United States* took deposits of $1,015,361, plus another $36,830 left by the *Franklin*, on which deposit fees of 1 percent netted Hull about $10,000. The *Peacock* and the *Dolphin* received lesser sums. In the last half of 1825 deposits in the frigate were only $253,425, and in 1826 they dwindled to $92,055.[95]

Hull's business affairs in America were still in the hands of Amos Binney. Most of the revenue from the rental properties in Charlestown was being plowed into retiring the mortgages, although, like all property owners, Hull met the usual setbacks: the Woodward house roof was "rotten as a pear and as open as a sieve"; the new one cost over $1,000. The brick house remained empty for a year or more. Binney reported that "Charlestown has improved in her streets and buildings, but nothing in the feelings and manners of her sons."[96]

There were other causes of friction between Hull and Michael Hogan besides Mrs. Hogan's gossiping tongue. Hogan's manner made him unpopular with the Chileans and was perhaps one of the reasons for the issuing of a decree in the spring of 1826 that would require foreign governments to pay duty on provisions imported for their public ships. Hull got much better terms from Peru: stores were to be landed there and reshipped free of charge, subject only to customs inspection. Remarking wryly to Allen that "I am not so unpopular with the government as some would endeavour to make me," Hull ordered that all supplies henceforth be sent directly to Callao. He recommended the same course to the Navy Department, suggesting that a permanent storeship be located at that port. This was sure to cut off Hogan's commissions as navy agent for the Pacific, and since he had come to Valparaiso in the first place to recoup his shattered fortunes, he was not pleased with Hull's actions. He complained that "Hull lay so long at Chorrillos that the sails would rot on the yards" and that the frigate was being kept there as a floating bank. Hogan brooded over the matter for a long time; finally, in 1833, he issued a series of charges against Hull that led to a brief investigation by a committee of Congress.[97]

Leaving Valparaiso on 23 March, the *United States* made a leisurely month's passage back to Callao, stopping at Coquimbo, Huasco, Arica, and Quilca. Hull was surprised not to find the *Dolphin* at Callao. Her six-month cruise had lengthened to eight, and there was no word of her except an alarming rumor started by a passenger who had come from Panama in the British sloop of war *Mersey* that there had been a mutiny on board. Hull investigated and found there was no basis to it; apparently the fact that the *Dolphin* had gone in search of mutineers had been twisted to a mutiny in the schooner herself. Still, he was disturbed. He had planned to send the *Peacock* to the islands after the *Dolphin* returned, but the plan of her cruise would depend partly on Percival's report. He waited another month; when there was no news by mid-May, he decided to dispatch the *Peacock* anyway. His orders to Thomas ap Catesby Jones were to get livestock and fresh food on the coast of Peru and then proceed to the Marquesas, Tahiti, and the Sandwich Islands; and, if time permitted, to run down the coast of California and Mexico on his return. Although he affected not to be alarmed by the *Dolphin's* delay, he was fearful for her, as his instructions to Jones show: he was to speak as many vessels as possible and to inquire at the islands for news of the *Dolphin*, "and in the event of your hearing that any disaster has happened to her . . . you will do all in your power to relieve her, even should you be compelled to abandon your present cruise."[98]

The *Peacock* was reduced to one surgeon's mate, and the *United States* had only one. Hull could create acting lieutenants and sailing masters out of midshipmen readily enough, but doctors' skills were not so easily come by. The *Peacock's* crew, however, were healthy and were eager for a cruise to the "isles beneath the wind." All but seven of them gladly reshipped to the end of March. The sloop's sailing and accommodations were also of the best. At Jones's request, Hull's workmen had built a roundhouse to keep her from shipping following seas, and had altered her to her original rig as a barque, with fore-and-aft sails on the mizzen. Jones claimed that her speed had greatly improved as a result.[99]

The cruise was very successful, but, like the *Dolphin*, the *Peacock* was absent nearly a year and did not leave Callao for the United States before July 1827. Jones made himself much more popular with the missionaries than had Percival; in fact, he took their side completely. As soon as he had opportunity to send a confidential letter, from San Blas in late February, he wrote to Southard that

> the foul stains which Lieut. P's transactions had left upon the American naval and national character, and their deleterious effects upon our future intercourse with the Sandwich Islands, were too manifest and humiliating to escape the attention of the most casual observer, and, I regret to add, were but too well calculated to establish that inferiority which the British agents have so strenuously endeavoured to attach to the American character.[100]

The *Dolphin* finally appeared at Valparaiso on 23 July and rejoined Hull at Callao a month later. Hull was pleased to have his old friend back with him, and he wrote immediately to Southard that "the cruise of the Dolphin has been a most fortunate one." A week after the schooner's return he fulfilled a promise to Beverly Kennon, who was senior to Percival and had been turned out of his command in the *Peacock* by the arrival of Jones, by giving Kennon command of the *Dolphin* and taking Percival again as executive officer of the *United States*. But he assured Percival that "it has not been done with a view that the least possible censure can be attached to you . . . on the contrary, so far as your conduct has come to my knowledge and particularly during your long and interesting cruise to the islands in the Pacific Ocean, it meets my approbation." He was loyal to Mad Jack through all his subsequent difficulties, as Percival had been to him.[101]

After their return from Valparaiso the whole Hull family had remained on board ship or at San Lorenzo for a couple of months, taking occasional horseback rides on shore for diversion. But in June the ladies rented a house at the village of Miraflores, where Isaac was able to visit them only occasionally; on 19 July he wrote wistfully that he had seen Ann only once in five weeks. It may have been during this winter that, if the family story is true, Augusta, now twenty-three years old, attracted the eye of the romantic Liberator. The *Connecticut Courant* carried a story in September reporting that the two were married, but there is no word even of a romance in Isaac Hull's letters. Perhaps his wife kept it from him, on the theory that he had enough to worry about. At any rate, Harriet Augusta Hart returned to Connecticut still single.[102]

What makes this romantic tale least likely to have much basis in fact is the serious state of the Peruvian and Colombian governments at this period, which must have occupied most of Bolívar's time and attention. He cannot have had much leisure for romantic involvement with nubile Norteamericanas if Isaac Hull's running commentary on Peruvian politics is any true indication of the situation. There had been a revolt in Chiloé in May said to have been engineered and financed by Bernardo O'Higgins, who was at Lima, and the rumor was that Bolívar was intriguing to restore O'Higgins to power in Chile.[103] Further rumor had it in July that Bolívar would declare himself emperor of Peru, but as Hull told Allen:

> he has given another name to the head of the government, that of President for life, and he of course to be the first and to name his successor. . . . [H]owever, disturbances have arisen in Colombia and we now hear that he is to leave soon for that part. . . . It is thought by some that Bolivar, finding he is losing his popularity, has been at the head of the troubles in Colombia that he might be called there to save them. I cannot believe anything we hear, there are so many stories.[104]

The assessment he wrote to Condy Raguet, United States chargé at Rio, a few days later was thoroughly pessimistic:

> I am heartily tired of the coast and of the people and I regret to say I leave Peru, in my opinion, in as unsettled a state in their political concerns and as far from having a settled government as when I came here. It is true great changes have taken place and what government they have is in other hands, but it will be many years before they get a settled government of any sort and I am much mistaken if they have not blood to spill before they arrive at that point. And poor as the country now is, it is doomed to be much poorer, indeed they appear to me to be like the dog in the manger: they will not work the mines nor let others work them, and their resources are buried in the bowels of the earth and someone must dig them out.[105]

Hull still believed that Bolívar would try to make himself emperor of Peru and, with the cooperation of O'Higgins, annex Chile, but if he had any such plans they did not materialize. The election of Hull's old nemesis, Admiral Blanco, as president of Chile evidently had a stabilizing effect in the southern republic.[106] By mid-August, Tudor was advising Hull to have his family at Miraflores ready to leave at a moment's notice, for Bolívar was soon to depart and anarchy was to be feared thereafter. Admiral Guise and many other former officials were under arrest.[107] On 3 September, Hull gave Allen a general description of the state of affairs in Peru:

> President Bolivar leaves Lima in the morning for Colombia with all his family, he will leave about five hundred troops here, Colombians, to keep order but I much doubt whether we shall not have trouble, at any rate I do not think that Chile will soon have a visit from this quarter.
>
> A large transport ship has this moment anchored and a brig is in the offing with troops on board, Colombians, they no doubt are to be landed here. I have now no doubt but an attempt will be made by Colombia and Mexico against Cuba and I am told that Bolivar has said our government has prevented his doing it for six months but now he will make the attempt.
>
> The Lima papers have come out this morning and speak of the United States as being friendly to Spain, and state that we have sent a large force to the West Indies to aid the Spaniards in defending Cuba and charges us with interfering with the affairs of South America in Europe and many other ridiculous things.
>
> Shooting and banishment is now the order of the day here; more than one hundred of the most respectable men, citizens and officers have been arrested and have been or will be banished; Admiral Guise is among them and is now confined and no one knows what their crime is, indeed it is said that nothing has been proven against them. Some would be allowed to remain by giving heavy bonds for their good conduct, yet there is no proof that they have committed a bad act.

> Mr. Tudor is again gone to the mountains and we are left as before without any one to look after our affairs. He will be absent five or six weeks.[108]

The next day the *United States* stood over to Callao and made all preparations for manning yards and saluting Bolívar on his departure, but apparently the *Congreso* sailed with him during the night without fanfare.[109] The Colombian troops left behind numbered four thousand or five thousand instead of five hundred, and they kept the lid on Peru pretty effectively; Hull speculated three weeks later on reports from Guayaquil about a declaration of independence in that province:

> no doubt Bolivar (as he is now on his way there) will be president and the constitution of Peru will be received there, and no doubt but an attempt will be made to give Colombia the same constitution; that done, perhaps they will invite Chile to follow them. Time only will show what is to be done.[110]

By this time Admiral Guise had been exonerated and reinstated; Hull had sent him hearty congratulations, and the two men were now friends.

Hull was, above all, eager to be on his way home. Despite all his pleas to the Navy Department, nothing had been done about a relief for the squadron in time to allow it to return within the three-year enlistment period; when Southard received a letter from Hull written in May, suggesting that the *United States* spend some time in the West Indies on her return to avoid reaching the coast in winter, he callously endorsed it: "No order is necessary. He cannot arrive before March or April." On 21 August he wrote Hull casually: "It was intended to relieve you at an earlier day, but has been found impracticable."[111] The flagship of the relief squadron, the frigate *Brandywine*, commanded by Jacob Jones, did not sail from New York until 3 September.

By that time most of the enlistments of Hull's squadron had expired, and he had a harsher word for the delay than "impracticable." He had called his crew to muster on the morning of 1 August and had given them a little talk on the benefits of returning home in the spring and being reunited with their families; and he had promised to every man who would agree to remain with the ship until her return a shore liberty of four or five days with a partial advance on his pay. With this inducement all but about twenty reenlisted in August for the duration of the cruise. The process was repeated on the first days of September, October, and November, with the loss of about ten more men. But Hull was thoroughly angry about being reduced to this expedient, and he relieved his feelings by writing a little homily on the subject to Heman Allen:

The term of service of nearly all my crew has expired, and I am left here at their mercy, but thank God they have been treated in a way that they have become attached to the ship and nearly all of them remain until she gets home, but you cannot imagine a more trying and unpleasant situation for a commander to be placed in than that of having a crew he can have no control over legally, and where the whole force in the Pacific is in a situation to be abandoned by the seamen, and if they could do better for themselves, or if they had been treated in a way to cause them to be dissatisfied they would leave to a man, and what a disgrace would it be to our country to see our ships left on a foreign station and laid up for want of seamen, and what a triumph to other nations to see our ships placed in that situation.[112]

Hull did himself only justice in saying that he had treated his men well. He was known in the navy as a humane commander. Throughout the cruise he was solicitous for his crew, seeing to it that they had fresh meat and vegetables several times a week in port, careful of their health, and generous in affording shore liberty. Punishments were infrequent and very mild. Two dozen lashes were the maximum inflicted during the cruise, and that was unique; the man was also dismissed from the ship for mutinous conduct. The usual sentence, even for serious offenses like striking an officer or desertion, was six lashes; sometimes it was three. He gave them plenty of praise, too. At the end of the cruise he told the secretary that "I can say with great truth that I have never seen a better crew or better disposed men in any ship that I have commanded or visited in our service, or that of any other country." He singled out some for special rewards. In May 1826 the *United States* broke her chain cable in Callao harbor and lost one of her bower anchors, which was so deeply embedded in the mud that it seemed impossible to retrieve. (The frigate had then been at anchor about four weeks.) But a few weeks later, through the ingenuity of Boatswain James Evans, the anchor was fished up. Hull ordered Purser Beale to pay Evans twenty dollars for his zeal and perseverance, adding that if the Navy Department would not allow the payment he would pay it himself. He commended Evans to the secretary as "one of the best if not the very best boatswain in the service."[113]

Part of the secret of Hull's success was that he kept his crews busy. Although an examination merely of dates shows the *United States* lying in port for long periods, these weeks were not spent in idleness. The men were constantly occupied watering ship; going to market for fresh provisions; repairing; cleaning; washing; painting; boarding vessels as they came and went; hauling the seine to provide fresh fish; and practicing sail handling, gunnery, and small-arms drill. On only one or two days were the officers reduced to ordering the busywork of picking oakum and making mats. Often the frigate maneuvered around the bay for an afternoon; or she went to sea and returned, to give the crew and the young officers practice. Luckily for all of them Isaac Hull, that precise ship handler, was not on board on 6 November 1825 when the *United States* went around from Chorrillos to Callao: "At 3 attempted to tack but finding she would not come round, boxhauled her round on the larboard tack."[114] Hull would have had plenty to say about that piece of sloppiness.

The order and discipline of the *United States* were attested by the officers of the *Cambridge,* who respected Isaac Hull as a true naval hero. One of them, John Cunningham, rhapsodized in his journal after a visit on board:

> The Commodore's appearance pleased me much. He is a stout, thick set, rather shortish man, has a pleasing, rather handsome, honest-looking countenance, and very much beloved by his officers and men. Indeed, he brought to my recollection several of the captains of the *old school.* . . . His honest tar-like habits, the substantial fittings of the ship—her shrouds, stays and rigging generally possessing more scantling than that of the *Cambridge,* an 80-gun ship—the physical strength and excellent discipline of her crew. . . . [A]ll brought forcibly to my mind the Golden Days of our irresistible Navy before the Peace of Amiens.

British naval minds still played on the theme of the immense size of the American frigates, which had so easily overmatched their own in the recent war, and Cunningham was no exception:

> The *States* is a tremendous frigate . . . and what may be called a bed of timber. Her scantling throughout is considerably above that of the *Cambridge,* according to actual measurement. Her sides are thicker by several inches. . . . Their fighting arrangements are admirable; and, having seen them at quarters, I could not help admiring several of their appointments. One especially— their boarding cap. It is of helmet form, the frame of pretty stout iron, covered outside with a stout, hard leather. Unless a cutlass were laid on by a very heavy arm, the head would scarcely be wounded. They are decidedly the best preservative I ever saw before in any service. . . .
>
> I had not been five minutes on board before I ceased to wonder that my friend, Capt. Carden in the *Macedonian,* was forced to succombe to her. . . . Positively if she had closed the *Macedonian,* as she ought to have done, she ought to have blown her out of the water in 20 minutes.

But in another part of his journal, Cunningham mentions a circumstance that had more to do with the American victories than the size of their ships: in July 1825 Captain Maling ordered a general gun exer-

Commodore Hull

cise in the *Cambridge,* "the second since the ship was commissioned!!!"[115]

Not least among the duties of officers and crew of the *United States* and other foreign warships in the Pacific was providing assistance to their own and other countries' whalers and traders. Gangs of hands from the *United States* and other vessels of the squadron towed merchant ships in and out of harbors; helped them get their anchors up; quelled mutinies; caulked, rigged, watered, and stowed; and performed every service the new country could not provide. Many a ship would have gone ashore or simply sunk at her moorings for want of caulking if it had not been for the navy. Hull himself aided merchant and whaling captains in settling disputes with their crews and took mutinous sailors on board for confinement. Moreover, on several occasions he helped American firms recover sums from captains who, once around Cape Horn, felt themselves free to do what they liked with their owners' property. Hull personally recovered a sum of money from a Captain Gelston for Colin Auld of Baltimore, and through the adroitness of John Percival he was able to return to another Baltimore firm, Hammond & Newman, the proceeds of their schooner *Adonis.* Captain Leonard Sistare had sold the *Adonis* and simply "skipped" with the money, but Percival ran him down at Honolulu and impounded the funds for the owners. The pursuit of the *Globe* mutineers was also a valuable service to the mercantile community, even though the two men recovered were innocent, because as Hull observed, it "will show our seamen that for acts of mutiny they have no escape from justice, and that they will be searched for in the remotest parts of the world."[116]

Hull encouraged the consuls and other Americans in South America to help him collect seeds, plants, and other curiosities that might be beneficial to "our dear country." His particular contributions to the collection were some skulls and an Araucanian Indian boy.[117] He also "collected" some 160 American seamen who were stranded in Peru and Chile, many of them in bad health (11 died). With this addition, much as he regretted losing 30 men by discharge, he had an ample crew with which to return.

But, in reenlisting his men, Hull had assured them that they would be on the way home by September or October. When the days stretched on into November the crew grew restless, and so did Hull. He fully understood their plight; many of them had left half-pay tickets or "allotments" for their dependents at home. Once the three-year period was up, the navy agents would stop payment on these, and the men's wives and children would be left with no income through the winter. Condy

Raguet had written from Rio a horror story about the state of the *Franklin*'s crew on her homeward passage three years earlier:

A number of her men presented themselves to the Commodore, as we learn, in a body and demanded their discharge. This of course was refused, but in order to avoid a repetition of complaint, the ship was actually got under way, a day before the intended period of her departure, and laid at anchor outside the harbour, exposed to the danger of a storm, should one have taken place. But this was not the worst of it. This little adventure, laid the foundation for a report, which after the departure of the ship exposed us Americans here to the deepest mortification. It was stated that the crew of the Franklin were in a state of mutiny, and that they wanted to enter into the Brazilian service!!![118]

Hull did not want that sort of scene repeated in his ship.

Ann Hull had been ill in late winter, and in October and November Isaac was also under the weather. On 1 December he wrote Allen that "as for myself I hardly have strength to walk." He had sent word to Valparaiso that he would leave Callao by 15 December if no relief arrived and would be in the Chilean port by 10 January. The other foreign warships were withdrawing from Callao. Captain Maling sailed for Valparaiso on 9 December, leaving only three or four sloops of war on the coast; Admiral Rosamel had already gone to the Atlantic side. Peru was still quiet, and Hull thought it would remain so as long as there was money to pay the soldiers, but on his final visits to Lima he saw a riot of extravagance that revolted his Yankee sensibilities: "The officers of the army are covered with gold lace and the soldiers are as well dressed as any I have ever seen. The officers of the government are constantly giving dinners and balls and are spending the public money in a way that cannot last long."[119]

On the afternoon of Friday, 15 December 1826, Admiral Guise paid Commodore Hull a farewell visit on board the *United States.* Next morning at daylight all hands were called to weigh anchor, and the frigate filled away, returning a salute of thirteen guns from the British sloop of war *Eclair* and the cheers of the *Dolphin,* which was remaining at Callao for another ten days. At noon she was becalmed off the harbor mouth, but from then it was fair weather and clear sailing until she reached Valparaiso on 6 January 1827. To Hull's immense relief he sighted the *Brandywine* and sloop of war *Vincennes* in the bay. As the *United States* stood in, "the Brandywine fired a salute of 13 guns, let fall her topsails and hauled down the blue and hoisted the red pendant."[120] The *Dolphin* came in on the nineteenth. Commodore Jones had brought new officers and crew for her, as she was to remain part of his squadron. Kennon with his officers and men transferred to the

United States. Hull also acquired a much-needed surgeon for his ship, Dr. Gerard Dayers. Southard had sent extra doctors in the *Brandywine* to help out in Hull's ships, and Dayers was particularly anxious to be one of those returning in the *United States,* as Jacob Jones remarked wryly to the secretary: "The Doctor's case was peculiarly distressing, for being engaged to marry (and the age for such a purpose being nearly passed with the Doctor) he was under the most melancholy apprehensions, so much so, that some of his messmates expressed a belief that he would die of anxiety."[121] The Allens were not going home in the frigate, despite entreaties from the Hulls; Heman Allen felt that he had to remain a few months longer. They would come in the *Peacock.*

There was quite a gathering of warships to see the "Old Wagon" off: the British *Cambridge, Blanche,* and *Eclair,* the American *Brandywine, Vincennes,* and *Dolphin.* On Tuesday afternoon, 23 January, "at 1:30 called all hands up anchor for home. Answered the cheers of the Vincennes, Dolphin and the English squadron and a salute of H. B. Majesty's Ship Cambridge of 13 guns. At 2 filled away and stood out of the harbour, the frigate Brandywine in company." The *Brandywine* went out to try her sailing against the *United States,* but Acting Master William G. Woolsey's log entry was noncommital about the result. After all, the *Brandywine* was a famous ship for speed, and she was light, while the *United States* was loaded for a cruise. At sunset the *Brandywine* hove to, saluted the departing ship with thirteen guns, and hauled up for the harbor; the *United States* ran off to the westward.[122]

It was a good passage home; high summer at Cape Horn and the "Old Wagon" went around under her royals. On 6 March she anchored at Bahia, forty-two days from Valparaiso. There was no hard work here; on 11 March the men went swimming. A few days later the new sloop of war *Boston* arrived, commanded by one of Hull's old lieutenants from the *Constitution,* Beekman V. Hoffman. Early the next morning the frigate was under way again. Hull had decided to show the flag in the West Indies, so he laid a course past Fernando de Noronha to Barbados, and from there ran up the Windward chain, touching at Martinique and St. Thomas. On 9 April the *United States* slipped through Sail Rock passage east of Porto Rico and ran off northward for New York. By the twenty-first she was off Sandy Hook and had her pilot on board, but head winds and a low tide kept her at sea for two more days.

At last, at 1:00 P.M. on Tuesday, 24 April 1827, she anchored in the North River. As soon as the moorings were secure and the upper yards sent down, the crew came aft in a body to tell the commodore they wanted to go on shore. "Finding them determined to go, and their term of service having expired for several months," Hull explained, "I did not think proper to detain them by force, for had I attempted it I am confident the ship would have been in great confusion."[123] To add to the confusion, civil officers came off and arrested Mad Jack Percival and his officers from the *Dolphin* on charges of extortion leveled by Alfred P. Edwards, who had beaten the frigate back to New York. On the twenty-ninth two steamboats came down to carry the *United States* to the navy yard, but she did not have enough men to raise her anchors. Isaac Chauncey had to send down sixty men from the yard before the Old Wagon could be brought up and delivered to the yard the next morning. She was in fine shape despite her long service, and Hull boasted that she could make another three-year cruise immediately, if needed:

> after my having been under orders to her for more than three years and six months and have not lost a spar, sail, cable, or anchor or even a boat since I joined her, indeed not the slightest accident has occurred by which the ship has in any way been injured and I have more than ordinary pleasure in having returned without an officer suspended or a man confined, nor has there been a duel fought or the slightest misunderstanding between the officers under my command and those of foreign ships of war on the coasts we have visited, but on the contrary they have at all times been on the most friendly footing and I believe I can say without fear of being contradicted that I have left the coasts of Chile and Peru with the authorities of those countries friendly disposed towards the United States, and I indulge the hope that they have not had just cause of complaint against me individually since I took the command on that station. My duty has been at times arduous and embarrassing and frequently involved a responsibility that I should have been happy to have avoided, but should I be so fortunate as to have my conduct during the cruise receive your approbation and that of the President of the United States I shall be more than compensated for the many troubles I have had growing out of the many changes that have taken place in the governments of those countries.[124]

14

At Home and Abroad

It was early spring of 1827 when the *United States* anchored at New York, but the days had lengthened into midsummer before Isaac Hull was free of responsibility for the squadron. After the crew were paid off, he asked orders to go to Washington to settle his accounts. (By getting orders to go he could charge his traveling expenses to the government.) Southard replied that "such *orders* have been *invariably declined,* but you have permission to come . . . if the Auditor shall certify that your presence is necessary."[1] Tobias Watkins, the fourth auditor, was accommodating in that respect, and Hull was at Washington by 14 May. He had already asked his friend at the Treasury Department, Thomas H. Gillis, to keep him informed: "we are again in the land of the living," he wrote from off Sandy Hook,

> which I am sure you and Mrs. Gillis will be pleased to hear. . . . Should you know or hear of any evil doings going on at Washington against me I am sure you will give me a hint; I know of none, yet this world has some wicked people in it, particularly attached to the Navy, and one hardly knows when he is safe, or who [are] his friends or who his enemies.[2]

The wounds from the Charlestown affair still throbbed.

Mad Jack Percival was out of the clutches of the law for the moment, so he accompanied Hull to Washington to try to mend his fences at the Navy Department. He did not fare well. Samuel Southard was an efficient administrator, but he had no talent for dealing with subordinates; he had already decided that Percival was a villain on the basis of reports from the missionaries, and there was no changing his mind.

At Washington, Hull also had to confer with the commissioners about the ships of the squadron and their outfits and to discuss with the secretary the character and accomplishments of his officers. He spent a good deal of time over the next few months writing testimonials for the midshipmen. Some he recommended more enthusiastically than others, but the worst he would say about any of them was that "being young he sometimes allows his temper to get the better of his usual feelings, but I have no doubt a few years' experience will overcome his quick temper and that he will make an intelligent and valuable officer."[3] He also wrote to the anxious fathers of the young men; for example, to John Boyle of the Navy Department, whose son Junius was still out in the *Peacock*, "if you had a dozen such boys you would have reason to be proud of them," and to Richard Cutts, second comptroller of the treasury, about his son Walter: "He has been most of the time in my boat and his conduct has been more immediately under my observation than the other young midshipmen and I have great pleasure in saying that his temper is mild and amiable, his manners gentlemanly and his conduct as an officer has been correct."[4] Midshipman Charles A. Thompson of Baltimore had been the frigate's pet:

> he has generous and good feelings, and was a favourite with the officers of the ship generally, particularly so for the first two years owing to his being the youngest midshipman in the ship, and uncommonly quick to learn his duty as an officer; the last year he required occasionally some hints and advice relative to his dress and choice of company suitable to his situation and family, but all that I am sure in a short time will be remedied.[5]

The *Peacock* had been an unhappy ship from the beginning, and Hull had had to bring home with him two officers, Lieutenant James M. Williams and Midshipman Joseph R. Blake, under arrest. Lieutenant Ramsay had chosen to return alone via Panama. Williams had been suspended because a court of inquiry had found him at fault in letting the *Peacock* collide with the merchant ship *Georgia Packet* off Callao harbor in April 1826. Hull persuaded the secretary that his being suspended for a whole year was punishment enough. The reasons for Blake's suspension were not clear, and Hull gave him a glowing testimonial: "Mr. Blake has been on duty many months in this ship and I have great pleasure in bearing testimony to his correct conduct as an officer as well as to his moral character, which has been unexceptionable."[6] Blake, too, was released from arrest. Even the unpleasant Ramsay came in for a good word from the commodore:

> Lieut. Ramsay is a promising officer and no doubt a few years more experience will make him an ornament to the service; and notwithstanding I consider his conduct in many instances very improper I should have great pleasure in seeing the difficulty between him and Master Commandant Jones brought to a close without a court martial if it could be done consistent with your views and the good of the service.[7]

Hull even took a fatherly interest in the two young refugees from the *Globe*, Cyrus Hussey and William Lay, who had still to undergo legal examination for their part in the mutiny. He was evidently convinced of their innocence, for he had given them shore liberty at Lima with the rest of the crew. Lay was from Saybrook and apparently was known to the Hart family. Hussey, who had been granted leave to visit his family in Nantucket after the crew of the *United States* were paid off, returned to New York to face the court proceedings and was counseled by Hull:

> [Take] some friend with you and state your case to Judge [Smith] Thompson and take his opinion or be examined by him should he think proper to examine you. Was I in your situation I should wish a discharge from the proper authority [so] that nothing could be said hereafter. I hope you found your friends well and that you will remember the advice I have so often given you. Your friends are respectable and you should look forward to a situation above a common sailor.[8]

Hull could make only a temporary settlement of accounts because the auditors required certificates from agents and merchants in the Pacific showing the rate of exchange on Peruvian currency. It was clear, though, that he had $6,000 or $7,000 coming to him from his pay, and as he was in need of cash he was able to secure a Treasury draft for $4,000 before he left the capital, about 2 June.[9] He had decided to take a year's leave of absence, for he had to settle his father's estate and take care of his own business interests, and as he had written Amos Binney from the Pacific, "it will take at least a year to collect my little all when I return."[10] As soon as Southard heard of Hull's arrival in the United States, he had offered him a seat on the Board of Navy Commissioners, to replace Charles Morris, who was going to the Charlestown yard. The secretary added tactfully: "It is probable that Commo. Bainbridge will in two or three months resign his place, which will be supplied by Commo. Rodgers."[11] But Hull was not taking any chances. He did not care to be Bainbridge's subordinate for a single day. Besides, for once in his life he had money enough to enable him to take a leave of absence, and by attending to his business affairs exclusively for a year or two he hoped he might secure a continuing income from his properties that would ensure the security of his wife and dependents for the future. Another excellent reason for not going to Washington in the summer of 1827 was that the political campaign was hotter than the weather; if Isaac Hull continued to be identified with the fortunes of John Quincy Adams, he might find himself "on a lee shore" very quickly. It was far better to be on leave for the time being.[12]

From Washington, Hull returned to New York to wind up the squadron's affairs, and from there he traveled to Boston by way of Derby. By the end of July he had settled at Saybrook, Connecticut, for a few weeks. At Derby the commodore and his "Doña" made a lasting impression on Mary and Levi's two little daughters. Sarah remembered for years how dazzling the couple were:

> My first recollection of Uncle Commodore Hull and wife was their landing from a small boat (in which they had crossed the river) at the wharf near my father's house. Papa, my sister and myself went to the shore to meet them. I was about eight years old. They impressed me greatly as I had never seen any one in navy uniform before. Mrs. Hull wore a bright red Spanish cape which looked very gay to my childish eyes. We all walked to the house and I can see Uncle now sitting by our parlor window and looking out upon the river which flowed so calmly by. The next time I saw them was in the old Derby Church which was a mile from the landing; from there they walked to the church. As we owned the first pew in the church, they were very conspicuous. I remember staring at my aunt, for I thought her the most beautiful person I ever saw.[13]

In the early fall the Hulls left Saybrook to take the still ailing Jannette on a tour of the springs. They visited Lebanon Springs and Saratoga and were at Albany, at Cruttenden's Hotel, on 14 September when they met Captain and Mrs. Basil Hall, whose book on South America Ann had recommended to her sisters as an accurate description of the continent. Mrs. Hall wrote to a friend that

> At the door [of the hotel] we met Commodore Hull, one of the most eminent officers in the United States Navy. Mrs. Hull was not visible, but her two sisters the Miss Harts I saw and have not before seen anything so dashing in America. They are very pretty girls and have just returned with their brother-in-law and sister from South America where the Commodore was employed. They were dressed Spanish fashion and have quite a Spanish air. I hope I shall meet them again.[14]

Her hope was fulfilled. The Hull family passed the winter in Philadelphia and were staying at the home of George Harrison, the navy agent, when the Halls came to dinner. Margaret Hall's observation was acute:

> they are on the whole the pleasantest set we have met with. There is Commodore Hull with his very pretty wife, and two sisters, the Miss Harts, but the elder of the two [Jannette] is confined to her room by sickness and I have never seen her. The Commodore is a good-natured, excellent man, an excellent sailor but deaf as a post. The ladies are not generally popular, I don't know why, but I believe they are considered as giving themselves airs and appearing to think themselves above their associates, which as they are *nobody* won't do in this aristocratic country. They are very civil to me, of course.[15]

Affairs at Derby were settled in the fall. Isaac, who, despite his choice of a seagoing career never lost his nostalgia for the old farm, had bought out all the heirs, giving Levi and Mary the Huntington farm and establishing Joseph's widow at Derby with her daughters, with his brother Henry, who apparently was doing nothing productive, as nominal overseer. Joseph B. Hull, now a lieutenant, was also on leave after a cruise in the West Indies that had undermined his health, and he came to Derby to spend the winter with his mother. Isaac wrote him from Philadelphia to see about getting the farm property rented for the coming year:

> And should you not be ordered away you must commence early in the spring and see what you can do in the way of gardening and setting out fruit trees. Indeed, I shall expect the place to be in fine order by midsummer. . . . Is all the grain threshed out and the stock well taken care of? And how have you made out for wood? Tell me all about it.[16]

Among the heirs Isaac bought out was that shadowy figure, Freelove Hull, old Joseph's third wife. One gets the impression that as soon as Joseph Hull became too ill to protest the family had hustled her out of the way, for it was the old man's granddaughter, Sarah Ann, who was keeping house for him when he died. Freelove was written off the family books with finality on 2 October 1827 when she gave Isaac Hull a quitclaim for her share in the estate for $150. That was certainly no widow's third; Freelove got short shrift from the Hulls.[17]

Isaac and his ladies remained at Philadelphia until March, and after the *Peacock's* return in February they were joined by Elizabeth Allen. Both she and Jannette were placed in the care of the celebrated Dr. Philip Syng Physick. Everyone had great confidence in him; he was perhaps the best-known American physician of his day. But he was a disciple of Benjamin Rush and was, therefore, a firm believer in the efficacy of blood-letting. Whatever benefit the sisters derived from his care was probably psychological. In January Isaac Hull was confined by a lame foot, but he was suffering more from agonies of the pocketbook, for he cautioned Joseph:

> My hopes have been that with the house furnished as it now is and what we can get from the farm when let, with what you will be able to spare from your pay . . . the family would have a comfortable support. Indeed, they must in some way live within those limits for with my expensive family it will be impossible for me to allow more than the use of the farm for them, for my other property is so unproductive that I have not anything to spare from it and my pay.

With regard to the repairs being done about the place during the winter he advised: "See that the men work well and be constantly with them and do all you can yourself. You can save much by attention."[18]

Leaving Jannette and Elizabeth in Philadelphia, the Hulls returned to

Derby for the spring of 1828. In early May, Isaac made a business trip to Boston, from which he sent Ann the latest and most titillating piece of navy gossip: Evalina Anderson Porter, whose husband was still at Vera Cruz in command of the Mexican navy, had eloped with her cousin, Midshipman A. A. Anderson, who had been one of the officers in the *United States*. Porter returned a few months later and reclaimed his wife, but when he left the United States for good in 1830 to become chargé d'affaires at Constantinople, Evalina stayed behind.[19]

The Hulls were supposed to rejoin Jannette at Burlington, New Jersey, in late May. They thought of going to Europe, but Ann felt that she could not leave her sisters; nor could she take so many of them away from their father "in his declining life." Isaac probably thought of the cost. At any rate, they were back at Derby in July where Isaac answered an inquiry from the secretary of the navy about suitable officers for a proposed exploring expedition. He could think of none who was particularly qualified for a scientific endeavor but mentioned Hiram Paulding and J. Collings Long. Both of them, however, were in poor health after their Pacific cruise. William Woolsey, newly promoted to lieutenant, "is an excellent seaman and mathematician, keeps a most vigilant watch and in seasons of difficulty and danger is very useful, and endures exposure and privation without a thought of self—but he is rough and uneducated in the extreme." That could almost have been a description of the young Isaac Hull, had he not worked so hard at acquiring gentlemanly manners. He also discussed the vessels that should be employed: a sloop of war outfitted for sturdiness and comfort, not speed and, if funds allowed, a merchant ship and a high-decked schooner as consorts. As for the crews, they should be Americans—preferably from whaling ports like New London, Nantucket, and New Bedford—who might be experienced in long Pacific voyages. Moreover, "the seamen from that part of the country have usually families, and I have always found those who have that tie to their country more faithful and less troublesome, and in foreign ports less liable to desert or seek adventure."[20]

At the same time, he asked for another year's leave of absence, with the proviso that "should my services be particularly required I shall always be ready to accept such a situation as my rank and services entitle me to." He was eager to get Joseph back into active employment, however, and at the end of July he asked that the young man be ordered to the frigate *Hudson* or any other vessel not going to the West Indies. That letter didn't bear fruit, so in November he wrote again from New Haven, where he and Ann were spending the winter of 1828–29. This request brought Joseph orders to the *Guerrière*, which was going to relieve Jacob Jones as flagship in the Pacific. The commodore of the squadron was Charles C. B. Thompson, an acquaintance of Hull's; also going out in the frigate, to take command of the *Dolphin,* was Master Commandant Joseph Smith. Hull told his nephew that Smith "is a good seaman and correct officer." This was the same Joseph Smith who would have been cashiered at Boston in 1809 except for Hull's kindhearted intervention.[21]

Joseph was on his way by early January 1829. He sailed from Norfolk before receiving his uncle's letter of 7 January, written from New York:

> You will be surprised to know that I am here for the purpose of attending the funeral of my brother Charles. He died on Monday last and will be buried tomorrow at three o'clock. His charming little wife is, as you may suppose, in great affliction, but conducts with great propriety.

Charles, the youngest Hull, was just thirty-seven when he died. Of the seven brothers, that left only Isaac, Levi, and Henry. Lavinia Mann Hull, Charles's widow, was now one more potential damsel in distress for Isaac Hull to care for, the more so when her father's business failed soon afterward.[22]

With all these responsibilities in mind, Hull was on the lookout for another suitable command, so when his old friend Thomas Tingey died at Washington on 23 February he wasted no time on sorrow. On 17 March he asked for the Washington Navy Yard, which Tingey had commanded. The orders were given by the new secretary of the navy, John Branch, on 31 March 1829, and on 11 April, at 11:00 A.M., Isaac Hull entered the yard as commandant under a salute of thirteen guns.[23]

Isaac Hull found his new command in poor condition. Thomas Tingey had been the first and only commandant of the Washington Navy Yard from its inception in 1801. In the last years, with age and illness overtaking him, he had let the yard go to seed. Hull set about a vigorous cleanup program, but it took him all summer to get the place as shipshape as he liked. It was August before he had the commandant's house ready to receive his family; in the meantime, they remained in Connecticut, and Isaac lived in a rented house near the navy yard. The commandant's house had to be painted inside and out, and all the fireplaces had to be repaired. Dampness from the cellar had crept up the house walls, damaging the plaster; it had to be patched and a new drain installed in the cellar to prevent future damage. Very few pieces of furniture or household utensils were usable. Hull bought a curled maple bedstead, a mahogany sideboard and bureau, a pair of pier tables, two mantel glasses in gilt frames, and thirty parlor chairs with rush seats.

There were no carpets, but new painted oilcloth was put on the floors in the public rooms.[24]

The house for the master commandant of the yard also needed work. Soon after Hull took command, Master Commandant Thomas Holdup Stephens got a transfer to the New York yard; Hull asked for and got his old second in command, William B. Shubrick, as his replacement.[25] When Shubrick and his family arrived in July, the two men agreed that the house was uninhabitable. In damp weather the inside walls dripped moisture; the plaster and paper were damaged; and the house needed new stairs—all amounting to about $450 worth of labor and materials. Hull told John Rodgers that "'tis the filthiest house I ever saw, that had been occupied by decent people."[26]

Hull was delighted to have Shubrick. The lieutenant of the yard was none other than William W. Ramsay, but he and Hull got along well until Ramsay went on leave in April 1830 and was replaced by Hull's choice, Alexander Gordon. Some of the other officers were less than satisfactory. Edward Barry, the sailing master, was old and feeble; he died the following May. In the meantime, Hull took on Passed Midshipman William D. Porter, son of his old friend, to assist him. Benjamin King, the master blacksmith, was also an old man. Perhaps he was senile at sixty-nine, though officers at Washington had been complaining about him for many years. Hull found him intolerable. Before he had been ten days in the yard he told the commissioners, "I find Mr. King so excessively stupid that I cannot get at time or anything else from him."[27] By mid-July he had had all he could take of King, and he told Rodgers that "from some cause he appears deranged in his mind, and not to know what he is doing. . . . I have informed Mr. King that his services were no longer required in the shop until your pleasure could be known." The commissioners ordered Hull to reduce King to journeyman status and to put someone else in charge of the blacksmith shop, but the old man protested that he could not do the work of a journeyman; as head of the shop he had only had to supervise. No one wished to fire him, so he was allowed to putter on at reduced pay for the time being.[28]

Hull tried to get his secretary, John Etheridge, made purser of the yard, but was unsuccessful. Etheridge continued as commandant's clerk, but Hull managed to boost his pay to $1,000 a year, just a little less than he would have received as purser. Hull was still drawing $100 per month and sixteen rations per day for an aggregate of $3,466.75 per year.[29]

The Washington Navy Yard was somewhat different from the other yards. Because of the shallow water in the Potomac, it was a poor location for building and repairing ships, and although the commissioners continued to stockpile timber for frigates and sloops there—the lion's share of building appropriations during Hull's tenure was for timber sheds—ship construction declined. The frigate *Columbia,* on the stocks, remained there until 1836; the only vessels built under Hull's command were a naval schooner and a revenue cutter. Activity at the yard increasingly centered on ironwork, blocks, and what were called laboratory stores—the various items accessory to guns. Not yet embarked on its long service as the navy's gun factory, it kept its steam engine, tilt hammer, and a force of more than two hundred workmen, most of them hired by the day, busy making blocks, anchors, chain cables, and cambooses (ships' galleys). After 1830 most of these items were supplied to the other yards from Washington.

Hull discovered one violation of navy regulations in the Washington yard right away: the employment of slaves, some of them belonging to yard officers. But he took it for granted that this was the accepted routine at Washington, since in southern society whites would not perform menial tasks. It was certainly the expected thing that the officers' servants would be black, and Hull himself bought one slave, John Ambler, whom he freed when he left the yard in 1835. But early in 1830 John Rodgers, on a visit to the yard, told Master Commandant Shubrick that by regulation slaves belonging to officers of the yard were not to be employed except as servants. When Hull heard about it, he protested to Rodgers that he could discharge all the blacks if ordered to do so, but "I fear we could not find a set of men white or black, or even slaves belonging to poor people outside the yard to do the work the men now do in the anchor shop. . . . I have considered them the hardest-working men in the yard."[30] There the matter rested. Of the black workmen, three were free, seven were slaves of yard master workmen and officers, and six belonged to women (five widows and a child).[31]

One thing Hull did not observe, at least overtly, was the effect of the slave economy on his workmen. Whereas laborers at the Charlestown yard had received, on the average, $1.00 a day and sometimes more, the men at Washington, white and black, were getting $0.72. In June 1829 Hull asked permission to raise the rate, at least for the summer months, to $0.80, since there was for the moment some competition for workmen from the Chesapeake and Ohio Canal and the Baltimore & Ohio Railroad. His request was granted, but this still left Washington laborers receiving 20 percent less than those in Boston. The usual custom at all yards was to lay off a number of workers when winter weather made it unprofitable to employ them outdoors, and to reduce the wages of the remainder. Hull, however, did his best to keep as many as possible on the rolls through the winter, for he observed that "they have large families, and not a cent to support them except what they receive for their labour at this yard; if I discharge them now, I see no way for them to live through the winter." In the spring of 1830 there was a brief protest: Hull had given orders to raise wages to the summer rate as of 1 April, but on 23 March the laborers "stood out" for a week to show that the raise should have been granted sooner. Serious labor protests, however, would not occur for several years.[32]

In contrast to the laborers, Hull thought the mechanics, or skilled workmen, at Washington were overpaid and underworked. He observed in them a tendency to put what is now called Parkinson's law into effect, by stretching their work to last the whole summer—not surprising, since when the job was completed they would be laid off. But, to Hull's eye, it was a very un-Yankee way of behaving. In April 1831, in answer to the commissioners' question whether new buildings in the yard should be erected by hired workmen or by contract, he wrote:

if the men employed by the day would perform fair days work, it would be much to the public interest to have the work done in that way, [rather than by contract] but experience has shewn me that all the care and attention possible to give them and all driving and encouragement is thrown away on the mechanics of this place, for if they are at work by the day on a building that there is the least chance of keeping through the whole season they will be sure to do so, though it might be completed by mid-summer.[33]

There were only two ships in ordinary at the Washington yard: the frigates *Congress* and *Potomac*. The former was an old veteran; the *Potomac*, launched in 1822, was a sister of the *Brandywine*, built by William Doughty, who at this time was still naval constructor at Washington. Hull thought the *Potomac* a fine ship, but both frigates were sadly in need of care. They had been allowed to lie in one position so long that their larboard sides, exposed to the sun, were cracked and open, with oakum hanging in strings from the gaping seams; the *Congress* was in such shallow water that she grounded at every low tide, and a sandbar was building up around her keel. At the end of July, Hull put his men to work on them, so that by autumn the *Congress* was ready to be sent down to Norfolk as a receiving ship. The *Potomac* was, by order, to be given a coat of varnish after caulking, but Hull asked if he couldn't paint her instead: "the difference of expense . . . would not be very great, and I wish her to look well." The commissioners, however, opted for varnish.[34] The sloop of war *Florida* also came and went from time to time, and in the spring of 1831 the yard outfitted three small purchased schooners, the *Fourth of July* (renamed the *Ariel*), the *Spark*, and the *Sylph*, which were to cruise on the Florida coast for the protection of the precious live oak that was used in constructing the navy's wooden ships.

The navy commissioners could sometimes be penny wise and pound foolish. In January 1830 they received an inquiry from William R. Nimmo, a citizen of Baltimore, about the wrecks near the navy yard, remains of the ships burned there when the Americans had fled from the British in 1814. The only one still visible was the old frigate *New York*, and Nimmo proposed to remove her if the navy would give her to him. Evidently the commissioners thought that if Nimmo would find it practical to raise the *New York*, the navy could, too. So Hull was ordered to see to it.[35] Hull pointed out that he couldn't explore the depths of the Potomac in February, but as soon as the weather would allow, he sent down divers. On the strength of their report, the commissioners ordered him to raise the hulk. Men worked on her nearly every day from 1 July to 5 November 1830, and getting her up was no picnic, as attested by the log for 1 September:

> succeeded in raising the wreck about 3 feet. At high tide tore away one of the timber heads to which a screw was attached on the larboard side which brought a sudden strain on the two small chains shackled to the upper rudder brace, tore it off, the whole weight then coming on the large chain which was brought to the Spanish windlass snapped it in the centre (the windlass) and the whole stern of the wreck sunk about 8 feet. Her stern post previous to sinking at high tide was about 22 inches [above?] the surface of the water.[36]

When, after all that exertion, they got the *New York* up, the commissioners decided that the whole enterprise was too expensive, and she was allowed to settle back into the Potomac ooze.

The only naval construction project at Washington during Hull's tenure was the *Experiment*, one of three schooners built for the navy in 1831–32. She was indeed an experimental vessel, for she was built without an interior frame, on the principle of lamination. Her designer, William Annesley of Albany, had been trying to sell this idea to the navy since 1816, but the commissioners had always rejected it as not being strong enough for a warship. Since these small schooners were not expected to do any serious fighting, however, they decided to allow Annesley to design one of them. The designer supervised the construction, beginning in the fall of 1831. The *Experiment* was 88½ feet long and 23½ feet wide, measuring $176^{30}/_{95}$ tons. Her hull was formed of five courses of white oak plank; the inner course ran fore and aft and was temporarily fastened to the molds, which acted as a building frame. Successive courses of plank were laid at right angles to one another, interspersed with coats of oiled paper; aggregate thickness of the hull was about 5 inches. The *Experiment* was launched on the afternoon of 14 March 1832. She proved to be a buoyant vessel and fast off the wind, but on the wind her tubby shape made her slow and inclined to fall off to leeward. She was not a successful vessel, but her fault was more in her stars than in herself: officers were afraid to sail in her and therefore criticized her at every opportunity; and the naval constructors, particularly Chief Constructor Samuel Humphreys, condemned her out of hand because they were jealous of Annesley. The *Experiment* ran a few seasons on the coast and was then made a receiving ship at Philadelphia, where she was sold in 1848. Hull seems to have been a neutral observer; he neither went out of his way to praise the *Experiment* nor joined in the general denunciation. He probably agreed with John Rodgers that the idea was worth the trial.[37]

Life at Washington was by no means all work and no play. Ann Hull and her sisters were particularly delighted to be in the social swim again; evidently Jannette as well as Augusta lived with the Hulls during most of their years in the capital. They had to tread lightly at first. Hull took over the Washington Navy Yard just a few weeks after Andrew Jackson's inauguration, and by the time the ladies joined him in September 1829 the Peggy Eaton scandal was tearing the cabinet apart; navy officers were in an uncomfortable corner because their secretary, John Branch, was one of the anti-Eaton faction and belonged to the Calhoun coterie.[38] January 1830 saw the Webster–Hayne debate in the Senate, and Hull almost surely attended the Jefferson's birthday dinner on 13 April at which "Old Hickory" challenged John C. Calhoun with his toast: "Our Federal Union: it must be preserved."

Hull survived the ordeal very well. On the morning of 2 January 1830 he called on his old friend, former president John Quincy Adams, who was revisiting the capital after having left it in ignominious defeat nine months earlier. Hull went with General Alexander Macomb as a committee to invite Adams to the ball on 8 January commemorating the battle of New Orleans. The startled Adams declined and noted in his diary: "The invitation itself surprised me. I suppose it is a well-intentioned proposition of General Macomb as a compliment to me, and as an effort to give the ball itself some color of a celebration not entirely sycophantic."[39] Hull was keeping his connection with the Adamses alive without losing favor among the Jacksonians. A measure of his success is the fact that during Jackson's first administration he succeeded in getting, first, the long-desired purser's appointment for his former clerk, John Adams Bates, and even more surprising, an appointment as acting midshipman for the ex-president's nephew, Joseph Harrod Adams. The Hulls were on good terms with Jacksonians like Secretary of State Edward Livingston—although Mrs. Hull and Mrs. Livingston did not hit it off—but their guest list also included members of the Adams circle like Edward Everett. Mrs. Livingston, as the wife of the secretary of state, assumed her right to be the leading lady of Washington society; Ann Hull had other ideas. This kind of rivalry did not, however, disrupt relations with the French minister, Louis Sérurier, and his wife, nor with Sir Charles Vaughan, the British envoy. The ladies called Vaughan "the old knight" and counted him their best friend in Washington.[40]

At Washington, Hull was frequently in the company of John Rodgers and the other navy commissioners; they and the secretary, John Branch (replaced by Levi Woodbury in May 1831), visited the yard from time to time to witness experiments in proving cables, canvas, and other articles, or to consult with Hull about improvements to be made in the buildings and facilities. On some days everyone stopped work for militia muster, the Fourth of July, or a celebration like the one of 28 October 1830:

> This day the citizens of Washington celebrated the late revolution in France, which has resulted in the establishment of a system of government favoring, as conceived by them, the progress of universal liberty. All business was suspended—the President, heads of Departments, officers of government, the local authorities, militia, and citizens generally attended the celebration—and the office of Navy Commissioners was shut.[41]

The Hulls also visited Connecticut at least once a year, usually in August. They had just returned from their summer holiday when Isaac wrote to Joseph in September 1830 to say that they had found everyone well at Saybrook and Derby. The Allens were settled in Burlington, Vermont, where Heman Allen was president of the branch Bank of the United States. But Isaac Hull was worried about Joseph on two counts: first, that he might become embroiled in intraservice quarreling, as so many officers were doing; second, because of reports that Joseph's ship, the *Guerrière*, was rotten and might not be able to return safely around Cape Horn. Uncle Isaac cautioned him:

> should there be any difficulty in the squadron you will keep out of it. There has been many and constant troubles among the officers in the Mediterranean and on the coast of Brazil; many have come home arrested and others broke on the station by court martial, and from the last account from the Mediterranean there is another batch of them under arrest and one of the charges against a midshipman is for having threatened to horsewhip the commander of the squadron. They have indeed come to a pretty pass.[42]

Before the end of the year, as a result of Commodore Thompson's report of the bad condition of the *Guerrière*, Hull received orders to fit out the *Potomac* as quickly as possible. Because of his anxiety about Joseph, he had extra incentive to get her ready rapidly, but even so it was summer before she was able to sail. Thompson, meanwhile, had left the coast of Peru without waiting for his relief in order to bring the *Guerrière* around Cape Horn in summer weather. In December 1831 the family at Washington were relieved to hear that Joseph was safely back at Norfolk. Isaac urged him to come to Washington as soon as possible and to bring along a barrel of fresh oysters. Joseph had arrived at a fortunate time, for Lieutenant Joseph Cross, who had succeeded Alexander Gordon as lieutenant of the yard a few months earlier, was going on sick leave and the post was vacant. Isaac suggested:

> I think it will be well for you to be here a short time as you have never spent much time at Washington. There will be in a few days a vacancy at this yard which if you would like I hope I could get it for you. There are one or two now looking out for it. When you come up you can make up your mind. But in the mean time you need not mention it, for the moment a place is vacant there are fifty applications for it.[43]

On 15 December he requested the post for Joseph, and it was immediately granted. Lieutenant Hull remained under his uncle's command until October 1833.

The summer visit to Connecticut in 1831 had been somewhat prolonged because Hull had to spend some time in New York where he had a case in chancery. This unhappy affair involved two of his oldest friends, Oliver Wolcott and George Sullivan. Wolcott had moved to New York in 1827 after being defeated for reelection as governor of Connecticut, and Sullivan had also moved his law practice from Boston to New York. He had leased offices at 30 Pine Street from Wolcott, and in early 1828 when Hull gave Sullivan $5,000 to invest for him in some safe property, Sullivan had taken a mortgage on the premises he occupied but had not told Wolcott that Hull owned the mortgage. Since then, the two men had had a dispute about repairs to the building. Sullivan had refused to pay rent and eventually moved out, and Wolcott was now offering to settle the mortgage for $4,115, deducting damages and rent owed from the original sum. At the same time, Sullivan had been skating on the edge of bankruptcy, and Hull, alarmed by the whole proceeding, had placed his business affairs in the hands of George and Francis Griffin. Hull had, of course, hoped to make money on his $5,000, so he refused Wolcott's offer of settlement, resulting in the chancery suit. Sullivan reproached Hull for his ingratitude in transferring his legal business to the Griffins, recalling his own steadfastness to Hull in the dark days of 1822:

> you made me a poor return for the confidence I cherished in your honor, when you falling under the suspicion of dishonorable conduct in your official station, the government directed an inquiry, and you were abandoned and left alone by all your friends, save only one, and that one who came to you and proferred his services and had the happiness to aid you in your vindication, and did by the course he pursued restore you completely to your honor, was myself.[44]

Hull, on the advice of the Griffins, went to New York in late July to attend the trial of the suit, but the case dragged on until 1837, when Hull finally won it, recovering his $5,000 plus $2,100 interest, at a cost of $530.61 in attorneys' fees.[45]

From New York the Hulls traveled to Derby, Saybrook, Boston, and Burlington, Vermont, and did not return to Washington until 19 September 1831. This prolonged absence caused them to miss one of the most horrifying episodes of the Jackson period, the panic following the Southampton slave uprising in August. On 22–23 August a group of slaves led by Nat Turner rose in Southampton County, Virginia, and killed fifty-eight whites before their force was broken up. Turner remained at large until 30 October. The whole slave-owning society went into a panic at this largest and most successful slave uprising to date, and Washington was very much a part of that society. It was popularly, though falsely, believed that Turner had been inspired by reading William Lloyd Garrison's new paper, the *Liberator,* and that a widespread conspiracy was being organized through its columns. Consequently, Secretary of the Navy Levi Woodbury received a note on 27 August, written in a disguised backhand:

> It is reported in this city that the principal messenger of your office, who is a Col.^d man, is the receiver and *one* of the *agents* for a papaper printed in Boston, called the "Liberator." It is considered of such dangerous principles as tending to produce *Rebellion* amongst our slave population, of which the late affair in Virg.^a is sufficient evidence, that the retaining of people of colour as messengers in any of the Departs. (particularly when engaged in sowing the seeds of bloodshed in our Southern states) may be well questioned. . . . A. Citizen.[46]

A few days before Hull returned to the capital, as a result of the continuing panic, the president ordered the whole force of sailors and workmen in the navy yard to be organized to repel attacks on the yard or arsenal; however, this was to be done "silently, and without creating alarm among the citizens." Similar orders were given to Colonel Archibald Henderson, commanding the marine barracks. How secrecy was to be maintained, considering that the yard workmen were themselves "citizens," is not quite clear. A week later, in answer to the secretary's inquiry, Hull reported that he had plenty of arms and ammunition and that 214 men were in the yard, but many of them belonged to the District of Columbia militia. Thus, in the event of a mobilization, they would have to join their companies rather than the yard defense. By that time, however, the panic had subsided, and the southern volcano returned to its dormant state.[47]

At this time Hull was on very good terms with most of his fellow officers. Some of his enemies were dead. John Shaw had passed from the scene while Hull was in the Pacific, and Arthur Sinclair died in February 1831. And his friends, some of whom had been rather silent in his time of troubles, had recovered their warmth. In March 1831 William B. Shubrick was promoted to captain and left the Washington yard to assume a command of his own; on his departure he wrote Hull that

> the course of service having separated me from your command, I cannot leave an association from which I have derived so much benefit in the acquirement of professional knowledge and so much pleasure in personal intercourse without expressing in the only manner in my power my sense of your many kindnesses. I beg you to be assured that they will never be forgotten by me, and that, from the time of our first association in service, I have been, am now, and shall continue *under all circumstances* your constant and faithful friend.[48]

Hull missed the South Carolinian but was pleased to see him get his promotion. About the same time he succeeded in getting Lieutenant J. Collings Long, who had served with him in the Pacific, made commander of the *Dolphin* in the next squadron. He told the secretary that "as a seaman, in my opinion there are few on the list of lieutenants who stand so high, having commanded an East India ship several years belonging to his father."[49]

Shubrick's replacement at the yard was John H. Aulick, with whom Hull worked in harmony for the next three years. Aulick had been at the Philadelphia yard and was eager to leave because of a troubled situation there. His letter asking Hull to recommend him for Washington revealed that the commandant, William Bainbridge, was being summarily removed by Secretary of the Navy John Branch. Hull was astonished and genuinely sorry. He and Bainbridge had been reconciled since Hull's return from the Pacific; still, there was a tinge of the old feeling in his confidential letter to Bainbridge, written as soon as he learned of the removal: "What are you going about? I hope all this has been done at your own request, and without injury to your feelings in any way. How is your health? I hope better than it has been for some years past." He had never forgiven Charles Morris for his coldness ten years before, and he wrote Bainbridge: "Morris was here some time since and you may be assured that he made good use of every moment he remained. This is indeed a strange world or there are strange people in it." Morris was, in fact, preparing the way for resigning command of the Charlestown Navy Yard to resume a seat on the Board of Navy Commissioners.

With regard to Bainbridge, Hull had forgiven and forgotten all the injury done him, and he treated the other man as if their long friendship had never been interrupted:

> I wish I could give you some good news from this quarter, but I cannot. All is kept as still as death and all the news we get comes from Norfolk or some other station, and generally from some young officer. They now have all the secrets.
>
> Will you write and say what your object is and how you are? Why not come on and see how the land lays? You and myself are not so good managers as some of our friends are; it is now out of fashion to act *above board.* All is done under hatch.[50]

Bainbridge had been a little too free with John Branch, who was not as complaisant as B. W. Crowninshield or Smith Thompson had been. His fortunes improved after Levi Woodbury replaced Branch; in the subsequent round of musical chairs, Charles Morris replaced Lewis Warrington on the Board of Navy Commissioners; Warrington replaced James Barron as commandant of the Norfolk Navy Yard; Barron took Bainbridge's place at Philadelphia; and Bainbridge ended up at his favorite spot, Charlestown. But he was still a bitter man when he died in July 1833.

In the summer of 1832 Washington suffered a devastating epidemic of cholera, which brought tragedy to some of the Hulls' oldest and closest friends. Benjamin Lincoln Lear, the son of their longtime friend Frances Lear, died of cholera, and John Rodgers caught the disease, while attending at his deathbed. Though Rodgers recovered enough to return to work by the fall, he had suffered irreparable brain damage. His memory gradually failed him, and by 1835 he was nearly helpless. In the meantime, he had other troubles to contend with, including the enmity of the powerful fourth auditor, Amos Kendall. Hull hinted at these animosities in a note on 2 January 1833, covering one just received from George Harrison in Philadelphia:

> It gives me pleasure to know that H. is so much your friend. And it would give me pleasure to have the rascals that are endeavouring to injure you. Depend upon it, those fellows are led on by some fellow that dare not appear in

the business. I much suspect the man near the *bank* of the river and I have no doubt but others are with him.[51]

Hull had his own troubles with Amos Kendall. When he came to Washington in April 1829 to take command of the navy yard, he had learned, to his chagrin, that he was expected to act as navy agent as well, for which no other consideration was allowed by law than double rations, or an extra two dollars per day. Every other major city had a separate agent who received 1 percent of his disbursements as a commission. Hull had protested and had been promised that he would not have to continue long as navy agent; in the meantime, he could employ an extra clerk to handle the agency. But it was more than three years before Elias Kane was appointed to be navy agent at Washington, in July 1832. By that time Hull had learned that Thomas Tingey had received 1 percent of his disbursements as agent, and he thought he should have the same allowance. Since he had not deducted the commission from his accounts, the only way he could recover it was by petition to Congress for a "relief" bill. But Kendall refused to concede that Hull was entitled to the commission, and he wrote to Representative Ben Hardin opposing the claim. To add insult to injury, in settling Hull's accounts as navy agent, Kendall disallowed $604.84 that Hull had paid for timber on a specific order from the Board of Navy Commissioners but that Kendall said was in excess of the contracted price and therefore illegal. This sum also had to be requested from Congress. In all, Hull asked $6,500 for his services as agent for three years, plus the sum for the timber. Bills on his behalf were introduced in one or both houses of Congress in 1832, 1833, 1834, 1835, 1837, 1840, 1842, and 1843. The money paid for the timber was finally voted him in 1842; for his services as navy agent he never received a penny.[52]

The winter of 1832–33 saw Washington agitated by the election campaign and, following Jackson's reelection, by the terrible crisis of Nullification. Through January 1833 crowds jammed the streets as people tried to get to the Capitol to hear the debates on the tariff and the Force Bill. But Isaac Hull remained aloof from the agitation, concerned with more mundane affairs at the yard. The mechanics continued to trouble him. John Judge, the head machinist, was proving incapable of keeping the steam engine in operation, and after a year's hesitation Hull finally dismissed him in October 1833. Benjamin King was also a thorn in his side. In January 1833 his wages had been further reduced to one dollar per day, and he had called on his friends in Congress, including Senator

Samuel Smith of Maryland, to have him restored to his old position. Smith wrote Secretary Woodbury that

> Mr. King of the Navy Yard has been known to me for more than thirty years. He did my work in Baltimore, and was in good and profitable business when, *seduced by vanity,* he accepted the call made upon him to come to the Navy Yard. He is now old and somewhat infirm and complains that his pay has been [reduced] too low for the support of his family. This cannot be right: the orange has been squeezed and the rind is to be thrown away.[53]

Woodbury referred the matter to the commissioners, who passed it along to Hull. Hull replied that he had put King in the blockmaking shop out of charity, but the master workman reported that he did little or no work and was seldom there. Under other circumstances he would have fired him, but instead he had reduced his wages, content to overlook his behavior as long as it was not too costly to the government.[54]

Incidents like this pointed to the real problems of living for workingmen in an era of rising prices and stable wages. When their working lives ended, because of either old age or accident, they had nothing to fall back on except their savings, which were hard to set aside in an inflationary period. Hull generally thought, however, that a journeyman should be self-reliant. His sympathy went to the unskilled, to Jack Tar, and to the even poorer victims of the mechanics' imposition. In May 1832 he discharged some men who had used their employment in the yard as a means of running up debts to poor women who ran shops and taverns near the gate and then claimed the protection of the insolvency act. On the other hand, he defended himself for sometimes having more seamen on the yard books than were allowed, because in the winter some men came to him in distress and he would not turn them away. The case of James Williamson is typical of Hull's attitude toward such men. Hull reported:

> Williamson came to this yard about nine months since, bringing a note from Mr. Woodbury requesting me to give him such employment as I could find for him, he being a pensioner. When he handed me the note, I found that he had been drinking freely, and directed him to call again, that I could not say any thing to him unless he came to me perfectly sober. In two or three days, he returned and I received him and directed his name to be put on the books of the Ordinary at ten dollars a month but the next day he was taken extremely ill, and was sent to the hospital where he remained some time. When returned to the Yard, finding that he would be serviceable to the Gunner, and that the work would be light, I placed him under his direction, where he has remained ever since, and has I believe conducted himself well, and has been useful.[55]

Isaac Hull was sixty years old in 1833, and he had begun to think about his place in history. Among his belongings scattered about in

Derby, Saybrook, and Boston were a number of paintings, some of which he had commissioned to depict his exploits, others that he had bought in Paris and elsewhere. In January 1832 he suggested to Joseph that he take the large pictures at Derby, which had been damaged in storage, to New York for Isaac Chauncey's evaluation:

> I have requested the Commodore to allow his sons [to] look at them and see whether many of the heads would not be worth cutting out and framing; indeed, I am sure there are many, and perhaps three or four heads of some of them might be kept in one group. . . . Take the Commodore's advice and whatever you may do, let him take such of them as he likes. He is a good judge of painting and would say which he thinks worth the frames.[56]

In the summer of 1833 he participated in an event that made him even more conscious of his historic role: the docking of "Old Ironsides." Not long after Hull left Charlestown, Congress had at last agreed to appropriate money for naval dry docks, one each at Gosport and Charlestown. These monumental pieces of engineering were completed, under the supervision of Loammi Baldwin, in the spring of 1833. It was decided that the *Constitution*, lately the subject of Oliver Wendell Holmes's spirited poem, "Old Ironsides," would be the first vessel docked at Boston. The event, coming so soon after the Nullification crisis, was to be made the occasion for an emphasis on the Constitution and the Union. President Jackson and Vice-President Van Buren would attend. And what would be more fitting than that the captain who had led the favorite frigate to the pinnacle of glory should take the quarterdeck once more?

Hull felt the honor very consciously. It was doubly gratifying to be cheered in Boston again, when he stood with Andrew Jackson in the portico of the Tremont House on the evening of 21 June. The weekend was filled with entertainments, and President Jackson's health was not equal to the pace. He missed the big event that, because of the time of high tide, took place at 5:00 A.M. on Monday, the twenty-fourth. In the predawn hours special barges carried the dignitaries from Boston to the frigate: Vice-President Van Buren; the secretaries of war and navy; Governor Levi Lincoln of Massachusetts; Joel R. Poinsett, representing South Carolina where the *Constitution*'s live oak had grown; Captain Jesse D. Elliott, now the commandant at Charlestown; and as many more as could crowd into the boats. It was a miserable, rainy morning, but the event drew a large crowd. The docking, which took about fifteen minutes, went off without a hitch, and according to the newspapers:

> The conqueror of the Guerrière stood on the quarter deck, trumpet in hand, and gave orders with that firmness and strength of lungs which has so often raised his voice above the roar of cannon and the noisy strife of the elements.

He was all animation—the pride that nestled at the heart, beamed at the eye. The multitude caught the inspiration, and responded in loud and long continued shouts.[57]

After the ship had entered the dock, accompanied by salutes from the navy yard battery and the ship of the line *Columbus*, the water was pumped out, leaving her dry-hulled on the cradle. The gentlemen on her deck were far from dry by this time, and they beat a hasty retreat up the hill to the commandant's house to shed their dripping cloaks and to have breakfast. After the meal Hull gave ceremonial canes made of the *Constitution*'s live oak to Secretary Woodbury for presentation to Vice-President Van Buren for the absent president, to Governor Lincoln, and to Joel R. Poinsett. He kept his remarks brief, as always. After mentioning the recipients, and the fact that the canes were made of the *Constitution*'s original live oak, he concluded: "In looking to the support which the instrument (after which this ship derived her name) has received at their hands, I trust that an equal support may be rendered to them when arrived at the same age."

Levi Woodbury, however, did not miss the occasion to make a long speech adorned with political allusions, concluding,

> Long, like our political Constitution . . . may she continue to triumph over all assailants; and as one of the most distinguished defenders of the former once [said] in terms which have become a nation's motto, that in respect to *the Union, it must be preserved*—I trust all who hear me will heartily unite in declaring as to this Constitution—the legitimate and worthy representative of our whole Navy—that she *must be preserved.*

Governor Lincoln referred emphatically to the *former* devotion of South Carolina to the country's cause and to "the recent noble manifestation of unshaken fidelity to the Constitution, by many of her distinguished sons." Poinsett, who had been one of the Unionists alluded to, nevertheless ruffled a bit in defending his state:

> It is the land of a brave, and generous, and patriotic people; and while I have ever felt proud of being a citizen of this great Republic, and never more so than on this occasion . . . I love and revere the land of my birth, and must vindicate its character from the aspersions which have been unjustly cast upon it. . . . [T]he people of South Carolina . . . feel no hostility towards their fellow citizens here, or elsewhere, and are ardently attached to the Union. They regard it as the foundation of the liberty and peace of the country, and stand prepared, if ever circumstances should require the sacrifice, to cement it with their blood.[58]

When Poinsett and Lincoln had finished glaring at each other, Hull stepped forward with a few words of thanks to Jesse D. Elliott for his hospitality at the navy yard, ending the party on a harmonious note.

Hull returned to Washington by 1 July, but he did not leave the *Constitution* entirely behind. During the next several years he was busy dispatching souvenir canes and snuffboxes, which were made from the wood taken out of the ship during her rebuilding, to most of the distinguished men in America. He also had a few items made for himself. In September 1834 he wrote to Joseph that

> I saw when in Boston a handsome vase or urn made of the wood of the Constitution. If you could get a piece that would work sound large enough to make one I should like to have one made. You can find out the man that carves them by calling at Jones's the jeweller on Cornhill as you turn up to go to the Tremont House. Mr. Jones no doubt would take the superintendence of its being made if he could get the timber, or Mr. Greenleaf that keeps a book store opposite would get it done for me. . . . I believe the man charges 25 dollars for making the urn, and I should want Mr. Jones to put some work on it in his way.[59]

There was a general stirring of interest in "Old Ironsides" and her career throughout the country. Peter Force made up a sheet of trophy flags from the war, framed in her timber. Hull began to get requests for his autograph, and he received a number of letters asking for his recollections of the chase and battle, including a serious inquiry from Professor Benjamin Silliman of Yale in July 1835 and a rather more frivolous one from Captain George W. Courtenay, British consul in Haiti, who asked him in September 1834 to settle a wager on the length of the engagement from the time the *Constitution* opened fire until the *Guerrière*'s colors were hauled down. As Hull was not a journal keeper, he had to refer to Charles Morris for confirmation of his impressions on that point. In his letter to Silliman, Hull enclosed one of the printed copies he had had made of Silas Talbot's letter praising him for cutting out the *Sandwich* from Puerto Plata; all his later achievements never dimmed that incident in his eyes. He had ordered a painting of it by Robert Salmon that, together with Corné's of the escape of the *Constitution*, he deposited at the Boston Athenaeum in 1835.[60]

He also undertook to retrieve his papers and one important souvenir from Derby. In December 1833 he instructed Joseph:

> I have hanging up in one of the rooms in the house the register of the ship that Dakers endorsed a challenge on to one of the commanders of our large frigates to meet him at sea. I wish you to take it carefully from the frame and roll it on a piece of wood in a way that it cannot be injured in traveling, and send it on to me by someone coming on. If you cannot find a private conveyance, direct it to Commodore Rodgers and it will come safe by the mail. Take care that you put a strong cover over it. I intend to get three or four copies of it from the Treasury Department and deposit the original in some place for safekeeping.

He was beginning to give some thought to future biographers, for when he heard that Dr. David Hull, the last of his father's generation, was near death he told Joseph:

> I think you had better call down and see him and see whether you cannot in some way serve him. Whilst you are there, if he is well enough to converse, I should like to have you ask him whether he has any knowledge about our origin, what part of England we came from, and any other information he may be in possession of on the subject. Should he be able to give you anything in writing, take care of it, or write down what he may tell you.[61]

Ann Hull did not accompany her husband to Boston for the ceremony. At some time in the spring or summer of 1833 she suffered an accident to her foot that evidently tore the ligaments and perhaps broke some bones. In October, Isaac took her to a bonesetter in New York and thought she would recover, but she remained bedridden or confined to her room for two years. Thus, the family's social life was considerably limited during this time. This situation also prevented Ann from accompanying Isaac and Jannette on a sad mission to Vermont in May 1834 to console Heman Allen after the sudden death of Elizabeth on 1 May. Now there were five Hart sisters: Amelia at home in Saybrook with their father; Augusta with Ann in Washington; Jannette (or, as she now spelled her name, Jeannette), sometimes at one place and sometimes at the other; and Sarah in Europe, where her husband had moved his family after his troubles at Boston in 1826. Jeannette had astonished the family in 1832 by converting to Catholicism, under the magnetic influence of Charles Constantine Pise, chaplain of the Senate. According to that splendid Washington gossip, Margaret Bayard Smith, "His zeal, his eloquence and his personal beauty combine to give him an influence no priest has before had amongst us." Sarah was very upset by her sister's conversion, but Ann accepted it more philosophically:

> Hers is no common mind and she has made it a matter of long consideration and enquiry. She says she is *now* happy and satisfied. God grant it. I think every one is accountable alone to God for their religion and I have so many friends of the purest and most exalted character who are Catholics that I have the utmost charity for all—yet in the instance of Jeannette I have mourned about.[62]

Isaac Hull maintained generally good health despite his advancing years. In November 1832 he was bled for a cough, and in January 1834 he suffered another severe cold, but apart from his susceptibility to chest infections he was a hale old man. His summer trip north was never neglected, though in 1834 he had to go without Ann. As compensation, he took her to the Virginia springs in September, but her foot would not heal. Her continued ill health worried him, and at this time he began to think of leaving Washington, though it was another year before he did so. The very severe winter of 1834–35 helped him to decide. It was so intensely cold and snowy that little work could be done outdoors, and Hull set up a soup kitchen at the yard for the destitute families of the neighborhood.[63] By April he had decided to resign the command of the yard. Ann described their plans to Sarah:

> So soon as Amelia is recovered from an inflammatory sore throat Jeannette will come to me with Mr. Allen and remain until my foot is strong enough to go away and then we propose to go to Bedford Springs for a few weeks, and then to Newport to invigorate me for I so love the ocean waves, and then to Boston for three or four weeks for the Comdr. to look after his private affairs. He will resign this command in July. It is in all respects a beautiful residence and agreeable, but expensive, having required $1000 more than his salary every year. We have been here seven years, never changed one of our servants or horses or carriages and we think it expedient to get rid of all now. Independent of every consideration is the Comdr's own feelings and he is anxious to be free from all care after having devoted so many years of his life to the most responsible situations and arduous and important duties. He wishes, he says, to devote himself *to me*. He will get leave of absence for a certain period, and has always intended when he accomplished that to go abroad.[64]

But they did not get away quite as soon as they planned. In the summer Isaac Hull was busy arranging to sell the furniture and to deposit paintings and books at repositories like the Boston Athenaeum and the Naval Lyceum and generally getting ready to travel. But before he could leave the yard he had to deal with a serious labor crisis that, compounded by a concurrent racial incident, turned into a dangerous situation.

The master workmen had complained so often about the disappearance of tools and other small items that in the summer of 1835 Hull ordered a watch set in the workshops at mealtimes. Not long afterward a laborer was caught hiding a copper spike in his lunch basket, and a search of his house turned up a collection of similar articles. Consequently, Hull, careful of the public property and not at all eager to give any opening for the kind of accusations that had plagued him at Charlestown, issued regulations on 29 July prohibiting mechanics and laborers from going into the workshops during meal hours and forbidding them to bring their meals into the yard. But, when the clerk read out these regulations, the workmen, insulted at this slur on their integrity, put down their tools and left the yard. Hull protested to John Rodgers and to Secretary of the Navy Mahlon Dickerson that "the regulations ... contain no reflection upon the men, do not impose any hardship on them, and I apprehend are absolutely necessary for the safekeeping of the public property in this yard." He speculated that the mechanics "have been acted upon by other causes," and he was probably right, because the movement for a ten-hour workday was at its height, and the navy commissioners' resistance to the ten-hour system, until overruled by President Van Buren in 1840, was a cause of bad feeling among workingmen. The Washington mechanics had recently received a circular letter from the shipwrights of Philadelphia, complaining that working in navy yards was "worse than Egyptian bondage" and proposing a general strike.[65] To make matters worse, Naval Constructor William Doughty denounced Hull's regulations, telling the men that Hull "must think them all rogues or thieves."[66]

On 31 July, when Francis Barry stood up to call the roll of workmen after breakfast, the strikers stood outside the gate and shouted to the men inside: "Don't answer! Don't answer!" Many of those in the yard left work and joined the strike, but 123 remained, and work went on after a fashion. The strikers formed a committee to petition the secretary and to go to the Rip Raps in Virginia, where President Jackson was vacationing, to present their case to him. They stated their objections to Hull's behavior as commandant:

> The very first step of his administration was marked by his despotic power by parading us all before him to try the tempers of the men swearing in a most blasphemous manner that if the men did not march before him he would march them out of the Yard dam'd quick and he has from time to time during his administration either in a direct or an indirect manner accused us publicly of stealing the public property. He has now gone so far that forbearance has ceased to be a virtue.

Further complaints included Hull's having prevented them from working on militia muster days, though more than half were exempt from militia duty, and on other "frivolous holidays merely because a few wished to recreate themselves on those days and on all those occasions contrary to the wishes of the industrious portion." Hull had also, they alleged, docked men's pay a half day or more when they missed muster because of "the bustle of the time" and had refused to pay for quarter days when the men were absent the remainder of the day. They referred in general terms to his treatment of John Judge and of Benjamin King: "He has caused men who have spent their youth and prime of life working as mechanics in the Navy Yard to be reduced to want either by discharging them or curtailing their wages and for no other cause save that of old age." And finally, he had often promised pay increases that he did not deliver and, when approached on other subjects, "has treated them with silent contempt."[67]

The grievances reveal something of the slackness into which the yard had fallen under Thomas Tingey and the resentment caused by Hull's efforts to transform it speedily into a "tight ship." They also show his methods of exacting the most work for the least money on behalf of the government, by refusing to allow only a small part of the work force to be on the job when the majority were at militia muster or on holiday, since the remaining few could not work efficiently. There was no way for the men to know about his frequent petitions on their behalf for increased wages or about his efforts to keep infirm men on the payroll even at reduced pay; his "silent contempt" was probably the result of his deafness. The executive, of course, declined to interfere, and after a week of stalemate a group of gentlemen headed by Dr. Alexander McWilliams undertook, with Hull's consent, to mediate the dispute. But Hull was offering no concessions. On 10 August the mechanics' committee reminded him that "while you have the power to make laws for the protection of the public property we have it in our power to refuse our services when those laws oppress us." They offered to return to work provided that Hull would alter his order in such a way that it would not impute dishonesty to them and that all the strikers were taken back "without any distinction of persons." Hull was not prepared to go quite that far, but he let it be known that those who had left the yard might return "on their expressing to the officers of the Navy Yard the impropriety of and regret for their conduct against the regulations of the Yard and promising to respect in future the regulations of that establishment."[68]

By 11 August all the mechanics had returned to work except the ship carpenters and a few blockmakers. The carpenters were still out because of the influence of Naval Constructor William Doughty, who had advised them to hold out for higher wages.[69] Doughty, it seems, also had a hand in drawing the navy yard into the dangerous riot, which in that same week spread from Baltimore to Washington.

Baltimore's uproar in the second week of August 1835, the worst in the history of the city, was due to the monetary crisis provoked by Nicholas Biddle's retaliation against Jackson's war on the Bank of the United States. This had brought about the failure of the Bank of Maryland the previous year, and the depositors, who had waited seventeen months for some settlement, finally took to the streets. The riot went on for almost a week and saw the demolition of the homes of Bank Directors Reverdy Johnson; John Glenn; J. B. Morris; and several others, including Mayor Jesse Hunt, who resigned from office when it became clear that the city government had collapsed. The mob was finally dispersed by the influence of Samuel Smith and his son, John Spear Smith, but before the tumult died at Baltimore the excitement had spread to Washington, where the trigger was not money but race. On Tuesday, 11 August, just when peace was being restored at the navy yard, the Georgetown police arrested a white man named Reuben Crandall on a charge of "circulating incendiary publications among the Negroes of the District." He was examined and committed for trial the next day, Francis Scott Key appearing as the government's attorney. By 8:00 P.M. two of the yard foremen, William Ellis and John Cassidy, had reported to Hull that

> there was a great excitement both in Washn. and Georgetown, and large collections of persons around the jail and elsewhere and that . . . many say that they would hang the man committed that day, commit violence upon Francis S. Key and that then Commd. Hull might look out.[70]

It appears that Doughty had excited further feeling against Hull in connection with the racial incident because Hull had brought a gang of black caulkers from Baltimore to caulk the frigate *Columbia.* Doughty had told the carpenters that this action violated the city ordinance forbidding blacks to come to Washington to reside—which was untrue, as the men were brought in only for temporary work—but in the existing state of things it was enough to bring the threat of violence on the yard.

For the next two nights mobs roamed the city, setting fire to as many black-owned houses and buildings as they could find. Hull put the yard in a state of defense and asked the secretary if he could shelter his caulkers there, but Dickerson chose to throw them to the mob: "for the present I should think it best not to admit any coloured people in the Navy Yard at night."[71]

By Sunday the excitement had ended; as usual, the blacks were the chief sufferers. In Baltimore the city council voted to compensate the gentlemen whose houses had been sacked; but the black people of Washington got nothing except a new ordinance aimed at them: they (not their attackers) were forbidden to assemble after sundown.

These events made the Hulls content to leave Washington. Immediately after the riots Isaac took Ann and Augusta to Fauquier White Sulphur Springs to stay for several weeks; on 10 September he formally requested to be put on leave of absence for a year, with permission to travel in Europe. In mid-September he rejoined the ladies for a few days, then brought them back to Washington and settled them at the National Hotel. His formal resignation of command was scheduled for 1 October. This departure, despite the difficulties in August, would be much happier than that from Charlestown; the day before his resignation he wrote a testimonial to his officers:

It would perhaps be sufficient to say that during my command, a period of nearly seven years, I have not had cause to suspend from duty, for any cause, any officer placed under my command; but it may be necessary for me to say something more definite in relation to those now attached to the Yard, and it is with pleasure I state to the Department that the officers now attached to the Yard have met my fullest approbation and I doubt not, whoever may succeed me in the command, will find them all that officers and gentlemen should be.[72]

A day or two after he formally surrendered command of the yard to Master Commandant John Gallagher, Hull and his family boarded the train for New York, where they would embark for Europe. Louis Sérurier had told him that they could live in the Place Vendôme cheaper than at Washington, and the prospect was welcome. A week at the National Hotel prior to departure had cost him eighty-eight dollars, which equaled one and one-half weeks' income including his regular pay and the income from his Boston properties. The farm at Derby continued to be an expense; the fields were rented out, but the income from them was not sufficient to support Joseph's mother and sisters in expensive idleness. Sarah Ann Hull had married a young lawyer, Ira Ufford, in the winter of 1833 and was now, as Isaac told Joseph, "in the way that women are generally after marriage." But Ufford seemed content to live in the household at Isaac's expense, and Isaac, disgusted at his idleness, decided to sell the farm and invest the proceeds for the support of Joseph's mother and his other sister, Eliza, who was exhausting her feeble strength in keeping house for all of them. He told Joseph that

I find that Mr. Ufford is very willing to live there and take all that the farm produces—a share of the money you allow your sisters—for that and many other reasons I am confident that it will be better to sell the farm and let him see what he can do for himself.

But, although he found a buyer before he sailed, the family raised such a cry of distress that he relented and postponed the sale until his return.[73]

The family—Isaac, Ann, and Augusta—embarked at New York on 19 October in a ship bound for Gibraltar, where they arrived, after a long and boisterous passage, at the end of November. They were disappointed at not finding Joseph there. His ship, the Potomac, was still part of the Mediterranean squadron and was enjoying a harmonious cruise. Isaac had written anxiously to Joseph in the summer to advise him to avoid trouble, particularly in his treatment of the crew:

You have only to do your duty and treat everyone kindly and all will be well, or at any rate, if it is not it will not be your fault. And above all, let me advise you to treat the men and all under your command with as much kindness as you can consistent with your duty and do not punish anyone except as the law directs. You cannot imagine what excitement there is throughout the town about Captain Read's treatment to one of his midshipmen, and many other officers have been severely handled for their treatment to the seamen and for their overbearing spirit and the Navy is much injured by it. . . . Let me beseech you to be careful not to suffer yourself or any under you to punish the men unnecessarily.[74]

Evidently Joseph had taken the advice to heart, for he was now the *Potomac's* first lieutenant. But the ship had gone to Cadiz when the Hulls reached Gibraltar. They stayed only briefly at the cape before moving on to Malta to spend the remainder of the winter. The tiny island provided splendid society, and it was of a sort especially congenial to Isaac Hull, for a British squadron of seven large ships was based there. There was plenty of shop talk, and there was at least one acquaintance to renew, for the captain of the *Edinburgh,* 74, was James Richard Dacres. It was the first meeting of the two former foes since Dacres had left Boston in 1812, but they had no difficulty striking up a cordial friendship. Mrs. Hull was still on crutches; nonetheless, they all made the rounds of parties and balls and went sightseeing. One of Hull's oldest friends, Joshua Blake, was importuning them to join him and his family at Palermo, but he had to admit that

here there is very little good society, but after the round of visiting (and probably I might not be much out of the way in saying dissipation) which you have had in Malta, the *quiet* of this place would not be disagreeable. . . . I am delighted that you and Dacres have met, and in the way you have at Malta. The pleasure you are enjoying in the society of the naval officers and others now at Malta is but a just return . . . for your merits as an *officer* and *gentleman,* and worth as a *man.*[75]

It was late March before the family left Malta in the steamer *Ganges* for Palermo, Sicily, to join the Blakes. The year's leave of absence was passing swiftly, and they wanted to extend it for a year, but at this time there seemed an imminent threat of war with France, due to a misunderstanding between President Jackson and the French government over payments owed to the United States under the treaty of 1831. If war came, Hull certainly did not want to find himself and his family stranded in Europe. But soon after he reached Palermo he learned from a friend at Malta that Horatio Sprague, the United States consul at Gibraltar, had sent word that the crisis was over. Accordingly, on 15 April, Hull requested an extension of his leave to October 1837; it was granted routinely.[76] The party stayed a month at Palermo, then moved on to Naples, from which they made excursions to the excavations at Pompeii. The relative interest of these sights to the ladies and to the commodore was suggested by a parting letter Hull had received from Amos Binney: "I wish your lady and family a prosperous voyage . . . and all the delights which cultivated minds cannot fail to derive from a journey in a country so full of natural beauties and glorious recollections as Italy is; to yourself I wish all happiness and good fortune."[77] Hull cheerfully escorted his ladies through ruin after ruin, but within a few months he could not help saying he would rather see buildings going up than falling down. Otherwise, his only complaint was the cost of postage for letters that followed them about the Continent—in June ten letters arrived via Le Havre, Naples, and Palermo with postage of a dollar apiece: "O, how husband scolded!" said Ann.

From Naples the party continued along the coast to Leghorn, where they found the American squadron and Joseph Hull. The illuminations at nearby Pisa were pronounced splendid, and Isaac had the pleasure of visiting naval ships and talking with navy men. But Ann had to give up her hope of going with the squadron to Constantinople, for Isaac decided that the long waits during quarantine would take too much time. Leaving Leghorn in late June, they made the short journey to the Baths of Lucca. By this time Ann was able to walk and to take the baths. She and Augusta were disappointed in the Italian shops. They could find nothing that could not be had better and cheaper in America, thanks to the low duty there on French goods. Even Isaac's socks, bought in Naples, were inferior: "his toes *poke* through directly."[78]

The group moved on to Florence and Venice, then settled for the winter in Rome. There, like typical American tourists, the Hulls spent their time visiting other Americans—Calhouns, Binneys, Harpers, Schermerhorns, Hares, Gibbses, and Ticknors. They repeatedly made the round of the sights with each new arrival—the Colosseum, the Vatican marbles by torchlight, and so on. But Isaac found one thing at Rome he truly enjoyed—visiting the sculptors' studios. There were quite a few Americans as well as Italians sculpting at Rome at the time. It was an Italian, Lorenzo Bartolini, who was engaged to do Ann's bust, but Isaac sat for Thomas Crawford. The artist told his friend James Freeman, after one sitting, that his subject had been "in a very jocose humor and remarkably amusing. As I was working with my modeling-tool about his eyes, he cried out as if he were hurt. 'I say, signor Tommaso, don't poke that stick into my peepers that way, I can't stand it; Softly, my lad, softly.'" Freeman also remembered seeing Hull and Dacres walking together in Rome during that winter, arm in arm, "and we used to call them Light and Shadow, Commodore Hull being preposterously bulky, and his companion notably thin and bony."[79]

In the spring of 1837 Isaac and his ladies went to Paris, where they enjoyed a long-awaited reunion with Sarah Jarvis and her children, whom they had not seen since the Hulls left Boston for the Pacific thirteen years before. Isaac also found old friends, including David Baillie Warden, who had crossed with him in the *Constitution* in 1811. He received indirect greetings from Louis Philippe by the hands of a peer who was instructed to show him the city and all the royal palaces. But he could not remain for the summer fêtes; by the end of May it was time to start for home if he was to be there in September. The diligence, or its successor, took the party to Rouen and Le Havre, where Isaac engaged cabin space in the packet *Poland* for the three of them, for 2,250 francs. News from home was disturbing: the panic of 1837 had struck, and the cities were in disorder. Early in June came news that Welles & Co. at Paris, who had been Hull's agents on the Continent to handle his drafts for traveling expenses, had closed their doors. By that time the Hulls had expected to be well at sea, but they had had a narrow escape when the *Poland,* only a few hours out of Le Havre, went aground. Luckily, the weather was calm; all the passengers were put ashore, and the ship was towed back to Le Havre for repairs. In spite of this alarming mishap, Isaac decided to sail in the *Poland* when she was ready rather than look for another packet. As Augusta told Sarah, "we were comfortable on board—a kind, attentive maid. Most of those passengers who were disagreeable have taken places in the Louis Philippe and it is uncertain if the captain will be able to fill their rooms; so much the better for us!"[80] When they finally got under way they had a relatively short summer passage and arrived at New York before the end of July.

Hull was relieved to find his business affairs in good order at New York and Boston; the trip had been more expensive than he expected, and his New York broker, Stephen Whitney, had been forced to borrow $1,800 for him in December. But the $6,600 realized by the settlement of the old chancery suit left him fairly comfortable in the midst of the country's distress. The American cities were in miserable condition, and Washington was in an uproar with a special session of Congress debating President Van Buren's Sub-Treasury plan. Hull wanted to visit Washington to see what sort of command he might be able to get, but John Etheridge advised him to wait until Congress adjourned, as the city was mobbed and rooms were at a premium: "I understand Captain Shubrick has been in search of rooms and he can get none he likes for less than $80 per week."[81] In the meantime, Etheridge kept him up to date on political news. He wrote in July:

The political affairs of our country I trust are about to undergo a change. It is believed that Mr. Van Buren is well disposed to rid himself of the cabal by which he is surrounded but that he has so far committed himself to Gen.

Jackson and the party that he cannot act immediately. What his course will be cannot be inferred even, until after the meeting of Congress. Kendall, it is believed, has d——d himself by his tyrannical edicts, contempt of the acts of Congress and violation of the laws of the land. God grant he may receive what I consider his deserts! the indignation of a much abused and injured people, even should it be expressed by an effigy execution and a garment of tar and feathers.[82]

Hull and his friends, like many old Adams Republicans, were appalled by locofocoism and were swinging in the direction of Whiggery. In September, as the special session neared its end, Etheridge reported that

what was the administration party is now divided and the suggestions of the President in relation to the currency are not received as sound. The attempt to avoid a National Bank will probably succeed, but the next thing to it in my opinion is about to be established, by giving authority to Govt. to issue 20 millions in Treasury notes; this must form a part of the currency of the country and will be made use of for remittances from one part of the country to another, affording great advantages to banks, brokers and money dealers. . . . The Benton humbug of a currency to consist of nothing but gold and silver is at its last gasp and it now remains for the people at large to shew their abhorrence of mountebanks and charlatans.[83]

Hull therefore made only a very brief visit to Washington in August. He stayed just long enough to learn that there was no desirable command available. The big navy appropriations and the high hopes of 1836 had been dashed by the panic and the keynote now was retrenchment. Hull wished his family at Derby would think of retrenching a bit. His opinion of Ira Ufford was lower than ever, and after a visit to Derby in early August he told Joseph that they must come to some resolution about the farm: "whether the farm is sold or not my own opinion is that they cannot live as they now do without ruin to all." By the time he returned from Washington it seemed that they had finally decided to hold on to the farm, but he wrote his nephew in disgust: "as they look to you for support they should leave to you the choice of the best way to give it them. I have had so much trouble and vexation about [it] that I am tired of hearing it named. And I feel that I have been driven from my own home, nor can I even think of visiting it again."[84]

Joseph succeeded in bringing the matter to an issue by the end of September. The outlands of the farm were to be sold and the house and garden retained for the use of the family; Isaac would deed it to Joseph in trust for them. He thought they should be able to manage with strict economy, "which they owe to themselves to observe in all things. They must know the sacrifices you have made to provide for them, and that even now you are depriving yourself of domestic happiness for their sake." For Joseph, like his uncle before him, wanted to get married and found himself short of means. The Hulls had returned from Europe to find that romance had bloomed between Joseph Hull and Amelia Hart, the last sister at Saybrook. Both were well into their thirties, so the marriage could not be too long delayed, but Joseph would have to get a good shore station first.

That was one of his uncle's reasons for going to Washington for the winter. The Hulls spent a short holiday at Sachem's Head, in Connecticut, in early September and moved to the capital in late October after Congress adjourned. Isaac was also still on the lookout for a new command for himself, for as he remarked to his nephew, "I am, like yourself, on shore pay; my living exceeds my pay, and my means are small."[85] But nothing turned up during the winter except two weeks' service in December as presiding officer of a board to review plans for the South Sea Exploring Expedition. That was over by Christmas, and the Hulls moved to Baltimore for the rest of the winter. In March, Isaac got word of a possible situation for Joseph. J. Collings Long wrote from Portsmouth, New Hampshire, that he was being promoted to commander and consequently would vacate his post as lieutenant of the yard there; Joseph would be acceptable to Captain William M. Crane, the commandant. Isaac sent the letter on to Joseph with a note: "I have . . . written to [Mr. Long] saying that I did not think that climate would suit you, but you had better write immediately and thank him for the information and say what you think as the place will be given away."[86] Instead, Joseph got a berth in the *Columbus*, the receiving ship at Boston, where the climate was not much better than at Portsmouth.

In April 1838 Hull was appointed with two friends, Captains John Downes and Joseph Smith, as a board to revise the tables of outfits and stores for the different classes of naval vessels. They were to meet at Boston on 1 May, and they held sessions there until early September. But Isaac Hull probably knew before he left for Boston, as a near certainty, that he was about to be given the best command the Navy Department could bestow: the Mediterranean squadron, with his flag in the ship of the line *Ohio*.

Return to the Mediterranean

The beautiful *Ohio*, the finest ship ever built for the American sailing navy, was Henry Eckford's masterpiece. After she was launched at the Brooklyn Navy Yard in 1820, Eckford had gone to Constantinople to build ships in her image for the Ottoman Empire. She was 208 feet 8½ inches long, 53 feet 10 inches molded beam, measured 2,542 tons, and mounted 84 guns. The *Ohio* was not the equal in size of the mammoth *Pennsylvania*, which carried 132 guns and was the largest American sailing warship, but she had the edge in everything but size. No warship of her day surpassed her in beauty, speed, and handling. Howard Chapelle said of her that she was "long considered one of the finest vessels of her rate in the world, if not the finest, and by far the best liner in the American Navy. Not only was she a handsome ship of her type, but she was a remarkably good sailer and a good seaboat, carried her guns high, and stowed her allowances with ease. It was often said that she handled like a frigate."[1] In the Mediterranean she showed her heels to every vessel that challenged her in any but the lightest breeze. She was the pride of the navy, and the command of her long-delayed maiden voyage was given to the most honored of the navy's living officers, Isaac Hull.

As soon as it became known that Hull was to take the *Ohio*, officers began to clamor for places in her for themselves, their sons, and their relatives. Hull was given the usual courtesy of selecting his senior officers. He chose Joseph Smith as flag captain and submitted a list of lieutenants, but he was told that his first choice for executive officer, Alexander B. Pinkham, was too junior. Garret Pendergrast was made senior lieutenant, followed by Samuel Mercer, Samuel F. DuPont, William L. Howard, Robert L. Browning, John S. Missroon, John W. Cox, Alfred Taylor, and Guert Gansevoort. As a matter of course, Hull called on his old friend John Etheridge to join him as secretary, and he appointed a young Bostonian, John Peirce, Jr., as professor of mathematics to the midshipmen. It was probably Peirce who wrote a book about the cruise under the pseudonym "F. P. Torrey."[2]

Hull accepted the command with apprehension. He was sixty-five years old and not in good health. During the previous winter Dr.

Thomas Harris had operated on his throat to relieve a persistent cough, and it is probable that he was suffering from a progressive lung disease, or possibly from heart failure. Because of this, and because of his deafness, he depended a great deal on Ann, who was always at his side. In another time, Hull would have retired from the active service under these circumstances, but there was no navy retirement pay in the 1840s; off-duty officers went on half pay, and Hull's finances were no more able to sustain that reduction in wages than they had ever been. Conscious of his failing strength and consequent decline in emotional resilience, he acknowledged his orders to the *Ohio* with trepidation:

> I feel that the command you have been pleased to honour me with is one of importance, and involves great responsibility. I therefore enter upon the duty assigned me with anxiety, fearing that with my best endeavours and constant attention, and an ardent wish to do all in my power to serve the best interest of the department, and to meet your views and wishes, I may not with the many perplexing difficulties before me, so conduct the squadron in all things as to meet your approbation.[3]

These were unhappily prophetic words.

On 11 October 1838 the navy yard commandant at Boston, John Downes, turned over the *Ohio* to Captain Smith, and Hull's blue broad pendant was hoisted on board. Leaving Smith to bring her around to New York for her guns and final outfitting, the commodore started overland by way of Saybrook and New Haven. His entourage included Ann and Augusta, as well as Sarah Jarvis, recently returned, with Hull's financial assistance, from her exile in Paris. He left the ladies at Saybrook with Amelia and their father and went on to New York, where Lieutenant Joseph Hull was to join him. The family at Derby had finally agreed to the sale of the farm but with so much bitterness that Isaac refused to visit Derby on his way south. He lamented to Joseph that "it would give me much pleasure to visit my home and the home of my father and mother before I leave the country—but I cannot, nor do I believe I shall ever again see that delightful valley and visit the graves of my father, mother and brothers."[4]

Hull reached New York on 16 October, the same day the *Ohio* sailed from Boston. He found Secretary of the Navy James Kirke Paulding in the city, and when Mrs. Hull and her sisters joined him a few days later he presented his wife to the secretary and obtained informal permission for her to accompany him on the cruise. The cabin entourage was to include as well Captain Karl August Gosselman of the Swedish navy, who had been visiting the Americas on a trade mission for his government. Hull had invited David Porter to join them, too. The ex-commodore had left his legation at Constantinople for a visit to America and was improving his health at the Warrenton Springs, but he wrote Hull that he intended to stay in the United States until spring rather than make a winter crossing of the Atlantic.[5]

The *Ohio* entered New York harbor on 23 October and was towed to the navy yard by the steamboats *Hercules* and *Samson*. She was in good order except for her green and seasick crew, though much of her outfit remained incomplete. But the promise of a happy cruise was shattered on 30 October when, during the secretary of the navy's formal visit to the ship, First Lieutenant Garret Pendergrast handed Commodore Hull a letter for the secretary signed by the wardroom officers.

The cause of the officers' grievance was a decision by the Board of Navy Commissioners, several years earlier, to berth the wardroom officers on the orlop deck (the lowest deck in the ship) in line-of-battle ships. This would keep the lower gun deck, where they had their mess, clear of their personal belongings and, it was thought, cause them less inconvenience when the ship cleared for action. But the orlop had drawbacks. Located below the water line, it was dark, stuffy, and smelly. The arrangement had never been put to the test because, in the last line-of-battle ship to visit the Mediterranean, the *North Carolina*, there had been no flag captain. The commodore occupied the poop cabin, and the captain's cabin on the main deck had been taken over by the lieutenants. In the *Ohio* there were both a commodore and a captain; therefore, both cabins were occupied and the officers were relegated to the lower decks. The *Ohio*'s officers asserted to the secretary that Fleet Surgeon Benajah Ticknor was sure their health would be ruined by living on the orlop deck. But this, they protested, was a small sacrifice; their real concern was that they would be last on deck when all hands were called and that they could be too easily battened under hatches in case of mutiny. Secretary Paulding referred the matter to the navy commissioners, who decided that the officers' objections were farfetched. The arrangement would stand.

But the lieutenants were not defeated. They had alleged in their letter that they had not objected to the orlop quarters while at Boston because they were "desirous to give the new arrangement a fair trial." In fact, before they reached New York they had still hoped that Hull and Smith would share the main cabin. When they learned that Mrs. Hull and Augusta Hart were to go in the ship, their hopes vanished. Failing to move the secretary or the commissioners, they began sending anonymous letters to the newspapers, attacking Hull for giving women pride of place to naval officers.

Isaac Hull was wounded by these attacks. Still an officer of the old school, he could not understand how these men could so far forget themselves, and the discipline of the service, as to resist orders by writing to the newspapers, and especially by attacking women. Their manners and temperament were foreign to him: nearly all the officers were southerners, and none except Ticknor was from New England. They saw their commander as a crabbed old Yankee and his middle-aged wife and sister-in-law as by no means ideal companions for the cruise. The newspaper campaign was a partial success. Secretary Paulding, who had returned to Washington, was alarmed by the outcry and wrote Hull at the last minute that he had understood that only Mrs. Hull was to go with her husband.

> I have, however, just been informed that Miss Hart, if not two Miss Harts, are to go out with you in the Ohio. This, certainly, was not my intention; but as any interference on my part at this late moment would probably disarrange your motions, produce great disappointment, and probably delay the sailing of your ship, I am induced to acquiesce in this addition to your party, with the express understanding that the ladies are to reside on shore during your cruise.
>
> I feel assured that, in order to quiet the clamors and dissatisfaction expressed *in every quarter*, as well as for the benefit of the service generally, you will willingly make this sacrifice to my wishes, and those of the President.[6]

Hull could not have obliged his officers if he had wanted to. Even without his wife and sister-in-law, his cabin would have been crowded by Captain Gosselman's suite, and the Navy Department had just ordered Commander Robert L. Stockton to the *Ohio* to act as executive officer and to share Captain Smith's cabin. He readily acceded to the commissioners' suggestion that in warm weather the officers should be permitted to swing their cots in the wardroom, and he arranged to have ventilator pipes installed in the orlop deck while the ship lay at New York. These measures, however, did not quiet dissension. The officers objected that they were entitled to better than makeshift and temporary sleeping quarters, and they intimated that the ventilator pipes would weaken the ship.

Hull felt himself unable to sustain a long quarrel with his subordinates. On the eve of the *Ohio*'s sailing he addressed a letter both pathetic and proud to the secretary, asking to be relieved from command as soon as another commodore could be sent to the Mediterranean:

> At the time I accepted the command of the U.S. naval force in the Mediterranean, it was with the hope that I might do something for the good of the naval service of my country, and that the officers selected for the flag ship of the squadron would extend towards me that courtesy due to my rank and that consideration which is due to long services. But from the circumstances

which have already developed themselves . . . it is but too evident, however ardently I desire to preserve harmony in this ship, all my efforts will be unavailing; and the attacks which have already been made upon myself and family show but too conclusively how little I have to expect from the sea lieutenants and other wardroom officers of this ship, either of consideration or respect. . . . I feel myself impelled by a sense of duty to the service, from a sense of self respect, and from a consideration of my own honor and standing, to ask and to claim to be relieved from a command, commenced under so unfavorable aspects, already irksome to my own feelings and one which, under the present arrangement, can only eventuate in discredit to our country and in irreparable injury to its naval service.

I . . . trust the Department will properly estimate the necessity of protecting an officer who has served his country long, and with some credit, but who, if he is to be assailed by those young in the service and placed under his command, by misstatements and wrong impressions, at least sanctioned by them, has lived *too long*.[7]

The commodore's anguish could not be allowed to stand in the way of the amenities. On 30 November, before dropping down to the outer harbor, the *Ohio* held open house for the "quality" of New York. Abigail Chew described the day's events:

Mrs. Hull, Mrs. Jarvis and the Miss Harts were all ready to receive company. Soon after the steam boat arrived with the mayor and many other invited guests from New York—all looked pleased. The Countess of Westmoreland and niece [were] of the number. We looked to our hearts' content, then, seeing all of the ship, were again introduced to the cabin and a table of refreshments were in waiting. . . . The mayor made a speech and then Mr. [Philip] Hone with a few remarks gave the toast, "The original defender of the Constitution"—drank and cheered. After leaving the ship, the yards were manned and cheers given and responded to from the ship and boat.[8]

A week later the *Ohio* passed the bar through Gedney's Channel and began her passage of the Atlantic. The voyage was stormy, as might be expected in December. On the twenty-first, Seaman James Morse was killed when he fell from the topsail yard during a gale. Lieutenant John S. Missroon broke his leg in a fall from the horse block, and Lieutenant Robert L. Browning suffered a bad sprain while working on deck in another storm. The *Ohio* passed Gibraltar on 27 December in such squally weather that Hull did not attempt to enter the harbor but pressed on to the squadron rendezvous at Port Mahon, Minorca, where the ship anchored on 4 January 1839. Besides Morse and the injured lieutenants, the only casualty of the outward passage was Assistant Surgeon Edward Van Wyck, who suffered an apoplectic stroke the day after the *Ohio* left Sandy Hook. Fleet Surgeon Ticknor, though forced to admit in his official report of 28 December that "the accommodations of the officers, with respect to temperature and ventilation, have been comfortable," insisted that Van Wyck's stroke had been directly caused by a single night of sleeping on the orlop deck near the noxious vapors from the pump wells, and he warned the rest of the wardroom mess that the same thing might well happen to them.[9]

At Port Mahon, Hull found one other unit of his squadron, the new sloop of war *Cyane*, which had already been some months in the Mediterranean under the command of his old friend, Mad Jack Percival. The Navy Department had been more than usually vague about the makeup of Hull's squadron, and he left the United States knowing only that he would have "a frigate, a sloop of war and a dispatch vessel." The frigate was to have been the *Constitution*, but she was sent to the Pacific instead and was replaced by the *Brandywine*, which finally reached Mahon on 28 November 1839. The dispatch vessel never arrived.

The commodore and his ladies went on shore soon after the *Ohio*'s arrival and took up quarters in the town of Mahon overlooking the harbor. With the aid of Consul and Storekeeper Obadiah Rich, and the facilities of Mahon's navy yard, the *Ohio* was put under overhaul to make her a showpiece for the summer cruising season. On 23 February 1839 Lieutenant Sylvanus W. Godon reported to Hull for duty. He had been traveling in Europe, and Hull had promised Godon's mentor, William Short of Philadelphia, that he would receive the young man on board. For Short's sake he welcomed him cordially and made him flag lieutenant of the *Ohio*, a very fine compliment, in that the flag lieutenant was the commodore's personal aide. Godon was flattered and surprised, for, as he wrote to Short,

> it was well known the terms on which I stood with several officers of the wardroom mess and I suppose you cannot have forgotten the letters written by those gentlemen to the Secretary of the Navy about their rooms &c. Those letters have created a heart burning which will be difficult to get rid of for some time: It was a great object with the Commodore to find out how I felt on that matter. I had a difficult game to play, but here I am, I hope for the cruise. The appointment of Flag Lieut. is all very fine, but I like keeping my watch better; this business of *playing the gentleman* too much I don't care about, although it will do very well for the present and for one summer cruise on the coast of Italy.[10]

The "heart burning" was indeed still active. Garret Pendergrast had a second complaint against Hull. Commander Stockton had been detached from the ship to go on a diplomatic mission to London as soon as the *Ohio* reached Mahon, leaving Pendergrast again as executive officer. The lieutenant contended that, since the post had been held by a commander, he himself should be allowed a commander's pay according to navy regulations. Hull did not agree and refused to sanction his claim, which only helped to nurture Pendergrast's grudge against the commodore.[11] Moreover, Surgeon Ticknor had written a letter to his brother on 19 January, dated "U.S. Ship Ohio, Port Mahon, Cell No. 10," which was published a few months later in the *New York Courier and Enquirer*. Ticknor wrote that he and his brother officers expected release by an order from the Navy Department; in the meantime,

> Our CELLS are as dark as Egypt; but I expected that in port, our wardroom would be light enough to admit of reading and writing by daylight. I find, however, I was mistaken. In a cloudy day we require candles almost constantly, even in our wardroom, and in a clear day I can make use of the daylight only when the sun shines in at the stern ports. Thus I am making a painful sacrifice; but I thank God it cannot be forever. The day of deliverance will surely come.[12]

For the time being, however, Hull had something much more serious to worry about than the comfort of his officers' sleeping quarters. Anglo-American relations were in a very bad state because of incidents on the Canadian border. Involvement of Americans in the insurrection in Upper Canada had led to the burning of the American steamer *Caroline* in December 1837. Tempers had not yet cooled over this matter when a boundary dispute arose betwen Maine and New Brunswick. Late in 1838 there was actual fighting between borderers in this "Aroostook War," provoking Congress on 3 March 1838 to pass a bill authorizing the enlistment of fifty thousand volunteers and appropriating $10 million for the protection of American interests. President Van Buren countered by sending General Winfield Scott to Maine to arrange a truce, but the newspaper reports reaching the Mediterranean were so bellicose that, early in April, Hull decided to take his squadron outside the Straits, so that he would not be bottled up in the event of a sudden war. At the same time, he wrote for advice to the American ministers at Paris and London, Lewis Cass and Andrew Stevenson, respectively.

The *Ohio* and the *Cyane* sailed from Mahon on 15 April. Hull sent Percival to Marseilles with his letters to Paris and London and to obtain funds for the squadron while the *Ohio* proceeded directly to Gibraltar. Hull was particularly piqued that he had received only one letter from the secretary of the navy since sailing from New York. On 19 April he wrote Isaac Chauncey at the Board of Navy Commissioners that "I have now been from the United States nearly five months and am without information as to the time when other vessels are to join the squadron under my command, if at all."[13] The *Ohio* beat around Europa Point on the afternoon of 21 April and clawed up to her anchorage in Gibraltar

Bay at 2:00 P.M. Here again Hull was disappointed to find no letters, but the wardroom was agog with war talk. Lieutenant Godon wrote home that

> the last acts of Congress . . . give us some hope that we may yet have some work, that will give us a chance of making our way ahead. We will probably remain here but a day or two; if the packet that is to arrive tomorrow from England confirms the present appearances, that a difficulty is likely to take place between the U.S. and England, we will get underway at once and cruise outside of the Mediterranean, or run to Cadiz until further news will show the Commodore how to act. We are all in fine spirits at the present prospects, and dream of nothing but promotion. Our guns work well, our crew in good discipline, and willing, and headed by such officers as we have on board would we are [sure] find few vessels on the ocean that could stand before us.[14]

Hull was less sanguine. His crew were inexperienced; many of them were foreigners ("though shipped as 'Americans,'" he noted); and although they made a smart show of gunnery exercise, they had as yet done no actual firing. He was a good deal less disappointed than his juniors, therefore, when the next day's packet brought word from England of General Scott's peace mission.[15] Since there were still no letters from Washington, however, he decided to take the ship to Lisbon, and after a stormy week at Gibraltar, during which the *Ohio* broke an anchor chain and collided with an English merchant brig, he sailed again on 29 April. The westerly gales battered the *Ohio* up the coast; she did not make Lisbon until 16 May. During the passage, Hull took occasion to ask his officers for their opinion of the *Ohio* for transmittal to the Navy Department; the reports were received and summarized by Captain Smith. Neither officer could fail to notice that all the senior lieutenants used the opportunity to derogate the orlop sleeping arrangements. Samuel F. DuPont was particularly vehement:

> in my most unqualified opinion, an experience of seven months has stripped this system of berthing lieutenants and some other officers on the orlop of even the shadow of a palliative, that its manifold evils and palpable military impropriety continue unmitigated, that it is unrelieved by a single redeeming feature, and is wholly indefensible.[16]

The commodore put these letters aside for the time being. From 17 to 26 May, while the *Ohio* lay at Lisbon, he was engaged in a continual round of visits, dinners, and other activities with the government at Lisbon and the other foreign officials in the port. Ordinarily, Ann would have taken much of this strain on herself by arranging the parties and receptions on board the *Ohio*, but she and Augusta had been left at Mahon because of the war threat. The only coolness felt at Lisbon was from the British naval officers; on 18 May when Hull visited Rear Admiral Sir John Ommaney in his flagship, the *Donegal*, he was not received on the quarterdeck and was given no salute. Therefore, when Admiral Ommaney returned the visit on the nineteenth, he too was shown below to the cabin and was not saluted. John Etheridge, keeping a memorandum of these exchanges, noted: "Quid pro quo." But on 23 May the *Ohio* saluted Queen Victoria's birthday, and the next day Hull was invited to dine on board the *Donegal*. On the twenty-fifth Hull and his officers were presented to the queen of Portugal, and they concluded the festivities with a grand dinner on board the *Ohio*. By that time the *Cyane* had joined the *Ohio*. Percival had had a miserable voyage; the *Cyane* had been slowed by head winds, and Percival had had a painful attack of quinsy, but he brought letters from Cass and Stevenson, both assuring Hull that there was no likelihood of war with England. The two ships weighed anchor on the twenty-seventh and returned to Mahon.[17]

Now Hull had time and opportunity to deal with his officers. The one letter he had received from Secretary Paulding, dated 27 December, was a response to his parting letter in which he had offered to resign the command of the squadron. Paulding urged him to retain his command and seemed to back him up wholeheartedly:

> the Department expects that . . . you will retain your command until by a firm and steady assertion of authority, in which you may rely on it for support, you have suppressed that spirit of discontent which, if permitted to triumph, will, it is feared, be fatal to the future character and discipline of the service.

The secretary went on to praise Hull and to censure the officers in very severe terms. He said that Hull, "the man who first broke the charm of British naval superiority," had been chosen for the Mediterranean command in order to revive old-fashioned discipline, and that the choice of officers was made both as a compliment to them and as a spur to emulation of the navy's traditions. But instead of this,

> a spirit of discontent, approaching to insubordination, has prevailed among a portion of the officers which manifested itself in disrespect to their commander, in appeals to the public as void of foundation as they were destitute of all manly consideration for the feelings of himself and the ladies of his family, and in a violation of the regulations of the service, by publishing an official correspondence without permission of this Department. Had it not been believed that the Ohio would have left New York before the order could be received, every Officer of the Ward Room, who sanctioned or participated in those publications, including the Purser and Surgeon, would have been detached from that ship.

Paulding expressed a hope that, by this time, the officers would have become reconciled to the situation. But if this were not the case, and Hull still wished to resign the command, he would be allowed to do so. If he were to resign, however, he should have the secretary's letter read to the assembled officers on the *Ohio*'s quarterdeck,

> in order that all may know why it is, that the man who has contributed as much as any other living or dead, to raise them and their profession in the estimation of their country and the eyes of the world, has found himself forced to relinquish what he once considered the crowning honour of his life, that of being their commander.[18]

On 7 June, Hull sent extracts of this letter to his wardroom officers, suppressing the compliments to himself, the concluding paragraph, and the words "for the feelings of himself and the ladies of his family." He asked them for a response, hoping that they would apologize and put an end to the matter, for he did respect them as officers. Godon had just remarked that "the Commodore says himself that he has never met with so good and so capable a set of officers since he has been in service." But the officers stood their ground:

> Whatever we have urged against the messing and sleeping apartments of the ship, has been the offspring of feelings very different from discontent, insubordination or disrespect: we were actuated by a sense of what we conceive to be due to our rank; as well as by a desire to call attention to a system of accommodation without precedent, we believe, in any other naval service.[19]

Although he was far from satisfied with this reply, Hull was content to let the question rest for the moment. He forwarded the correspondence to Paulding with the comment,

> The Department expects me to retain my command with a firm and steady assertion of authority in which I may rely on it for support. To retain command whilst there shall be extended to me the necessary support, is felt not only a duty to my country and to the Navy, but which shall receive my best and strongest exertions; but in the absence of that support, pride for the service must cease, mortification will ensue, and that interest in its welfare which inspires me, will no longer exist. . . .

He expressed the opinion that the orlop deck arrangements might well be objectionable; but the objections should be voiced "at proper times, in a proper manner and without interfering with public duty or private reputation," and the ultimate decision must be left to the navy department.[20]

The ultimate responsibility for this and all the subsequent unhappiness in the *Ohio* must be considered Secretary Paulding's. He was a very poor administrator, as is evidenced by his failure to write to his squadron commander for months at a time or to keep him informed about serious diplomatic crises. (Van Buren's appointment of Paulding to the cabinet has been called "pure self-indulgence.") Moreover, he was vacillating: he tended to blow hot and cold and to side with the person he talked to last. When the *Ohio* sailed, he was upset about the women on board, and besides his letter to Hull on the subject, he evidently let it be known that he would make some changes in the ship. Ticknor had hinted in his letters that the officers expected some "relief" from the Navy Department; this, of course, stiffened their determination to hold out for their supposed "right" to different quarters. After receiving Hull's letter of 5 December, Paulding changed tack and gave Hull carte blanche to exercise authority while condemning the officers' conduct. By the time Hull had need to exercise the authority he thought had been given him, however, Paulding had changed his mind again; the result was much suffering on both sides.

At sunrise on 13 June 1839 the *Ohio* got under way from Mahon, followed by the *Cyane*, for her first summer cruise in the eastern Mediterranean. By the next afternoon she was at Marseilles; from there she proceeded to Leghorn, where she was visited by the grand duchess of Tuscany. She then went to Naples, called off Malta and Hydra, and anchored at Athens on 2 August. There, a week later, the Hulls entertained King Otho and his queen with appropriate ceremony. Next, the squadron crossed to Urla, near Smyrna, to check out reports of pirates in the Greek archipelago. All was quiet. Hull had applied to David Porter to secure permission for the *Ohio* to visit Constantinople, but the unsettled state of Turkish politics and the terms of a treaty between Turkey and Russia made it impossible for an American warship to pass the Dardanelles. Hull, disappointed, and with the ship's provisions going bad, turned back to Mahon, sending the *Cyane* to call at Tunis and Tripoli.

It was an unusually hot summer in the eastern Mediterranean. As the *Ohio* rounded the Italian boot, and the thermometer on the main deck rose past eighty degress, a chorus of complaints broke out again. Surgeon Ticknor's meteorological report for June was marked "Suf" on eleven days, with the notation, "These letters are inserted to denote the peculiarly suffocating and oppressive state of the atmosphere in my room on the orlop deck." On 26 July, Captain Smith inspected the staterooms at 4:00 P.M. and at midnight. He reported the atmosphere as being "close and confined," as was to be expected, but not "suffocating." He recommended that the officers be allowed to sleep on the gun decks during the hot weather, a suggestion Hull readily agreed to. But this did not satisfy the complainers; they insisted that they were entitled by rank to suitable *permanent* quarters. Samuel F. DuPont was the most vocal member of the group. He wrote Smith that he would refuse to occupy temporary quarters; since Hull declined to change the arrangement established by the commissioners, "I prefer remaining where the Navy Department have placed me, as long as my health will endure it, rather than occupy quarters which I deem unfit for an officer holding the third rank known in our service, and from which he may be ejected at any moment."[21] Smith passed this letter on to Hull with the remark that "The tenor and character of this communication, as well as the course he has taken . . . develop a spirit of dictation in its author too clearly, to my view, to require comments from me."[22] But Hull and Smith had the last word in this exchange. On 14 September, after the *Ohio*'s return to Mahon, DuPont asked permission to return to the United States for "reasons of a domestic nature." Hull flatly refused the request and forwarded DuPont's protest to the secretary without comment. If DuPont wanted to stay on the orlop, then stay he should.

Hull was never able to understand how his lieutenants could become so upset about their quarters. In his youth a lieutenant had slept where he was told, taken the watch assigned to him, and never opened his mouth. What he did not realize was that these minor questions loomed large in the minds of men who had few other ways of distinguishing themselves or determining their precarious status in a peacetime service oversupplied with officers. When Hull entered the navy, officers were few, action was plenty, and promotion was swift. He had joined the service as a lieutenant at twenty-five, and by the age of thirty-three he was a captain. Many of these lieutenants, however, were nearing forty, with no immediate prospect of promotion and no way of maintaining their slender dignity but by guarding jealously their rights to quarters, uniform, and other forms of deference.

Another truth that would have surprised Hull was that the very achievements of which he was so proud made him an object of hatred to some of his juniors. When David G. Farragut, in later years, praised Hull's capture of the *Guerrière* and added, "I always envied Hull that piece of good fortune," he expressed the positive side of a feeling that had more negative implications in less distinguished minds. Juniors like Godon and DuPont, who perceived quite correctly that it was that event which had brought Hull to the top of his profession, came to believe that it had been mere luck, not evidence of skill or daring on the part of a man they knew only as old and ill. They wanted the old commodore and others of his generation out of their way, and they longed for a war that might make *them* the new sons of fortune. Most of them would achieve their ambition, but they had twenty years to wait.

By the time the *Ohio* reached Mahon a rupture had also occurred between Hull and Godon. The commodore expected his flag lieutenant, as his personal aide, to dance attendance on his ladies, to escort them in the different ports, and to do some of their errands. This was far from unusual, but Godon found it—and them—outrageous. He wrote to William Short that

> so far as going with the Commodore and doing everything which could please him on duty went, I was not only willing but pleased to do, but. . . . The women themselves are two of the most uninteresting that it has ever been my lot to be cast among, and frequently their want of *tact*, to say no more, mortified me. I, however, managed as long and as well as I could and everybody was surprised that I got along with them so long. However, all things must have an end; because I was not always hanging at their heels the Commodore was offended, [and] an explanation took place, in which I found that *going* with the women was a *sine qua non* to my being Flag Lieut. I could not understand this to be a part of my duties and after a month or so I was at last relieved from that duty.[23]

Some of the malcontents, Godon among them, were thinking of asking a transfer to the *Cyane*. Percival, ridden with gout, was going home, and William K. Latimer had been ordered as his replacement. The lieutenants knew that they would have no better life under Percival, whose views of naval service were definitely "old school." He had recently written that "the spirit which is in many instances manifested in the service, to question or animadvert on orders generally, their propriety or impropriety, together with frequent appeals made through the public prints to public opinion, is striking at, if not sapping the very foundation of the service."[24]

On the other hand, they were afraid they might catch a Tartar in Latimer as well. Godon had heard that Latimer "is one of our martinets in service and is no favorite with anyone."[25] But he still thought that the *Cyane* might be a desirable berth, since she would see more active service than the *Ohio* and would go home six months sooner. Nevertheless, Godon managed to find it "outrageous" when, on 1 October, he was transferred to the *Cyane*, together with Lieutenants Browning and Taylor.

> The Commodore had time after time said that the Lieuts. were the best he had ever sailed with, that he would not wish to have one of them changed, and indeed expressed his entire satisfaction of their manner of doing their

duty and their moral deportment; he knew too that we were very happy among ourselves and that there was a rare unity of feeling in this mess. We were indeed very happy. This very happiness was a source of annoyance to him, he could never find fault with us *on duty,* but he did find fault that after he had done a number of things to discontent us with the ship and the cruise, that we should not feel very cordial to him and his family, when not on duty. . . . I had long foreseen that troubles would grow out of women being on board the ship and particularly such women as *they* are, and placed on such delicate ground as they were.[26]

The lieutenants believed that Hull had received orders at Mahon "to land the women . . . at all events the women *were* landed." There had been no such orders, other than Paulding's letter at the commencement of the cruise; the women went on shore because the summer cruise in the Levant was over and the *Ohio* was bound on less pleasant duty in the Atlantic.

Despite the lateness of the season, the *Ohio* was going to Tenerife because Hull had received word of the detention there of an American vessel, the *Two Friends,* suspected of being a slaver. The *Two Friends* had sailed from Cuba to New Orleans, back to Cuba, from there to the coast of Africa and—her cargo not being ready—had put in at Santa Cruz de Tenerife to avoid British cruisers. By various sales and resales between Spanish and American owners, and by carrying two crews, her nationality had been clouded. At Tenerife the non-Spanish crew, a motley lot containing only one American, had fled to the protection of their consuls, and the American representative, Joseph Cullen, had called on Hull to take charge of the vessel as a slaver operating contrary to United States law. However, by the time the *Ohio* reached Santa Cruz on 26 October, the Spanish authorities had seized the *Two Friends* and referred the question to Madrid. There it rested, and none of the efforts of Hull, United States Minister John H. Eaton, or anyone else could extricate the question from the somnolent Spanish court.[27]

Not only was this expedition fruitless; it was exhausting to all on board the *Ohio* as well. Outward bound the ship encountered a terrific gale, which the pseudonymous chronicler, "F. P. Torrey," recorded in superlative terms, describing

the Commodore, on the poop, supporting himself by holding on to the brass railing, and gave his orders with great coolness. The old veteran never shows to better advantage, than when surrounded by danger.—The carpenter reported the main mast in danger; the sea was running mountains high, the decks all floating with water, and torrents rushing over the forecastle. For some time fear was plainly depicted on the countenance of many a gallant Tar. Never was a ship's crew more active in performing their orders with cheerfulness and alacrity, or more attentive to their duties. Many an uncertain hour passed the wind so strong, it would seem to sweep into destruction every thing in its course. A fine French frigate was dashed upon the rocks, impossible to sustain itself against the violence of the elements. But our noble ship worked and labored like a thing of life, and rode the storm in safety.[28]

In returning from Tenerife, the *Ohio* had to put into Gibraltar because of a fault in her rudder. Adequate iron was not to be had, so that only temporary repairs could be made. The stormy passage to Mahon, against continued easterly gales, was thus even more tense than the passage out. The flagship anchored at last on 28 November and was followed into the harbor within minutes by the long-delayed *Brandywine*. The *Cyane* was absent. Shortly after the *Ohio* sailed for Tenerife, William K. Latimer had reached Mahon to take over the sloop from Percival. Mad Jack ended his command in his usual eccentric style. According to Midshipman Henry A. Wise,

> all hands being called old Jack came out of the cabin, with the ever to be remembered shoes made out of the boot legs on, took out the *yaller* handkerchief, blew his horn, hopped up on the wardroom combing and said: "I render unto God the things that are God's and unto Latimer the things that are Latimer's. Gentlemen, step in the cabin and I'll give you some wine." "Pipe down," says the new skipper, and so ended the dynasty.[29]

The *Cyane* then went off to cruise the Italian ports. There was a continuing rumor at Mahon that Minorca might be ceded to France. In that case, it would no longer be a proper rendezvous for the American fleet, and Hull asked Latimer to survey several harbors, including Ferrajo on the island of Elba, as possible alternatives. The only one that seemed feasible, other than Preble's old base at Syracuse, was La Spezia. Mahon had the drawbacks of any sailors' haven. Liquor was all too plentiful, and during the carnival season of 1840 there was a serious riot in a theater between American and Spanish officers, leading Hull, the following year, to forbid the midshipmen to attend the masquerades. Communications between Minorca and the mainland were slow and uncertain. But the harbor was excellent; the former navy yard was completely at American disposal; and relations with the government were generally amicable. In the end, Minorca remained Spanish, and the American rendezvous stayed at Mahon.

The *Cyane's* officers were, for the time being, contented with their new captain. Godon wrote that "he will never be a great favorite with either officers or crew; still I think he will do very well. His great selfishness is his strongest objection." This charge of selfishness was one Godon threw at all his commanders, it seems. He repeated again and again that Hull was "selfish" or "mean" and wrote that "the Ohio has not left a very good character behind her in the different ports she visited last summer. . . . I am really glad that I am no longer in her, to be identified with her present reputation, that is the reputation which the Commodore is getting for her. . . . All this is owing to the women."[30] On his return to Mahon he found the *Ohio*'s lieutenants still complaining, this time because they had not been allowed to go on shore at Tenerife. Godon carried on about Hull's character: "I was so repeatedly disgusted with the old gentleman and his meanness in his intercourse with foreigners of rank that I felt that all my respect for him was gone. . . . I felt that he *used* me but did not care the snap of his finger for me or my interest in any way."[31]

Godon and his friends never understood, or attempted to understand, their commodore's situation. For one thing, he must have seemed cold and aloof to them because he was deaf. Thus isolated, he felt keenly his exclusion from the camaraderie of the junior officers, and he must continually have suspected them of whispering behind his back—suspicions that were evidently justified. In charging him with "meanness," they overlooked the fact that Hull was still a poor man. His business interests in Charlestown were in the same sad state as were all such interests in the post-1837 depression. Early in 1840 he learned, moreover, that a suit had been filed to take away part of his wharf, an action that was likely to succeed, or that could be averted only by the payment of several hundred dollars on his part. He had nothing to depend on but his pay, which, as his accounts and bills for the cruise show, barely covered his own expenses and those of his family. He was fortunate to be able to keep his wine supply up to par for visiting dignitaries; lavish entertainment was quite beyond his means. Worst of all, the old charges that he had taken a watch for passage in the *Constitution* were still as lively as ever and were being repeated in the wardrooms of his squadron as late as 1841. Godon believed that "his *Victory* has saved him on two occasions from ignominious punishment, for offenses which he could not have defended in any way."[32]

Isaac Hull—anxious, angry, and ill—ground his teeth in frustration at his impotence in this situation. The lieutenants would give him no ground for action under navy regulations. They were polite when they saw him, but they generally managed to avoid him. Throughout the winter of 1839–40, none called at his home in Mahon. He knew that they were spreading the old gossip about him; even "F. P. Torrey" recorded his impressions of the reasons behind Godon's transfer from the *Ohio*:

> rumor says . . . that he grossly slandered the character of our venerable commander whilst attending a dinner party on board the English flag ship when

laying in the harbor of Lisbon. The English officers told G. he was no gentleman in slandering the character of an absent and distinguished officer, that they were acquainted with him for years, and knew him to be a man of honor and patriotism. His sinking the Guerriere, preserving his own gallant ship when surrounded by the whole English fleet, his long and faithful services to his country when the patriotism of men were put to a severe trial, all these deeds of glory and honor seem to have no effect to soften the bitter malice and impotent hatred of this G., whose services, in comparison to the Commodore's, is like comparing an angel of light to a demon of darkness.[33]

For Hull, it was like living through the old Charlestown nightmare over again. Isolated from the lieutenants, the old commodore spent more time with the younger officers, who had always been his favorites, leading Godon to sneer that "he frequently holds conversations with *young midn.* of the *lieuts.,* in which he frequently forgets the dignity of his station so far as to speak *disrespectfully* of them."[34] Evidently, in Godon's mind, it was all right for him to speak disrespectfully of his commanding officer to whomever he pleased, even to foreign officers, but it was unthinkable that Hull should criticize a lieutenant before a midshipman. The particular case in point was probably that of Passed Midshipman Carter B. Poindexter, who had run afoul of John S. Missroon, one of the lieutenants Hull particularly disliked. A general court-martial that tried all the squadron's offenders during January and February 1840 sentenced Poindexter to twelve months' suspension; Hull refused to approve an additional clause that required the sentence to be read at all naval stations, and pointedly told the secretary that

> I consider the punishment very severe for the degree of culpability proven. Mr. Poindexter is a correct officer and his conduct has met my approbation generally, and the necessity of confirming even a part of the sentence of the court has given me much pain. I used my best exertions to prevent his being brought to trial, which were met by him, but his prosecutor [Missroon] evincing much obstinacy I was obliged to lay the case before the court.[35]

The lieutenants were more cautious than Poindexter had been. Cold and hostile they might be, but on duty they were scrupulously correct, giving him no excuse to arrest them.

The attitude of Godon and the others toward the naval service may be gauged by some remarks made by the former on 19 February, shortly after the *Cyane* sailed from Mahon to carry letters to Gibraltar and to look for some Arab cruisers reported to be on the Spanish coast. He evidently believed that Hull had ordered the *Cyane* to sea expressly to spoil the pleasure of her officers in the Mahonese society.

> the incessant pestering of the Commodore made our sailing uncertain from day to day; as it was, the Mahonese had invited us to a ball, among the first

ever given in Mahon by the natives; no sooner were the invitations out, than the C. gave out our orders to sea. We sailed on the 17th, the ball took place on the 18th. The Governor applied for our ship to remain one day, but the Co. refused and here we are.[36]

Lieutenant Robert Browning thought he had outfoxed the commodore; a few hours before the *Cyane* sailed he secured a certificate from the surgeons stating that his health could not sustain a winter cruise, and he was left behind. But he found that he had fooled himself. Hull was only too happy to take this opportunity to relieve himself of one troublemaker. He told the lieutenant that since it was so necessary for him to avoid exposure he had better return to the United States. To the Secretary Hull remarked that

Lieut. Browning has been sufficiently well to attend balls and evening entertainments since the arrival of the Cyane in December last and was at a theatrical representation last evening on board ship and has never complained, that I have heard, of that "kind of exposure." . . . His absence from the squadron will produce no detriment to the service, but on the contrary, I think, will be beneficial to my command.[37]

Browning protested that he was quite well enough for *summer* cruising, but Hull was adamant; the lieutenant could wait a few weeks for spring weather for his passage home, but he was no longer part of the squadron.

Finally, on 18 March, Hull received what appeared to be a solution to his dilemma about the other offenders. The storeship *Dromo* brought him a letter from Paulding, dated 16 December 1839, that denounced the reported conduct of the wardroom officers, and their proved actions in writing to the newspapers, in the strongest terms. The secretary concluded:

For yourself Commodore, I have only to say, you are Commander in Chief of the Mediterranean Squadron; the Laws and Regulations of the Service give you ample power to protect yourself from disrespect and to enforce subordination. Exert that power to the utmost, and so long as you do not go beyond your lawful authority, you may rely on my cooperation and support. . . . You must enforce your own rights, at the same time that you respect those of others, and oblige every man to do his duty as the best means of entitling him to the full enjoyment of those rights.[38]

To Hull this letter seemed to give him clear authorization to remove the disrespectful lieutenants from his squadron. He was fortified in his resolve by a letter received next day from Commander Latimer, immediately on the *Cyane*'s return from her mission, asking him to remove Lieutenants Samuel Lockwood and Sylvanus Godon from his ship. Latitimer was incapable of getting along with any executive officer. Hull merely removed Lockwood to the *Ohio*, but he was far from displeased to have additional evidence against Godon, of whom Latimer had written: "I find him so much disposed to treat with indifference my orders, and a manifest desire on his part to cavil at all restraints imposed upon him requiring an obedience of them." He implied that, if Godon remained in his ship, he would soon put him under arrest, "as he seems to require more, than, in my opinion, is proper to yield to a subordinate officer."[39]

Godon, meanwhile, had already caught the rumors that were flying about the squadron, to the effect that the commodore had received permission from the navy department to make whatever changes in the squadron he wished. It was reported that officers would be transferred among the ships, and that some would be sent home. Godon averred that he hoped to be one of those sent to the United States: "I would look upon a leave of absence at this time as the greatest piece of good fortune that could happen to me. I shall be careful how I say so however for fear that if such a thing is in contemplation I might be balked."[40]

On 20 March, Hull made one more attempt to effect a reconciliation with this recalcitrant. He invited Godon for a private interview in his office at Mahon, but Godon was not disposed to bend. On Monday the twenty-third, Hull assembled the original ten lieutenants of the *Ohio* and had Etheridge read to them the censure contained in the secretary's letter. The lieutenants prepared a formal written remonstrance to Hull and to the secretary, disavowing any intention of contempt or disrespect toward the commodore. Hull would have been wise to accept their declaration and leave them with a warning, but he could not. Captain Joseph Smith was going home, an invalid. This would leave Hull to command the *Ohio* for the summer, and the thought of the daily contact with the lieutenants that this would entail was unbearable, particularly since Hull's health was again poor. He made up his mind by 27 March to order Lieutenants Pendergrast, DuPont, Missroon, and Godon back to the United States. Surgeon Ticknor had already been relieved by the Navy Department; Browning would go with them as well. Hull apologized to William Short for having to detach Godon, explaining

> When Lt. Godon arrived from Paris I was very happy to comply with your request and received him on board the Ohio although she had her complement of officers. As the officers of that ship had protested against the arrangements ordered for them by the Government before I received Mr. Godon I told him as he knew that fact to examine well and judge for himself that there might be no discontent afterwards. He assured me of his perfect satisfaction and earnest wish "to join the ship on any terms." I therefore made him my

Flag Lieutenant, took him into my family with the cordiality and kindness that I would have shewn a son or brother. Almost immediately he joined those disaffected officers, repaid me with disrespect, ingratitude and treachery! It was only by great forbearance that I kept from sending him home under arrest, but removed him to the sloop of war Cyane.

There he has exhibited the same spirit and set examples that produce insubordination and the worst results to the Navy.

I now feel compelled to send him home to report himself to the Secretary of the Navy. I regret these things, my dear Sir, and feel that this statement is due yourself after your application to me in behalf of Mr. Godon. It was a pleasure to comply with your wishes and I now only regret that he has proved unworthy the interest taken for him.[41]

The storeship *Dromo* was chartered to carry home the returning officers and the invalids of the squadron. She sailed on 14 April. A few days later the vessels of the squadron scattered to carry out their summer cruising: the *Brandywine* was sent westward to sweep as far as Lisbon, the *Cyane* to the Levant, and the *Ohio* northward to cruise the coasts of France and Italy.

It should, perhaps, be noted that the Mediterranean squadron was rarely a happy one. There was not enough activity for the officers; a great deal of the duty was social, as Hull's encounters with assorted royalty indicate. This was the kind of situation in which status and "honor" became particularly important in the minds of some. Boredom and heat added their irritations. One may recall Hull's shocked letter to Joseph in 1830 about a midshipman who was supposed to have threatened the Mediterranean commodore with a horsewhip. That was presumably James Biddle, who commanded in the Mediterranean from 1829 to 1832, or possibly his immediate predecessor, William M. Crane. At least six duels were fought in Biddle's squadron;[42] there was none in Hull's. Apparently, his lieutenants were too interested in maintaining a united front against their commander to bicker among themselves; and Hull kept a weather eye on his midshipmen. While his squadron was not a harmonious one, it was not unique in that respect.

The summer cruise of 1840 was a happy interlude in this unhappy squadron. Hull, relieved of the obnoxious lieutenants, rather enjoyed taking direct command of his ship again. The crew were happy, too, for Isaac Hull was as sparing of the lash as ever, and floggings were few. Not a single instance of public punishment occurred in May and only one in June.[43] The *Ohio* visited La Spezia and Genoa and called at Toulon. She left the last port somewhat precipitately on 1 June when a case of smallpox was found on board. But the victim was left on shore, and by the time the ship reached Palermo on the seventeenth there were no new cases. She then returned to La Spezia so that Purser Sinclair could purchase a stock of tea for the crew and also engage a new cook for the commodore; on 11 July she anchored again at Mahon, where the *Brandywine* joined her on the thirty-first. On the twenty-seventh a new captain for the *Ohio*, Elie A. F. Lavallette, reached Mahon, and after a six-day quarantine he took command of the ship on 2 August. According to the squadron's chronicler, "Commodore Hull made a few remarks suitable to the occasion. He appeared much affected; he said the ship was the finest one in the world, and an excellent ship's company, and all possible indulgence should be granted them."[44] Lavallette, in turn, reported home that "the inspection of [the *Ohio*] enables me to pronounce her the most perfect ship of war I have ever seen. The high order and fine discipline . . . are worthy of all example."[45] Hull, for his part, felt that the "ship is now in perfect order, her condition in every respect is such as to give me great pride and satisfaction; her officers give me entire satisfaction, and her crew is under good discipline, strictly subordinate and attend to their several duties with cheerfulness and alacrity; I trust nothing will occur to mar the happiness or to interfere with the contentment which now reign on board."[46]

But by that date decisions had been made in Washington that would shatter this brief reign of peace. The dismissed officers arrived in the United States early in June and lost no time in appealing their case to the secretary of the navy. Pendergrast, who had done some research, remarked pointedly that "I believe but one other instance of the kind has occurred in the service, and this took place under Com. Hull, while commanding the Pacific squadron. The first Lieut. of the Peacock was displaced by him, but upon his appearing before the Department, he was immediately restored to his ship by Mr. Secretary Southard."[47] Pendergrast was partly right; although it was by no means the only such instance in the service, it was true that Hull had been called down for sending Lieutenant Ramsay home in 1824, and he had repeated his mistake by detaching these men without preferring charges against them. By 10 June, Pendergrast, Godon, Missroon, and Browning were at Washington, joined briefly by DuPont, whose wife was ill in Delaware. Their combined pressure soon worked the desired effect on Paulding's changeable mind. On the twelfth Godon reported that

> [The secretary] appears to regret the course which the Commodore has taken, and finds after reading all that Commodore Hull has written to him on the subject of our return to the U.S. that he cannot uphold him; but at the same time he wishes us to be quiet. He is willing to do something for us but fears to mortify the Commodore and yet he begins to find that something must be done.

According to Godon, all the naval captains at Washington were on the side of the aggrieved lieutenants, but were afraid that if Hull were disciplined, the authority of captains would be weakened. He also wrote that several members of Congress had offered to bring the subject up there, but the lieutenants had so far declined the offer, since "the Secretary desired that we should allow the subject to remain in his hand entirely for the present."[48]

By 24 June, Paulding had made his decision. He ordered Pendergrast, DuPont, Missroon, and Godon back to the Mediterranean, instructing Hull that "there are no specific acts or definite charges exhibited in the documents transmitted to the Department, and no official misconduct alleged against the wardroom officers of the Ohio generally, that would authorize or justify the censure which the Department passed on these gentlemen in the letter of the 16th December, 1839."[49] Hull was required to reinstate the lieutenants and to have this letter read as publicly as the letter of 16 December had been. Word of this decision spread quickly up and down the seaboard. James Fenimore Cooper wrote to William B. Shubrick: "Old Hull has got himself in a scrape. Those women of his are—but you know them better than I do."[50] Mad Jack Percival commiserated his friend: "I regret you should have ordered them home, more particularly after they made the disclaimer of never having intended to treat you with disrespect, unless you had authority from the Dept. to do so. It will be placing you very unpleasantly."[51]

Years later, in 1856, Paulding attempted to justify his action, and in doing so revealed the allegations the lieutenants had made in their conversations with him. In a letter to Senator John M. Clayton he wrote:

> The circumstances attending the case of Captain DuPont and his brother officers occasioned me more painful perplexity than anything that occurred during my administration of the Navy Department. But a thorough examination of the whole case, convinced me that all the difficulties came from my having injudiciously permitted Mrs. Hull to accompany the Commodore merely in his voyage to Italy, which permission she made use of to take up her abode in the Ohio during the whole cruise, and in fact to assume the command of the ship. In short, I became satisfied I had been misled, and thought it better to retrieve an error than perish in a wrong.

A week later he became alarmed at the prospect of Clayton's publishing his letter and begged him to keep it private:

> The vindication of his officers carries with it almost inevitably a reflexion on honest brave old Commodore Hull, and I should think I was robbing my country by detracting in any way from the merits of a man who perhaps did more to influence the destinies of this republic than any other since the advent of Washington. . . . I beseech you, Sir, not to touch a hair of his head if you can help it.[52]

Clayton ignored the request, and the allegations were printed in the public record. That Ann Hull played a greater role on board the *Ohio* than was customary for the commodore's wife is probably true. Her husband's deafness and increasingly serious illness during the cruise made him depend heavily on her and on John Etheridge in drafting correspondence and in conducting daily intercourse with his subordinates. That she shared his distaste for his unruly lieutenants is undoubted, especially as they had attacked her in the newspapers. On the other side, the lieutenants' attitude toward her was never uncolored by their expectation that getting her out of the ship would get them off the orlop deck.

The first news of Paulding's action reached Hull at Trieste on 27 August. He could hardly believe it and attempted to put the implications out of his mind:

> A state of happiness and harmony exists [in the *Ohio*] which assures me that in any case in which the united efforts of all on board might be required, such results would be produced as our country would expect. . . . There is, however, I have noticed, an announcement in a Paris paper of the arrival of Lieutenant G. S. Pendergrast & S. W. Godon at Havre, the former as bearer of dispatches to our Legation at Paris, & hence a probability that those officers and perhaps others of the discontented, who were detached from the squadron in the Mediterranean by my order of the 31st March last, may have been directed to rejoin the Ohio. Perhaps I ought not to anticipate the circumstances under which those officers are ordered back to my command (I trust not with an express or implied censure to myself or the course which I have pursued towards them). But I feel that I may call upon the Department for that support which has been so liberally promised and which I ought not to doubt will be readily yielded, and as some months will elapse before this ship will return to Mahon and perhaps before those officers will report for duty, I ask of the Department the discretionary power to dispose of them in the squadron in such way as will separate them from this ship, and in such a way as I may deem will best conduce to the good of the service.[53]

Neither party was ready to compromise. Pendergrast, Godon, and Missroon, rather than taking the first steamer to Mahon, spent the summer months in Italy, half assured that they were trying to get to the *Ohio* faster in that way, because they had heard reports that Hull might bring her to La Spezia for quarantine. At the same time, they were suspicious that Hull was keeping his flagship in the Levant just to avoid them. Hull, for his part, when he returned to Mahon in the early days of November, was crushed by the secretary's letter of 24 June and irritated at not finding the lieutenants there. When they finally appeared on 18 November, he angrily demanded of them a detailed account of their travels and an explanation of why they had not gone directly to Mahon. He forwarded these to the Navy Department with a despairing lament, referring bitterly to his lacerated feelings, his shattered hopes of "restoring the discipline of the Navy by honestly carrying out the views of the Department,"—an ironic reference to Paulding's letter of December 1838—and admitting to "the complete overthrow and frustration of all my hopes."[54]

Lieutenant Godon had barely touched ground at Mahon before he was ordered to rejoin the *Cyane*. She had recently returned from a summer in the Levant, where she was present at the bombardment of Beirut by the British, French, and Turkish forces allied against Mehemet Ali, pasha of Egypt. Latimer had evacuated the American missionaries and consular families from Beirut to Cyprus. When Godon rejoined the *Cyane*, she was under sail again for Toulon. By this time Commander Latimer had quarreled with two first lieutenants, so that Godon found himself executive officer. Latimer was even more astounded than Hull that the officers had been ordered back. According to Godon, "when he heard it he exclaimed, 'well I suppose they have been severely reprimanded.' He could not believe the contrary."[55] Godon was certain that Hull would not allow him to remain executive officer of the *Cyane*, but he was mistaken. Hull had given up. As soon as the *Cyane* returned to Mahon, he had Captain Lavallette assemble the *Ohio*'s original lieutenants again and read aloud the letter of 24 June. He then sent Paulding a long letter, casting in the secretary's teeth all his own censures of the officers, threats to remove them from the squadron, and pledges of support for Hull. The style of the letter suggests that it was drafted by Ann Hull. It concluded:

> That any immediate evil will come to the Navy generally, or to my immediate command, remains to be seen, but I must say I much fear that my reputation and authority as a commander of a foreign squadron have received a shock from which they will not speedily recover.
> It is somewhat remarkable that this station, the Mediterranean, was the scene of my early services in our then infant Navy; I witnessed its rise, its progress and its advancement, bound myself to it, and hoped its course would ever be onward. And that now, it is the scene of my last services and I am here, I fear, to be a witness, of its fall, retrogradation and ruin, but my hopes and wishes are, to live long enough to see harmony and union, discipline and subordination, restored among its officers.[56]

Circumstances suggest that it was at about this time that Hull suffered a stroke, or "attack of apoplexy," that incapacitated him for the remainder of the winter months. He remained at his house in Mahon, sad and withdrawn, attended by his wife and secretary, until the spring of 1841.

The *Cyane* left the Mediterranean on 13 December 1840. Latimer and Godon managed to tolerate each other on the voyage homeward, partly at least because Latimer already faced charges, brought by the *Cyane's* surgeon, for having at various times beaten and kicked members of the crew.[57] But Latimer was only biding his time; as soon as the *Cyane* reached the United States he brought charges against Godon for insubordination and neglect of duty. In May a court-martial at Norfolk tried nearly every officer of the *Cyane*, from the captain down. Meanwhile, a rash of quarrels broke out in the *Brandywine*. Captain William C. Bolton had sent his first lieutenant, John Kelly, home the previous spring after a trivial quarrel. Now there was a row between Surgeon James M. Greene and First Lieutenant Richard S. Pinckney that led to Greene's being tried and sent on shore and Pinckney's being detached to await trial. Among the original charges Greene laid against Pinckney was having talked of Hull's taking a watch for passage in the *Constitution*, but Hull told him flatly that he was not going to allow that to be hashed over in another public trial, so Greene revised his charges, emphasizing drunkenness and oppression. There were also charges, trial, and countercharges between Passed Midshipman John B. Randolph of the *Brandywine* and Purser Grenville C. Cooper. Randolph was sentenced by a court-martial to two years' suspension, but Cooper was not tried. On 18 February, Hull got the last word in the orlop controversy by having Captain Lavallette read to the lieutenants two more brief letters from the Navy Department, urging him to retain command of the sqaudron and denying any intention to censure him by sending the lieutenants back.[58]

These were among the last letters received from James K. Paulding. News had already reached the Mediterranean that the fall elections of 1840 had returned the Whigs victorious, and a new administration under William Henry Harrison came into office in March 1841. But before anything could be heard from a new secretary of the navy, the Anglo-American crisis again assumed frightening proportions. There were now two points of contention: the Maine boundary and the arrest of a British subject, Alexander McLeod, in New York State in connection with the *Caroline* affair of 1837. In mid-March Hull sent the sloop of war *Preble*, which had replaced the *Cyane*, to Toulon for funds for the summer cruising. She returned on 23 March with a most alarming letter from the United States minister to England, Andrew Stevenson:

> Although I am ignorant of your plans and take it for granted you hear regularly from our government, I yet deem it proper to write and apprize you of the excitement which prevails here, and the fears which many entertain that we

may be *forced into war with Great Britain*. Although in my opinion such will not be the immediate result, it is by no means improbable that this may be the case. . . . I hasten to apprize you of the present state of things to enable you to decide what steps it may be proper to take with our Squadron in the Mediterranean. Would it not be the most judicious course to get nearer home, and within reach of orders from the Department? Unless you have strong reasons for remaining and of which I know nothing, I should think it the safer and more prudent course to return.[59]

There was a second, equally excited letter from John Hare Powel, an American resident at London:

When war is threatened, the Hero of the Constitution is present to the mind of every American. . . . I regret to find that in private, as well as in debate, the most decided tone of hostility prevails through all parties [in Parliament]. . . . Notice the preparations for defence—the violent and warlike report of the committee on foreign relations—the reports and resolutions in the Legislature of Maine—the paragraphs of the Ministerial Journal—the Chronicle, stating that workmen are employed *in relays* by night and by day to force into readiness the steam Frigates for the American coast; read the "report that 10 sail of the line are ordered to assemble at Gibraltar in consequence of the trial of McLeod.". . . You will pardon an American, whose intrusion proceeds from the desire that Hull shall but be prepared for his Enemy, to add lustre to his name and glory to his country.[60]

Hull did not, of course, "hear regularly from [the] government." At the time he did not know who might be the new secretary of the navy or what policy the incoming administration planned to pursue toward England. These cries of alarm from London were, therefore, all the more disturbing. The morning following receipt of these letters, with their accompanying extracts from the English and French papers, Hull called a council of commanders in his cabin. He presented them with three alternative courses of action: to go to Toulon for later news; to sortie from the Mediterranean and try to avoid being blockaded there, while seeking more recent news outside; or to return home. The last Hull did not recommend, and after some discussion it was decided to take the second course, as had been done in the summer of 1839. The three vessels got under way the next morning, leaving the sick, a few officers, and probably the ladies behind. Hull gave the following orders to Bolton for the *Brandywine* and to Commander Ralph Voorhees of the *Preble:*

Circumstances have rendered it necessary to make rather a hasty movement in the squadron under my command; I have therefore to direct that you proceed to sea and make the best of your way out of the Mediterranean; You will endeavour, either by speaking Vessels or by touching at some port, to ascertain the state of affairs between the United States and Great Britain. In case of war,

Isaac Hull, 1841. By Louis Jean-Baptiste Hyacinthe Pellegrin. U.S. National Portrait Gallery, Smithsonian Institution, Washington, D.C.

you will use every exertion to protect yourself and command and to annoy the enemy, cruising as long as your provisions and other circumstances will admit of, and when a favorable opportunity offers you will run into some port of the United States and report to the Secretary of the Navy; much however must be left to your own judgment. Should you ascertain that quietness has been restored, you will return to the Mediterranean, touching at Mahon where you will probably hear from me.[61]

By 1 April the squadron, battling head winds, was off Cape de Gat, and Hull ordered Voorhees to take the *Preble* into Málaga for fresh news. Two nights later the *Brandywine* parted company during a westerly gale. On the sixth the *Preble* was seen standing out of Málaga; she brought letters from Horatio Sprague, the consul at Gibraltar, and French papers with the latest news from America, both of which indicated that war would not be declared immediately, if at all. Immensely relieved, Hull put about for Toulon, sending the *Preble* to Mahon for an overhaul and with orders for the *Brandywine*, on her return to the base, to prepare for a cruise in the Levant. But Bolton never came back. Somehow he had convinced himself that war was inevitable; when he touched at Gibraltar and found no British squadron there, he decided they had all gone to blockade the American coast, and he made straight for home without any further attempt to communicate with Hull. By 9 May, to everyone's surprise, he was at New York.[62]

Of course, Hull had no way of knowing that his frigate had decamped. He had government business to transact at Marseilles: orders to charter a vessel to transport Horatio Greenough's mammoth statue of George Washington from Italy to the United States. The statue was too large to go through the hatches of the *Ohio*, and Hull was glad enough not to have to take it on board anyway. At Marseilles he secured the ship *Sea* for $500 and sent her to Leghorn where, with assistance from the *Preble*, she loaded the huge, toga-clad Washington and carried it home to its anything-but-enthusiastic reception in the United States. While the *Ohio* was at Toulon, Hull also had his own portrait done by Louis Pellegrin. This final likeness, a quick sketch, shows a once corpulent man now apparently emaciated by illness. The mouth no longer laughs, as in the Stuart portrait, but the eyes are as determined as ever, and the wavy hair, though gray, has not lost its spring.[63]

On 4 May news reached Toulon of the death of President William Henry Harrison. This event, which would inevitably throw the government into an uproar, reinforced Hull's determination to return home without waiting for a relief vessel. The *Ohio*'s crew were already discontented; thinking they were bound home when the squadron left Mahon, they had raised an outcry when the flagship put about for Toulon, and Hull had addressed them, promising to sail for America in June or July. They trusted him to keep his word. As "F. P. Torrey" wrote, "The man who says that Commodore Hull is not a good friend to his ship's company, and one who does all in his power to promote their comfort, is a liar and the truth is not in him."[64]

The *Ohio* left Toulon on 8 May and reached Mahon the following afternoon. Hull proudly forwarded to the Navy Department a paragraph from the Toulon paper, comparing his ship most favorably with the vessels of the mighty French squadron:

> The American vessel the Ohio . . . is a true type of order and cleanliness in a vessel of war. She has no guns in mahogany cases with large pullies well varnished and polished placed upon pins in front of the poop, but her batteries are ready for action from stem to stern, and their gear is substantial and well painted. Artisans in visiting her will perceive, without doubt, that she is far superior to the neatest vessel in our squadron.[65]

However, during the war scare Hull had expressed his regret that his vessel was not equipped with the explosive Paixan shot available to the British and French captains. He was not one of those antiprogressives like John Rodgers and James K. Paulding who had retarded the navy's technological development. When it came to fighting, he wanted the best he could get.

On 29 May the *Ohio* was towed out of Mahon harbor and set her course homeward to the band's rendition of "Home, Sweet Home," which, with "Hail Columbia!" formed the principal items in its repertoire. No one was happier to see the end of the cruise than Isaac Hull. His health, bad to begin with, had been further undermined by the stresses of the past three years. On 23 May he had suffered another mild stroke, and his chronic cough persisted. The *Ohio,* after calling at Málaga and Gibraltar, made a quick passage of thirty-one days to Boston, taking time on the Grand Banks for Hull and his men to indulge in his favorite sport, fishing. She anchored in President Roads on 17 July. Ten days later Commodore Hull's broad pendant was struck, and the old sailor went on shore for the last time. "F. P. Torrey" concluded his book with an encomium to his commander, now known generally in the navy as "the old Commodore":

> I cannot in justice, close this small volume, without noticing the warm feeling and manner every man of the Ohio's crew speaks in favor of Commodore Hull; never was a ship's company more devoted to their commander. . . . [E]very man of his crew honor and admire him, for his love of justice and clemency, and a devotion he always manifested in behalf of their happiness and welfare.[66]

16

Haven

From July 1841 to February 1843 Isaac Hull spent much of his time in a vain search to recover his health, so badly undermined by the three years in the Mediterranean. He tarried a few weeks at Boston, where his nephew Joseph was now attached to the receiving ship *Columbus*. Joseph, having settled his mother and sisters at last, had realized his heart's desire in July 1839 by marrying Ann Hull's younger sister, Amelia Hart, and by the time the *Ohio* returned to Boston, Amelia was pregnant. Fortunately for the growing family, Joseph was promoted to commander in September. Isaac and Ann spent the late summer at New Haven, then moved to the Carlton House, New York, where Hull was to testify at the court of inquiry into Captain Bolton's conduct in leaving the Mediterranean without orders. Bolton had tried to ingratiate himself with Hull on the latter's return by drawing an analogy between his action in sailing without orders and Hull's similar course in 1812:

> In my route homeward I sought information, but procured none, nor did I know until we made Long Island that war did not exist. Suppose it had? Then I would have been called a most admirable officer, for coming so promptly to the country's succour: and might, by chance, have been the first to bring a frigate into the contest.[1]

Isaac Hull, on his part, cared nothing about the affair so long as his integrity was not impugned. What did upset him was Bolton's publication in the newspapers of Andrew Stevenson's and John Hare Powel's letters as part of his justification. These letters had raised a hornet's nest in Congress, and John Quincy Adams was using the whole incident as a stick with which to beat the Democrats for their undue bellicosity. Hull, having visited Washington in the fall, before the trial, was as repelled as ever by political goings-on, and especially by the chaos of the Tyler administration. He confined himself, however, to remarking that "all is dull as death at Washington."[2]

Bolton's court of inquiry decided that he ought to be tried by a court-martial, but by this time the Hulls had established winter quarters at New Haven, and Hull persuaded the Navy Department to let him answer any further questions by deposition. He presented a letter from Fleet Surgeon Thomas Williamson to show that his "severe pulmonary affection . . . and the two premonitory attacks of apoplexy" required medical care, abstemious diet, and above all, peace and quiet.[3] As it turned out, Bolton was convicted by court-martial of disobedience of Hull's orders, but because of the circumstances he was given only a mild reprimand.

The courts-martial of the *Cyane*'s officers had taken a different and surprising turn. The court, sitting at Norfolk, had given Latimer a mild rebuke and a suspension that the president reduced to one year, but it had cashiered some of the junior officers and sentenced Sylvanus Godon to two years' suspension. Godon, of course, was not one to take this lying down. "It appears," he wrote to William Short, "that the Court has *dared* to suspend me for two years." He went immediately to Washington, where he met Pendergrast and other friends, and they opened their combined artillery on Secretary of the Navy Abel P. Upshur, who proved even more pliant than Paulding had been. The result was that the court's sentences on every one of the junior officers were overturned, and Latimer was ordered for trial on new charges.[4] Whereas Upshur had assured Latimer, immediately after his first trial, that the sentence would in no way impede his promotion, he was passed over for advancement to captain in 1842. Hull kept clear of all this, except to send two letters to the Navy Department in testimony to Latimer's character and competence. But he was so disgusted by the whole business that he thought very seriously of resigning from the navy, even of quitting the United States for good. He mentioned this plan to the Navy Department and to friends in the service, but they dissuaded him. His former lieutenant, John B. Nicolson, wrote him that life in Europe was no cheaper than in the United States, and besides, America was his home.

> I hope you may ultimately determine to continue among your countrymen and friends, where your worth is known and appreciated, rather than abandon your country to live among people whose language you are not familiar with, as I feel confident you will find a great difference as Com. Hull with a command, and as Ex. Comd. Hull a plain citizen of the U.S.
>
> I confess, my dear Comd., that I am too proud of you, as among our most distinguished officers to lose you from among us. You belong to your country, and I know you love our institutions; then, why should you after your many years of services leave your country and your connexion among your Navy friends, where your experience may be required by them to give stability to our service.[5]

Another friend, Gilbert Davis of New York, wrote after a visit to Washington that Commodores William M. Crane and Lewis Warrington had inquired about him, as had Commodore Edmund P. Kennedy, "the man that eats all kinds of animals. I asked him how the monkey tasted. He replied, 'the same flavour as a cat.'"

> [N]o man in my travels but what speak well of the *Old Commodore;* most men in this *homely* or good feeling of soul *reply* when your name is mentioned "well, the Old Commodore is at the top of the heap; he is a devilish fine old man. I wish we had more such men in the Navy; then we should have but little trouble." I hope you will by spring come out like a second edition of a good old work, *as good as new.*[6]

Charles Bradbury, Hull's business agent at Boston, was also distressed at the old man's low spirits. He had a hard time convincing Hull that his business concerns were doing well and that, as he told him, "you have nothing to give you uneasiness, as your income is ample to meet all your reasonable wishes."[7]

Hull must have felt like the last leaf on the tree. All his old friends were gone. Isaac Chauncey and Daniel Todd Patterson had died while he was in the Mediterranean; David Porter was dying in faraway Constantinople. Of the eight captains who had ranked him in 1812, only two were left: James Barron and Charles Stewart. Neither had ever been his particular friend. Hull's gregarious heart felt the loneliness keenly. Then, in December 1841, tragedy struck within the household. Augusta, the little sister-daughter, fell suddenly ill at New Haven. Isaac sent to New York for a doctor and urged Joseph to keep the news from Amelia, who was nearing her confinement. But in a few days Augusta was dead.[8]

This shock, and the protracted illness of Ann's father at Saybrook, removed any thoughts of moving to Europe. Although confined to the house throughout the winter, Isaac was in slightly better spirits by early February when he congratulated Joseph and Amelia on the birth of their daughter: "we should be happy to get a letter from the young lady."[9] He was more resigned than happy, though, and expressed the state of his thoughts most fully in a letter to John Etheridge, who was now employed in the fourth auditor's office at Washington:

> you know so well my feelings as relates to the Navy and my anxiety for its being restored to what it was, and at any rate to prevent its going still lower. . . . [F]rom the state of my health and the trouble and vexation I have had together with the affliction we have had if you should find me at times a little *nervous* you must let it pass. . . . [Y]ou see how I have been annoyed on all sides, and have had all sorts of troubles, but now I am determined to let all pass and take things as they come for I do not feel that I have long to remain and my wants will be few.

After inquiring about Etheridge's own prospects and urging him to keep up his spirits, he concluded: "I do not get letters from anyone that interests me. Our country is indeed in a dreadful state. What will be done, God only knows."[10]

The Hulls remained at New Haven past the middle of June 1842. They then visited Saybrook, where Hull caught a cold that gave him another setback, then traveled to New York, intending to go from there to Boston and then on to Washington. Hull wrote Etheridge from New York that

> for several days my health and spirits were below par like everything else in our beloved country. . . . My stay in Washington will be short, not more than a day or two, for there is not many people or things that I care about seeing and if I were to look for friends I should not know on what side I should find them. All appears in confusion, and in that confusion they have set country, patriotism and honour aside for party purposes, and happy I am that I can pass by.

There was a tidbit of gossip from the Mediterranean: the young daughter of Consul Rich at Mahon had married the squadron commander, Charles W. Morgan. Hull did not think much of the match: "It does appear to me that the world is mad or some way deranged. Poor little girl, she will wish herself back. Bad as was her situation, I feel much for her. But all does no good. The Mediterranean station is indeed in a very bad state, and we shall be fortunate if we do not get into trouble, if some person is not sent out that knows how to act and sense to act with."[11]

After the brief Washington visit the Hulls spent August at Saratoga and Sharon Springs in New York. From the latter place they made an excursion to Lake Otsego, where they met James Fenimore Cooper. Hull was just finishing the first volume of Cooper's latest naval novel, *The Two Admirals*, and the novelist seized the chance to check up a piece of nautical usage that had been disputed by William B. Shubrick:

> I told him of your criticism, about "bowsing *up* his jib," and asked him how it ought to be, "bowse *up*," or bowse *out*." "We say both, " was his answer, "but they mean different things. Bowse *out* the real jib, on the traveller, is right; but, we say bowse *up* when a fellow is *drunk*." There's nicety for you, and I hope you'll give in. Do you think a drunken man is expected to be right? Even Madam said *she* knew better. I blush for you, since I feel certain you are too lazy to do it for yourself.[12]

From the springs the couple returned to the Carlton House in New York city about 10 September. They had decided to spend the winter in Philadelphia, and perhaps to reside there permanently. Hull wrote in advance to George Harrison: "if I can get a house to please us, I think I shall establish myself there as a quiet Quaker inhabitant. . . . I thought one of the Girard houses (if the rent be not too great) would suit us— for my wife says she will not 'live anywhere but in Chestnut Street.'"[13] By 1 October they were established at the Jones Hotel in Philadelphia, from which Hull wrote to the secretary of the navy declining his offer of the command afloat at Boston. "I have a bad cough of long standing," he explained, "that is greatly increased by the climate of the east."[14] Later in the month he visited Washington, where the smaller of his long-standing claims arising out of his service at the navy yard there had at last been approved by Congress. He secured a leave of absence for another twelve months and returned to Philadelphia, where he and Ann had furnished a house at 5 Portico Square, the first house, other than navy yard residences, they had ever had. Purchases of furniture alone amounted to more than $2,000, but Hull by this time was so sure that he did not have long to live that he was resigned to a measure of extravagance. He had given up hope of making his Charlestown investments productive; they had yielded nothing for the past two years. But there had been a financial debacle at Charlestown in which others were much greater losers than he: the failure of Wyman's Bank.

> It is indeed a blow up and not a timber head of it can be found. Poor *Percival* has lost his all. He is "in" for fifteen thousand. . . . I shall lose about three hundred. My concerns are all in a bad way there. . . . Percival writes that Wyman is the damnedest rascal on earth. It is indeed a hard case for him.[15]

Early in December, Hull caught another bad cold that confined him to his room for most of the month. Just before Christmas he was well enough to write to Etheridge that he had been more or less in pain through the entire ordeal and under the daily care of two naval surgeons, Thomas Harris and C. W. Ruschenberger.[16] Gilbert Davis was urging him to get well: "We want all the old war commanders made admirals, before we lose them."[17]

But of the war commanders, only Charles Stewart would live to wear an admiral's stars. Isaac Hull was in his last illness. On 3 February 1843 he made his will, leaving his estate to his wife and, after her death, to be divided between Mary Wheeler Hull and her daughters and his wife's sisters Jeannette and Amelia. Ten days later, at five in the morning of Monday, 13 February, he died quietly at his home, "without a groan or struggle," sensible and lucid to the last.[18] His friends and naval brethren gave him a large public funeral, and his body was laid temporarily in a vault belonging to Horace Binney. In May, in accordance with his instructions, it was buried at Laurel Hill Cemetery, high above the Schuylkill River. The sailor was home from the sea at last.

The long life that closed so quietly had been a naval life through and through. Isaac Hull first trod a frigate's deck at the age of twenty-five, but for at least ten years before that he had been preparing himself, as if consciously, for an officer's career. Thereafter, his whole identification was with the navy: in a service of forty-five years he was off duty but three. His business ventures were merely supplementary and were always handled through agents. Isaac Hull's time and attention belonged to one thing only: the building up of the navy.

The navy, in his eyes, existed to defend his country's rights and honor, not to embellish the reputations of its officers. He was proud of his achievements, especially the conquest of the *Guerrière*, yet they were darkened by their bloody price. No one rejoiced more than he at the conclusion of peace, and he always hoped to see the United States behave internationally in such a way as to keep clear of war, so long as that could be done with honor. Hull was equally pacific in his personal relations. Though his profession was arms, aggression was a trait totally lacking in his character. But, as history would have it, he is best remembered for a single hour at war.

Some of his later subordinates attributed Hull's success to luck. That was not the case. He knew from the outset that he had only his own abilities to carry him forward, for his family influence was tenuous at best and his fortune nonexistent. He had a talent for ship handling, a good head for organization, and a love for people—even the rough sailors whose life he had tasted as a boy. If he was, at least sometimes, in the right place at the right time, it was because he had prepared the way.

Hull's pleasures were nautical: sailing and fishing. His speech was so salted with nautical metaphor that he could not even take a wife without comparing her to a ship. He thus came, by the end of his life, to symbolize what seemed a simpler era—a time when one's life was all of a piece. The quarrel with his juniors in the *Ohio* was symptomatic of the change, for they regarded the navy as their career: for him, it was his whole existence. This air of old-fashioned simplicity made Isaac Hull a monument while he was still alive. It is clear from his late correspondence that he had an uncomfortable sense of the fact. For he was no monument, but a man—a man with faults and follies—but also a man of courage, generosity, goodwill, and a kind of innocence. So let him be remembered.

Notes

Abbreviations Used in the Notes

Adams MSS	Adams Papers, MassHS. Used with permission of the editors of *The Papers of John Adams.*
AHA	American Historical Association.
ASP	*American State Papers: Documents Legislative and Executive, 1789–1838.* 38 vols. (Washington, D.C., 1832–61).
Barbary Wars	U.S. Office of Naval Records and Library. *Naval Documents Related to the United States Wars with the Barbary Powers.* 6 vols. (Washington, D.C., 1939–44).
BWC Papers	Benjamin W. Crowninshield Papers, Peabody Museum of Salem, Massachusetts.
CL	Captains' Letters, NA, RG 45. Letters Received by the Secretary of the Navy from Captains.
Comm. LB	NA, RG 45. Letters Sent by the Secretary of the Navy to Commandants of Navy Yards and Navy Agents.
ConnHS	Connecticut Historical Society, Hartford.
Elliot Coll.	Isaac Hull Papers, Collection of Mrs. Roger C. Elliot, *USS Constitution* Museum, Boston, Massachusetts.
FDR Lib.	Franklin D. Roosevelt Library, Hyde Park, New York.
General LB	Miscellaneous Letters Sent by the Secretary of the Navy.
HSPa	Historical Society of Pennsylvania.
LC	U.S. Library of Congress.
MassHS	Massachusetts Historical Society, Boston.
MeHS	Maine Historical Society, Portland.
NA	U.S. National Archives.
NCLB	Navy Commissioners' Letterbook.
NYHS	New-York Historical Society, New York City.
OL	NA, RG 45. Letters received by the Secretary of the Navy from Officers.
OSW	NA, RG 45. Letters Sent by the Secretary of the Navy to Officers, Ships of War.
Quasi-War	U.S. Office of Naval Records and Library. *Naval Documents Related to the Quasi-War between the United States and France.* 7 vols. (Washington, D.C., 1935–38).
RG	Record Group.
Talbot MSS	Papers of Silas Talbot, Mystic Seaport, Connecticut.
TennHS	Tennessee Historical Society, Nashville.
WLCL	William L. Clements Library, University of Michigan, Ann Arbor.

Introduction

1. LC, Short Family Papers: Sylvanus Godon to William Short, 17 Nov. 1841.

Chapter 1

1. There has been only one full-length biography of Isaac Hull: Bruce Grant, *Isaac Hull, Captain of Old Ironsides* (New York, 1947). A brief and partly accurate sketch appeared in Fletcher Pratt, *Preble's Boys* (New York, 1950). Leo T. Molloy has compiled *Commodore Isaac Hull, U.S.N., His Life and Times* (Derby, Conn., 1964), which is not so much a life of Hull as a collection of interesting lore relating to the Derby locality and its notable personalities.

Documentary materials on Hull's life are like the proverbial feathers from the pillow opened on top of a windy hill: they are to be found in virtually every major research library from coast to coast, and many are in private collections. Two sizable groups of manuscripts of particular value for Hull's early life as well as for later periods are the family collection, whose use was opened to me by the late Haviland Hull Platt, and a large group of papers, mainly personal and business records, in the Boston Athenaeum. The Platt collection of papers and memorabilia was deposited by H. H. Platt's daughter, Pamela Elliot, in the USS *Constitution* Museum in 1982. A selection of the Athenaeum collection was published by Gardner W. Allen, *Papers of Isaac Hull* (Boston, 1929). Another important group of Hull manuscripts is in the New-York Historical Society, whose collections on the Rodgers family are also a valuable source of Hull material. Items from these three collections are used by permission, respectively, of Mrs. Roger C. Elliot, the Trustees of the Boston Athenaeum, and the New-York Historical Society, New York City.

Near the end of his life Hull wished to have his biography written by Dr. Thomas Harris, who had done a like service for William Bainbridge. With that in view, he prepared a series of memoranda on his early life, which are in the Elliot Collection. Written fifty years or more after the events described, these documents might be suspect, but in all major respects they correspond closely to the available contemporary evidence. I have therefore relied on the memoranda as a supplement to other documentary sources.

For date and place of Hull's birth see NA, Navy Department Records, ZB File, Leo T. Molloy to Captain F. K. Loomis, and also Molloy's *Commodore Isaac Hull*, pp. 4–5, 18, 23. Bruce Grant did thorough research on this point; he reviews the whole controversy in *Captain of Old Ironsides*, pp. 7, 363–364. Grant suggests that after Hull's marriage to a much younger woman he deliberately tried to lower his age, but it seems that Hull was genuinely uncertain when he was born. Five years after his marriage he wrote to his stepsister: "Mary, when you write me again will you take from the Good Book the year in which I was born. I am not sure how old I am" (Elliot Coll.: Hull to Mary Wheeler Hull, 8 Sept. 1818). In that year the Navy Department was attempting to establish a record of the ages of all officers.

For the four Joseph Hulls see Charles J. Hoadly, ed., *Public Records of the Colony of Connecticut*, 15 vols. (Hartford, 1890; reprint, New York, 1968), vols. 10–15.

Notes to Pages 3–8

2. Puella F. H. Mason, *A Record of the Descendants of Richard Hull* (Milwaukee, 1894), p. 32; also Grant, *Captain of Old Ironsides*, pp. 364–365. The seven Hull sons were: Joseph, 1771–1810, m. Susan Bartone (or Bartine), 1800; Isaac, 1773–1843, m. Ann McCurdy Hart, 1813; Levi, 1775–1848, m. Mary Wheeler, 1811; William, 1781–1812; Daniel, 1784–1817; Henry, 1788–1833; and Charles, 1792–1829, m. Lavinia Mann.

Their mother, Sarah, was the daughter of Deacon Daniel Bennett and Elizabeth Bennett of Huntington Landing. She was born about 1751 and died in 1803. Joseph Hull subsequently married Lucy Smith Wheeler, widow of Joseph Wheeler and the mother of Mary Wheeler, and (in 1821) widow Freelove Nichols. Joseph died in 1826.

3. Mason, *Descendants of Richard Hull*, p. 22; Grant, *Captain of Old Ironsides*, pp. 365–366; Elliot Coll.: Memorandum in Mrs. Hull's handwriting; NA, M247, Roll 28, Item 19, vol. 5, p. 87: Jonathan Trumbull to Secretary of War, 8 Feb. 1784.

4. Elliot Coll.: Memoranda; Mason, *Descendants of Richard Hull*, p. 23; Louis F. Middlebrook, *History of Maritime Connecticut during the American Revolution* (Salem, Mass., 1925), 2: 212.

5. Mason, *Descendants of Richard Hull*, p. 23.

6. Mason, *Descendants of Richard Hull*, p. 32; Harvard University, Houghton Library: Samuel C. Clarke, MS "Recollections of Isaac Hull." Mrs. Clarke must have got the stories from her parents, for she herself was born in 1790.

7. Elliot Coll.: Hull memorandum, and Isaac Hull to Joseph Hull, 25 Oct. 1791.

8. Elliot Coll.: Hull memoranda; NA, RG 36, New Haven Registers, Enrollments and Licenses, Issued and Surrendered, 1785–1791; List of Foreigners Outwards, 1787–1790, and List of Foreigners Inwards, 1787–1790; *Connecticut Journal* (New Haven), 13 Aug. 1788; see also George Coggeshall, *Second Series of Voyages to Various Parts of the World, made between the years 1802 and 1841* (New York, 1852), pp. 17–19, for comparable accounts of this Connecticut trade with the West Indies.

9. Elliot Coll.: Hull memoranda, and Isaac Hull to Joseph Hull, 9 Nov. 1791; *Columbian Centinel* (Boston), 5 Oct. 1791.

10. Elliot Coll.: Isaac Hull to Joseph Hull, 8, 25 Oct., 9 Nov. 1791.

11. Elliot Coll.: Hull memoranda; LC: George H. Stuart Coll., receipt, 10 Mar. 1792.

12. NA, RG 36, Newport, Rhode Island, Record of Sea Letters Received and Issued, 1793–1796; Abstract of Temporary Registers Issued and Surrendered in the District of Newport, 1 Jan.–31 Mar. 1794, Register No. 11; Manifest of *Liffey*, 12 Mar. 1794; Oaths Taken by Owners and Masters of Vessels, Prior to Registry, 1794: oaths of Thomas English and Isaac Hull; NA, RG 36, Boston, Registers, No. 328; Elliot Coll.: Hull memoranda.

13. NA, RG 36, New London, Registers, No. 324; WPA Survey of Federal Archives, Ship Registers and Enrollments of Boston and Charlestown, vol. 1 (1789–1795), p. 140; Boston, Registers, No. 883, Daily Record of Clearances, No. 9 (24 Jan.–26 Nov. 1795); *Connecticut Gazette* (New London), 15 Oct. 1795.

14. NA, RG 36, Boston Registers, No. 1100; New London Registers, No. 324, No. 386, No. 402.

15. NA, RG 36, New London Registers, No. 386, No. 402; Manifest of *Minerva*, 21 Nov. 1796; *Connecticut Gazette*, 9 Feb. 1797.

16. Gardner W. Allen, *Our Naval War with France* (Boston, 1909), pp. 32–35.

17. NA, RG 36, New London, Manifest of *Minerva*, 13 Apr. 1797; Inspection Certificate of *Minerva*, 24 Mar. 1797; *Connecticut Gazette*, 21 June 1797; NA, RG 123, U.S. Court of Claims, French Spoliation Case No. 3267, *Minerva*, including insurance records, depositions of Benjamin Paine, Benjamin Ames, Hezekiah Kelley, and Isaac Hull, as well as extracts from a report of Victor Hugues.

18. Court of Claims, Case No. 3267; NA, RG 36, New London Registers, No. 411; Manifest of *Beaver*, 4 July 1797; Certificate of Inspection, 24 June 1797; *Connecticut Gazette*, 15 Nov. 1797.

19. *Quasi-War* 1: 21, Pickering to Samuel Sewall, 27 Dec. 1797, and 1: 113, Pickering to Josiah Parker, 13 June 1798; *Columbian Centinel*, 8 Nov. 1797.

20. NA, RG 36, New London Registers, No. 27, No. 439; Manifest of *Favorite*, 8 Feb. 1798; Certificate of Inspection, 9 Feb. 1798.

21. Elliot Coll.: Hull memoranda; *Connecticut Journal* (New Haven), 13 June 1798.

22. Elliot Coll.: Hull memoranda, and James McHenry to Isaac Hull, 13 Mar. 1798; NA, RG 36, New London Registers, No. 439.

Chapter 2

1. *Quasi-War* 1: 7–9.

2. Adams MSS, Reel 386, Undated memorandum in McHenry's hand with additions by Adams. Hull may have enlisted Federalist influence also, in the person of David Humphreys, a fellow native of Derby, close friend of George Washington's, and Adams's minister to Spain.

3. NYHS: Hull to Bainbridge, 11 Apr. 1808.

4. Christopher McKee, *Edward Preble: A Naval Biography* (Annapolis, 1972), p. 50; Elliot Coll.: Nicholson to Hull, 17 June 1798; *Quasi-War* 1: 11, Uniform Regulations, 24 Aug. 1797. All the ship's officers were from Massachusetts. Even Hull was listed in McHenry's memorandum as a Massachusetts man, which strengthens the conviction that he owed his appointment to his uncle William.

5. NA, RG 59, Letters of Application and Recommendation during the Administration of John Adams, 1797–1801 (Microcopy no. 406): Benjamin Beale to John Adams, 30 Aug. 1797; Adams MSS, Reel 387: Benjamin Beale to John Adams, 19 Mar. 1798.

6. *Quasi-War* 1: 65.

7. *Quasi-War* 1: 73–74, Nicholson's recruiting ad, 12 May 1798.

8. *Quasi-War* 1: 106–107.

9. *Quasi-War* 1: 111.

10. *Quasi-War* 1: 107.

11. *Quasi-War* 1: 107, 109.

12. AHA *Annual Reports*, 1889– (Washington, 1890–), 1896, 1: 806, Higginson to Pickering, 9 June 1798.

13. WLCL: John Roche, Jr., to John Roche, Sr., 19 June [1798], edited by Christopher McKee, "*Constitution* in the Quasi-War with France: the Letters of John

Roche, Jr., 1798–1801," *American Neptune* 27 (1967), pp. 135–149, at 138. Several years later the heavy long guns on the *Constitution*'s upper deck were replaced by 32-pounder carronades.

14. *Quasi-War* 1: 69.
15. *Quasi-War* 1: 171, Nicholson to [Henry Jackson], 6 July 1798.
16. *Quasi-War* 1: 187, 197–198, Stoddert to Nicholson, 12 July 1798.
17. *Quasi-War* 1: 233, Stoddert to Fletcher, 23 July 1798.
18. *Quasi-War* 1: 236, Pitts journal, 23 July 1798.
19. *Quasi-War* 1: 240, Pitts journal, 24 July 1798.
20. *Quasi-War* 1: 245, Pitts journal, 27 July 1798.
21. *Quasi-War* 1: 295–296, Stoddert to Nicholson, 13 Aug. 1798.
22. *Quasi-War* 1: 370, Pitts journal, 1 Sept. 1798.
23. *Quasi-War* 1: 373, Pitts journal, 3 Sept. 1798.
24. *Quasi-War* 1: 374, Pitts journal, 4 Sept. 1798.
25. *Quasi-War* 1: 377, Pitts journal, 5 Sept. 1798.
26. *Quasi-War* 1: 378, Pitts journal, 6 Sept. 1798.
27. This and following from Pitts journal, passim, and from *Quasi-War* 1: 393–396, Nicholson to Stoddert, 12 Sept. 1798; also from statement of Captain George du Petit-Thouars, 1: 414–417.
28. McKee, ed., "Roche": John Roche, Jr., to John Roche, Sr., 15 Sept. 1798, pp. 139–140.
29. *Quasi-War* 1: 400, Pitts journal, 12 Sept. 1798.
30. *Quasi-War* 1: 449, Stoddert to Adams, 24 Sept. 1798.
31. *Quasi-War* 1: 436, Pitts journal, 21 Sept. 1798, and 1: 454, Pitts journal, 25 Sept. 1798.
32. Adams MSS, Reel 391: Nicholson to Stoddert, 26 Sept. 1798, encl. in Stoddert to Adams, 5 Oct. 1798; *Quasi-War* 1: 555, Pickering to Thos. Nelson, 22 Oct. 1798.
33. *Quasi-War* 1: 493, Stoddert to Nicholson, 5 Oct. 1798. This letter, not received by Nicholson, was recalled and replaced by a milder one, *Quasi-War* 1: 504, Stoddert to Nicholson, 8 Oct. 1798.
34. Adams MSS, Reel 391: Nicholson to Stoddert, 26 Sept. 1798.
35. Pitts journal, passim.
36. Allen, *Our Naval War with France*, p. 71.
37. *Quasi-War* 1: 495, Stoddert to Adams, 5 Oct. 1798.
38. *Quasi-War* 1: 555, Pickering to Nelson, 22 Oct. 1798.
39. Adams MSS, Reel 392: Cyrus Griffin to [John Adams], 10 Nov. 1798. The owners appealed the judgment and were eventually awarded $11,000 damages. See Allen, *Our Naval War with France*, p. 71.
40. This may have concerned the men's pay, which apparently was being partly withheld by the Navy Department on the curious pretext of preventing desertion. See *Quasi-War* 2: 37–38, Stoddert to Higginson, 19 Nov. 1798.
41. *Quasi-War* 2: 47, Pitts journal, 23 Nov. 1798; Talbot MSS: Affidavit of John Hunt, 24 Dec. 1798.
42. *Quasi-War* 2: 61–62, Stoddert to Higginson, 3 Dec. 1798.
43. *Quasi-War* 2: 241, Stoddert to Barry, 16 Jan. 1799.
44. AHA *Annual Report*, 1896, pp. 816–817: Higginson to Pickering, 1 Jan. 1799.

45. *Quasi-War* 2: 202, Pitts journal, 2, 12 Jan. 1799. The appointment of a warrant officer to act as lieutenant was unusual.

46. *Quasi-War* 2: 247, Pitts journal, 16 Jan. 1799; McKee, "Roche": Roche, Jr., to Roche, Sr., 16 Mar. 1799, pp. 142–143; Allen, *Our Naval War with France*, p. 105.

47. *Quasi-War* 2: 253, Pitts journal, 17 Jan. 1799.

48. *Quasi-War* 2: 447, Circular Instructions to the Captains and Commanders of Vessels in the Service of the United States, 12 Mar. 1799.

49. *Quasi-War* 2: 419, Pitts journal, 2–3 Mar. 1799.

50. James Fenimore Cooper, "Old Ironsides," *Putnam's Monthly* 1 (1853), pp. 473–487, 593–607.

51. *Quasi-War* 2: 467–468, Stoddert to Barry, 15 Mar. 1799; *Quasi-War* 2: 473–475, Barry to Stoddert, 16 Mar. 1799.

52. *Quasi-War* 2: 519–520, Stoddert to Higginson, 26 Mar. 1799.

53. *Quasi-War* 2: 523, Pitts journal, 27 Mar. 1799; *Quasi-War* 3: 32, *Constitution* log, 8 Apr. 1799.

54. Pitts journal, *passim*.

55. HSPa, Carey Papers, Gardner Coll.: Nicholson to Barry, 16 May 1799.

56. *Quasi-War* 3: 667, Stoddert to Adams, 19 Apr. 1799.

57. Adams MSS, Reel 119: Adams to Stoddert, 27 Apr. 1799.

Chapter 3

1. For letters concerning this controversy see, among others, *Quasi-War* 1: 510, 542; 2: 249, 313, 315; 3: 132, 157, 158, 340, 400, 401, 463, 474, 475, 479, 490–492, 495, 528–532, 542, 567, 568. Truxtun eventually resigned in March 1802 because as commodore of the Mediterranean squadron he was not permitted a flag captain for his ship.

2. Talbot MSS: Midshipmen of the *Constitution* to Stoddert, 21 May 1799.

3. *Quasi-War* 3: 274, Stoddert to Talbot, 29 May 1799. Original in Talbot MSS.

4. *Quasi-War* 3: 350, Stoddert to Adams, 17 June 1799.

5. *Quasi-War* 3: 350, Stoddert to Talbot, 17 June 1799.

6. Adams MSS, Reel 119: Adams to Stoddert, 28 June 1799; Reel 393: Chas. Adams to John Adams, 19 Feb. 1799.

7. *Quasi-War* 3: 317–318, 359, Stoddert to C. Talbot, 8, 18 June 1799; Talbot MSS: Stoddert to Silas Talbot, 18 June 1799.

8. *Quasi-War* 3: 369, Stoddert to Higginson, 19 June 1799.

9. Adams MSS, Reel 119: Adams to Stoddert, 8 July 1799. Talbot's letter of 7 June is not extant.

10. *Quasi-War* 3: 349–350, Stoddert to Adams, 17 June 1799.

11. Adams MSS, Reel 395: Talbot to Adams, 3 June 1799.

12. *Quasi-War* 3: 438–439, *Constitution* Muster Roll, 22 Sept. 1798–July 1799.

13. *Quasi-War* 3: 412–420, Cordis Court Martial, 27 June 1799, *passim*; 4: 198–199, Stoddert to Cordis, 17 Sept. 1799; Adams MSS, Reel 119: Adams to Stoddert, 8 July 1799.

14. NYHS: Nicholson to Hull, 21, 27 May 1799; U.S. Naval Academy Mu-

seum: Nicholson to Hull, 22 May 1799; reference to "humoring the Johns" from *Quasi-War* 1: 50, Truxtun to John Rodgers, Apr. 1798. Cf. Nathaniel Haraden's Journal of the frigate *Constitution*, 6 Dec. 1798–20 Oct. 1800, in NYHS; and NA, RG 217, Letters Sent by the Accountant of the Navy, Mar. 1801–May 1802, "Remarks on the recruiting accounts of Lieutenant Isaac Hull dated July 1799."

15. Talbot MSS: Hull to Talbot, 24 June, 2 July 1799; Harvard University, Houghton Library: Hull to Talbot, 25 June 1799.

16. Talbot MSS: Hull to Talbot, 20 June 1799.

17. Harvard University, Houghton Library: Hull to Talbot, 9 July 1799; see Haraden's journal for presence of at least one black sailor. One probable reason why captains like Talbot were unwilling to have free black sailors in their ships was that they often took on board one or more of their own slaves as body servants. The usual reluctance to allow free blacks to associate with slaves was strongly reinforced by conditions of shipboard intimacy.

18. Talbot MSS: Hull to Talbot, 29 June, 5 July 1799.

19. Talbot MSS: Hull to Talbot, 15 July 1799; a second letter of the same date is in RG 217, Letters Sent by the Accountant of the Navy, Mar. 1801–May 1802.

20. Talbot MSS: Talbot to Higginson, 20 July 1799.

21. *Quasi-War* 3: 392, Stevens to Pickering, 24 June 1799; 3: 408–410, Proclamation of President Adams, 26 June 1799, and Circular to Collectors of Customs, 26 June 1799. For a full discussion of the negotiations with Toussaint see Alexander DeConde, *The Quasi-War* (New York, 1966), pp. 206–211. For background on the situation in the island see Thomas O. Ott, *The Haitian Revolution, 1789–1804* (Knoxville, 1973).

22. *Quasi-War* 3: 462, Stoddert to Talbot, 3 July 1799.

23. *Quasi-War* 4: 63–64, 74, *Constitution* log 11, 14 Aug. 1799; Talbot MSS: Hull to Talbot, 15 Aug. 1799.

24. Talbot MSS: Talbot to Hull, 15 Aug. 1799.

25. *Quasi-War* 3: 480–481, Carmick to William W. Burrows, 9 July 1799.

26. *Quasi-War* 4: 91–92, Carmick to Burrows, 18 Aug. 1799.

27. McKee, "Roche": John Roche, Jr., to John Roche, Sr., 17 Aug. 1799, p. 143.

28. *Quasi-War* 4: 122–123, Carmick to Burrows, 24 Aug. 1799.

29. *Quasi-War* 3: 553–554, Stoddert to Talbot, 27 July 1799; 4: 124, *Constitution* log, 26 Aug. 1799.

30. No regulations for the *Constitution* are extant. For details of ship's routine cf. *Quasi-War* 5: 546–550, Rules and Regulations to be observed on board the U.S. Frigate *Congress*, 22 May 1800; *Barbary Wars* 3: 32–41, Internal Rules and Regulations for U.S. Frigate *Constitution*, [sic] 1803–1804; *Barbary Wars* 2: 29–40, U.S. Navy Regulations, 25 Jan. 1802; WLCL: Robert Rogers MSS, Isaac Hull and Silas Talbot to Midshipmen of the frigate *Constitution*, 15 Dec. 1800. For a full description of a day on board the *Constitution* in 1803–4 see chap. 12 in McKee, *Edward Preble*, pp. 214–219.

31. *Quasi-War* 4: 189, 195, *Constitution* log, 15–16 Sept. 1799; Talbot MSS: Silas Talbot to G. W. Talbot, 15 Sept. 1799, and King & Talbot to Silas Talbot, 20 Jan. 1800; *Quasi-War* 5: 399–400, Judge Washington's opinion in the case of the *Amalia*, 9 Apr. 1800, reported in *New Hampshire Gazette* (Portsmouth), 22 Apr. 1800. For salvage regulations see *Quasi-War* 5: 572–573, Stoddert to D. M. Clarkson, 29 May 1800; 6: 242–243, case of the prize *Amalia*, reported from

Connecticut Courant (Hartford), 1 Sept. 1800. The ship's name is spelled variously *Amalia* and *Amelia* in the documents.

32. Talbot MSS: G. W. Talbot to Silas Talbot, 18 Aug. 1801; *Quasi-War* 7: 462–473, Rules and Regulations for the Government of the United States Navy, 23 Apr. 1800; *U.S. Statutes* 2: 16–18, Act of 3 March 1800, Providing for Salvage in Cases of Recapture; *U.S. Reports*, 4 Dallas 34–36, 1 Cranch 1–44, *Talbot* v. *The Ship Amelia.*

33. *Constitution* log, passim.

34. Talbot MSS: Levy to Talbot, 17 Oct. 1799.

35. *Quasi-War* 4: 349, *Constitution* log, 1, 3 Nov. 1799; McKee, "Roche": Roche, Jr., to Roche, Sr., 26 Nov. 1799, p. 144.

36. *Constitution* log, passim; Talbot MSS: Talbot to Levy, 19 Nov. 1799.

37. *Quasi-War* 4: 479–480, *Constitution* log, 3 Dec. 1799.

38. *Quasi-War* 4: 487–488, Stevens to Little, 4 Dec. 1799, two letters; *Constitution* log, passim; McKee, "Roche": Roche, Jr., to Roche, Sr., 7 Dec. 1799, pp. 144–145.

39. *Quasi-War* 4: 503–506, Stevens to Pickering, 9 Dec. 1799.

40. *Quasi-War* 4: 570, Stevens to Pickering, 27 Dec. 1799.

41. *Constitution* log, passim.

42. *Quasi-War* 4: 468–469, C. R. Perry to a Gentleman of Providence, R.I., 5 Dec. 1799.

43. Ott, *The Haitian Revolution*, chap. 6.

44. *Quasi-War* 5: 250–251, Letter from an Officer of the *General Greene*, 14 Apr. 1800; cf. Allen, *Our Naval War with France*, pp. 180–181; *Quasi-War* 5: 309–310, Toussaint Louverture to Edward Stevens, 16 Mar. 1800. Allen erroneously places the surrender on 27 February.

45. *Quasi-War* 5: 1–3, Stevens to Talbot, 1 Jan. 1800; see Talbot MSS: Maley to Talbot, 3 Jan. 1800.

46. The *Experiment* was an unhappy vessel. While she was in company with the *Constitution* late in February her officers accused their commander, Lieutenant William Maley, of cowardice. Maley seems to have been inefficient, possibly tyrannical, but not pusillanimous. Talbot, to ease the situation, transferred Lieutenant Boss and his son to the *Experiment* and made Lieutenant David Porter of the *Experiment* master of the *Amphitrite*. See *Quasi-War* 5: 259, *Constitution* log, 1 Mar. 1800; 5: 252, *Experiment* journal, 27 Feb. 1800. The correspondence on this subject is in Talbot MSS.

47. *Quasi-War* 5: 163–164, Talbot to Porter, 3 Mar. 1800; 6: 410, sale of *Les Deux Anges*, 30 Sept. 1800; Talbot MSS: Talbot to Stevens, 5 Feb. 1800. See these MSS, passim, for the wrangle over the proceeds of *Les Deux Anges*. In the end, nobody realized anything for her because her proceeds were refunded under the Convention of Mortefontaine: see *Quasi-War* 6: 410.

48. *U.S. Statutes* 2: 10.

49. Talbot MSS: Talbot to Stevens, 1 Apr. 1800.

50. *Quasi-War* 5: 446–447, Talbot to Stoddert, ca. 25 Apr. 1800.

51. *Quasi-War* 5: 470, *Constitution* log, 2 May 1800; Talbot MSS: Talbot to captain of polacre, 2 May 1800.

52. Talbot MSS: Talbot to Commandant of Puerto Plata, 2 May 1800.

53. Talbot MSS: Commandant of Puerto Plata to Talbot, 2 May 1800.

54. *Quasi-War* 5: 495–496, *Constitution* log, 9 May 1800, Isaac Hull journal, 9 May 1800; *Quasi-War* 5, *Ester* log, passim.

55. *Quasi-War* 5: 495–496, 499, *Constitution* log and Hull journal, 9–10 May 1800.

56. *Quasi-War* 5: 501–502, Deposition of Captain Thomas Sandford of the *Sally*, 19 May 1800. Poor Sandford suffered most in this affair. The *Constitution* landed him at Cap Français, from which he took passage in a French ship to return to Puerto Plata and reclaim his remaining property. The French ship was taken by the *Alarm*, and Sandford was put on shore sixty miles from his destination, which he reached overland by an arduous trek in the course of which he contracted yellow fever. When he reached Puerto Plata, where he lay ill for a month, he found that the inhabitants blamed him for the misfortune to the *Sandwich* and that all his property had been confiscated. In fact, when he mentioned the subject, he was threatened with the guillotine! He returned, disconsolate, to Cap Français where he appealed to Talbot for the restoration of his ship; see Talbot MSS: Sandford to Talbot, 12 July 1800.

57. *Quasi-War* 5: 500–506, documents concerning the capture of *Sandwich* grouped at 11 May 1800. See also several items in Talbot MSS. Hull commissioned a painting of the incident by the marine artist Robert Salmon; it is now in the collection of the Boston Athenaeum. (See illustration on page 48.)

58. Talbot MSS: Talbot to Hamilton, 1 June 1800; *Quasi-War* 6, *Constitution* log and Hull journal, passim.

59. *Quasi-War* 6: 153–154, Talbot to Russell, 15 July 1800; *Constitution* log, passim.

60. *Quasi-War* 6: 166, reprinted from *Massachusetts Mercury* (Boston) 5 Sept. 1800.

61. *Quasi-War* 6: 169.

62. NYHS: *Constitution* log, 24–29 Aug. 1800.

63. Sources for the *Constitution*'s second cruise under Talbot are nearly all in Talbot MSS. *Quasi-War* 6 and 7 have a sharply declining number of relevant documents. Nathaniel Haraden's *Constitution* log ends 20 Oct. 1800, and no log for the subsequent cruise survives.

64. *Quasi-War* 6: 285, Talbot to Stoddert, 25 Aug. 1800.

65. Talbot MSS: Memorandum of Silas Talbot, 17 July 1800, and correspondence with Collins dated 20, 21, and 28 July; 4 Aug.; and 2 Nov. 1800.

66. *Quasi-War* 6: 285, 422, Talbot to Stoddert, 25 Aug., 1 Oct. 1800.

67. Talbot MSS: Hull to Talbot, 27 Oct. 1800.

68. Talbot MSS: Wm. Hunt to Talbot, 3 Sept. 1800. It was a sound decision. Thomas Hunt served honorably in the navy until his early death in 1807.

69. Talbot MSS: Talbot to Hull, 11 Sept. 1800.

70. Talbot MSS: *Constitution* log.

71. Talbot MSS: Hull to Talbot, 27 Oct. 1800.

72. DeConde, *The Quasi-War*, pp. 255–256, 283.

73. *Quasi-War* 6: 536, Stoddert to Talbot, 18 Nov. 1800.

74. Talbot MSS: Talbot journal, 14–20 Dec. 1800.

75. *Quasi-War* 7: 53, "Extract from a Letter Written on board the *Constitution*," 2 Jan. 1801, as published in *Mercury & New England Palladium* (Newport, R.I.), 6 Feb. 1801.

76. Ott, chaps. 6 and 7; Talbot MSS: Talbot to Toussaint, 31 Jan. 1801; Talbot to Stevens, 4 Feb. 1801 (two letters).

77. Talbot MSS: Talbot to Stevens, 4 Feb. 1801.

78. *Quasi-War* 7: 80–84, Stoddert to Chairman, Committee on Naval Affairs, 12 Jan. 1801; 7: 134–135, Act Providing for a Naval Peace Establishment, 3 Mar. 1801.

79. Talbot MSS: Talbot to Stevens, 23 Mar. 1801.

80. Talbot MSS: Talbot to Samuel Smith, 15 June 1801.

81. *Quasi-War* 7: 315–358, Register of Officers. John Roche had been transferred to the *Scammel* as acting lieutenant. He resigned in July.

82. *Quasi-War* 7: 190, Truxtun to [Burr], 13 Apr. 1801; 7: 158–162, J. H. Nicholson to [Thomas Jefferson?], 27 Mar. 1801; 7: 164, Stoddert to C. Talbot, 30 Mar. 1801; 7: 271, 286, Robert Smith to S. Talbot, 28 July, 21 Sept. 1801; *Barbary Wars* 1: 488–489, Acting Secretary of the Navy to Truxtun, 11 June 1801; 1: 622–623, [R. Smith] to C. Talbot, 18 Nov. 1801.

83. MassHS: Hull to James Prince, 21 Aug. 1801.

84. Talbot MSS: Hull to Talbot, 15 Jan. 1802; Peter St. Medard to Talbot, 28 Nov. 1801.

85. Talbot MSS: Hull to Talbot, 20 Nov., 30 Dec. 1801.

86. Talbot MSS: Hull to Talbot, 15, 25 Jan., 9 Feb. 1802; Harvard University, Houghton Library: Hull to Talbot, 27 Mar. 1802.

87. *Quasi-War* 7: 135–138, List of Officers Retained in U.S. Navy, after the passage of the Peace Establishment Law, of 3 Mar. 1801; Talbot MSS: Hull to Talbot, 29 Jan. 1802.

88. Talbot MSS: Hull to Talbot, 3 Mar. 1802.

89. See note 1 above. Truxtun claimed that when he asked leave "to quit the service" he meant only the Mediterranean command, but Secretary of the Navy Robert Smith, who had no patience with resignation as a tool for obtaining favors, interpreted him to mean that he resigned the naval service altogether. *Barbary Wars* 2: 76, Truxtun to Smith, 3 Mar. 1802; 2: 83, Smith to Truxtun, 13 Mar. 1802.

90. Harvard University, Houghton Library: Hull to Talbot, 27 Mar. 1802.

91. *Barbary Wars* 2: 101, Smith to Hull, 1 Apr. 1802.

Chapter 4

1. *Barbary Wars* 2: 62–63, Preble to Smith, 20 Feb. 1802. The *Adams* now mounted a lower battery of twelve-pounders and a spar-deck battery of nines. Cf. *Barbary Wars* 2: 332, A. Murray to John Graham, 14 Dec. 1802.

2. *Barbary Wars* 2: 141–142, Smith to Hull, 3 May 1802.

3. OSW: Smith to Campbell, 1 May 1802.

4. *Barbary Wars* 1: 465–469, Samuel Smith to Richard Dale, 20 May 1801.

5. Gardner W. Allen, *Our Navy and the Barbary Corsairs* (Boston, 1905), p. 91; *Barbary Wars* 1: 455–460, Cathcart to Secretary of State, 16 May 1801. Cathcart, who had once been a prisoner in Algiers, retired forthwith to Leghorn.

6. *Barbary Wars* 1: 177–180, Treaty with Tripoli, 4 Nov. 1796, 10 June 1797.

The dey of Algiers had gotten nearly $1 million in cash plus an annual tribute; the bey of Tunis received $107,000. Yusuf got only $46,000 and another $23,000 when Cathcart was received as consul in 1799: Allen, *Our Navy and the Barbary Corsairs,* p. 60; *Barbary Wars* 1: 338–341, Cathcart to David Humphreys, 14 Dec. 1799.

7. Allen, *Our Navy and the Barbary Corsairs,* pp. 94–97.

8. McKee, *Edward Preble,* pp. 93–94.

9. *Barbary Wars* 2: 268–269, Campbell to Robert Smith, 7 Sept. 1802; routine details of movements of the *Adams,* and later of the *Enterprize,* are drawn from the Journal of Jonathan Thorn, FDR Lib.

10. *Barbary Wars* 2: 271, O'Bannon to William W. Burrows, 10 Sept. 1802.

11. Albert Gleaves, *James Lawrence* (New York, 1904), pp. 35–36; Memorandum in Elliot Coll.

12. *Barbary Wars* 2: 283, United States Passport issued to the Ship *Meshuda,* 27 Sept. 1802; 2: 284–286, Simpson to James Madison, 28 Sept. 1802; 2: 286–287, Campbell to R. Smith, 1 Oct. 1802.

13. *Barbary Wars* 2: 320, Wm. H. Allen to Wm. Allen, 23 Nov. 1802.

14. *Barbary Wars* 2: 335, Campbell to Wm. W. Burrows, 16 Dec. 1802.

15. *Barbary Wars* 2: 387–388, Smith to Morris, 6 Apr. 1803. Realizing its mistake in selling the small cruisers, the Navy Department was building three brigs and a schooner as auxiliary vessels, but none of these would reach the Mediterranean for many months.

16. NA, RG 45, *Enterprize* Muster Roll, 1802–1803.

17. Howard I. Chapelle, *History of the American Sailing Navy* (New York, 1949), pp. 145–146.

18. *Barbary Wars: Register of Ships' Data,* p. 71.

19. Elliot Coll.: Isaac Hull to Joseph B. Hull, 7 June 1835.

20. *Barbary Wars* 2: 389–390, Journal of Henry Wadsworth, 12 Apr. 1803.

21. *Barbary Wars* 2: 403–404, Wadsworth journal, 12 May 1803; FDR Lib.: Thorn journal, 25 Apr. 1803.

22. *Barbary Wars* 2: 400–402, 405, 407, 409, Journal kept on board the *John Adams,* 7–19 May 1803; 2: 408–409, Morris to Simpson, 19 May 1803.

23. *Barbary Wars* 2: 416–417, Wadsworth journal, 22 May 1803; FDR Lib.: Thorn journal, 22–23 May 1803.

24. *Barbary Wars* 2: 425–426, Wadsworth journal, 27 May 1803.

25. *Barbary Wars* 2: 432, Wadsworth journal, 31 May 1803; McKee, *Edward Preble,* pp. 118–119.

26. *Barbary Wars* 2: 430–432, Wadsworth journal, 30 May 1803; *John Adams* journal, 30–31 May 1803; FDR Lib.: Thorn journal, 1 June 1803.

27. *Barbary Wars* 2: 432, 435–437, Wadsworth journal, 31 May, 2 June 1803; FDR Lib.: Thorn journal, 1–3 June; C. W. Goldsborough, *U.S. Naval Chronicle,* excerpted in *Barbary Wars* 2: 529–531.

28. McKee, *Edward Preble,* pp. 129–131; *Barbary Wars* 2: 449, Wadsworth journal, 9 June 1803; FDR Lib.: Thorn journal, passim.

29. *Barbary Wars* 2: 439–440, Nissen to Cathcart, 4 and 8 June 1803.

30. *Barbary Wars* 2: 459–460, Rodgers to R. Smith, 22 June 1803; 2: 465–466, Rodgers to R. V. Morris, 30 June 1803; 2: 459–460, *John Adams* journal, 21–22

NOTES TO PAGES 81–91

June 1803; FDR Lib.: Thorn journal, 22 June 1803; MeHS: Extract from journal of Lieut. James Lawrence, 22 June 1803; Archives du Ministre des Affaires Étrangères, Correspondance Consulaire, Tripoli de Barbarie 32: B. Beaussier to Talleyrand, 5 Messidor an onze [24 June 1803].

31. *Barbary Wars* 2: 457–458.

32. *Barbary Wars* 2: 457.

33. *Barbary Wars* 2: 489, *John Adams* journal, 16–18 July 1803; FDR Lib.: Thorn journal, passim.

34. *Barbary Wars* 2: 509, *John Adams* journal, 11–12 Aug. 1803; FDR Lib.: Thorn journal, 12 Aug. 1803.

35. *Barbary Wars* 2: 521–522, Wadsworth journal, 27 Aug. 1803.

36. *Barbary Wars* 3: 27–28, Somers to W. J. Keen, 11 Sept. 1803; 3: 29, *Constitution* log, 12 Sept. 1803; 3: 30, Wadsworth journal, 13 Sept. 1803.

37. *Barbary Wars* 3: 30, Wadsworth journal, 12 Sept. 1803; 3: 56–59, Preble to R. Smith, 18 Sept. 1803. The editors of *Barbary Wars* are incorrect in interpreting references in *John Adams* journal for September to "the schooner" as the *Enterprize*; this was the *Nautilus*, which joined Rodgers and Morris at Málaga on 11 September.

38. *Barbary Wars* 3: 46–47, exchange of letters between Rodgers and Preble, 15 Sept. 1803; McKee, *Edward Preble*, pp. 139–148.

39. *Barbary Wars* 3: 65–66, 71–72, Preble to Hull, 19 and 22 Sept. 1803.

40. *Barbary Wars* 3: 75, Wadsworth to Nancy Doane, 24 Sept. 1803; 3: 77, *Constitution* log, 25 Sept. 1803.

41. *Barbary Wars* 3: 129–130, Preble to Hull, 12 Oct. 1803, Preble to Somers, 12 Oct. 1803; 3: 155, *Constitution* log, 19 Oct. 1803; McKee, *Edward Preble*, pp. 160–172.

42. *Barbary Wars* 3: 161, Preble to Smith, 23 Oct. 1803.

43. *Barbary Wars* 3: 206, *Constitution* log, 7 Nov. 1803; 3: 203, Preble to Decatur, 7 Nov. 1803; 3: 211, *Argus* log, 9 Nov. 1803.

44. *Barbary Wars* 3: 209, Preble to Smith, 9 Nov. 1803.

45. Chapelle, *American Sailing Navy*, pp. 184, 532.

46. *Barbary Wars* 3: 220, 225, *Constitution* log, 13, 16 Nov. 1803.

47. *Barbary Wars* 3: 210, Preble to Smith, 9 Nov. 1803.

48. *Barbary Wars* 3: 466, Hull to Preble, 3 Mar. 1804; 4: 27, Preble to Livingston, 15 Apr. 1804. Cf. McKee, *Edward Preble*, pp. 224–226.

49. *Barbary Wars* 3: 204–205, Preble to Hull, 7 Nov. 1803.

50. *Barbary Wars* 3: 219, *Argus* log, 13 Nov. 1803.

51. Elliot Coll.: *Argus* log, passim; *Barbary Wars* 3: 237–238, Hull to Preble, 26 Nov. 1803.

52. *Barbary Wars* 3: 320, Hull to Preble, 9 Jan. 1804; 3: 261, Preble to Hull, 10 Dec. 1803.

53. *Barbary Wars* 3: 339, Preble to Smith, 17 Jan. 1804.

54. *Barbary Wars* 3: 329, Hull to Joseph Yznardi, 14 Jan. 1804; 3: 360, Hull to Smith, 26 Jan. 1804.

55. *Barbary Wars* 3: 466, Hull to Preble, 3 Mar. 1804; 3: 438, Preble to Smith, 19 Feb. 1804.

56. *Barbary Wars* 3: 466, Hull to Preble, 3 Mar. 1804; Elliot Coll.: *Argus* log, 12 Mar. 1804.
57. *Barbary Wars* 3: 356, Smith to Hull, 24 Jan. 1804; 3: 399–400, Smith to Hull, 9 Feb. 1804.
58. *Barbary Wars* 3: 514, Hull to Smith, 22 Mar. 1804.

Chapter 5

1. *Barbary Wars* 4: *Argus* log, passim.
2. *Barbary Wars* 4: 27, Preble diary, 15 Apr. 1804.
3. *Barbary Wars* 4: *Argus* log, passim.
4. McKee, *Edward Preble*, pp. 245–246.
5. McKee, *Edward Preble*, p. 249.
6. *Barbary Wars* 4: 137, Hull to William Higgins, 31 May 1804.
7. *Barbary Wars* 4: 163, Preble diary, 7 June 1804; 4: 204–205, Preble to George Davis, 19 June 1804; 4: 216–217, Davis to Don Joseph Noguera, 22 June 1804.
8. *Barbary Wars* 4: 186–190, Preble to Robert Smith, 14 June–5 July 1804.
9. *Barbary Wars* 4: 233–234, Wadsworth to "Jack," 28 June–16 July 1804; 4: 254, Stewart to Preble, 8 July 1804; 4: *Argus* and *Syren* logs, passim.
10. McKee, *Edward Preble*, pp. 266–267; Linda and Christopher McKee, eds., "An Inquiry into the Conduct of Joshua Blake," *American Neptune* 21 (1961), pp. 130–141.
11. McKee, *Edward Preble*, pp. 276–283; *Barbary Wars* 4: 389, 390, Preble diary and *Argus* log, 9 Aug. 1804.
12. McKee, *Edward Preble*, pp. 285–307.
13. Allen, *Our Navy and the Barbary Corsairs*, p. 88; *Barbary Wars* 4: 152–154, Smith to Samuel Barron, 6 June 1804.
14. NA, RG 59, Letters of Application and Recommendation during the Administration of Thomas Jefferson, 1801–1809.
15. L. B. Wright and J. H. Macleod, *The First Americans in North Africa* (Princeton, 1945), p. 114.
16. McKee, *Edward Preble*, pp. 186–188, 210–212, 330–331.
17. *Barbary Wars* 5: 20, S. Barron to Hull, copy dated 15 Sept. 1804, attested by Hull and Eaton.
18. *Barbary Wars* 5: 23–24, *Constitution* log, 14 Sept. 1804; 5: 26, *Argus* journal and Eaton journal, 15 Sept. 1804; 5: 32, Eaton journal, 17 Sept. 1804.
19. *Barbary Wars* 5: 2–3, Eaton to Cathcart, 7 Sept. 1804.
20. *Barbary Wars* 5: 100, Barron to Hull, 26 Oct. 1804; 5: 32–38, Eaton to Smith, [18 Sept.] 1804.
21. *Barbary Wars* 5: 116, Lear to Madison, 3 Nov. 1804.
22. See *Barbary Wars* 5: 139, Barron to Lear, 13 Nov. 1804; Earl Gregg Swem Library, College of William and Mary, Barron Papers: S. Barron to Joseph Clery, April 1806.
23. *Barbary Wars* 5: 136–137, Bainbridge to Lear, 11 Nov. 1804.
24. *Barbary Wars* 5: 167, Eaton journal.

25. *Barbary Wars* 5: 222, Hull to Eaton, 27 Dec. 1804; 5: 248, Hull to Briggs, 2 Jan. 1805; 5: 270, Briggs to Hull, 9 Jan. 1805.

26. *Barbary Wars* 5: 171, Eaton to Hull, 2 Dec. 1804.

27. Hull believed this as well. He had acquired from Preble the idea that Bonaventure Beaussier at Tripoli was a secret enemy of the Americans and a general belief that French policy in the Mediterranean was hostile. The suppositions about Beaussier were false, but apparently the French consul at Alexandria, Bernardino Drovetti, did act against the Americans, perhaps because they were so friendly to the English agents. Cf. *Barbary Wars* 5: 210–212, Hull to Barron, 23 Dec. 1804; 5: 254–255, Hull to Eaton, 5 Jan. 1805; 5: 300–305, Eaton to Preble, 25 Jan.–16 Feb. 1805.

28. *Barbary Wars* 5: 197, Eaton to Hull, 17 Dec. 1804.

29. *Barbary Wars* 5: 214–215, Hull to Eaton, 24 Dec. 1804; 5: 210–212, Hull to S. Barron, 23 Dec. 1804.

30. *Barbary Wars* 5: 223–225, Eaton to Hull, 29–31 Dec. 1804; 5: 341–342, Eaton to Hull, 9 Feb. 1805.

31. *Barbary Wars* 5: 332–333, Hull to Eaton, 5 Feb. 1804.

32. *Barbary Wars* 5: 348–350, Eaton to Smith, 13 Feb. 1805.

33. *Barbary Wars* 5: 382, Muster Roll, 1 Mar. 1805; 5: 398–399, Eaton journal, 8 Mar. 1805.

34. Earl Gregg Swem Library, College of William and Mary, Barron Papers: Statement of James Barron, 12 Apr. 1806; *Barbary Wars* 5: 438–441, S. Barron to Eaton, 22 Mar. 1805. See also 5: 209–210, Hamet Caramanli to Thos. Jefferson, 5 Aug. 1805.

35. *Barbary Wars* 5: 440–441, S. Barron to Eaton, 22 Mar. 1805.

36. *Barbary Wars* 5: 438–441, S. Barron to Eaton, 22 Mar. 1805; 5: 446–447, S. Barron to Hull, 23 Mar. 1805.

37. *Barbary Wars* 5: 529–530, Hull to S. Barron, 22 Apr. 1805; 5: 538, 540–541, Eaton journal, 24–25 Apr. 1805.

38. *Barbary Wars* 5: 540, Hull to Dent, 25 Apr. 1805; 5: 542, Dent to Eaton, 26 Apr. 1805.

39. *Barbary Wars* 5: 542, Eaton to Governor of Derna, 26 Apr. 1805.

40. *Barbary Wars* 5: 547–548, Hull to S. Barron, 27 Apr. 1805; 5: 550–555, Eaton to S. Barron, 29 Apr. 1805.

41. *Barbary Wars* 5: 550–555, Eaton to S. Barron, 29 Apr. 1805.

42. *Barbary Wars* 5: 555–556, Hull to S. Barron, 29 Apr. 1805.

43. *Barbary Wars* 6: 5, Eaton journal, 3 May 1805; 6: *Argus* journal passim.

44. *Barbary Wars* 6: 14–15, Eaton to S. Barron, 15–17 May 1805.

45. *Barbary Wars* 6: 22–23, S. Barron to Lear, 18 May 1805.

46. *Barbary Wars* 6: 25–26, S. Barron to Eaton, 19 May 1805.

47. *Barbary Wars* 6: 24–25, S. Barron to Hull, 19 May 1805.

48. *Barbary Wars* 6: 46–47, *Argus* journal, 24–25 May 1805; 6: 47–48, Eaton journal, 25 May 1805.

49. *Barbary Wars* 6: 58–63, Eaton to S. Barron, 29 May–11 June 1805.

50. *Barbary Wars* 6: 58–63, Eaton to S. Barron, 29 May–11 June 1805; 6: 107, *Argus* journal, 10 June 1805.

51. *Barbary Wars* 6: 117–118, *Argus* journal, 13 June 1805.

52. *Barbary Wars* 6: 116–117, Eaton to Rodgers, 13 June 1805.
53. Wright and Macleod, *First Americans,* pp. 200–201.

Chapter 6

1. LC, Jefferson Papers: Smith to Jefferson, 27 Mar. 1805.
2. LC, Jefferson Papers: Jefferson to Smith, 31 Mar. 1805; Smith to Jefferson, 19 Apr. 1805.
3. *Barbary Wars* 6: 258–259, Rodgers to Hull, 31 Aug. 1805.
4. Elliot Coll.: Lawrence to Hull, Saturday 1 p.m., n.d. [1805].
5. Elliot Coll.: Rodgers to Hull, 11 Sept. 1805.
6. Elliot Coll.: Richard Cheeseman to Masters of Transports at Syracuse, 4 Nov. 1805; Cheeseman to H. F. Woodman and T. McCulloch, 5 Nov. 1805; Cheeseman to Hull, 6 Nov. 1805.
7. *Barbary Wars* 6: 325–326, Hull to Rodgers, 25 Dec. 1805.
8. *Barbary Wars* 6: 331–333, Rodgers to Smith, 3 Jan. 1806.
9. *Barbary Wars* 6: 290–291, Smith to Rodgers, 12 Oct. 1805.
10. *Barbary Wars* 6: 412–413, Hull to Rodgers, 3 Apr. 1806; Elliot Coll.: Wm. M. Crane to Hull, 25 Mar. 1806; W. Lewis to Hull, n.d. [1806]; Hull to Crane, 3 Apr. 1806.
11. Elliot Coll.: Hull to Hethcote J. Reed, 29 May 1806.
12. *Barbary Wars* 6: 431–433, Rodgers to Smith, 23 May 1806.
13. *Barbary Wars* 6: 420, Smith to Stewart, Hull and Chauncey, 24 Apr. 1806; 6: 453, Smith to Nathaniel Ingraham, 14 July 1806. The appointments were interim because Congress was not sitting; they were confirmed by the Senate in January 1807.
14. Gardner W. Allen, ed., *Papers of Isaac Hull* (Boston, 1929), p. 8.
15. HSPa: Hull to Eaton, 1 Sept. 1806.
16. Charles O. Paullin, *Commodore John Rodgers* (Cleveland, 1910), p. 178.
17. LC, Edward Preble Papers, vol. 19: Hull to Preble, 27 Nov. 1806.
18. HSPa: Hull to Eaton, 1 Sept. 1806.
19. LC, Edward Preble Papers, vol. 18: Hull to Preble, 16 Oct. 1806; vol. 19: Hull to Preble, 27 Nov. 1806.
20. CL: Hull to Smith, 8, 11 Nov. 1806.
21. LC, Jefferson Papers: Smith to Jefferson, 13 Feb. 1807; Jefferson to Smith, 7 Mar. 1807.
22. CL: Hull to Smith, 3 Sept. 1807; OSW: Smith to Hull, 17 Sept. 1807.
23. CL: Hull to Smith, 8 Sept. 1807.
24. Boston Public Library: Hull to Goldsborough, 27 Dec. 1807.
25. CL: Hull to Smith, 10 Apr. 1808.
26. NYHS: Hull to Bainbridge, 11 Apr. 1808. Connecticut was known as "the land of steady habits."
27. CL: Hull to Smith, 17 Oct. 1808.
28. NA, RG 45, Contracts, I: Contract between Joseph Hull and Simeon North, [30 June 1808].
29. CL: Hull to Smith, 22 Apr. 1808, 27 Sept. 1808.

30. Elliot Coll.: Wm. Hull to Mary Wheeler, 10 Dec. 1808.

31. U.S. Navy Dept., Naval History Division, ZB File: Hull to Campbell, 19 Mar. 1809.

32. CL: Hull to Paul Hamilton, 15 Aug. 1809.

33. CL: Hull to Hamilton, 3 Sept. 1809.

34. CL: Hull to Hamilton, 12 Nov. 1809.

35. CL: Hull to Hamilton, 30 Aug. 1809.

36. Elliot Coll.: Isaac Hull to Joseph Hull, 7 Aug. 1809.

37. OSW: Hamilton to Hull, 19 July 1809.

38. Elliot Coll.: Isaac Hull to Joseph Hull, 24 Apr. 1809.

39. U.S. Naval Academy Museum, Annapolis: Hull to Campbell, 21 Aug. 1809.

40. NYHS, *Collections* 1868– (New York, 1868–), 1931, Diaries of William Dunlap, 3 vols., vol. 3 (16 Mar. 1832–31 Dec. 1834), entry for 19 June 1833. There is no portrait by Edwin extant. The reference is probably to Edwin's engraving of the Stuart portrait for the *Analectic Magazine,* in which the eyelids have a distinct droop.

41. Elliot Coll.: Isaac Hull to Joseph Hull, 11 May, 20 July, 7 Aug. 1809.

42. Elliot Coll.: Isaac Hull to Mary Wheeler, 27 Oct. 1809. In the "arrival from Europe" allusion, Hull is evidently making a play on the standard newspaper cliché by which important news was announced.

43. Elliot Coll.: Isaac Hull to Mary Wheeler, 28 Nov. 1809.

44. NA, RG 45, Naval Records Collection, Area 7 file: Hull to Bainbridge, 31 Dec. 1809.

45. NYHS: Hull to Porter, 23 Feb. 1810.

46. Elliot Coll.: Mary Wheeler to Levi Hull, 3 Mar. 1810.

47. Elliot Coll.: Isaac Hull to Mary Wheeler, 21 Mar. 1810. Miss J. may have been one of the prominent Jacksons of Boston.

48. NYHS, Hull LB: Hull to Hamilton, 16 Apr. 1810.

49. NYHS, Hull LB: Hull to Hamilton, 1 Apr. 1810.

50. OSW: Hamilton to Hull, 8 Apr. 1810.

51. NYHS, Hull LB: Hull to Hamilton, 16 Apr. 1810.

52. OSW: Hamilton to Hull, 7 May 1810.

53. Elliot Coll.: Isaac Hull to Mary Wheeler, 12 July 1810.

Chapter 7

1. NYHS: Charles Morris to Lemuel Morris, 20 July 1810.

2. NA, RG 45, Circulars: Hamilton to Decatur and Rodgers, 9 June 1810; Elliot Coll.: Rodgers to Hull, 19 June 1810.

3. Elliot Coll.: Rodgers to Hull, 4 Aug. [sic] 1810.

4. Lilla M. Hawes, ed., "Letters of Henry Gilliam, 1809–17," *Georgia Historical Quarterly* 38, no. 1, 54–55: Gilliam to William Jones, 25 June 1810.

5. LC, Rodgers Family Papers: John Rodgers to Minerva Rodgers, 27 June 1810.

6. Elliot Coll.: Hull to Mary Wheeler, 12 July 1810.

7. NYHS, Hull LB: Hull to Hamilton, 24 July 1810.

8. NYHS, Frederick Rodgers Coll. (microfilm): Hull to Rodgers, 22 Aug. 1810.

9. NYHS, Hull LB: Hull to Hamilton, 18 Aug. 1810.

10. NYHS, Hull LB: Hull to Rodgers, 3 Sept. 1810.

11. NA, RG 45, Acceptances, Midshipmen, 1810–1814: English to Hamilton, 20 July 1810.

12. NYHS, Hull LB: Hull to Charles W. Morgan, 17 Oct. 1810.

13. OSW: Hamilton to Hull, 24 Oct. 1810, enclosing copy of Hamilton to Rodgers, 22 Oct. 1810.

14. OSW: Hamilton to Hull, 30 Oct. 1810.

15. Elliot Coll.: Hull to Mary Wheeler, 26 Oct. 1810.

16. NYHS, Frederick Rodgers Coll. (microfilm): Hull to Rodgers, 3 Nov. 1810.

17. NYHS, Hull LB: Hull to Hamilton, 3 Dec. 1810; *The War* 1, no. 29 (9 Jan. 1813), p. 123. *The War* was a weekly newspaper.

18. Paullin, *Commodore John Rodgers*, p. 219; NA, RG 24, *Constitution* log, 14 Mar. 1811.

19. NYHS, Hull LB: Hull to Rodgers, 20 Feb. 1811.

20. NA, RG 24, *Constitution* log, 10 Mar. 1811.

21. NYHS, Hull LB: Hull to Morris, 22 Dec. 1810.

22. NYHS, Hull LB: Hull to Morris, 5 Jan. 1811.

23. Elliot Coll.: Hull to Mary Wheeler, 24 Jan. 1811.

24. Elliot Coll.: Hull to Mary Wheeler, 23 Feb. 1811.

25. NYHS, Hull LB: Hull to James Biddle, 5 Mar. 1811.

26. NA, RG 24, *Constitution* log, 20 Mar. 1811.

27. NYHS, Hull LB: Hull to Rodgers, 25 Feb. 1811.

28. Harvard University, Houghton Library: "Recollections" of Samuel C. Clarke; Hull to Samuel Clarke, 18 Apr. 1811. S. C. Clarke placed the dinner in 1812, but Hull's letter to the senior Clarke shows it was 1811. Christopher Gore was governor of Massachusetts from 1809 to 1810.

29. LC, Naval Historical Foundation, Elliott Snow Coll., box 2: Hull to Morris, [8 May 1811]. Photostat.

30. NYHS, Hull LB: Hull to Rodgers, 26 May 1811.

31. NYHS, Hull LB: Hull to Hamilton, 26 June 1811.

32. OSW: Hamilton to Hull, 19 July 1811.

33. NYHS, Hull LB: Hull to Hamilton, 25 July 1811.

34. NYHS, Hull LB: Hull to Rodgers, 26 May 1811.

35. Elliot Coll.: Hull to Mary Wheeler Hull, 26 July 1811.

36. NYHS, Hull LB: Hull to Barlow, 21 June 1811.

37. Elliot Coll.: Stewart to Hull, 7 July 1811.

38. Elliot Coll.: Hull to Mary W. Hull, 22 June 1811.

39. Elliot Coll.: Hull to Mary W. Hull, 26 July 1811.

40. Journal of David Baillie Warden, *Maryland Historical Magazine* 11, no. 2 (June 1916).

41. Moses Smith, *Naval Scenes in the Last War; or, Three Years on Board the Frigate Constitution, and the Adams; including the Capture of the Guerriere* (Boston, 1846), pp. 11–12.

42. Probably *Fanny and Julia* or some other work of Sophie de la Roche (1731–1807).

43. Smith, *Naval Scenes*, pp. 7–8.

44. NYHS, Hull LB: Hull to Barlow, 22 Sept. 1811.

45. LC, David Baillie Warden Papers: Hull to Warden, 24 Sept. 1811.
46. LC, Warden Papers: Hull to Warden, 29 Sept. 1811.
47. Elliot Coll.: Warden to Hull, 21 Sept. 1811.
48. LC, Warden Papers: Hull to Warden, 29 Sept. 1811.
49. Smith, *Naval Scenes*, p. 18.
50. LC, Warden Papers: Hull to Warden, 10 Sept. 1811.
51. LC, Warden Papers: Hull to Warden, 24 Sept. 1811.
52. *Trial of Captain John Shaw, by the General Court Martial, Holden on Board the U.S. Ship Independence, at the Navy Yard, Charlestown, Massachusetts, upon Charges and Specifications Preferred against Him by Captain Isaac Hull* (Washington, 1822), pp. 23–31, 50–65 (hereafter *Trial of Shaw*).
53. NYHS, Hull LB: Hull to Hamilton, 19 Nov. 1811.
54. CL: Curtis to Hull, 19 Nov. 1811.
55. NYHS, Hull LB: Hull to Russell, 20 Nov. 1811.
56. Smith, *Naval Scenes*, p. 17.
57. LC, Warden Papers: Hull to Warden, 22 Nov. 1811; MassHS: Journal of Frederick Baury; cf. *Trial of Shaw*, p. 88: Leonard Jarvis to Hull, 22 Mar. 1822.
58. LC, Warden Papers: Hull to Warden, 22 Nov. 1811.
59. LC, Warden Papers: Hull to Warden, 1 Dec. 1811.
60. Elliot Coll.: Warden to Hull, 18 Nov. 1811; Hull diary.
61. LC, Warden Papers: Hull to Warden, 15 Dec. 1811.
62. LC, Warden Papers: Hull to Warden, 20 Dec. 1811.
63. LC, Warden Papers: Hull to Warden, 28 Dec. 1811; 6, 8, 9 Jan. 1812.
64. Morristown (N.J.) Historical Society: Hull to George A. Otis, 13 Mar. 1812.
65. CL: Hull to Hamilton, 23 Feb. 1812.
66. CL: Hull to Hamilton, 28 Mar. 1812.
67. For an account of heaving down the *Constitution* in 1803 see McKee, *Edward Preble*, pp. 123–127.
68. Elliot Coll.: Hull to Mary W. Hull, 15 Apr. 1812.
69. Elliot Coll.: General William Hull to Joseph Hull, 16 Apr. 1812.
70. Elliot Coll.: Isaac Hull to Joseph Hull, 10 June 1812. The final vote in the Senate was 19–13.
71. Elliot Coll.: Hamilton to Hull, 18 June 1812.

Chapter 8

1. CL: Hull to Hamilton, 20 June 1812; OSW: Hamilton to Hull, 22 June 1812.
2. OSW: Hamilton to Hull, 1 July 1812.
3. [Lucy Brewer West], *An Affecting Narrative of Louisa Baker, a Native of Massachusetts, Who, in Early Life having been Shamefully Seduced, Deserted her Parents, and Enlisted, in Disguise, on Board an American Frigate, as a Marine, Where, in Two or Three Engagements, She Displayed the Most Heroic Fortitude, and was Honorably Discharged Therefrom a few Months Since, Without a Discovery of her Sex Being Made* (Boston, n.d.; reprint, New York, 1816), p. 19.
4. Smith, *Naval Scenes*, p. 24.
5. FDR Lib.: Hull to Thomas Beatty, 28 June 1812.
6. CL: Hull to Hamilton, 2 July 1812.

7. OSW: Hamilton to Hull, 3 July 1812.

8. Elliot Coll.: Isaac Hull to Joseph Hull, 5 July 1812.

9. CL: Hull to Hamilton, 10 July 1812.

10. CL: Hull to Hamilton, 12 July 1812.

11. Smith, *Naval Scenes*, p. 25.

12. Smith, *Naval Scenes*, p. 27.

13. George Coggeshall, *History of the American Privateers, and Letters-of-Marque, During our War with England in the Years 1812, '13 and '14* (New York, 1856), p. 12.

14. Coggeshall, *American Privateers*, p. 15.

15. Abel Bowen, *The Naval Monument, Containing Official and Other Accounts of all the Battles Fought Between the Navies of the United States and Great Britain during the Late War; and an Account of the War with Algiers, with Twenty-Five Engravings. To Which is Annexed a Naval Register of the United States, Revised and Corrected, and Brought Down to the Year 1836* (Boston, 1836), p. 9.

16. Great Britain, Public Record Office, Admiralty: Broke to Croker, 30 July 1812.

17. Smith, *Naval Scenes*, p. 28.

18. Coggeshall, *American Privateers*, p. 19.

19. CL: Hull to Hamilton, 21 July 1812.

20. *Niles' Register* (Philadelphia), 2: 381.

21. NA, RG 217, Letters Received by the Accountant of the Navy: Chew to Thomas Turner, 26 July 1812.

22. Charles Morris, *The Autobiography of Commodore Charles Morris, U.S. Navy* (Annapolis, 1880), p. 163.

23. Amos A. Evans, *Journal Kept on Board the United States Frigate Constitution, 1812* (n.p., 1928), entry for 28 July 1812 (hereafter Evans journal).

24. Benson J. Lossing, *Pictorial Field-Book of the War of 1812* (New York, 1868), p. 439.

25. CL: Hull to Hamilton, 28 July 1812.

26. OSW: Hamilton to Hull, 28 July 1812.

27. Elliot Coll.: Hamilton to Hull, 29 July 1812.

28. Elliot Coll.: Isaac Hull to Joseph Hull, 1 Aug. 1812.

29. CL: Hull to Hamilton, 2 Aug. 1812; NA, RG 217, Fourth Auditor Accounts, Alphabetical Series: Bemis & Eddy to Amos Binney, bill for charts furnished frigate *Constitution*, 29 July 1812.

30. Caroliniana Library, University of South Carolina, Hamilton MSS.: Hamilton to Morton Waring, 21 July 1812.

31. *The War* 1: 79, 24 Oct. 1812.

32. *The War* 1: 51, 12 Sept. 1812. See also Coggeshall, *American Privateers*, p. 20.

33. Evans journal, 10–11 Aug. 1812.

34. Smith, *Naval Scenes*, p. 30.

35. Coggeshall, *American Privateers*, p. 26.

36. Smith, *Naval Scenes*, pp. 30–31.

37. Hawes, ed., "Letters of Henry Gilliam": Gilliam to William Jones, 7 Sept. 1812. There is an old and popular story to the effect that Hull and Dacres, before

the war, had wagered a hat on the outcome of a contest between their two ships and that Hull, on this occasion, told Dacres he would not accept his sword, "But I will trouble you for that hat!" Alas for romance; investigation has shown that the two men never met before the war and could not have made the wager. Moreover, Isaac Hull sternly disapproved of dueling between individuals; it is scarcely possible to imagine him setting a wager on a duel between ships. That would have been, for him, tantamount to gambling with the lives of his men.

38. NA, RG 24, *Constitution* log, 20 Aug. 1812. Details of the battle are drawn from many sources, including Hull's official letters (see notes 43 and 45 below); Morris's *Autobiography* and an extract from his journal in the Elliot Coll.; Smith's *Naval Scenes*, Evans's journal and Gilliam's letter; MassHS: Journal of Frederick Baury; Coggeshall's *American Privateers*, Bowen's *Naval Monument*, contemporary newspaper items in *The War*, and *Niles' Register*; a letter from Captain William B. Orne to Phineas Sprague in the G. H. Stuart Coll., LC; letter of Lt. John Contee, U.S.M.C., to Col. Franklin Wharton, 31 Aug. 1812, in NA, RG 45, Area 9 file; and Dacres's court-martial in Public Record Office, Admiralty 1/502.

In his book on the frigate *Constitution, A Most Fortunate Ship* (Chester, Conn., rev. ed. 1982), Tyrone G. Martin has presented an account and a diagram of the *Constitution–Guerrière* battle, based on his own knowledge of the behavior of floating bodies, which differ widely from my account and from Isaac Hull's diagram, reproduced on page 187. Commander Martin and I have had extensive correspondence on the subject, but agreed to disagree. Although his book as a whole is the result of thorough research as well as his own expertise, it is not documented. Therefore I would like to explain our respective positions for the reader.

Commander Martin reasons that, when the *Guerrière's* mizzenmast went over the side, the resulting drag in the water would have turned her bow *away* from the *Constitution*, and that the *Constitution* could not have crossed her bow, been caught aback, and begun a turn back to larboard before the ships collided. He thinks, therefore, that the *Constitution* actually lay on the *Guerrière's* *starboard* beam, and that the fall of the mizzen brought the *Guerrière* directly around into the *Constitution's* quarter, resulting in the collision. He has drawn a new diagram of the battle accordingly. The main problem with all this is the unanimous testimony of the contemporary witnesses against it. Martin has to account for Hull's different version of the battle by postulating an attempt on his part to make himself look better by inventing some fancy maneuvering. (This does not, however, account for the agreement of the other witnesses with Hull.) I differ with Martin in both his speculations for the following reasons:

1. The historian must rely on eyewitness accounts of past events unless there is some very serious reason to doubt them. When the eyewitness accounts come from a number of unrelated sources, as is the case here, it is almost impossible to disregard their testimony. As John Dickinson said at the Constitutional Convention: "Experience must be our only guide. Reason may mislead us." In this case, reasoning about what *should* have happened has, in my opinion, misled Martin.

2. In addition to the sources mentioned in this note, and in notes 43 and 45 below, we have the evidence of the series of four paintings of the battle by

Michel Corné, which were done immediately after the battle *under Hull's direction,* and which were widely circulated as engravings. (For full-color reproductions of these paintings, see Linda McKee [Maloney], "By Heaven, that Ship is Ours," *American Heritage* 16, no. 1 (Dec. 1964), pp. 4–11. See also note 63 below.) It is out of the question that Hull could have given such full publicity to an incorrect account of the battle at a time when some five hundred eyewitnesses could have refuted him. It should be noted that one of the most important witnesses in favor of Hull's account was Charles Morris, who had already been promoted to Captain and had absolutely nothing to gain by currying favor with Hull.

3. There is one document that speaks of the *Constitution* as approaching on the *Guerrière's* starboard beam. That is Dacres's court-martial. But here it should be kept in mind, first, that Dacres certainly had to make himself look good (to avoid being cashiered), and second, that he reckoned the battle as lasting more than two hours, i.e., from the time the first long-range shots were fired. At that time, and during the subsequent maneuvering, the *Constitution* may indeed have approached the *Guerrière's* starboard beam, but she did not do so during the close action, as later parts of Dacres's own account show.

4. Finally, there is no shred of evidence that Hull could have made himself look better by falsifying an account of the battle, nor that he wanted to. He actually suggested that the secretary of the navy suppress his first, longer account of the battle on the principle of "the less said the better." If he had been making up a story, surely he would not have fabricated the embarrassing details of being caught aback and colliding with the *Guerrière!* In fact, twenty years later it was suggested that Hull had sacrificed the advantage of the windward position by taking station on the *Guerrière's* larboard side—that is, he would have done better to say he had placed the *Constitution* to starboard. He denied this, saying that both ships were running before the wind, and therefore there was no advantage to be gained in taking one side or the other. But it would seem that Commander Martin's version of the battle would in fact have made Hull look better than his own account did!

Martin thinks that Hull was lucky to have won this engagement—that it could have gone either way. There is some truth to that, but it cannot be denied that "luck" comes more often to the skillful and the daring. Hull knew his advantages, and he used them: he demanded close action, where his big guns would do the most damage, and where, if his ship should be disabled, he could board and overthrow his enemy by means of his larger, better-equipped crew. He made his luck and he won his laurels. Gilding the lily was not his style.

39. Theodore Roosevelt calculates these percentages in elaborate detail; see his *The Naval War of 1812* (New York, 1897), p. 70. Figures on the *Guerrière's* crew vary.

40. Edmund Quincy, *Life of Josiah Quincy of Massachusetts* (Boston, 1867), pp. 262–263, quoted in Allen, *Papers of Isaac Hull,* pp. 28–29.

41. Smith, *Naval Scenes,* p. 35.

42. Quincy, *Life of Josiah Quincy,* p. 264, quoted in Charles Francis Adams, "Wednesday, August 19, 1812, 6:30 P.M.: the Birth of a World Power," *American Historical Review* 18: 519–520.

43. Bruce Grant, *Isaac Hull, Captain of Old Ironsides*, pp. 394–397, n. 2: Hull to Hamilton, 28 Aug. 1812.
44. Quoted in *The War* 1: 114, 28 Dec. 1812.
45. CL: Hull to Hamilton, 30 Aug. 1812.
46. CL: Hull to Hamilton, 1 Sept. 1812.
47. CL: Bainbridge to Hamilton, 2 Sept. 1812.
48. OSW: Hamilton to Hull, 9 Sept. 1812.
49. MassHS: Wm. Sullivan to Isaac Hull, 10 Sept. 1812.
50. MassHS: Hull to Arnold Welles, Wm. Sullivan, Francis J. Oliver, and Henry Purkitt, 12 Sept. 1812.
51. HSPa: Hull to C. A. Rodney, 9 Sept. 1812.
52. Elliot Coll.: Sir James Jay to Hull, 12 Sept. 1812.
53. Evans journal, 11 Sept. 1812.
54. OSW: Hamilton to Hull, 9 Sept. 1812.
55. Smith, *Naval Scenes*, p. 38.
56. CL: Bainbridge to Hamilton, 17 Sept. 1812.
57. LC, Warden Papers: Hull to Warden, 16 Sept. 1812.
58. NA, RG 45, Area 11 file: Hamilton to Hull, 10 Oct. 1812.
59. CL: Hull to Hamilton, 15 Oct. 1812.
60. Elliot Coll.: Isaac Hull to Joseph Hull, 21 Oct. 1812.
61. CL: Hull to Hamilton, 4 Nov. 1812.
62. OSW: Hamilton to Hull, 12 Nov. 1812; *The War* 1: 133–135, 26 Jan. 1813.
63. Hull to Chew, 14 Nov. 1812. A copy of this letter was furnished me in 1963 by the courtesy of its owner, Mr. J. William Middendorf II. The original is now in the Philadelphia Maritime Museum. It was once part of a collection of seventeen letters from Hull to Chew, dated from 28 July 1812 to 14 June 1817. The remaining sixteen letters were sold by Parke-Bernet Galleries in April 1963 to an unknown collector who has declined all requests to examine them. I have been forced to rely on the snippets from the sale catalogue for the contents of these important letters, several of which give minute descriptions of the *Constitution–Guerrière* engagement for the guidance of the painter, Corné.
64. NA, RG 45, Area 7 file: Hull to Theodore Hunt, 2 Dec. 1812.
65. NYHS; Hull to Bullus, 4 Dec. [1812].
66. Quoted in Oliver W. Larkin, *Art and Life in America* (New York, 1956), p. 110.
67. Quincy, *Life of Josiah Quincy*, p. 262, in Allen, *Papers of Isaac Hull*, p. 29.
68. *The War* 1: 118–119, 4 Jan. 1813.
69. See NYHS, *Collections*, 1931, Diaries of William Dunlap, vol. 3, entry for 23 June 1833; Hull to Chew, 14 Nov. 1812 (see note 63 above).
70. R. S. Guernsey, *New York City and Vicinity during the War of 1812–15*, 2 vols. (New York, 1889), 1: 152–156.
71. NA, Naval History Division, ZB file: Hull to Bullus, 7 Jan. 1813, partial typescript.
72. NA, RG 45, Area 7 file: Hull to Rodgers, 7 Jan. 1813.
73. Quoted in Allen, *Papers of Isaac Hull*, p. 31.
74. Quoted in Allen, *Papers of Isaac Hull*, p. 39.
75. *Samuel F. B. Morse; his Letters and Journals*, ed. and supplemented by

his son *Edward Lind Morse* (Boston and New York, 1914), 1: 112: J. Hillhouse to S. F. B. Morse, 12 July 1813.

76. Elliot Coll.: Henry Hull to Mary W. Hull, 17 Jan. 1813.

77. Elliot Coll.: Ann Hull to Mary W. Hull, 27 Feb. 1813.

78. CL: Hull to Wm. Jones, 11 Mar. 1813; OSW: Jones to Hull, 15 Mar. 1813.

79. Elliot Coll.: Isaac Hull to Joseph Hull, 21 Mar. 1813; Ann Hull to Mary W. Hull, 22 Mar. 1813.

80. *Oracle* (Portsmouth), 3 Apr. 1813.

Chapter 9

1. *ASP,* Naval Affairs, 1: 326.

2. *ASP,* Naval Affairs, 1: 90–91.

3. *ASP,* Naval Affairs, 1: 85. Final purchase price was $5,500.

4. CL: Preble to Robert Smith, 6 Oct. 1806.

5. CL: Hull to William Jones, 3 Apr. 1813.

6. *ASP,* Naval Affairs, 1: 326.

7. Chapelle, *American Sailing Navy,* pp. 80–83.

8. CL: Hull to Jones, 3 Apr. 1813.

9. CL: Hull to Jones, 20 Apr. 1813.

10. CL: Hull to Jones, 20 May 1813. Captains in the navy received $1,200 per annum, but they also drew eight rations per day. A ration being computed at $0.20, this added a comfortable $600 per year. *ASP,* Naval Affairs, 1: 255; General LB: Schedule of Pay and Rations, enclosed in Jones to A. Glennie & Sons, 4 Jan. 1814.

11. CL: Hull to Jones, 20, 29 Apr. 1813.

12. Comm. LB: Jones to Hull, 9 Apr. 1813; NYHS, Hull LB: Hull to Bainbridge, 22 Apr. 1813; CL: Hull to Jones, 23 Apr. 1813.

13. Chapelle, *American Sailing Navy,* p. 131.

14. Comm. LB: Jones to Hull, 9 Apr. 1813; Jones to Bainbridge, 9 Apr. 1813.

15. CL: Hull to Jones, 2 Nov. 1813.

16. Comm. LB: Jones to Bainbridge, 28 Apr. 1813; CL: Hull to Jones, 5 May 1813; Bainbridge to Jones, 11 May 1813. On this subject, Jones became philosophic: "The formation of floating bodies, their relative dimensions and complicated connection with the multifarious objects of force, activity, capacity, strength, stability, ease and safety requires a life of study and practice tested by the experience of those nations who have attained the highest eminence in the art, illustrated by that of our own, in which every variety of form and fancy has been indulged even to excess." Obviously, he thought he was just the man to remedy the situation.

17. CL: Hull to Jones, 23 Apr. 1813.

18. CL: Hull to Jones, 28 Apr. 1813, enclosure.

19. NYHS, Hull LB: Hull to Bainbridge, 12 June 1813.

20. CL: Hull to Jones, 6 July 1813.

21. CL: Hull to Jones, 24 July 1813.

22. H. A. S. Dearborn, *The Life of William Bainbridge* (Princeton, 1931), p.

188; Thomas Harris, *The Life and Services of Commodore William Bainbridge* (Philadelphia, 1837), p. 184. Harris gives the date of Bainbridge's letter as 21 Aug. 1813. Hull's suggestion was made on 24 July. See David F. Long, *Ready to Hazard: A Biography of Commodore William Bainbridge, 1774–1833* (Hanover, N.H., 1981), p. 171.

23. NYHS, Hull LB: Hull to Bainbridge, 9 Aug. 1813.

24. Comm. LB: Jones to Hull, 10 Aug. 1813.

25. Walter E. H. Fentress, *Centennial History of the United States Navy Yard, at Portsmouth, N.H.* (Portsmouth, 1876), pp. 40, 80. The *New Hampshire* was originally called the *Alabama* but was rechristened before the launching.

26. NYHS, Hull LB: Hull to Bainbridge, 23 Sept. 1813.

27. NYHS, Hull LB: Hull to Binney, 7 Oct. 1813.

28. NYHS, Hull LB: Hull to Bainbridge, 13 Oct. 1813.

29. CL: Hull to Jones, 20 Apr., 7 May 1813.

30. NYHS, Hull LB: Hull to Bainbridge, 1 Oct. 1813.

31. NYHS, Hull LB: Hull to Bainbridge, 2 Nov. 1813.

32. Chapelle, *American Sailing Navy*, p. 269.

33. CL: Hull to Jones, 24 Nov. 1813.

34. CL: Bainbridge to Jones, 15 Dec. 1813; Hull to Jones, 17 Dec. 1813.

35. Elliot Coll.: Ann Hull to Mary W. Hull, 16 May 1813.

36. Elliot Coll.: Isaac Hull to Mary W. Hull, 14 Apr. 1813.

37. Elliot Coll.: Ann Hull to Mary W. Hull, 16 May 1813.

38. Elliot Coll.: Isaac Hull to Charles Hull, 19 May 1813.

39. LC, Rodgers Family Papers: Hull to Rodgers, 11 Apr. 1813.

40. LC, Rodgers Family Papers: Ann Hull to Minerva Rodgers, 25 May [1813]; Paullin, *Commodore John Rodgers*, p. 279.

41. Elliot Coll.: Isaac Hull to Mary W. Hull, 20 June 1813.

42. Elliot Coll.: Eliza Hart to Mary W. Hull, 1 July 1813.

43. CL: Hull to Jones, 24 May 1813.

44. CL: Hull to Jones, 23 Aug. 1814.

45. NA, RG 217, Letters Received by the Accountant of the Navy: T. Craven to [T. Turner], 9 Feb. 1813.

46. CL: Hull to Jones, 20 Apr. 1813.

47. Charles W. Brewster, *Rambles About Portsmouth* (Portsmouth, N.H., 1859–1869), 2d ser., Ramble 120.

48. *New Hampshire Gazette* (Portsmouth), 28 Dec. 1813; WLCL, Neil Family Papers: G. Andrews to W. Neil, Mar. 1814.

49. *Intelligencer* (Portsmouth), 21 Oct. 1813.

50. CL: Hull to Jones, 27 Dec. 1813.

51. WLCL, Hubert S. Smith Coll.: Isaac Hull to Gen. William Hull, 26 Feb. 1814.

52. LC, Rodgers Family Papers: Hull to Rodgers, 21 Feb. 1814.

53. LC, Rodgers Family Papers: Bainbridge to Rodgers, 9 Mar. 1814.

54. CL: Hull to Jones, 7 May 1813.

55. Comm. LB: Jones to Hull, 14 May 1813.

56. CL: Hull to Jones, 20 May 1813.

57. New Hampshire Archives, Executive Docs.: Plumer to Clement Storer, 20 May 1813; W. Marshall to J. T. Gilman, 14 Oct. 1813.

58. CL: Hull to Jones, 5 June 1813.
59. NYHS, Hull LB: Hull to Bainbridge, 9 June 1813; Hull to Blake, 10 June 1813.
60. Brewster, *Rambles About Portsmouth*, 2d ser., Ramble 130.
61. New Hampshire Archives, Executive Docs.: Votes of Portsmouth town meeting, 2 Aug. 1813; *Intelligencer* (Portsmouth), 1 July 1813; *Oracle* (Portsmouth), 17, 24 July, 21 Aug. 1813; *War Journal* (Portsmouth), 30 July 1813.
62. NA, RG 45, Miscellaneous Letters Received by the Secretary of the Navy: W. Widgery to J. Monroe, 10 May 1813 (hereafter Misc.).
63. CL: Hull to Jones, 24 June 1813; Comm. LB: Jones to Hull, 5 July 1813.
64. CL: Samuel Storer to Hull, 6 Sept. 1813; NYHS, Hull LB: Hull to Bainbridge, 5 [i.e., 6] Sept. 1813.
65. NYHS, Hull LB: Hull to S. Storer, 12 Oct. 1813.
66. William Goold, *Portland in the Past* (Portland, 1886), pp. 489–491; Misc.: J. Thompson to Jones, 21 Jan. 1814. The "passing stranger" was Silas M. Burrows of New York, no relation to William Burrows.
67. NYHS, Hull LB: Hull to Bainbridge, 23 Sept. 1813.
68. OL: H. B. Rapp, Peter Gamble, J. H. Aulick, and Thos. Newell to William Jones, 22 Nov. 1813.
69. CL: Hull to Jones, 13 Jan. 1814.
70. CL: Creighton to Hull, 10 Dec. 1813; D. Yeates to Jones, 10 Nov., 12 Dec. 1813; OSW: Jones to Hull, 22 Dec. 1813; CL: Hull to Jones, 1 Jan. 1814.
71. LC, Rodgers Family Papers: Bainbridge to Rodgers, 9 Mar. 1814.
72. CL: Blakeley to Bainbridge, 20 Dec. 1813, encl. in Bainbridge to Jones, 21 Dec. 1813.
73. CL: Stoodley to Hull, 28 Apr. 1814, encl. in Hull to Jones, 27 [i.e., 28] Apr. 1814.
74. CL: Hull to Jones, 1 Mar. 1814.
75. Brewster, *Rambles About Portsmouth*, 2d ser., Ramble 130.
76. CL: Hull to Jones, 7 Dec. 1813.
77. Comm. LB: Jones to Hull, 3 Feb. 1814.
78. NYHS, Hull LB: Hull to Bainbridge, 3 July 1813.
79. NYHS, Hull LB: Hull to J. S. Williams, 3 July 1813.
80. Letters Received by the Accountant of the Navy: Hull to Turner, 2 Jan. 1813; [i.e., 1814]; Accountant's LB: Turner to Hull, 18 Jan. 1814.
81. Brewster, *Rambles About Portsmouth*, 1st ser., Ramble 51.
82. NYHS, Hull LB: Hull to J. J. Nicholson, 12 Mar. 1814.
83. NA, RG 127, Service Records, Marine Corps: Aaron Smith.
84. OSW: Jones to Hull, 18 Apr. 1814.
85. OSW: Jones to Hull, 26 Apr. 1814.
86. See Henry Adams, *History of the United States of America*, 9 vols. (New York, 1889–1891), 7: 385–390.
87. CL: Hull to Jones, 5 May 1814.
88. CL: Hull to Jones, 25 June 1814; NYHS, Hull LB: Hull to Bainbridge, 3 Aug. 1814.
89. NYHS, Hull LB: Hull to Bainbridge, 25 May 1814; CL: Hull to Jones, 26 May 1814.
90. Comm. LB: Jones to Hull, 14 Jan. 1814.

91. CL: Hull to Jones, 23 Jan. 1814.

92. CL: Hull to Jones, 25 Jan. 1814.

93. LC, Isaac Hull Papers: Jones to Hull, 31 Jan. 1814.

94. NYHS, Hull LB: Hull to Walbach, 25 Mar. 1814.

95. NYHS, Hull LB: Hull to J. Mason, 25 Mar. 1814.

96. New Hampshire Archives, Executive Docs.: Anonymous to Hull, 7 Apr. 1814.

97. CL: Hull to Jones, 9 Apr. 1814.

98. *New Hampshire Gazette,* 12 Apr. 1814.

99. *New Hampshire Gazette,* 19 Apr. 1814; New Hampshire Archives, Executive Docs.: Votes of the Town of Portsmouth Presented to the Governor by a Committee, 25 Apr. 1814.

100. NYHS, Hull LB: Hull to L. DeForrest, 11 May 1814. The boats of *La Hogue,* 74, had landed at Pettipague, or Pettipaug Point, Connecticut, a village of about fifty houses forming part of the town of Saybrook, in April, and burned the shipping. *The War,* 19 Apr. 1814.

101. Detroit Public Library, Burton Historical Collection, Henry Burbeck LB: Burbeck to Hull, 13 May 1814.

102. *New Hampshire Gazette,* 24 May 1814.

103. Walter M. Whitehill, ed., *New England Blockaded in 1814; the Journal of Henry Edward Napier, Lieutenant in H.M.S. Nymphe* (Salem, 1939), p. 18. Italics added.

104. *New England Blockaded,* pp. 18–19; CL: Hull to Jones, 29 May 1814.

105. *New England Blockaded,* p. 20.

106. Comm. LB: Jones to Hull, 17 June 1814.

107. See Henry Adams, *History of the United States* 8: 220–221, 287–288; 9: 45; *New England Blockaded,* p. 60, n. 17.

108. *New Hampshire Gazette,* 28 June 1814; NYHS, Hull LB: Hull to Walbach, 22 June 1814.

109. *New Hampshire Gazette,* 28 June 1814; *Oracle,* 23 July 1814; CL: Hull to Jones, 9 July 1814.

110. Elliot Coll.: Isaac Hull to Mary W. Hull, 22 Aug. 1814.

111. NYHS, Hull LB: Hull to Henry Dearborn, 3 Sept. 1814.

112. CL: Hull to Jones, 5 Sept. 1814.

113. CL: Hull to Jones, 8 Sept. 1814.

114. *New Hampshire Gazette,* 13 Sept. 1814.

115. CL: Hull to Jones, 11 Sept. 1814.

116. NYHS, Hull LB: Hull to Bainbridge, 15 Sept. 1814.

117. *New Hampshire Gazette,* 27 Sept. 1814.

118. Comm. LB: Jones to Bainbridge, 26 Sept. 1814; CL: Bainbridge to Jones, 1 Oct. 1814.

119. *Oracle,* 8 Oct. 1814.

120. Letters Received by the Accountant of the Navy: T. A. Beatty to Thomas Turner, 21 Oct. 1814.

121. *Oracle,* 8 Oct. 1814.

122. CL: Hull to Jones, 2, 4 Oct. 1814.

123. CL: Hull to Jones, 3 Oct. 1814.

124. Comm. LB: Circular to Navy Agents, 15 Sept. 1814.

125. Letters Received by the Accountant of the Navy: Morris to W. S. Rogers, 1 Nov. 1814.

126. CL: Hull to Jones, 2 Nov. 1814; Comm. LB: Jones to Hull, 10 Nov. 1814.

127. Elliot Coll.: Isaac Hull to Mary W. Hull, 15 Nov. 1814.

128. NYHS, Hull LB: Hull to J. B. Walbach, 29 Nov. 1814.

129. NYHS, Hull LB: Hull to J. Mason, 28 Nov. 1814.

130. ConnHS: Hull to Wolcott, 29 Nov. 1814; Wolcott to Hull, 8 Dec. 1814.

131. CL: Hull to Jones, 3 Dec. 1814.

132. LC, Rodgers Family Papers: Bainbridge to Rodgers, 21 Dec. 1814.

133. WLCL, Chew Papers: Lyde to Thomas Chew, 14 Jan. 1815.

134. Peabody Museum of Salem, Mass., B. W. Crowninshield Papers: Rodgers to Crowninshield, 13 Feb. 1815.

135. NYHS, Hull LB: Hull to Samuel Storer, 21 Feb. 1815.

Chapter 10

1. *ASP*, Naval Affairs, 1: 324.

2. Junior "commodores" and their reasons for so styling themselves included:
David Porter, who had commanded the gunboat flotilla at New Orleans and had then created his own "fleet" of captured merchant vessels in the Pacific in 1813. Subsequently he was given command of one of the "flying squadrons" of brigs and schooners being put together in the winter of 1814–1815;
John Shaw, who had succeeded Porter at New Orleans; in 1815 he would be left in charge of the Mediterranean squadron by Bainbridge;
Isaac Chauncey, Oliver H. Perry, and *Thomas Macdonough*, who had held the wartime commands on Lakes Ontario, Erie, and Champlain, respectively;
Daniel Todd Patterson, wartime commander at New Orleans.
Perry and Macdonough were commissioned captains in September 1814, Patterson on 28 February 1815. Jesse D. Elliott, still a master commandant in 1815, succeeded Perry as "commodore" on Lake Erie.

3. NA, RG 233, Records of the House of Representatives, HR 11A–F6.1, Petition of the Navy Officers of the United States, 1808, 1810. Several copies of the petition are present, each evidently signed by the officers of a different part of the country. The signatures on the Boston copy were headed by that of Isaac Hull.

4. NYHS, Hull LB: Hull to D. Daggett, 18 Nov. 1814.

5. *ASP*, Naval Affairs, 1: 324.

6. NYHS, Hull LB: Hull to Daggett, 24 Nov. 1814.

7. Yale University Library: Hull to Daggett, 20 Nov. 1814.

8. NYHS, Hull LB: Hull to J. Mason, 28 Nov. 1814.

9. NYHS, Hull LB: Hull to W. Reed, 1 Dec. 1814.

10. WLCL, Chew Papers: Hull to Chew, 30 Dec. 1814.

11. NYHS: Hull to Bullus, 26 Feb. 1814 [i.e., 1815].

12. Peabody Museum of Salem, Mass., B. W. Crowninshield Papers: H. A. S. Dearborn to Crowninshield, 7 Jan. 1814 [i.e., 1815].

13. NYHS, Hull LB: Hull to J. Mason, 28 Nov. 1814.

14. The canceled word is so lightly crossed off in the original that it was obviously intended to be read by the recipient.

15. Peabody Museum, BWC Papers: Rodgers to Crowninshield, 11 Feb. 1815.

16. Peabody Museum, BWC Papers: Rodgers to Crowninshield, 13 Feb. 1815.

17. LC, Rodgers Family Papers: Hull to Rodgers, 8 Mar. 1815.

18. NYHS, Frederick Rodgers Coll. (microfilm): Hull to Rodgers, 9 Mar. 1815.

19. Indiana University Library: Hull to Porter, 9 Mar. 1815.

20. CL: Hull to Crowninshield, 11 Mar. 1815; NYHS, Hull LB: Hull to S. Storer, 11 Mar. 1815.

21. WLCL, Charles Morris Papers: Tingey to Morris, 15 Mar. 1815.

22. Comm. LB: Crowninshield to Hull, 18 Mar. 1815.

23. *New Hampshire Gazette*, 21 Mar., 4 Apr. 1815.

24. NYHS, Frederick Rodgers Coll. (microfilm): Hull to Rodgers, 23 Mar. 1815.

25. WLCL, Porter Papers: Hull to Porter, [5 Apr.] 1815.

26. Misc.: Commissioners to Crowninshield, 25 Apr. 1815.

27. NYHS, Frederick Rodgers Coll. (microfilm): Hull to Rodgers, 23 Mar. 1815. On Paulding's resignation in 1823 Goldsborough moved up to the secretaryship, where he remained for twenty years.

28. NA, RG 45, Letters Sent by the Secretary of the Navy to the Board of Navy Commissioners: Crowninshield to Rodgers, 23 May 1815.

29. NA, RG 45, Letters Sent by the Board of Navy Commissioners to the Secretary of the Navy: Rodgers to Crowninshield, 19 May 1815; Hull, Rodgers, and Porter to James Madison, 25 May 1815 (hereafter Comm. to SecNav). This attempted "power grab" by Rodgers and Porter is not surprising, given the personalities involved. As incumbents of a newly created office, they were determined to acquire for themselves as much authority as possible. Moreover, they were testing the mettle of a new secretary. Crowninshield, however, proved not quite as pliant as they had expected.

30. MeHS, Fogg Autograph Coll.: Hull to John Bullus, 24 May 1815.

31. Comm. to SecNav: Commissioners to Crowninshield, 2 May 1815. There can be no doubt at all that Isaac Hull, who had built gunboats in Rhode Island and Connecticut and whose father was still navy agent for Connecticut, suggested seeking a navy yard site in that area.

32. *National Intelligencer*, 23 May 1815; MeHS, Fogg Autograph Coll.: Hull to Bullus, 24 May 1815.

33. Although often referred to as the Boston yard, the facility is actually located in Charlestown, across the Mystic River.

34. NA, RG 45, Letters Received by the Board of Navy Commissioners: Hull to Rodgers, 27 Sept. 1815 (hereafter Comm. Rec.).

35. Elliot Coll.: Isaac Hull to Mary W. Hull, 15 Dec. 1815.

36. CL: Hull to Crowninshield, 5 Nov. 1815. Rates of pay for lake service were higher because there was little prospect of prize money on those stations.

37. NYHS: Bainbridge to Porter, 6 Sept. 1815.

38. NYHS, Frederick Rodgers Coll. (microfilm): Hull to Rodgers, 20 Nov. 1815.

39. Comm. Rec.: Bainbridge to Crowninshield, 19 Nov. 1815 (copy).

40. WLCL, Chew Papers: A. H. Chew to T. J. Chew, 22 Nov. [1815]; T. J. Chew to A. H. Chew, [23 Nov. 1815].
41. CL: Hull to Crowninshield, 20 Nov. 1815.
42. NYHS: Bainbridge to Porter, 20 Dec. 1815.
43. CL: Bainbridge to Crowninshield, 23 Dec. 1815.
44. NYHS: Bainbridge to Porter, 24 Jan. 1816.
45. NYHS, Frederick Rodgers Coll. (microfilm): Hull to Rodgers, 3 Mar. 1817.
46. Chapelle, *American Sailing Navy*, p. 312.
47. Comm. Rec.: Hull to Rodgers, 12 Dec. 1816.
48. *Minutes of Proceedings of the Court of Enquiry into the Official Conduct of Capt. Isaac Hull, as Commandant of the United States Navy Yard at Charlestown, in the State of Massachusetts, Convened at the Navy-Yard in Charlestown, on the 12th day of August, A.D. 1822* (Washington, 1822), appendix, pp. 49–50 (hereafter *Hull Court*).
49. Elliot Coll.: Isaac Hull to Mary W. Hull, 15 Dec. 1815.
50. Comm. Rec.: Hull to Rodgers, 18 Oct. 1816.
51. Comm. Rec.: Hull to Rodgers, 30 Mar. 1817.
52. Comm. Rec.: Hull to Rodgers, 20 Apr. 1817; Navy Commissioners' Letter Book: Rodgers to Hull, 28 Apr. 1817 (hereafter NCLB).
53. Comm. Rec.: Hull to Rodgers, 20 May 1817.
54. Comm. Rec.: Hull to Rodgers, 10 June 1817. The shortage of workmen, and consequent employment of all available hands for whatever tasks needed to be done, could produce unfavorable impressions. Samuel F. Holbrook, a naval carpenter briefly attached to the yard in 1817, wrote in his autobiography, "I noticed very soon after I had joined the yard, the boatswain and gunner with one of the master's mates, were often busy about the commodore's house, and frequently about the kitchen: and at one time I saw the boatswain go over to Boston with a wheelbarrow, and bring home the commodore's marketing, which was derogatory to their rank." Samuel F. Holbrook, *Threescore Years: an Autobiography* (Boston, 1857), p. 194.
55. Sarah H. Jarvis to Samuel F. Jarvis, 31 July 1817, copy in possession of Eleanor T. Tilton.
56. Sarah H. Jarvis to Samuel F. Jarvis, 27 July 1817, copy in possession of Eleanor T. Tilton.
57. Elliot Coll.: Isaac Hull to Mary W. Hull, 2 Nov. 1817. This was certainly *not* Johnston Blakeley's widow.
58. Elliot Coll.: Isaac Hull to Mary W. Hull, 7 Mar. 1818.
59. Elliot Coll.: Isaac Hull to Mary W. Hull, 12 June, 8 Sept. 1818.
60. NA, RG 181, Daily Journal of Transactions at the Navy Yard, Charlestown, Mass. (hereafter Charlestown Journal), 2–6 July 1817.
61. Charles Francis Adams, ed., *Memoirs of John Quincy Adams, Comprising Portions of his Diary from 1795 to 1848*, 12 vols. (Philadelphia, 1874–1877), 4: 6; Charlestown Journal, 30 Aug. 1817.
62. Pierpont Morgan Library: Hull to G. C. Read, 4 Nov. 1817.
63. ConnHS: Copy of resolutions of the legislature, 28 Oct. 1817; Hull to Wolcott, 8 Jan. 1818.
64. ConnHS: Hull to Wolcott, 6 July 1818.

65. Comm. Rec.: Hull to Rodgers, 29 July 1818.
66. WLCL: Hull to T. Aspinwall, 26 Jan. 1818; Comm. Rec.: Hull to Rodgers, 11, 23 Dec. 1818.
67. NYHS, Hull to S. W. Dana, 17 Nov. 1818.
68. Charlestown Journal, 26 Oct. 1818; Harvard University, Houghton Library: "Recollections" of Samuel C. Clarke.
69. CL: Hull to Crowninshield, 26 Mar. 1818; Comm. LB: Crowninshield to Hull, 3 Apr. 1818.
70. Chicago Historical Society: Hull to Bainbridge, [23 Jan. 1819].

Chapter 11

1. See above, chapter 10.
2. LC, John Shaw Papers: Miles King to John Shaw, 10 July 1819. There were three orders of broad pendants: blue for the senior commodore present, red for the second, and white for the third. "Pendant," rather than "pennant" was the nineteenth-century usage, and it was accurate: the short "broad pendant" was hung from a central swivel, as was the narrow "long pendant" that a captain flew.
3. FDR Lib.: Isaac Hull to Samuel W. Dana, 8 Mar. 1820.
4. Comm. LB: Circular, 1 May 1820.
5. CL: Hull to Thompson, 10 May 1820.
6. Comm. LB: Thompson to Hull, 17 May 1820.
7. NA, RG 125, Records of the Judge Advocate General (Navy), Records of General Courts-Martial and Courts of Inquiry (microcopy no. 273), Trial of P. A. J. P. Jones, 28 July–5 Aug. 1818; second trial 8–13 May 1820. Jones planned to bring countercharges against Macomber, but the master commandant was accidentally drowned in March 1820.
8. Misc.: Hull to Thompson, 11 Feb. 1820. A peculiarity of the law made warrant officers, including midshipmen and sailing masters, exempt from prosecution for debt.
9. Peabody Museum of Salem, BWC Papers: Crowninshield to Constant Freeman, 1 July 1817.
10. Trial of Lieutenant Joel Abbot, by the General Court Martial, Holden on Board the U.S. ship Independence, at the Navy Yard, Charlestown, Massachusetts. On Allegations made against him, by Captain David Porter, Navy Commissioner (Washington, 1822), p. 115 (hereafter Trial of Abbot); Abbot, Caldwell, and Ferguson to Smith Thompson, 2 Jan. 1821; Thompson to Abbot, Caldwell, and Ferguson, 16 Jan. 1821. The fact that many lieutenants were married helps to account both for their poverty and for their unwillingness to live on shipboard.
11. Trial of Abbot, testimony of William M. Caldwell, pp. 58–63.
12. Trial of Abbot, pp. 120–122.
13. Comm. LB: Crowninshield to Hull, 4 Jan. 1816.
14. Comm. LB: Crowninshield to Hull, 18 Jan. 1816; Trial of Abbot, testimony of Charles F. Waldo, pp. 75–76. In 1821 Hull and Navy Agent Amos Binney strongly supported a claim by Waldo, ultimately successful, for yard housing and full allowances.

15. *Trial of Lieutenant Joel Abbot, by the General Naval Court Martial, Holden on Board the U.S. ship Independence, at the Navy Yard, Charlestown, Massachusetts, on Allegations made against him, by Capt. David Porter, Navy Commissioner. Reported by F. W. Waldo . . . To which is added, an Appendix, containing sundry documents in relation to the management of affairs on the Boston station* (Boston, 1822), appendix D, pp. 4–8. This version of the trial was printed privately by Abbot and his friends.

Samuel Holbrook's autobiography (see above, chapter 10, note 54) provides an illuminating example of Hull's dealings with yard subordinates. Holbrook was at the yard in 1817, a time when the establishment was desperately shorthanded. Unwilling to perform duty he considered beneath his rank as a carpenter, and knowing Hull would not release him because of the shortage of men, Holbrook secured a berth for himself on board an Indiaman, then went directly to Secretary of the Navy Crowninshield at Salem to obtain his furlough. Only afterward did he confront his commanding officer with the fait accompli: "and when I first named it to him, he was quite astonished at my not having first applied to him. . . . He seemed to regret my leaving the yard" (p. 196). Rodgers's or Bainbridge's reaction to such a confrontation would have been audible in Salem without amplification. But Hull, who according to Joel Abbot was guilty of "oppressing" his subordinates with unusual meanness, took it as a matter of course. Despite this lenity, Holbrook passed critical judgment on Hull: "Commodore Hull was an excellent seaman, and as all the world knows, a brave naval officer: yet he was evidently lacking in one point, and that was, a proper respect for his officers" (p. 194). It is difficult to know what more respect Hull could have shown; however, Holbrook's particular criticism seems to have been that the captain was *too* intimate with some of the subordinate officers and master workmen, a relationship that, in Abbot's mind, pointed to a sinister conspiracy.

16. Comm. Rec.: Hull to Rodgers, 7 Nov. 1818; OL: Bates to Secretary of the Navy, 11 Dec. 1818.

17. Elliot Coll.: assorted deeds and mortgages, 1816–1821; Boston Athenaeum, Isaac Hull Papers: translation of a letter enclosed in John A. Merle to Isaac Hull, 1 Sept. 1821. Francs were then about 5.30 to the dollar.

18. WLCL, Smith Naval Collection: Hull to T. Aspinwall, 26 Jan. 1818; *Trial of Abbot*, testimony of John Percival, pp. 71–72.

19. *Trial of Abbot*, testimony of Samuel R. Trevett, p. 80. In fact, Percival's pay account was receipted 5 Sept. 1818; he paid the money to Hull, through Sailing Master Waldo, on 11 Sept. Receipts in trial appendix. Percival denied this conversation under oath in 1822.

20. NYHS; Percival to Aspinwall, 21 May 1821.

21. Hull to Samuel W. Dana, 4 July 1820. Copy furnished from Goodspeed's Bookshop, Nov. 1961.

22. HSPa: Mortgage note of Isaac Hull to Rowleff Classen, 29 Apr. 1820.

23. Elliot Coll.: Isaac Hull to Mary W. Hull, 17 Jan. 1821.

24. WLCL, Porter Papers: Hull to Porter, 20 Sept. 1820.

25. Comm. Rec.: Hull to Rodgers, 22 Sept. 1820.

26. *Trial of Shaw*, appendix, p. 91: Shaw to Chauncey, 9 Oct. 1820; LC, Shaw Papers: Arthur Sinclair to Shaw, 17 Aug. 1821.

27. Chicago Historical Society: Hull to Porter, [4 Nov. 1820], partial MS. The

Navy Commissioners' Journal, 29 Sept. 1820, records "replied at large to [Captain Hull's] letter upon the subject of the relative authorities and duties, of commandants of yards and commanding officers afloat," but the letter is not copied in the commissioners' letterbook.

28. LC, Rodgers Family Papers: Shaw to Hull, 7 Oct. 1820. Also printed in *Trial of Shaw*, p. 4. The reference to "emoluments" has to do with the allowance of double rations to squadron commanders, which commuted at an extra two dollars per day. The end effect of the course Hull was pursuing was clear to Shaw, though perhaps not to Hull. If the senior officer on a station were entitled to give orders to all those junior to him, the dual command would be destroyed and there would cease to be a "commander afloat" and a "Navy Yard commandant." Instead, each station would have but one commander. Hull's aim was to get into a position from which he could order Shaw to haul down his broad pendant; Shaw and Sinclair saw themselves potentially deposed from their commands.

29. Chicago HS: Hull to Porter, [4 Nov. 1820].

30. LC, Shaw Papers: Chauncey to Shaw, 19 Oct. 1820.

31. LC, Shaw Papers: Sinclair to Shaw, 22 Oct. 1820.

32. MassHS, *Proceedings*, 3d ser., vol. [41]– (1907/8–), 45: 29–30: Hull to Nathaniel Silsbee, 29 Nov. 1820.

33. NCLB: Rodgers to Hull, 13 Dec. 1820.

34. Charlestown journal. Carpenters began work on the *Alligator*'s frames on 26 June; she was launched on 4 November.

35. NA, RG 45, Letterbook of the Philadelphia Navy Yard: J. J. Nicholson to Isaac Hull, 2 Jan. 1821; Alexander Murray to Hull, 22 Jan. 1821.

36. *Hull Court*, testimony of Josiah Barker, p. 8.

37. *Hull Court*, testimony of Barker, p. 9. Wyman's duty was to witness and countersign the workmen's signatures on the weekly payroll. He died before the courts-martial of 1822.

38. *Hull Court*, testimony of Keating, pp. 104–105; testimony of Binney, pp. 204–205. Fosdick had covered his fraud very cleverly. The men were divided into categories according to the type of work they did, and a separate roll was kept for each item of expenditure (increase of the navy, improvement of yards, etc.). Fosdick would alter the men's time on a different roll each pay period, so that if one were selected at random for checking, as Binney and Keating had done in 1819, the odds were that no discrepancy would be found. Misc.: Charles Morris to Smith Thompson, 25 May 1822.

39. CL: Hull to Thompson, 22 Feb. 1821.

40. *Hull Court*, depositions of Ogden, Chew, Tillotson, and Livingston.

41. CL: Hull to Thompson, 10, 22 Feb. 1821.

42. *Hull Court*, testimony of Charles Bradbury, p. 185.

43. *Hull Court*, testimony of Asa Bucknam, p. 194.

44. *Hull Court*, testimony of Asa Bucknam, pp. 193–194. There is one anomalous document in Hull's papers (Elliot Coll.): a mortgage, dated 26 June 1821, when the investigation was nearing its end, by which Hull mortgaged a piece of property to Fosdick/Hichborn for $1,700, subject to repayment, which was eventually made in 1825. It is evident from the testimony of Fosdick/Hichborn's old friends and business associates that he was neither disgraced nor excluded from polite society by his fraudulent activities; still, it was indiscreet of Hull to enter

into business dealings with him at that time. Curiously, the fact of the mortgage was never uncovered by the busy "investigators," or if it was, they did not consider it derogatory to Hull. Probably Bradbury, who sometimes acted as agent for Hull's properties, made the mortgage without telling Hull who held it. It is certain that Hull was short of money at the time and needed to mortgage property to raise funds. However, had he been, as his detractors alleged, in need of money to repay his share of the embezzled funds, that is, to give to Fosdick/Hichborn, he certainly could not have borrowed it from the latter. Nor would he have preserved the discharged mortgage among his papers, if he had considered it evidence of collusion in fraud.

45. LC, Isaac Hull Papers: George Blake to Isaac Hull, 3 July 1821.

46. NA, RG 45, Letters Sent by the Board of Navy Commissioners to Officers: John Rodgers to John Shaw, 14 May 1821 (hereafter Commissioners to Officers); Comm. Rec.: Shaw to Rodgers, 15 May 1821. Article 3 stated: "The senior officer afloat shall always be entitled to wear the pendant of the first order; and all officers entitled to a broad pendant shall, when not in the presence, or in sight of a superior officer, also entitled to a pendant, wear the pendant of the first order." Article 5 read: "No officer shall wear a broad pendant, of any kind, unless he shall have been appointed to command a squadron of vessels on separate service." These articles are reprinted in *Trial of Shaw*, appendix, p. 101.

47. Commissioners to Officers: Rodgers to Shaw, 16 May 1821; Miscellaneous Letters Received by the Board of Navy Commissioners: Percival to Rodgers, [16 May 1821].

48. CL: Shaw to Thompson, 16 May and [28 May] 1821.

49. NYHS, Frederick Rodgers Coll. (microfilm): Shaw to Hull, 22 May 1821.

50. NYHS, Frederick Rodgers Coll. (microfilm): Hull to Rodgers, 27 May 1821.

51. Elliot Coll.: Isaac Hull to Joseph B. Hull, [2 or 3 Sept. 1821].

52. Elliot Coll.: Isaac Hull to Joseph B. Hull, 16 Sept. 1821.

53. The report simply reproduced the secretary's language: to "investigate the whole transactions of Mr. Hichborn from the time of his first entering upon duty, the day on which he was first entrusted with paying the mechanics and laborers and others under Commodore Bainbridge, to the period of his leaving the public service." Comm. LB: Thompson to Hull, 1 Mar. 1821; LC, Isaac Hull Papers: Hull, Binney, and Blake to Thompson, 14 July 1821.

54. CL: Bainbridge to Thompson, 29 July 1821; OSW: Thompson to Bainbridge, 3 Aug. 1821.

55. CL: Hull, Binney, and Blake to Smith Thompson, 6 Aug. 1821.

56. CL: Bainbridge to Thompson, 8 Aug. 1821. Bainbridge was extraordinarily anxious to keep his name out of the Fosdick/Hichborn affair.

57. CL: Hull to Thompson, 22 Feb. 1821. If one were disposed to be circumstantial, it could be pointed out that Bainbridge was at Boston during nearly the entire period of Fosdick's service at the navy yard, except for his three-month cruise in 1815, and during that whole time the two were on intimate terms. It was Bainbridge who had given Fosdick the exceptional task of paying the men, contrary to regulations. Bainbridge left Boston in November 1819, and within two months Fosdick resigned from the yard. There would be just as good circumstantial grounds, therefore, for accusing Bainbridge of complicity with Fosdick as for laying the charge against Isaac Hull—better, if one considers the relative

financial health of the two officers. I do not believe, however, that either was privy to the theft.

58. CL: Bainbridge to Thompson, 20 Aug. 1821.

59. CL: Bainbridge to Thompson, 22 Oct. 1821.

60. Bainbridge's family consisted of a wife, a son, and four daughters; Hull had a wife, a niece, and one or more sisters-in-law in residence or at school.

61. LC, Shaw Papers: Sinclair to Shaw, 7 June, 17 Aug. 1821.

62. CL: Hull to Thompson, 6 Oct. 1821.

63. WLCL, Porter Papers: Hull to Porter, 7 Oct. 1821.

64. Huntington Library: Hull to Porter, [12 Nov. 1821].

65. Comm. Rec.: Hull to Rodgers, 11 Oct. 1821.

66. Comm. Rec.: Bainbridge to Hull, 16 Nov. 1821; Hull to Bainbridge, 17 Nov. 1821.

67. WLCL, Porter Papers: Hull to Porter, 17 Nov. 1821.

68. NA, RG 45, Appointments: Circular, 1 Feb. 1822.

69. *Hull Court*, testimony of Abbot, pp. 33–41, 42–54; testimony of Shubrick, pp. 5, 187–190. It is ironic that one of Abbot's main charges against Hull was that yard surveys were not properly conducted, since he himself always managed to be out of the way when surveys were scheduled.

70. OL: Abbot to Thompson, 4 Oct. 1821.

71. *Trial of Abbot*, appendix T, p. 126: Thompson to Abbot, 12 Nov. 1821.

72. *Trial of Abbot*, appendix A, pp. 106–110: Abbot to Thompson, 11 Jan. 1822.

73. At the next survey the copper was weighed and was found to *exceed* the estimate by two thousand pounds because that quantity, allocated to one of the new ships, had not actually been used yet. The account book was not lost; it was produced at Hull's court of inquiry.

74. CL: John Shaw to Smith Thompson, 14 Jan. 1822.

75. CL: Shaw to Thompson, 22 Jan. 1822. Shaw managed, in this letter, to get most of the facts wrong: for example, he had Joel Barlow going as minister to England and the *Constitution* carrying his dispatches from there to France.

76. *Trial of Abbot*, appendix D, p. 111: Abbot to Trevett, 19 Jan. 1822.

77. The "Elliot story" was that Dr. Ephraim Elliot, a Boston apothecary, had been forced against his will to bill to the government for medicines he had provided for the ladies of the Hull family. It was subsequently established that, up to May 1821, this was standard practice at all naval stations. A circular order of that month put an end to the custom. Cf. *Hull Court*, testimony of Usher Parsons, pp. 41–42; testimony of Ephraim Elliot, pp. 131–135; *Trial of Abbot*, appendix R, p. 124.

78. *Trial of Abbot*, appendix E, pp. 111–112: S. R. Trevett to Smith Thompson, 22 Jan. 1822.

79. CL: Shaw to Thompson, 25 Jan. 1822.

80. OSW: Smith Thompson to David Porter, 26 Jan. 1822.

81. CL: Porter to Thompson, 31 Jan. 1822 (two letters).

82. *Trial of Shaw*, testimony of Shubrick, pp. 8–9; LC, Shaw Papers: Shaw to Hull, 27 Jan. 1822.

83. CL: Porter to Thompson, [4] Feb. 1822. See also *Trial of Abbot*, testimony of Porter, pp. 35–36.

84. CL: Porter to Thompson, [4] Feb. 1822.
85. *Hull Court*, testimony of Percival, pp. 119–120; *Trial of Abbot*, p. 123; and testimony of Percival, pp. 7–10.
86. CL: Porter to Thompson, 5 Feb. 1822; *Trial of Abbot*, testimony of Porter, p. 36.
87. CL: Porter to Thompson, 5, 6, 11, 12 Feb. 1822.
88. OL: Abbot to Thompson, 12 Feb. 1822, enclosing James T. Austin to Abbot, 9 Feb. 1822.
89. *Evening Gazette* (Boston), 8, 16 Feb. 1822.
90. CL: Hull to Thompson, 14 Feb. 1822; *Trial of Shaw*, pp. 4–7.
91. CL: Porter to Thompson, 17 Feb. 1822.
92. Comm. Rec.: Porter and Blake to Smith Thompson, 25 Feb. 1822.
93. *Trial of Abbot*, pp. 4–7. Porter sent the charge to Abbot, and to the prospective judge advocate of the court, William C. Aylwin, on 9 March, but Aylwin thought that some of the specifications were not sufficiently exact as to time and place, and he returned the document to Porter for alterations while withholding Abbot's copy. Abbot did not, therefore, receive his copy of the charge until about three weeks before his trial began, and he complained that he had not been allowed sufficient time to prepare his defense.

Chapter 12

1. CL: Shaw to Thompson, 7 Mar. 1822; LC, Shaw Papers: memorandum of witnesses, n.d.
2. OSW: Thompson to Shaw, 13 Mar. 1822.
3. HSPa: Hull to Porter, 18 [Mar.] 1822.
4. *Trial of Shaw*, p. 88: Leonard Jarvis to Isaac Hull, 22 Mar. 1822.
5. *Trial of Abbot*, p. 17.
6. *Trial of Abbot*, p. 150.
7. *Trial of Abbot*, p. 105.
8. CL: Hull to Smith Thompson, 9 May 1822.
9. *New England Galaxy* (Boston), 3 May 1822.
10. CL: Hull to Thompson, 11 May 1822.
11. OSW: Thompson to Hull, 23 May 1822; *Galaxy*, 25 Oct. 1822.
12. WLCL, Porter Papers: Hull to Porter, 11 May 1822.
13. *Galaxy*, 10 May 1822.
14. *Hull Court*, testimony of Elliot. Thomas Waine was a purser attached to the *Java*. He died in December 1820.
15. WLCL, Porter Papers: Hull to Porter, 11 May 1822.
16. LC, Shaw Papers: Elliott to Shaw, 11 May 1822.
17. *Galaxy*, 17 May 1822.
18. Haverford College Library: Hull to Porter, 18 May 1822.
19. CL: Shaw to Thompson, 28 May 1822; OSW: Thompson to Shaw, 1 June 1822.
20. LC, Shaw Papers: Bainbridge to Shaw, 17 June 1822.
21. HSPa: Hull to Porter, 13 May 1822.
22. NYHS; Percival to Aspinwall, 27 May 1822.

23. Haverford College Library: Hull to Porter, 18 May 1822.
24. Elliot Coll.: Thompson to Hull, 21 May 1822.
25. *Boston Patriot*, 13 June 1822.
26. *Galaxy*, 14 June 1822.
27. CL: Porter to Thompson, 3 June 1822.
28. WLCL, Smith Naval Coll.: Hull to Porter, 9 June 1822.
29. *Galaxy*, 7 June 1822.
30. *National Intelligencer*, 24 June 1822. Porter was right on this point. A comparison of the two versions of the trial reveals a consistent pattern of variation that tends, in the Waldo copy, to make the testimony more favorable to Abbot. In addition, documents ruled inadmissible at the trial are appended, with commentary.
31. *National Intelligencer*, 6 July 1822.
32. NYHS: Hull to [Porter], 15 June 1822; Trinity College Library, Hartford, Conn., Archives of the Episcopal Diocese of Connecticut, Samuel F. Jarvis papers (microfilm): Jarvis to Hull, 12 June 1822.
33. *Galaxy*, 21 June 1822.
34. NYHS: Hull to [Porter], 15 June 1822.
35. NA, RG 45, Misc.: Morris to Thompson, 25 May 1822; Blake to Thompson, 1 June 1822 (two letters); Blake to Thompson, 7 Sept. 1822; CL: Morris to Thompson, 1 Aug. 1822 (two letters); *American Statesman* (Boston), 8 Apr. 1822. The *Statesman*'s editor soon recovered his "neutral" stance and apparently forgot that he had ever published this outburst.
36. NA, RG 45, Area 7 file: Morris to Porter, 13 June 1822.
37. WLCL, Porter Papers: Hull to Porter, 29 June 1822; see also HSPa: Hull to Porter, 22 June 1822.
38. Commissioners, Miscellaneous Letters Sent: Porter to several publishers, 1 July 1822.
39. *National Intelligencer*, 27 June 1822; *Boston Patriot*, 2 July 1822; *Columbian Centinel*, 3 July 1822.
40. *National Intelligencer*, 20 July 1822; *Columbian Centinel*, 3 July 1822; *Galaxy*, 5 July 1822. The "ten-footers" were tenements built on Hull's Charlestown lots, allegedly by navy yard workmen.
41. *Daily Advertiser* (Boston), 20 July 1822; *The Repertory* (Boston), 20 July 1822; WLCL, Porter Papers: Hull to Porter, 21 July 1822.
42. *Galaxy*, 5 July 1822; *Columbian Centinel*, 6 July 1822; *American Statesman*, 8 July 1822. The latter reference is to Elliot's apothecary bills.
43. CL: Hull to Thompson, 13 July 1822.
44. *Boston Patriot and Daily Mercantile Advertiser (BP&DMA)*, 16 July 1822.
45. *Independent Chronicle and Boston Patriot (IC&BP)*, 17 July 1822. Ballard and Wright published the *BP&DMA* in the evening, the *IC&BP* in the morning, with essentially the same content.
46. Misc.: J. T. Austin and S. L. Knapp to Smith Thompson, 17 July 1822.
47. WLCL, Porter Papers: Hull to Porter, 21 July 1822.
48. *Boston Patriot*, 17 July 1822; *National Intelligencer*, 30 July 1822.
49. Albert J. Beveridge, *The Life of John Marshall*, 4 vols. (Boston and New York, 1919), 4: 239.
50. WLCL, Porter Papers: Hull to Porter, 30 July 1822. There is a touch of

irony in the fact that William Sullivan, one of those Hull named in this letter as his enemies, had headed the committee that offered Hull a public dinner in 1812. See above, chapter 8, notes 49 and 50.

51. NYHS, Havemeyer Coll.: Hull to Porter, 2 Aug. 1822.

52. *American Statesman*, 8 Aug. 1822; *Galaxy*, 9 Aug. 1822.

53. *Hull Court*, p. 145. Subsequent references are to the proceedings of the court unless otherwise indicated.

54. *Hull Court*, p. 147.

55. *Hull Court*, passim; *Boston Evening Gazette*, quoted in *Boston Commercial Advertiser*, 7 Oct. 1822.

56. NA, RG 125, Records of the Judge Advocate General (Navy), Records of General Courts-Martial and Courts of Inquiry (microcopy no. 273), Reel 15: Minutes of proceedings of the Court of Enquiry ordered by the Secretary of the Navy on the application of Capt. James Biddle.

57. WLCL, Chew Papers: Hull to Chew, 14 Oct. 1822.

58. LC, Rodgers Family Papers: Porter to Rodgers, 5 Oct. 1822. What would Bainbridge have said if he had seen the mention of him in Hull's defense: "a man who, whatever may be his personal feelings towards me, is as much above [Abbot], as the proud Lion is superior to the Jackal"? The interpretation of Bainbridge's role in the whole Charlestown business in Long, *Ready to Hazard* (see chapter 9, note 22, above), agrees substantially with mine.

59. *Hull Court*, pp. 243–244.

60. *National Intelligencer*, 22, 25 Oct. 1822.

61. *National Intelligencer*, 29 Oct. 1822; *Boston Patriot*, 23 Oct. 1822; *Boston Weekly Recorder*, 31 Oct. 1822; *Columbian Centinel*, 7 Sept. 1822.

62. CL: Hull to Thompson, 26 Oct. 1822; WLCL, Porter Papers: Hull to Porter, 4 o'clock Friday [8 Nov. 1822].

63. *Salem Gazette*, ca. 15 Nov. 1822; cf. also *New England Galaxy*, 15 Nov. 1822, and *Essex Register*, about the same date. These clippings are in the Shaw Papers, LC.

64. CL: Hull to Thompson, 28 Nov. 1822.

65. WLCL, Porter Papers: Hull to Porter, 2 Dec. 1822. Ward left the yard in January to escort some men for Porter's expedition against the West Indian pirates, but he did not go out on the cruise; by August he was back in the yard as lieutenant commandant under Bainbridge.

66. NYHS, Frederick Rodgers Coll. (microfilm): Morris to Rodgers, 15 Dec. 1822.

67. Elliot Coll.: Isaac Hull to Joseph B. Hull, 23 Dec. 1822.

68. CL: Hull to Thompson, 4, 27 Mar. 1823.

69. CL: Hull to Thompson, 16 Apr. 1823.

70. CL: Bainbridge to Thompson, 28 Apr. 1823.

71. OSW: Thompson to Hull, 24 May 1823; CL: Hull to Thompson, 29 May 1823.

72. OSW: Thompson to Hull, 3 June 1823.

73. CL: Hull to Thompson, 17 June 1823.

74. CL: Hull to Thompson, 4 Mar. 1823.

75. CL: Hull to Thompson, 18 June 1823.

76. NA, RG 45, Muster Rolls, Charlestown Navy Yard, 1823.

77. NYHS, Frederick Rodgers Coll. (microfilm): William Crafts to John Rodgers, 30 July 1823; Adams, ed., *Memoirs of John Quincy Adams*, 6: 169.
78. *Boston Evening Gazette*, 9 Aug. 1823.
79. *Boston Evening Gazette*, 16 Aug. 1823.
80. *Charlestown Journal*, 23 Aug. 1823.

Chapter 13

1. For a good general treatment of this period see Edward B. Billingsley, *In Defense of Neutral Rights: The United States Navy and the Wars of Independence in Chile and Peru* (Chapel Hill, N.C., 1976). A summary account of the cruise of the *United States* and an assessment of its importance will be found in Linda M. Maloney, "The U.S. Navy's Pacific Squadron, 1824–1827," in United States Naval Academy History Symposium (1977), *Changing Interpretations and New Sources in Naval History*, ed. Robert William Love, Jr. (New York, 1980), pp. 180–191.
2. Ann Hart Hull to Sarah H. Jarvis, Tuesday [about 6 Oct.] 1823, copy in possession of Eleanor T. Tilton.
3. CL: Bainbridge to Smith Thompson, 1 Sept. 1823 (2 letters); John Percival to Smith Thompson, 1 Sept. 1823; Hull to Percival, 5 [Oct.] 1823, copy furnished by Goodspeed's Book Shop, Oct. 1958.
4. NCLB: Chauncey to Warrington, 15 Sept., 9 Oct. 1823; Ann Hull to Sarah H. Jarvis, [about 6 Oct. 1823], copy in possession of Eleanor T. Tilton; CL: Hull to Southard, 25 Oct. 1823; Hull to Smith Thompson, 22 Aug. 1823, enclosing H. E. Ballard to Hull, 19 Aug. 1823.
5. CL: Hull to Southard, 3 Nov. 1823.
6. OSW: Southard to Hull, 24 Nov. 1823.
7. Chapelle, *American Sailing Navy*, pp. 130, 356.
8. CL: George Kennon to Hull, 23 Nov. 1823; Arthur Sinclair to Southard, 27 Nov. 1823; Hull to Southard, 28, 30 Nov. 1823.
9. NYHS: Log of frigate *United States*, Nov. 1823–Apr. 1827 (hereafter *US* log), 20–21 Nov. 1823. With the departure of Smith Thompson, the title "commodore" returned to official usage and remained. Hull, no longer plagued with junior officers placing themselves over him, did not object.
10. *US* log, 27 Nov. 1823.
11. Ann Hull to Sarah H. Jarvis, 26 Nov. [1823], copy in possession of Eleanor T. Tilton; *US* log, 26 Nov. 1823.
12. CL: Hull to Southard, 30 Nov., 3 Dec. 1823.
13. OSW: Southard to Percival, 12 Dec. 1823.
14. CL: Hull to Southard, 14 Dec. 1823.
15. Misc.: Southard to Daniel Campbell, 16 Dec. 1823; Southard to Hull, 16 Dec. 1823; Southard to Henry Clay, 16 Dec. 1823; Thos. Cromwell to Isaac Hull, 24 Dec. [1823]; Daniel Campbell to Hull, n.d.; Campbell to Hull, 26 Dec. 1823; John Bubier et al. to Hull, 27 Dec. 1823; *US* log, 28 Dec. 1823.
16. CL: Hull to Southard, 20 Dec. 1823; Porter to Southard, 9 Jan. 1824.
17. NYHS, Hull LB: Hull to Porter, 3 Jan. 1824.

18. NYHS, Frederick Rodgers Coll. (microfilm): Porter to Rodgers, 27 Dec. 1823.

19. LC, Rodgers Family Papers: Porter to Rodgers, 6 Jan. 1823 [i.e., 1824]; cf. David F. Long, *Nothing Too Daring: A Biography of Commodore David Porter, 1780–1843* (Annapolis, 1970), pp. 222–224.

20. CL: Hull to Southard, 24 Dec. 1823.

21. *US* log, 28 Dec. 1823, 2 Jan. 1824; OSW: Southard to Hull, 24, 27 Dec. 1823.

22. CL: Hull to Southard, 2, 4 Jan. 1824; *US* log, 5 Jan. 1824.

23. CL: Hull to Southard, 16 Feb. 1824.

24. *US* log, 4–31 Jan. 1824; CL: Samuel Larned to Hull, 31 Mar. 1824; Ann Hull to Sarah H. Jarvis, 1 May 1824, copy in possession of Eleanor T. Tilton.

25. OSW: Southard to Hull, 24 Dec. 1823; Adams, ed., *Memoirs of John Quincy Adams*, 6: 210.

26. OSW: Southard to Hull, 24 Dec. 1823.

27. NA, RG 45, Hull LB: Hull to Percival, 26 Jan. 1824.

28. *US* log, 17 Feb.–27 Mar. 1824.

29. *US* log, 27 Mar.–4 Apr. 1824; NA, RG 59, Dept. of State, Consular Dispatches: Stanhope Prevost to Michael Hogan, 11 Feb. 1824; Hogan to J. Q. Adams, 12 Mar. 1824.

30. *US* log, 4 Apr.–3 May 1824; Ann Hull to Sarah H. Jarvis, 1 May 1824, copy in possession of Eleanor T. Tilton.

31. OSW: Southard to Hull, 24 Dec. 1823; NA, RG 59, Letters from Diplomatic Agents, Chile: Allen to J. Q. Adams, 29 Apr. 1824; OL: Hull to Conner, 20 Apr. 1824; Conner to Southard, 30 Oct. 1824; Billingsley, *In Defense of Neutral Rights*, pp. 156, 185.

32. CL: Stewart to Latimer, 30 Sept. 1824; Latimer to Stewart, 5 Oct. 1824; Stewart to Southard, 5 Oct. 1824; OL: Latimer to Southard, 30 Oct. 1824.

33. NYHS, Hull LB: Hull to Carter, 30 Aug. 1824; Hull to Southard, 1 Sept. 1824.

34. NYHS, Hull LB: Hull to Ramsay, 17 Sept. 1824 (2 letters); Hull to Southard, 17, 18 Sept. 1824; NA, RG 45, Letters Received by the Secretary of the Navy from Commanders: Interrogatories to be proposed to J. Armstrong, encl. in W. Carter to Southard, 29 Mar. 1825.

35. OSW: Southard to Hull, 23 Mar. 1825.

36. CL: Hull to Southard, 22 Sept. 1825, enclosing Ramsay to Hull, 31 July 1825.

37. FDR Lib.: Hull to Thos. ap Catesby Jones, 1 May 1826; George Beale to Hull, 8 May 1826; OL: Hull to Joseph Smoot, 11 May 1826; Huntington Library: Jones to Hull, 12 May 1826; OL: Ramsay to Southard, 1 Oct. 1826.

38. *US* log, 1 June 1825; NYHS, Hull LB: Hull to Southard, 28 July 1825.

39. Boston Athenaeum, Isaac Hull Papers: Smith Thompson to Charles Stewart, 8 Sept. 1821, copy.

40. Letters from Diplomatic Agents, Chile: Allen to J. Q. Adams, 29 Apr. 1824.

41. Boston Athenaeum, Hull Papers: Tudor to Hull, Friday morning [28 May 1824].

42. Athenaeum, Hull Papers: Tudor to Hull, 24 May 1824.

43. NYHS, Hull LB: Hull to Allen, 9 July 1824; Hull to Prevost, 25 May 1824; Hull to Bolívar, [26 May 1824], 28 May 1824.

44. NA, RG 59, Letters Received from Ministers, Chile: Allen to Hull, 4 Aug. 1824, copy.

45. *US* log, 23 July 1824; William R. Manning, ed., *Diplomatic Correspondence of the United States Concerning the Independence of the Latin-American Nations* (New York, 1925), 3: 1760, Wm. Tudor to J. Q. Adams, 24 Aug. 1825 (hereafter Manning); CL: Hull to Southard, 2 Oct. 1824.

46. NYHS, Hull LB: Hull to Southard, 1 Aug. 1824.

47. Manning, 3: 1764, Tudor to Rodil, 6 Sept. 1824; NA, RG 45, Area 9 file: Andrew H. Foote to [Wm. A. Brown], 15 Sept. 1824; *US* log, 5 Sept. 1824.

48. Manning, 3: 1759, Tudor to J. Q. Adams, 24 Aug. 1824; Boston Athenaeum, Hull Papers: Tudor to Hull, 19, 20 Aug. 1824; NYHS, Hull LB: Hull to Rodil, 21 Aug. 1824.

49. Area 9 file: Andrew H. Foote to [Wm. A. Brown], 15 Sept. 1824; *US* log, 12 Sept. 1824; Area 9 file: Hull to Southard, 29 Sept. 1824.

50. NYHS, Hull LB: Hull to T. J. Maling, 17 Sept. 1824; Area 9 file: Maling to Hull, 17 Sept. 1824; Hull to Southard, 29 Sept. 1824.

51. Manning, 3: 1796, Tudor to J. Q. Adams, 17 Oct. 1824; Donald Worcester, *Sea Power and Chilean Independence* (Gainesville, Fla., 1962), p. 81; *US* log, 7–8 Oct. 1824.

52. NYHS, Hull LB: Hull to Southard, 19 Oct. 1824.

53. Worcester, *Sea Power*, p. 80. Percival was a Patriot partisan. He wrote to his old friend Thomas Aspinwall at London that "the long oppression of the too amiable natives is beyond any description *yet ever given* and the conduct of the Turks towards the Greeks does not surpass it." NYHS: Percival to Aspinwall, 9 Oct. 1824.

54. Worcester, *Sea Power*, p. 81; CL: Percival to Hull, 7 July 1825.

55. Manning, 3: 1770, Tudor to J. Q. Adams, 17 Oct. 1824; NYHS, Hull LB: Hull to Southard, 10 Nov. 1824.

56. *US* log, 3 Nov. 1824; NYHS, Hull LB: Hull to Rodil, 3 Nov. 1824; Hull to J. Q. Adams, 13 Nov. 1824.

57. CL: Hull to Southard, 4 Nov. 1824.

58. *US* log, 4–11 Nov. 1824; NYHS, Hull LB: Hull to Rodil, 5, 9 Nov. 1824. Paulding did not return to the ship until 11 November.

59. NYHS, Hull LB: Hull to Southard, 12 Nov. 1824.

60. NYHS, Hull LB: Hull to Tudor, 30 Nov. 1824. Hull was probably too sanguine about the disinterestedness of the American mercantile community; for them, it wasn't the principle but the money.

61. NYHS, Hull LB: Hull to Southard, 5 Dec. 1824.

62. NYHS, Hull LB: Hull to Southard, 16 Dec. 1824; Hull to Heman Allen, 17 Dec. 1824.

63. NYHS, Hull LB: Hull to Southard, 16 Dec. 1824.

64. NYHS, Hull LB: Hull to Allen, 17 Dec. 1824.

65. NYHS, Hull LB: Hull to Bolívar, 18 Dec. 1824.

66. Ann H. Hull to Sarah H. Jarvis, 28 Jan. 1825, copy in possession of Eleanor T. Tilton.

67. *US* log; Area 9 file: Andrew H. Foote to Wm. A. Brown, 12 Aug. 1825.

68. *US* log, 22–23 Feb. 1825; Boston Athenaeum, Hull Papers: Tudor to Hull, 28 Feb. 1825, 23 Apr. 1826.

69. *US* log; Boston Athenaeum, Hull Papers: Tudor to Hull, 29 Mar., 8 June 1825; NA, RG 45, Hull LB: Hull to Percival, 28 Apr. 1825.

70. CL: Kennon to Hull, 11 Apr. 1825, enclosing Kennon to Blanco, [6 Apr. 1825]; Blanco to Kennon, 7 Apr. 1825; Thos. Espora to Blanco, 6 Apr. 1825; Blanco to Kennon, 8 Apr. 1825; and Kennon to Blanco, 10 Apr. 1825.

71. CL: Hull to Southard, 27 Aug., 22, 26 Sept. 1825; Hull to José de Morales, 27 Aug. 1825; Morales to Hull, 28 Aug. 1825; Hull to Morales, 1 Sept. 1825; Hull to S. Prevost, 1 Sept. 1825; NYHS, Hull LB: Hull to Heman Allen, 27 Sept. 1825; Hull to Hogan, 27 Sept. 1825.

72. NYHS, Hull LB: Hull to Allen, 25 Sept. 1826. Manuel Blanco Encalada was, by that time, president of Chile.

73. Letters Received from Ministers, Chile: Allen to Clay, 16 Sept. 1825.

74. NYHS, Hull LB: Hull to Hogan, 10 June 1825.

75. NYHS, Hull LB: Hull to Southard, 14 Dec. 1824.

76. CL: Hull to Southard, 10 June 1825; Comm. Rec.: Hull to Bainbridge, 30 July 1825. After all his clamor to obtain the Boston command, Bainbridge had remained there less than two years.

77. CL: Hull to Southard, 30 July 1825, 22 Aug. 1825.

78. NYHS, Hull LB: Hull to Hogan, 31 July, 2 Nov. 1825; Hull to J. Illingworth, 6 Dec. 1825.

79. NYHS, Hull LB: Hull to Allen, 4 Aug. 1825.

80. CL: Hull to Percival, 10 Aug. 1825; Percival to Hull, [11 Aug. 1825] (2 letters); NYHS, Hull LB: Hull to Southard, 22 Aug. 1825; NA, RG 45, Hull LB: Hull to Percival, 14 Aug. 1825; Area 9 file: Andrew H. Foote to Wm. A. Brown, 12 Aug. 1825; Elliot Coll.: Petition of merchants and others engaged in the whale fishery, Dec. 1824; Petition of same, Nantucket, 5 Apr. 1825; Petition of citizens of New Bedford, n.d. [1825].

81. See Linda McKee [Maloney], "Mad Jack and the Missionaries," *American Heritage* 13, no. 3 (Apr. 1971), pp. 30–37, 85–87; OSW: Southard to Percival, 20 Jan. 1829. One of the *London*'s owners was Commodore Charles Stewart.

82. *US* log, 20 Aug.–1 Sept. 1825; CL: Hull to Southard, 24 Aug., 24 Sept. 1825. Dr. Fitzhugh sailed for the United States on a sick ticket in 1826, but only a few days' sail from home he shot and killed himself.

83. *US* log; NYHS, Hull LB: Hull to Allen, 2 Nov. 1825.

84. NYHS, Hull LB: Hull to Allen, 2 Dec. 1825.

85. CL: Hull to Southard, 22 Aug. 1825; Letters Received from Ministers, Chile: Allen to Hull, 14 Oct. 1825, extract.

86. NYHS, Hull LB: Hull to Allen, 2 Dec. 1825; Harvard University, Houghton Library: Hull to Tudor, 15 Jan. 1826.

87. Boston Athenaeum, Hull Papers: Tudor to Hull, 25 Jan. 1826.

88. Elliot Coll.: Wm. Hull to Isaac Hull, 25 Aug. 1825.

89. NYHS, Hull LB: Hull to Allen, 12 July 1826; Misc.: Henry Hull to Southard, 13 Feb. 1826; Jannette Hart to Southard, 20 Feb. 1826; LC, Isaac Hull Papers: A. Binney to Hull, 1 May 1826; Elliot Coll.: Memorandum, n.d.

90. *US* log, 19 Nov. 1826.

91. CL: Hull to Southard, 30 Dec. 1825.

92. NYHS, Hull LB: Hull to Lewis Warrington, 21 Jan. 1826; CL: Hull to Southard, 24 Jan. 1826; NA, RG 59, Letters Received from Ministers, Chile: Allen to Clay, 20 Mar. 1826; Heman Allen to S. F. Jarvis, 4 Apr. 1826, copy in possession of Eleanor T. Tilton.

93. Allen to S. F. Jarvis, 4 Apr. 1826, copy in possession of Eleanor T. Tilton.

94. Mrs. Hogan to Mrs. Allen, 15 Mar. 1826; Mrs. Allen to Mrs. Hogan, 16 Mar. 1826, copies in possession of Eleanor T. Tilton; NYHS, Hull LB: Hull to Thos. ap Catesby Jones, 24 Apr. 1826; Hull to Ramsay, 27 Apr. 1826; Hull to Allen, 13 July 1826.

95. CL: Hull to Southard, 21 Sept. 1826, 25 June 1826, 23 Jan. 1827.

96. LC, Isaac Hull Papers: Binney to Hull, 1 May 1826.

97. NA, RG 59, Letters Received from Ministers, Chile: Allen to Clay, 20 Mar. 1826; NYHS, Hull LB: Hull to Allen, 18 May 1826; Boston Athenaeum, Hull Papers: Lawrence Pennington to Hull, 2 Feb. 1833. As an indication of Hogan's attitude, consider the following, addressed to Z. W. Nixon in October 1826: "I have received your explanation of an *indelicate* thing (to say the least of it) done towards me, in which you conceive yourself borne out, by being requested so to do by Commodore Hull. That officer in doing so has made a direct attack upon my integrity, both as an officer of the U. States, and as a man and merchant, of which he will hear from me; for I despise all underhand work, as well as those I find concerned in it. The evil consequences to me in a variety of ways, of the exposition of such a want of confidence in the consul of the U. States are endless—it is only a part of the plan, matured for my ruin, in the opinion of the government, and the destruction of my private character, in which you are made an instrument." The matter at issue? Nixon's having, at Hull's direction and while Hogan was ill and not doing any business, forwarded some letters directly to the squadron without first giving them to Hogan. Hogan to Nixon, 18 Oct. 1826, copy in possession of Eleanor T. Tilton.

98. Misc.: Tudor to Southard, 11 Apr. 1826; CL: Hull to Southard, "No. 24," 25 Apr. 1826; Hull to Jones, 27, 29 May 1826.

99. NA, RG 45, Hull LB: Hull to Smoot, 11 May 1826; Comm. Rec.: Jones to Hull, 23 Jan. 1826; Jones to President, Board of Navy Commissioners, 28 Feb. 1826; CL: Hull to Southard, 26 May 1826.

100. OL: Jones to Southard, 26 Feb. 1827.

101. NYHS, Hull LB: Hull to Southard, 24 Aug. 1826; NA, RG 45, Hull LB: Hull to Percival, 1 Sept. 1826.

102. Curiously, every modern writer who has treated this titillating subject has supposed that the lady in question was Jannette Hart. The most cursory review of the documents shows that only Augusta accompanied her sister. See Elliot Coll.: John R. Fenwick to Hull, 5 Feb. 1828.

103. CL: Hull to Southard, "No. 34," 17 June 1826.

104. NYHS, Hull LB: Hull to Allen, 12 July 1826.

105. NYHS, Hull LB: Hull to Condy Raguet, 17 July 1826.

106. NYHS, Hull LB: Hull to Allen, 19 July 1826.

107. Boston Athenaeum, Hull Papers: Tudor to Hull, 10 Aug. [1826].

108. NYHS, Hull LB: Hull to Allen, 3 Sept. 1826.

109. *US* log, 4–5 Sept. 1826.

110. NYHS, Hull LB: Hull to Allen, 25 Sept. 1826.

111. CL: Hull to Southard, 27 May 1826; OSW: Southard to Hull, 21 Aug. 1826.

112. NYHS, Hull LB: Hull to Allen, 25 Sept. 1826; *US* log, 7 Aug. 1826. Interestingly, the first man who stepped (or hopped) forward to sign the articles was Hull's one-legged pensioner from the *Constitution*, Richard F. Dunn. There must have been some subterfuge in enlisting Dunn, since he was on pension and one-legged men were not usually received on board navy ships. But he had been Hull's faithful shadow for fifteen years. Only at the end of this cruise, when Hull went on leave of absence, did Dunn separate from him at last to settle in Portsmouth.

113. *US* log; CL: Hull to Southard, 21 Apr. 1826; NA, RG 45, Hull LB: Hull to Beale, 17 June 1826; CL: Hull to Southard, 12 Sept. 1826.

114. *US* log, 7 Nov. 1825.

115. "John Cunningham's Journal," *The Mariner's Mirror* 9 (1923), pp. 334–335.

116. NYHS, Hull LB: Hull to T. H. Gillis, 12 Sept. 1826.

117. NYHS, Hull LB: Hull to Samuel Larned, 15 July 1826; Hull to Condy Raguet, 9 Sept. 1826. The seeds and skulls went to the New York Horticultural Society, the Massachusetts Historical and Agricultural Society, and Dr. James Warren of Boston, but there is no trace of the boy.

118. Boston Athenaeum, Hull Papers: Raguet to Hull, 13 Nov. 1826.

119. NYHS, Hull LB: Hull to Allen, 1 Dec. 1826; CL: Hull to Southard, 10 Dec. 1826.

120. *US* log, 16 Dec. 1826–6 Jan. 1827.

121. CL: Jones to Southard, 16 Jan. 1827. The hardworking *Dolphin* remained as part of seven squadrons before being sold in 1835.

122. *US* log, 7–24 Jan. 1827.

123. *US* log; CL: Hull to Southard, 24 Apr. 1827.

124. CL: Hull to Southard, 4 May 1827.

Chapter 14

1. CL: Hull to Southard, 1 May 1827; OSW: Southard to Hull, 5 May 1827.

2. NYHS, Hull LB: Hull to T. H. Gillis, 21 Apr. 1827.

3. NYHS, Hull LB: Hull to Southard, 9 June 1827.

4. NYHS, Hull LB: Hull to John Boyle, 21 Apr. 1827; Hull to Richard Cutts, 21 May 1827.

5. Elliot Coll.: Hull to —— Thompson, 9 June 1827.

6. CL: Hull to Southard, "No. 64," 21 Apr. 1827.

7. CL: Hull to Southard, "No. 61," 21 Apr. 1827.

8. NYHS, Hull LB: Hull to Cyrus M. Hussey, 20 May 1827.

9. NA, RG 217, Records of the Fourth Auditor of the Treasury: Tobias Watkins to [Southard], 24 May 1827; Hull to Watkins, 6 June 1827; Boston Athenaeum, Hull Papers: Disbursements by Commo. Isaac Hull during his Command of the Squadron in the Pacific Ocean, 1824–5–6–7.

10. NYHS, Hull LB: Hull to Binney, 11 Sept. 1826.

11. OSW: Southard to Hull, 25 Apr. 1827.

12. CL: Hull to Southard, 2 May 1827. An officer on leave of absence received full pay but no rations; when on duty, Hull got eight rations per day, or sixteen as squadron commander, so by going on leave he sacrificed $730 to $1,460 per year, besides allowances for quarters, servants, firewood, and candles.

13. Elliot Coll.: Recollections of Sarah Hull Galpin, n.d.

14. Margaret Hall, *The Aristocratic Journey, Being the Outspoken Letters of Mrs. Basil Hall Written during a Fourteen Months' Sojourn in America 1827–1828*; edited and with a preface by Una Pope-Hennessy (New York, 1931), p. 61. Margaret Hall was slightly confused. She either mistook Ann Hull for one of her sisters, or else supposed one of the other sisters, probably Amelia Hart, had been one of the party in South America.

15. Hall, *The Aristocratic Journey*, p. 147. Hull was equal in acumen to any modern expense account traveler. He charged the Navy Department his expenses for traveling from Derby to Philadelphia and back in November to attend William Carter's court-martial, 350 miles at $0.15 per mile ($52.50). But he probably took his family to Philadelphia at that time and stayed. Boston Athenaeum, Hull Papers: Account, 2 Nov. 1829.

16. Elliot Coll.: Isaac Hull to Joseph B. Hull, 11 Jan. 1828.

17. HSPa: Quitclaim of Freelove Hull, 2 Oct. 1827.

18. Elliot Coll.: I. Hull to J. B. Hull, 23 Jan., 11 Jan. [sic: Feb.] 1828.

19. Ann Hull to Heman Allen, 2 May 1828; Eliz. Allen to H. Allen, 1 June 1828, copies in possession of Eleanor T. Tilton; cf. Long, *Nothing Too Daring*, pp. 277–278, 302.

20. CL: Hull to Southard, 3 July 1828.

21. CL: Hull to Southard, 3, 24 July, 23 Nov. 1828; Elliot Coll.: I. Hull to J. B. Hull, 7 Jan. 1829. At the same time, Isaac and Ann began a long series of unsuccessful applications for a midshipman's warrant for another nephew, John Abraham Jarvis: OSW: Chief Clerk, Navy Dept., to I. Hull, 5 Jan. 1829.

22. Elliot Coll.: I. Hull to J. B. Hull, 7 Jan. 1829, 27 Sept. 1830.

23. CL: Hull to SecNav, 17 Mar., 11 Apr. 1829; TennHS: Hull to SecNav, 17 Mar. 1829, "Private"; NA, RG 45, Appointments: Branch to Hull, 31 Mar. 1829; NA, Washington Navy Yard log, 11 Apr. 1829 (hereafter Washington log).

24. Comm. Rec.: Philip Inch to T. H. Stephens, 11 Apr. 1829; John Dunn to T. H. Stephens, 13 Apr. 1829; Hull to President, Board of Navy Commissioners, 15 Apr. 1829; Boston Athenaeum, Hull Papers: Inventory of furniture, 31 Oct. 1829; Account, 2 Nov. 1829.

25. CL: Hull to John Branch, 13 June 1829.

26. Comm. Rec.: Hull to Rodgers, 1 Aug. 1829.

27. Comm. Rec.: Hull to President, Board of Navy Commissioners, 20 Apr. 1829. The Barrys seem to have been a numerous clan. Besides Edward Barry, the master, the yard employed Richard Barry, second clerk to the commandant; Francis Barry, clerk of check; and Thomas Barry, gunner, who was made keeper of the magazine in 1828.

28. Comm. Rec.: Hull to Rodgers, 18 July 1829; Shubrick to Rodgers, 2 Sept. 1829; NCLB: Warrington to Hull, 3 Sept. 1829; Comm. Misc. Letters Rec.: B. King to John Rodgers, 3 Aug. 1829.

29. NA, RG 45, Commissioners' Book of Estimates, II: Estimates, Washington Navy Yard, 1832.

30. Comm. Rec.: Hull to Rodgers, 8 Apr. 1830.

31. Hull told Rodgers that he had discharged "many" slaves since he took command, but as a matter of fact the list he enclosed with his letter showed thirteen slaves employed, while a report of May 1829 has only eight. Two of them, Charles Washington, slave to Mrs. [Bailey?] Washington, and Alexander Taylor, slave to Mrs. Wailes, were missing from the 1830 list, but one freeman had been added and seven slaves enlisted as "ordinary men." Commissioners' Reports, Estimates and Surveys, Washington, 1829: List of persons employed at Washington Navy Yard, 8 May 1829.

32. Comm. Rec.: Hull to President, Board of Navy Commissioners, 23 June 1829; CL: Hull to Levi Woodbury, 19 Dec. 1831; Navy Commissioners' Journal, 24 June 1829 (hereafter NC journal); Washington log, 23 Mar.–1 Apr. 1830.

33. Comm. Rec.: Hull to Rodgers, 5 Apr. 1831.

34. Comm. Rec.: Hull to Rodgers, 31 July, 30 Oct. 1829; NC journal, 2 Nov. 1829.

35. Comm. Misc. Letters Rec.: William R. Nimmo to [John Branch], 23 Jan. 1830; Comm. Rec.: Hull to Rodgers, 2 Feb. 1830.

36. Washington log, 1 Sept. 1830; CL: Hull to Branch, 30 Oct. 1830; Comm. Rec.: Hull to Rodgers, 5 Nov. 1830.

37. For a detailed account of the schooner *Experiment* see Linda McKee Maloney, "A Naval Experiment," *The American Neptune* 34 (1974), pp. 188–196. The Washington yard also built the revenue cutter *Jackson* for the Treasury Department later in 1832.

38. Tensions between Jackson and Calhoun factions in the administration were exacerbated when Secretary of War John H. Eaton married his reputed mistress, Margaret O'Neill Timberlake, and Mrs. Calhoun and her set refused to receive her socially. Jackson, who identified the attacks on Mrs. Eaton with those directed at his late wife during the campaign, sided with Eaton.

39. Adams, ed., *Memoirs of John Quincy Adams*, 8: 160–161.

40. Elliot Coll.: Louisa C. Adams to Hull, 9 May 1831; John Adams to Hull, 26 June 1831; CL: Hull to Levi Woodbury, 10 Dec. 1831; MassHS: Invitation from Hulls to Edward Everett, 14 Feb. 1831. Hull's first intention was to seek a warrant for Isaac Hull Adams, born in 1812, but his aunt, Louisa Catherine Adams, thought him too old at nineteen to be a midshipman, and suggested his younger brother Joseph. On the Livingstons and the "old knight" see Ann Hull to Sarah H. Jarvis, 25 Apr. [1835], and Augusta Hart to Amelia Hart, 30 June 1835, copies in possession of Eleanor T. Tilton.

41. NC journal, 28 Oct. 1830.

42. Elliot Coll.: I. Hull to J. B. Hull, 27 Sept. 1830.

43. Elliot Coll.: I. Hull to J. B. Hull, 4 Dec. 1831.

44. Boston Athenaeum, Hull Papers: Sullivan to Hull, 2 June 1831.

45. Boston Athenaeum, Hull Papers: Sullivan to Hull, 28 Jan. 1831; Francis Griffin to Hull, 7 Feb. 1831; Griffin to Hull, 20 May 1831; Sullivan to Hull, 2 June 1831; Griffin to Hull, 16 June 1831; Sullivan to Hull, 27 June 1831; Griffin to Hull, 20 July 1831, 29 July 1837.

46. Misc.: A. Citizen to Woodbury, 27 Aug. 1831. This was a none-too-subtle way of eliminating competition of free blacks for government jobs, however menial.

47. OSW: John Boyle to Hull, 17 Sept. 1831; Woodbury to Hull, 23 Sept. 1831; NA, RG 127, Hist. Coll. *USMC:* John Boyle to A. Henderson, 17 Sept. 1831; CL: Hull to Woodbury, 24 Sept. 1831; Washington log, 17 Sept. 1831.

48. HSPa: Shubrick to Hull, 25 Mar. 1831.

49. CL: Hull to Branch, 18 Mar. 1831.

50. Haverford College Library: Hull to Bainbridge, Sunday [13 Mar. 1831].

51. LC, Rodgers Family Papers: Hull to Rodgers, 2 Jan. 1833. The reference is obscure. It may be to Nicholas Biddle, who headed the United States Bank in Philadelphia, or to Rodgers's old enemy, James Barron, now at the navy yard in that city. See also Paullin, *Commodore John Rodgers,* pp. 393–394; Augusta Hart to Amelia Hart, 30 June 1835, copy in possession of Eleanor T. Tilton.

52. NA, HR 27A–G14.2, Claims, Committee on Naval Affairs, bundle docketed: Commodore Isaac Hull.

53. Misc.: Smith to Woodbury, 2 Feb. 1833; King to Woodbury, 4 Feb. 1833.

54. Comm. Rec.: A. Woodward to Hull, 22 Apr. 1833; Hull to Rodgers, 23, 25 Apr. 1833.

55. NA, RG 181, Hull LB: Hull to Woodbury, 20 May 1833.

56. Elliot Coll.: I. Hull to J. B. Hull, [29 Jan. 1832].

57. *Boston Evening Transcript,* 22, 24 June 1833; *Boston Courier,* 25 June 1833.

58. *Columbian Centinel,* 29 June 1833.

59. Elliot Coll.: I. Hull to J. B. Hull, [8 Sept. 1834]. There is a photograph of a bowl, apparently the same one, in Allen, *Papers of Isaac Hull.*

60. Comm. Misc. Letters Rec.: Peter Force to John Rodgers, 1 Jan. 1834; Elliot Coll.: Lewis J. Cist to Hull, 15 Aug. 1833; G. W. Courtenay to Hull, 30 Sept. 1834; Yale University Library: Hull to B. Silliman, 28 July 1833.

61. Elliot Coll.: I. Hull to J. B. Hull, 8 Dec. 1833. The death of Henry Hull in 1833 left but two brothers in Isaac's own generation.

62. Ann Hull to Sarah H. Jarvis, 25 Apr. 1835, copy in possession of Eleanor T. Tilton; Margaret (Bayard) Smith, *The First Forty Years of Washington Society, portrayed by the Family Letters of Mrs. Samuel Harrison Smith,* ed. Gaillard Hunt (New York, 1906), p. 340.

63. Ann Hull to Sarah H. Jarvis, 25 Apr. 1835, copy in possession of Eleanor T. Tilton; Boston Athenaeum, Hull Papers: Resolutions of Distributing Committee for the Poor of the Sixth Ward, 26 Feb. 1835.

64. Ann Hull to Sarah H. Jarvis, 25 Apr. 1835, copy in possession of Eleanor T. Tilton.

65. Comm. Rec.: Hull to Rodgers, 1 Aug. 1835; RG 181, Hull LB: Hull to Dickerson, 1 Aug. 1835; Boston Athenaeum, Hull Papers: Circular Letter from mechanics of Philadelphia, n.d.

66. Boston Athenaeum, Hull Papers: Wm. P. Piercy to Hull, 10 Aug. 1835.

67. NA, RG 45, Misc.: Mechanics of Washington Navy Yard to Mahlon Dickerson, 1 Aug. 1835.

68. Boston Athenaeum, Hull Papers: Geo. Lyndall and others to Hull, 10 Aug. 1835; Alexander McWilliams and others to Hull, 12 Aug. 1835; CL: Hull to

Dickerson, 11, 12 Aug. 1835; Comm. Letters Rec. from the Secretary of the Navy: Dickerson to John F. Stump, 24 Aug. 1835.

69. Boston Athenaeum, Hull Papers: Wm. J. Belt to Hull, 21 Aug. 1835.

70. *National Intelligencer*, 13 Aug. 1835; Boston Athenaeum, Hull Papers: Ellis and Cassidy, certificate, 12 Aug. 1835.

71. *National Intelligencer*, 12–15 Aug. 1835; Washington log, 12–14 Aug. 1835; CL: Hull to Dickerson, 14 Aug. 1835; OSW: Dickerson to Hull, 14 Aug. 1835; Boston Athenaeum, Hull Papers: undated statement on the actions of William Doughty.

72. CL: Hull to Dickerson, 30 Sept. 1835.

73. Boston Athenaeum, Hull Papers: National Hotel bill, 2 Oct. 1835; I. L. Ufford to Hull, 11 Oct. 1835; G. Perry to Hull, 12 Oct. 1835; Clark Elliott to Hull, 12 Oct. 1835; Elliot Coll.: I. Hull to J. B. Hull, 7 June, 2 Dec. 1835, 5 Mar. 1836.

74. Elliot Coll.: I. Hull to J. B. Hull, 7 June 1835.

75. Boston Athenaeum, Hull Papers: Blake to Hull, 8 Feb. 1836; Bills for calash hire, 5–12 Feb., 17 Feb.–1 Mar., 1836; Memorandum of warships at Malta, 1836.

76. Boston Athenaeum, Hull Papers: P. Eynaud to Hull, 2 Apr. 1836; CL: Hull to Dickerson, 15 Apr. 1836.

77. Boston Athenaeum, Hull Papers: Binney to Hull, 12 Oct. 1835.

78. Elliot Coll.: I. Hull to J. B. Hull, 25 June 1836; Ann Hull to Sarah H. Jarvis, 27 June [1836], copy in possession of Eleanor T. Tilton; Boston Athenaeum, Hull Papers: Fitch Bros. to Hull, 30 Aug. 1836; S. Whitney to Hull, 31 Dec. 1836.

79. James E. Freeman, *Gatherings from an Artist's Portfolio* (New York, 1877), 1: 244.

80. Augusta Hart to Sarah H. Jarvis, 10 June 1837, copy in possession of Eleanor T. Tilton.

81. Boston Athenaeum, Hull Papers: Etheridge to Hull, 6 Oct. 1837; S. Whitney to Hull, 29 July 1837; F. Griffin to Hull, 29 July 1837.

82. Boston Athenaeum, Hull Papers: Etheridge to Hull, 27 July 1837.

83. Boston Athenaeum, Hull Papers: Etheridge to Hull, 25 Sept. 1837.

84. Elliot Coll.: I. Hull to J. B. Hull, 7 Aug., 1 Sept. 1837.

85. Elliot Coll.: I. Hull to J. B. Hull, 26 Sept. 1837.

86. Elliot Coll.: J. Collings Long to I. Hull, with autograph note to J. B. Hull by I. Hull, 5 Mar. 1838. The expedition referred to is the one commanded by Charles Wilkes.

Chapter 15

1. Chapelle, *American Sailing Navy*, p. 314.

2. F. P. Torrey, *Journal of the Cruise of the United States Ship Ohio, Commodore Isaac Hull, Commander, in the Mediterranean, In the Years 1839, '40, '41* (Boston, 1841). This book was plagiarized by Roland F. Gould, *The Life of Gould, An Ex-Man-of-War's-Man* (Claremont, N.H., 1867).

3. CL: Hull to Paulding, 18 Sept. 1838.

4. Elliot Coll.: Isaac Hull to Joseph B. Hull, [9 Oct. 1838].

5. Elliot Coll.: Porter to Hull, 17 Oct. 1838; Boston Athenaeum, Hull Papers: Christopher Hughes to Hull, 19 Nov. 1838.
6. Paulding to Hull, 20 Nov. 1838, in Ralph M. Aderman, ed., *The Letters of James Kirke Paulding* (Madison, Wis., 1962), p. 239.
7. CL: Hull to Paulding, 5 Dec. 1838.
8. WLCL, Chew Papers: Abigail H. Chew to Elisabeth H. Chew, [4 Dec. 1838].
9. Boston Athenaeum, Hull Papers: Ticknor to Smith, 26 Dec. 1838; CL: Hull to Paulding, 16 June 1839.
10. LC, Short Family Papers: Sylvanus Godon to William Short, 1 Mar. 1839.
11. Boston Athenaeum, Hull Papers: Pendergrast to Hull, 7, 14 Feb. 1839.
12. Boston Athenaeum, Hull Papers: copy in Etheridge's hand.
13. Comm. Rec.: Hull to Chauncey, 19 Apr. 1839; CL: Hull to Paulding, 18 Apr. 1839.
14. LC, Short Family Papers: Godon to Short, 20–21 Apr. 1839.
15. CL: Hull to Paulding, 22 Apr. 1839.
16. CL: DuPont to Smith, 7 May 1839, encl. in Hull to Paulding, 16 June 1839.
17. CL: Hull to Paulding, 27 May 1839 (Nos. 93 and 94); Elliot Coll.: Cass to Hull, 21 Apr. 1839; Boston Athenaeum, Hull Papers: Andrew Stevenson to Hull, 24 Apr. 1839.
18. Elliot Coll.: Paulding to Hull, 27 Dec. 1838.
19. LC, Short Family Papers: Godon to Short, 7 June 1839; Boston Athenaeum, Hull Papers: Officers of the *Ohio* to Joseph Smith, 8 June 1839.
20. CL: Hull to Paulding, 16 June 1839.
21. Boston Athenaeum, Hull Papers: DuPont to Smith, 29 July 1839; see also Benajah Ticknor, Meteorological Journal for June 1839; Smith to Hull, 26 July 1839; Officers of the *Ohio* to Smith, 27 July 1839; and Smith to Officers, 28 July 1839. On 9 September, Hull reported that "the past summer has been unusually warm; at every port we touched at, in the Levant and Archipelago, it was the general remark that so warm weather had not been known for several years." CL: Hull to Paulding, 9 Sept. 1839.
22. Boston Athenaeum, Hull Papers: Smith to Hull, 30 July 1839. This was not the first time that DuPont had quarreled with a Mediterranean commodore. He had sailed as a midshipman with John Rodgers in the *North Carolina* in 1825. As senior midshipman, he was made sailing master of the flagship, which he considered an honor until his promotion to lieutenant in 1826. Then he declined to consider serving in a "subordinate grade" and, after "some little dispute" with Rodgers, obtained a transfer to the *Porpoise*. He clearly felt contempt for the navy's senior commander afloat and concluded his cruise with the remark that "I can never feel any regard or esteem for him." (See James M. Merrill, "Midshipman DuPont and the Cruise of the *North Carolina*, 1825–1827," *American Neptune* 40 [1980], pp. 211–225.) Twelve years later, thirty-six years old and still a lieutenant, DuPont was no more inclined to suffer the "impositions" of his superiors gracefully.
23. LC, Short Family Papers: Godon to Short, 20 Sept. 1839.
24. Letters Received by the Secretary of the Navy from Commanders: Percival to Paulding, 25 July 1839.
25. LC, Short Family Papers: Godon to Short, 20 Sept. 1839.
26. LC, Short Family Papers: Godon to Short, 21 Oct. 1839. To put Godon's

attitude in perspective, it should be noted again that in peacetime officers' wives on board ships of the American and British navies were the rule rather than the exception. Even lieutenants sometimes brought their wives on board. In the 'tween decks there were always women, whether in peace or in war. They were only officially invisible. That a flag lieutenant, as the commodore's aide, would escort his family went without saying. But obviously Isaac Hull's family was not to Lieutenant Godon's taste.

27. The documents on this affair are in the Hull Papers, Boston Athenaeum. Several of the principal items are printed in Allen, *Papers of Isaac Hull*, pp. 277–295.

28. Torrey, *Journal of the Cruise*, p. 37.

29. NA, RG 45, Area 7 file: Henry A. Wise to George Wells, 16 Feb. 1840.

30. LC, Short Family Papers: Godon to Short, 8 Dec. 1839.

31. LC, Short Family Papers: Godon to Short, 5 Jan. 1840.

32. LC, Short Family Papers: Godon to Short, 19 Feb. 1840.

33. Torrey, *Journal of the Cruise*, p. 48.

34. LC, Short Family Papers: Godon to Short, 5 Jan. 1840.

35. CL: Hull to Paulding, 12 Feb. 1840.

36. LC, Short Family Papers: Godon to Short, 19 Feb. 1840.

37. CL: Hull to Paulding, 18 Feb. 1840.

38. Elliot Coll.: Paulding to Hull, 16 Dec. 1839.

39. Boston Athenaeum, Hull Papers: Latimer to Hull, 17 Mar. 1840.

40. LC, Short Family Papers: [Godon] to Short, 18 Mar. 1840.

41. LC, Short Family Papers: Hull to Short, 27 Mar. 1840.

42. David F. Long, *Sailor-Diplomat: A Biography of Commodore James Biddle, 1783–1848* (Boston, 1983), pp. 148–152, 164.

43. Boston Athenaeum, Hull Papers: Samuel Mercer to Hull, 31 May, 30 June 1840.

44. Torrey, *Journal of the Cruise*, p. 67.

45. CL: Lavallette to Paulding, 2 Aug. 1840.

46. CL: Hull to Paulding, 1 Aug. 1840.

47. OL: Pendergrast to Paulding, 5 June 1840.

48. LC, Short Family Papers: Godon to Short, 12 June [1840].

49. Aderman, ed., *Letters of Paulding*, pp. 277–279.

50. James F. Beard, ed., *The Letters and Journals of James Fenimore Cooper*, 6 vols. (Cambridge, Mass., 1960–68), 4: 53, Cooper to Shubrick, 2 Aug. 1840.

51. Boston Athenaeum, Hull Papers: Percival to Hull, 5 July 1840.

52. Aderman, ed., *Letters of Paulding*, pp. 561–562, 563–567.

53. CL: Hull to Paulding, 27 Aug. 1840.

54. CL: Hull to Paulding, 20 Nov. 1840.

55. LC, Short Family Papers: Godon to Short, 20 Nov. 1840.

56. CL: Hull to Paulding, 5 Dec. 1840.

57. Charges and countercharges are in Boston Athenaeum, Hull Papers.

58. CL: Paulding to Hull, 1, 8 Oct. 1840.

59. LC, Stevenson Papers: Andrew Stevenson to Isaac Hull, 8 Mar. 1841. Recipient's copy in Boston Athenaeum, Hull Papers.

60. Boston Athenaeum, Hull Papers: John Hare Powel to Hull, 11 Mar. 1841.

61. CL: Hull to Secretary of the Navy, 25 Mar. 1841.

62. CL: Hull to Secretary of the Navy, 6 Apr. 1841; Comm. Rec.: Bolton to Navy Commissioners, 9 May 1841.

63. Comm. Letters Rec. from Secretary of the Navy: Hull to Secretary of the Navy, 1 May 1841. The portrait by Pellegrin is now in the National Portrait Gallery at Washington, the gift of James H. Welch.

64. Torrey, *Journal of the Cruise*, p. 93.

65. CL: Hull to Secretary of the Navy, 12 May 1841.

66. Torrey, *Journal of the Cruise*, p. 114.

Chapter 16

1. CL: Bolton to Hull, 21 July 1841.

2. Elliot Coll.: Isaac Hull to Joseph B. Hull, 29 Oct. 1841.

3. CL: Hull to Upshur, 23 Oct. 1841.

4. LC, Short Family Papers: Godon to Short, 23, 28 Oct., 17 Nov. 1841.

5. Elliot Coll.: J. B. Nicolson to Hull, 13 Nov. 1841.

6. Boston Athenaeum, Hull Papers: Gilbert Davis to Hull, 4 Dec. 1841.

7. Boston Athenaeum, Hull Papers: Bradbury to Hull, 7 Dec. 1841.

8. Elliot Coll.: Isaac Hull to Joseph B. Hull, 9 Dec. 1841; CL: Hull to Jacob Jones, 12 Dec. 1841.

9. Elliot Coll.: Isaac Hull to Joseph B. Hull, 5 Feb. 1842.

10. Elliot Coll.: Hull to J. Etheridge, 18 Feb. 1842.

11. Elliot Coll.: Hull to Etheridge, [26] June 1842.

12. Beard, ed., *Letters of James Fenimore Cooper*, 4: 310, Cooper to Shubrick, 4 Sept. 1842.

13. HSPa: Hull to G. Harrison, 12 Sept. 1842.

14. CL: Hull to Upshur, 8 Oct. 1842.

15. Elliot Coll.: Hull to Etheridge, 8 Oct. 1842.

16. Elliot Coll.: Hull to Etheridge, 22 Dec. 1842.

17. Elliot Coll.: Davis to Hull, 26 Dec. 1842.

18. Elliot Coll.: Jeannette Hart to Levi Hull, [14 Feb. 1843]. The letter is dated from 188 Chestnut St., Philadelphia.

Index

Isaac Hull is abbreviated IH

Index

Index

Index

Index

Hull, Joseph (*cont.*)
483n2; Revolutionary services, 3–4;
trading voyages, 5–6; marries Lucy
Wheeler, 120; Navy agent for Connecticut, 124–25, 143, 146; and widow
Blakely, 286; marries Freelove Nichols,
300; illness of, 352, 359, 399; IH takes
leave of, 365; death of, 400; IH's attitude toward, 132, 150, 170, 181, 286,
400
Hull, Joseph (5) (IH's brother) 3, 4, 6, 7,
120, 128, 145, 285, 483n2
Hull, Joseph B., USN (IH's nephew), 128;
IH's advice to, 74, 360–61, 440–41,
465; IH offers to take on board, 145;
should be at school, 201; receives midshipman's warrant, 227; at Portsmouth,
249–50, 255; sails in *Washington,* 283;
will not attend to his books, 286; in
Franklin, 312, 359, 374; cruises in West
Indies, 417; in *Guerrière,* 418–19, 425–
26; at Washington, 426; cares for IH's
paintings, 432; and *Constitution* souvenirs, 434–35; and sale of Derby farm,
440, 444, 447; in Mediterranean, 441–
42; hopes to marry, 445; marries Amelia Hart, 475; birth of daughter, 477
Hull, Julia, 399
Hull, Lavinia Mann, 419, 483n2
Hull, Levi (IH's brother), 3, 135, 419,
483n2; farms at Derby and Huntington,
120, 285–86, 300, 359, 416; marriage to
Mary Wheeler, 143, 145, 150, 158;
health of, 146
Hull, Sarah (IH's niece), 416
Hull, Sarah Ann (IH's niece), 128, 145,
201, 255, 272, 285–87, 312, 359–60,
417, 440, 475
Hull, Sarah Bennett (IH's mother), 3, 120,
483n2
Hull, Susan Bartone (IH's sister-in-law),
128, 145, 201, 300, 360, 417, 440, 475,
483n2
Hull, William (IH's uncle), 54, 208–9,
222, 224; and IH's childhood, 4–6; and
IH's appointment to Navy, 13–14,
484n4; and Republican politics, 13–14,
24, 116, 123, 315; governor of Michigan
territory, 147; to command troops in
Northwest, 165–66; surrenders Detroit, 198; court-martial of, 227–28;
owes IH money, 399; death of, 400
Hull, William (IH's brother), 200, 201,
210, 483n2; in business at New York,
120, 125, 128; health of, 146; IH's favorite, 150; in charge of IH's business

affairs, 163, 170; illness of, 181; death
of, 196; IH holds up as example, 221
Humphreys, Daniel, 3
Humphreys, David, 128, 484n2
Humphreys, Joshua, 211–13
Humphreys, Samuel, 213, 424
Hunt, Jesse, 438
Hunt, John, 23, 32–33
Hunt, Theodore, USN, 203
Hunt, Thomas, USN, 54, 489n68
Hunt, William, 54
Hunt, William E., USN, 380
Hunter, Harry D., USN, 362, 373, 376
Hussey, Cyrus, 397, 414–15

Ica, privateer (ex-*Esther*), 385
Iggulden, Edward, 156
Illingworth, John, 395
Ilsley, Isaac, 237
Independence, USS, 243, 265, 268, 271,
274, 279, 282–84, 287–88, 291, 293–94,
297, 301, 310–11, 329
Ingersoll, Jared, 38
Ingersoll, Joseph, 346–47, 357
Insurgente, frigate, 25
Intrepid, ketch, 96
Irvine, Dr., RN, 190–92
Isabella, frigate, *See O'Higgins*
Israel, Joseph, USN, 96
Ivan, Miss, 287
Izard, Ralph, Jr., USN, 86, 118

Jackson, Andrew, 315, 424–25, 427, 432–
33, 437–38, 441, 443–44, 525n38
Jackson, Mr., 20–21
Jackson, revenue cutter, 525n37
James (IH's servant), 131
Jarvis, Jannette, 286, 443
Jarvis, John Abraham, 286, 443, 524n21
Jarvis, John Wesley, 205, 206
Jarvis, Leonard, 160, 330
Jarvis, Philip, USN, 24, 30–31
Jarvis, Samuel F., 206–7, 286, 341, 399,
435
Jarvis, Sarah Hart, 436; Ann Hart visits,
206; Henry Hull comments on, 207;
visits Hulls at Charlestown, 286; living
in Europe, 435; meets Hulls at Paris,
443; IH helps to return to US, 447; re-
ceives guests on board *Ohio,* 450
Java, HMS. 200, 204, 208, 285
Java, USS, 236, 283, 334, 515n14
Jay, Sir James, 156–57, 160, 198
Jay, John, 156
Jay's Treaty, 8, 9
Jefferson, Thomas, 227, 424; Nicholson

Index

Index

Constitution, 166; rejoins *Constitution*, 168; suggests kedging maneuver, 172; remarks on escape from British squadron, 176, 178; IH praises, 177–78, 193; receives letter at Boston, 183; boards *Lady Warren*, 184; requests permission to fire on *Guerrière*, 188; wounded, 189; convalescent, 196; called to Washington, 202; promoted to captain, 203; commands *Adams*, 251; and losses on Treasury notes, 254; Rodgers praises, 264; fits out *Congress*, 266; at Boston with wife, 274; surveys *Macedonian*, 283; commands Portsmouth station, 301; and Shaw–Abbot trials, 328–29, 342, 344; and Binney investigation, 328, 342–43; IH suspects of enmity, 343, 429; and inquiry on IH, 349–50, 356, 359; and Board of Commissioners, 415, 429; confirms IH's memory of *Constitution–Guerrière* battle, 434, 501n38

Morris, J. B., 438

Morris, Richard V., USN, 95; commands *Constitution*, 63; transfers to *Chesapeake*, 63; commands Mediterranean squadron, 68, 72, 80, 492; and Moroccan crisis, 70; Murray reports on inactivity of, 73; at Tripoli, 76–77; withdraws from Tripoli, 79; birth of son at Malta, 79; dismissed from command, 81; takes squadron to Gibraltar, 82–83; ignored by Rodgers and Preble, 84; Eaton's hatred of, 97

Morse, James, 450

Morse, Samuel, F. B., 207

Moyana, privateer, 382, 384

Moyse, General, 50, 52

Mungo (slave), 61

Murray, Alexander, USN, 51, 73, 81, 97, 124, 138, 269, 304, 313

Murray, Robert, 87

Mustapha (governor of Derna), 107, 109–10

Nancy, brig, 7–8

Nancy, merchant vessel, 382, 387

Napier, Henry Edward, RN, 247–48

Nautilus, USS, 231; in Morris squadron, 81, 492n37; in Preble squadron, 83–84, 86, 89, 92, 94, 97; in Barron squadron, 99, 107–8, 110–11; at Hampton Roads, 151; in Rodgers's squadron, 171; captured by Broke's squadron, 175; cartel returns crew to Boston, 198–99; court of inquiry on loss of, 200; in British service as *Young Emulous*, 232

Nease, John, 146–48

Nelson, Admiral Horatio, RN, 244

Nelson, Thomas, 22

Neutrality, schooner, 27

New Hampshire, USS, 217, 504n25

New York, USS: in Morris squadron, 72–75, 77–79, 81–84, 86; explosion in, 75; attempts to raise wreck of, 423

Nichols, Captain, 185

Nichols, Freelove (Mrs. Joseph Hull), 300, 417, 483n2

Nicholson, James, USN, 13

Nicholson, Joseph H., 60

Nicholson, Joseph J., USN, 242

Nicholson, Samuel, Jr., USN, 21

Nicholson, Samuel, USN, 138; political nature of appointment, 13–14, 60; commands *Constitution*, 13–28; and choice of officers, 13–14; Federalist hatred of, 16–17; and *Niger* case, 19–22, 485n33; and death of son, 21; SecNav wants to replace, 23–24, 27, 29; and race with *Santa Margaretta*, 26; sent on shore, 27–28; and officers, 30, 32–33; and marines, 36; commands Charlestown Navy Yard, 136, 271; death of, 196–97

Nicholson, William C., USN, 362, 390

Nicolson, John B., USN, 476

Niger, private armed vessel, 20–23, 25, 27, 31

Nimmo, William R., 423

Nissen, Nicholas C., 79

Nixon, Zachariah W., USN, 374, 376, 382, 522n97

Norfolk, steamboat, 367

Norfolk, USS, 39–40

North, Simeon, 127–28, 288

North Carolina, USS, 268, 304, 448, 528n22

North Point, merchant vessel, 387

Nymph, brig, 46

Nymphe, HMS, 247

O'Bannon, Presley N., USMC, 71–72, 101, 103, 106, 108, 112

O'Brien, Richard, 93

Ogden, David B., 307

O'Higgins, Bernardo, 390, 404–5

O'Higgins, frigate, 387, 391

Ohio, USS, 268, 480; flagship, Mediterranean squadron, 445–80; qualities of, 446, 474; IH's pendant hoisted in, 447; arrives at New York, 448; controversial arrangements in, 448–49, 453, 455–57; arrives at Mahon, 450; overhauled at Mahon, 451; sails for Gibraltar, 452; at

Index

Index

Wadsworth, Mrs., 267
Wailes, Mrs., 525n31
Waine, Thomas, USN, 334, 515n14
Wainwright, R. D., USMC, 287
Walbach, John, 223
Walbach, John Baptiste de Barth, USA, 223, 244, 247, 249, 255, 258
Waldo, Charles F., USN, 297–98, 323, 510n14, 511n19
Waldo, F. W., 333, 339–40, 343–44, 347–49, 358, 516n30
Wall, Albert G., USN, 377
Wallace, William (John Burns), 160–61
Ward (master's mate), 23
Ward, Henry, USN, 334, 349, 351, 358–59, 517n65
Warden, David Baillie, 149, 151–56, 158–59, 162, 200, 443
Warren, James, 523n117
Warrington, Lewis, USN, 329, 366, 429, 476
Washington, Bushrod, 38
Washington, Charles (slave), 525n31
Washington, George, 4, 14, 382, 392, 467, 473, 484n2
Washington, Mrs. (Bailey?), 525n31
Washington, USS, 252, 254–55, 263, 265–66, 268, 272, 274, 276–77, 279, 283
Wasp, USS, 232, 236–38, 262, 274
Waters, Kervin, USN, 233
Watkins, Tobias, 413
Watson, Joseph, 211, 225, 239–40, 307, 309
Webster, Daniel, 226, 229, 354, 357
Webster–Hayne debate, 424
Welsh (pilot), 170
West, Lucy Brewer (Louisa Baker), 169
Westmoreland, Countess of, 450
Wetmore, William S., 374
Wheeden, Isaac, 333–34, 367, 398
Wheeler, Joseph, Jr., 136, 399
Wheeler, Joseph, Sr., 483n2
Wheeler, Lucy Smith, 120, 150, 285, 483n2

Wheeler, Mary, 482n1, 483n2; mother marries Joseph Hull, 120; characterized, 120; friendship with IH, 120; teaches at Litchfield, 133; and IH's affairs of the heart, 133, 135–36, 138, 146, 150, 165; IH tells of his ship, 140–41; engagement to Levi Hull, 143, 145; marriage, 150, 158, 165; friendship with Ann Hull, 207–8, 210, 220; has IH's miniature, 208; William Hull praises, 209; IH writes of his married happiness, 222, 249–50, 272; IH writes of concern for Joseph's children, 250, 255, 286–87; IH writes of his navy yard activities, 283; cares for Joseph Hull, 286, 300; at Huntington Landing farm, 416; Hulls visit, 416; IH wills estate to, on wife's death, 479
Whipple, Joseph, 213
Whitney, Stephen, 443
Widgery, William, 230
Wilkes, Charles, USN, 527n86
Williams, James M., USN, 414
Williams, John Shirley, 239
Williams, Miss, 146
Williamson, James, 431
Williamson, Thomas, USN, 476
Willink & Van Staphorst, 155
Wilson, John, 34
Wilton, John, 109
Wise, Henry A., USN, 460
Wolcott, Oliver, Jr., USN, 288–89
Wolcott, Oliver, Sr., 256, 288–89, 426
Woodbury, Levi, 425, 427–29, 431–33
Woodrop Sims, storeship, 91
Woodward, Mrs., 226
Woolsey, William G., USN, 411, 418
Wyman, Francis, 305, 512n37

Yeates, Donaldson, USN, 235
Young Emulous, HMS (ex-USS *Nautilus*), 232